Seafaring, Trade, and Knowledge Transfer

Crossroads – History of Interactions across the Silk Routes

Edited by

Angela Schottenhammer
(*Catholic University of Leuven, Belgium*)

VOLUME 9

The titles published in this series are listed at *brill.com/cros*

Seafaring, Trade, and Knowledge Transfer

Maritime Politics and Commerce in Early Middle Period to Early Modern China and South East & East Asia

Edited by

Angela Schottenhammer
Mathieu Torck
Wim De Winter

BRILL

LEIDEN | BOSTON

This research was supported by, and contributes to the project "Seafaring, Trade, and Knowledge Transfer: Maritime Politics and Commerce in Early Middle Period to Early Modern China", sponsored by the German Gerda Henkel Foundation (GHF, grant agreement number AZ/31/F/13). It also contributes to the ERC AdG project TRANSPACIFIC which has received funding from the European Research Council (ERC) under the European Union's Horizon 2020 Research and Innovation Programme (Grant agreement No. 833143).

Cover: Chart of the mouth of the Pearl River (part). Van der Hem 41:18; *Grote Atlas van de Oost-Indische Compagnie* (*VII*), 89. Courtesy of ANNO/Austrian National Library.

Library of Congress Cataloging-in-Publication Data
Names: Schottenhammer, Angela editor | Torck, Mathieu editor | Winter, Wim de editor
Title: Seafaring, trade, and knowledge transfer : maritime politics and commerce in early middle period to early modern China and South East & East Asia / edited by Angela Schottenhammer, Mathieu Torck, Wim De Winter.
Description: Leiden : Brill, 2026. | Series: Crossroads : history of interactions across the silk routes, 2589–885X ; volume 9 | Includes bibliographical references and index.
Identifiers: LCCN 2025030018 (print) | LCCN 2025030019 (ebook) | ISBN 9789004730557 hardback | ISBN 9789004740556 ebook
Subjects: LCSH: Navigation—Asia—History | Trade routes—Asia—History | Culture diffusion—Asia—History—To 1500 | Asia—Commerce—History
Classification: LCC HC412 .S426 2026 (print) | LCC HC412 (ebook)
LC record available at https://lccn.loc.gov/2025030018
LC ebook record available at https://lccn.loc.gov/2025030019

Typeface for the Latin, Greek, and Cyrillic scripts: "Brill". See and download: brill.com/brill-typeface.

ISSN 2589-885X
ISBN 978-90-04-73055-7 (hardback)
ISBN 978-90-04-74055-6 (e-book)
DOI 10.1163/9789004740556

This book is printed on acid-free paper and produced in a sustainable manner.

Contents

Figures and Tables

Figures

Tables

Notes on Contributors

Leonard Blussé

Ph.D. (1986), Leiden University, is Professor Emeritus of History of European-Asian Relations at that university. His extensive publication record includes *A Colonial Tragedy: The Chinese Massacre at Batavia, 1740* (Leiden University Press 2025).

Cai Ellen Xiangyu

Ph.D. (2012), Guangzhou University, is Associate Professor of History at that university. Her publications include " The Origin of the Dutch Embassy to China in 1794," in Thijs Weststeijn (ed.), *Foreign Devils and Philosophers: Cultural Encounters between the Chinese, the Dutch and Other Europeans, 1590–1800* (Brill, 2020).

Patrizia Carioti

Ph.D. (1994), is Full Professor of History of East Asia, and of History and Civilisation of Far East Asia, and President of the Centre for East Asian Studies at L'Orientale University of Napoli. Her publication record includes "A Bitter Defeat for the VOC: The Conquest of Taiwan by Zheng Chenggong, 1661–1662" (Keisuisha, 2017).

John Chaffee

Ph.D. (1979), Binghamton University, is SUNY Distinguished Service Professor Emeritus of History and Asian and Asian American Studies at that university. His extensive publication record includes *The Muslim Merchants of Premodern China* (Cambridge University Press, 2018).

Cheng Weichung

Ph.D. (2012), Academia Sinica, is Associate Research Fellow and Deputy Director at its Institute of Taiwan History. He has published monographs, book chapters and many articles on VOC in East Asia, including *War, Trade and Piracy in the China Seas (1622–1683)* (Brill, 2013).

Wim De Winter

Ph.D. (2021), KU Leuven, is postdoctoral researcher of Early Modern Asian, world-, and maritime history on the Indian Ocean and the Pacific. His publications include "Merchants, Sailors and Privateers: Maritime Affairs between Spain and England during Wartime as Revealed by the Prize Papers" (Routledge 2024).

Ubaldo Iaccarino
Ph.D. (2014), "L'Orientale" University of Napoli, is Senior Researcher at the Department of Asian, African and Mediterranean Studies, where he teaches History of South-East Asia. His publications include a monograph titled *Comercio y diplomacia entre Japón y Filipinas en la era Keichō (1596–1615)* (Harrassowitz, 2017).

Kimura Jun
Ph.D. (2011), Tokai University, maritime archaeologist and associate professor of the Department of Maritime Civilizations at that university. His publications focus on East Asian, Southeast Asian and trans-Pacific maritime archaeology and include *Archaeology of East Asian Shipbuilding* (University Press of Florida, 2016).

Li Man
Ph.D. (2010), Vasco Da Gama European Institute of Diplomacy and International Relations, is Senior Lecturer at that institute. His publications include "Where is 'Yingyou': the 'Tea Route' between Khitan and Southern Tang and its ports of departure" (National Maritime Research, 2016).

Ma Guang
Ph.D. (2016), Macao Polytechnic University, is Associate Professor of East Asian Maritime History at that university. His publications include *Rupture, Evolution, and Continuity: The Shandong Peninsula in East Asian Maritime History during the Yuan-Ming Transition* (Harrassowitz, 2021).

Elke Papelitzky
Ph.D. (2017), University of Oslo, is Associate Professor of Chinese History at that university. Her extensive publication record on Chinese mapmaking and maritime history includes *Writing World History in Late Ming China and the Perception of Maritime Asia* (Harrassowitz, 2020).

Angela Schottenhammer
Ph.D. (1993), KU Leuven, is Full Professor of Chinese Middle Period and early modern world history. Her publications include *China and the Silk Roads (ca. 100 BCE to 1800 CE) Role and Content of its Historical Access to the Outside World* (Brill, 2023).

Mark Staniforth

Ph.D. (1999), Flinders University of South Australia, is a retired (honorary Adjunct) Associate Professor of Maritime Archaeology at that university. He has an extensive publication record which includes a book chapter such as "Abandoned Ships in Australia" (Kaveri, 2015).

Mathieu Torck

Ph.D. (2006), KU Leuven/Ghent University, is postdoctoral researcher of Early Modern Chinese and world maritime history at KU Leuven and lecturer at Ghent University. His publications include "Surgeons and Physicians on the Move in the Asian Waters (15th to 18th Centuries)" (2022).

Xu Zhexin

is a doctoral researcher who specializes in maritime commerce and local society in Chinese coastal regions, social network of communities in medieval Chinese urban spaces, animals in maritime commerce and cultural communication.

INTRODUCTION

Seafaring, Trade, and Knowledge Transfer: Maritime Politics and Commerce in Early Middle Period to Early Modern China

Angela Schottenhammer

Maritime politics in China changed over time.* Sometimes these changes were quite significant, while during other periods we can observe more continuities. One of the major research questions that we pursued with our research project, which has generously been sponsored by the Gerda Henkel Foundation, was the question of if or not such changes can be related to dynastic cycles or what kind of impact dynastic shifts had on a continuity or discontinuity of maritime politics in China. Based on a comparative analysis of textual (including maps and sea routes) and recently discovered archaeological sources (such as shipwrecks with their cargoes, grave objects, tombs, and tomb inscriptions) from China and her "neighbouring countries", we intended to examine the interrelationship between maritime politics and commerce and comparatively analyse the development of maritime trade and its impact on state politics and vice versa in the *longue-durée*, that means, from the first peak of maritime trade during the Tang period to the early and high Qing, in other words, from approximately 750 to 1750. In this chapter, I will bring together results and conclusions including those that have been published elsewhere.[1] I seek to provide

* This project, entitled "Seafaring, Trade, and Knowledge Transfer – Maritime Politics and Commerce in Early Middle Period to Early Modern China", has been sponsored by the Gerda Henkel Foundation since January 2014. In a special issue of our journal *Crossroads – Studies on the History of Exchange Relations in the East Asian World*, issue 11 (2015), we have already introduced first joined research results and we have published a series of articles and book chapters since then. In this publication, we are providing a *resumé* of our research results and also include new aspects to the topic, including those that were originally presented on a conference in Het Pand in Gent in summer 2017.

1 In addition to our special issue of *Crossroads* in 2015, this chapter draws heavily on my recent research on this topic, in particular on the following publications: Angela Schottenhammer, "China's Gate to the Indian Ocean – Iranian and Arab Long-distance Traders", *Harvard Journal of Asiatic Studies* (2016), 135–179; item, "The Song 宋 Dynasty (960–1279) – A Revolutionary Era Turn?", in Kósa Gábor (ed.), *China across the Centuries* [Budapest Monographs in East Asian Studies] (Budapest: ELTE University, Department of East Asian Languages, 2017), 133–173; item, "China's Rise and Retreat as a Maritime Power", in Robert Antony, Angela

 | DOI:10.1163/9789004740556_002

a *resumé* of our research results and to critically reassess the role and importance of dynastic transition periods for changes and/or continuities in China's maritime trade politics.

Significant transitions occurred (1) at a time period when maritime commerce experienced a significant upswing in the course of the late Tang to mid Song, (2) during the Southern Song and Yuan, when China rose as a real maritime power, (3) during the shift from the Yuan period promotion of maritime trade to the early Ming maritime trade proscription, and (4) eventually during a period when once again a foreign people (Manchus) ruled China, and who allegedly concentrated only on continental borders and border security with little to no interest in maritime commerce and defence:

(1) Tang-Song transition (c. 750–1150);
(2) Song-Yuan transition (c. 1150–1350);
(3) Yuan-Ming transition (c. 1350–1500);
(4) Ming-Qing transition (c. 1550–1750);

The ascendency of China as a maritime power was very obvious by the thirteenth century, when large battle ships sent by the Mongol rulers of the Chinese Yuan 元 court (1271–1368), initiated a series of military offensives, specifically against Japan (in 1274 and 1280) and the kingdoms of Champa (in 1281) and Java (in 1292–1293). But maritime relations have already flourished since the fourth century at the latest.[2] The great upswing of maritime trade and com-

Schottenhammer (eds.), *New Discourses on China's Role in East Asian Maritime History* (Wiesbaden: Otto Harrassowitz, 2017), 189–211; item, "Foreign Trade, 1000–1800", in Debin Ma, Richard von Glahn (eds.), *The Cambridge Economic History of China* (Cambridge: Cambridge University Press, 2020), 637–675; A.S., *China and the Silk Roads (ca. 100 BCE to 1800 CE). Role and Content of Its Historical Access to the Outside World* Series [Crossroads – History of Interactions across the Silk Routes, 6] (Leiden: E.J. Brill, 2023); item, "China's Increasing Integration into the Indian Ocean World Until Song 宋 Times: Sea Routes, Connections, Trades", in Angela Schottenhammer (ed.), *Early Global Interconnectivity Across the Indian Ocean World* [Palgrave Series in Indian Ocean World Studies], 2 vols. (London: Palgrave Macmillan), vol. 1, *Commercial Structures and Exchanges*, 21–52; item, "The Emergence of China as a Maritime Power", chapter 7 of vol. 5 of *The Cambridge History of China*, vol. 5, part Two, *The Five Dynasties and Sung China, 960–1279*, ed. by John W. Chaffee und Paul J. Smith (Cambridge: Cambridge University Press, 2014), 437–525. A.S. "Imperial Maritime China", in *Oxford Research Encyclopedia, Asian History*, https://oxfordre.com/asianhistory/view/10.1093/acrefore/9780190277727.001.0001/acrefore-9780190277727-e-209.

2 In this context, the Chinese historian Liu Shufen even suggested that due to the prosperous maritime trade in China's coastal regions at that time, the Southern Dynasties (420–589) experienced an "impressive" commercial and urban development. See Liu Shufen, "Jiankang and the Commercial Empire of the Southern Dynasties: Change and Continuity in Medieval Chinese Economic History", in Scott Pearce, Audrey Spiro, and Patricia Ebrey (eds.), *Culture*

merce, however, occurred during the mid-Tang (618–906) to early/mid Song 宋 (960–1279) – the so-called Tang-Song transition period (*c.*750–1150).[3]

While, on the one hand, Chinese politics and society experienced a Neo-Confucian reorientation during the Song Dynasty, which was partially accountable for some quite negative attitudes among the intellectual élites, especially towards the northern "barbarians", maritime borders, in particular, became increasingly permeable and foreign traders welcomed rather than banned. By the Southern Song Dynasty (1127–1279), as we have long known, China's maritime trade reached an unforeseen prominence; China had become the economic motor of the whole Asian region. With the Mongol Yuan conquest, when China became part of the Mongolian Empire, new avenues in the exchange of knowledge, products, and human migration emerged. And to an unforeseen extent, maritime space also served military purposes, as the offenses of the Yuan navy against Japan, Champa and Java show (Song-Yuan transition). While the Tang-Song transition in terms of maritime politics can be characterized as a political, ideological and socio-economic change, the Song-Yuan transition appears more like a shift towards an increasing role of the military.

With the founding of the Ming Dynasty (1368–1644), Chinese rulers suddenly officially implemented a new policy, which was strongly influenced by the first Ming emperor's security calculations, permitting trade and exchange only under strict government control. Strict regulations were established for interaction both with China's northern and north-western neighbours, and their sea border (maritime prohibition policy between 1371 and 1567). Historians even speak of a kind of "rupture" between a period of pro trade policy and a sudden anti-foreign and anti-maritime commerce policy. Definitely, this is only partly true; in terms of China's view of "the others", of foreigners, we have to distinguish between official ideology and local practice.

The shift from the Yuan period promotion of maritime trade to the early Ming maritime trade proscription, raises the question as to what extent maritime commerce was actually maintained – after all, it was in the course of the Ming when "international" trade relations experienced another unforeseen peak – and which characteristics the inter-relation between military and commercial activities possessed during this "Yuan-Ming transition" (*c.*1350–1500).

---

and Power in the Reconstitution of the Chinese Realm, 200–600 (Cambridge and London: Harvard University Asia Center, 2001), 35–52.

3 The motives for a general shift of trade routes from the traditional overland to maritime routes have to be sought for the political instability in Inner, North and East Asia, and, last but not least, in China herself.

This transitional period is an almost absolute white sheet in maritime history, a fact that obviously has much to do with the underestimation of the importance of maritime commerce for both the Yuan and the Ming.

In the late sixteenth century, a semi-nomadic people, the Manchus, rose in Northeast Asia and eventually invaded China and established their own dynasty, the Qing, as rulers. Again ruled by a foreign people, China largely extended her borders into north and northwest Central Asia and colonized new territories. Consequently, maritime relations and commerce seemingly played only a minor role, with its main focus basically on border security. While this is not absolutely incorrect, recent scholarship has already started to show that maritime commerce was much more important for the Qing than hitherto suspected.[4] But exactly because continental space was more important for the Manchu rulers than maritime space, the latter has still rather been neglected and underestimated in historical research, both in terms of commercial and cultural exchange, as well as human interaction.

Although the focus of our research clearly lies on maritime interactions, one has of course also to thoroughly consider developments in Central Asia and along China's continental borders, in order to be able to examine how land and sea trade were interconnected and how the latter influenced the former and *vice versa*. For, with the increasing ascendancy of China as a maritime player, the quality of exchange relations via the East China Sea and the Indian Ocean as well as via Central Asia underwent a major shift. In our project, Chinese and East Asian maritime space is consequently also treated as a part of Asia's macro-regional structures. Research, thus, also focuses on the investigation of China's multifaceted trading networks, including aspects of the migration of people to and from China. Here, the role of Muslim/Islamic commercial networks receives special attention, as it was Iranian and Arab merchants who were among the most active traders in China's long-distance maritime commerce during the initial period under investigation here, and who were the ones who actually initiated the era of a *more routinized long-distance maritime trade*[5] – for example in port cities such as Guangzhou 廣州 or Quanzhou 泉州, as I have argued elsewhere.[6]

4 See, for example, Angela Schottenhammer, "Characteristics of Qing China's Maritime Trade Politics, *Shunzhi* through Early *Qianlong* Reigns", in Angela Schottenhammer (ed.), *Trading Networks in Early Modern East Asia* [East Asian Maritime History, 9] (Wiesbaden: Harrassowitz, 2010), 101–154; Zhao Gang [Zhao Gang 趙岡]. *The Qing Opening to the Ocean: Chinese Maritime Policies, 1684–1757* (Honolulu: University of Hawai'i, 2013).

5 Angela Schottenhammer, "China's Gate to the South".

6 Angela Schottenhammer, *Das songzeitliche Quanzhou im Spannungsfeld zwischen Zentralregierung und maritimem Handel. Unerwartete Konsequenzen des zentralstaatlichen Zugriffs*

1 The Tang-Song Transition

Tang China found herself confronted with various strong emerging powers, and that Tang rulers had to see how best to secure their borders and interests. Although the balance of power was in favour of China up to the Battle of Talas, Tang China was not dominant. And after the battle and the An Lushan 安祿山 Rebellion (755–763), China struggled to survive. In marching west, China definitely sought to gain control over trade routes, and access to peoples and countries from where the foreign goods originated. The Tang court established protectorates in Annam, and in Korea. At the same time, Tang China wanted to secure its borders and prevent foreign countries and people harming Chinese territoriality. Most of the time, China shifted between a militarily forward position, on the one side, and defence and cultural persuasiveness or soft power, on the other, as Wang Zhenping has termed it,[7] trying to appease her neighbours by offering material, cultural, or ideological (such as Tang titles, *etc.*) advantages, and expecting peace and respect for Tang interests and especially its territorial integrity in response.

Tang rulers were already "opening a route to India", and to obtain access to the larger Indian Ocean world was of major importance to Tang rulers. The Indian Ocean world was of interest primarily for economic reasons, but there were also political-diplomatic circumstances that mattered. Tang China applied what one may call a "soft power policy", a policy that tried to appease foreign rulers by providing access to China's material and intellectual wealth. Such a policy is, from its starting point, a negative, defensive, not an offensive approach. Soft power policy was a means of responding to border security problems, and get along with peoples of other ethnicities who were settling along China's borders, and constituted a potential source of trouble and insecurity for Chinese ruling élites. From the beginning, the Tang government adopted such measures in order to integrate non-Han people into its empire, to win their allegiance by attempting to convince them of an allegedly superior Chinese culture, by bestowing them the royal surname, official and noble titles, or arranging inter-ethnic marriages and, in this way, to maintain and guarantee the *status quo* in a multi-polar macro region. Tang foreign policy, as Wang Zhenping has shown, "could barely be a binary choice between peace and war, negotiation and rejection, pacification and assimilation, or coercion

---

auf den Reichtum einer Küstenregion (Wiesbaden: Otto Harrassowitz, 2002), esp. 53–59, 57; item, "China's Gate to the South".

7 Wang Zhenping, *Tang China in Multi-Polar Asia. A History of Diplomacy and War* (Honolulu: University of Hawai'i Press, 2013), 10.

and engagement. The Tang court needed to manage problems in multi-polar Asia by a variety of policies based on appropriateness".[8] This politics applied to both land and sea borders.

Interestingly, it was Arab and Iranian, in other words, foreign, merchants, or "Persian Gulf traders", as I have argued elsewhere, who can actually be considered as the initiators of the era of long-distance maritime trade in China.[9]

Maritime trade dominated by Iranian merchants prospered especially from the late seventh and first half of the eighth century until approximately the 750s. The development would imply that the reign period of Wu Zetian 武則天 (r. 690–705) actually had a relatively positive impact on the development of maritime trade – an issue that certainly needs further research. We know that Iranian in China supported Wu Zetian as ruling empress.[10] And there is indeed evidence that Wu Zetian may indeed have been indeed influenced by the "migrant" and merchant cultures of Iranians and Sogdians in her obviously pro-foreign-commercial policy.[11] Interestingly, not long after her rule, some time during the early eighth century, 714 at the latest, the position of a maritime trade officer (*shiboshi* 市舶使) was created. This creation provides further evidence of the Tang court's interest in overseas trade.

In the 750s, maritime trade was subject to its first incursion, probably due to corruption and over-taxation. Raids and massacres certainly contributed to a decline of maritime trade. Dissatisfaction with local conditions, including the burden imposed on foreign merchants by corruption, obviously constituted the cause for a raid on Guangzhou by Iranians (Bosi 波斯) and Arabs (Dashi 大食) in 758, who "looted the storehouses, burned residential homes, and then sailed away on the sea."[12] The eunuch maritime trade officer Lü Taiyi 呂太一 (in office 763–767) is said to have organized a rebellion, although his exact motivations remain unclear: he conscripted a group of soldiers, burnt three thousand overseas vessels, set fire to two thousand residential homes, and expelled the

8 Wang Zhenping, *Tang China in Multi-Polar Asia*, 10.

9 Angela Schottenhammer, "China's Gate to the Indian Ocean", 137; item, *Das songzeitliche Quanzhou im Spannungsfeld zwischen Zentralregierung und maritimem Handel. Unerwartete Konsequenzen des zentralstaatlichen Zugriffs auf den Reichtum einer Küstenregion.* Habilitationsschrift [Münchener Ostasiatische Studien, 80] (Stuttgart: Steiner 2002), 53–39, 57.

10 Rong Xinjiang 荣新江, *Sichou zhi lu yu Dongxi wenhua jiaoliu* 丝绸之路与东西文化交流 (Beijing: Beijing daxue chubanshe, 2015), 70; Rong Xinjiang, *Zhonggu Zhongguo yu wailai wenming* 中古中国与外来文明 (Beijing: Sanlian shudian, 2011), 204–221.

11 Antonio Forte even speaks of her "Internationalist and pacifist policy". Antonio Forte, *The Hostage An Shiguo ad His Offsprings* [Italian School of East Asian Studies, Occasional Papers, 6] (Kyōto: Italian School of East Asian Studies, 1995), 97.

12 *Jiu Tangshu* 舊唐書, by Liu Xu 劉昫 (Hou Jin) (Beijing: Zhonghua shuju, 1997), 198.5313.

military commissioner of Lingnan, Zhang Xiu 張休.[13] Besides Guangzhou, obviously Yangzhou was a major port for exportation. In the late 750s to early 760s, several thousand Arab and "Persian" (Bosi 波斯) traders were killed during local unrest, when the military governor and general of the imperial troops, Tian Shengong 田神功 (d. 776), turn against wealthy foreign merchants.[14] *Xin* and *Jiu Tangshu* explicitly state that Tian Shengong plundered the wealth and fortunes of the ordinary people and of merchants.[15]

In terms of maritime commerce, we consequently observe a *caesura* in the wavelike (with ups and downs) but still relatively steady development. The massacres but also rampant corruption prompted many foreign merchant families to migrate to China's peripheries and beyond in Southeast Asia, such as Champa, Thailand, or places in the thalassocratic state of Śrīvijaya, which comprised the Malay Archipelago, Sumatra, and later, also parts of Java. Were the court and the central government really interested in fomenting maritime trade, they had to act and especially reduce the burden of foreign merchants.

The first incursion, consequently, happened exactly during the initial phase of the Tang-Song transition, around 750. But soon afterwards we observe measures of the court to reactivate maritime trade. In 834, Emperor Wenzong 文宗 (r. 827–840) issued an edict providing protection for foreign "guests" in the provinces of Lingnan and Jiangnandong (Fujian, and Yangzhou). Wenzong pointed out that foreign ships and merchants had been overtaxed for many years and decreed that "except for the *bojiao* 舶脚 [anchorage-fee], *shoushi* 收市 [government monopoly duty], and *jinfeng* 進奉 [tribute payment], no additional taxes should be imposed on them."[16] This decree certainly has to be seen against a series of drop backs in maritime trade.

A second incursion occurred during and after the Huang Chao 黄巢 (?–884) Rebellion (878/879). Foreign merchant culture definitely influenced Chinese social and ruling elites in the *longue-durée* in their attitude towards foreign trade and commerce. This aspect will require a more thorough investigation in the future.

The period of the Song Dynasty (960–1279) was characterized by fundamental changes in almost all parts of China's society (culture, economy, politics, religion and ideology, science and technology). Most significant was the official

---

13 *Jiu Tangshu*, 11, 274; *Zizhi tongjian* 資治通鑑, ed. Hu Sanxing 胡三省 (1230–1302) (Beijing: Zhonghua shuju, 1956), 223.7157.

14 *Xin Tangshu* 141.4655.

15 *Jiu Tangshu* 124.3533; *Xin Tangshu* 144.4702.

16 For this decree, see *Quan Tangwen* 全唐文, ed. Dong Gao 董誥 (1740–1818) (Beijing: Zhonghua shuju, 1983), v. 1, 75.976.

appraisal of trade and commerce. Emperor Shenzong 神宗 (r. 1068–1085) explicitly intended to facilitate merchants to conduct trade and commerce in order to assist to fill the state coffers. Both domestic and foreign trade were promoted to help the state increasing its income, in particular in face of growing expenditure.[17] Commercial expansion, in addition to technical progress, inventions and scientific development, had their roots at least partly in the introduction of a new state ideology (*raison d'état*) and a new or revised reference of the state to its economic resources. Trade and commerce were assessed increasingly positively as a source to be tapped and not the parasite of society. This, of course, had decisive influences on China's maritime politics.

During the early Song, maritime politics was increasingly bureaucratized and institutionalized. In all ten Maritime Trade Offices (*shibo si* 市舶司), respectively Superintendencies of Maritime Trade (*shibo tiju si* 市舶提舉司) and Maritime Trade Bureaus (*shibo wu* 市舶務) were opened. *Maritime trade thus officially entered the government's bureaucratic structures and Maritime Trade Offices were integrated step-by-step into China's central finance administration*.[18]

As China was suddenly confronted with an unprecedented geo-political situation in East Asia, being no longer the undisputed empire surrounded by only loosely organized nomad tribes or loyal state organizations, it was a country among equals, neighboured by strong, well organized states in the north and northwest. China found herself confronted with a multi-state order and political instability, thus a geopolitical order that lead to what has been called an "arms race",[19] since the Khitan 契丹, Jurchen 女真 and later the Mongols all proved adept at acquiring and utilizing Song technological advances. In this context, also the traditional concept of the weak dynasty has been reviewed – definitely, the Song was not a militarily speaking strong dynasty but its capacity to survive and flourish in "the most multipolar East Asian world in Chinese imperial history" was remarkable.[20]

With the consolidation of the Song dynasty, China eventually emerged as a much more important participant in international trade than ever before,

17 For example *Song huiyao jigao* 宋會要輯稿, by Xu Song 徐松 [1781–1848] *et al.*, comp. (Taibei: Shijie shuju, 1964), Zhiguan 44/27a–b.

18 On this development see Angela Schottenhammer, "The Emergence of China as a Maritime Power".

19 John W. Chaffee, "Song China and the multi-state and commercial world of East Asia", *Crossroads – Studies on the History of Exchange Relations in the East Asian World* 1.2 (2010), 33–54.

20 John W. Chaffee, "Introduction: Reflections on the Sung", in John W. Chaffee and Paul J. Smith (eds.), *The Cambridge History of China*, vol. 5, part Two, *Sung China, 960–1279* (Cambridge: Cambridge University Press, 2014), 1–18, 3.

it became the motor of Asian maritime commerce.[21] Of course, the system of international maritime trade was still not yet a highly sophisticated and global one, but it was substantially more complex in organization and greater in volume than anything the world had previously known.[22]

Which role did the Tang-Song transition period play?

Very obvious is the *close interrelationship between political and military developments, and commerce*. The former are directly linked to China's geopolitical situation and integration in Asia. During the transition period, especially the tenth century, the ruling elites' struggle to survive and to guarantee their access to wealth in a politically, socially, and economically difficult situation had them seek for and mobilize new and/or other resources. China was split up in five dynasties and ten kingdoms. In order to guarantee the economic underpinnings of their regimes, especially the coastal kingdoms did what they could to foster maritime trade. *The Tang-Song-transition meant a significant expansion of official and private maritime commerce and the official appraisal of maritime trade as a source to be tapped.*

Initially, during the Tang, maritime trade was still *basically* used and sponsored in order to primarily satisfy the *private* interests of the Chinese social and ruling élites. A gradual shift of trade routes from traditional overland routes to maritime routes has also to be seen against the background of political instability in Central, North, and East Asia, and, last, but not least, in China itself. Starting in the tenth century, rulers and emperors began to treat maritime trade increasingly as a way to underpin the economic foundation of their regimes. They sought to use the profits derived from this trade not only for their own private consumption needs, but to pay for the political and economic maintenance of the state.[23] We know that the local rulers of China's south and southeast coastal regions – the Min 閩 (909–945), covering large parts of modern Fujian province, and later the independent rulers of the Quanzhou 泉州 region (945–978) and the Southern or Nan Han 南漢 (917–971) – during the

21 John W. Chaffee, "Song China and the multi-state and commercial world", 33–54.

22 Cf. Janet Abu-Lughod, *Before European hegemony: The world system A.D. 1250–1350* (New York and Oxford, 1989), 353.

23 Angela Schottenhammer, "Quanzhou's Early Overseas Trade: Local Politico – Economic Particulars During its Period of Independence", *Journal of Song-Yuan Studies* 29 (1999), 1–41; item, *Das songzeitliche* Quanzhou; Schottenhammer, "China's Emergence as a Maritime Power", in John W. Chaffee and Paul J. Smith (eds.), *The Cambridge History of China*, vol. 5, part Two, *Sung China, 960–1279* (Cambridge: Cambridge University Press, 2014), 437–525. This latter development has also been described by Lo Jung-pang, "Maritime Commerce and its Relation to the Sung Navy", *Journal of the Economic and Social History of the Orient* 12 (1969), 57–101.

period of division of the Five Dynasties. This was a decisive and far-reaching change in the attitude of Chinese rulers towards maritime trade. The reasons for this active sponsorship of maritime trade since the tenth century have to be sought for in (external) geopolitical circumstances and in the subsequent reassessment of the role of trade and commerce. In this context, *the Tang-Song transition was an accelerating period that prompted the fundamental changes* briefly addressed above. And it wonders little that within this geopolitical environment both China and the neighbouring countries sought to acquire more knowledge to improve their situation.

Kimura Jun 木村淳 and Mark Staniforth demonstrate this shift from the archaeological perspective, focussing on the increasingly active role of Chinese seafarers and merchants in the region of modern Vietnam. Again, politics, wars, and commerce are interrelated. And the navy played an ever-increasing role. The greatest period of advancement in Chinese shipbuilding technology occurred during the Song and Yuan dynasties.[24] The navy played a major role in winning the war against the kingdoms of Later Shu 後蜀 (934–965) and the Southern Tang and eventually subjugated Southern Han in 974. Afterwards, the importance of the navy gradually declined. But after the fall of the Northern Song dynasty in 1126 greater efforts were made and China finally possessed a permanent, sea-going imperial navy.[25] Many contemporary government officials advocated adoption of a strong naval policy, transforming the navy from a more or less mere defensive instrument into a weapon of offense. Li Gang 李綱 (1083–1140), chief councillor under Emperor Gaozong 高宗 (r. 1127–1162), and one of the leaders of the so-called "war party", played a major role in building up a strong imperial navy, and in mobilizing provincial naval units. We can observe such technological advances as both floating and graving docks (below ground level) in the shipyards, and the use of models and blueprints to standardize the production of government ships. Much of the shipbuilding was aimed at supplying the needs of the Song navy and domestic commerce, but the demand for seagoing ships was also great, especially since, beginning in the eleventh century, Chinese-style junks came to supplant the Arab dhows

24 Jacques Dars, "Les jonques chinoises de haute mer sous les Song et les Yuan", *Archipel* 18 (1979), 41–56; Pierre-Yves Manguin, "Trading ships of the South China Sea: Shipbuilding Techniques and their Role in the Development of Asian Trade Networks", *Journal of the Economic and Social History of the Orient* 36 (1993), 253–280.

25 These developments are described in Lo, "Maritime commerce and its relation to the Sung navy."

that had long dominated transoceanic trade in the Indian Ocean and southeast Asia.[26]

Li Man 李漫 introduces an economic aspect of the contemporary growing trade relations, focussing on trade relations between Southeast Asian, especially Javanese, merchants with the Southern or Nan Han kingdom in south China. He examines the question why Southeast Asian businessmen accepted valueless lead coins from the Southern Han.

Nan Han elites were active both militarily and commercially. They greatly sponsored maritime commerce. Our recent research has shown that we have to critically reassess and start to revise the traditional picture of the rulers of the Nan Han that official historiography has so far comported. We especially have to revise our picture of an ignorant, uneducated ruling élite with partly barbaric characteristics. Interesting to note is also the fact that obviously women played a much more important and active role also in politics than Song sources make us believe.[27] Both textual and archaeological evidence suggests that the Nan Han court "was certainly actively involved in maritime trade in the sense that it purchased and sold goods and received envoys. But we have no records that members of the Nan-Han court sent embassies abroad. Nor do we have evidence of Nan Han merchants privately sailing abroad with own ships. The evidence we have at least strongly suggests that both, the contemporary court and the local social élites, as well as private merchants basically still depended on foreign traders and ships to provide them with commodities from overseas. Hopefully, future archaeological evidence will cast more light on these aspects."[28]

The Tang-Song transition period was, thus, definitely an important phase in the development of maritime trade. Whereas in and for South and Southeast China long-distance maritime trade was of major importance, Northeast Asia during the time of separation and the existence of the Khitan Empire relied rather on what Li Man has called "jump-over contacts".[29]

---

26 Tansen Sen, *Buddhism, Diplomacy, and Trade: The Realignment of Sino-Indian Relations, 600–1400* (Honolulu: University of Hawaii Press, 2003), 177–178.

27 Angela Schottenhammer, "China's Gate to the South: Iranian and Arab Merchant Networks in Guangzhou During the Tang-Song Transition (c. 750–1050), Part 2: 900–c. 1050", *AAS Working Papers in Social Anthropology/ÖAW Arbeitspapiere zur Sozialanthropologie* 29 (2015), 1–30.

28 Angela Schottenhammer, "China's Gate to the South", 22f.

29 Li Man 李漫, "Tea, Fierce-Fire Oil and Maps: Northeastern China during the Tang-Song Transition", *Crossroads – Journal of the History of Exchange Relations in the East Asian World* 11 (2015), 31–44, 43.

2 The Song-Yuan Transition

After the conquest of China and the founding of the Yuan dynasty (1271–1368), the Mongols encouraged both overland and maritime trade, especially with the Islamic and Turkic worlds. They pursued ambitious geopolitical goals and had a strong interest in strengthening their role throughout Eurasia and the Indian Ocean world. Access to the Indian Ocean was of particular importance and can be designated an early "belt policy".[30]

During a transition from Han Chinese to Mongol rulers, one would expect great changes. But the dramatic turning point – in the past often considered as one from a heyday to dark age – was neither so dramatic or that much a fundamental change. In terms of maritime trade in particular, the active promotion continued, even though with special characteristics. Also the exchange of knowledge, products, and human migration, both on land and sea routes, actually achieved an unforeseen peak. The Yuan government re-established maritime trade offices, designated Quanzhou as the primary port for the South Seas trade, and sent numerous diplomatic missions abroad as far afield as India inviting tribute and trade. Overseas expeditions to Vietnam, Champa, Java, and Japan were intended to extend Mongol authority abroad and to impose control over important trading hubs throughout the Indian Ocean. Troops and military were supposed to implant Mongol hegemony in these regions, following which trade could commence. In order to be able to build up and govern their vast empire, they needed a massive accumulation and distribution of wealth and tried to attract merchants and goods from every corner of the world that they could gain access to.[31] This explains the close interrelationship between politics, military and trade that we have observed above. Many, or perhaps most, of their actions were commerce-driven.

That the Yuan Mongols were not only a continental power, but were very active in the maritime realm as well, is now accepted and has increasingly become a topic of research. Most recently, seeking for an explanation, scholars have emphasized global climatic changes – the "little Ice Age" – as a particular motor for their movements southward.[32] Environmental change, including falling temperatures, and the drying-up or loss of traditional grasslands, prompted

30 Angela Schottenhammer, *China and the Silk Roads* (*ca. 100 BCE to 1800 CE*).
31 See also Thomas T. Allsen, *The Steppe and the Sea*, 140, 168, and passim.
32 See, for example, Mukai Masaki, "The Interests of the Rulers, Agents and Merchants behind the Southward Expansion of the Yuan Dynasty", in *Academia Turfanica, Journal of the Turfan Studies: Essays on The Third International Conference on Turfan Studies, The Origins and Migrations of Eurasian Nomadic Peoples* (Shanghai: Shanghai guji chubanshe, 2010), 428–445.

various nomadic tribes to move further southwards and migrate from the Eurasian Inner Asian steppe regions to settle in parts of northern China, or even further southwards. Social and political developments in turn, principally the conquest of south China, also prompted another kind of southward movement, an active maritime endeavour in the Chinese seas and farther south, in the Indian Ocean in particular.

In terms of maritime trade, we may characterize this as a "continuous expansive transition", alluding also to the unforeseen militarization of maritime space in the area and the attempts to control important sea routes. *Definitely, the Song-Yuan transition meant both a further commercialization and a militarization of maritime politics.*

The militarization was of course a direct consequence of the Mongols' ambitious geopolitical interests and their aggressive push to get access to the countries overseas. The attempts of Qubilai Khan (r. 1260–1295) to subdue Japan are well known. But their maritime interests took the Mongols as far as Southeast and South Asia.[33]

It is interesting to see that maritime commerce was obviously so important to the Yuan rulers that they did not prohibit maritime trade, even when as early as 1309, Wokou 倭寇 pirates began to raid the Chinese coasts, and in the following years, the coasts of Zhejiang 浙江, Fujian 福建, and even of northern China (areas such as Shandong 山東 and Liaodong 遼東) were frequently raided. Nevertheless, the Yuan government did not close its doors and continued to permit Japanese merchants to conduct trade along the coasts of China, as Ma Guang 馬光 shows.

This early rise of piracy is closely linked to environmental changes and the "little Ice Age". In the thirteenth century, the temperature in Japan became colder, what significantly affected grain production and caused food shortage. There were many times famines, which not only caused domestic turbulences in Japan, but also forced Japanese people to plunder their neighbours, the Korean Peninsula and China. It was precisely around the time when the temperature began to drop in the 1220s, that *Wokou* started to raid the Korean Peninsula. From the 1350s to the 1380s, the temperature reached its lowest point, and at the same time, the *Wokou* raiding activities in Korea and China, too, climbed to a peak.

Whereas we can observe a strong government sponsorship of maritime trade during early Yuan times, most notably during the reign of Qubilai Khan,

33 Tansen Sen, "The Yuan Khanate and India: Cross-Cultural Diplomacy in the Thirteenth and Fourteenth Centuries", Asia Major, 3rd Series, 1/2:19 (2006), China at the Crossroads: A Festschrift in Honor of Victor H. Mair, 299–326.

the later Yuan maritime world is more characterized by private commerce and entrepreneurship. State sponsorship of ships, for example, was terminated in 1323. The selection of a special group of merchants, called *ortoγ* ("partnership" in Turkish), comprised mainly of Uighurs and Central Asian Muslims, with a kind of trading monopoly, was actually an attempt to strengthen government control over foreign trade. The *ortoγ* served as agents of foreign trade for the Yuan state and individual Mongol nobles, who provided them with ships and capital (mostly silver) to engage in commerce. The economy of Yuan China, to a large extent, rested on its sea power, as Lo Jung-pang has concluded.[34] They possessed extraordinarily high demands for such valuable tribute offerings, mainly gold, silver, pearls and precious stones, as well as for other precious objects. Such luxury items as gold, silver, or pearls played a significant role in their social hierarchies and, thus, in the administration and managing of their empire. Exerting tribute from foreign countries was considered a regular source of state income. Commercial interests, access to the wealth of the south, was the major motivation behind many of these missions. Embassies sent to southern coastal states of India successfully persuaded ten states to send commercial and tributary missions to China.[35] And in order to build up their commercial empire, the Mongols relied heavily in particular on private Muslim merchants and their networks. *We consequently also observe a privatization and a certain liberalization in maritime politics.*

In this historical context, cross-cultural knowledge transfer, namely state-sponsored knowledge collection, often of a military nature, about other countries, is a case in point. States have, of course, always collected military knowledge when confronted by potentially hostile neighbours, and during the Song, spying and intelligence gathering directed at the Liao, Xi Xia and later the Jin were common. However, there is little evidence of it in Song maritime relations except with regard to the Jin navy, and in the last years of the Song, to the Mongols. By contrast, John Chaffee argues that during the Yuan, intelligence gathering was an important part of its relations with the maritime states of Asia, and that this involved merchants and merchant organizations in addition to envoys, for whom this was an expected role. *The Song-Yuan transition also implied a more intense knowledge and technology transfer (military, geographical, cartographic, medicinal, mechanical, and many more) and intelligence gathering.*

34 Lo Jung-pang, *China as a Sea Power*, 319.

35 Lo Jung-pang, *China as a Sea Power*, 311.

3 The Yuan-Ming Transition

With the establishment of Ming rule, centuries of active promotion of foreign trade came to an end. But that did not mean that trade relations no longer existed, nor that China was suddenly isolated. The Ming initiated a tribute system that linked all trade to diplomatic relationships which subordinated tributary subjects to the nominal suzerainty of the Ming emperor. The first Ming ruler, Emperor Hongwu 洪武 (r. 1368–1398), was convinced that "if he did not prohibit private trade, the people could be lured by profit from trade and eventually be punished by law."[36] Against this background he permitted foreign trade only as part of the official tribute system while imposing a ban on private maritime trade, a political measure that had far-reaching consequences for the entire maritime region. For nearly two hundred years, from the enactment of the maritime trade prohibition in 1371 until its abolition in 1567, Ming subjects were prohibited from going to sea or contacting foreigners or face capital punishment. Hongwu, explained in his "Ancestral Injunctions" (*Huang Ming zuxun* 皇明祖訓, 1373): to maintain peaceful coastal borders and frontiers, China should not trouble overseas countries "lying far away in a corner", whose "lands would not produce enough for [China] to maintain", and whose people would not usefully serve China if integrated into the Empire. He furthermore uttered his dislike for military operations against these countries.[37] In a later version of the ancestral injunctions from 1395, fifteen countries were designated as "not to be invaded", namely Vietnam (Annam), Champa (Zhancheng), Korea, Japan, the Ryūkyūs, Taiwan (Lesser and Greater Liuqius), Siam, Cambodia, South India (Western Oceans), Samudra-Pasai, Java, Pahang, Baihua (Battack or West Java), Śrīvijaya, and Brunei.[38] Hongwu certainly was well aware of the fact that the primary purpose of foreign rulers behind sending "tribute missions" to China was trade, "but he wanted foreign rulers to be circumspect about it".[39]

The logic behind this prohibition policy is difficult to understand at first glance. Maritime trade, encouraged by authorities in China for centuries, suddenly came to a halt. Seagoing merchants were now deemed "pirates" who violated the laws by continuing to trade, or – in the eyes of the authorities – to

36 *Ming shilu*, *Taizong shilu* 太宗實錄, 70.8b.

37 Taizu Zhu Yuanzhang 太祖朱元璋 (1328–1398, r. 1368–1398), *Huang Ming zuxun* 皇明祖訓, 5b–6a (167–168), in *Xuxiu Siku quanshu*, fasc. 264, 165–189.

38 Wang Gungwu, "Ming Foreign Relations: Southeast Asia", in Denis Twitchett and Frederick Mote (eds.), *The Ming Dynasty, 1368–1644*, Part 2, vol. 8 of *The Cambridge History of China* (Cambridge: Cambridge University Press, 1998), 301–332, 312.

39 Wang Gungwu, "Ming Foreign Relations", 312.

smuggle. The effort to fight against these "pirates" also strained the state's fiscal resources. The response to this riddle has to be sought in the Confucian political ideology of the first Ming emperor.[40] Foreign trade for profit, for *purely* commercial purposes in other words, was incompatible with this political ideology.

The Yuan-Ming transition, as Ma Guang shows for Northeast China, *was not only a transition period from private maritime trade to official tribute trade but also a transition from the active, aggressive strategies of the Yuan rulers to more passive defence structures.* The military element remained present but the aggression came rather from abroad, from pirates. To this end, Ma Guang particularly focuses on the relation between natural disasters, climate change, and the outbreak of *Wokou* raids. Piracy during the Yuan-Ming transition can, consequently, not only to be traced back to domestic political-economic reasons, the subjective decision of the first Ming emperor to curtail all private maritime trade, but also had objective environmental reasons. In addition, I would add, *the transition theoretically also moved along the lines from a primacy of commerce to a primacy of ideology and security calculations.* In reality, certainly much more trade was conducted that official authorities would concede – much of it as contraband trade or "piracy". *Compared to the earlier dynastic transitions, in terms of maritime politics, the Yuan-Ming transition was consequently the most pronounced period of change.*

Nevertheless, we cannot speak of a complete rupture. While the Yuan-Ming transition constituted a kind of "rupture" in some aspects, we can observe a gradual transition of developments in other aspects. The sea transportation system or the Wokou problem, for example, continued. And changes in the coastal defence system took decades. To link the two dynasties Yuan and Ming, Richard von Glahn and Paul Jakov Smith have advanced the idea of a Song-Yuan-Ming transition.[41] stating that "the three centuries between the Tang-Song transformation and later imperial China (roughly 1100 to 1400) remain a black hole".[42] In their eyes, the Yuan and Ming dynasties show similar characteristics and can be considered part of the same phase. Li Bozhong 李伯重 has pointed out that the evolution of agriculture in the Jiangnan 江南 region during the thirteenth and fourteenth centuries "was marked not by a

40 For a detailed analysis see especially the PhD dissertation of Li Kangying, *The Ming Maritime Trade Policy in Transition, 1368–1567* [East Asian Maritime History, 8] (Wiesbaden: Otto Harrassowitz, 2010).

41 Paul Jakov Smith, Richard von Glahn (eds.), *The Song-Yuan-Ming Transition in Chinese History* (Cambridge: Harvard University Press, 2003).

42 Richard von Glahn, "Imagining Pre-modern China", in Paul Jakov Smith, Richard von Glahn (eds.), *The Song-Yuan-Ming Transition*, 35–70, here 35.

sudden or dramatic rupture but by cyclical fluctuations and spatial variations", and has demonstrated that "the Song-Yuan-Ming transition was not a turning point but merely a phase in a continuous process of development".[43] As Ma Guang shows in his PhD dissertation, also Li Zhi'an 李治安 and Zhao Shiyu 趙世瑜 have articulated the same point, namely that there was no great shift between the two dynasties.[44]

In terms of maritime trade politics, I think we can definitely speak of a rupture, but it was gradual and not sudden and it varied depending on certain aspects of maritime administration. Looking at the politics towards Japan, where many Wokou originated, we can, for example, observe significant changes during this transition period. In the beginning, Hongwu adopted a diplomatic strategy toward Japan, and only when all his diplomatic advances failed, he disillusioned shifted from "Wokou diplomacy", as Ma Guang has called it, to the breach of relationship, turning his attention to strengthening and fortifying the coastal defence system.

The Yuan-Ming transition period definitely had a far-reaching influence not only for China, but for the development of the entire East Asian macro region. With the initiation of the maritime prohibition policy foreign merchants took over large parts and great percentages of the maritime trade that had formerly been conducted by Chinese. Official maritime trade became part of the tribute system and was "ritualized".

As mentioned above, we also observe a strengthening of Confucian ideology. In this context, many Ming Chinese literati had little interest in maritime affairs. But, especially from the later Ming period, when overseas commerce again boomed, especially because of the advent of the Europeans, who possessed a sheer insatiable demand for Chinese products, we do have Chinese texts on the maritime world, including sea route descriptions. Prominent examples are Zhang Xie's 張燮 (1574–1640) *Dongxi yangkao* 東西洋考 (ca. 1617), Yan Congjian's 嚴從簡 *Shuyu zhouzilu* 殊域周咨錄 (Record of the Dispatches Concerning Various Regions), completed 1574, printed 1583; Shen Maoshang's 慎懋賞 *Siyi guangji* 四夷廣記 (Extensive Records of all Barbarians), early seventeenth century, or the Zheng He 鄭和 map included in Mao Yuanyi's 茅元儀

43 Li Bozhong, "Was There a 'Fourteenth-Century Turning Point'? Population, Land, Technology and Farm Management", in Paul Jakov Smith, Richard von Glahn (eds.), *The Song-Yuan-Ming Transition in Chinese History*, 175.

44 Li Zhi'an 李治安, "Yuandai ji Ming qianqi shehui biandong chutan" 元代及明前期社會變動初探, *Zhongguo shi yanjiu* 中國史研究, special issue (2005), 83–98; Zhao Shiyu 趙世瑜, "Ming qingshi yu Song Yuan shi: shixue shi yu shehui shi shijiao de fansi" 明清史與宋元史：史學史與社會史視角的反思, *Beijing shifan daxue xuebao* (*shehui kexue ban*) 北京師範大學學報(社會科學版), No. 5 (2007), 87–95.

Wubei zhi 武備志 of 1621. Another text, although we do not know the author, is the rutter *Shunfeng xiangsong* 順風相送 (Fair Winds for Escort), probably late sixteenth century,[45] which describes historical routes from Japan to Java and from Timor to Hormuz.[46] Much of this knowledge was of course orally transferred.

It springs to mind that many of the texts that were produced in the Ming, at least partly copied from each other as well as from other texts. Some contain various mistakes, giving the impression that their authors possessed a pure encyclopaedic or philosophical rather than a geographical or technological interest in their topic. Even mythical and fantastic countries still appear in some works. Elke Papelitzky addresses the questions of which kind of literati were interested in this kind of technical knowledge and to what extend they really understood the topics they were writing about.

Texts of a more practical, for example, military nature, such as the just mentioned *Wubei zhi* or rutters used for navigation, of course required correct knowledge. How can you organise military defence strategies against pirates, if the knowledge transported is not reliable, both in terms of geographical and technological expertise? *In the field of maritime politics against piracy, that experienced a peak at the beginning of the Ming-Qing transition in the 1550s, we can in fact observe a re-militarization and an increasing importance of security calculations that was to endure at least until the reign period of the Yongzheng* (r. 1723–1735) emperor. Mathieu Torck examines the correlation between the gradual intensification of continental and seaborne warfare on the one hand and an increasing number of military treatises characterized by an inclusive approach that also addressess topics such as health, diet and sanitation in the armies and navies of the era. With a focus on the works of Qi Jiguang 戚繼光 (1528–1588), a prominent army commander, official, and prolific military writer, he analyses the systematization of practical instructions and explores their innovative character and unique value.

Against the same background of a need for practical and objective knowledge, we also have to understand China's politics in face of diseases and

45 Originally, the text had been dated to approximately 1430. But the *Shunfeng xiangsong* mentiones some place names that definitely have to be dated into the sixteenth century. See the entry on the website by Chen Jiarong 陈佳荣, http://www.world10k.com/blog/?p=2028 (accessed on September 23, 2020).

46 John Guy, "China in India: Porcelain trade and attitudes in collecting in early Islamic India", in Geoff Wade, James K. Chin (eds.), *China and Southeast Asia: Historical Interactions* (London, New York: Routledge, 2019), 44–84, 51–52. That these routes are described in a sixteenth-century text does not mean that the Chinese were actually sailing along these routes at that time.

epidemics, many of which were results of natural disasters or were "imported" from abroad. In the coastal region of Fujian considerably more epidemic diseases broke out than in other regions in south China; Fujian – together with Guangdong a door towards the maritime world – was one of the most seriously affected regions in terms of epidemic diseases.[47] The frequency of widespread diseases reached a peak in the late fifteenth and early sixteenth centuries, and in many cases, we can observe a clear correlation with natural disasters (such as floods, typhoons, and droughts) and seasonal changes. A major pandemic disease that crossed oceans during the Ming-Qing transition period were smallpox, and we can observe both in the late Ming and the early Qing period that rulers and local authorities/officials were concerned about the treatment of people and the procurement of cheap medicines with simple ingredients. The publication and dissemination of medicinal texts and handbooks with recipes, for example against regional diseases like malaria, dysentery, and cholera, was also sponsored.[48] Xu Zhexin introduces the compilation, printing, and spread of medical texts in the coastal region of Fujian. People living during the Ming-Qing transition were consequently, probably to a greater extent than during any other transition period before, confronted with new risks – the transfer of hitherto unknown diseases. Causes have at least partly to be sought for in the increasing mobility of people worldwide.

New risks and challenges definitely arrived with the advent of the Europeans just during that time period. The Dutch VOC authorities intended to exploit the politically complicated circumstances, when the new rulers of China, the Manchus, sought to consolidate their new regime against the Ming loyalist Zheng 鄭 family (Zheng Zhilong 鄭芝龍, Zheng Chenggong 鄭成功 (1624–1662), alias Coxinga,[49] and Zheng Jing 鄭經). The conflict with Coxinga, who passed away in 1662, and his successors, in 1661, prompted Kangxi not only to prohibit private people to sail abroad but even to order an evacuation

47 In Fujian, for example 136 times, while in Guangdong and Guangxi respectively only 4 and 47 times. See Wang Shuanghuai 王雙懷, "Mingdai Huanan de ziran zaihai jiqi shikong tezheng", 明代華南的自然災害及其時空特征, *Dili yanjiu* 18 (1999), 152–160, 158; also Xu Zhexin, "The Environment, Perceptions, and Publication of Medical Texts in Fujian during the Ming Period (1368 to 1644)", in Angela Schottenhammer, Mathieu Torck and Wim De Winter (eds.), *Seafaring, Trade, and Knowledge Transfer. Maritime Politics and Commerce in Early Middle Period to Early Modern China* (Leiden: Brill, 2026), 154–179.

48 Xu Zhexin, "The Environment, Perceptions, and Publication of Medical Texts"; Wang Zunwang 王尊旺 and Cai Hongxin 蔡鴻新, *Fujian yiji kao* 福建醫籍考 (Xiamen: Xiamen University Press, 2016).

49 This is a westernization of the Chinese expression "Guoxingye 國姓爺", literally "Lord (permitted to carry) the surname of the imperial family".

of the coastal population from the coasts to the hinterlands, in order to cut off Coxinga and his successors, the Zheng "rebels" on Taiwan, from their human and material resources on the mainland. This evacuation or relocation of the entire southeastern coastal strip, referred to as "*qianjie ling*" 遷界令 in Chinese, was implemented between 1656 and 1669. Seeking to expand along the Chinese coast and intensifying trade relations, the Dutch offered the Manchus (the arch enemies of the Zhengs) their maritime military force to facilitate trade with China. At the same time, the Dutch profited from the Manchus' coastal evacuation policy, and carried out detailed investigations along the China coast, while no official or private individuals could oppose their hydrographical charting activities. These nautical investigation activities of the Dutch are introduced by Cheng Weichung 鄭維中. They clearly show an entirely new challenge that directly prompted a reinforcement of security calculations. The Kangxi emperor was well aware of potential dangers. Antoine Gaubil (1689–1759) recorded in his memories from a court meeting with Kangxi soon after the emperor's death:

"The Portuguese [*i.e.* the Spanish] of Luzon have many Chinese, and they could easily become very powerful in the countries neighbouring China and Japan. Their king in Europe is extremely rich and possesses great states far from Europe. He is of the same family as the king of France, a powerful and bellicose nation which is esteemed and respected on land and sea throughout the world."[50]

"The Russians, Dutch, and the Portuguese, like the other Europeans, are able to accomplish whatever they undertake, no matter how difficult. They are intrepid, clever, and know how to turn a profit. As long as I reign, there is nothing to worry about from them for China ... But if our government were to become weak, if we were to weaken our vigilance over the Chinese in the southern provinces, and over the large number of boats that leave every year for Luzon, Batavia, Japan, and other countries, or if divisions were to erupt among us Manchus ... what would become of our Empire? With the Russians to the north, the Portuguese from Luzon to the east, the Dutch to the south, (they) would do with China whatever they want."[51]

Maritime trade prohibition policy in Japan had long-lasting socio-economic impacts on the emerging Tokugawa world, as well as on the overseas communities that were cut off from the motherland. Still, trade relations were not

---

50 Antoine Gaubil, S.J., *Correspondance de Pékin, 1722–1759* (Geneva: Librairie Droz, 1970), 710 (letter to P. Berthier 1752). This correspondence is also quoted in Laura Hostetler, Qing Colonial Enterprise. Ethnography and Cartography in Early Modern China (Chicago: University of Chicago Press, 2001), 39–41.

51 Antoine Gaubil, S.J., *op. cit.*, 711.

necessarily severed and were continued in alternative ways through Chinese and Dutch mediators. For some time, Japanese merchant communities continued to uphold their position in Southeast Asian societies and to play a meaningful role. Leonard Blussé investigates the fate of Japanese trade with the area of what is now Vietnam and the economic activities of Japanese merchant communities there after the instalment of the *kaikin*.

The Philippine Archipelago remained a region of concern in terms of security considerations during the early Qing. An edict of 1716 also reflects official concerns about maritime security, stating that "after hundreds of years, we are afraid that [China] will suffer from overseas countries, for example, from the European countries";[52] intellectual elites, too, uttered their fears. But relations were not only characterized by suspicions from the Chinese side. The Kangxi Emperor was generally speaking very open and curious and maintained good relationships with various Jesuit missionaries. And Manila, the city founded by the Spaniards between 1565 and 1571, within just a couple of years, developed as one of the most important crossroads for merchants from many places worldwide, but especially from China, Japan, and New Spain. Ubaldo Iaccarino discusses the role of the Chinese and the Japanese merchants in Manila and in the other ports of the Philippine Archipelago at the end of the sixteenth century and in the first decades of the seventeenth century, focusing on the nature of their trade and on the identities of the several traders, smugglers and adventures who crossed the seas between China, Japan and the Philippines on behalf of Chinese Mandarins, Japanese local rulers (*daimyōs*) and international merchant guilds.

Flourishing trade notwithstanding, violence was frequently involved in contacts between Chinese and Europeans. A bloody massacre the Chinese residing in the Parian in Manila was committed by the Spanish in 1604. In 1656, Coxinga declared an embargo on all Chinese shipping to Manila.[53] After he had seized Taiwan from the Dutch in 1662, he demanded from the Spanish authorities in

52 Lo-Shu Fu, *A Documentary Chronicle of Sino-Western Relations* (1644–1820) (Tucson: The University of Arizona Press, 1966), 106, with reference to *DaQing lichao Shengzu Renhuang shilu* 大清歷朝聖祖仁皇實錄 (Kangxi) (Taibei: Huawen shuju, 1964), 160.26–27 (November 24, 1693).

53 Cheng Wei-chung, *War, Trade and Piracy in the China Seas 1622–1683* [TANAP Monographs on the History of Asian-European Interaction, 16] (Leiden: E.J. Brill, 2013), 177. During a short truce between Manchu troops and Coxinga the same year, even false rumours spread around Mindanao that Coxinga was preparing a large fleet to conquer the Philippines. A galleon that was expected from Acapulco that year ran aground on the northern tip of Luzon. The Spanish later tried to salvage the silver from the wreck (pp. 175–176).

Manila to pay him tribute – a demand that resulted in another bloody massacre of Chinese in Manila.[54]

Especially the Dutch tried for some time to use a policy of shock and awe to force the Chinese to open its borders for trade. This does not mean that diplomacy was unimportant, on the contrary. It was clear that special rules and official rituals had to be followed and had to accompany or precede any trading relations. The process dictated the need for a specific use of language and etiquette in order to obtain or to negotiate trade permissions, for which intercultural linguists and writers often fulfilled a crucial role. One basic requirement was an official letter addressed to the emperor and written in perfect classical Chinese. How could the Dutch prepare such a qualified letter of credence to the Chinese authorities? This is an aspect Ellen Cai Xiangyu addresses. In terms of authorship, for example, although the chief of the Dutch factory at Canton, the High Government of the Dutch East India Company (VOC), Andreas Everard van Braam Houckgeest, had insisted that the letter of credence should be issued by the Commissioners-General in Batavia in the name of the 'King of the Netherlands' (the stadtholder Willem V of Orange Nassau), it came to bear merely the signatures of the four Commissioners-General when it was presented to the Chinese officials in Canton. In other words, it meant that the Dutch embassy was dispatched by functionaries of a commercial company rather than the King of a state. Such an arrangement was institutionally unacceptable for the tribute system of the Qing court and therefore caused further negotiation between the Chinese officials and the Dutch ambassadors in Canton. The Hong 行 merchants (see below) and native interpreters were also involved. Ellen Xiangyu Cai reconstructs the process of the negotiation, pointing out that the re-rendering of the letter of credence was, for the Chinese authorities, both an important step to assist and discipline the Dutch ambassadors, and a necessary procedure to integrate the Dutch embassy into the tribute system of the Qing dynasty.

The complicated interaction between Chinese merchants and official authorities and European agents is also addressed by Wim De Winter. In a comparative analysis of the practical interaction of the Austrian-Netherlandish Ostend Company in China and Bengal, Wim De Winter shows that this was basically a learning process, shaped in the cradle of foreign customs and policies established over a *longue durée*, which often clashed with European ideologies and preconceptions. Relations were often marked by both commercial and political obligations, as well as debts, which required a context of power in order to

54 Cheng Wei-chung, *War, Trade and Piracy*, 225.

be enforced. The particular enforcement of such courtly power relations also carried a long precedent, going back to seventeenth-century or earlier customs, and clearly defined the space for commercial and non-commercial exchange in both China and Bengal. Chinese authorities seem to have enforced their rules more strictly than the Bengali or Mughal authorities. Hierarchical elements played an essential role in both contexts, while at the same time local interaction demonstrates that there was space for individual interpretation and that we should be careful to characterize China's (and also other countries') maritime politics generalized from a Sino- or Eurocentric perspective. Agents on the practical micro-level did of course have to act according to government rules, but these examples show that concrete results in negotiations were frequently also a result of interaction on individual levels.

Trade between China and European merchants slumped in the mid-seventeenth century during the Ming-Qing dynastic transition and the Qing maritime ban, and remained modest before 1700. But the eighteenth century witnessed significant growth in European demand for Chinese goods such as porcelains and silks, and increasingly for tea. During the late seventeenth and early eighteenth centuries, China sold at least one million pieces of porcelain to the British East India Company alone. After an incident in 1757, European traders were restricted to the single port of Guangzhou (or Canton, as European referred to it). The so-called "Canton system", which governed European trade with China from 1760 until the outbreak of the Opium War in 1839 confined all maritime trade with Western countries to Guangzhou/Canton. European merchants – most of whom had been obliged to join "East India Companies", which acted as national cartels for Asian trade – were required to conduct their business with a consortium of twenty-odd Chinese merchant firms (*hang*, or *hong* or in Cantonese), who became known as the Cohong 公行 merchants. The major purpose of the Cohong was not, as previously thought, to eliminate competition and disadvantage foreign commerce, but on the contrary to preserve competition so that the trade with the Europeans could continue and foreigners would not be discouraged from returning to China. Paul Van Dyke has concluded that the Cohong "provided the means whereby [a select group of Chinese] partnerships could gain more control and channel foreign investments to China's production areas to finance expansion, and all without sacrificing competition and growth." Prices remained competitive, and increasing numbers of foreigners were attracted. Van Dyke thus considers the Cohong a "market managing group," not a monopoly.[55] But when the triple

55 Paul A. Van Dyke, *Merchants of Canton and Macao*, vol. 2, *Success and Failure in Eighteenth-Century Chinese Trade* (Hong Kong, Hong Kong University Press, 2016), 4, 6.

alliance began to fall apart after Cai Hunqua's death in 1770, the Cohong had outlived its purpose and was abolished the following year.

Patrizia Carioti finally demonstrates how the Ming and Qing authorities lost direct control over coastal and overseas trade during the Ming-Qing conquest. Many Chinese escaped the chaos in China and migrated to Southeast Asia and to Japan, giving birth to many Chinese overseas communities. In Japan they scattered all over the entire archipelago, especially in Kyūshū, and formed the *Tōjin machi* 唐人街. The overseas Chinese played a significant role in the historical intercourse between China and Japan, and exerted profound influence on the Japanese decisions in foreign policy, first of all with regard to China, but also in general on the political and economic strategies pursued. Her contribution can attest to the fact that developments in one of China's most important trading partner, Japan, especially the increasing migration of Chinese to Japan, could influence China's maritime politics and that the large Chinese community in Nagasaki, conversely, also influenced Japan's maritime politics. Actually, both under the Kangxi and the Yongzheng reign spies were sent to Japan to inquire about the economic and political situation in Japan.[56] Whereas Kangxi was still primarily concerned about economic issues, decreasing imports of copper exports from Japan, Yongzheng was more worried about possible military threats. In 1728, the governor-general of Zhejiang, Li Wei 李衛 (1687?–1738),[57] in a memorial reported about all kinds of illegal activities in the East Asian waters. Li Wei recalled the historical situation during Ming times, when Japanese pirates suddenly attacked the country and caused devastation.[58] He thereupon officially inspected important ports and ordered officials from the coastal prefectures to demonstrate Qing power and make inspection tours in order to prevent any possible perils from the sea. At the end of his memorial he comes to a clear conclusion: "Although Japan is a tiny dwarf barbarian island, it relies on its big copper cast cannons

56 Angela Schottenhammer, "Japan – the tiny Dwarf? Sino-Japanese Relations from the Kangxi to the Early Qianlong Reigns", in Angela Schottenhammer (ed.), *The East Asian Mediterranean – Maritime Crossroads of Culture, Commerce, and Human Migration* [East Asian Maritime History, 6] (Wiesbaden: Otto Harrassowitz, 2008), 331–388; Angela Schottenhammer, "Empire and Periphery? The Qing Empire's Relations with Japan and the Ryūkyūs (1644–c. 1800), a Comparison", *The Medieval History Journal* 15.2 (2012), 139–196.

57 He has a brief entry in Arthur W. Hummel, *Eminent Chinese of the Ch'ing Period* (Taiwan: SMC Publishing, 1991), 2 vols., vol. 2, 720–721.

58 *Huangchao zhanggu huibian* 皇朝掌故彙編, by Zhang Shouyong 張壽鏞 (1876–1945) (Beijing: Qiushi shushe, 1902), Waibian 外編, *juan* 14 (Riben guo 日本國), quoted by Guo Yunjing, "Views of Japan and Policies Toward Japan in the Early Qing", in Joshua Fogel (ed.), *Sagacious Monks and Bloodthirsty Warriors: Chinese Views of Japan in the Ming-Qing Period* (Norwalk: EastBridge, 2002), 88–108, 104.

which can attack from a far-away distance and its extraordinarily sharp Wodao swords; already in the former Ming Dynasty [Japan] belonged to the evils of the seas (*haihuan* 海患); in the Eastern Seas (*Dongyang* 東洋) it was considered a violent invader (*qiangkou* 強寇). Our dynasty has a majestic spirit, and they [i.e. the Japanese] have prostrated themselves from fear and hidden, so that for many years they have had no way to offend against China (*zhonghua* 中華)."[59]

This was an obvious warning to pay more attention to developments there. The use of the term "powerful invader" alone suggests, as Guo Yunjing also emphasizes, that during the Yongzheng reign Chinese authorities had "reached a deeper realization of Japan's expansionist ambitions".[60] But Qing China also looked further into the Asia-Pacific region. Through the trade, especially of Fujian merchants, with the Spanish in the Philippine, China was eventually linked up with the new Spanish provinces in the New World, both via the Pacific, and the Atlantic and Indian Ocean. A "Pacific Silk Road" came into existence, and the economic importance of the Philippine trade and the influx of silver into China grew significantly. In this context, we also observe an increasing geographic awareness of the Pacific world, beyond the Philippines. Already the Italian Jesuit missionary Matteo Ricci (1552–1610) marked the famous early modern 'silver city', Potosí, on his world map for China's Wanli Emperor (r. 1572–1620), *Kunyu wanguo quantu* 坤輿萬國全圖 (*Map of the Myriad Countries of the World*). In the mid- and late eighteenth century, we see a country like Peru in Spanish America drawn as a square or circles into maritime space opposite of China's southeast coastal regions. An untitled Chinese map of 1743, for example, shows a Beiduxi 北度西 Mountain (that is, Potosí), said to contain many silver mines, and states that the silver is used for exchange.[61] The mountain is drawn as a three-peak mountain in the middle of the water east of Wenzhou 溫州 on the Southeast Chinese coast, as if the map drafter wanted to symbolically emphasise the importance of this silver mountain for China. And a square text block below says that this mountain contains many silver mines, and the silver is extracted for exchange. Also Transpacific routes, although some existed already shortly after the Spanish Manila galleon

59 *Shizong Xianhuangdi zhupi yuzhi*, 174.25 a–b (201), section 8.

60 Guo Yunjing, "Views of Japan and Policies Toward Japan in the Early Qing", 105.

61 See Richard J. Smith, "Mapping China's World: Cultural Cartography in Late Imperial Times", in Wen-hsin Yeh (ed.), *Landscape, Culture, and Power in Chinese Society*, 71–77; Marcel Destombes, Wang P'an, Liang Chou et Matteo Ricci: Essai sur la cartographie chinoise de 1593 à 1603", in Appréciation par l'Europe de la tradition chinoise *a partir du XVIIe siècle; actes du IIIe Colloque International de Sinologie*; Centre de Recherches Interdisciplinaire de Chantilly (CERIC), 11–14 septembre 1980 (Paris: Les Belles Lettres, Cathasia, 1983), 47–65.

trade started in the second half of the sixteenth century, become more popular only by the mid-eighteenth century.[62]

At the same time – and undoubtedly fostered by the mediation of European and New Spanish missionaries, not only Jesuits, but also Augustinians, Dominicans, or Franciscans – knowledge and technology exchange was gradually intensifying, for example in the field of medicine.[63] *The Ming-Qing transition, consequently led to a further commercialization, privatization and opening towards the maritime world that we may call 'internationalisation' or 'globalisation', even though this was not an entirely linear process.*

It is interesting to observe that more or less around the same time, with the ascension of the Qianlong emperor to the throne in 1736, China's maritime politics gradually started to change. Increasingly less serious efforts were obviously undertaken any more to comprehend the situation in other countries overseas. In the late eighteenth century, the maritime realm gradually seems to have disappeared almost completely from Qianlong's political agenda in the last perhaps three to four decades of the eighteenth century – what may at least partly explain why the late Qianlong emperor was obviously surprised by various actions of Europeans. The reasons for this new passivity have mostly been traced back to personal reasons, a "loss of impulse"[64] or a tiredness and exhaustion, as Mark C. Elliott explains: Qianlong, other than Kangxi, was "both proud and insecure. Decades of responsibility for affairs of so diverse and huge a realm, perhaps had worn him out."[65] Definitely, I would argue, the political and economic success China had reached in the mid-eighteenth century, the consolidation of its continental borders, especially the successful wars against and the subsequent extinction of the Dzungars (China had reached its greatest territorial extension in 1759), treaties with the Russians,

62 This is attested to by first research results from our ERC AdG project TRANSPACIFIC, which has received funding from the European Research Council (ERC) under the European Union's Horizon 2020 Research and Innovation Programme (Grant agreement No. 833143).

63 See, for example, Angela Schottenhammer, "'Peruvian balsam': an example of transoceanic transfer of medicinal knowledge", *Journal of Ethnobiology and Ethnomedicine* 16:69 (2020), 1–20, https://doi.org/10.1186/s13002-020-00407-y.

64 Jonathan Spence speaks of an undercurrent "running through many of Qianlongs's pronouncements and actions" – "that of a man who has been praised too much and has thought too little, of someone who has played to the gallery in public life, mistaken grandeur for substance, sought confirmation and support for even routine actions, and is not really equipped to make difficult or unpopular decisions." (p. 101); Jonathan Spence, *The Search for Modern China* (New York: W.W. Norton & Company, 1990), 99.

65 Mark C. Elliott, *Emperor Qianlong. Son of Heaven, Man of World* [Library of World Biography, ed. by Peter N. Steams] (New York, San Francisco, Boston: Longman, 2009), 140.

and the economic prosperity of the country, played a major role in the shift from a centuries-old active maritime politics to a passive one, partly even characterized by ignorance – a tendency that is also reflected in the knowledge of the social elites about the maritime world. Scholars certainly knew more about the maritime world beyond in the sixteenth and seventeenth centuries than in the nineteenth century. That a prominent Qing scholar specialized in philology and textual studies, including history, Yu Yue 俞樾 (1821–1907), in the late nineteenth century claims that he does "not know where the country of Peru is located", nor "what kind of tree this balsam is",[66] that was mentioned on the 1743-map we introduced above, seems difficult to understand. But it obviously reflects a tendency among Chinese intellectual elites who, especially after the Opium Wars (1839–42 and 1856–60), were no longer interested in Western knowledge and traditions if it could not be used for practical use, and promoted instead a "return to antiquity" (*fugu* 復古) and to Chinese traditions *Zhongxue wei ti, Xixue wei yong* 中學為體，西學為用). But this was part of late imperial China's modernisation process.

4 China's Maritime Politics in the *Longue-durée*

Sinological scholarship has long emphasized China's land orientation, giving the impression that the Chinese were not interested in the seas, or in foreign trade as a commercial undertaking, and that all that they would tolerate was a form of official tribute trade. This assumption has undergone a fundamental reassessment in the last decades. It is now clear that even during maritime trade prohibitions trade relations were continued. Lo Jung-pang 羅榮邦 (1912–1981), a famous Chinese maritime historian, was well ahead of his time in acknowledging the essential role maritime space played for the Chinese, especially in the period between the eleventh century and the Yuan-Ming transition (roughly 1350–1400).[67] Since the 1980s and 90s, gradually more and more scholars have come to see that from early times on we have evidence of China's specific interest in, and use of the seas for political, military and commercial

66 *Chaxiang shi congchao* 茶香室叢鈔, by Yu Yue 俞樾 (1821–1907), in Zhen Fan 貞凡, Gu Sheng 顧馨 and Xu Minxia 徐敏霞, annotated version of *Chaxiang shi congchao* 茶香室叢鈔 (Beijing Zhonghua shuju. 2006), vol. 4, 1819, https://archive.org/stream/02097536.cn#page/n60/mode/2up.

67 I particularly want to recommend his both path-breaking and excellent overview, see Lo Jung-pang, *China as a Sea Power, 1127–1368: A Preliminary Survey of the Maritime Expansion and Naval Exploits of the Chinese People During the Southern Song and Yuan Periods*, edited by Bruce A. Elleman (Singapore: National University of Singapore Press, 2011).

purposes, that maritime trade developed continuously and that we can observe a first peak during what we have called the Tang-Song transition.

The political defragmentation as well as political instability along the traditional overland routes, I would argue, rather fostered an active maritime politics of both the Tang, local coastal kingdoms, and the Song. In addition, ideological changes, too, were conducive to a more positive reference of Chinese governments to maritime trade, especially the reassessment of the role of trade. Political instability within China, conversely, frequently had negative effects but, in the *longue-durée*, prompted governments to actively sponsor maritime trade and recruit foreign merchants, as we can observe in many occasions particularly during the tenth and eleventh century. Confronted with an unprecedented geo-political situation in East Asia, the founders of the Song Dynasty sought for new solutions to strengthen the country and guarantee long-term stability to re-unify China after it had fallen apart into several competing polities in the early tenth century.

We can consequently observe a gradual shift from maritime trade satisfying primarily the *private* interests of the Chinese social and ruling élites, to a maritime trade policy that focused more on serving the interests of the state as a whole. This was a decisive and far-reaching change in China's maritime politics, and it became especially obvious in the tenth century when China fell apart into several smaller dynasties and kingdoms that sought new material and financial means to guarantee the underpinning of their regimes.[68] But we can discern the first signs of this shift already in Tang times.

Considering the Tang-Song-Yuan transition, we observe a cautious but growing liberalization, commercialization, privatization, and bureaucratization; at the same time, it is obvious that at least until early to mid-Yuan times, the ruling elites sought for a strict control of maritime trade. How much liberty was possible and how much central control necessary, this had been a continuous debate among Song officials in the eleventh century in particular.[69]

Developments and politics were not always steady but were sometimes changed or experienced setbacks. Four times in total, for example, the Yuan rulers imposed a maritime ban, suspending foreign trade, prohibiting merchants from sailing abroad, and abolishing the Superintendencies of Maritime Trade. They even forced private merchants to enter government service. But,

68 See for example Hugh Clark, "The Southern Kingdoms between the T'ang and Sung", in vol. 5, part One, Denis Twittchett and Paul J. Smith (eds.), *The Five Dynasties and Sung China, 960–1279*, 133–205; Angela Schottenhammer, "Quanzhou's Early Overseas Trade".

69 Angela Schottenhammer, "China's Emergence as a Maritime Power", 479–482.

after 1325, regulations were again liberalized and maritime relations experienced a new peak.

During the Tang-Song-Yuan period, we also observe a slow but growing militarization of maritime politics that reached a peak in Yuan times and continued into the early Ming. From late Song to early Ming dynasties (1368–1644) China was definitely also a naval power. The Mongol rulers used their navy to assert political claims across the entire macro region. The early Ming period, under Emperor Yongle, is characterized by unforeseen political, military, and commercial maritime expansion. Like during the Yuan, China actively and often aggressively expanded overseas. In this context, it has convincingly been argued that it was the Yuan's expansive maritime politics that actually enabled or "paved the way" for the Yongle emperor to launch the famous Zheng He expeditions (1405–1433).[70] After 1435, China *officially* retreated from the seas and prohibited all private maritime commerce, until internal socioeconomic and financial problems and the great demand of foreigners – after 1500 also including the Europeans – for Chinese products urged the government to "reopen" its borders for trade.

It should also be mentioned that while the first Ming rulers attempted to treat foreign trade as part of an official tribute system and subordinated it to the ministry of rites (*libu* 禮部), in general the ritual dimensions of maritime politics decreased over time. In 1685, foreign traders received permission to trade in Chinese ports and the authority for levying taxes was transferred from the ministry of rites – which supervised tribute embassies – to the ministry of revenue (*hubu* 戶部). Again, we see that developments were not always steady or went into one direction. During Song times, for example, the maritime trade offices were subordinate to the central state's fiscal institutions such as the regional fiscal commissioners (*zhuanyun si* 轉運司) or the ministry of revenue, and not the ministry of rites.

Which role, finally, did defence strategies play? Security calculations, I would argue, hardly mattered in China's early maritime politics but became more and more important during Ming and Qing. The rampant piracy at the beginning of the Ming-Qing transition required political measures, as we have seen above. And security calculations remained essential for various reasons during the Qing. As early as 1659, the Shunzhi 順治 emperor (r. 1644–1662) ordered a detachment of Manchu troops to move permanently to Hangzhou. During the coastal wars against the Zheng clan (see above), they were temporarily moved to Fuzhou, but returned to Hangzhou in 1683. In 1728, another 1,600

70 Tansen Sen, "The Yuan Khanate and India", 301.

Manchu troops were stationed at the naval base at Zhapu 乍浦, the port of Hangzhou. The Qing court assigned special personnel to complete the building of warships and the navy was ordered "to repair weapons such as artillery and practice offensive military strategies". The Yongzheng emperor in particular clearly sought to strengthen the navy and China's self-defence capacity.[71] Nonetheless, the Qing navy remained basically a coastal navy that was never intended to attack or invade another country, not even against the background of a lack of monetary metals, such as copper, as the Japan trade shows.[72]

That maritime security and defence was less important before, has to do with the fact that whereas China had from ancient times continuously been challenged from her continental borders, no serious threats came from overseas until the fourteenth/fifteenth centuries, but especially the late fifteenth and early sixteenth centuries – with the rise of piracy and powerful maritime merchants, and later the advent of the Europeans who initially joined the so-called pirates to get access to Chinese markets. To secure its maritime borders was, consequently, over long periods only of secondary importance.

Despite their interest in and promotion of maritime trade, rulers of many dynasties, perhaps except for the Mongols, maintained a fair degree of suspicion towards private commerce. This notwithstanding, from the tenth until the late eighteenth century, the private sector played an increasingly important role. But no historical Chinese government, including the Song or Yuan, considered private trade as *the* basis of its political power.[73] Private commerce,

71 See Guo Yunjing, "Views of Japan and Policies Toward Japan in the Early Qing", 103–104; or my "Empire and Periphery?", 166–167.

72 The increasing demand for copper already in 1699 induced Kangxi to promote maritime trade with Japan in order to purchase Japanese copper, so-called "*yangtong*" 洋銅 in the sources. Between 1684 and 1723 China more or less completely relied on Japanese copper. Liu Hsü-feng (Liu Xufeng) 劉序楓, "Qing Kangxi~Qianlong nianjian yangtong de jinkou yu liutong wenti 清康熙~乾隆年間洋銅的進口與流通問題", in T'ang Hsi-yung 湯熙勇 (ed.), *Zhongguo haiyang fazhan shilun wenji* 中國海羊發展史論文集, vol. 7, *j.* shang (Taibei: Zhongyang yanjiuyuan, 1999), 93–144; Angela Schottenhammer, "Japan – the tiny Dwarf?"; item, "Empire and Periphery?".

73 It has become very popular to point to all kinds of private business activities among Chinese to show that early modern China was in fact not so different from European countries. All these "arguments", however, deliberately ignore the specific different nature and history of the European countries during the initial phase of capitalism. In Europe during the Middle Period the Emperor increasingly handed over to the merchants the liberty to enrich themselves according to their own criteria. Impressed by the sheer quantity of wealth that merchants amassed, the ruling emperors regarded this wealth as a tool also for their own enrichment, namely by benefitting from the merchants' capital via taxes. The enrichment of merchants was in fact so successful that together with the bourgeoisie, a class, which developed from the merchant class, they eventually represented the greatest part of national wealth, on which the aristocratic rulers had become dependent.

consequently, never received the same government support as it did in early modern European states. And its maritime politics consequently differed significantly from the maritime politics of European states in the early phase of capitalist development, from their motivations and goals. This brings us to a final question.

5 Was Traditional China's Maritime Politic (Proto-)Colonialist?

This question is not new. It has been debated for decades. But related academic discussions about China's treatment of foreign peoples, polities and territories, have continued to advance the argument that China, like the Europeans in the early modern period, was a colonialist or proto-colonialist power. Conversely, I want to argue that such a characterization does not advance our understanding, and actually blurs the specific content of China's historical and imperial maritime politics. China has never developed a colonialism that is comparable to that of the early modern European states. Of course, this does not mean that no violence was used.

China's traditional economy tended to be self-sufficient, aiming at providing a mostly agrarian population with a modest survival income and the ruling élites with enough surplus for the state to siphon off. The production of use values – and *not* the production of exchange values to serve for the increase of capital accumulation (that is, money with an entitlement for profit; resulting from a credit-financed production and sale of ever-increasing quantities of commodities for money in its abstract form) as the sole criterion of the economy – continued to be the ultimate purpose of China's economy. Imperial China did not seek to overcome the barriers to national (capital) accumulation by turning state power outwards, getting access to foreign wealth to integrate it into a country-wide abstract value production with capital increase as the only valid purpose of production. This latter production rationale simply did not exist in imperial China. The *politico-economic* contents of China's imperial expeditions and expansions were thus qualitatively different from the *colonialist* undertakings as perhaps best represented by the later British Empire.[74]

During the famous Zheng He expeditions, Ming China did use lots of violence to secure sea routes or to punish local rulers who did not accept Ming

---

Subsequently, merchants and bourgeoisie no longer saw and accepted why they should support and nourish an emperor, a person who in their eyes only sponged from their wealth. Instead, in the French Revolution they took over the power of state themselves.

74 For a more detailed discussion, I would like to refer the interested reader to my book *China and the Silk Roads (ca. 100 BCE to 1800 CE)*.

China's political claim for superiority in the wider region of maritime Asia. Representatives of the Ming court locally exchanged Chinese products, like silks, for desired foreign goods, like pepper. But Chinese rulers and merchants (or their representatives) never robbed alien wealth to integrate it into the building up of local industries in their home country, China, nor did they systematically rob foreign riches like, for example, the Spanish did in the newly discovered American world.

The degree of systematic colonialism of the Europeans of course differed; and while the motivations of the Portuguese and the Spanish were also religious – the Portuguese in particular wanted to spread Christianity and rollback Islam – the Dutch and the British were no longer driven by religious motivations. They all, however, wanted to get access to foreign material wealth (spices, gold, ivory, slaves) to integrate it into their own economy and transform it into monetary wealth – precious metals in the case of the Portuguese and Spanish, credit financed monetary advances in the case of the Dutch and, in a much more sophisticated way, the British. The "age of discovery" was initiated by the search for a domination of the spice routes and the forceful extraction of wealth from other parts of the world, pepper, gold, silver, *etc*.

Decisive in the early phase of colonialism (and primitive accumulation) was not only the specific use of the robbed wealth in the mother countries, but the degree of privatization of production means, in order to enable private owners to accumulate wealth in its abstract form, as (credit) money. Large quantities of the gold and silver the Spanish extracted from their new colonies in the Americas was eventually "consumed" by the Spanish court, spent for the financing of wars and private interests of the ruling elite, and not successfully turned into capital. The discovery of gold and silver in America at the same time exacerbated competition among the early capitalist European countries and the world oceans turned into a battlefield of navies, capers, "pirates" and pirate-merchants. The birth of the world market as a competition of capitalist states was characterized by an enormous degree of violence, force, coercion, and murder.

With the Dutch East India Company (VOC; that is, Vereenigde Oostindische Compagnie), one of the most powerful merchant organizations of the time, supported by the state, we can first observe a systematic accumulation of capital, and it was the Dutch who first more and more successfully ousted the Spanish and the Portuguese in the Asian waters.[75] Holland was the country which first fully developed the colonial system.

---

75 The independent development of merchant's capital is inversely proportional to the degree of development of capitalist production. The principal profits of the Dutch (as was

The behaviour of merchant's capital wherever it ruled over production is, consequently, strikingly illustrated by the colonial economy and the methods of the VOC. The rule of trade is to buy cheap and to sell dear, *not* to exchange equivalents. Profits, consequently, are made in the circulation process and realized in the sale, they constitute, therefore, "profit upon alienation". Merchant's capital exploits the differences between prices of products from various countries, appropriating an over-whelming portion of the surplus-product, partly as a mediator between communities, which still substantially produce for use-values, and for whose organisation the sale of their products is of only secondary importance. The development of commerce and merchant's capital brings about a tendency towards an increasing production of exchange values, makes it cosmopolitan and develops money into world-money. In this respect it has a dissolving influence on traditional production spheres. But to which extent old modes of production are dissolved, depends on their internal structure and solidity.[76] The VOC actually initiated a credit system of shares and stock certificates to finance their overseas purchases. They also, as did the British, continued to apply traditional methods, such as violently enforced monopolies, unfair trade agreements, and warfare.[77]

Undoubtedly did the great revolutions that took place in the sphere of commerce with the European overseas discoveries and expansion and that accelerated the development of merchant's capital "constitute one of the principal elements in furthering the transition from a feudal to a capitalist mode of production. *The sudden expansion of the world-market, the multiplication of circulating commodities, the competitive zeal of the European nations to possess themselves of the products of Asia and the treasure of America, and the colonial system* – all contributed materially towards the destruction of the old modes

the case earlier in history among the Venetians or Genoese, for example) were not made by exporting domestic products but by promoting the exchange of products of commercially and otherwise economically rather undeveloped societies, and by exploiting both countries. See, for example, the description of Adam Smith, *An Inquiry into the Nature and Causes of the Wealth of Nations* (MetaLibri: Amsterdam, Lausanne, Melbourne et al., 2007), Book III, Chapter III, 313–314 (G.ed. p. 407). Capital, here, appears in the process of circulation, *not* of production.

76 Karl Marx, *Capital. A Critique of Political Economy* (London: Lawrence & Wishart, 1959), Book III, Chapter XX, 331–332.

77 For the Dutch activities in the Indian Ocean, I can recommend René J. Barendse, *The Arabian Seas. The Indian Ocean World of the Seventeenth Century* (New York, London: M.A. Sharpe, 2002). In Chapter 7, Barendse also discusses the difference between the Portuguese Estado da India and the VOC and their economic undertakings in the Indian Ocean. In contrast to the Portuguese, for example, the VOC was able and willing "to sacrifice immediate profits to long-term ones" (p. 362).

of production. But the transition towards modern mode of production took only place where the conditions for it had taken shape already in the Middle Ages (compare for example Holland with Portugal or Spain)." And the rise of capitalist production, favoured by the expansion of commerce and the new 'world-market', took place only on the basis of an already existing capitalist mode of production, but it acted revolutionary only where domestic industry subordinated merchant's capital and the supremacy of commerce under industrial capital. "The history of the decline of Holland as the ruling trading nation is the history of the subordination of merchant's capital to industrial capital".[78] Since merchant's capital is restricted to the circulation sphere, its function consisting in the promotion of the exchange of commodities, it requires no other condition for its existence except those necessary for the simple circulation of commodities and money.

This historical development has been described in an excellent manner by the famous German economist Karl Marx (1818–1883)[79] approximately 150 years ago. The colonies, eventually, secured a market for the sprouting manufactures, and, "through the monopoly of the market, an increased accumulation. The treasures captured outside Europe by undisguised looting, enslavement, and murder, *floated back to the mother-country and were there turned into capital* [italics are mine]. Holland, which first fully developed the colonial system, in 1648 stood already in the acme of its commercial greatness. … The system of public credit, *i.e.*, of national debts, whose origin we discover in Genoa and Venice as early as the Middle Ages, took possession of Europe generally during the manufacturing period. The colonial system with its maritime trade and commercial wars served as a forcing-house for it. Thus it first took root in Holland. National debts, *i.e.*, the alienation of the state – whether despotic, constitutional or republican – marked with its stamp the capitalistic era. … Public credit becomes the *credo* of capital … and public debt becomes one of the most powerful levers of primitive accumulation."[80] With national debt also an international credit system arose.

"The different moments of primitive accumulation distribute themselves now, more or less in chronological order, particularly over Spain, Portugal, Holland, France, and England. In England at the end of the 17th century, they

78 Karl Marx, *Capital*, Book III, Chapter XX, 333.

79 Especially in the successful modern capitalist countries it has become quite outdated, old-fashioned, even come under criticism, to quote Marx. Actually, a careful analysis of his works helps a lot to better understand the historical process and emergence of our modern global economy and the separation of industrially successful and underdeveloped countries.

80 Karl Marx, *Capital*, Book I, Chapter XXXI, 705–706.

arrive at a systematical combination, embracing the colonies, the national debt, the modern mode of taxation, and the protectionist system. These methods depend in part on brute force, *e.g.*, the colonial system. But, they all employ the power of the State, the concentrated and organised force of society, to hasten, hot-house fashion, the process of transformation of the feudal mode of production into the capitalist mode, and to shorten the transition."[81]

Historically speaking, thus, the comprehensive validity of private property, of the exclusive disposal of all means of consumption and production in the hands of private owners, consequently first had to be established by a stately power monopoly. With the requisite violence the state destroyed traditional forms of production, created a separation between propertied and unpropertied social classes and subordinated all forms of labour and all life under the private power of money. Money became the binding measure of private property and the whole society became obliged to gain money.[82] In this way, the private power of property came to reign the entire society and all economic production. And the propertied classes, in this way officially entitled to use the private power of money, came to command the productive labour of the whole society. It is obvious – and evident from the history of the successful European capitalist countries – that this kind of production only came into force and existence because a political power, using its power monopoly, first subordinated all its citizens under such rules of the private power of money and thus first created the class of so-called employers and the majority who possess nothing than their work force. And it is obvious that imperial Chinese governments never wanted to establish the private power of property in the form of money as the only legal measure to rule the entire economic life of its society.

In China, the dissolving influence of commerce and merchant's capital on its organisation of production, primarily small-scale agriculture and home industry, remained initial at best. The dissolving or corrosive influence of merchant's capital on local modes of production was particularly weak in China, because it was not reinforced by political power. Instead did the substantial subsistence economy and the association of agriculture with manufacture in China "put up a stubborn resistance to the products of the big industries,

81 Karl Marx, *Capital*, Book I, Chapter XXXI, 703. He continues: "Force is the midwife of every old society pregnant with a new one. It is itself an economic power. ... The history of the colonial administration of Holland – and Holland was the head capitalistic nation of the 17th century 'is one of the most extraordinary relations of treachery, bribery, massacre, and meanness'."

82 Who would ever voluntarily work in a factory if he/she did not have to because he/she simply does not dispose of anything else than his/her workforce.

whose prices include the *faux frais* of the circulation process which pervades them",[83] as can be observed in the intercourse of the English with China.

The search for material wealth overseas to integrate it into their economy and transform it into money and capital accumulation, in other words, to "have treasures captured floated back to the mother-country and turn it into capital",[84] never existed as a political purpose of China's imperial political power. Even the expansive expeditions, such as the Zheng He expeditions, should not be considered as *colonialist* undertakings in the sense of European colonialism. The politico-economic quality behind these expeditions – as violent as they were at times[85] – was decisively different from what we know as (European) colonialism.

It is, furthermore, an immanent necessity of the capitalist mode of production to produce on an ever-increasing scale and to continually extend the world-market, gradually completely converting into a resource for one's own capital accumulation. This becomes strikingly evident when we look at the Opium Wars (1839–1842 and 1856–1860) and the causes of the confrontation of the English with China. Such a necessity never existed in imperial China – not even against the background of a need for money metals.

83 Karl Marx, *Capital*, Book III, Chapter XX, 334.

84 Karl Marx, *Capital*, Book I, Chapter XXXI, 705.

85 It is another popular and unscientific accusation against those who argue that China was not a *colonialist* country like early modern capitalist European countries that they would conceal (or even deny) the violence involved in Chinese undertakings. Actually, these are two pairs of boots. Because colonialism involved violence, the absence of colonialism does not mean the absence of violence.

CHAPTER 1

Maritime Archaeological Evidence for Trade in the Early and Medieval South China Sea and Political Events in Vietnam

Jun Kimura and Mark Staniforth

1 Introduction

Studies in maritime archaeology have contributed to our understanding of how the inhabitants of Vietnamese coastal regions have engaged with natural inland waterways as well as sea environments. The waters, both shallow and deep, off modern Vietnam's long coast have functioned as sea routes, and estuaries have provided gateways to the trading centres and polities that have developed along inland waterways and in river deltas. Being positioned on a delta on the Indochina Peninsula, Óc Eo first arose as a prominent trading trading centre from the polities along the Vietnamese coasts and its inlets. The long-distance maritime trade to transport Chinese merchandise from East to West was already being facilitated by Southeast Asian and Indian Ocean seafarers before the tenth century. It is a common misconception that the emergence of water transport by Chinese traders began to transform the South China Sea trading system internally at an early period. In fact, shipwreck archaeology shows that this occurred around the eleventh-twelfth centuries.[1]

The salvaging of the Châu Tân shipwreck in Bình Sơn, Central Vietnam, which dates from the Champa period, has caused controversy over its implications for the protection of underwater cultural heritage. However, findings suggest that the region might have been involved in the long-distance maritime trading system that exported Chinese products to Muslim markets in the early ninth century.[2] In the north, the development of an offshore port for maritime trade is considered to have occurred along with the emergence of Đại Việt (a polity in North Vietnam) in the eleventh century, government-controlled trading first being centralized at the ancient port of Vân Đồn 雲屯 (modern Quan

1 Jun Kimura, *Archaeology of East Asian Shipbuilding* (Gainesville: University Press of Florida, 2016).

2 Noriko Nishino et al., "Nishimura Masanari's Study on the Oldest Known Shipwreck Ever Found in Vietnam", *Asian Review of World Histories* 5:2 (2017), 106–122.

 | DOI:10.1163/9789004740556_003

Lan island).[3] An archaeological survey has revealed human settlement on the island since prehistoric times, but the large-scale growth of the island's population and extensive environmental changes coincided with the development of the port as well as its utilization as a strategic point for naval defense. This highly populated trading hub eventually became a centre for naval and military activity in the thirteenth century, following the expansion of imperialism by the Mongol Empire. Geopolitically northern Vietnam had been exposed to the threat of fleets from Chinese territories as early as the Han 漢 Dynasty (206 BCE–220 CE), but the area experienced the most powerful territorial expansionism during the Yuan 元 Period (1279–1368) of the Mongol Empire in the thirteenth century. To confront this threat, the Trần Dynasty of Đại Việt had to intercept invading fleets.[4] In this chapter, we investigate the material remains of early and medieval voyages, including different types of anchor remnants, port facilities and naval battlefields. The archaeological evidence which has been identified in the coastal and underwater environments provides an overview of the maritime commerce and political events in the South China Sea.[5] Recently this thematic study has been facilitated by the support of the Gerda Henkel Foundation and financial aid from institutes in Japan. This chapter covers arguments about significant transitions in the history of the South China Sea regarding Vietnamese involvement in maritime commercial activities and naval conflicts between the eighth and thirteenth centuries.

2 Archaeological Examination of Vietnam's Coasts and Waters

The maritime archaeological heritage beneath Vietnamese waters is linked to early and medieval water transport for purposes of trade and naval campaigns

---

3 Yamamoto Tasuro 山本達郎, "Annan no bōekiko Unton" 安南の貿易港雲屯, *Tōho Gakuhō* 東方学報 9 (1939), 277–309. Kikuchi Yuriko 菊池百里子 suggested that Quan Lan might not have been a major port during the Nhà Trần period. See her book *Vietnam hokubu ni okeru bōekikō no kōko gakuteki kenkyū: Vūandon to Fōhien o chūshin ni* ベトナム北部における貿易港の考古学的研究：ヴァンドンとフォーヒエンを中心に (Tōkyo: 雄山閣, 2017), 57–69. However, in addition to existing scholarship based on historical accounts that insist on the identification of Quan Lan as a major port, our archaeological and geological investigations also suggest a long-term occupation of the Quang Lan Island during the Nhà Trần period.

4 Jun Kimura and John Pollack, "Preliminary study on Van Don: Lost ports and lost fleets in northern Vietnam", In: N.H. Tan (ed.), *Advancing Southeast Asian Archaeology 2013* (Bangkok: SAMEO SPAFA Regional Centre for Archaeology and Fine Arts, 2015), 385–393.

5 Mark Staniforth, Jun Kimura and Le Thi Lien, "Defeating the fleet of Kublai Khan: the Bach Dang River and Van Don Naval battlefields research project", *Archaeologica Postmedievale* 18 (2014), 29–44.

in the South China Sea. The importance of Vietnamese involvement in the region's maritime trading networks has been well acknowledged. Historians have shifted from the study of maritime polities in Central and Southern Vietnam to the significance of the ports in the north, emphasizing the weight of the country's maritime commerce.[6] This has resulted in a re-evaluation of the usual view of Vietnam's socio-economic development as relying firmly on agricultural systems. From an archaeological point of view, in the north the Red River delta had facilitated the use of primitive watercraft since the prehistoric period, as indicated by finds of the remains of dugout canoes.[7] Water transport aided the formation of citadels along the delta systems, including at Cổ Loa and Lũng Khê. The Lũng Khê citadel is considered to have been the political centre of the Jiaozhi 交趾 Commandery of the Han Dynasty, identified as either Luy Lâu (Leilou 羸𨻻) or more likely Long Biên (Longbian 龍編).[8] The political regime based in the Lũng Khê Citadel was involved in maritime exchanges with India and China during the second and third centuries CE, though the role of the delta as a maritime entrepot gradually declined from the fourth century onwards,[9] as a direct sailing route developed around the fourth century between southern China and the central Vietnamese coast.

The use of seaworthy ships built drawing on Austronesian boatbuilding traditions allowed early seafarers to conduct long-distance voyages and facilitated the growth of maritime polities in Central Vietnam. Existing historical and archaeological studies have examined the formation and structure of the Champa citadels and political centres that emerged on the coasts.[10] The phrase "Champa kingdom", in actuality was composed of a number of maritime polities which could control maritime activities along the coasts. But the archaeological study of ships' remains has so far been limited to the early

6 Shiro Momoki, "Dai Viet and the South China Sea Trade: from the 10th to the 15th century", *Crossroads: An Interdisciplinary Journal of Southeast Asian Studies* 12:1 (1998), 1–34; Momoki Shiro 桃木至朗, "Vietnam hokubu to kitachuubu ni okeru minatoshi no ichi ベトナム北部・中北部の港湾都市の位置, in Murai Shōsuke 村井章介 (eds.), Rekishigaku kenkyukai 歴史学研究会 (2005), 179–205; John K. Whitmore, "The Rise of the Coast: Trade, State and Culture in Early Dai Viet", *Journal of Southeast Asian Studies* 37:1 (2006), 103–122.

7 Peter Bellwood et al., "Ancient Boats, Boat Timbers, and Locked Mortise-and-Tenon Joints from Bronze/Iron-Age Northern Vietnam", *International Journal of Nautical Archaeology* 36:1 (2007), 2–20.

8 Masanari Nishimura, "Reexamination of the Lung Khê Citadel in the Red River Delta", *Southeast Asia: History and Culture* 30 (2001), 46–71.

9 Nishimura, "Reexamination of the Lung Khê Citadel in the Red River Delta", 46–71.

10 Đỗ, T.G., "Champa Citadels: An Archaeological and Historical Study", *Asian Review of World Histories* 5:2 (2017), 70–105.

shipping and seafaring of Champa people. Wreck sites in Vietnamese waters are well known, but only recently has exploration started for archaeological purposes. Throughout the 1990s and 2000s, the ceramic cargo of merchant ships dating from the fifteenth to eighteenth centuries have been recovered for commercial salvage. However, awareness of the loss of underwater cultural heritage has slowly emerged with a series of findings of earlier wreck sites in Bình Sơn District in Quảng Ngãi Province, Central Vietnam, including of a wreck that was carrying a number of Chinese export wares produced during the Tang-Five Kingdom periods.[11] The coast areas of Central Vietnam that were occupied by the Champa Kingdom provided a number of anchorages for merchants from the Indian Ocean World and for Southeast Asian seafarers engaged in the Maritime Silk Route trade. Champa's main ports included Đại Chiêm (Hội An) in Quảng Nam Province, Cổ Lũy in Quảng Ngãi Province and Thi Nại – Nước Mặn in Bình Định Province. These wrecks from the early Champa period are direct evidence of the international trading in the region.

Given that none of the wreck sites had necessarily been investigated for their safeguarding underwater before, our project team first aimed to improve the protection and management of the shipwreck sites and to enhance scientific approaches to maritime heritage. This researcher-led initiative first focused on investigations of the medieval naval battlefield sites related to the Khubilai Khan invasions of the Trần Dynasty Đại Việt during the late thirteenth century because of their historical significance to the country.[12] Approaches in naval battlefield archaeology have been pursued since 2008 and have led to the successful identification of new sites, as well as raising awareness about the protection of such sites in the context of maritime archaeology (Map 1). In 2013, the Institute of Archaeology established the Department of Underwater Archaeology (DUA) in co-operation with VMAP (Vietnam Maritime Archaeology Project). Shipwreck archaeology and maritime archaeological surveys are now growing fields in Vietnam. The following sections will provide an overview of the sites of early medieval and medieval wrecks that have been identified and the overall maritime cultural landscape in Vietnam, as well as discussing the material evidence for maritime commercial activities and naval conflicts in the South China Sea.

---

11 Noriko Nishino et al., "Nishimura Masanari's Study on the Oldest Known Shipwreck Ever Found in Vietnam", 106–122.

12 Jun Kimura and John Pollack, "Preliminary study on Van Don: Lost ports and lost fleets in northern Vietnam", 385–393; Mark Staniforth, Jun Kimura and Thi Lien Le, "Defeating the fleet of Kublai Khan: the Bach Dang River and Van Don Naval battlefields research project", 29–44.

3 Discovery of an Anchorage for Ships on the Maritime Silk Route in Central Vietnam

Despite the fact that terrestrial archaeological investigations and cultural heritage management have been practiced in Vietnam for a long time, surveys of the sites of maritime wrecks for scientific purposes have only been introduced recently. The deficiencies in protecting wreck sites became apparent when a remarkable find of a concentration of wreck sites was made in the waters near Cổ Lũy in Bình Sơn District, Quảng Ngãi Province, Central Vietnam. This indicated that there was an anchorage on the delta of the Trà Khúc River, the largest river in Quảng Ngãi Province, but records concerning a possible port at Cổ Lũy are very limited. Bình Sơn District has long sandy beaches between capes, and today there are a few villages and communes along these beaches. Off the beaches one can see Lý Sơn Island, probably an important landmark for sailors, and it is even possible that the island was used as an outer port. The spatial situation of the area as a polity could be similar to Trà Kiệu, the early capital of Champa and a political centre related to the religious centre of Mỹ Sơn, the port city of Hội An and the outer port at Cù Lao Chàm. The location of a religious centre in the Bình Sơn area is uncertain since the nearest monument is the Chiên Đàn towers, more than 67 kilometres north of the area.

In the past, quite a few merchant ships presumably approached the shore of the Bình Sơn area and then became entrapped in the waters for various periods of time. This is indicated by the fact that many pieces of salvaged Chinese ceramics from the seabed span the time periods from the Tang to the mid-Qing dynasties. Efforts by the Quảng Ngãi provincial government have been largely limited to the protection of heritage on land that actually supports the thesis of the development of a Cham polity reliant on maritime trading. The shipwreck resources were not necessarily considered to be among their archaeological assets. There is the remnant of an old citadel only four kilometres from the present-day coast. The Châu Sa citadel at Tịnh Châu in Sơn Tịnh District is located near the delta of the Trà Khúc River. Very little of its structure is left inside the citadel, but its ramparts are well-preserved to a height of about four metres, and the moats are still visible (Figure 1). The fortified area was believed to have been established around the eighth century and developed up until the eleventh century, coinciding with the growth of the area as a maritime entrepot and commercial hub as part of the Maritime Silk Route.

In 2009, a local collector salvaged a quantity of Tang 唐 Dynasty (618–906) ceramics from the water not far from the Châu Sa citadel.[13] These salvaged

13 Noriko Nishino et al., "Nishimura Masanari's Study on the Oldest Known Shipwreck Ever Found in Vietnam", 106–122.

ceramics include Yue 越 ware and Changsha 長沙-Tongguan 銅官 ware (Figure 2.). They were apparently buried beneath the seabed only thirty metres off the coast of Châu Tân village in Bình Sơn District. The mass salvage of Changsha-Tongguan ware from the Châu Tân shipwreck resembled what happened when the ninth-century Belitung ship was found in Indonesia. Both were merchant ships involved in transporting Chinese ceramics to the Indian Ocean World. Notably, the assemblage and quality of the ceramics from the two shipwrecks are quite distinct from each other. The motif and design of the Changsha-Tongguan ware recovered from the Châu Tân wreck are geometric, being intended for export to Islamic markets. Many shards of the bowls and jars have more than five hundred and eighty-five incised and ink inscriptions in different scripts, Chinese, Arabic and Indic. Arabic ink scripts with a Star of David inscribed on some jar pieces indicates that a Hebrew-speaking individual or group may have been on board or involved in the transportation of these materials. Apart from the ceramics and other objects, forty-nine ship's timbers were salvaged simultaneously from the same spot, though archaeologically this can no longer be proved. The on-going study of the shipwreck material is limited to post-archaeological analysis to examine the contexts between the ceramics and the ship's timbers. The radiocarbon dating on the keel demonstrates that the timber was cut sometime between the late seventh and the middle of the eighth centuries. The result of the radiocarbon dating on the fibre cordage, made of arenga palm, to reinforce the planking indicates that the ship was constructed sometime between the late eighth and early ninth centuries. The gap in the dating analysis reflects the gap between the time of construction and the ship's operational period. The link between the recovered material and the ship's timbers is considered to be fairly valid, but further examination of it is needed. Based on the length of the keel and the characteristics of the planks, which show a lashed-lug technique that is specific to Southeast Asian shipbuilding,[14] the Châu Tân ship is considered to have been a trading vessel about twenty-five metres long operated by South China Sea seafarers. The ship might have carried fifty to eighty tons of cargo. The Châu Tân shipwreck provides a clue to understanding how the long corridors for transporting seaborne commodities that are represented as the Maritime Silk Route functioned. The Châu Sa citadel and the Châu Tân shipwreck are mutually

14 G. Adrian Horridge, *The lashed-lug boat of the eastern archipelagoes, The Alcina MS and the Lomblem whaling boats. Maritime Monographs and Reports* (London: Trustees of the National Maritime Museum, 1982); Ligaya Lacsina, "The Butuan Boats of the Philippines: Southeast Asian edge-joined and lashed-lug watercraft", *Journal of the Australasian Institute for Maritime Archaeology* 39 (2015), 126–132.

related in a way that helps us to understand early maritime commerce conducted by the Champa people of Central Vietnam.

4 Medieval Maritime Trade and Cargoes Salvaged from Wrecks

Maritime activities in Bình Sơn District were stimulated by the introduction of Chinese merchant ships into the South China Sea and led the continuous growth in maritime trade throughout the medieval period. This may have happened before the eleventh century, and it also transformed the trading system within the South China Sea. On the other hand, a limited number of wrecks dating back to the eleventh to fourteenth centuries have been found in waters off the coasts of the Indochina Peninsula. Concerns emerged when looting was reported at multiple wreck sites found in Quảng Ngãi Province in Central Vietnam, which were dated to the thirteenth to fourteenth centuries.[15] These wreck sites were located in a very shallow water at a depth of approximately four metres about two hundred metres off the beach near Bình Châu commune in Bình Sơn District. The discovery of artefacts under a sandy seabed in different places indicated the existence of a few sunken ships, but no archaeological data positioning these wrecks has ever been produced. Anecdotal evidence suggests that the hull of the Bình Châu shipwreck No. 2 was well preserved. According to a government report, the exposed hull measured approximately twenty-five metres long and amidships was about 5.6 metres. Twelve bulkheads divided the hull into thirteen holds in which mast structure also remained. Iron nails seem to have been used for planking, which indicates that the ship could have been built in China, but the details of the planking methods have not been reported. Some of the ship's timbers show evidence of fire, though the reason why the shipwreck was sunk in such shallow waters has not been clarified. Approximately four thousand objects were recovered from the wreck site (Figure 3). Among them, the recovered metal objects include bronze mirrors, bronze scales and copper coins produced in the late thirteenth century. Most of the salvaged objects consisted of ceramics, including brown grazed pots and jars with four handles. The recovered celadon products are diverse in type, including plates, bowls, incense burners with three legs and cups. Among the large plates is one with a distinctive dragon motif. Other ceramics are of blue and white porcelain and white porcelain.

15 Mark Staniforth, "First wrecked, now pillaged: Vietnam's underwater treasure", *The Conversation*, 2012. To be consulted at: http://theconversation.edu.au/first-wrecked-now-pillaged-vietnams-underwater-treasure-10219.

The proposed date for the Bình Châu shipwreck No. 2 assigns the ship's operational period to the early- and mid-fourteenth centuries, but this needs further scientific examination. There were political tensions between the polities in medieval Asia caused by the rise to maritime hegemony of the Yuan Dynasty, which substantially impacted on maritime trading networks in Asian regions. Khubilai Khan (r. 1260–1294), founder of the Yuan Dynasty in China, led maritime campaigns to Kamakura period's Japan, Singhasari in Indonesia, Đại Việt and Champa, which resulted in a temporary decline in overseas diplomatic exchanges between China and these countries. However, private merchant ships from China could probably sail sporadically to the coasts of Champa, and at least the trading port in Bình Châu may have been actively involved in shipping goods from China after the Mongol invasions. By that time transregional maritime commerce was firmly established to satisfy the demand for commodities in Central Vietnam.

5 Northern Islets as Medieval Maritime Trading Hubs and Naval Bases

The Tonkin Gulf region has been important to China geopolitically for more than two millennia in providing coastal sailing routes, while geographically, the Red River Delta provided important access routes for water transport.[16] Nanyue (Nam Việt) 南越, which had a large shipyard in modern Guangzhou 廣州, was the first polity that controlled the Red River Delta region systematically. In the first millennium CE, the Tonkin Gulf region formed part of the Han dynasty's province known as the Jiaozhi Commandery.[17] During the provincial era, a sort of inter-state shipping network was developed linked with the Chinese imperial court in the north, but in northern Vietnam the international maritime trade and its communication routes developed more during the Đại Việt period than during previous periods. Maritime ports such as Vân Đồn served the entrepot trade and grew as important hubs for merchants from

16 James A. Anderson, "Slipping through Holes: the late tenth century and early eleventh century Sino-Vietnamese Coastal Frontier as Subaltern Trade Network", in James Anderson (ed.), *The Tongking Gulf through History* (Philadelphia: University of Pennsylvania Press, 2012), 87–100.

17 Anderson, "Slipping through Holes", 91; Tana Li, "Jiaozhi (Giao Chi) in the Han period – Tongking Gulf", in James Anderson (ed.), *The Tongking Gulf through History* (Philadelphia: University of Pennsylvania Press, 2012), 39–52; Keith Weller Taylor, *A History of the Vietnamese* (Cambridge: Cambridge University Press, 2013), 14–50.

various places, including India, the Middle East and the Mediterranean to the West, China and East Asia to the East and island Southeast Asia.[18]

The state formation of Đại Việt in the tenth century resulted in decreased political interference from China and led to the growth of maritime commerce. The trading system of the Red River Delta developed along with the establishment, by King Lý Anh Tông (Ly dynasty), of the port of Vân Đồn as an international trading port of the Đại Việt in 1149 CE. It has been suggested that Vân Đồn existed not as a single dominant port but as a network of several trading ports in Halong Bay.[19] The volume of the maritime trade in the Bay certainly expanded from time to time, but the result of recent maritime archaeological surveys is persuasive that international hub ports were probably centred on the islands of Cái Lân and Quan Lan in modern Vân Đồn District at least through the medieval and post-medieval periods. These islands are positioned on the fringes of the eastern part of Halong Bay, and they would have been ideal for controlling trade as the outermost harbors, as well as for defense against a maritime power in the neighboring regions in east.

The importance of Quan Lan Island in relation to medieval international trading was examined in the 1930s in early archaeological investigations of the middle part of the island.[20] More recent maritime archaeological surveys of material evidence found in a sand dune in the middle part of the Island (Động Chơi area) suggest that Quan Lan was inhabited from the Halong cultural period and was continually occupied. Among the identified artefacts are Han-period ware, Đông Sơn culture (2500–2000 BP) artefacts and a thick cultural layer containing Halong cultural type pottery and grinding stones (4000–3500 BP). Less than two kilometres to the south is a residential area known as *Sơn Hảo*, which is a coastal settlement adjacent to the bay of Sông Cái. In the bay, the remnants of a small harbour composed of mooring stones, retaining walls, flat building pads and a well for water supply have been identified. Archaeological evidence suggests that Sông Cái was used temporarily to store supplies and to camp military forces during the Mongol Empire's invasion of the Trần Dynasty

18 Tansen Sen, "The formation of Chinese maritime networks to Southern Asia, 1200 to 1450", *Journal of the Economic and Social History of the Orient* 49:4 (2006), 421–453 (2006); Li, "Jiaozhi (Giao Chi) in the Han period – Tongking Gulf", 39; Kenneth R. Hall, "Revisionist study of Cross-Cultural Commercial Competition on the Vietnamese coastline in the fourteenth and fifteenth centuries and its wider implications", *Journal of World History* 24:1 (2013), 82.

19 Nguyen, V.K., "Hệ thống thương cảng Vân Đồn qua các nguồn tư liệu lịch sử, điền dã và khảo cổ học (The Harbor System of Vân Đồn as Seen through Historical and Archaeological Materials), *Khảo cổ học* (Journal of Archaeology) 4 (2006), 48–65.

20 Yamamoto, "Annan no bōekiko Unton", 277–309.

in the thirteenth century, as illustrated by the considerable number of ceramic fragments, all of approximately the same date, on the shore (Figure 4). Vân Đồn, centered on the middle part of Quan Lan Island, had a dual function as a trading hub and naval base, its latter role being especially important during the historical naval campaign in the thirteenth century.

6 Cargo Salvage of "Gulf Trader" Traders in Central and Southern Vietnam

The unique historical value of sunken ships in Vietnamese waters was first recognized through the commercial salvaging of seaborne ceramics in the 1990s. The substantial cargoes of five shipwrecks were salvaged for commercial benefit. A large portion of the recovered ceramics were scattered throughout the world by sale at auction. These ships were considered to be merchant ships engaged in trade during the fifteenth to seventeenth centuries. Some of these shipwrecks are defined as belonging to the Southeast Asian Gulf trade and represent Vietnamese coastal engagement with the Southeast Asian maritime economy. The waters off the coasts of Central and Southern Vietnam include some landmark islands that were regularly sighted by seafarers and were used as a trading hub. Historically known islands include Cu Lao Cham off Hội An, the Côn Đảo islands in the south and Phú Quốc Island in the Gulf of Thailand, all of which attracted South China Sea traders. The Vietnam Salvage Corporation (Visal), in conjunction with foreign salvage enterprises, has conducted salvage at the following wreck sites since 1990.

Phú Quốc (Hon Dam) shipwreck. This shipwreck was found in waters at a depth of 15 m near Phú Quốc Island in Kiên Giang province. The date of the shipwreck was determined based on the fifteenth-century Thai ceramics it contained (more than 15,000 pieces of Sawankhalok ware) and a Ming Dynasty coin of the Yongle Emperor reign period (1402–1424).[21] The well-preserved hull was 25 metres long and 5 metres wide in the midship section. The cargo holds were divided by bulkheads, and the characteristic construction method of using wooden dowels for planking indicated that the ship was a locally built merchant vessel.

21 Kikuchi Seiichi 菊池誠一, "Betonamu kaiiki no chinbotsusen" ベトナム海域の沈没船, in Kikuchi Seiichi 菊池誠一 and Abe Yuriko 阿部百里子 (eds.), *Umi no michi to kōkogaku: Indoshina hantō kara Nippon e* 海の道と考古学：インドシナ半島から日本へ (Tōkyō: Koshi shoin, 2010), 127–138.

Hội An shipwreck. This wreck was found at a depth of 70–72 m in the waters 15 km away from Cham Island (Cu Lao Cham) in Quảng Nam province. It was dated to the late fifteenth century based on radiocarbon dating of the ship's timbers and the date of the ceramics. The length of the remaining hull was about 29 m and the width was 7 m. The holds of the hull were divided by bulkheads, and as the ship's timbers are of Thai wood, the ship was presumably built somewhere on mainland Southeast Asia. More than 240,000 pieces of intact ceramics were found at the wreck, besides hundreds of thousands of broken shards, the majority Vietnamese blue and white porcelains produced in the Hải Dương region (Chu Dau).

Bình Thuận shipwreck. This shipwreck was found off the southeast coast of Phan Thiết in Bình Thuận province. It has been dated to the early seventeenth century based on the study of the ceramics it was carrying. The excavation revealed that the remaining structure of the hull measures about 23 m long and 7 m wide. The hull has bulkheads, but the structural details of these have not been clarified. A total of over 61,000 objects were recovered, most of them from the Chinese kilns of Fujian and Guangdong, including the Zhangzhou kiln.

Vũng Tàu (Côn Đảo) shipwreck. This wreck was the first shipwreck to be salvaged in Vietnamese waters. It was found at a depth of 40 m off Côn Đảo Island in Ba Rịa – Vũng Tàu province. The assemblage of ceramics and copper coins identified it as a merchant ship that had been lost around 1690.[22] The remnants of the keel timbers indicate that that the hull of the ship was 25 meters in length. Based on the bulkhead structure and planking methods, the ship was probably built somewhere in the South China Sea region. The salvaged objects comprised 34,710 pieces of porcelain and 28,556 pieces of stone and earthen ware. The majority of the porcelain was Chinese in origin, including blue and white ware from the kilns of Jingdezhen 景德鎮 dated to the Kangxi 康熙 period (1662–1722), and bowls and dishes from the kilns of Fujian and Guangdong.

Cà Mau shipwreck. This shipwreck was found in the waters off the coast of Trần Văn Thời district in Cà Mau province. The date of the shipwreck was identified based on the examination of the assemblage of the ceramics it was carrying to the era of the Yongzheng 雍正 Emperor (r. 1723–1735) of the Qing 清 Dynasty in China. Although the Vietnamese salvage team reported that the hull's remains were 24 meters long and 8 meters wide, the structural details have not yet been described. The recovered ceramics comprised blue

22 Kikuchi Seiichi "Shipwrecks in Vietnamese Waters", 127–138.

and white porcelain produced in the kilns of Jingdezhen and Dehua 德華 and various types of other ware, including bowls, cups, vessels and dishes, as well as some European-style ceramics.[23]

Of the five salvaged shipwrecks, the Phú Quốc shipwreck, in being assigned to the fifteenth century, has been dated to the oldest period for such a find in Vietnam. Looking at the whole of Southeast Asia, only a few sunken merchant ships have been dated to the same period, including the Santa Cruz shipwreck and the Lena Shoal shipwreck excavated in the Philippines.[24] These were merchant traders that were mainly used for long-distance voyages in the inter-regional trade in Southeast Asia. By this time, construction methods for Southeast Asian sailing vessels had achieved a standardization that allowed seaworthy hulls to be built using a hybrid of the shipbuilding technologies of Southeast Asia and East Asia. The growth in shipbuilding along the South China Sea's coasts occurred through contact with shipbuilding traditions developed in the East China Sea. The coasts of the Gulf of Thailand were major suppliers of Gulf Traders, large freighters, whose construction may date back to as early as the fourteenth century and which have been continuously developed since then. The structural remains of these Vietnamese shipwrecks should have been preserved appropriately, but none of those described above have been protected or investigated since their commercial excavation.

7 Conclusion

There is a diverse range of archaeological evidence of Vietnamese involvement in maritime commerce and in political events in the South China Sea in the early and medieval periods. An overview of the identified wreck sites and maritime cultural heritage of Vietnam leads to insights into the importance of shipping and maritime hubs in the region's maritime history. There is some evidence of early seafarers on the Vietnamese coast who could conduct long-distance voyages is recorded in historical accounts. The recent identification of the significance of the Châu Tân shipwreck, found off the coast of Bình Sơn District, is important in terms of compensating for the absence of material evidence of shipwrecks dating back to the eighth and ninth centuries in Central Vietnam. Further comprehensive study of hull remains and shipwreck cargoes needs to be scientifically pursued in order to provide a

23 Kikuchi Seiichi "Shipwrecks in Vietnamese Waters", 127–138.

24 Franck Goddio, M. Crick et al., *Lost at Sea: the strange route of the Lena Shoals junk* (London: Periplus Publishing, 2002).

better understanding of how the maritime polity in modern Bình Sơn District emerged and developed. The increase in data has been beneficial, but as of today what has been dismissed in past salvage operations includes a failure to consider a wreck as archaeological heritage. Vietnam therefore needs to move away from simply focusing on the value of the cargo in the wrecks. The Bình Châu shipwreck No. 2 dating to the early- and mid-fourteenth centuries found in Bình Sơn is worthy of examination in relation to the impact of the Mongol invasions on the trading systems of Champa's ports. This theme needs to be synergistically pursued with the Đại Việt ports in the north. Vietnamese involvement in the commerce of the South China Sea was represented by the discovery of the Southeast Asian Gulf Traders. However, protection and management of the hulls and wreckage that comprise archaeological contexts have not been implemented since the underwater salvage at the sites. The notion of specific Gulf Traders, Southeast Asian merchant ships which made outstanding contributions to the South China Sea's maritime networks and Southeast and East Asian consumer societies, needs to be made more explicit through studies of wreck sites in the future.

CHAPTER 2

Southern Han's "Bad Money" in the Java Sea: Possible Reasons for the Southward Flow of Money in the Early Tenth Century

Li Man

In 1997, a shipwreck was excavated off the northwestern coast of Java, Indonesia, near the waters of the Intan oilfields.[1] In the wreck, there was a large number of commercial cargoes of different origins, including Chinese silver ingots and coins. Some of the ingots had inscriptions like "*Guiyang jian*" 桂陽監 (Guiyang industrial prefecture) and "*yanshui shangse yin*" 鹽稅上色銀 (Superior quality silver for the salt tax). There was also a small amount of lead coins from the Southern Han 南漢 Dynasty (917–971) known as "*Qianheng zhongbao*" 乾亨重寶. In 2003, also in Indonesia, northwest of Cirebon, another shipwreck was discovered from which "hoards of" Chinese coins were excavated, among them a great number of Southern Han "*Qianheng zhongbao*" 乾亨重寶.[2]

This has attracted the attention of many scholars, but their interest has been mainly concentrated on speculations about the age of the wreck based on coin inscriptions, which, of course, is a very important and very relevant approach.[3] However, this chapter is more interested in another question: why and how did Southeast Asian businessmen treat Southern Han lead coins as "bad" money? This chapter will therefore examine the acceptance and circulation problems of lead coins as "bad" money by analysing the coinage mechanism and trade system of the Five Dynasties and Ten States (907–960), as well as the overseas trade networks of the Southern Han over a period of several decades. This will allow us to understand the historical logic behind the appearance of Southern Han lead coins in Southeast Asia.

---

1 This article is part of the project "Seafaring, Trade, and Knowledge Transfer: Maritime Politics and Commerce in Early Middle Period to Early Modern China", which has been supported by the Gerda Henkel Foundation from 2014 to 2020.

2 Horst Hubertus Liebner, "The Siren of Cirebon: A Tenth-Century Trading Vessel Lost in the Java Sea", PhD dissertation, University of Leeds (2014), 196–97.

3 See, for example, Denis Twitchett and Janice Stargardt, "Chinese Silver Bullion", *Asia Major (third series)*, 15.1 (2002), 23–72; Michael Flecker, *The Archaeological Excavation of the 10th century Intan Shipwreck* (Oxford: Archaeopress, 2002).

 | DOI:10.1163/9789004740556_004

1 General Situation of Trade and Currency Circulation in the Five Dynasties and Ten States and the Origin and Circulation of Lead Coins

Although the general picture during the period of the Five Dynasties and Ten States is one of separate regimes, trade connections and the circulation of currencies continued to function among the various political powers involved. As a result, a general pattern of economic and monetary circulation was formed: on the one hand there was the prosperity of inter-state trading among all these regimes, while on the other there was an overall shortage of money.

Firstly, despite overt and covert struggle between the different political powers, trade between them had never been interrupted. Rather, because of these conflicts and occasional small-scale wars, the lack of goods domestically caused by the situation increased the demand for cross-border trade. The markets between countries were exceptionally active. The Chu 楚 (896–951), Nan Ping 南平 (924–963), Min 閔 (909–945), Wu Yue 吳越 (907–978) and Southern Tang 南唐 (937–975) states, among others, traded with each other, regardless of distance and obstacles, and even traded with the Khitan across the sea. The Southern Tang established a long-term official post inside Khitan territory in order to manage bilateral political and trade relations. The Later Zhou Dynasty (951–960) enacted specific laws on commercial activities so as to facilitate the smooth conduct of trade. At that time, all regimes paid a great deal of attention to the development of commerce. Some of them even introduced tax-free measures to attract business travellers and strictly prohibited behavior interfering with business contacts. Some states counted on commercial revenues as economic pillars, such as Nan Ping and Chu. Most of these powers set up a large number of trade commissions, such as the Market Exchange Office (*boyi wu* 博易務) and the Recovery Office (*huitu wu* 回圖務),[4] both monopsony offices, on their borders to supervise and encourage commercial transactions. In addition to official trade, a variety of types of non-governmental trade and smuggling activities also prospered.

Secondly, since the end of the Tang Dynasty, the problem of the shortage of money had never been solved, and during the period of the Five Dynasties and Ten States, it deteriorated still further. There were two fundamental reasons for this shortage. First, due to conflicts occurring since the late Tang Dynasty, quartermaster finance and warfare seriously harmed the overall economic situation, which was characterized by a lack of goods. Therefore, not surprisingly,

4 *Zizhi tongjian* 資治通鑑, by Sima Guang 司馬光 (1019–1086), Hu Sanxing 胡三省 [ed.] (Beijing: Zhonghua shuju, 1956), 266.8702.

goods became both expensive and cheap. This economic situation gradually drove copper coins out of circulation. The most obvious symptom of this was that the intrinsic material value of the copper coins was higher than their monetary face value: in other words, the legal value of the copper coins was less than the cost of the material used for their production. Despite repeated prohibitions, this resulted in copper coins being melted down to produce copper utensils for profitable sale. For example, in the first year of the Tiancheng 天成 reign of the Later Tang Dynasty (926), the Imperial Secretariat (*zhongshu sheng* 中書省) and the Chancellery (*menxia sheng* 門下省) reported:

> After recently visiting and hearing from various prefectures, superior prefectures and circuits, [we know that] the copper wares for sale are highly priced, therefore more copper cash has been melted [for producing copper utensils], in order to get generous profit
>
> 訪聞近日諸道州府所賣銅器價貴, 多是銷熔見錢, 以邀厚利.[5]

This illegal profit was extremely high, to the extent that, if one "melted money to make copper wares, the profit is ten times [the monetary value of the copper coins]" 銷錢為器，其利十倍.[6] The profit was thus so high that, although the government had introduced stringent laws to prohibit such illegal commercial conducts and had made efforts to stabilize the prices of copper wares, the illicit trade still remained active. At that time the situation was, as an official reported in his memoires:

> At first, because of the high value of copper wares, a lot of businessmen melted coins to cast copper utensils. Bans were issued but not observed. Then [the price of copper utensils] was ordered to decrease, and the former ban was set up again, but [the illegal behavior] could still not be [successfully] prohibited.
>
> 先以銅器貴，市人多銷錢以為器，下令禁之，令不行。又降之，乃再行前敕，亦不能禁.[7]

---

5 *Wudai huiyao* 五代會要, by Wang Pu 王溥 [922–982] (Shanghai: Shanghai guji chubanshe, 1978), 27.434; *Wenxian tongkao* 文獻通考, by Ma Duanlin 馬端臨 [1254–1323] (Beijing: Zhonghua shuju, 1986), 9.93.

6 *Wenxian tongkao*, 9.93.

7 *Cefu yuangui* 冊府元龜, by Wang Qinruo王欽若 [962–1025], Zhou Xunchu 周勛初 et al. [eds.] (Nanjing: Fenghuang chubanshe, 2006), 501.5693.

The second reason for the shortage of money was the proliferation of bad money, i.e. iron coins, tin coins, pewter coins and even clay coins.[8] This situation is described in the *Wenxian tongkao* 文獻通考:

> Coins are classified in two ranks, namely, copper and iron ones. The Five Dynasties continued to use the coins of the Tang dynasty. In separatist regimes, [for instance] in Jiangnan (namely, the Southern Tang), coins are known as *Tangguo tongbao* 唐國通寶. And [in addition to this, they] cast new coins according to the Tang numismatic system, with inscriptions in seal script on the back of the coins. Later, iron coins were cast, in every ten coins, there were six iron coins, which equaled four copper coins. Since the Qiande 乾德 reign (963), only iron coins were used for trade, every ten iron coins equaled one copper coin. In Liangzhe (namely, Eastern Zhe and Western Zhe, modern Zhejiang) and Hedong (modern Shanxi) region, they cast their own iron coins, also in conformity with the Tang numismatic system.
>
> 錢有銅、鐵二等。五代相承用唐錢。諸國割據者，江南曰唐國通寶。又別鑄如唐制，而篆文其後。其後鑄鐵錢，每十錢，以鐵錢六，權銅錢四而行。乾德後，只以鐵錢貿易，凡十當銅錢一。兩浙、河東自鑄鐵錢，亦如唐制.[9]

Undoubtedly, these coins, which were made from low-quality and less valued material instead of copper, once entering the market, would further worsen the already very serious economic situation caused by the shortage of copper coins. It is understandable that people were often reluctant to spend coins of good quality and preferred to save them, first spending money of bad quality to get it off their hands. This resulted in a process of less and less good money circulating in local markets. Jia Yi 賈誼 (200–168 BCE), more than a thousand years earlier, had commented on this phenomenon, saying that "bad money prospers day by day, and good money dies out gradually" (奸錢日繁，正錢日亡).[10] This is what modern economists call "Gresham's Law", namely, that bad money drives good money out of circulation.[11]

---

8 *Jiu Wudaishi* 舊五代史, by Xue Juzheng 薛居正 [912–981] (Beijing: Zhonghua shuju, 1976), 1802.

9 *Wenxian tongkao*, 9.93.

10 *Xinshu jiaozhu* 新書校注, by Jia Yi 賈誼 [c.200–168 BCE], Yan Zhenyi 閻振益, Zhong Xia 鐘夏 [eds.] (Beijing: Zhonghua shuju, 2000), 4.167.

11 Peter Bernholz and Hans Gersbach, "Gresham's Law: Theory", in *The New Palgrave Dictionary of Money and Finance*, vol. 2 (London and Basingstoke: Macmillan, 1992), 286–288.

The circulation of social commodities is proportional to the amount of money invested in market circulation. Since there was a lot of cross-border trade, international currencies were bound to circulate. Therefore, the shortage of currency and the production of bad money had become a vicious circle of mutual cause and effect. This problem was not really solved until the early Song. It was against this historical, political and economic backdrop that the lead coins found on the Cirebon and Intan wrecks had been cast and were circulating at that time among the southern regimes. In fact, the Southern Han was not the first regime to cast lead coins.

The first regime to cast lead coins was the Min 閩 kingdom (909–945) in the reign of Wang Shenzhi 王審知 (862–925). According to the record in the *Zizhi tongjian* 資治通鑒, "(In the second year [of the Zhenming 貞明 reign, namely, 917]), lead coins were cast in Min, to circulate together with copper coins" (梁貞明二年; 閩鑄鉛錢，與銅錢並行).[12] This is the first time in Chinese history that lead coins were cast officially with governmental approval. This was because of the strong market demand for currency in circulation and the fact that, according to *Taiping guangji* 太平廣記,

> when Wang Shenzhi of Min first entered the town of Jin'an, he set up a regime with various administrative costs, therefore he was running short of funding.
>
> 閩王審知初入晉安。開府多事，經費不給.[13]

In order to continue raising taxes, Wang cast coins using lead discovered in Ninghua 寧化 county. In 918, Wang Shenzhi set up thirteen furnaces for casting lead coins in the southwest of Fuzhou for three main reasons. Firstly, during his reign, he continued to use old coins of the collapsed Tang dynasty, which were definitely not enough to satisfy the demand for circulation in the region. Secondly, foreign trade also had urgent demands for large amounts of coins. Thirdly, Wang Shenzhi built a lot of temples and cast many copper Buddhas, but Fujian had always lacked copper and iron deposits. Casting copper Buddha statues could consume large quantities of copper. For instance, to cast just one Maitreya statue, sixty thousand *jin* of copper and three hundred *liang* of gold were needed.

12 *Zizhi tongjian*, 269.8808.

13 *Taiping guangji* 太平廣記, by Li Fang 李昉 [925–996] (Beijing: Zhonghua shuju, 1961), 126.895.

> Wang used sixty thousand *jin* of copper (approx. 38,400 kg) and three hundred *liang* of gold (approx. 12 kg) to cast a statue of Maitreya, with a height of three *zhang* and six *chi* (approx. 12 m).
>
> 王氏用銅六萬斤、黃金三百兩鑄彌勒，方三丈六尺.[14]

In the second year of the Qianheng reign, namely 918, only one year after Wang Shenzhi's trial circulation of lead coins, the Southern Han started casting lead coins as well. It seems that Wang's action had a certain impact in this respect. The *Nanhan shu* 南漢書 records that:

> [In the first year of Qianheng, 917], [copper] coins were cast, with the inscription *Qianheng zhongbao*, seven *fen* (roughly 2.3 cm) in diameter, three *zhu* and six *lei* in weight [roughly 2.34 *g*].... [In the first year of Qianheng, 918], lead coins were cast, with the inscription *Qianheng zhongbao*, ten of these lead coins equalling one copper coin in value. The larger [version of these lead coins] had a diameter of one *cun* [roughly 3.33 *cm*] and weighed three *zhu* and nine *lei* [roughly 2.54 *g*], while the inscribed character *bao* was swapped [with *zhong*, in terms of their position]. The smaller [version of these lead coins] had a diameter of seven *fen* [roughly 2.33 *cm*] and weighted the same as the copper coin.
>
> (乾亨元年)鑄錢。文曰乾亨重寶, 徑七分，重三銖六參。……(乾亨二年)鑄乾亨重寶鉛錢, 十當銅錢一。大, 徑寸, 重三銖九參, "寶" 字傳形;[15] 小，徑九分，重如銅錢).[16]

Therefore, before 917, the money used in the Southern Han region should have consisted of the old coins from the Tang Dynasty. In 917, the first year of the Qianheng reign, copper coins were cast, but the amount of copper coins with the inscription *Qianheng zhongbao* remains unknown. Due to the

14 *Sanshan zhi* 三山志, by Liang Kejia 梁克家 [1128–1187], Fuzhou shi difangzhi bianzuan weiyuanhui 福州市地方志編纂委員會 [eds.] (Fuzhou: Haifeng chubanshe, 2000), 33.517.

15 "寶"字傳形 means "重寶"二字傳形, according to *Nanhan ji* 南漢記, by Wu Lanxiu 吳蘭修 [*juren* 1808], *Wudai shishu huibian* 五代史書彙編, vol. 10 (Hangzhou: Hangzhou chubanshe, 2004), 2.6618.

16 *Nanhan shu* 南漢書, by Liang Tingnan 梁廷枏 [1796–1861] (Guangzhou: Guangdong renmin chubanshe, 1981), 2.7, and *Nanhan shu* 南漢書, by Liang Tingnan 梁廷枏 [1796–1861], *Wudai shishu huibian* 五代史書彙編, vol. 10 (Hangzhou: Hangzhou chubanshe, 2004), 6362.

fact, however, that the shortage of both copper resources and copper coins in market circulation remained unsolved, and also that no further records were discovered of the casting of copper coins except in 917, the quantity of copper coins cast in that year was presumably not large. In 918, after lead coins were cast, three kind of coins might have circulated simultaneously in the territory of Southern Han, namely old Tang dynasty copper coins, *Qianheng zhongbao* copper coins and *Qianheng zhongbao* lead coins. This situation lasted for more than twenty years, until the Qianhe 乾和 reign (first year of Qianhe, i.e. 943).

Shiguo chunqiu 十國春秋 records clearly describe the situation with the economy and currency in the Southern Han state:

> [In the fifth year of the Dabao 大寶 reign, 962], within the city, *Qianheng* [*zhongbao*] lead coins were used, and outside the city *Qianheng* [*zhongbao*] copper coins were used. Violators [were to be sentenced] to death. If any official's salary was paid in copper coins, in most cases he was bestowed with a superior gift. [*Hanshi* 漢史 of *Shiguo jinian* 十國紀年 records: After the reign of Qianhe, [the government] gathered more copper coins. Inside the city lead coins were used, and outside the city copper. [Copper] entering the city or [lead] leaving the city were forbidden; any violator would be executed. Salaries of officials were not paid in copper coins unless a special act of grace was being bestowed.
>
> (大寶五年)是時，城以內行乾亨鉛錢，城以外行乾亨銅錢，犯禁者罪至死。凡百官俸祿給銅錢者，多出自上恩焉。(十國紀年漢史曰：乾和後多聚銅錢，城內用鉛，城外用銅，禁其出入，犯者抵死。俸祿非特恩，不給銅錢).[17]

From this source, we can see that, from the Qianhe reign until the end of the regime in the fourteenth year of the Dabao reign (971), for nearly three decades, lead coins were used as a major currency in the Southern Han state.

However, the puzzling point is this: now that these lead coins were only allowed to circulate within the cities under Southern Han regime and are rarely found elsewhere in archaeological discoveries in other regions of China, how did they make their way to Southeast Asia? If this bad money only had purchasing power within the Southern Han realm, why should a ship in Southeast Asia carry it? Especially in the case of the Cirebon shipwreck, a lot of lead coins from the Southern Han dynasty were discovered. The reason given by Denis

17 *Shiguo chunqiu* 十國春秋, by Wu Renchen 吳任臣 [1628–1689] (Beijing: Zhonghua shuju, 1983), 863.

Twitchett and Janice Stargardt does not seem to explain this case at all reasonably, namely that the lead coins of the Southern Han discovered in the Intan shipwreck functioned as change used in bulk trading: "the coins may, since the value of such lead coins was so trivial – one tenth of that of copper cash – equally well represent 'small change' left after trading was concluded, perhaps kept for use on a future voyage to Guangzhou."[18]

2 The Flow of "Bad Money"

According to archaeological information, low-quality coins of the southern kingdoms during the period of the Five Dynasties and Ten States, including the *Qianheng zhongbao* 乾亨重寶 lead coins of the Southern Han, the *Guangzheng tongbao* 廣政通寶 iron and lead coins of the Later Shu 後蜀 (934–965), the *Qianfeng quanbao* 乾封泉寶 and the *Qianyuan zhongbao* 乾元重寶 iron and lead coins of Ma Chu 馬楚 (926–951), were very rarely, if ever, discovered far away from where they had been cast. This fact indicates that the circulation of low-quality coins was mainly limited to those regions. Although small amounts of bad money might cross borders and flow into other regions, neither archaeological evidence nor historical records indicate the possibility of large-scale cross-border flows of bad money.

This is not only the case for the period of the Five Dynasties and Ten States. Even under the early Song Dynasty, after the reunification of China, being dissatisfied with the incomplete central monetary system, the Song central government allowed certain regions to use their old money, i.e. low quality coins, in the short term, but only limited for local circulation. Ma Duanlin 馬端臨 (1254–1323) described this in his *Wenxian tongkao* 文獻通考:

> Since the conquest of Guangnan and Jiangnan, old money from these regions were allowed to be used expediently, without crossing the border of their Circuit.
>
> 自平廣南、江南, 聽權用舊錢, 勿得過本路之境. [19]

Therefore, these low-quality coins could only be used with difficulty in trading with other countries and was not even allowed. As they could not be used beyond a limited territory, lead coins as bad money could therefore have a

18 Twitchett and Stargardt, "Chinese Silver Bullion in a Tenth-Century Indonesian Wreck", 59.
19 *Wenxian tongkao*, 9.93.

value for circulation only in a specific region for general equivalent exchange. Here we are faced again with the two questions raised at the end of the previous section. Firstly, why did the lead coins of the Southern Han not flow into neighbouring Chinese regimes, yet appeared in Southeast Asia. Secondly, what was the purpose of the low-quality lead coins being carried on board the Intan and Cirebon shipwrecks? Answering the second question is hindered by lack of information concerning the ethnicity, country of origin and identity of the ship owners.

The tentative answer to these two questions offered in this chapter is based on two arguments. Firstly, the Five Dynasties, namely, the self-esteemed orthodox Central dynasties, the Later Liang 後梁 (907–923), the Later Tang 後唐 (923–936), the Later Jin 後金 (936–946), the Later Han 後漢 (947–950) and the Later Zhou 後周 (950–960), all rejected lead coins, therefore making a northward flow of lead coins much less likely. Secondly, the Southern Han regime to a large extent money inherited the maritime trade network of the late Tang Dynasty and enjoyed frequent trade contacts with Southeast Asia. Moreover, Southeast Asian currencies developed comparatively very slowly and emerged very late. Because the use of large, high-value units of precious metals was only suitable for large quantity trading, but not for fragmented transactions, foreign coins, including Chinese, Arabian and Persian coins, circulated widely in Southeast Asia.

3 Monetary Policy Differences between the Five Dynasties and the Ten States

In the late Tang period, after repeated trials and contests among a number of military commissioners, an evenly matched situation arose between the different armed separatist regimes. On the one hand, the five central dynasties, namely the Later Liang, the Later Tang, the Later Jin, the Later Han and the Later Zhou, consecutively claimed and were more or less acknowledged to be officially legitimate empires, having inherited their legitimacy from the Tang. As for the Ma Chu 馬楚 (926–951), the Nan Ping, Min and Wu Yue, they all accepted royal titles granted by the Five Dynasties. Together they formed a central dynastic system with the Five Dynasties as the successor suzerain state, while the Chu, Nan Ping, Min, and Wu Yue served as satellite states. On the other hand, the Southern Tang, the Southern Han, the Northern Han 北漢 (951–979), the Former Shu 前蜀 (907–925) and the Later Shu 後蜀 (934–965), as well as other neighboring non-Han regimes, formed another system that competed with the central dynastic system, in accordance with their own ways and interpretations of political legitimacy. Although all the states in these two systems, to protect their own interests, disputed with each other from time to time, they maintained mutual recognition and a system of checks and balances and did not embark rashly on warfare. Therefore, more than half a century of roughly peaceful separatist coexistence was maintained. Therefore, the Five Dynasties and the Ten States coexisted, being largely independent from one another, but the greatest difference between these two groups of regimes is that the five central dynasties, self-esteemed orthodox dynasties, believed themselves to be legitimate successors of the Tang Dynasty, while the ten states were satisfied with being politically independent and did not consider claiming official legitimacy.

This difference, once reflected in monetary policy, reflects the fact that the five dynasties, as self-claimed officially legitimate dynasties, paid more attention to government credit and image. In casting coinage, they acted more responsibly. Almost all the coins they cast were made of copper, reflecting more sophisticated craftsmanship, and low-quality coins were far fewer. Firstly, the coins cast by the Five Dynasties were made of copper, generally of high quality, i.e. more valuable mint metal, the purity and craftsmanship of the coin being of high quality, while no low-quality coins of lead, tin, iron or other inferior materials were permitted. Secondly, most coins had the denomination "1" (known as *xiaoping qian* 小平錢), and coins with larger denominations were generally not cast. Thirdly, each of the Five Dynasties cast just one kind of coin, and therefore the phenomenon of coins made from a variety of materials and with a variety of denominations appearing simultaneously in circulation did not happen. The Later Liang and Later Tang cast only very small amounts of coins, just for symbolic reasons, and as old Tang coins were mostly used, there was no numismatic chaos at that time. The Later Jin Dynasty, out of good intentions, once loosened its casting policy for a short period of time, allowing local non-government exploitation of copper mines and the casting of cooper coins in compliance with a specific royal stipulation, resulting the fact that the quantity of lower-value alloy coins increased, while their quality decreased. But even during this short-lived situation, coins with large denominations were very rarely seen, let alone lead or iron coins. The coinage of the Later Han Dynasty and the Later Zhou Dynasty increased significantly, using high-quality copper and delicate crafting with beautiful inscriptions. The quality of coins from these two dynasties is generally recognized as comparable to that of the *Kaiyuan tongbao* 開元通寶 coins of the Tang dynasty, therefore representing the peak of coinage among the Five Dynasties.[20]

20 *Wenxian tongkao*, 9.93; *Jiu Wudai shi*, 135.1802; *Jiu Wudai shi*, 146.1948; *Zizhi tongjian*, 274.8953.

By contrast, the ten states and the warlord regimes competed in casting low-quality coins. Two points concerning their attitudes towards coinage are to be noted. Firstly, inferior metal was used competitively in casting coins. Metals with low value and easy access were heavily used for coinage: for instance, lead, tin, iron and other base metals becoming the main materials used for the national coinage. The Wu Yue, Min, Yin, Chu, Southern Han and Later Shu states, among others, cast large amounts of lead and iron coins. These regimes rarely used copper for their coinage. Liu Shouguang 劉守光 (?–914), the son of Liu Rengong 劉仁恭 (?–914), even used clay for coinage.[21] Secondly, a large quantity of coins with insufficient intrinsic value were cast by these regimes. There were two kinds of undervalued coins: coins with overvalued denominations, and coins with less, or less valuable, metal. Both methods led to the nominal value of the coin being seriously out of line with its intrinsic value.[22]

Therefore, in regions controlled by the central dynasties, finely crafted copper coins with the denomination "1" (*xiaoping qian*) were used, and lead or iron coins were strictly prohibited from circulating. Two separate zones of the circulation of good money and bad money were formed, so that the distinction between purity and impurity was clear. Copper coins from the Five Dynasties certainly enjoyed greater purchasing power in the Ten States. Merchants from the south who traded in the north usually either carried inferior quality coins to buy goods or sold goods for high-quality copper coins. Some regimes even took to exporting inferior coins to rival regimes as an economic strategy. For instance,

> at the beginning, when [Ma] Yin, the king of Chu, annexed Hunan, he did not levy tax from merchants [in his territory], therefore businessmen gathered from all directions in [Chu]. Hunan is rich in lead and iron ore, therefore [Ma] Yin adopted the strategy of Gao Yu, the Military Chief Administrative Assistant, to cast iron and lead into coins. Businessmen could not use these coins outside of Chu's territory, therefore, all of them exchanged [these lead and iron coins] into goods. Thus [Chu] could trade in a variety of goods from other places with its remnant goods, and the state became rich.
>
> 初，楚王殷既得湖南，不征商旅，由是四方商旅輻湊。湖南地多鉛鐵，殷用軍都判官高郁策，鑄鉛鐵為錢，商旅出境，無所用之，皆易他貨而去，故能以境內所餘之物易天下百貨，國以富饒.[23]

21 *Jiu Wudai shi*, 135.1802.

22 *Wenxian tongkao*, 9.93; *Jiu Wudai shi*, 135.1802.

23 *Zizhi tongjian*, 274.8953. See also Biography of Ma Yin, in *Jiu Wudai shi*, 133.1757.

The fact that low-quality lead coins illegally entered circulation while high-quality copper coins were stealthily carried over the borders worsened the shortage of coins in the central dynasties. This problem became even more serious in the Later Tang Dynasty. In the second year of the Tongguang 同光 reign (924),

> when shops and stores were counting coins, there were a lot of tin and pewter coins with small denominations to be picked out which were all brought in by wholesalers from Jiangnan [regions south of the Yangtze River].
>
> 市肆間點檢錢帛，內有錫鑞小錢，揀得不少，皆是江南綱商挾帶而來.[24]
>
> High quality coins were exchanged and stored by rich families. This is really a harmful behaviour [to the economy], and counter measures should be planned [against it].
>
> 換易好錢，藏貯富室，實為蠹弊，須有條流.[25]

All dynasties repeatedly condemned the perniciousness of bad money publicly and spared no effort in banning it. For instance, in the capital cities and all prefectural capitals, coins used in shops and markets had to be carefully examined, and all counties along the river had to check all ships pulling ashore in order to prevent bad money from being brought in for the purpose of trading it against good money.[26] Checkpoints were set up at the city gates, and "copper coins amounting to more than five hundred were forbidden to take out of the city" (五百已上，不得放出).[27] The best way of countering the use of bad money was to cast enough high-quality coins to meet the needs of commercial circulation, supplemented by the necessary legal sanctions, thus driving low-quality coins out of circulation. Thus, by controlling the inflow of bad money on the one hand and providing sufficient good money on the other, by the reign of Shizong of the Later Zhou 周世宗 (921–959), there were enough coins of high quality in circulation, removing the threat of bad money.

Therefore, in general, the Five Dynasties successfully curbed any large-scale northward flow of bad money from the south. In this context, lead coins of the Southern Han were basically limited to circulating within their own territory

24 *Jiu Wudai shi*, 14.1948.
25 *Jiu Wudai shi*, 146.1948.
26 *Jiu Wudai shi*, 146.1948.
27 *Wudai huiyao*, 27.434.

and could not flow northward in larger amounts. To the south of the Southern Han is naturally Southeast Asia, linked to the north by sea. Did the Southern Han maintain sufficient trade links with Southeast Asia, thus making currency exchange with this region possible?

4 The Southern Han Regime and Its Commercial Networks

The founders of the Southern Han Dynasty were two brothers, Liu Yin 劉隱 (873–911) and Liu Yan 劉龑 (889–942). Liu Yin was originally the Military Commissioner of the Qinghai Army (*Qinghai jun jidushi* 清海軍節度使), i.e. the Military Commissioner of the East Lingnan Circuit (*Lingnan dongdao jidushi* 嶺南東道節度使), during the Tang Dynasty. Because of the decline of the Tang regime, he became a local separatist power, patronizing it as a local overlord. In 907, Zhu Wen 朱溫 (852–912, also called Zhu Huang 朱晃 or Zhu Quanzhong 朱全忠) usurped the throne of the Tang Dynasty and proclaimed himself emperor of the Later Liang Dynasty. Liu Yin was nominated by Zhu Wen, consecutively Commandery Prince of Dapeng (*Dapeng jun wang* 大彭郡王), the Prince of Nanping (*Nanping wang* 南平王) and the Prince of Nanhai (*Nanhai wang* 南海王). While acknowledging the suzerainty of the Later Liang, the two brothers took advantage of the chaotic situation in central China and availed themselves this precious opportunity to develop their own sphere of political and military influence. Supported by descendants of officials and elites of the Tang dynasty and those who were living in exile in this territory but could not return to central China due to the fall of the Tang dynasty, the Liu brothers gradually annexed territories controlled by different separatist forces in the circuits of Eastern and Western Lingnan, and occupied parts of Guangdong, Guangxi and Yunnan. The territory of the Southern Han encompassed as many as sixty prefectures in its heyday.

The capital of the Southern Han regime was located in Xingwang Prefecture 興王府, now Guangzhou, a hub of maritime commerce under the Tang dynasty. According to Arabic sources, Guangzhou was a distribution center for Arab and Chinese goods.[28] Chinese records also unsparingly praised the prosperity of Guangzhou at that time.

---

28 *Aḫbār aṣ-Ṣīn wa l-Hind*, by Abū Zayd Ḥasan ibn Yazīd al-Sīrāfī [fl. 916]. French translation: Jean Sauvaget (tr., ed.), *Aḫbār aṣ-Ṣīn wa l-Hind Relation de la Chine et de L'Inde redigee en 851* (Paris: Belles Lettres, 1948). Chinese translation cited: Mu Genlai 穆根來, Wen Jiang 汶江, Huang Zhuohan 黃倬漢 (trs.), *Zhongguo yindu jianwenlu* 中國印度見聞錄 (Beijing: Zhonghua shuju, 1983), 7.

> Foreign goods arrive every day, and pearls, spices, ivory, rhinoceros horn, hawksbill and other rare treasures overflow in China, all in endless supply.
>
> 外國之貨日至，珠香象犀玳瑁奇物溢於中國，不可勝用.[29]

Even in the under the already collapsing late Tang dynasty, some officials described the bustling scene of Guangzhou as an international commercial hub:

> Nanhai [i.e., Guangzhou] is in fact a land of chartered business, abundant in precious goods, such as gold, pearls, shells, carapaces, ivory and rhinoceros horn.
>
> 南海實筦榷之地，有金珠貝甲修牙文犀之貨.[30]

Therefore, Guangzhou at that time, according to another record, perhaps somewhat exaggerated, was still the most prosperous commercial maritime port city in China. Guangzhou is

> the interior of Zhanghai [ancient name for the South China Sea], a giant enclosure in the Panyu region. It boasts of foreign valuable goods, and its prosperity dwarfs other cities in the Wu and Yue regions [present day Jiangsu, Zhejiang, Fujian and Guangdong].
>
> 漲海奧區，番禺巨屏，雄蕃夷之寶貨，冠吳越之繁華.[31]

This prosperity owes a lot to the Guangzhou's geographical location, which "is an important intersection [of transportation] and is popularly known as prosperous. Merchants are always gathering in this place." (廣州地當要會，俗號殷繁，交易之徒，素所奔湊).[32]

Although in the sixth year of the Qianfu 乾符 reign (879), Huang Chao's 黄巢 (835–884) capture of Guangzhou was a major blow to commercial activities in this port city for a short period, the city gradually restored its stability

29 *Han Changli wenji jiaozhu* 韓昌黎文集校注, by Han Yu 韓愈 (768–824), Ma Qichang 馬其昶 [ed.] (Shanghai: Shanghai guji chuban she, 1986), 284.

30 *Quan Tang wen* 全唐文, by Dong Gao 董誥 [1740–1818] (Beijing: Zhonghua shuju, 1983), 789.8254.

31 *Quan Tang wen*, 827, 8717.

32 *Lu Xuangong quanji* 陸宣公全集 by Lu Zhi 陸贄 [754–805] (Shanghai: Shijie shuju, 1936), 110.

and brought its business and transportation back to prosperity. *Xin Wudai shi* writes:

> In the late Tang period, Nanhai was the last place to fall into chaos. Therefore, since Xizong, ministers who were selected to be local governors could only be appointed to Nanhai because all other places in the empire were out of control, except Nanhai.
>
> 唐末，南海最後亂。僖宗以後，大臣出鎮者，天下皆亂，無所之，惟除南海而已.[33]

Owing to a relatively stable political situation, trade activities in Guangzhou were quickly restored to their previous level. The Southern Han inherited the maritime commercial hub of Guangzhou from the Tang Dynasty. Therefore, after the fall of the Tang Dynasty, to a great extent it continued to trade with the rest of the world.

Judging from the tribute paid to Zhu Wen by Liu Yin and Liu Yan, we can easily see these precious goods being obtained through maritime trade, normally from southeastern Asian and Arab merchants. For instance, in 907, the year when Zhu Wen proclaimed his ascent to the throne, Liu Yan offered precious tribute on several occasions. In the first month of 907, "Guangzhou offered exotic treasures and famous medicines, of many different varieties" (廣州進奇寶名藥，品類甚多).[34] In the tenth month, he "furthermore offered *longnao*,[35] belts, pearl pillows, hawksbill, spices, etc." (又進龍腦、腰帶、珍珠枕、玳瑁、香藥等).[36] In the seventh month of 910, "Guangzhou paid a tribute of rhinoceros horn, and jade, and offered rose water perfume [which had arrived by] ship" (廣州貢犀、玉，獻舶上薔薇水).[37] In the twelfth month of 911, "Guangzhou offered rhinoceros, elephants, rare treasures, gold, and silver, etc."

33 *Xin Wudai shi* 新五代史, by Ouyang Xiu 歐陽修 [1007–1072] (Beijing: Zhonghua shuju, 1974), 6.811.

34 *Jiu Wudai shi*, 3.52.

35 The use of the term *longnao* 龍腦 (lit. "Dragon brains") in Chinese literature is a complex issue, as it is often used interchangeably with *longnao* incense (*longnao xiang* 龍腦香). *Longnao* refers to the resin or resin products of dipterocarp trees (also called borneol). In terms of its chemical composition, the main chemical composition of Dragon brains is borneol. Of them, the main component of natural borneol is almost pure d-borneol, the main component of moxa is l-borneol, and the main component of mechanized borneol is dl-borneol.

36 *Jiu Wudai shi*, 3.55.

37 *Jiu Wudai shi*, 5.84.

(廣州貢犀、象、奇珍及金銀等).[38] Gifts of exotic treasures from the Southern Han to the Later Liang were unparalleled at that time and showed that the Southern Han continued to highlight maritime commerce and maintained a high level of international trade. In 1069, in his handwritten edict to his feudatories, Song Shenzong 宋神宗 (r. 1067–1085) commented on the maritime trade of the Wuyue and the Southern Han regime as follows:

> [talking about] the pillars for the economy of the southern and eastern regions, maritime commerce is also one of them. When Qian and Liu stealthily claimed sovereignty over Zhejiang and Guangdong, they managed to be sufficiently rich inside [their regimes], and strong enough to confront central dynasties from the outside. One of the reasons for this is that they won maritime merchants over by proper means. You should initiate creative strategies, not only to earn a substantial annual profit, but also to attract outlying countries to converge on China. That would be something spectacular.
>
> 東南利國之大，舶商亦居其一焉。昔錢、劉竊據浙、廣，內足自富，外足抗中國者，亦有籠海商得術也。卿宜創法講求，不惟歲獲厚利，兼使外藩輻中國，亦壯觀一事也.[39]

Wuyue mainly developed maritime trade with Japan, while the Southern Han focused on maritime trade with Southeastern Asia. The Southern Han actively extended their overseas contacts to acquire maximum control of the trade in the South China Sea region, sometimes even with military power. In the autumn of the second year of the Qianheng reign (918), Liu Yan sent General Liang Kezhen 梁克貞 (birth and death unknown) with a fleet to attack Champa, thus

> coercing [Champa] with military power and returning with the treasures on board. Evermore, all overseas states [in the South China Sea region] succumbed to [the Southern Han].
>
> 脅以兵威，載寶以還。自是，海外皆懾服.[40]

---

38 *Jiu Wudai shi*, 6.100.

39 *Xu zizhi tongjian changbian shibu* 續資治通鑑長編拾補, by Huang Yizhou 黃以周 [1828–1899] (Beijing: Zhonghua shuju, 2004), 5.239–240.

40 *Nanhan shu* (ed. 1981), 11.56, see also *Nanhan shu* (ed. 2004), 11.6471.

Under the strict control of the central dynasties on the north, Southern Han coins as bad money were prevented from flowing north. The above outline of Southern Han's maritime ties with overseas merchants and the archaeological discoveries in the Intan and Cirebon shipwrecks show that the Southern Han regime maintained a considerably larger scale of trade with overseas merchants, although understandably less than the previous Tang and later Song dynasties. Large-scale trade also means inevitable currency exchanges. These commercial exchanges provided possibilities for the lead coins of the Southern Han to flow southward. The question remains: what role did the currency of the Southern Han play in their foreign trading activities?

5 The Reasons for the Flow of Lead Coins to Southeast Asia

When people use gold, silver or copper coins to effect the exchange of goods, they will calculate and value them according to the actual valuation of the metal. For example, if one catty (*jin* 斤) of wheat is worth one tael (*liang* 兩) of copper, then one tael of copper will be weighed in exchanging one catty of wheat. Because repeated weighing is very inconvenient, a tael of copper is forged into a special shape, its weight marked on its surface. This is the standardization of weighing, and in this way, the original currency is born. The standardized and weighed metal quickly became the most important medium in trade because of the saving of energy and time involved in weighing and cutting the metal. However, in addition to a considerable level of casting technology and the necessary metal deposits, the numismatic development of a region also requires a certain level of economic activity, government control of coinage and much else. Therefore, for a small and ancient regime, organizing all the necessary conditions for casting its own currency is normally beyond its capacity. That is why the coins of big states were usually directly imported and used by neighbouring small states in ancient times, especially in Asia.[41]

41 Peng Xinwei 彭信威, *Zhongguo huobi shi* 中國貨幣史 (Shanghai: Shanghai renmin chubanshe, 1958), 6. Weng Dongling, "Overseas Circulation of Ancient Chinese Currency on the Silk Road and Its Enlightenment", *Journal of Shihezi University* (*Philosophy and Social Sciences*) 32.6 (2018), 90. Here we are mainly talking about Asia, but similar cases also can be found in European history. For instance, in Scandinavia, coins from England were used on quite a large scale, and at times foreign coins circulated there extensively, passing by weight. Many English coins – since found in Scandinavian hoards (Danegeld payments) – have characteristic peck-marks where the fineness of the silver was tested. John Chown, *A History of Money: From AD 800* (London and New York: Routledge / Taylor & Francis, 1994/1996), 28.

Therefore, in the ancient international trade and commercial exchange, coins, as a measure of value and a means of exchange, flow easily across borders and circulate in countries where there is a demand for international media for purposes of exchange. Archaeological discoveries show that, in the countries and regions along the Silk Road, many large or small zones of circulation have existed for the use of international currencies. For instance, from the fourth to seventh centuries, from the east of Persia to the Hexi 河西 Corridor of China, there was a circulation zone for Persian Sassanid silver coins. Similarly, from the 670s to the 740s, in the Hexi area, which was deeply influenced by the Tang dynasty's coin regulations, a special currency zone for gold and silver coins was established. Historically, in remoter areas of China, such as the Lingnan area (south of the Five Ridges), before the Tang dynasty, the use of metal currencies, especially in coined form, was very rare because, during the Six Dynasties, "in the Lingnan prefectures, salt, rice and cloths were used for exchanges; no coins were used" (其嶺南諸州，多以鹽米布交易，俱不用錢云).[42]

> In the Tang dynasty, people used more cloths and silks than coins [for the exchange of goods.] Before the Dali reign (766–779), in Lingnan, in addition to coins, [people] used gold, silver, cinnabar and ivory [for exchange].
>
> 唐時民間用布帛處多，用錢處少。大歷以前，嶺南用錢之外，雜以金銀、丹砂、象齒.[43]

At that time, in Southeast Asia, the situation was yet more primitive. Until around the tenth century, the monetary system of Southeast Asian countries was yet to be developed, and some countries did not even have their own coins. For instance, in Samboja (Sanfoji 三佛齊, Sri Vijaya),

> [there exist] no stringed coins; according to local custom, [people] traded with gold and silver in exchange for all kinds of things.
>
> 無緡錢，土俗以金銀貿易諸物.[44]

---

42 *Suishu* 隋書, by Wei Zheng 魏徵 [580–643] (Beijing: Zhonghua shuju, 1973), 24.690.
43 *Huang Zongxi quanji* 黃宗羲全集, by Huang Zongxi 黃宗羲 [1610–1695] (Hangzhou: Zhejiang guji chubanshe, 1985), vol. 1, 36.
44 *Songshi* 宋史, by Tuo Tuo 脫脫 [1313–1355] (Beijing: Zhonghua shuju, 1977), 489.14088.

In Java (Dupo 闍婆),

> [people] cut silver slices as money for trading. And one *hu* (60 kg) and two *dou* (12 kg) of millet is officially regarded as equivalent to one *qian* (5 g) of metal.
>
> 剪銀葉為錢博易，官以粟一斛二斗博金一錢.[45]

In Sukadana (Sujidan 蘇吉丹),

> for daily trading, alloy silver, chiselled into dice-shaped coins, with their official stamp sealed on, was used. Sixty-four pieces of these coins are allowed to be exchanged for one *liang* (50 g) of metal. Each coin can be used for the exchange of thirty *sheng* (one *sheng* = 0.75 kg) of rice, or forty *sheng*, or even to one hundred *sheng* of rice. It is used also in all other transactions.
>
> 民間貿易，用雜白銀鑿為幣，狀如骰子，上鏤番官印記。六十四隻準貨金一兩，每隻博米三十升，或四十升至百升，其他貿易悉用是。[46]

During the period of the Five Dynasties and Ten States, the money system in Java, where both Intan and Cirebon shipwrecks were discovered, was still very primitive, and strictly speaking there was no coinage. However, by the eighth to ninth centuries ritualized transactions had become monetized, and gold and silver metage coins, i.e. coins with a value corresponding to their weight, had appeared, though in very scarce quantities and with a very high nominal value. The high-value gold and silver coins recovered archaeologically were not suitable for small-scale purchases and were therefore scarcely found in circulation. Until the eleventh or twelfth centuries Javanese ports, smaller weight units were gradually adopted and smaller units appeared, for instance, the *kupang* (*kupang* = 0.603 g).[47] Even though the Javanese were able to produce coins with primitive tools, they were not able to produce sufficient quantities of coins to meet the circulation demand. Because of their

45 *Songshi*, 489.14091.

46 *Zhufan zhi jiaoshi* 諸蕃志校釋, by Zhao Rugua 趙汝適 [1170–1231], Yang Bowen 楊博文 [ed.] (Beijing: Zhonghua shuju, 1996), 60.

47 Jan Wisseman Christie, "Money and Its Uses in the Javanese States of the Ninth to Fifteenth Centuries A.D.", *Journal of the Economic and Social History of the Orient*, 39.3 (1996), 243–86; and Robert S. Wicks, "Monetary Developments in Java Between the Ninth and Sixteenth Centuries: A Numismatic Perspective", *Indonesia* 42 (1986), 43–77.

exquisite craftsmanship, portability, convenience for measurement and rich cultural connotations, Chinese coins were generally highly favoured by many Southeast Asian countries. This situation basically remained unchanged until the Ming Dynasty: for instance, the *Yingya shenglan* 瀛涯勝覽, a book written in Ming Dynasty (1368–1644), recorded that:

> [in Java,] Chinese copper coins from past dynasties are generally in common use … [In Palembang,] Chinese copper coins are also used for daily trade in the market, together with cloths and silks [functioning as general equivalent exchange] etc. … [In Sri Lanka,] Chinese musk, fine silk, colorful spun silk, celadon wide mouth bowls, *copper coins* [my emphasis], and camphor are especially welcome. Jewellry would be used in exchange for them.

> [爪哇國]中國歷代銅錢通行使用[48]…… [舊港國]市中交易亦使中國銅錢，并用布帛之類。[49]…… [錫蘭國]中國麝香、紵絲、色絹、青磁片碗、銅錢、樟腦，甚喜。則將寶石珍珠換易.[50]

Java and Palembang are both in present-day Southeastern Asia, Sri Lanka in South Asia. This record shows that, at that time, Chinese copper coins were in common use in those regions. During that period in South and Southeast Asia, there were many large and small regimes. For domestic and international trade, they urgently needed a creditable currency in order to do business successfully with other countries. For coinage, control over copper ores, or at least a stable source of copper, was needed, and at the same time, alongside a sufficient casting technology. This was already too difficult for many small countries. Moreover, shoddily minted coins can easily damage confidence in the currency. Therefore, producing one's own coins in these conditions of insufficient technology and cooper deposits is not feasible. As a result, if these small countries themselves cannot mint coins, how can they solve the problem of circulation demand? Of course, the best way is to use the coins from a country where there is confidence in the currency, such as China, so that Chinese coins are imported as a special commodity. For instance, according to the description of Bao Hui 包恢 (1182–1268), in the Song Dynasty, Japanese merchant ships

48 *Yingya shenglan jiaozhu* 瀛涯勝覽校注, by Ma Huan 馬歡 [1414–1451], Feng Chengjun 馮承鈞 [ed.] (Beijing: Zhonghua shuju, 1955), 8.

49 *Yingya shenglan*, 18.

50 *Yingya shenglan*, 37.

> first pass by the territory of Wen[zhou] and Tai[zhou], pulling along to the shore. Rich people openly trade with them. These Japanese are only fond of copper coins, anchoring at sea [for them], while what the [Chinese] coastal dwellers are fond of are the precious treasures onboard Japanese ships. Those worth one hundred *guan* [1 *guan* = 1,000 pieces of copper coins] can be obtained only for ten *guan*; and those worth one thousand *guan* of copper coins can be obtained only for one hundred *guan*.
>
> 預先過溫[州]、台[州]之境，擺泊海涯，富豪之民，公然與之交易。倭所酷好者銅錢，而止海上，民戶所貪嗜者，倭船多有珍奇，凡值一百貫文者，止可十貫文得之；凡值千貫文者，止可百貫文得之.[51]

This clearly shows that Japan favoured Song copper coins, and therefore dumped low-priced Japanese goods on to Chinese markets in order to obtain more Chinese coins. These Japanese merchants

> claimed to ship other sundry goods, but in fact [they] sail with tall, big, deep and wide ships, therefore [they] can carry away tens of thousands of *guan* of copper coins in one ship.
>
> 雖曰他有雜貨，其實以高大深廣之船，一船可載數萬貫文而去.[52]

In fact, from the Tang Dynasty to the Qing Dynasty (1644–1911), the continuous outflow of Chinese coins remained basically unchanged. According to Zhao Rugua's [also romanised as 'Rukuo'] 趙汝适 (1170–1231) records, in the Song Dynasty, Chinese businessmen often violated the law and secretly took copper coins abroad to trade in overseas states.[53] The *Yingya shenglan* records:

---

51 *Quan Songwen* 全宋文, ed. by Zeng Zaozhuang 曾棗莊, Liu Lin 劉琳 (Shanghai: Shanghai cishu chubanshe and Anhui jiaoyu chubanshe, 2006), 319.282.

52 *Quan Songwen*, 319.283.

53 See *Zhufan zhi*, 55: "There is a vast store of pepper in this foreign country and the merchant ships, in view of the profit they derive from that trade, are in the habit of smuggling [out of China] copper cash for bartering purposes. Our court has repeatedly forbidden all trade [with this country], but the foreign traders, for the purpose of deceiving [the government], changed its name and referred to it as Su-ki-tan." (此蕃胡椒萃聚，商舶利信蓰之獲，往往冒禁潛載銅錢博換。朝廷屢行禁止興販。番商詭計，易其名曰蘇吉丹。) Translation of this quote from Robert S. Wicks, *Money, Markets, and Trade in Early Southeast Asia: The Development of Indigenous Monetary Systems to* A.D. *1400* (Ithaca: Cornell University Press, 1992), 284.

> There are a lot of rich men among the barbarians, and they use Chinese copper coins from past dynasties for buying and selling and trading transactions.
>
> 番人殷富者甚多，買賣交易行使中國歷代銅錢.[54]

This is testified by archaeological discoveries of ancient Chinese coins as a kind of proof in various South Asian and Southeastern Asian countries. In some countries, a coin's value in circulation or its exchange value was far more important than its material value. The prevalence of lead-tin alloy coins in Kmir (Khmer) consisting of 90% lead is a good example. In places like Java, where coinage was underdeveloped, high-value precious metals appear to have been useless in small market transactions. Although the lead coins of the Southern Han were a kind of bad money, they were no doubt usable as a means of circulation. And as Wicks has shown, money was not used as money in Java, but as a commodity, a special commodity to be used for exchange, but not yet the so-called "universal equivalent".[55] Thus, as a result, the lead coins of the Southern Han could be welcomed as a currency with a lower value than copper coins.

> Most of the Chinese coins imported between the tenth and twelfth centuries by the Javanese must have circulated as much-needed small change in the domestic markets, and thus equivalencies between the indigenous and imported coins must have been standardized well before the fourteenth century.[56]

Although the lead coins of the Southern Han could not flow north because this was blocked by the northern dynasties, it was more likely that they travelled south to Southeast Asia through the maritime trade routes and the network that the Southern Han regime had inherited from the Tang dynasty. Because in Southeast Asia the demand for coins was very large, while the region's own coinage was underdeveloped, the exchange value of coins was far more important the value of their material alone. Therefore, lead coins were more likely

54 *Yingya shenglan*, 14.

55 Wicks, *Money, Markets, and Trade*, 43–77. On the function of lead coins and for a discussion of *picis* or *caixa* in early seventeenth-century Java, see Leonard Blussé, *Strange Company: Chinese Settlers, Mestizo Women and the Dutch in VOC Batavia* (Dordrecht: Foris Publishers, 1986), 35–48.

56 Wisseman Christie, "Money and Its Uses", 269.

welcomed in Southeast Asia, in contrast to the central Chinese dynasties that boycotted them.

6 Conclusion

In conclusion, it can be argued that the discovery of Southern Han lead coins in Javanese shipwrecks is not accidental, but a consequence of a variety of factors. Firstly, during the period of the Five Dynasties and Ten States, the monetary system of the Five Dynasties in central China was generally orthodox and creditable, proper copper coins being cast in line with their face value, while in the peripheral Ten States monetary systems were quite chaotic, many regimes, such as Min, Southern Han or Chu, issuing lead coins and other low-quality coins. Therefore, the two heterogeneous monetary systems of the Five Dynasties and Ten States formed two closed circles. The central dynasties exhausted all efforts to prevent the outflow of high-quality coins or the inflow of low-quality coins, and to a large extent their efforts were effective and successful. As a result, the ability of the lead coins of the Southern Han to flow north was very limited. At the same time, due to their geographical advantage and complete inheritance of the maritime trade network from the Tang dynasty, the Southern Han were able to maintain a relatively frequent maritime trade with Southeast Asian regions. Southeast Asia, at that period of time, was still underdeveloped in not having its own coinage system, therefore small change was in great demand for small-scale daily trading and transactions. Against this backdrop, in a place where cowry and foreign coins were widely used, lead coins from the Southern Han, disdained as bad money by the central dynasties of China, were quite readily accepted by Southeast Asian peoples. Lead coins of the Southern Han discovered in Javanese shipwrecks, including the Cirebon and the Intan wreck, are direct evidence of the trade between Southern Han and Southeast Asia, confirming the popularity of Chinese coins in Southeast Asia to a degree that even Chinese bad money was acceptable.

CHAPTER 3

Yuan Maritime Activities and the Role of Knowledge

John Chaffee

This paper is devoted to a particular form of cross-cultural knowledge transfer, namely state-sponsored knowledge collection, often of a military nature, about other countries. Such knowledge, of course, is something that states have always collected when confronted with potentially hostile neighbours, and during the Song, spying and intelligence-gathering directed at the Liao, Xi Xia and later the Jin were common.[1] However, there is little evidence of it in Song maritime relations except with regard to the Jin navy, and in the last years of the Song, the Mongols. By contrast, I will argue that during the Yuan, intelligence-gathering was an important part of its relations with other Asian maritime states, and that this involved merchants and merchant organizations in addition to envoys, for whom this was an expected role.

For a highly militarized dynasty and one that maintained a large navy and fought many foreign wars, the Song approach to maritime trade, especially trade with the South Seas, was remarkably pacific. Zhu Yu 朱彧 (1075–after 1119) describes how naval stations extending to Ru Island 溽洲 (seven hundred *li* west of Guangzhou) would spot ships approaching from the south and provide an escort for their passage to Guangzhou.[2] But that role was purely defensive. Likewise, the elaborate procedures of the Maritime Trade Superintendencies in Guangzhou, Quanzhou and elsewhere were aimed at managing the trade – inventorying cargoes, collecting revenues and treating foreign merchants well. But there were no attempts to make use of the powerful Song navy beyond the

1 The literature on spying in premodern China is sparse. Noteworthy are two books by the military historian Ralph D. Sawyer: see Ralph D. Sawyer, *The Tao of Spycraft: Intelligence Theory and Practice in Traditional China* (New York: Basic Books, 2004); Ralph D. Sawyer, *The Tao of Deception: Unorthodox Warfare in Historic and Modern China* (New York: Basic Books, 2007). They offer little for the purposes of this paper, for Sawyer's focus is exclusively on the military functions of spying and deception in the context of warfare, and not their role in foreign relations. In addition, the former deals exclusively with the pre-Qing period of ancient China. In the latter, the lengthy section on the Song deals exclusively on writings about these topics, and it has nothing on the Yuan.

2 *Pingzhou ketan* 萍洲可談, by Zhu Yu 朱彧 (Shanghai: Shanghai guji chubanshe, 1989), 2.25.

 | DOI:10.1163/9789004740556_005

coastal waters of the empire, to extend the influence of the superintendencies beyond the coast of China, or even to make use of the increasing numbers of Chinese merchants venturing abroad as sources of information. It is true that the Quanzhou superintendency was the site of the single most important Song compendium of information about the countries of maritime Asia, the *Zhufan zhi* 諸蕃志 (Description of Foreign Lands). Compiled by Zhao Rugua 趙汝适 (1170–1231) when he was the superintendent there in 1224–1225, it presents wide-ranging information he collected from merchants and mariners visiting Quanzhou, much of it representing new knowledge.[3] However, the *Zhufan zhi* was a personal undertaking of Zhao's; there is no evidence of proactive or systematic collection concerning maritime Asia on the part of the Song government, even while it was providing unprecedented support for trade with that part of the world.

This passive approach can also be seen in Song diplomacy with maritime states.[4] The dynasty was the recipient of large numbers of tribute missions, almost two hundred from maritime states during the Northern Song alone. However, the diplomatic missions that it sent abroad were few in number and were used mainly for announcements: four during the Yongxi 雍熙 era (984–987), when it invited states from the South Seas (Nanhai 南海) to engage in maritime trade with the newly reunified empire; and several missions in 1132 reaffirming the dynasty's ties with those states in the wake of its loss of northern China.[5]

Although most discussions of Yuan maritime activities stress continuities with the Song in its support of maritime trade, it should be recognized that the Mongols' objectives throughout the reign of Khubilai Khan (r. 1260–1294) were fundamentally different. Commercial concerns were of course important, for the Mongols were ever mindful of opportunities for economic gain. However, throughout the last decades of the thirteenth century military

3 *Zhufan zhi jiaoshi* 諸蕃志校釋, by Zhao Rukua 趙汝适 (Beijing: Zhonghua shuju, 2000); Frederick Hirth and W.W. Rockhill (trans.), *Chau Ju-kua: His Work on the Chinese and Arab Trade in the Twelfth and Thirteenth Centuries, Entitled* Chu-fan-chi (St. Petersburg: Imperial Academy of Sciences, 1911; reprinted: Taibei: Ch'eng-wen Publishing Company, 1971).

4 By contrast, in Song relations with the Liao and Jin, spying or the gathering of military intelligence was an important task of envoys. See Herbert Franke, "Sung Embassies: Some General Observations", in Morris Rossabi (ed.), *China Among Equals: The Middle Kingdom and Its Neighbors, 10th–14th Centuries* (Berkeley: University of California Press, 1983), 116–148, at pp. 137–139.

5 *Songshi* 宋史, by Tuo Tuo 脫脫 [1311–1355] (Beijing: Zhonghua shuju, 1977), 186.4559; Lo Jung-pang, *China as a Sea Power, 1127–1368: A Preliminary Survey of the Maritime Expansion and Naval Exploits of the Chinese People during the Southern Sung and Yuan Periods*, Bruce Elleman (ed.) (Hong Kong: Hong Kong University Press, 2012), 200.

activities predominated. Continuing his predecessors' drive for world conquest, Khubilai secured the submission of Koryŏ by 1270 and had his greatest success with the conquest of the Southern Song, which was completed in 1279. However, his ambitions and his actions extended beyond continental Asia. These included his 1274 and 1281 invasions of Japan, with plans for a third invasion that continued until late in his life; the ill-fated invasions of Champa and Annam in the 1280s, again with plans for another invasion continuing into the 1290s; and the invasion of Java in 1293.[6]

Even apart from invasions, Yuan maritime activities throughout the last third of the thirteenth century were all framed in terms of political domination backed by the threat of military conquest.[7] Numerous diplomatic missions were dispatched to Japan and to the countries of southeastern and southern Asia, with the envoys being given titles such as "Commissioner of the Pacification Office" of the target country, as well as the task of securing their "conditions of surrender" (*jiangbiao* 降表), which typically took the form of tribute missions from that country. In the case of Japan, they also created a Japan Branch Secretariat (日本行省) in anticipation of its successful conquest. The reports from these envoys included recommendations as to the advisability of conquest, as well as assessments of military capabilities. In 1273, the envoy Zhao Liangbi 趙良弼 reported on a mission to Japan with a recommendation that Khubilai ignored, with disastrous consequences.

> He had stayed a year in Japan, where he performed another function of an ambassador, which was to spy. On his return he presented to the khan a detailed report on the government and political situation of Japan, the location and number of towns, description of roads and fortifications, manners and customs of the people, and the spirit of the nation. He cautioned against launching an invasion of Japan because, he said, the country was not wealthy, but the people were warlike.[8]

---

6 Lo Jung-pang, *China as a Sea Power*, chapters 7 and 8. Mention should also be made of the Burmese campaigns of the 1270s.

7 See Mukai Masaki's 向正樹 excellent treatment of this period in Mukai Masaki 向正樹, "The Interests of the Rulers, Agents and Merchants Behind the Southward Expansion of the Yuan Dynasty", *Journal of the Turfan Studies: Essays on the Third International Conference on Turfan Studies, The Origins and Migrations of Eurasian Nomadic Peoples* (Shanghai: Shanghai guji chubanshe, 2010), 428–45. Mukai notes the pressure for continued conquest on the part of various groups in the Mongol power structure as one of the factors behind the military activities of this period.

8 Lo Jung-pang, *China as a Sea Power*, 253; *Yuanshi* 元史, by Song Lian 宋濂 [1310–1385] (Beijing: Zhonghua shuju, 1976), 208.

Zhao's advice was obviously ignored, but in other cases peaceful proposals prevailed. Tansen Sen has described the advice of the Uighur official Karandas (Jialu'nadasi 迦魯納答思) concerning the possibility of invading Siam and other southeast Asian states:

> All these are petty states. Although we can [easily] invade them, what can be gained [by belligerence]? The initiation of military operations will lead to the destruction of people's lives. [It would be] better to send embassies [to these kingdoms and] discuss the calamities [of warfare] and benefits [of submitting peacefully]. It is not too late to subjugate [these kingdoms] without waging a war.[9]

The active Yuan diplomacy with south Asia can also be viewed through this prism of Mongol aspirations, though mention should also be made of Khubilai's ongoing struggles with Khaidu (1235–1301) and the western khanates, which made the maritime link to the Ilkhanate in Persia of strategic importance. From 1272 to 1296, sixteen missions were dispatched from the Yuan court to India, primarily to the kingdoms of Ma'bar and Kollam. Four of the early missions were led by the military official Yang Tingbi 楊庭璧, but the second, in 1281, was especially interesting. For a 1281 mission to Kollam, a major port on the southwestern coast of India, the envoy Qasar Qaya (Hasaerhaiya 哈撒兒海牙) was given the title of "Commissioner of the Pacification Office [in-charge of] Kollam", a clear sign of the Mongols' intent to bring the maritime world under their sway. In fact, he and his fellow envoy Yang Tingbi only made it as far as Ma'bar, on the east coast of India, and reported that their inquiries about how to reach Kollam by land were rebuffed by local Ma'bar officials. More remarkably, a month after this interaction, and while they were still in Ma'bar, they were secretly visited by two men claiming to represent a local leader who claimed to be in danger from the rulers of Ma'bar (a group of five brothers). The men informed the Yuan envoys that the Ma'bar rulers were planning an attack on Kollam and promised, on behalf of their patron, that if the rulers surrendered he would send envoys to the neighbouring states persuading them to submit to the Yuan.[10]

This incident, which so far as we know did not result in major political changes in the Indian subcontinent, has been the subject of extensive analysis,

9 Tansen Sen, "The Yuan Khanate and India: Cross-Cultural Diplomacy in the Thirteenth and Fourteenth Centuries", *Asia Major*, Third Series, 19 (2006), 299–326, here 305–306; *Yuanshi*, 134.3260.

10 *Yuanshi*, 210.4669–4670.

to which I have little to add.[11] Rather, I raise it as an example of the kind of political intelligence that envoys were expected to obtain. But what of those who had no such political status? Were they also intelligence gatherers or spies? I will argue below that merchants in the service of the Mongols in fact had just such a role.

From the very beginnings of the Mongol empire, merchants had played a special and highly valued role, for it was they who could turn war booty into usable goods through trade. Those who served the Mongols were known as *ortoy* or "partners" (from the Turkish *ortaq*; in Chinese *wotuo* 斡脫). They came from all across Asia, though Uighurs and Turkestani Muslims were prominent. They were given capital by the *khans*, princes or court nobles, and upon their successful return they gave the bulk of the profits to their patrons while keeping the remainder for themselves. Educated, often cultured and necessarily multi-lingual, the *ortoy* came to perform a number of functions, for example, as commercial agents and tax farmers in northern China. And since they crossed political borders and ventured far beyond the Mongol domains, they could also serve as spies, that is, providing intelligence about the Mongols' enemies, actual and potential. In fact, the use of merchants as spies represented a major turning point in the history of Mongol conquest.

In 1215, Chinggis had concluded a treaty of friendship with the sultan of the Khwarazm Empire providing for freedom of trade between the two empires: "… from both sides let merchants (*tujar*) and caravans come and go and let the fineries and wares of my lands be brought to thou and let those of thy lands likewise be directed [to mine]."[12] When, four years later, Chinggis launched his invasion of the Khwarazms – a crucial step in the Mongol creation of the "world empire" – it was in retribution for the actions of a Khwarazm governor who had seized a large caravan sent by Chinggis, massacring the caravan members, including its four Muslim merchant leaders. The reason? The governor claimed that they were provocateurs and spies.

Before moving on, mention should be made of the size of the caravan. Persian sources describe it as consisting of 500 camel loads of "elegant wares from China", as well as gold, silver, silk and precious firs, and that 450 men were killed. According to a Chinese source, one hundred merchants (*guren* 賈人) died.[13] The caravan's enormous value may well have been a more important

11 See the extensive and detailed analysis of this episode by Tansen Sen, "The Yuan Khanate and India", 313–19.

12 Thomas T. Allsen, "Mongolian Princes and Their Merchant Partners, 1200–1260", *Asia Major*, Third Series, 2.2 (1989), 83–126, here 88, quoting Juvayni.

13 Allsen, "Mongolian Princes", 89–92.

cause of Chinggis's wrath than the injury to commerce, but it also indicates that the four merchant leaders were no ordinary traders, but rather great merchants, commanding wealth and followers. So it was with the *ortoy* generally: they were a merchant elite, wealthy, visible and trusted by their Mongol overlords, though undoubtedly hated by many others.

Following the conquest of the Southern Song, the Yuan court quickly expressed interest in maritime trade, establishing maritime trade offices in Quanzhou, the primary port handling the South Seas trade, as early as 1277, as well as Qingyuan (modern Ningbo), Ganpu 澉浦 and Shanghai.[14] In theory the terms of trade were quite liberal: merchants arriving with their goods were required to pay a percentage levy (*choujie* 抽解, or more commonly *choufen* 抽分) of 1 part in 10 (10 percent) for fine goods and 1 part in 15 (6.5 percent) for coarse goods – a rate that compared favourably with that of the Song – and then were free to sell their goods.[15] The problem was that the free trade upon which this was predicated often did not exist.

Our sources are frustratingly incomplete, but this much is clear. A request to invite merchants from abroad to come and trade was accepted in 1278 then reversed in 1279.[16] In 1284 the trade ban prohibiting Chinese merchants from going abroad was lifted, but as we shall see they were still subject to various restrictions. The task of supervising this new order was given to a new office, the maritime trade and salt administration office (*shibo du zhuanyun si* 市舶都轉運司).[17] In 1294 a ban on private maritime trade was lifted, then for some reason it was lifted again in 1298, reinstated in 1314, lifted in 1320, reinstated in 1322 and lifted permanently in 1323.[18]

This erratic history of trading activities can be explained in large part by the *ortoy*. In 1268, as the defeat of the Song became increasingly certain, the Yuan institutionalized the *ortoy* through the creation of the Wotuo zongguanfu 斡脫總管府 (General administration for the supervision of the *ortoy*), and in 1272 regional *ortoy* offices (Wotuosuo 斡脫所) were established. Then in 1280 the Wotuo zongguanfu was replaced by the Quanfusi 泉府司 ("supervising money office"), which was charged with managing the affairs relating to the incomes and expenditures of the emperor, empresses and imperial princes, and

14 *Yuanshi*, 94.2401. The entry reports the establishment of the Quanzhou office in one sentence and that of the other three in another, with different officials listed as overseeing them. This may reflect the special status of the Quanzhou office as the one most concerned with the South Seas.

15 Ibid., 13.296 and 43.2401–2402.

16 Ibid., 10.204, 211.

17 Ibid., 94.2402. Two such offices were created, the other being located in Hangzhou.

18 Ibid., 94.2401–2403.

overseeing the activities of the *ortoy*.[19] In 1284/4 the Quanfusi was subsumed under the Ministry of Finance (Hubu 戶部), but then was reinstated in 1285/8.[20] The record is spotty for the *ortoy* activities in Quanzhou, but we know that in 1286 the maritime trade offices were placed under the *ortoy* affairs office.[21] Then in 1288 the provincial *ortoy* affairs office (Xing-quanfusi 行泉府司) was given the task of managing naval relay stations between Quanzhou and Hangzhou.[22] We have a reference to the functioning of the quanfusi in 1290 and to the re-establishment of the provincial Quanfusi in 1291.[23] In 1297 provincial office was abolished, but in 1308 a Quanfuyuan 泉府院 (Supervising Money Bureau) was established, again with authority over the maritime trade offices.[24]

Also revealing in this regard is a regulation from 1292, part of a detailed set of regulations related to maritime commerce from the *Yuan dianzhang* 源典章:

> Officials are to provide the ships and capital and select the people to go abroad to trade in all kinds of goods. As to the profits, officials take 7 parts out 10 and the traders 易人 receive 3. Rich and powerful families are all prohibited from using their own money to go abroad and trade. Those who disobey will be punished: half of their family property is to be confiscated. The foreign guests travelling on the government ships to come and trade are subject to the percentage levy.[25]

Although there is no reference to *ortoy*, the procedures described for the conduct of trade conform closely to our understanding of *ortoy* practices, particularly the provision by the officials of the ships and capital and the seven-to-three split, the latter being much greater than the ten percent percentage levy paid by the foreign merchants. It is also noteworthy that wealth alone on the part of merchants in China was not sufficient for participation in this trade; only "selected traders", presumably the *ortoy*, could take part in it.

---

19 Ibid., 10.227.

20 Ibid., 10.265, 278.

21 Ibid., 14.292.

22 Ibid., 15.320.

23 Yokkaichi Yasuhiro, "The Structure of Political Power and the Nanhai Trade: From the Perspective of Local Elites in Zhejiang in the Yuan Period". Paper presented to the annual meetings of the Association for Asian Studies, San Francisco, March 2006, 3. For the 1290 reference see the account concerning Lizhiliwei below.

24 *Yuanshi*, 94.2401–2403.

25 Ibid., 43.2402. Franz Schurmann, *Economic Structure of the Yuan Dynasty* (Cambridge, MA: Harvard-Yenching Institute, 1956), 231. Presumably this division was made after the initial capital had been returned.

Of course, the 1280s and 1290s were not peaceful, trade-oriented years along the coast of China, for, as we noted earlier, the dynasty was on a wartime footing, engaged in multiple attempts at maritime conquest, and this necessarily affected commerce. In 1279 Yangzhou 揚州, Hunan 湖南, Ganzhou 贛州 and Quanzhou had been ordered to provide six hundred warships for a new invasion of Japan, of which two hundred were to come from Quanzhou. In 1281 Pu Shougeng 蒲壽庚 (fl. *c.*1250–1281) managed to get this number reduced to fifty on the grounds of the hardships that were being imposed upon the people.[26] Of course ship construction was not the same as maritime commerce, but it is noteworthy that Khubilai's refusal to grant Pu's request to invite foreign merchants to come and trade occurred just three months after the command for the six hundred ships, suggesting that his attention was focused on the invasion.

More important than this issue of ship requisitions is the fact that merchants and officials, especially Yuan military officials, were all involved in *ortoy* activities. Yokkaichi Yasuhiro 四日市康博 has described a number of hierarchical patronage networks that operated through the *ortoy* structure, in which wealthy merchants answered to Yuan generals and other high officials, who in turn answered to the emperor, imperial princes and the like. He identifies several such networks, but one of the most noteworthy was that of Pu Shougeng, already mentioned above, a Sino-Muslim Quanzhou merchant of great wealth and political influence who was linked to two of the leading generals from the conquest – Soyudu (Soudu 唆都, d. 1285) and Möngtei (Mangwudai 忙兀歹) in the 1280s–and above them to Shihāb al-Dīn (Shafuding 沙福丁), a high official with close ties to the court.[27]

26 *Yuanshi*, 10.209 and 11.230.

27 Another important network consisted of Zhu Qing and Zhang Xuan, who in the late Song were a salt merchant and pirate respectively, and their patron Sayyid Ajall Shams al-Dīn, a Muslim native of Bukhara who gained fame as an administrator in Yunnan. Both Sayyid Ajall and Shihāb al-Dīn had large families with numerous relatives who became important players in the maritime trade. Yokkaichi Yasuhiro, "The Structure of Political Power", 7–8. Mukai Masashi treats this same collection of individuals from a slightly different perspective, emphasizing the vertical and horizontal ties that connected them with both the Yuan court and each other in ways that allowed them to dominate the maritime trade. See Mukai Masaki, "Contacts between Empires and Entrepots and the Role of Supra-regional Network: Song-Yuan-Ming Transition of the Maritime Asia 960–1405", in *Empire, Systems, and Maritime Networks: Reconsidering Supra-regional Histories in Prenineteenth Century Asia Working Paper Series* (2010), 1–24; Fujita Kayoko (ed.), *Asian Empires and Maritime Contacts before the Age of Commerce*. 2009–2011, JSPS Grants-in-Aid for Scientific Research (B) No. 90454983, Empires, Systems, and Maritime Networks: Reconstructing Supra-Regional Histories in Pre-19th Century Asia, Working Paper Series 1 (Osaka, 2010), 13–16.

This was a remarkable constellation of individuals. Not only were Soyudu and Möngtei between them responsible for many of the victories against Song forces (one Fujian battle also involving none other than the envoy-to-be Yang Tingbi as a general under Soyudu), but it was to them that Khubilai turned in his campaign against Champa and Annam. Soyudu's *Yuan History* biography states that, "Seeing the submission [of the Song forces], the emperor considered Jiangnan to have been pacified and prepared for ventures abroad. [Soyudu] was promoted to minister of the left in the Quanzhou Branch Secretariat and was invited to discuss the countries of the southern barbarians 南夷諸國."[28] Although as early as 1280 Khubilai had begun active mobilization for a campaign against Champa, Soyudu argued in favour of achieving its submission through diplomacy, and led a mission that year to Champa to confer the title of King of Champa upon Indravarman VI. However, Khubilai established a Branch Secretariat of Champa with Soyudu as its minister of the right in 1281, and then, after the Champa government detained several Yuan envoys who were on their way south in 1282, in early 1283 the Yuan launched a punitive expedition against it under Soyudu's command.[29] From then until his death fighting Annamese troops in 1285, Soyudu was involved first in the unsuccessful campaign against Champa, and then in the failed first and second campaigns against Annam in 1284 and 1285. In the second campaign he was joined by Möngtei, who briefly commanded the Yuan land troops.[30]

Given the exclusively military nature of his activities in his last years, it is unlikely that Soyudu's *ortoy* activities extended beyond 1282, but this was not the case with Möngtei, who is known to have cooperated closely with Pu Shougeng, as well as with Shihāb al-Dīn, a financial bureaucrat who emerged with his brothers as one of the primary *ortoy* families of the 1280s and 1290s.[31] Möngtei, it should be noted, was also involved in the second Annamese campaign, where he commanded the land troops in 1285, though unlike Soyudu he returned to Quanzhou and, in conjunction with Pu Shougeng and Shihāb al-Dīn, played a dominant role in maritime trade well into the 1290s.

Returning to the question of intelligence from abroad, in this period of continuing military campaigns, this intermingling of generals and great merchants in the *ortoy* patronage networks would have provided an ideal vehicle

28 *Yuanshi*, 129.3152.

29 Lo Jung-pang, "China as a Sea Power", 287–89. The Cham court had become a magnet for Song loyalists, who convinced it to oppose the Yuan.

30 Lo Jung-pang, "China as a Sea Power", 289–95.

31 Yokkaichi Yasuhiro, "The Structure of Political Power", 6–11.

for intelligence gathering on the part of the *ortoy* merchants. Jung-pang Lo was categorical in asserting the merchants' roles as spies:

> The merchants served the Mongols as spies to gather information and as agents provocateurs to weaken the enemies' will to resist. They gave financial support to the Mongols to enable them to build their war machine, and they excited the cupidity of the Mongols to want to conquer foreign lands.[32]

Lo also notes that spying in this period was not limited to the Mongols. Describing the events of 1283, when the Mongols were preparing for a third invasion of Japan, he writes:

> Later in the year (1283), a Japanese spy ring was uncovered in South China. According to the confession of a captured spy, he and other spies were soldiers of the South China Division taken prisoner by the Japanese and recruited for espionage work. Sent back to China on Japanese merchant ships, their jobs were to find out about shipbuilding and the concentration of troops, and to infiltrate into the ranks of the New Attached Army.[33]

But by far the best evidence is the epitaph of the Tangut official Ligirqui (Lizhiliwei 立只理威, 1254–1310), who in 1290 supervised the *Ortoy* affairs office (Quanfusi) and uncovered financial records that detailed the funding of spying activities, records which he had been ordered to leave alone:

> As for the Quanfu, at the beginning of the dynasty it disbursed from and took into the [imperial] treasury valuables. The western merchants ("dog merchants") traded among the people [within China] as well as among the overseas barbarians. They made use of dynastic documents in order to travel without interruption far and wide. No one dared to impede them. For they used this as a pretext to penetrate remote and dangerous areas to spy. It was not really for profit.[34]

32 Lo Jung-pang, "China as a Sea Power", 308.

33 Ibid., 275–76, citing *Yuanshi*, 11.246.

34 *Daoyuan lei gao* 道園類稿, by Yu Ji 虞集 (1272–1348), in Yuanren wenji congkan 元人文集珍本叢刊 (Taibei: Xinwenfeng chuban, 1985), 42.30a, cited by Elizabeth Endicott-West, "Merchant Associations in Yuan China: The "Ortoy", *Asia Major* Third Series 2.2 (1989) 127–154, here 134. The translation is adapted from hers.

This passage is remarkable for at least two reasons. First, it illustrates the unique ability of merchants – in this case specifically *ortoy* merchants – to travel to distant places that were inaccessible to the military or even to envoys and gather intelligence. It should be obvious that these merchants were not major figures like Pu Shougeng or Möngtei but rather trusted subordinates who actually engaged in the trade. Second, it describes a secret programme of spying activity extending back in time in which the merchants were supposedly not simply reporting or passing on information about where they had visited, but were actually spies using trade as a pretext.

While I have not been able to find accounts illustrating this programme of *ortoy* spying or the specific nature of the intelligence gained, there are some indications of the particular value placed upon maps. In 1284, as Soyudu's Champa campaign was stalling, the Jianghuai Secretariat obtained a map of Champa that led to an attempted land invasion of this kingdom via Annam.[35] The source of the map is unclear, but it quite possibly came from merchants. Eight years later, at the end of the unsuccessful invasion of Java, the returning Yuan fleet reported booty consisting of prisoners from the Javanese royal family, large quantities of spices, batik cloth, gold, silver, ivory and rhinoceros horn, but also maps of the country and a population register.[36]

The early post-Song Yuan period was unique in Chinese history. Never before had south China been ruled by an alien people, and never before or since was the country to experience this combination of maritime trade encouraged by the state and a policy of naval and political expansion, albeit one that largely failed. In concluding this very preliminary paper, I would make two points, one structural, the other about the nature of the information flows that were involved in this period.

Despite the apparent similarities between Song and Yuan in their approach to maritime commerce – the active encouragement of overseas trade and the use of maritime trade offices – in practice the differences were great. The Song government was essentially passive, welcoming foreign merchants and tribute missions and permitting Chinese merchants to venture abroad. But it made no effort to extend its influence diplomatically or militarily, this despite the fact that it possessed a navy of unprecedented size and power. By contrast, the Yuan remained in conquest mode through Khubilai's reign through both active diplomacy and invasions, the latter involving frequent naval build-ups.

---

35 *Yuanshi*, 13.268; *Xin Yuanshi* 新元史, by Ke Shaomin 柯劭忞 [1848–1933] (Changchun: Jilin renmin chubanshe, 1996), 11; Lo Jung-pang, "China as a Sea Power", 290.

36 Lo Jung-pang, "China as a Sea Power", 307–8, citing Su Tianzhuo 蘇天爵, *Guochao wenlei* 國朝文類, 41.

It should be noted that the vital sea link with the Ilkhanate in Persia provided yet another reason for emphasizing naval power and political influence.

In the realm of commerce, the early Yuan also departed sharply from Song practices. Behind the confusing and at times contradictory institutional changes and regulations, the reality was the domination of trade by the *ortoy*, particularly the *ortoy* patronage networks. This should not be surprising: the Mongols were used to conducting trade through the *ortoy*, a system that emphasized trust between the rulers and merchants and which funnelled the major profits of the trade to the court (with all of those involved benefiting handsomely in the process). It was also a system that privileged the foreign servants of the Mongols, Muslim officials and merchants in particular.

In the post-Khubilai period, this constellation of military, diplomatic and commercial interests seems to have disintegrated. Both the conquests and the diplomatic missions ended. Discerning changes in the commercial realm is more difficult, though I would suggest that the constant changes to the private trade ban in the early fourteenth century reflects a breakdown in *ortoy* dominance of the trade, and that the permanent lifting of the ban in 1323 brought about a period of relatively free trade. This would accord with Ibn Battuta's (1304–1368/9) account of his time in China, which praises the role of the maritime trade office and contains not a hint of *ortoy* domination.

Turning to the flow of information, in this paper I have described a structure that allowed the Yuan government under Khubilai to engage in a widespread programme of intelligence gathering. I say "structure" because examples of this process are frustratingly difficult to obtain, given the secrecy that was involved. Still, we can surmise that the military was engaged in operational intelligence related to its campaigns, that the envoys provided political intelligence like that related to the intrigues in Ma'bar, as well as reports on the wealth and military strength of the countries that they visited, and that the *ortoy* merchants, with their ability to travel far and wide – behind the lines of potential enemies, as it were – provided kinds of information that were otherwise unobtainable.

Among the kinds of intelligence that the Mongols obtained in this manner, maps were undoubtedly among the most important, given their value to seafarers and military operations. We have seen how the appearance of a map of Champa led to the launch of a new military campaign in 1284 and how maps were prominently mentioned as being among the booty after the Java expedition. This leads me to a speculation with which I shall close. In the early fifteenth century, Zhu Di 朱棣 (1360–1424, r. 1403–1424), the Yongle 永樂 emperor, embarked on a series of foreign ventures in the south that bore an interesting resemblance to those of Khubilai: the invasion of Annam in 1406 and the great Zheng He 鄭和 (1371–1433) expeditions of 1403–1433. For the second and last time in Chinese imperial history, China's political and military power extended across maritime Asia. For nineteen years prior to the civil war that secured his emperorship, Zhu Di, as the Prince of Yan 燕王, had lived in the palaces of the Mongol emperors and governed Beiping 北平 (Yuan Dadu 元大都). He must therefore have had access to the Yuan government archives, including those resulting from Khubilai's intelligence-gathering operations. Could those records have played a role in his decision to launch the Zheng He voyages and perhaps in the operation of the voyages themselves?

CHAPTER 4

The *Wokou* 倭寇 Problem in Yuan China, 1300s–1360s

Ma Guang

As early as the Yuan dynasty, the *wokou*, literally "Japanese pirates" or "dwarf pirates", began to raid the coastal regions of China. In Ming times, the *wokou* raided China more frequently, inflicting great suffering on its residents and becoming a major threat to the regime, especially during the Jiajing reign (1522–1566). The *wokou* problem not only influenced the military, economic and social interests of China, it was also the central issue in diplomatic, military and commercial exchanges between China, Japan and Korea.

Although this early period is of great importance in tracing the origins of the *wokou*, most scholars have focused almost exclusively on the *wokou* during the Jiajing period but have paid little attention to the serious *wokou* problem during the Yuan and early Ming dynasties. There is no doubt that during the Jiajing reign the *wokou* were its most serious problem, which is important and deserves our attention. However, the *wokou* problem lasted for almost four centuries (from thirteenth to sixteenth centuries) in East Asia, and there is a big difference between the *wokou* in the early period and the later period from the 1520s to the 1560s in China. For example, some scholars have argued that it was the policy of prohibiting maritime trade that caused the outbreak of *wokou* in Jiajing times.[1] However, while the Chinese markets were open and the

1 There are numerous books and articles on the *Wokou* in the Jiajing period, including Merrilyn Fitzpatrick, "Local Interests and the Anti-pirate Administration in China's South-East 1555–1565", *Ch'ing-shih wen-t'i* 4:2 (1979), 1–50; Roland L. Higgins, "Pirates in Gowns and Caps: Gentry Law-breaking in the Mid-Ming", *Ming Studies* 1 (1980), 30–37; James Geiss, "The Chia-ching Reign, 1522–1566", in Frederick W. Mote and Denis Twitchett (eds.), *The Cambridge History of China, Vol. 7, The Ming Dynasty, 1368–1644, Part 1* (Cambridge: Cambridge University Press, 2008), 490–510; James K. Chin 錢江, "Merchants, Smugglers, and Pirates: Multinational Clandestine Trade on the South China Coast, 1520–50", in Robert J. Antony (ed.), *Elusive Pirates, Pervasive Smugglers: Violence and Clandestine Trade in the Greater China Seas* (Hong Kong: Hong Kong University Press, 2010), 43–57; Li Kangying 李康英, *The Ming Maritime Trade Policy in Transition, 1368 to 1567* (Wiesbaden: Harrassowitz, 2010); Chen Maoheng 陳懋恒, *Mingdai wokou kaolüe* 明代倭寇考略 (Beijing: Beijing renmin chubanshe, 1957); Chen Wenshi 陳文石, *Ming Hongwu Jiajing jian de haijin zhengce* 明洪武嘉靖間的海禁政策 (Taibei: Guoli Taiwan daxue wenxueyuan, 1966); Tanaka Takeo 田中健夫, *Wokou: Haishang*

 | DOI:10.1163/9789004740556_006

Yuan government permitted Japanese merchants to conduct maritime trade, there were still a lot of *wokou* raiding activities in the coastal regions of China. Why were the *wokou* so active even when there was an open market? A large number of Chinese people joined the *wokou* to plunder the coastal regions in the Jiajing period.[2] Were there also numerous Chinese people raiding the coast with the *wokou* in Yuan times? How can we explain the differences in the two different times? It is well known that the *wokou* raided southeast China, in areas such as Zhejiang, Fujian and Guangdong, during the Jiajing reign, but few historians realize that the *wokou* also seriously raided the coastal regions of northern China during the early Ming dynasty. None of the questions posed above have yet been answered sufficiently in studies of this theme. Therefore, in order to obtain a bigger picture of China's *wokou* problem, it is imperative to study their origins and then make a comparative analysis of the early *wokou* with those in the later Ming.

Since the *wokou*'s characteristics, such as members, places of origin and targeted areas varied across time, the first essential step in our approach is to explore their historical definition, origins and development before turning to other matters. *Wokou* is called *waegu* in Korean, and *wakō* in Japanese. Breaking down the word, generally speaking "*wo*" is a derogatory term for Japan, meaning "dwarf", while "*kou*" means pirates, bandits or enemy. Hence, *wokou* means Japanese pirates, marauders or "dwarf raiders." In Chinese, "*kou*" can also be used as a verb meaning to plunder, to raid, to invade or to rob. In the *Zhongguo lishi da cidian*, which is perhaps the most authoritative Chinese historical dictionary, *wokou* are defined as "Japanese pirates who harassed the coastal areas of China during the Ming dynasty",[3] while in the modern edition of the authoritative *Da cihai, wokou* are defined as "Japanese sea merchants

lishi 倭寇：海上歷史, Yang Hangqiu 楊翰球 (trans.) (Wuhan: Wuhan daxue chubanshe, 1987); Zheng Liangsheng 鄭樑生, *Zhong Ri guanxi shi yanjiu lunji* 中日關係史研究論集, vols. 1–11 (Taibei: Wenshizhe chubanshe, 1990–2001); Fan Zhongyi 范中義 and Tong Xigang 仝晰綱, *Mingdai Wokou shilue* 明代倭寇史略 (Beijing: Zhonghua shuju, 2004). Concerning the *Wokou* in Yuan China, see: Wang Ting 王頲, "Wokou gonglue" 倭寇攻掠, in *Shengwang zhaoye: Han Ri Zhong jiaosheshi kao* 聖王肇業：韓日中交涉史考 (Shanghai: Xuelin chubanshe, 1998), 241–259; Gao Rongsheng 高榮盛, "Yuandai 'wokou' lun" 元代"倭寇"論, in: *Yuanshi qianshi* 元史淺識 (Nanjing: Fenghuang chubanshe, 2010): 247–266. The paper has been revised based on Ma Guang, "Re-evaluating the *Wokou* Problem in East Asia During the 1220s and 1390s from the Perspective of Environmental History", *Journal of Asian History*, 54:2 (2020), 261–280.

2 So Kwan-wai 蘇均煒, *Japanese Piracy in Ming China During the 16th Century* (East Lansing: Michigan State University Press, 1975), 15–40.

3 Wang Yuquan 王毓銓, Cao Guilin 曹貴林 (eds.), *Zhongguo lishi da cidian: Mingshi juan* 中國歷史大辭典：明史卷 (Shanghai: Shanghai cishu chubanshe, 1995): 411; Zheng

and pirate groups who plundered the coastal areas of China during the fourteenth and sixteenth centuries."[4] Perhaps the definition of *wokou* in these two dictionaries is too narrow because they do not consider *wokou* activities in other periods and areas, such as the *wokou* on the Korean Peninsula. In the *Nihon shi daijiten*, the term is defined as "pirate groups including Japanese people who were active on the Korean Peninsula, the coastal areas and inland of China, and the South Seas".[5] Although this definition is broader, it seems to have been made at the cost of downplaying the role of Japanese pirates and their raiding activities.

Furthermore, although there are plenty of papers on the "*wokou* problem" in the sixteenth century, few scholars have examined their origins. In addition, some of their arguments are not correct.[6] For instance, some historians argue that the term "*wokou*" emerged as a noun in Korean sources in 1350 and that it was not used until the early Ming dynasty in China. However, I found that *wokou* was used as a noun in a poem in Korea as early as 1232, while from 1344–1345 it can be found in Chinese historical evidence dating from 1344–1345. Therefore, I will seek to fill the lacuna in the literature by properly investigating the origins of the *wokou* in China and Korea between the 1220s and the 1360s.

1 The First Evidence for Use of the Word "*Wokou*" in Korea

In fact, records mentioning *wokou* seem to date back to as early as the fifth century. According to Takeo Tanaka, the word first appears on a monument dedicated to King Kwangkaet'o 廣開土大王 (r. 391–413) of Koguryŏ 高句麗 (37 BCE–668 CE), erected by King Changsu 長壽王 (r. 413–491) as a memorial to his father in 414.[7] On this monument, which is now located in Ji'an City 集安市, Jilin Province 吉林省, China, it is stated that in 404, "the *wokou* were defeated, and [Koguryŏ soldiers] killed innumerable [*wokou*]".[8] In this context, "*wokou*"

Tianting 鄭天挺 et al. (eds.), *Zhongguo lishi da cidian* (*Yinxu ben*) 中國歷史大辭典(音序本) (Shanghai: Shanghai cishu chubanshe, 2007), 2818.

4 Xia Zhengnong 夏征農 (ed.), *Da cihai: Zhongguo gudaishi juan* 大辭海：中國古代史卷 (Shanghai: Shanghai cishu chubanshe, 2005), 147.

5 Heibonsha 平凡社 (ed.), *Nihon shi daijiten* 日本史大事典 (Tōkyō: Heibonsha, 1994), 6.1312–1313.

6 Shen Dengmiao 沈登苗, "Mingdai *Wokou* jianji Aomenshi yanjiu zhongwen lunzhu suoyin" 明代倭寇兼及澳門史研究中文論著索引, *Aomen yanjiu* 澳門研究 30 (2005), 208–229.

7 Tanaka, *Wokou*, 1.

8 *Haotaiwang bei yuanta ben* 好太王碑原拓本, collection of the Liaoning Provincial Museum, China.

refers to Japanese soldiers who invaded Koguryŏ. However, after this there are no other historical records employing the term for approximately another 800 years. This suggests that the term *wokou* was only used occasionally, in special cases, in early sources, rather than being a term in common usage at that time. Moreover, the meaning of *wokou* on the monument is very different from that applied to the term during the thirteenth to seventeenth centuries.

Nakamura Hidetaka 中村榮孝 (1902–1984) has argued that *wokou* emerged as a term during the fourth year of the reign of King Ch'ungnyŏl 忠烈王 (r. 1274–1308) of Koryŏ 高麗 (1278).[9] In the seventh lunar month of 1278, King Ch'ungnyŏl requested that Chinese soldiers in Korea should be retained for defence against the *wokou*. However, Kubilai Khan 忽必烈可汗 (r. 1260–1294) replied that there was no need for them to be retained because Korean soldiers alone should be strong enough to defeat any *wokou*.[10] This led Nakamura Hidetaka to argue that the word *wokou* emerged as a noun from 1278.

However, Takeo Tanaka and Zheng Liangsheng argued that *wokou* emerged as a term only in 1350, during the second year of the reign of King Ch'ungjŏng 忠定王 (r. 1348–1351) of Koryŏ. At that time, the *wokou* raided beyond coastal areas of the Korea Peninsula on several occasions. For instance, in the second lunar month they raided Kosŏng 固城 and Kŏjedo 巨濟島, and in the fourth, fifth, sixth and eleventh lunar months they also plundered official grain victualers, burned military camps and killed many people in coastal areas such as Namwŏn 南原, Kurye 求禮, Yŏnggwang 靈光, Changhŭng 長興 and Tongnae 東萊. This forced a number of coastal residents to leave their homes and move into the interior.[11] It is recorded in the *Koryŏsa* 高麗史 that the "*wokou* began to raid from this year",[12] the "*wokou* emerged in this year",[13] and "from this year onwards, the *wokou* would raid the coast every year".[14] The year 1350 was a *gengyin* 庚寅 year, and the words "the *wokou* emerged from *gengyin* year"

9 Tanaka, *Wokou*, 1.

10 *Koryŏsa chŏryo* 高麗史節要 (1452), by Kim Chong-sŏ 金宗瑞, Collection of the Gyujanggak 奎章閣, Korea, 20.11a.

11 *Koryŏsa chŏryo*, 26.4a–6a. Barbara Seyock, "Pirates and Traders on Tsushima Island During the Late 14th to Early 16th Century: As Seen from Historical and Archaeological Perspectives", in Angela Schottenhammer (ed.), *Trade and Transfer Across the East Asian "Mediterranean"* (Wiesbaden: Harrassowitz, 2005), 91.

12 *Koryŏsa* 高麗史 (1451), by Chŏng In-ji 鄭麟趾, Collection of the Gyujanggak, Korea, 37.21b–22a.

13 *Koryŏsa chŏryo*, 26.4a.

14 *Chaoxian shilüe* 朝鮮史略, Jingyin Wenyuange Siku quanshu 景印文淵閣四庫全書 (Shanghai: Shanghai guji chubanshe, 1987), 10.29b.

appears in these Korean historical records, which, in Takeo Tanaka's opinion, is evidence that people were familiar with the term *wokou* after 1350.[15]

An analysis shows that Nakamura's and Tanaka's respective arguments can be faulted on several points. There are at least two problems with their studies. First, the historical materials they employed, such as the *Koryŏsa* and the *Chosŏn wangjo sillok* 朝鮮王朝實錄, were compiled by historians in 1392 or even later.[16] There is no doubt that these editors would have used their own contemporary terminology, rather than that used by people active between 1278 and 1350. For example, the conversation between King Ch'ungnyŏl and Kubilai Khan in 1278, which is recorded in the *Koryŏsa chŏryo* 高麗史節要, was written by historians. In reality King Ch'ungnyŏl and Kubilai Khan might not have conversed with each other in Chinese. If we cannot determine whether "*wokou*" was originally used by people at the time, or only by later historians, these later historical materials should not be used to study the origins of *wokou* as a noun.

Second, the statements in the *Koryŏsa* and similar records that "the *wokou* began to raid from this year" are simply not correct. As early as the fifth lunar month of 1223, "the *wokou* plundered Kimju 金州." In this Chinese sentence, "*wokou*" is not a single noun but a word that is composed of a noun "*wo*" and a verb, "*kou*", its meaning being that Japanese marauders attacked some places.[17] Moreover, the *wokou* raided many times in the following years. For instance, in the fourth lunar month of 1225, they raided Kyŏngsang-to 慶尚道[18] and plundered it again the following year.[19] In 1226 and 1227, they raided the coastal regions of Korea again.[20] Kiyoshi Inoue points out that the *wokou* of the time were adventurous warriors along with their companions from the coast of Kyūshū 九州 and the Seto Inland Sea 瀨戶內海 in Japan. Even while peacefully trading with local people, they looked for opportunities to plunder coastal residents. In the 1220s the *wokou* problem became so serious that Koreans were terrified of them.[21] Thus, *wokou* raiding activities began in 1223, not 1350, and the statement that "the *wokou* began to raid from this year" in the *Koryŏsa* only

15 Tanaka, *Wokou*, 8.

16 The *Koryŏsa* was edited from 1392 to 1451. The *Chosŏn T'aejo sillok* 朝鮮太祖實錄 was completed in 1413.

17 *Koryŏsa*, 22.23b; *Koryŏsa chŏryo*, 15.28a.

18 *Koryŏsa chŏryo*, 15.30b.

19 *Koryŏsa chŏryo*, 15.33a.

20 *Koryŏsa chŏryo*, 15.33b–35b.

21 Inoue Kiyoshi 井上清, *Riben lishi* 日本歷史, translated by Tianjin shi lishi yanjiu suo 天津市歷史研究所 (Tianjin: Tianjin renmin chubanshe, 1974), 1.166.

indicates that the *wokou* raids entered another such phase of increased activity, not that the word emerged as a noun that year because of *wokou* activities.

If we want to study the origins of *wokou* as a term, we should explore original materials, such as diaries, poems, memorials, steles and letters written by contemporary witnesses. According to all the historical evidence we currently possess, *wokou* appeared as a term for the first time in the "Taechangkyŏng tochangŭm ch'ansi" 大藏經道場音讚詩 written by Yi Kyu-bo 李奎報 (1168–1241), a famous Korean literary figure. In this poem, Yi records that "a piece of Buddhist chant [will make] thousands of disasters disappear, and it is not difficult to suppress those few *wokou*". There are small-character notes showing that "the poem was written in the year of capital relocation".[22] According to the chronological biography of Yi Kyu-bo, the capital was moved in the sixth lunar month of *renchen* 壬辰 year (1232).[23] The poem must therefore have been composed by 1232, giving expression to the reality of *wokou* raiding activities, which we know occurred from 1223 onwards.

2 The First Written Evidence for *Wokou* in China

In China, earlier scholars using the *Ming shilu* have argued that *wokou* as a noun emerged there in the fourth lunar month of 1369.[24] However, the *Ming shilu*, like the *Koryŏsa* and the *Chosŏn wangjo sillok*, was compiled by later historians. Even the earliest part, the *Ming Taizu shilu* 明太祖實錄, was not written until the brief Jianwen 建文 era (1399–1402). It is possible that the term *wokou*, as used in these historical materials, was not the (only) word used by contemporary witnesses. However, historical evidence suggests that the term emerged in Chinese documents as early as the Yuan dynasty. The earliest Chinese evidence comes from a biographical sketch of Elezhetu 諤勒哲圖 (Öljeitü, 1299–1344) written by Cheng Duanli 程端禮 (1271–1345) sometime between 1344 and

22 *Tongguk Yi Sang-guk chip* 東國李相國集 (1251), by Yi Kyu-bo 李奎報, collection of Waseda University Library, Japan, 18.1a–4a.

23 *"Tongguk Yi Sang-guk munjip yŏnbo"* 東國李相國文集年譜, in *Tongguk Yi Sang-guk chip*, 14.

24 Zheng Liangsheng 鄭樑生, *Mingdai Zhong Ri guanxi yanjiu* 明代中日關係研究 (Taibei: Wenshizhe chubanshe, 1985), 274–275; Fan Zhongyi and Tong Xigang, *Mingdai Wokou shilue, qianyan*, 3; *Ming Taizu shilu* 明太祖實錄 (Taibei: Taiwan zhongyang yanjiu yuan shiyu suo, 1962), 41.5b.

1345.[25] Elezhetu was appointed Huaiyuan general-in-chief (*Huaiyuan dajiangjun* 懷遠大將軍) and upper brigade chief (*shang wanhu* 上萬戶) of Qi County 蘄縣 in 1320, and was then promoted to Dingyuan General because of his success in restoring peace to the coastal areas. In 1344, he was promoted to commander-in-chief of the Pacification Commission of the Zhedong Circuit (*Zhedongdao xuanweishi duyuanshuai* 浙東道宣慰使都元帥) and made Grand Master of Palace Attendance (*zhongfeng daifu* 中奉大夫). Cheng, the author, claimed to have known Elezhetu intimately. In his biography of Elezhetu, Cheng recorded that in the 1320s the *wokou* repeatedly swept through Yin County 鄞縣 burning and plundering, which greatly troubled the coastal people. In order to pacify the *wokou*, Elezhetu strengthened the military, but also allowed fair trade. Cheng also relates the following story:

> One night, more than forty *wokou* with weapons came to the port. They plundered commercial and private goods and wealth, and captured and enslaved boatmen. After receiving the news, Elezhetu set off in a formidable ship to capture them. However, when he caught up with the *wokou*, instead of attacking them, Elezhetu negotiated and reasoned with them, convincing them to stop their raiding.[26]

This biographical sketch is perhaps the earliest historical evidence of its sort from China to use the term *wokou*. However, it is worth noting that Cheng used not only this word, but also *Wonu* 倭奴, which literally means Japanese slaves. It seems that *wokou* was not a standardized term at that time and that other, similar words, such as *Wonu*, were also used simultaneously to designate Japanese pirates.

Besides the biographical sketch, there is a collection of four poems written by Nai Xian 迺賢 (1309–1368)[27] to commemorate General Wanzhedu 完者都.

---

25 Cheng Duanli, a famous educationist, lived in Yin County his whole life. His courtesy name is Jingshu 敬叔, and his literary name is Weizhai 畏齋. He wrote two works, the *Dushu fennian richeng* 讀書分年日程, and the *Weizhai ji* 畏齋集.

26 "Gu zhongfeng dafu Zhedongdao xuanwei duyuanshuai jian Qixianyi shangwanhufu Aolezhetu gong xingzhuang" 故中奉大夫淛東道宣慰都元帥兼蘄縣翼上萬戶府謌勒哲圖公行狀, by Cheng Duanli, in *Weizhai ji*, in Jingyin Wenyuange Siku quanshu, 6.12a–14b; "Gu zhongfeng dafu Zhedongdao xuanwei duyuanshuai jian Qixianyi shangwanhufu dalugaqi Aolezhetu gong xingzhuang" 故中奉大夫淛東道宣慰都元帥兼蘄縣翼上萬戶府達嚕噶齊謌勒哲圖公行狀, by Cheng Duanli, in *Weizhai ji*, in Siming congshu 四明叢書 (Ningbo: Zhangshi yueyuan, 1932), 6.10b–12b.

27 Nai Xian was a Semu 色目人, and his family name is Gelolu 葛邏祿, Halalu 哈剌魯, or Helu 合魯, all of which are transliterated from Kurluk. He has different names, such as Na Xin 納新, Na Yan 納延, Nai Xian 乃賢, Nai Xian 迺賢, Geluolu Yizhi 葛邏祿

In these four poems, Nai Xian records that, when the *wokou* raided Zhedong, general Wanzhedu sailed out on a large ship and suppressed them. Wanzhedu died in Siming 四明 (nowadays Ningbo 寧波) and was buried in Yehuling 野狐嶺. After his death, many people erected monuments to commemorate his achievements.[28]

There were literary accolades as well, but the collection of four poems uses different titles and employs various names, according to the edition. In the Wenyuange *Siku quanshu* 四庫全書 edition, Nai Xian is changed to Na Yan 納延, Wanzhedu to Elezhedu 諤勒哲都, in the title of the poems.[29] In the *Chizaotang siku quanshu huiyao* 摛藻堂四庫全書薈要, Nai Xian became Na Xin 納新, and Wanzhedu became Wangzhaletu 旺扎勒圖.[30] In the *Siku quanshu zhenben* 四庫全書珍本 and *Yuanshi xuan chuji* 元詩選初集, two of four poems were deleted, so "sishou" 四首 became "ershou" 二首 in the title.[31] Meanwhile, Zhang Xian 張憲 (1320–1373?),[32] a famous poet living at the end of the Yuan and early Ming dynasties, also wrote a poem, "Huai Wanzhetu

---

易之, and Ma Yizhi 馬易之. His courtesy name was Yizhi 易之, and his literary name Heshuo waishi 河朔外史. Shanghai bowuguan 上海博物館 (ed.), *Zhongguo shuhua-jia yinjian kuanshi* 中國書畫家印鑒款識 (Beijing: Wenwu chubanshe, 1987), 737–738; X. Nai 廼賢, "Nancheng yonggu" 南城詠古. In Qi Gong 啟功 and Wang Jingxian 王靖憲 (eds.), *Zhongguo fatie quanji* 中國法帖全集 (Wuhan: Hubei meishu chubanshe, 2002), 15.216–217; Chen Gaohua 陳高華, "Yuandai shiren Nai Xian shengping shiji kao" 元代詩人廼賢生平事蹟考, *Wenshi* 文史 32 (1990), 247; Xing Han 星漢, "Nai Xian shengping kaolüe" 迺賢生平考略. *Xinjiang daxue xuebao* (*zhexue shehui kexue ban*) 新疆大學學報 (哲學社會科學版) 1998.4, 77–82.

28 "Song cishangren gui Xuedou zhuiwan Zhedong Wanzhe duyuanshuai sishou" 送慈上人歸雪竇追挽淛東完者都元帥四首, Nai Xian 廼賢, in *Jintai ji* 金臺集 (1638), reprinted in Haiwang cun guji congkan 海王邨古籍叢刊, Beijing: Zhongguo shudian, 1990), 1.30a–31b.

29 "Song cishangren gui Xuedou zhuiwan Zhedong Elezhedu yuanshuai sishou" 送慈上人歸雪竇追挽淛東諤勒哲都元帥四首, by Na Yan 納延, in *Jintai ji*, in Jingyin Wenyuange Siku quanshu, 1.31a–32a.

30 "Song cishangren gui Xuedou zhuiwan Zhedong Wangzhaletu yuanshuai sishou" 送慈上人歸雪竇追挽淛東旺扎勒圖元帥四首, by Na Xin 納新, in *Jintai ji*, in Jingyin chizao-tang Siku quanshu huiyao 景印摛藻堂四庫全書薈要 (Taibei: Shijie shuju, 1988), 1.31a–32a.

31 "Song cishangren gui Xuedou zhuiwan Zhedong Wanzhe duyuanshuai ershou" 送慈上人歸雪竇追輓浙東完者都元帥二首, by Na Xin 納新, in *Jintai ji*, in Siku quanshu zhen-ben shiyi ji 四庫全書珍本十一集 (Taibei: Taiwan shangwu yinshuguan, 1981), 1.32; "Song cishangren gui Xuedou zhuiwan Zhedong Wanzhe duyuanshuai ershou", by Nai Xian 廼賢, in Gu Sili 顧嗣立 (ed.), *Yuanshi xuan chuji* 元詩選初集 (Beijing: Zhonghua shuju, 1987), 1450–1451.

32 Zhang Xian lived in Shanyin 山陰 (now Shaoxing 紹興), Zhejiang Province. His courtesy name is Silian 思廉, and his literary name was Yusi 玉笥 or Yusisheng 玉笥生.

yuanshuai" 懷完者禿元帥, to commemorate General "Wanzhutu" 完者禿, who put down the *wokou* successfully.[33]

Who are Elezhetu, Wangzhaletu, Wanzhedu and Wanzhetu? Is it possible that they are the same person? Zhang Zhejun 張哲俊 points out that there were two individuals named Wanzhetu, one a member of the Korean royal family,[34] the other the fourth son of the Marquis of Sun 孫侯.[35] Zhang argues that the Wanzhetu in the poem by Zhang Xian was the latter, and that he was the same person as the Wanzhedu of Nai Xian's poems.[36] Yang Fuyou 楊富有 and Shi Haiguang 石海光, however, point out that the term "Wanzhe" could be used in both names and posthumous titles. For instance, Yang Guantong 楊貫通 was awarded Wanzhe as a posthumous title, and other individuals were named Wanzhetiemuer 完者帖木兒, Wanzhebuhua 完者不花 and Wanzhetu 完者禿. Yang and Shi argue that Nai Xian's Wanzhe was actually Hadasun 哈達孫, who was appointed commander-in-chief of the Pacification Commission of Zhedongdao in 1311 and died in Siming at the age of 65 after successfully defeating bandits.[37] The similarity of their activities in Zhejiang has led Yang and Shi to believe that Wanzhe and Hadasun may be one and the same person.[38]

However, Zhang Zhejun only explores the name Wanzhetu, overlooking other names such as Elezhedu and Wangzhaletu. And while Yang's and Shi's comparisons of Wanzhe's and Hadasun's achievements are useful, their names are very different in pronunciation, making any relationship between them unlikely. I suggest instead that the general in the poems by Nai Xian and Zhang Xian is neither Hadasun nor the fourth son of the Marquis of Sun but rather the Elezhetu of Cheng Duanli's biographical sketch. Wanzhedu and Elezhetu engaged in numerous similar activities. For example, they both had the same official title, enjoyed reading, set up a military camp at Dinghai 定海, once

33 "Huai Wanzhetu yuanshuai" 懷完者禿元帥, by Zhang Xian 張憲, in *Yusi ji* 玉笥集, in Congshu jicheng chubian 叢書集成初編 (Beijing: Zhonghua shuju 1985), 8.115; *Yusi ji* 玉笥集, by Zhang Xian 張憲, in *Yue yatang congshu* 粵雅堂叢書 (1851), 8.3b.

34 *Yuanshi* 元史, by Song Lian 宋濂 et al. (Beijing: Zhonghua shuju, 1976), 30.687.

35 "Da Yuan zhongdafu Yidu Banyang dengchu lu taojin zongguan Sunhou muzhiming" 大元中大夫益都般陽等處路陶金總管孫侯墓志銘, by Wu Cheng 吳澄, in *Wu Wenzheng ji* 吳文正集, in Jingyin wenyuange siku quanshu, 80.6b–8b.

36 Zhang Zhejun 張哲俊, *Zhongguo gudai wenxue zhong de Riben xingxiang yanjiu* 中國古代文學中的日本形象研究 (Beijing: Beijing daxue chubanshe, 2004), 178–180.

37 *Xin Yuanshi* 新元史, by Ke Shaowen 柯劭忞 (Shanghai: Kaiming shudian, 1935), 178.361–362.

38 Yang Fuyou 楊富有 and Shi Haiguang 石海光, "Nai Xian de yishou shi yu Yuandai Zhong Ri guanxi jiqi yiyi" 迺賢的一首詩與元代中日關係及其意義, *Yuwen xuekan* 語文學刊 5 (2013), 1–2.

sailed in a large ship to suppress the *wokou* and were buried at Yehuling. Besides these poems, there are two local gazetteers that record Wanzhedu's achievements, which are also the same as those of the Elezhetu in the biographical sketch.[39] In short, their activities are the same, and the pronunciation of their names is also similar, leading me to conclude that they are identical.

We must now ask why the same person had so many different names. In my opinion, this is due to different transliterations of Mongol names. Wanzhe 完者, Wanzhe 完哲, Elezhe and Wangzhale have similar pronunciations, as do Du 都, Tu 圖 and Tu 禿. Then, during the Qianlong 乾隆 reign (1736–1795), historians were forced to change the transliteration of Mongol names.[40] Below are some examples of this:

TABLE 4.1 Chinese transliterations of Mongol names

Original names	Modified names
Wanzhe 完者	Elezhe 鄂勒哲[a]
Wanzhe 完泽	Elezhe 鄂勒哲[b]
Wanzhedu 完者都	Elezhetu 諤勒哲圖[c]
Wanzhedu 完者都	Wangzhaletu 旺扎勒圖[d]
Wanzhedu 完者都	Elezhetu 鄂勒哲圖[e]
Wanzhetu 完者圖	Elezhetu 鄂勒哲圖[f]

a *Xu zizhi tongjian* 續資治通鑒, by Bi Yuan 畢沅 (Beijing: Zhonghua shuju, 1957), 199.5422.
b *Xu zizhi tongjian*, 206.5592.
c *Mingshi shilu* 明氏實錄, by Yang Xueke 楊學可, in Xuxiu Siku quanshu 續修四庫全書 (Shanghai: Shanghai guji chubanshe, 1996), 2b. However, in another edition his name was not changed. See *Mingshi shilu*, in Xuehai leibian 學海類編 (Shanghai: Shanghai hanfenlou, 1920), 28.2a.
d *Yupi lidai tongjian jilan* 御批歷代通鑑輯覽, by Fu Heng 傅恆 et al., in Jingyin Wenyuange Siku quanshu, 99.26a.
e *Xu zizhi tongjian*, 185.5047.
f *Xu zizhi tongjian*, 208.5678.

39 *Zhizheng Siming xuzhi* 至正四明續志 (1342), by Wang Yuangong 王元恭, in Song Yuan fangzhi congkan 宋元方志叢刊 (Beijing: Zhonghua shuju, 1990), 2.1a; *Jiajing Ningbofu zhi* 嘉靖寧波府志 (1560), by Zhou Xizhe 周希哲 et al., in Zhongguo fangzhi congshu: Huazhong difang 中國方志叢書：華中地方 (Taibei: Chengwen chubanshe, 1983), 25.1907–1908.

40 He Guanbiao 何冠彪, "Qianlong chao chongxiu Liao Jin Yuan sanshi pouxi" 乾隆朝重修遼、金、元三史剖析. *Menggu xue xinxi* 蒙古學信息 1 (1997), 26–34; Jin Xin 金鑫, "Qianlong chao gaiding Liao Jin Yuan sanshi yiming tanxi" 乾隆改定遼金元三史譯名探析. *Manyu yanjiu* 滿語研究 1 (2009), 58–62.

TABLE 4.1 Chinese transliterations of Mongol names (*cont.*)

Original names	Modified names
Wanzhedu 完泽笃	Elezhetu 鄂勒哲图[g]
Wulizhiduo 乌里质铎	Elezhetu 鄂勒哲图[h]
Wanzhedu 完者篤	Elezheyitu 額勒哲依圖[i]
Wanzhetiemuer 完者帖木兒	Wangzhaletemuer 旺扎勒特穆爾[j]
Wanzhebuhua 完者不花	Wangzhalebuha 旺扎勒布哈[k]
Wanzhehudu 完者忽都	Elezhehutuke 鄂勒哲呼圖克[l]
Wanzhetuohuan 完者脱歡	Wangzhaletuohuan 旺扎勒托歡[m]
Wanzhetiemuer 完者帖木兒	Elezhetemuer 鄂勒哲特穆爾[n]
Yangwanzhe 楊完者	Yang'elezhe 楊諤勒哲[o]
Wangwanzhetiemuer 汪完者帖木兒	Wang'Elezhetemuer 汪鄂勒哲特穆爾[p]

g *Xu zizhi tongjian*, 195.5318.
h *Xu zizhi tongjian*, 94.2447.
i *Nian'er shi zhaji: buyi* 廿二史劄記：補遺, by Zhao Yi 趙翼 (Beijing: Zhonghua shuju, 1984), 862.
j *Nian'er shi zhaji: buyi*, 865.
k *Nian'er shi zhaji: buyi*, 865.
l *Qinding gujin chuer jinjian* 欽定古今儲貳金鑒, in Jingyin Wenyuange Siku quanshu, 5.10a.
m *Yuding zizhi tongjian gangmu sanbian* 御定資治通鑑綱目三編, by Zhang Tingyu 張廷玉, in Jingyin wenyuange siku quanshu, 11.7a.
n *Xu zizhi tongjian*, 207.5638.
o *Guangxu Jiangxi tongzhi* 光緒江西通志 (1881), by Zeng Guofan 曾國藩 et al., in Xuxiu Siku quanshu (Shanghai: Shanghai guji chubanshe, 1996), 147.2b.
p *Jiaqing chongxiu yitong zhi* 嘉慶重修一統志, by Mu Zhang'a 穆彰阿 et al., in Sibu congkan xubian 四部叢刊續編 (Shanghai: Shangwu yinshuguan, 1934), 277.5a.

It is obvious that Wanzhedu was an original transliteration of Mongol names and that it was always used during the Yuan, Ming and early Qing dynasties, but it was changed from the Qianlong reign onwards. Wanzhedu was originally used in the Ming *Jintai ji*, but it was later changed to Elezhedu, or Wangzhaletu in Qing books. When scholars compiled the *Weizhai ji* by Cheng Duanli, they changed Wanzhedu to Elezhetu during the Qianlong reign. This clarification of the changes that resulted from transliterations makes it easier to understand why the same person had so many different names in different editions.

2.1 Wokou *during the Yuan Dynasty*

The *wokou* raids of the 1330s, mentioned earlier, were not unique: there were other *wokou* activities during the Yuan period that have thus far been ignored by scholars. Most *wokou* were related to Japanese merchants during the Yuan dynasty, especially the *wokou* in Qingyuan 慶元 (nowadays Ningbo). Although the Yuan government prohibited maritime trade four times, their prohibitions did not last long. The government encouraged people to trade overseas, and they also allowed foreign merchants to trade in China most of the time.[41]

However, some armed Japanese merchants did not obey the Yuan government's rules. At the end of 1308, some of them rioted. The local officials could not stop them, and these *Woren* 倭人, which literally means Japanese people, killed officials and commoners in Qingyuan.[42] *Wokou* also burned the venerable Tianning Temple 天寧寺, where Japanese merchants lived and traded during the Yuan dynasty.[43] Although they were merchants, they rioted with swords, spears, and halberds.[44] They were so aggressive that they even attacked the Pacification Commission of Zhedong, and officials only escaped with the help of a brave official named Zhang Fuchu 張復初.[45]

Following the *wokou* raids, the Mongol Yuan government realized that they had to strengthen the coastal defenses to protect the local population. In 1309, one third of the new soldiers in one coastal brigade, together with a Chinese army of the Qi County Brigade, were ordered to guard the coastal areas of the Jiangzhe Branch Secretariat (Jiangzhe xing zhongshusheng 江浙行中書省). In the tenth lunar month of 1311, the Bureau of Military Affairs (shumi yuan 樞密院) gave an order to dispatch more soldiers to strengthen the coastal areas at Qingyuan, which is very close to Japan.[46] In 1316, some ministers submitted a memorandum to the throne in which they suggested sending Chinese

41 Gao Rongsheng 高榮盛, *Yuandai haiwai maoyi yanjiu* 元代海外貿易研究 (Chengdu: Sichuan renmin chubanshe, 1998), 5–31; Hong Fuzhong 洪富忠 and Wang Liyuan 汪麗媛, "Yuanchao haijin chutan" 元朝海禁初探. *Qiannan minzu shifan xueyuan xuebao* 黔南民族師範學院學報 5 (2003), 59–63.

42 *Yuanshi*, 99.2548; "Yuan gu liang Zhe yunsi Pudongchang yansicheng Yangjun muzhiming" 元故兩浙運司浦東場鹽司丞楊君墓志銘, by Su Tianjue 蘇天爵, in *Zixi wengao* 滋溪文稿, in Congshu jicheng xubian 叢書集成續編 (Shanghai: Shanghai shudian, 1994), 20.6b.

43 The Tianning Temple was built in 851 as Guoning Temple 國甯寺. It was renamed to Chongning wanshou chan Temple 崇甯萬壽禪寺 in 1103, to Tianning wanshou Temple 天甯萬壽 in 1111, to Bao'en guangxiao chan Temple 報恩廣孝禪寺, and then to Bao'en guangxiao Temple 報恩光孝寺 in 1137. *Riben yijian: Qionghe huahai* 日本一鑑：窮河話海 by Zheng Shungong 鄭舜功 (1939), 7.16b; *Yanyou Siming zhi* 延祐四明志 (1320), by Yuan Jue 袁桷, in Song Yuan fangzhi congkan (Beijing: Zhonghua shuju, 1990), 16.13; *Jiajing Ningbofu zhi*, 22.1690.

44 "Lun wo" 論倭, by Wu Lai 吳萊, in *Yuanying Wu xiansheng ji* 淵穎吳先生集 (1577), in Sibu congkan chubian 四部叢刊初编 (Shanghai: Shangwu yinshuguan, 1929), 5.1b.

45 *Yibin ji* 伊濱集, by Wang Yi 王沂, in Jingyin Wenyuange Siku quanshu, 23.14b.

46 *Yuanshi*, 99.2548.

officials to placate the soldiers and common people of Fujian and Zhejiang, who were suffering from the disturbances resulting from the *wokou* problem in Zhedong.[47] As a result of these measures, the coastal regions returned to a state of calm for around twenty years. As noted previously, in the 1330s, *wokou* raided Zhedong before being pacified by Wanzhedu. But from 1358 onwards, they continued to raid the coastal regions. In the eighth lunar month of 1363, *wokou* raided Pengzhou 蓬州 but were defeated by Liu Xian 劉暹. It is recorded in the *Yuanshi* that the coastal regions then became peaceful again.[48]

However, this was not the case. In fact, the *wokou* did not stop their raiding activities. In the *Yuan gu mishu shaojian jiejun mubei* 元故秘書少監揭君墓, Song Lian 宋濂 (1310–1381), a very famous literary figure, records that Jie Hong 揭汯 (1304–1373) and his colleagues were attacked by the *wokou* in Tieshan 鐵山 in the Bohai Sea 渤海. Most of his associates were killed by the *wokou*, but Jie Hong escaped.[49] Based on the contents of the essay, we can estimate that this event took place sometime between 1362 and 1368, but it is difficult to narrow down the year or the names of all those involved. Fortunately, however, we have at our disposal another source containing details of the affair.

In the "Yuantingyu zhuan", Dai Liang 戴良 (1317–1383)[50] records that Jie Hong, Yuelubuhua 月魯不花 and Hu Jun 胡均 were attacked by the *wokou*; Yuelubuhua was killed, and his wife and concubines were captured.[51] In the essay, *wokou* is twice used as a noun. Based on the preface, we know that the draft of the *Jiulingshanfang ji* was completed in 1365, and it was reprinted and

47 *Yuanshi*, 122.3005.

48 *Yuanshi*, 46.964.

49 "Yuan gu mishu shaojian Jie jun mubei" 元故秘書少監揭君墓碑, by Song Lian 宋濂, in *Song xueshi wenji* 宋學士文集, in Sibu congkan chubian (Shanghai: Shangwu yinshuguan, 1929), 63.5b.

50 Dai Liang lived in Pujiang 浦江, Zhejiang. His courtesy name is Shuneng 叔能 and his literary name is Jiuling shanren 九靈山人, Xiaoxiao sheng 囂囂生, and Yunlin 雲林. *Mingshi* 明史, by Zhang Tingyu 張廷玉 et al. (Beijing: Zhonghua shuju, 1974), 285.7312; Yan Xuanjun 晏選軍, "Dai Liang Shandong Changle, Yidu xingji kaobian" 戴良山東昌樂、益都行跡考辨, *Wenxian* 文獻 3 (2008), 178.

51 "Yuan Tingyu zhuan" 袁廷玉傳, by Dai Liang 戴良, in *Jiuling shanfang ji* 九靈山房集, in Sibu congkan chubian (Shanghai: Shangwu yinshuguan, 1936), 27.20b. However, in another edition of the same text, Yuelubuhua was changed to Yiliebuha 伊埒布哈. See the edition published in Jingyin Wenyuange Siku quanshu, 27.33b–34b. The *Jiuling shanfang ji* was first published during the Hongwu reign. It was ignored by former scholars but was reprinted in 1445, 1771 and during the Tongzhi reign (1862–1874). Some contents vary between different editions. See *Bisonglou cangshu zhi* 皕宋樓藏書志 (1822), by Lu Xinyuan 陸心源 (1834–1894), in Xuxiu siku quanshu (Shanghai: Shanghai guji chubanshe, 2002), 108.9b–10a; Wang Zhongge 王忠閣, "*Jiuling shanfang ji* banben yuanliu kao" 九靈山房集版本源流考, *Wenxian* 文獻 1 (2001), 171–176.

recompiled several times during the following 600 years.[52] Is it possible that the essay in the book was completed before 1365? Unfortunately, there is no direct record of this, so we have to turn to its contents. In it, Dai records that Cheng Xu 程徐 (?–1370) was appointed vice minister of the Bureau of Appointments (*libu shilang* 吏部侍郎). According to the *Mingshi*, Cheng obtained this position in the second year of the Hongwu reign (1369).[53] Therefore, the essay cannot have been composed during the Yuan dynasty.

As discussed above, *wokou* raids occurred in about 1362–1368, but can this date be narrowed down further? According to Xiao Qiqing 蕭啟慶 (also Ch'i-Ch'ing Hsiao, 1937–2012), Yuelubuhua died in 1366, so the *wokou* raid should have occurred in that year.[54] In the *Yuanshi*, it is recorded that, after a fierce battle with the *wokou*, Yuelubuhua and more than eighty persons were killed by them during raiding,[55] which shows that there must have been a large number of *wokou* at that time.

3 Conclusion

Considering the above analysis, we can see that as early as 414 the Chinese word *wokou* had been used on King Kwangkaet'o's monument, but in the following more than 800 years, there is no record of the word being used. It therefore seems that the *wokou* on the monument was a special case, a word that was only used occasionally, not a term that was in frequent or common use at that time. Moreover, the meaning of *wokou* on the monument is very different from its meaning in the thirteenth to seventeenth centuries. Therefore, we should not take this earliest reference as the emergence of *wokou* as a term.

Moreover, I claim that the approach of certain scholars in using the *Koryŏsa*, the *Chosŏn wangjo sillok* or the *Ming shilu* to study the origins of *wokou* as a noun is methodologically flawed. After all, these books were written by later historians, not by contemporary witnesses. I argue that in Korea the first evidence for the use of the term *wokou* does not stem from 1278 or 1350, as is accepted by earlier scholars, but instead comes from the poem "Taechangkyŏng tochangŭm ch'ansi" written by Yi Kyu-bo in 1232. As far as Chinese historiography is concerned, the first use of the expression can be traced back to the

52 *Jiuling shanfang ji* (Sibu congkan chubian edition), Jie Hong xu.

53 *Mingshi*, 139.3982.

54 Xiao Qiqing, "Yuandai Menggu semu jinshi beijing de fenxi" 元代蒙古色目進士背景的分析, *Hanxue yanjiu* 漢學研究 18:1 (2000), 108.

55 *Yuanshi*, 145.3448–3451.

biographical sketch written by Cheng Duanli in 1344–1345, rather than to early Ming times.

After the invasions of Japan, the Mongol Yuan began to strengthen their coastal power against the Japanese, especially merchants going to China from the late thirteenth century onwards. However, the Yuan government did not close its markets. Although China permitted Japanese merchants to conduct trade on the coast of China freely, as early as 1309 the *wokou* began to raid Qingyuan in Zhejiang. In the following years, the coasts of Zhejiang and Fujian were frequently raided by the *wokou*. Even areas in the north of China, such as Shandong and Liaodong, were attacked seriously no later than the 1330s. Therefore, we can see that *wokou* activity was not necessarily related to whether maritime trade was prohibited or not during the Yuan dynasty, which was very different from the situation during the Ming Jiajing reign.

Most of the *wokou* in Yuan China were Japanese merchants going to China, but some of them were professional pirates. *Wokou* burned houses, plundered grain and treasure, and harmed, captured and even killed people, all of which had a highly negative impact on the coastal population. It is noteworthy that some Chinese people living in the coastal regions cooperated with the *wokou* to raid the coast. Although those Chinese residents were not many, it demonstrates once again the complexities of the *wokou* problem, the study of which requires a multifaceted approach addressing transnational socio-economic, political, terminological and historiographical issues.

CHAPTER 5

Seafaring Knowledge of Ming Literati: the Scholarly Dissemination of Sailing Route Descriptions

Elke Papelitzky

1 Introduction

In contrast to European navigators, who relied on portolan charts and rutters, Chinese seafarers used written instructions and oral knowledge to find their way around the oceans. Unfortunately, sources from the Ming period (1368–1644) on the technicalities of navigation composed by people who actually sailed are rare. To learn about sailing routes, we have to turn to sources written by literati who had access to records about nautical matters and included this knowledge in their own writings, adapting and changing it from the knowledge of the seafarers.

The technical aspects of Chinese navigation have long been an object of research. These studies describe the compass, the structure of sailing instructions, and the routes that were sailed during the Ming.[1] In this chapter, I will discuss their descriptions and place them in the context of intellectual history and the history of knowledge. I will examine the processes that lead to the creation of these texts, the transmission of knowledge, and the relationship between the compilers and their texts.

1 See, for example, J.V.G. Mills, *Ma Huan. Ying-Yai Sheng-Lan: The Overall Survey of the Ocean's Shores [1433]* (Cambridge: University Press, 1970); J.V.G. Mills, "Chinese Navigators in Insulinde about A.D. 1500", *Archipel* 18, no. 1 (1979), 69–93; J.V.G. Mills, "Arab and Chinese Navigators in Malaysian Waters in about A.D. 1500", *Journal of the Malaysian Branch of the Royal Asiatic Society* 47, no. 2 (226) (1974), 1–82; G.R. Tibbetts, "Comparisons between Arab and Chinese Navigational Techniques", *Bulletin of the School of Oriental and African Studies*, 36, no. 1 (1973), 97–108; Chen Jiarong 陳佳榮, Xie Fang 謝方, and Lu Junling 陸峻嶺, *Gudai Nanhai diming huishi* 古代南海地名匯釋 (Beijing: Zhonghua shuju, 1986); Chen Jiarong 陳佳榮 and Zhu Jianqiu 朱鑒秋 (eds.), *Duhai fangcheng jizhu* 渡海方程輯注 (Shanghai: Zhongxi shuju, 2013); Zhou Yunzhong 周運中, *Zheng He xiaxiyang xinkao* 鄭和下西洋新考 (Beijing: Zhongguo shehui kexue chubanshe, 2013); Joseph Needham, *Science and Civilisation in China. Vol. 4. Physics and Physical Technology. Part III: Civil Engineering and Nautics* (Cambridge: Cambridge University Press, 1971); Roderich Ptak, "Jottings on Chinese Sailing Routes to Southeast Asia, Especially on the Eastern Route in Ming Times", in Jorge Manuel dos Santos Alves (ed.), *Portugal e a China. Conferências nos encontros de história luso-chinesa* (Lisbon: Fundação Oriente, 2001), 107–131.

 | DOI:10.1163/9789004740556_007

Chinese sailing instructions are usually based on the use of the compass and give the direction a ship has to travel, as well as the length of travel in a unit called a "*geng*" 更 (watch), of which ten are equal to 24 hours.[2] Sometimes the texts provide information about the depth of the water and dangerous spots and give advice that might be useful for sailors. The beginning of the description of a route from China to Siam, for example, reads as follows:

> Sail into the ocean from Nantingmen 南亭門 [Dongguanxian 東莞縣, Guangdong]. Use the *kunwei* 坤未 compass bearing [217.5 °] and sail 5 *geng* until you reach Wuzhushan 烏豬山,[3] which is located on the *mahu* side 馬戶邊.[4] Use the *kunwei* compass bearing for 13 *geng* until you reach Qizhoushan 七洲山.[5] Use the *kunwei* compass bearing for 7 *geng* until you reach Duzhushan 獨豬山.[6] When you see Duzhushan, you can use the *dingwei* 丁未 compass bearing [202.5 °] for 20 *geng* and you

2 The Chinese compass rose is divided into 24 subsections named after heavenly stems and earthly branches. Two adjacent bearings can be combined to indicate the direction between the two bearings. The bearing *zi* 子, for example, points north (0 °), the bearing *gui* 癸 to 15 ° and the bearing *zigui* 子癸 to 7.5 °. For more information on the Chinese compass see, for example, Joseph Needham, *Science and Civilisation in China, Vol. 4. Physics and Physical Technology, Part 1: Physics* (Cambridge: Cambridge University Press, 1962), 279–292; Sun Guangqi 孫光圻, *Zhongguo gudai hanghaishi* 中國古代航海史 (Beijing: Haiyang chubanshe, 1989), 440f. Stephen Davies, however, has convincingly argued that an actual physical compass might not have been accurate enough for sailing and only the *concept* of the Chinese compass rose was used. See his articles "On Course and Course Keeping in Ming Dynasty Seafaring. Probabilities and Improbabilities", in Hong Kong Maritime Museum (ed.), *Mapping Ming China's Maritime World* (*Zhenlu lanlü* 針路藍縷) (Hong Kong: Zhonghua shuju: 2015), 289–336; "Routes, Rutters, Navigational Techniques and the Development of Navigational Aids in Traditional Chinese", *Artefact. Techniques, Histoire et Sciences Humaines* 8 (2018), 141–182.

3 Wuzhu island 烏豬洲. This is a small island and now part of the Chuanshan archipelago 川山群島, south of the coast of Guangdong, not far from Macau.

4 Geoff Wade believes that *mahu* refers to the starboard side, Chen Jiarong that it refers to the stern of a ship. Geoff Wade, "The Patani Region in Chinese Texts of the 6th to 19th Centuries", in Patrick Jory (ed.), *Ghosts of the Past in Southern Thailand. Essays on the History and Historiography of Patani* (Singapore: NUS Press, 2013), 53–84, here 80n115; Chen Jiarong 陳佳榮, "Zaishuo *Shunfeng xiangsong* yuanzi Wu Pu de *Duhai fangcheng*" 再說《順風相送》源自吳朴的《渡海方程》, *Haiyangshi yanjiu* 海洋史研究 10 (2017), 354–364, here 363. Judging from the passage here, "starboard" seems to be the more logical translation, as Wuzhushan would lie on the starboard side when sailing from Nantingmen to Qizhoushan.

5 The Qizhou archipelago west of Hainan.

6 This small island is now called Dazhoudao 大洲島. It is located south of the coast of Hainan (Haijun haiyang cehui yanjiusuo 海軍海洋測繪研究所 and Dalian haiyun xueyuan hanghaishi yanjiushi 大連海運學院航海史研究室 (eds.), *Xinbian Zheng He hanghaitu ji* 新編鄭和航海圖集 [Beijing: Renmin jiaotong chubanshe, 1988], 43).

> will reach Wailuoshan 外羅山.[7] Use the *bingwu* 丙午 compass bearing [172.5 °] for 7 *geng* until you reach Jiaopeiyu 校杯嶼[8]and Xinzhougang 新州港.[9]

This technical knowledge had little to do with the daily life of Ming literati, and one can imagine that reading page after page of such detailed descriptions was quite boring, especially compared to the far more exciting descriptions of the customs of faraway countries often found in the same texts. Nevertheless, several books with detailed sailing instructions have survived until today. The most famous are certainly the Zheng He Map (*Zheng He hanghai tu* 鄭和航海圖) included in Mao Yuanyi's 茅元儀 (1594–1640) 1621 military treatise *Wubei zhi* 武備志 (and also in the *Nanshu zhi* 南樞志),[10] and the 1617 work of historical geography *Dongxiyang kao* 東西洋考 by Zhang Xie 張燮 (1574–1640). Two other well-known sources are held in the Bodleian Library in Oxford: the rutter known as *Shunfeng xiangsong* 順風相送 and the Selden Map.

In total, at least 23 sources dated to the Ming that include sailing instructions with compass bearings are still extant today, and in addition we have some information on the now lost *Duhai fangcheng* 渡海方程 by Wu Pu 吳朴 (ca. 1500–ca. 1570).[11] For a list of all texts, see Table 5.1. As I am focusing on the

7 The Vietnamese island Culao Ré (Chen Jiarong, Xie Fang, and Lu Junling, *Gudai Nanhai diming huishi*, s.v. Wailuoshan 外羅山).

8 The exact identification of Jiaopeiyu (usually spelled Jiaobeiyu 交杯嶼) is debated. Mills believes it to be the islands Cù lao Hón Khô (Nui Ong Co) and Cù lao Xanh (Nui Ong Can) flanking the entrance to Qui Nhơn harbour. The editors of the *Gudai Nanhai diming huishi* give an alternative interpretation, according to which Jiaopeiyu is a part of the coast of Phương Mai Peninsula, east of Qui Nhơn (Mills, *Ma Huan*, 189; Chen Jiarong, Xie Fang, and Lu Junling, *Gudai Nanhai diming huishi*, s.v. Jiaobeiyu 交杯嶼).

9 Located at the modern port city of Qui Nhơn in Central Vietnam (Mills, *Ma Huan*, 197). The description is from *Siyi guangji* 四夷廣記 (ca. 1601–1603), by Shen Maoshang 慎懋賞, in Xuanlantang congshu xuji 玄覽堂叢書續集 (Nanjing: Guoli zhongyang tushuguan, 1947), *ce* 101.

10 Zhou Yunzhong 周運中, "Lun *Wubei zhi* he *Nanshu zhi* zhong de *Zheng He hanghai tu*" 論《武備志》和《南樞志》中的《鄭和航海圖》, *Zhongguo lishi dili luncong* 中國歷史地理論叢 22, no. 2 (2007), 145–152.

11 I have used Chen Jiarong and Zhu Jianqiu's book *Duhai fangcheng jizhu* and their more recent publication *Zhongguo lidai hailu zhenjing* to find the sources. In the first book, they compiled different sailing route descriptions sorted by region. They collected not only those sources that include detailed descriptions with compass bearings, but also those that base their description on land marks without using a compass. However, in this chapter, I will only discuss those routes and sources that include compass bearings. The *Zhongguo lidai hailu zhenjing* is an expanded version of the *Duhai fangcheng jizhu*. In this two-volume work, the editors included more descriptions concerning sailing routes. In particular, routes based on personal accounts not containing any references to the compass are added in this collection. In addition to the transcriptions of the sailing route

relationship between the compilers and their access to navigational knowledge in this chapter, I will omit some of the sources from the discussion that follows. This concerns the anonymous *Shunfeng xiangsong* and the Selden Map. The compilation and dissemination of local gazetteers also follows a different pattern than those of the other texts, with several compilers working on the same piece, so I will not discuss the biographies of the compilers of the three gazetteers *Guangdong tongzhi* 廣東通志, *Haiyanxian tujing* 海鹽縣圖經 or, and *Taicang zhouzhi* 太倉州志 in any detail.

2 The Texts

Some of the texts describe the routes between China and only one other country, while others take a more comprehensive approach and embed China in the sailing and trading networks of East and Southeast Asia. In the case of the Zheng He Map, the *Xiyang chaogong dianlu* 西洋朝貢典錄 and the *Shunfeng xiangsong*, the authors even extend routes into the Indian Ocean. Unsurprisingly, these differences are in line with the focus of each text. The *Chouhai tubian* 籌海圖編, describing the Japanese, only shows routes to Japan, the two *Shi Liuqiu lu* 使琉球錄 only to the Ryūkyūs. The *Haiyu* 海語 is only concerned with Siam and Malacca, the *Riben yijian* 日本一鑑 with Japan, and the *Annan tuzhi* 安南圖誌 with Annam. Only *Siyiguan kao* 四夷館考 is an exception. While the book discusses many of China's neighbours, such as Siam, Malacca, Cambodia, Mecca, Japan, and various countries on China's northern, southern, and western borders, only one sailing route for travelling from China to Siam is included.[12]

texts, these two volumes reproduced many maps. The *Zhongguo lidai hailu zhenjing* copies the routes of two texts with compass bearings not included in the *Duhai fangcheng jizhu*, namely those in Wang Zaijin's 王在晉 *Haifang zuanyao* 海防纂要and in Xie Jie's 謝杰 *Qiantai wozuan* 虔臺倭纂. All other routes with compass bearings are the same in both compilations (Chen Jiarong and Zhu Jianqiu, *Duhai fangcheng jizhu*; Chen Jiarong 陳佳榮 and Zhu Jianqiu 朱鑒秋 (eds.), *Zhongguo lidai hailu zhenjing* 中國歷代海路針經, 2 vols. [Guangzhou: Guangdong keji chubanshe and Quanguo youxiu chubanshe, 2016]). In addition to the routes introduced in these two compilations, I found sailings routes with compass bearings in the following sources: Tang Shunzhi's 唐順之 *Wubian* 武編, and the local gazetteers of Guangdong (*Guangdong tongzhi* 廣東通志, Wanli edition), Haiyan County (*Haiyanxian tujing* 海鹽縣圖經, Tianqi edition), and Taicang (*Taicang zhouzhi* 太倉州志, Chongzhen edition).

12 Wang Zongzai's interest in Siam is due to him talking to a Siamese envoy, as he states in the preface to the *Siyiguan kao*. His chapter on Siam includes far more detail than the other chapters. This suggests that he was not primarily interested in the sailing routes, but included as much as possible in his chapter on Siam (Xiang Da 向達, "Yingya suozhi. Ji Bali ben Wang Zongzai Siyiguan kao" 瀛涯瑣志．記巴黎本王宗載四夷館考, *Tushu*

All extant texts date to the sixteenth or seventeenth century, the earliest being the 1520 *Xiyang chaogong dianlu*. This means that today no original sailing instructions contemporary with Zheng He's voyages survive. The majority (13) of the 24 texts date to the fifty-year period between 1560 and 1610, during or shortly after the *Wokou* 倭寇 (lit.: Japanese pirates) crisis of the Jiajing era (1522–1566).[13] Of course, the authors' sources may be earlier. The *Wubei zhi* and the *Nanshu zhi* make this especially obvious, as the Zheng He Map includes sailing information originally dating to the early fifteenth century.

Several of these texts are preserved only in manuscript form, suggesting that their contents were not popular enough to be printed. Even if they were printed, not a large number survived. Only one print is left of *Qiantai wozuan* 虔臺倭纂 and of Xia Ziyang 夏子陽 (fl. 1589–1607) and Wang Shizhen's 王士禎 (fl. 1598–1607) *Shi Liuqiu lu* 使琉球錄. The *Nanshu zhi* is known in only one incomplete print, and the *Duhai fangcheng* is completely lost, as are the original prints of *Haiyu* and *Riben tuzuan* 日本圖纂. Huang Zhong's 黄衷 (1474–1553) *Haiyu* only survives because of its inclusion in several Ming and Qing source collections (*congshu*) and the *Siku quanshu* 四庫全書, although these *congshu* show that the text did become rather popular during the Qing.[14] Zheng Ruozeng's 鄭若曾 (1505–1580) *Riben tuzuan* now is known through the collection entitled *Zheng Kaiyang zazhu* 鄭開陽雜著, which was edited by its author's descendants during the Kangxi period (1662–1723).[15]

---

jikan 圖書季刊 Xin 新 2, no. 2 [1940], 181–186, here 183; Zhang Wende 張文德, "Wang Zongzai ji qi *Siyiguan kao*" 王宗載及其《四夷館考》, *Zhongguo bianjiang shidi yanjiu* 中國邊疆史地研究 no. 3 [2000], 89–100; Zhang Wende 張文德, "Cong Xianluoguan de shili kan Mingchao houqi yu Xianluo de wenhua jiaoliu" 從暹羅館的設立看明朝後期與暹羅的文化交流, *Dongnanya zongheng* 東南亞縱横 no. 11 [2009], 116–122).

13 Although the Chinese called these pirates "Japanese", most were not actually from Japan. On the issue of the *Wokou* during the Jiajing period, see for example, So Kwan-wai, *Japanese Piracy in Ming China During the 16th Century* (Michigan: Michigan State University Press, 1975); Ivy Maria Lim, *Lineage Society on the Southeastern Coast of China. The Impact of Japanese Piracy in the 16th Century* (New York: Cambria, 2010); Jurgis Elisonas, "The Inseparable Trinity: Japan's Relations with China and Korea", in John Whitney Hall and James L. McClain (eds.), *The Cambridge History of Japan, Vol. 4. Early Modern Japan* (Cambridge: Cambridge University Press, 1991), 235–300; Roland L. Higgins, "Piracy and Coastal Defense in the Ming Period, Government Response to Coastal Disturbances, 1523–1549" (Dissertation, University of Minnesota, 1981).

14 For a study of the circulation of the *Haiyu*, see Elke Papelitzky, "Editing, Circulating, and Reading Huang Zhong's *Hai yu*. A Case Study in the History of Reading and the Circulation of Knowledge in Ming and Qing China", *Ming Qing Yanjiu* 23, no. 1 (2019), 1–38.

15 That the *Riben tuzuan* had indeed been printed before its inclusion in the *Zheng Kaiyang zazhu* can be concluded through Mao Kun's 茅坤 (1512–1601) preface to the book entitled "Preface for the printed edition of the *Riben tuzuan*" 日本圖纂刻題辭 preserved in Mao Kun's collected writings (*Mao Lumen xiansheng wenji* 茅鹿門先生文集 (1588), by Mao Kun 茅坤, annotated edition as *Mao Kun ji* 茅坤集, by Zhang Dazhi 張大芝

Nevertheless, some of these texts were quite successful during the Ming and Qing. The extensive catalogue *Zhongguo guji zongmu* 中國古籍總目 lists fifteen still extant prints in three Ming editions of the *Chouhai tubian*, twenty Ming prints in five editions of the *Wubei zhi*,[16] eight prints of the original edition of the *Dongxiyang kao*, and seven of the *Haifang zuanyao* 海防纂要.[17]

TABLE 5.1 Ming sources, including sailing route descriptions with compass bearings

Name of text (and reference to route section in text)	Author	Date	Extent of routes	P or M[a]
Xiyang chaogong dianlu 西洋朝貢典錄[b]	Huang Xingzeng 黃省曾	1520	SE Asia, Indian Ocean	M
Duhai fangcheng 渡海方程 (lost)[c]	Wu Pu 吳朴	1537	SE Asia, Indian Ocean	P

a "P" stands for "printed", "M" for "manuscript". This refers to the work being printed during the Ming period. Some of the works were printed later: the *Xiyang chaogong dianlu*, for example, seems not to have been printed before being included in the 1808 *congshu Jieyue shanfang huichao* 借月山房彙鈔 (Xie Fang 謝方 (ed.), *Xiyang chaogong dianlu jiaozhu* 西洋朝貢典錄校注 [Zhongwai jiaotong shiji congkan 中外交通史籍叢刊] [Beijing: Zhonghua shuju, 2000 [1982]], 6). I marked books as being printed if no Ming print is extant anymore but it is known that the book was printed during the Ming.

b *Xiyang chaogong dianlu* 西洋朝貢典錄 (1520), by Huang Xingzeng 黃省曾, annotated edition as Xie Fang 謝方 (ed.), *Xiyang chaogong dianlu jiaozhu* 西洋朝貢典錄校注 [Zhongwai jiaotong shiji congkan] (Beijing: Zhonghua shuju, 1982), 1, 18, 33, 36f, 55, 64f, 71, 73f, 92, 115. For a discussion of the routes in the *Xiyang chaogong dianlu* and a list of routes see Mills, "Chinese Navigators", 74.

c No copy of the *Duhai fangcheng* has survived until today. However, a description of the work by Dong Gu 董穀 in his *Bili zazun* 碧里杂存 is still extant. He writes that the book contains

and Zhang Mengxin 張夢新, in Liangzhe zuojia wencong 兩浙作家文叢 [Hangzhou: Zhejiang guji chubanshe, 1993], 812).

16 Zhou Yunzhong, however, has suggested that some of the prints that are classified as Ming prints were actually produced during the early Qing, as they show some signs of censorship regarding information on the Jurchen. The actual number of Ming prints might therefore be lower. Nevertheless, the *Wubei zhi* can still be considered a successful text. The version dated to the early Qing by Zhou Yunzhong is preserved in the *Siku jinhuishu congkan* 四庫禁燬書叢刊. An original Ming print was reproduced in the *Gugong zhenben congkan* 故宫珍本丛刊 (Zhou Yunzhong, "Lun *Wubei zhi* he *Nanshu zhi*", 146; Zhou Yunzhong, *Zheng He xiaxiyang*, 70–72).

17 Zhongguo guji zongmu bianzuan weiyuanhui 中國古籍總目編纂委員會, *Zhongguo guji zongmu* 中國古籍總目 (Beijing: Zhonghua shuju, Shanghai: Shanghai guji chubanshe, 2009–2012), *shibu* 3395f, 4028, 4050; *zibu* 320.

TABLE 5.1 Ming sources, including sailing route descriptions with compass bearings (*cont.*)

Name of text (and reference to route section in text)	Author	Date	Extent of routes	P or M
Haiyu 海語[d]	Huang Zhong 黄衷	1536	Siam, Malacca	P
Wubian 武編[e]	Tang Shunzhi 唐順之	Before 1560[f]	Japan	P
Riben tuzuan 日本圖纂[g]	Zheng Ruozeng 鄭若曾	1561	Japan	P
Chouhai tubian 籌海圖編[h]	Zheng Ruozeng	1562	Japan	P
Liuqiu tushuo 琉球圖說[i]	Zheng Ruozeng	ca. 1561–1569[j]	Ryūkyūs	P

information from China and up to Hormuz, thus, the *Duhai fangcheng* likely also included routes into the Indian Ocean (*Bili zacun* 碧里雜存 (Wanli), by Dong Gu 董穀 [Shanghai: Shangwu yinshuguan, 1937], 2.9a–10b). See also Chen Jiarong and Zhu Jianqiu, *Duhai fangcheng jizhu*, 181f.

d *Haiyu* 海語 (1536), by Huang Zhong 黄衷, Lingnan yishu 嶺南遺書 edition in Zhongguo shixue congshu xubian 中國史學叢書續編 (Taibei: Taiwan xuesheng shuju, 1975), 1.1a, 1.3b.

e *Wubian* 武編 (mid-16th century), by Tang Shunzhi 唐順志, facsimile of edition printed in 1618 by Xu Xiangyun 徐象櫄 in Zhongguo bingshu jicheng 中國兵書集成 (Beijing: Jiefang jun chubanshe, Shengyang: Liaoshen shushe, 1989), *qianji* 6.44a–47a.

f Tang Shunzhi died in 1560, so the text must date to before that time. However, Tang Shunzhi never finished or printed the *Wubian*. Jiao Hong 焦竑 (1541–1620) received Tang Shunzhi's manuscript and edited it. In 1618 it was printed by Xu Yiangyun 徐象櫄 under the title *Tang Jingchuan xiansheng zuanji Wubian* 唐荊川先生纂輯武編.

g *Zheng Kaiyang zazhu* 鄭開陽雜著, by Zheng Ruozeng 鄭若曾, in Wenyuange Siku quanshu 文淵閣四庫全書 (Taibei: Taiwan shangwu yinshuguan, 1983), 4.47a–52b.

h *Chouhai tubian* 籌海圖編 (1562), by Zheng Ruozeng 鄭若曾, annotated edition by Li Zhizhong 李致忠 (Beijing: Zhonghua shuju, 2007), 158–161. This annotated edition of the *Chouhai tubian* does not reproduce the pictures of the island that are included in the original. For a reproduction of these pictures, see the facsimile edition of the 1562 print in Zhongguo bingshu jicheng 中國兵書集成 (Beijing: Jiefang jun chubanshe, Shenyang: Liaoshen shushe, 1990), 210–216. On the sailing routes in the *Chouhai tubian*, see Fujita Motoharu 藤田元春, "Chukai zuhen Nihon kōro kō (1)" 籌海圖編日本航路考（一）, *Jikyū* 地球 24, no. 2 (1935), 135–145; Fujita Motoharu 藤田元春, "Chukai zuhen Nihon kōro kō (2): tsuke gōresu kō" 籌海圖編日本航路考（二）：附ゴーレス考, *Jikyū* 地球 24, no. 6 (1935), 439–452.

i *Zheng Kaiyang zazhu*, 7.11a–12b.

j Zheng Ruozeng also wrote two books called *Annan tushuo* 安南圖說 and *Chaoxian tushuo* 朝鮮圖說, both included in the *Zheng Kaiyang zazhu*. In 1569 Lin Run 林潤 (1530–1569) printed the three *tushuo* together. This seems to be the first printed edition of the three works. Yu Xiangdong and Cheng Sijia, who discussed the *Annan tushuo*, believe the three *tushuo*

TABLE 5.1 Ming sources, including sailing route descriptions with compass bearings (*cont.*)

Name of text (and reference to route section in text)	Author	Date	Extent of routes	P or M
Riben yijian 日本一鑑[k]	Zheng Shungong 鄭舜功	ca. 1565–1567[l]	Japan	M
Shi Liuqiu lu 使琉球錄[m]	Xiao Chongye 蕭崇業 and Xie Jie 謝杰	1579	Ryūkyūs	P
Siyiguan kao 四夷館考[n]	Wang Zongzai 王宗載	1580	Siam	M

to be later than the *Chouhai tubian*. As Zheng Ruozeng's preface to the *Chouhai tubian* is dated 1561, the three *tushuo* should have been completed between 1561 and 1569 (Yu Xiangdong 於向東 and Cheng Sijia 成思佳, "Zheng Ruozeng yu *Annan tushuo* lüelun" 鄭若曾與《安南圖說》略論, *Zhongguo bianjiang shidi yanjiu* 中國邊疆史地研究 26, no. 3 [2016], 96–110, here 97). The *Annan tushuo* also includes three land and sea routes from China to Vietnam (via Guangxi, Yunnan, and Guangdong), but the sea route from Guangdong does not include any compass instructions (*Zheng Kaiyang zazhu*, 6.36b–38a).

k The *Riben yijian* was reproduced in 1939 in Shanghai. However, only a few libraries hold this reprint. I used the annotated version of the routes of the *Riben yijian* contained in Chen Jiarong and Zhu Jianqiu, *Duhai fangcheng jizhu*, 12–14; Chen Jiarong and Zhu Jianqiu, *Zhongguo lidai hailu zhenjing*, 248–264. On the routes in the *Riben yijian*, see Zhu Jianqiu 朱鑑秋, "*Riben yijian fuhai tujing* ji Mingdai ZhongRi haishang hanglu de yanjiu" 《日本一鑑桴海圖經》及明代中日海上航路的研究, *Haijiaoshi yanjiu* 海交史研究 no. 2 (2002), 31–38; Zheng Yongchang 鄭永常, "Zheng Shungong Riben hanghai zhi lü" 鄭舜功日本航海之旅, *Guojia hanghai* 國家航海 9 (2014), 144–165; Ōtomo Shin'ichi 大友信一 and Liu Zhenyu 刘震宇, "Nihon ikkan no banri chōka. Honyaku to oboekaki" 「日本一鑑」の「万里長歌」. 翻訳と覚え書き, *Okayama daigaku bungaku bu kiyō* 岡山大学文学部紀要 4 (1984), 83–97.

l The estimates for the date of the *Riben yijian* vary. Suganuma believes it to be finished in 1565, Chen Jiarong and Zhu Jianqiu around 1566 or 1567, and Kanbe Teruo estimates it to be completed between the Longqing (1567–1572) or early Wanli (1573–1620) periods (Unryu Suganuma, *Sovereign Rights and Territorial Space in Sino-Japanese Relations. Irredentism and the Diaoyu/Senkaku Islands* [Honolulu: University of Hawai'i Press, 2000], 64; Chen Jiarong and Zhu Jianqiu, *Zhongguo lidai hailu zhenjing*, 249; Kanbe Teruo 神戸輝夫, "Tei Shunkō cho *Nihon ikkan* ni tsuite (sei). *Fukai zukyō* to *Zettō shinpen*" 鄭舜功著『日本一鑑』について(正):「ふ海図経」と「絶島新編」, *Ōita daigaku kyōiku fukushi kagakubu kenkyū kiyō* 大分大学教育福祉科学部研究紀要 22, no. 1 [2000], 15–31, here 16).

m *Shi Liuqiu lu* 使琉球錄 (1579), by Xiao Chongye 蕭崇業 and Xie Jie 謝杰, in *Shi Liuqiu lu sanzhong* 使琉球錄三種, in Taiwan wenxian congkan 台灣文獻叢刊 (Taibei: Taiwan yinhang, 1970), 55–61.

n *Siyiguan kao* 四夷館考 (1580), by Wang Zongzai 王宗載, 1924 Dongfang xuehui edition in Zhongguo shaoshu minzu guji jicheng 中國少數民族古籍集成 (Chengdu: Sichuan minzu chubanshe, 2002), 2.22a.

TABLE 5.1 Ming sources, including sailing route descriptions with compass bearings (*cont.*)

Name of text (and reference to route section in text)	Author	Date	Extent of routes	P or M
Chouhai chongbian 籌海重編[o]	Deng Zhong 鄧鐘	1592	Japan	P
Qiantai wozuan 虔臺倭纂[p]	Xie Jie 謝杰	1595	Japan	P
Shunfeng xiangsong 順風相送[q]		Late 16th century[r]	East Asia, SE Asia, Indian Ocean	M
Siyi guangji 四夷廣記[s]	Shen Maoshang 慎懋賞	ca. 1601–1603	East Asia, SE Asia[t]	M

o *Chouhai chongbian* 籌海重編(1592), by Deng Zhong 鄧鐘, in Siku quanshu cunmu congshu 四庫全書存目叢書 (Jinan: Qilu shushe, 1997), 2.103a–105b.

p *Qiantai wozuan* 虔臺倭纂(1595), by Xie Jie 謝杰, in Xuanlantang congshu xuji 玄覽堂叢書續集 (Nanjing: Guoli zhongyang tushuguan, 1947), 1.22a–26b.

q *Shunfeng xiangsong* 順風相送 (late 16th century), in Xiang Da 向達 (ed.), *Liangzhong haidao zhenjing* 兩種海道鍼經 [Zhongwai jiaotong shiji congkan] (Beijing: Zhonghua shuju, 2000).

r The exact date of the *Shunfeng xiangsong* is unknown, but many scholars have speculated on the dating of the manuscript, ranging from the Yongle period until before 1639, when the Bodleian library received the manuscript. In recent years, Chen Jiarong has proposed the year 1593 for the completion of the manuscript. Zhang Rong and Liu Yijie believe it to date to the second half of the sixteenth century, or more specifically the Longqing and early Wanli periods (Chen Jiarong 陳佳榮, "*Shunfeng xiangsong* zuozhe ji wancheng niandai xinkao" 《順風相送》作者及完成年代新考, Nanmingwang 南溟網 2011, http://www.world10k.com/blog/?p=2028; Zhang Rong 張榮 and Liu Yijie 劉義傑, "*Shunfeng xiangsong* jiaokan ji biancheng niandai xiaokao" 《順風相送》校勘及編成年代小考, *Guojia hanghai* 國家航海 2 [2012], 78–96, here 90).

s *Siyi guangji*, *ce* 92, 94, 99–102.

t In its present state, the manuscript of the *Siyi guangji* only includes descriptions of the so-called "Western route" along the coast of Vietnam. Descriptions of the "Eastern routes", i.e. those connecting China with the Philippines and Brunei, are missing. It is, however, possible that the *Siyi guangji* originally also included information on those routes, as one volume of the text, which probably included information on the Philippines and Brunei, is now lost. See Elke Papelitzky, *Writing World History in Late Ming China and the Perception of Maritime Asia* (Wiesbaden: Harrassowitz, 2020), 30f, 69, 73; Elke Papelitzky, "An Introduction to *Siyi guangji* 四夷廣記", *Crossroads. Studies on the History of Exchange Relations in the East Asian World* 11 (2015), 85–95, here 88f.

TABLE 5.1 Ming sources, including sailing route descriptions with compass bearings (*cont.*)

Name of text (and reference to route section in text)	Author	Date	Extent of routes	P or M
Guangdong tongzhi (Wanli) 廣東通志(萬曆)[u]	Guo Fei 郭棐	1602	Siam	P
Shi Liuqiu lu 使琉球錄[v]	Xia Ziyang 夏子陽 and Wang Shizhen 王士禎	1607	Ryūkyūs	P[w]
Annan tuzhi 安南圖志[x]	Deng Zhong 鄧鐘	1608	Vietnam	M
Haifang zuanyao 海防纂要[y]	Wang Zaijin 王在晉	1613	Japan, Ryūkyūs	P
Dongxiyang kao 東西洋考[z]	Zhang Xie 張燮	1617	SE Asia	P
Wubei zhi 武備志[aa]	Mao Yuanyi 茅元儀	1621	SE Asia, Indian Ocean	P
Selden Map		Early 17th century[ab]	SE Asia	M

u *Guangdong tongzhi* (*Wanli*) 廣東通志(萬曆) (1602), in Airusheng – Zhongguo fangzhi ku 愛如生 – 中國方志庫, 70.51b.

v *Shi Liuqiu lu* 使琉球錄 (1607), by Xia Ziyang 夏子陽 and Wang Shizhen 王士禎, in *Shi Liuqiu lu sanzhong*, in Taiwan wenxian congkan (Taibei: Taiwan yinhang, 1970), 179–194.

w The version of this *Shi Liuqiu lu* I am using is based on a manuscript held in the National Central Library in Taipei. However, a reprint of the original Ming print conserved in the National Library in Beijing can be found in Huang Runhua 黃潤華 and Xue Ying 薛英 (eds.), *Guojia tushuguan zang Liuqiu ziliao huibian* 國家圖書館藏琉球資料匯編 (Beijing: Beijing chubanshe, 2000).

x *Annan tuzhi* 安南圖誌 (1608), by Deng Zhong 鄧鐘, in Sibu congkan xubian 四部叢刊續編 (Taibei: Taiwan shangwu yinshuguan, 1976), 30a–31a.

y *Haifang zuanyao* 海防纂要 (1613), by Wang Zaijin 王在晉, in Siku jinhui shu congkan 四庫禁燬書叢刊 (Beijing: Beijing chubanshe, 2000), 2.23a–26b, 2.38ab.

z *Dongxiyang kao* 東西洋考 (1617), by Zhang Xie 張燮, Xie Fang 謝方 (ed.) [Zhongwai jiaotong shiji congkan] (Beijing: Zhonghua shuju, 2000 [1981]), 170–185.

aa *Wubei zhi* 武備志 (1621), by Mao Yuanyi 茅元儀, in Siku jinhui shu congkan (Beijing: Beijing chubanshe, 2000), *j.* 240.

ab The dating of the Selden Map is debated. Guo Yusheng and Liu Yijie have proposed a date ranging from 1566 to 1602, James K. Chin supposes it dates to the late sixteenth or early seventeenth century, Timothy Brook suggested ca. 1608, Robert Batchelor ca. 1619, Chen Jiarong ca. 1624, and Lin Meicun 1633–1644 (Guo Yusheng 郭育生 and Liu Yijie 劉義杰, "*Dongxiyang hanghai tu* chengtu shijian chutan" 《東西洋航海圖》成圖時間初探,

TABLE 5.1 Ming sources, including sailing route descriptions with compass bearings (*cont.*)

Name of text (and reference to route section in text)	Author	Date	Extent of routes	P or M
Haiyanxian tujing 海鹽縣圖經[ac]	Fan Weicheng 樊維城, Hu Zhenheng 胡震亨, Yao Shilin 姚士麟	1624	Japan	P
Nanshu zhi 南樞志[ad]	Fan Jingwen 范景文 and Zhang Keshi 張可仕[ae]	ca. 1635–1638[af]	SE Asia, Indian Ocean	P
Taicang zhouzhi (Chongzhen) 太倉州志 (崇禎)[ag]	Qian Sule 錢肅樂, Zhang Cai 張采	1642	Japan	P

Haijiaoshi yanjiu 海交史研究 no. 2 [2011], 67–81; Qian Jiang [James K. Chin] 錢江, "Yifu xinjin faxian de Mingchao zhong ye caihui hanghaitu" 一幅新近發現的明朝中葉彩繪航海圖, *Haijioashi yanjiu* 海交史研究 no. 1 [2011], 1–7, here 6; Timothy Brook, *Mr. Selden's Map of China. Decoding the Secrets of a Vanished Cartographer* [New York et al.: Bloomsbury Press, 2013], 173; Robert Batchelor, "The Selden Map Rediscovered: A Chinese Map of East Asian Shipping Routes, *c.*1619", *Imago Mundi* 65, no. 1 [2013], 37–63; Robert Batchelor, *London. The Selden Map and the Making of a Global City, 1549–1689* [Chicago and London: The University of Chicago Press, 2014], 104; Chen Jiarong 陳佳榮, "'Mingmo jiangli ji Zhang Quan hanghai tongjiao tu' bianhui shijian, tese ji haiwai jiaotong diming lüexi" 《明末疆裡及漳泉航海通交圖》編繪時間、特色及海外交通地名略析, *Haijiaoshi yanjiu* 海交史研究 no. 2 [2011], 52–66; Lin Meicun 林梅村, "*Zheng Zhilong hanghai tu* kao. Niujin daxue Bodeli tushuguan cang *Xueerdeng Zhongguo ditu* mingshi bian" 《鄭芝龍航海圖》考. 牛津大學博德利圖書館藏《雪爾登中國地圖》名實辯, *Wenwu* 文物 no. 9 [2013], 64–82).

ac *Haiyanxian tujing* 海鹽縣圖經 (1624), in Airusheng – Zhongguo fangzhi ku, 7.14b–15a.

ad *Nanshu zhi* 南樞志 (ca. 1635–1638), by Fan Jingwen 范景文 and Zhang Keshi 張可仕, in Zhongguo fangzhi congshu 中國方志叢書 (Taibei: Chengwen chubanshe, 1983), *j.* 113.

ae The extant edition of the *Nanshu zhi* is incomplete, missing, among others, the first seven *juan*, and so no information on the author can be gathered from any prefaces or possible title pages. In addition, the book does not state the author at the beginning of a *juan*. From Qing book catalogues and the chapter on books in the *Mingshi*, the author can be assumed to be Fan Jingwen. The *Qianjingtang shumu* 千頃堂書目 lists Zhang Keshi as co-editor alongside Fan Jingwen. Zhang Keshi's biographies also note that he compiled the *Nanshu zhi* (*Qianqingtang shumu* 千頃堂書目 (17th century), by Huang Yuji 黄虞稷 [Shanghai: Shanghai guji chubanshe, 1990], 9.4a; Zhou Yunzhong, "Lun *Wubei zhi* he *Nanshu zhi*", 151). Lu Wenchao in his *Dushi zhaji* even claims that Mao Yuanyi also was one of the compilers (*Dushi zhaji* 讀史札記 (late 18th century), by Lu Wenchao 盧文弨, in Xuxiu Siku quanshu 續修四庫全書 [Shanghai: Shanghai guji chubanshe, 2002], 27a).

That Mao Yuanyi participated in the compilation of the *Nanshu zhi* is doubtful, as his biographies do not mention the *Nanshu zhi*. See also, Wu Enrong 吳恩榮, "Mingdai liangjing guanshu zhi de zuanxiu jiqi zhengzhi wenhua jiedu" 明代兩京官署志的纂修及其政治文化解讀, *Lishi dang'an* 歷史檔案 no. 2 (2015), 52–62, here 62n55.

af Wu Enrong supposes that the *Nanshu zhi* was completed between 1635 and 1638 as this was the period that Fan Jingwen was working as minister of war (Wu Enrong, "Mingdai liangjing guanshu zhi", 55, 62n55).

ag *Taicang zhouzhi* (*Chongzhen*) 太倉州志(崇禎) (1642 [1678]), in Airusheng – Zhongguo fangzhi ku, 11.20b–21a.

3 Organization and Presentation of the Route Descriptions

The sailing routes are either presented simply as text or are illustrated by a map. Aside from the Zheng He Map, the authors of both *Shi Liuqiu lu* incorporated the routes into maps. Zheng Ruozeng in his *Chouhai tubian* and *Riben tuzuan*, and Deng Zhong 鄧鐘 (fl. 1576–1614) in his copy of the *Chouhai tubian*, the *Chouhai chongbian* 籌海重編, illustrated the routes with views of the islands one passes along the way between China and Japan (see figs. 5.1 and 5.2). The *Annan tuzhi*, also by Deng Zhong, includes a map of the route from China to Annam copied from a book entitled *Pingjiao tushuo* 平交圖說.[18] However, this map only marks the route with dots: the sailing instructions with compass bearings are found in a different part of the text. These maps with sailing routes only provide a rudimentary representation of the coastline to serve as visual indices to the text and were not actually used for navigation. For Chinese navigators the important information was embedded in the text and not the image.[19] One could thus copy the texts of the instructions from the map, discard the graphical representation of space, and still have sensible information for navigating.

The texts that describe more than one route can be divided into two groups depending on how they present the routes. One way, found in the *Shunfeng xiangsong*, *Siyi guangji* 四夷廣記, and probably also the *Duhai fangcheng*, conserves the original structure of Chinese rutters. These texts have a description

18 This book is now lost, but according to Deng Zhong's preface, it was written by a certain Yu Douhu 俞都護, another name for General Yu Dayou 俞大猷 (1503–1597). In addition to the map, Deng Zhong copied another description of the sailing route between China and Annam from this book, but it includes no references to the compass (*Annan tuzhi*, *xu* 1a; 12a–26b).

19 See Elke Papelitzky "Shallow Water at China's Coast: Depicting Dangers on Early Modern Chinese Maps", *Isis* 112 (2021), 111–121; Elke Papelitzky, "Sailing the Waters of East and Southeast Asia: Chinese Navigators and their Material and Mental Tools", Journal of Chinese History (2025).

FIGURE 5.1 A section of the "Zheng He Map" showing the Strait of Malacca. The dots represent sailing routes that for some sections are annotated with information on how to use the compass
LIBRARY OF CONGRESS, GEOGRAPHY AND MAP DIVISION

for each section, for example, from China to Siam, or from China to Malacca. This results in redundant data, as there might be an explanation for a route from China to Champa and one from China to Siam. When sailing from China to Siam the ship also passes Champa, so the information on how to sail from China to Champa is given in both descriptions.

In his *Dongxiyang kao*, however, Zhang Xie changed the way he presented route descriptions. Instead of having multiple sections, he amended them to include two general routes, the so-called Western route (*xiyang zhenlu* 西洋針路) along the coast of Vietnam, and the Eastern route (*dongyang zhenlu* 東洋針路) along the Philippines and Kalimantan Island. For each of these two basic routes, he gives instructions for one trunk line and adds short descriptions for detours where an important harbour can be reached. Conceptually,

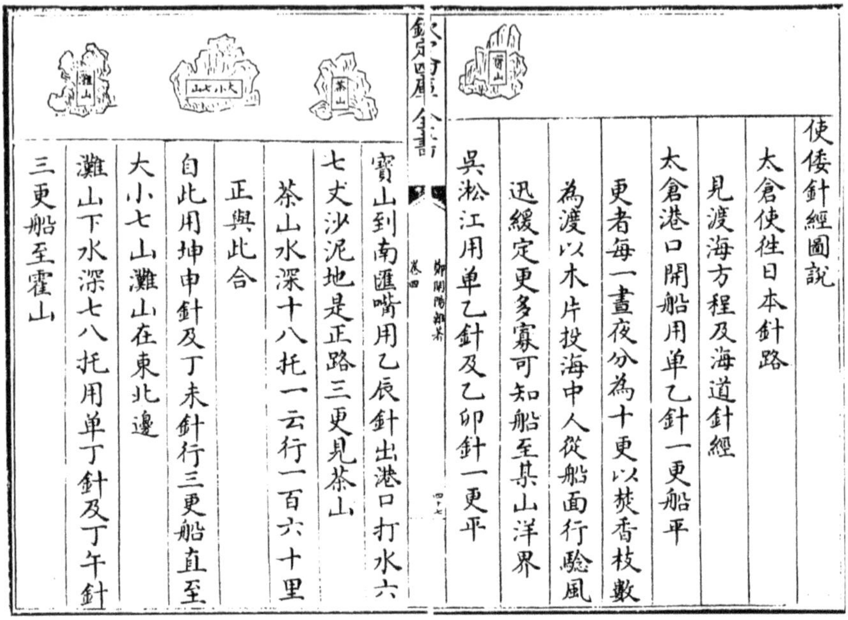

寶山

使倭針經圖說

太倉使往日本針路

見渡海方程及海道針經

太倉港口開船用单乙針一更船平

更者每一晝夜分為十更以焚香枝數

為渡以木片投海中人從船面行驗風

迅緩定更多寡可知船至某山洋界

吳淞江用单乙針及乙卯針一更平

寶山到南匯嘴用乙辰針出港口打水六

七丈沙泥地是正路三更見茶山

茶山水深十八托一云行一百六十里

正與此合

自此用坤申針及丁未針行三更船直至

大小七山灘山在東北邊

灘山下水深七八托用单丁針及丁午針

三更船至霍山

FIGURE 5.2 A page from the *Riben tuzuan* contained in the *Zheng Kaiyang zazhu* showing written sailing route instructions with profiles of islands in the upper register

this representation recalls the view of the routes in the Selden Map. Zhang Xie explains the process of restructuring the sailing route descriptions in the editorial principles (*fanli* 凡例) at the beginning of his book:

> From old times on, mariners had rutters[20] for going to sea. They are all written in jargon and are not easy to analyse. I have translated them [into standard language] and written them down. I have [written down] those historical records that can be recorded, so they can be spread and be appreciated. Originally, [the route books] recorded needle routes, in which every country was separated. [The information] was extremely fragmented, there were errors, and [the contents] did not fit together. [This is why] I merged [the information] into one piece. I narrate the journey straight along the route. If there are detours for entering certain harbours along the way, and then I explain how to take a different

20 The term used here for rutters is *Hanghai zhenjing* 航海針經. Xie Fang believes *zhenjing* to be part of the title of a book and *hanghai* being an attribute to this title, as he marks the term as "Hanghai *Zhenjing*" 航海《針經》 in his annotation of the *Dongxiyang kao*. It is also possible that *Hanghai zhenjing* is supposed to be the whole title of a book, or that the whole term refers generically to rutters.

> route from there to reach these certain countries. After that, I again follow the main route, straight and directly forward, and when there is a detour again, I follow the same pattern. This text has [information] on all oceans, so it is convenient to read.[21]

Zhang Xie's way of presenting data is in the form of an edited version that is not useful for seafarers but is "convenient to read", probably referring to his intended audience. His source for the sailing instructions must have originally been structured like the *Shunfeng xiangsong* and *Siyi guangji*. This editing process suggests that Zhang Xie was quite familiar with the way the routes were described, as changing and adapting the information requires a better understanding than is needed when information is simply copied word for word. In contrast, Shen Maoshang 慎懋賞 (fl. 1578–1607), the author of the *Siyi guangji*, had simply copied his source without understanding the geography of the descriptions, resulting in many errors.[22]

Shen Maoshang's way of describing the routes allowed him to attach the route descriptions to the chapters on the respective countries he was writing about, scattering the routes throughout the *Siyi guangji* and taking away the original context of a unified rutter. The *Dongxiyang kao*, on the other hand, collected all descriptions in one place and dedicates one *juan* to the routes.

4 Their Sources: Copying Old Texts, or First-hand Knowledge?

The authors obtained the information for their texts from a variety of sources. However, it is not always easy to determine the exact source for the descriptions of the sailing routes. In the context of the circulation of knowledge of sailing instructions, one can discern the following three types of knowledge:

1) First-hand knowledge resulting from the author having sailed the route himself
2) Second-hand knowledge from the author having talked to people who have first-hand knowledge of the route
3) Third-hand knowledge whereby the author simply copies information from a written source.

It is not always possible to assign a category for a text, as not all the authors reflected on their sources, and some authors used more than one type of source. Sometimes the authors explain that they used first- or second-hand

21 *Dongxiyang kao*, 20.

22 For a discussion of some of Shen Maoshang's errors, see Papelitzky, *Writing World History*, 122f.

knowledge in their prefaces, but it is unclear if this is also true for the sailing instructions or only for other parts of their books. Nevertheless, these categories can serve as a starting point for a discussion about the process of creating the texts and the dissemination of seafaring knowledge.

4.1 *First-hand Knowledge*

True first-hand knowledge is hard to find, as those who sailed the ships were usually not those who wrote the texts. However, including authors who were at least on a ship and might have had the opportunity to observe how the knowledge was applied leaves us with the authors of three reports of an official mission: Zheng Shungong's 鄭舜功 (fl. 1523–1566) *Riben yijian*, and the two *Shi Liuqiu lu*.

Zheng Shungong is very explicit about his sources in the preface to the *Fuhai tujing* 浮海圖經, the part of the *Riben yijian* that contains the sailing instructions. Two of his main sources were the *Duhai fangcheng* and a book called *Haidao jingshu* 海道經書, which, according to him, have the same content and record various compass routes. He complains that these two books were not detailed enough, as they focus too much on the routes to the southwestern ocean. In addition, he had access to a book called *Sihai zhinan* 四海指南 recording information from envoys travelling from Taicang (Jiangsu) 太倉 to Japan. He used these books as a basis and, when he went from Guangzhou to Japan himself, he collected more information, merging everything together in the *Riben yijian*.[23] Other books Zheng Shungong refers to are the *Haihang mijue* 海航秘訣 and *Hanghai quanshu* 航海全書, which, according to him, have similar contents.[24] Unfortunately, all these sources are now lost. It is clear that Zheng Shungong used both first-hand knowledge and previous written sources.

The authors of the two *Shi Liuqiu lu*, Xiao Chongye 蕭崇業 (ca. 1544–1586) and Xie Jie 謝杰 (1537–1604), like Xia Ziyang and Wang Shizhen, are less explicit about their sources and do not state whether their descriptions of sailing routes were based on first-hand information or not. Both books start with a map and the sailing route descriptions, and the authors also explain the importance of the compass for navigation.[25] Both accounts continue with a

23 For a translation of the relevant parts of the preface, see Zhou Yunzhong 周運中, "The Retrogression in Overseas Geographical Knowledge during the Mid-Ming Period", in Y.H. Teddy Sim (ed.), *The Maritime Defence of China. Ming General Qi Jiguang and Beyond* (Singapore: Springer, 2017), 145–161, here 159.

24 Zhu Jianqiu, "*Riben yijian fuhai tujing*", 33; Chen Jiarong and Zhu Jianqiu, *Zhongguo lidai hailu zhenjing*, 255; Chen Jiarong and Zhu Jianqiu, *Duhai fangcheng jizhu*, 187.

25 *Shi Liuqiu lu*, by Xiao Chongye and Xie Jie, 62; *Shi Liuqiu lu*, by Xia Ziyang and Wang Shizhen, 195.

short description of the personal journey they undertook, but these descriptions do not feature any compass bearings, although Xiao Chongye explains that shortly after departing from Meihuasuo 梅花所 (in Changle 長樂, Fujian) the ship lost the "compass-needle route" 針路 because of strong winds.[26] Xiao Chongye and Xie Jie include a poem about their voyage at the end of their report, also commenting on several stations along their route to the Ryūkyūs.[27]

That at least Xie Jie had been paying attention to the sailing route on the voyage to the Ryūkyūs can be ascertained from another book of his entitled *Qiantai wozuan*. While the routes in this book between China and Japan seem to be copied word for word from the *Chouhai tubian*, he adds a comment about his route to Naha 那覇:

> *Zhen* 針 (needle) refers to the needle pointing north or south of the water compass. The needle and the rudder [of the ship] are connected; wherever the needle points, the rudder follows. The persons in charge of the needle are called *huozhang* 夥長.[28] The persons in charge of the rudder are called *duogong* 舵工. When I was sent to the Ryūkyūs, there were eight huozhang and sixteen *duogong*. Two *huozhang* are one group, four duogong are one group. At day and night, they take turns resting, there is no gap. Those who are at work take care of things, those who are off work take a rest. The place of the persons in charge of the needle is very secluded, they cannot see a single thing from the outside. There is only an opening in a small wall facing the rudder door. This is so they can concentrate. A light is kept burning in the needle cabin, and so night and day cannot be discerned. A night is 5 *geng* long, a day is 5 *geng* long, and so the ship sails for 10 geng in 12 double hours. The route I took to the Ryūkyūs was from the mountains east of Meihua to the harbour of Naha. The tally ship was large, and its draught was deep, so we feared reefs. [Because of this], we did not see the places that are called Xiao Liuqiu 小琉球

26 *Shi Liuqiu lu*, by Xiao Chongye and Xie Jie, 129f; *Shi Liuqiu lu*, by Xia Ziyang and Wang Shizhen, 218–228.

27 *Shi Liuqiu lu*, by Xiao Chongye and Xie Jie, 157–170. For a discussion of the routes of Chinese envoys to Ryūkyū, see Azuma Yoshimochi 東喜望, "Chūgoku to Ryūkyū no kokkō II: sakuhōshi no rūto" 中国と琉球の国交 II： 冊封使のルート, *Shiraume gakuen tanki daigaku kiyō* 白梅学園短期大学紀要 31 (1995), 29–49, here 40–46; Wang Wenchu 王文楚, "Mingchao yu Liuqiu de haishang hanglu" 明朝與琉球的海上航路, *Shilin* 史林 no. 1 (1987), 29–34. For a discussion of Xia Ziyang's route, see also Maria Schreibweis, "Der Seeweg China – Ryūkyū am Beispiel des Gesandtschaftsberichts *Shi Liuqiu lu* 使琉球錄 von Chen Kan 陳侃 (1489–1538)", in Angela Schottenhammer (ed.), *Trade and Transfer Across the East Asian "Mediterranean"* [East Asian Maritime History 1] (Wiesbaden: Harrassowitz, 2005), 11–74.

28 Usually *huozhang* is written as 火長.

> (Taiwan), Jilongyu 雞籠嶼 (Keelung Island 基隆嶼), Pengjiashan 彭嘉山 (Pengjia Island 彭佳嶼), and Diaoyuyu 釣魚嶼. Only Gumishan 古米山 (Kume 久米 Island) did we see indistinctly [in the distance] before we arrived in [the capital of] the Ryūkyūs. The people from Zhangzhou are familiar with the way of the needle. We took the *danmao* 單卯 (90 °), *jiamao* 甲卯 (82.5 °), and *yimao* 乙卯 (97.5 °) needle to go [to the Ryūkyūs], and did not use the *genyin* 艮寅 (52.5 °) and other needles.[29] We did what is called to cross [the ocean] flying and did not look at the old texts. We sailed [like this] for eight days and then saw Rebi 熱壁 (Iheya island 伊平屋島), [this means that] we had already passed [the capital of] the Ryūkyūs for seven *geng*.[30] This is the unfortunate result of crossing [the ocean] flying. It took us another five days and nights to reach the harbour, at that time the favourable wind had changed into a headwind. It took us 50 *geng* to make a voyage of 7 *geng* to reach the harbour. Oh! [The voyage] was so dangerous! While I am writing this down, I remember this past event and I am low-spirited and feel dread. On the return route, we also only used three needles, *danyou* 單酉 (270 °), *gengyou* 庚酉 (262.5 °) and *xinyou* 辛酉 (277.5 °).[31]

This section shows that Xie Jie did gain at least some knowledge about sailing when he was an envoy to the Ryūkyūs. He seems to have talked to the sailors and carried a written description with him that he compared to his actual voyage. His comment shows that the instructions were not always followed exactly. Since the ship was too big and there was a strong wind, they could not stay close to the islands, as described in Xiao Chongye and Xie Jie's *Shi*

29 *Danmao*, *jiamao*, and *yimao* are directions that would have been used when sailing from Fuzhou, so they clearly refer to Xie Jie's voyage from Meihuasuo to Naha. *Genyin* would have been used when sailing from Zhangzhou – the sailors probably told Xie Jie that, when sailing from their home place, they first went in that direction. I am grateful to Stephen Davies for making me aware of this fact.

30 In their *Shi Liuqiu lu*, Xiao Chongye and Xie Jie talk about having lost the compass route after Meihua because of strong winds. In the *Qiantai wozuan*, Xie Jie attributes the change in course to the fear of sinking. There is, however, no reason to believe that one of the accounts is wrong – maybe due to a strong wind it was necessary for the ship to stay away from the coast. The rest of the account is the same in the *Shi Liuqiu lu* and the *Qiantai wozuan*. The ship sighted land too far away from Naha and had to turn back when the sailors discovered the land to be Rebi (called Yebishan 葉壁山 in the *Shi Liuqiu lu*) (*Shi Liuqiu lu*, by Xiao Chongye and Xie Jie, 129f). Rebi is an island belonging to the Ryūkyū kingdom but located further north of Naha, today called Iheya Island (Wang Wenchu, "Mingchao yu Liuqiu de haishang hanglu", 34n3).

31 *Qiantai wozuan*, 1.25a–26b. For an annotated version of this paragraph, see Chen Jiarong and Zhu Jianqiu, *Zhongguo lidai hailu zhenjing*, 278.

Liuqiu lu. Even though this was a perfectly good way to sail,[32] literati attached importance to the very literal meaning of the texts, so Xie Jie expressed surprise whenever the ship did not follow the route laid out in his written source, whether they were "crossing the ocean flying", i.e. not sailing close to the waypoints, or whether the last leg of the voyage took 50 *geng* instead of 7 *geng*, as it would with a favourable wind.

4.2 *Knowledge from Talking to Seafarers*

Zhang Xie, Huang Zhong, and Wang Zongzai 王宗載 (fl. 1562–1582) obtained at least part of their information by talking to people who possessed first-hand knowledge, although as in the case of Zheng Shungong, this more direct knowledge might have been supplemented by written sources. For his *Dongxiyang kao*, Zhang Xie interviewed merchants at his home place in Yuegang 月港, Zhangzhou, Fujian, and incorporated information he obtained from them into his work. However, it is quite difficult to discern which parts of the book are based on written sources and which on information obtained from the sailors and merchants. The chapter on Taiwan, for example, relies heavily on the latter's accounts.[33] As already mentioned above, in his *fanli* the author states that he rearranged the rutters of sailors to compose his own account, but unfortunately does not go into details as to whether he supplemented the written sources with accounts from his interview partners. Looking at the contents of the instruction, it is likely that he did indeed add information he received directly from the sailors. As Roderich Ptak has noticed, the sailing instructions in the *Dongxiyang kao* are far more up to date concerning the trade network in the late sixteenth and early seventeenth centuries than the instructions in other Ming texts.[34]

For his *Haiyu*, Huang Zhong also talked to seafarers in his native place Nanhai 南海 in Guangdong.[35] In his preface, he states: "I retired from public life and went out, I often met with sailors, I talked with them about things of the countries across the ocean and recorded [these things]. Gradually [the

---

32 Sailing this way ("high of course") would mean that arriving north of Naha was intentional and that they did not "pass" Naha, as Xie Jie claimed. I owe this insight to Stephen Davies, who helped me make more sense of Xie Jie's comment.

33 For a study on the sources for this section, see Zhang Caixia 張彩霞 and Lin Renchuan 林仁川, "Lun Zhang Xie 'Dongfan kao' de ziliao laiyuan" 論張燮《東番考》的資料來源, *Zhongguo shehui jingqi shi yanjiu* 中國社會經濟史研究 no. 2 (2009), 64–66.

34 Cf. Ptak, "Jottings on Chinese Sailing Routes", 119.

35 Cf. Donatella Guida, "Ming Images of Nanyang. Some Stories from *Haiyu* (Words of the Sea) [1536]", *Annali / Università Degli Studi Di Napoli l'Orientale* 54 (1994), 389–399, here 390.

account] became complete, and I collected it in [this book]."[36] Unfortunately, again, it is not certain whether the sailing instructions were solely based on oral accounts, but Huang Zhong gives no indication to believe otherwise.

Wang Zongzai received the sailing instructions from a Siamese envoy called Wowenyuan 握文源 when he was working at the *siyiguan* 四夷館, the office responsible for translating official correspondence between the court and the tributary states. A large portion of the chapter on Siam in the *Siyiguan kao* is based on this envoy's account, as Wang Zongzai explains.[37] The result is a description of the route from China to Siam that slightly differs in style and vocabulary from the routes in other sources, which can be explained by neither Wowenyuan nor Wang Zongzai being an expert in nautical matters.

One of the major differences between the route in the *Siyiguan kao* and most other routes is that the description does not stop at the Chao Phraya River estuary but continues the voyage up the river to the capital Ayutthaya. The only other Ming description I am aware of that includes this route is found in the *Haiyu*, but there is a copy of this route in the *Siyi guangji*, suggesting that information based on hearsay from sailors and travellers in the mid- to late Ming resulted in somewhat different knowledge than information based on written sources.[38]

This difference in the destination of the voyage could be explained by the focus of the text. Neither the *Haiyu* nor the *Siyiguan kao* aims to provide a detailed description for sailors, and neither of the authors was a sailor himself. For a scholar it is logical to ask for the route that led all the way to the capital. A sailor, however, would only need the route to the estuary of the correct river, as sailing up a river needs no special instructions. The rutters therefore did not

36 *Haiyu*, *xu* 1b. On the *Haiyu* being based on oral accounts, see also Duan Lisheng 段立生, "Huang Zhong jiqi *Haiyu*" 黄衷及其《海語》, *Dongnanya Nanya yanjiu* 東南亞南亞研究 no. 3 (1984), 48–52, here 50; Zhou Yunzhong, "Retrogression", 152.

37 Wang Zongzai first gives an introduction to the history of Siam and the country's relationship with Siam, mostly based on written sources. He also explains that Wowenyuan arrived in China and that an office of translation for Siamese was created. He ends the section on the history of Siam with the sentence: "Because I have time, I ordered the envoy Wowenyuan to tell me about his country's customs and products. [What he told me] is as follows." (*Siyiguan kao*, 2.22a). After this sentence, he starts narrating the sailing instructions and other information on Siam.

38 Other differences from the account in the *Siyiguan kao* include: 1) compass bearings are only given in two instances, which is a lot less than in the other texts. 2) the vocabulary for the use of compass is slightly different than in all other sailing route instructions. Wowenyuan used the term "to sail in the direction of a third between *wei* and *shen*, 未兼申三分 [220 °]." *Wei* and *shen* are not located directly next to each other on the compass, so giving the two bearings together is unusual. 3) The distances are provided in days, not in *geng*.

describe the way to the capital Ayutthaya, but Huang Zhong and Wang Zongzai had the opportunity to ask about this route from their interview partners.

4.3 *Knowledge from Copying Books*

Most of the books base their knowledge of sailing instructions on previously written sources. As already noted, even many of the authors who did have more direct knowledge, like Zheng Shungong, Zhang Xie, and the Ryūkyū envoys, mixed written sources with their own experiences.

Unfortunately, as already noted, few authors are explicit about their sources. Even those they do cite are often not extant anymore. The case is easily solved for the *Guangdong tongzhi* that copied from the *Haiyu*, as well as the *Chouhai chongbian* that relied completely on the *Chouhai tubian*. The *Chouhai tubian* in turn claims to have based its routes on the *Duhai fangcheng* and a text called *Haidao zhenjing* 海道針經. Scholarly opinion is divided on the nature of the *Haidao zhenjing*. It might be the same as the *Duhai fangcheng*, or it might be a text written by a certain Zhou Shuxue 周述學.[39]

The two gazetteers, *Taicang zhouzhi* and *Haiyanxian tujing*, record the same routes as *Chouhai tubian*, though there is no note of the source, namely *Duhai fangcheng* and *Haidao zhenjing*. Since the *Haiyanxian tujing* cites the *Chouhai tubian* elsewhere,[40] and since the *Chouhai tubian* circulated more widely than the *Duhai fangcheng*, it can be assumed that the gazetteers copied the information on the routes from the *Chouhai tubian*.

The routes in Tang Shunzhi's 唐順之 (1507–1560) *Wubian* 武編 also resemble the *Chouhai tubian* routes, although they vary in detail. While in his *Chouhai tubian* Zheng Ruozeng includes one route from Taicang to Japan and one from Fujian to Japan, Tang Shunzhi describes the route from Taicang to Taiwu 太武 in Fujian and back, as well as the route from Japan to Taicang and back. The route from Taicang to Japan is roughly the same in both *Wubian* and *Chouhai tubian*, but there are minor differences in wording. Unfortunately, Tang Shunzhi does not tell us where he copied the information from. Since the routes in the two texts are so similar, and since both Zheng Ruozeng and Tang Shunzhi worked

---

39 *Chouhai tubian*, 158, 979. Chen Jiarong argues that *Haidao zhenjing* is the title of the chapter of the *Duhai fangcheng* that includes the sailing routes. Zhu Jianqiu also draws a connection to the text *Haidao jingshu*, which, as Zheng Shungong stated, is the same as the *Duhai fangcheng*. Liu Yijie and Wang Ningjun, however, disagree. They believe the *Haidao zhenjing* to be a different text from the *Duhai fangcheng* created by Zhou Shuxue, as his biography in the *Mingshi* mentions him having written a *Haidao zhenjing* (Chen Jiarong, "*Shunfeng xiangsong* zuozhe"; Zhu Jianqiu, "*Riben yijian fuhai tujing*", 33f; Liu Yijie 劉義傑 and Wang Ningjun 王寧軍, "Haidao zhenjing shulun" 海道針經述論, *Guojia hanghai* 國家航海 14 [2016], 52–63, here 54).

40 *Haiyanxian tujing*, 16.12b.

for the supreme commander Hu Zongxian 胡宗憲 (1511–1565) and assisted him in his fighting against the *Wokou*, it is possible that Tang Shunzhi, like Zheng Ruozeng, used the *Duhai fangcheng* as a source and one of the two authors did not copy Wu Pu's text faithfully.

Wang Zaijin 王在晉 (fl. 1562–1582) includes routes in two sections of his *Haifang zuanyao*. The first routes are from China to Japan and were copied from *Chouhai chongbian*, as he clearly states at the end of the section.[41] The second section describes the route from China to the Ryūkyūs and back.[42] At first glance, they are very similar to the routes in Zheng Ruozeng's *Liuqiu tushuo* 琉球圖說, but some minor differences suggest that this part is not based on Zheng Ruozeng's work.[43] Wang Zaijin left some further clues in his bibliography. In a comprehensive list of the books he has used, Wang Zaijin mentions *Chouhai tubian* and *Chouhai chongbian*, the rutter *Haidao zhenjing*, and a *Haidao lucheng* 海道路程, probably another rutter.[44] It is likely that the section from China to the Ryūkyūs was based on one of the two rutters.

Deng Zhong names his source for the sailing route in the *Annan tuzhi*. In his preface, he lists many sources, among them *Pingjiao tushuo*, *Yuetong zhi* 粵通志, and a *Hanghai jing* 航海經.[45] He mentions this *Hanghai jing* again when explaining how to calculate the number of *geng*, right before describing the route from Fujian to Annam.[46] It therefore seems likely that the sailing instructions are based on this source. Judging from the preface, the *Annan tuzhi* might also contain first-hand knowledge. Deng Zhong mentions that he did take a ship from Annam to China.[47] However, comparing the sailing instructions in the *Annan tuzhi* with the *Siyi guangji* and the *Shunfeng xiangsong* shows that exactly the same instruction can be found in the *Siyi guangji* and nearly the same in the *Shunfeng xiangsong*, texts that are earlier than the *Annan tuzhi*.[48]

41 *Haifang zuanyao*, 2.26b.

42 *Haifang zuanyao*, 2.38ab.

43 These difference include a different starting point: in contrast to most other routes, including those in the *Liuqiu tushuo*, Wang Zaijin's route starts at Dongsha 東沙 instead of Meihuasuo 梅花所. The island Dongsha is not far from Meihua, both being in Changle, Fujian. However, usually this is the second stop after Meihua, as, for example, in the two *Shi Liuqiu lu*. In addition, Wang Zongzai uses some different place names. He does not call Taiwan Small Ryūkyū (Xiao Liuqiu 小琉球) but instead refers to the northern tip of Taiwan as Jilongshan 雞籠山.

44 *Haifang zuanyao*, *fanli* 1a, 4a.

45 *Annan tuzhi*, *xu* 1a.

46 *Annan tuzhi*, 30a.

47 *Annan tuzhi*, *xu* 1b.

48 *Siyi guangji*, *ce* 100; *Shunfeng xiangsong*, 49.

Shen Maoshang divided the routes in his *Siyi guangji* into two parts: the first, usually placed before the section on the history of the respective country, includes routes of which the source can be identified through a comparison with other texts. In this first part, Shen Maoshang copied all routes from the *Chouhai tubian* and *Haiyu*. The routes in the second part are unique to the *Siyi guangji* and cannot be found in any other source except for one route from Fujian to Annam, which we also find in Deng Zhong's *Annan tuzhi*. For this second part, Shen Maoshang probably copied from a now lost rutter. As Shen Maoshang does not often give the name of his sources, we unfortunately do not know which rutter he used, but the similarities between the route from Fujian to Annam with that from the *Annan tuzhi* suggests that he used the *Haidao jing* mentioned by Deng Zhong.[49]

Huang Xingzeng's 黄省曾 (1490–1540) exact source for the routes is unknown. In the preface to his *Xiyang chaogong dianlu*, he states: "I then collected the words of interpreters (*yiren* 譯人), like those who edited the *Xingcha* 星槎, *Yingya* 瀛涯, and *Zhenwei* 鍼位. …"[50] Without doubt, *Xingcha* and *Yingya* are references to the two accounts of Zheng He's voyages, *Yingya shenglan* 瀛涯勝覽 by Ma Huan 馬歡 (fl. 1413–1451), and *Xingcha shenglan* 星槎勝覽 by Fei Xin 費信 (1388–1436?). *Zhenwei* stands for a rutter, although it is not clear if it is the name of a rutter or a general term. Xie Fang believes it to stand for *Zhenwei bian* 鍼位編, denoting a now lost rutter that might have been based on Zheng He's voyages.[51] Huang Xingzeng wrote the *Xiyang chaogong dianlu* when he was staying in Nanjing at the invitation of the minister of war, Qiao Yu 喬宇 (1457–1524).[52] It is possible that he gained access to information on these routes at that time.

---

49 For more information on Shen Maoshang's sources, see Papelitzky, *Writing World History*, 169–172. For an evaluation of the distinctiveness of some of the routes in the *Siyi guangji*, see Elke Papelitzky, "Sea Routes to Thailand Described in Chinese Texts of the Ming Dynasty", in Chinese Maritime Museum 上海中國航海博物館 (ed.), *Silu de yanshen. Yazhou haiyang lishi yu wenhua. Guoji xueshu taolunhui lunwenji* 絲路的延伸：亞洲海洋歷史與文化國際學術研討會論文集 (Shanghai: Zhongxi shuju, 2015), 249–275, here 264–268.

50 *Xiyang chaogong dianlu*, 8. For a translation of the whole section and book into German, see Klaus Sonnendecker, "Huang Xingzeng. Verzeichnis der Akteneinträge zu Audienzen und Tributen vom Westlichen Meer (*Xiyang chaogong dianlu*) [黄省曾，西洋朝貢典錄, 1520 n. Chr.]" (Dissertation, Freie Universität Berlin, 2005), 3.

51 Xie Fang, *Xiyang chaogong dianlu jiaozhu*, 3. For a discussion of the early opinions on whether *Zhenwei* is the name of a rutter or just a term referring to a rutter, see Paul Pelliot, "Les grands voyages maritimes chinois au début du XVe siècle", *T'oung Pao* 30, no. 3/5 (1933), 237–452, here 345f.

52 L. Carrington Goodrich and Chaoying Fang (eds.), *Dictionary of Ming Biography. 1368–1644* (New York and London: Columbia University Press, 1976), 662.

The Zheng He Map was included in Mao Yuanyi's *Wubei zhi* and Fan Jingwen 范景文 (1587–1644) and Zhang Keshi's 張可仕 (1591–1654) *Nanshu zhi*. The question remains where the authors of the two texts obtained access to this map. Several scholars have theorized that Mao Yuanyi received it from his grandfather Mao Kun 茅坤 (1512–1601), who might have received it from Hu Zongxian, and so the map has often been called the "Mao Kun Map".[53] Zhou Yunzhong, on the other hand, suggested that Mao Yuanyi had access to the map when he was working in Nanjing at the Ministry of War.[54] Similarly, Fan Jingwen and Zhang Keshi had access to the archives of the Ministry of War, and so it is likely that the map came from there.

The source for Wu Pu's *Duhai fangcheng* is difficult to determine, as the text is now lost. However, if the *Shunfeng xiangsong* is based on the *Duhai fangcheng*, as T'ien Ju-K'ang, Chen Jiarong, and others have suggested, parts of the preface to the *Duhai fangcheng* might have survived in the form of the preface to the *Shunfeng xiangsong*.[55] Zhang Rong and Liu Yijie, on the other hand, disagree with this view and even suggested that Wu Pu saw a version of the *Shunfeng xiangsong*, thus inversing the relationship of the two texts.[56] The first part of the preface of the *Shunfeng xiangsong* reads:

> In bygone days, the Duke of Chou discovered and worked out the principles of the southpointing needle. Throughout the centuries from ancient times until to-day, these principles have circulated far and wide. Yet if you ignore the increase or decrease in the number of watches, or their divisions, you will be at fault. Thus it was that charts were drawn, and all details of voyages recorded.
>
> Now these old documents get worse worn every year, and it is difficult to judge from them what is the truth of the matter. If later people make

53 J.J.L. Duyvendak, *Ma Huan Re-Examined* [Verhandelingen Der Koninklijke Akademie van Wetenschappen Te Amsterdam] (Amsterdam: Noord-Hollandsche Uitgeversmaatschappij, 1933), 20–21; Mills, *Ma Huan*, 239; Fan Wentao 范文濤, "*Zheng He hanghai tu* diming kaoshi" 《鄭和航海圖》地名考釋, in Jinian weida hanghaijia Zheng He xiaxiyang 580 zhounian choubei weiyuanhui 紀念偉大航海家鄭和下西洋 580 週年籌備委員會 and Zhongguo hanghaishi yanjiuhui 中國航海史研究會 (eds.), *Zheng He yanjiu ziliao xuanbian* 鄭和研究資料選編 (Beijing: Renmin jiaotong chubanshe, 1985), 216–241, here 217; Xiang Da 向達 (ed.), *Zheng He hanghai tu* 鄭和航海圖 [Zhongwai jiaotong shiji congkan 中外交通史籍叢刊] (Beijing: Zhonghua shuju, 2000 [1961]), 4.

54 Zhou Yunzhong, "Lun *Wubei zhi* he *Nanshu zhi*", 151; Zhou Yunzhong, *Zheng He xiaxiyang*, 84.

55 T'ien Ju-K'ang, "The First Printed Chinese Rutter: Duhai Fangcheng 渡海方程", *T'oung Pao* Second Series, 68, no. 1/3 (1982), 76–90, here 87; Chen Jiarong, "*Shunfeng xiangsong* zuozhe"; Chen Jiarong, "Zaishuo *Shunfeng xiangsong*". See also Chen Jiarong and Zhu Jianqiu, *Duhai fangcheng jizhu*, 379–381.

56 Zhang Rong and Liu Yijie, "*Shunfeng xiangsong* jiaokan", 93.

> copies from these originals, they will, I fear, fall into error. (So) availing myself of leisure, I have made a comparison of the calculated (number of) watches for every day, and have investigated the respective (number of) days for (each) through voyage. And I have collected and written down the number of the watches, the directions of the compass-needle, the appearances of mountains and the conditions of the water, whether there are bays and islands, shoals and deeps; with regard to all the places from the directly governed (district) of the Southern Capital (Nanking) to Thai-Tshang and Wu-Li-Yang (the Gulf of Siam, the Sumatran Seas and the Indian Ocean) (where are) the barbarian countries and other such places – in order to hand down to later generations the way and manner of making good voyages.[57]

If the preface to the *Shunfeng xiangsong* is indeed based on Wu Pu's preface, it would show that, in compiling the *Duhai fangcheng*, Wu Pu relied on old rutters. It is also possible that Wu Pu received information from the sailors he met in his hometown, Zhangzhou. However, until a copy of the *Duhai fangcheng* surfaces, this remains speculation.

5 Biographies

The above discussion of these authors' respective sources has already provided initial insights into their biographies. Those who had first-hand knowledge were sent on missions, while those who obtained their knowledge by talking to people did so in their own home towns or workplaces. To further understand the motivation for compiling these texts, I will examine the biographies of our authors in more detail (see Table 5.2 for an overview). Thirteen of the eighteen authors are from coastal provinces and six from towns directly on the coast (Zheng Shungong, Zhang Xie, Wu Pu, Huang Zhong, Xie Jie, and Deng Zhong). These six authors from coastal towns did not just rely on written sources, they had all been on a ship or had incorporated second-hand knowledge in their books. Being connected to the coast as a starting point for the interest in nautical knowledge seems to be especially important for Huang Zhong and Zhang Xie, as they discussed matters regarding the sea with sailors in their hometown. None of our authors who was not from a coastal town was interested enough in sailing knowledge to travel to the coast to interview sailors.

As for their education, only half (9) of the authors had passed the *jinshi* examinations; Deng Zhong held a military *jinshi* degree. Two of the authors (Zhang Xie and Huang Xingzeng) held a *juren* degree, although Huang

57 Translation from Needham, *Science and Civilization 4.3*, 582.

Xingzeng obtained his ten years after having written the *Xiyang chaogong dianlu*. Like the fact that only a few copies of most of the books have survived, the lack of degree-holders shows that these books had a rather low profile and that no considerable market for selling them existed. This is especially true not only of those books that describe the route from China to one or two countries, but also of those that describe the routes within the greater region of Southeast Asia and the Indian Ocean (*Xiyang chaogong dianlu*, *Duhai fangcheng*, *Siyi guangji*, *Wubei zhi*, *Dongxiyang kao*, *Nanshu zhi*). Only Fan Jingwen had a *jinshi* degree while compiling his book, and Zhang Xie a *juren* degree. The others (Huang Xingzeng, Wu Pu, Shen Maoshang, Mao Yuanyi and Zhang Keshi) did not.

Many of the authors were connected to the military. Fan Jingwen was minister of war between 1635 and 1638, while Huang Zhong had been vice minister at the same ministry for some time before compiling the *Haiyu*. Deng Zhong was involved in campaigns in China's southern borderlands when he was Assistant Regional Commander of Guangdong. While he was writing the *Annan tuzhi*, he was a Regional Vice Commander and later became Regional Commander of Guizhou.[58]

Mao Yuanyi also followed a military career and was a military advisor to Sun Chengzong 孫承宗 (1563–1638) from 1621. He did outstanding work in the fighting against the Jurchen, which resulted in him being rewarded with the post of Regional Vice Commander in charge of the defence of Juehua Island 覺華島, Liaodong. However, his troops mutinied, and he was exiled to Zhangpu 漳浦, Fujian. In his interest in foreign affairs, Mao Yuanyi was also greatly influenced by his grandfather Mao Kun, a friend of Hu Zongxian.[59]

Not only Mao Yuanyi was connected to Hu Zongxian: Zheng Ruozeng and Tang Shunzhi (who are known to have been friends) both worked under the supreme commander fighting against the *Wokou*. Zheng Shungong, on the other hand, had less luck with Hu Zongxian. He was sent to Japan by Hu Zongxian's predecessor Yang Yi 楊宜 (*jinshi* 1523), but while Zheng Shungong was in Japan, Hu Zongxian took over the post of supreme commander with the help of Zhao Wenhua 趙文華 (died 1557) who had suggested to the emperor that he remove Yang Yi. After his return, Zheng Shungong was imprisoned for seven years due to his connections with Yang Yi.[60]

---

58 *Jinjiang xianzhi (Qianlong)* 晉江縣志(乾隆) (1765), in Airusheng – Zhongguo fangzhi ku, 7.21ab.

59 Goodrich and Fang, *Dictionary of Ming Biography*, 1053f.

60 Kanbe Teruo 神戸輝夫, "Tei Shunkō to Shō Shū. Ōtomo Sōrin to atta futari no Minjin" 鄭舜功と蒋洲：大友宗麟と会った二人の明人, *Ōita daigaku kyōiku fukushi kagakubu kenkyū kiyō* 大分大学教育福祉科学部研究紀要 21, no. 2 (1999), 109–124, here 117;

Shen Maoshang's father Shen Meng 慎蒙 (1510–1581) was also involved in a power struggle with Hu Zongxian, resulting in Shen Meng losing his title and position as an official.[61] The Shen family was from the same town as the Mao family – Gui'an 歸安 in Zhejiang – and Shen Meng passed the *juren* examinations together with Mao Kun. When Shen Meng died, Mao Kun took care of the Shen family, showing that there were ties between the two families. These relations might have influenced Shen Meng and his son in becoming interested in foreign affairs as well as nautical knowledge, but unfortunately we do not know enough about their lives to come to a decisive conclusion.[62]

Like Deng Zhong, Wu Pu was involved in military campaigns on China's southern border. He served as a military advisor to Lin Xiyuan 林希元 (1482–1567), who from 1536 was stationed in Qinzhou 欽州, Guangdong (today part of Guangxi), near the border with Vietnam. Lin Xiyuan proposed the conquest of Annam several times, but other officials at the court opposed this idea. In 1539, Wu Pu helped him when he raised troops for an attack on Annam, although this attack never took place.[63]

Lin Xiyuan and Wu Pu were both strong opponents of the ban on maritime trade, and Lin Xiyuan had contacts to the *Wokou*. T'ien Ju-K'ang believes it is possible that Wu Pu took part in smuggling activities as well. The gazetteer of Zhao'an 詔安 mentions Wu Pu being imprisoned at some point in his life without giving the reason. According to T'ien Ju-K'ang, the reason for his imprisonment might have been his connection to the *Wokou*.[64] Like Zheng Shungong and the Shen family, Wu Pu seems to have stood on the opposite side to Hu Zongxian.

Huang Xingzeng led a more scholarly live. He came from a well-known family of literati but himself repeatedly failed the examinations. Because of this failure, he started to travel around China. Hok-Lam Chan, in the *Dictionary of Ming Biography*, describes him as "a typical example of the 'pure' literary man

Suganuma, *Sovereign Rights and Territorial Space*, 64; Fang Jun, "The Military Functions of the Southern Capital in Ming China", *Monumenta Serica* 55 (2007), 133–155, here 146f.

61 *Yanzhou shiliao* 弇州史料 (1614), by Wang Shizhen 王世貞, in Siku jinhui shu congkan (Beijing: Beijing chubanshe, 2000), *houji* 20.7b–8a.

62 For a discussion of the relations between the Shen and Mao families, see Elke Papelitzky, "Gui'an as a Centre for Writing about the World during the Late Ming Dynasty", *Monumenta Serica* 68, no. 1 (2020), 107–135.

63 Kathlene Baldanza, *Ming China and Vietnam. Negotiating Borders in Early Modern Asia* (Cambridge: Cambridge University Press, 2016), 119f, 126; Chen Jiarong and Zhu Jianqiu, *Duhai fangcheng jizhu*, 190n4.

64 Goodrich and Fang, *Dictionary of Ming Biography*, 921; *Zhao'an xianzhi (Kangxi)* 詔安縣志(康熙), 1874 reprint, in Airusheng – Zhongguo fangzhi ku, 11.21ab; T'ien Ju-K'ang, "The First Printed Chinese Rutter", 83.

of his time".[65] However, even in Huang Xingzeng's biography we can see connections to the Ministry of War, as he was invited to come to Nanjing in 1517 by the minister of war and composed the *Xiyang chaogong dianlu* there.[66]

Wang Zongzai, Huang Zhong, Tang Shunzhi, Xiao Chongye, Xie Jie, Wang Zaijin, Wang Shizhen, and Fan Jingwen led the lives of typical bureaucrats, being promoted and changing positions from time to time, some more successfully than others. Of these bureaucrats, only Wang Zongzai, Wang Shizhen, and Xie Jie had held no positions connecting them to the military. Of all eighteen authors, only these three, Zhang Xie, and Shen Maoshang had no direct relations with the military, suggesting that military considerations played a major part in the inclusion of sailing routes and the interest in nautical knowledge. Of the five who were unconnected to the military, three were from coastal towns or had been on a ship as envoys to the Ryūkyūs. Only Wang Zongzai and Shen Maoshang do not fit into either of the two groups. Wang Zongzai's interest in nautical knowledge never seems to have been particularly strong, as he only included information in the chapter on Siam because the envoy Wowenyuan told him about it. Shen Maoshang, on the other hand, was from the same place as Mao Yuanyi and probably knew him and his grandfather, so he had contact with circles interested in military affairs and the affairs of foreign countries.

TABLE 5.2 The authors

Author	Degree	Career	Hometown
Huang Xingzeng (1490–1540)	1530 *juren*	1517 – ?: Compiling travelogues in Nanjing 1523: Student of Wang Shouren 王守仁 (1472–1529) No official career; traveller, poet, writer, publisher[a]	Wuxian 吳縣,Suzhou, Jiangsu
Wu Pu (ca. 1500–ca. 1570)		1530s: Advisor of Lin Xiyuan Afterwards sent to prison[b]	Zhao'an 詔安, Zhangzhou 漳州, Fujian

a For his biography, see Goodrich and Fang, *Dictionary of Ming Biography*, 662–663.
b His biography is contained in several gazetteers, including that of Zhao'an (*Zhao'an xianzhi* (*Kangxi*), 11.21ab). For a translation of the biography and further discussion, see T'ien Ju-K'ang, "The First Printed Chinese Rutter", 79f.

65 Goodrich and Fang, *Dictionary of Ming Biography*, 663.
66 Goodrich and Fang, *Dictionary of Ming Biography*, 662–663.

TABLE 5.2 The authors (*cont.*)

Author	Degree	Career	Hometown
Huang Zhong (1474–1553)	1496 *jinshi*	Several official positions, including: Secretary in the Nanjing Ministry of Revenue Vice director of the Nanjing Ministry of War Director in the Ministry of Rites Several posts in Zhejiang, Fujian, Guangxi, Yunnan, Hubei Vice minister in the Ministry of War Retired before writing the *Haiyu*[c]	Nanhai 南海, Guangdong
Tang Shunzhi (1507–1560)	1529 *jinshi*	Several official positions, including: 1529–1530: Secretary in the Ministry of War 1533–1535; 1539–1541: Compiler at the Hanlin Academy 1558: Director in the Ministry of War 1558–1559: Assistant to Hu Zongxian 1559: Vice Minister at the Court of the Imperial Stud[d]	Wujin 武進, Jiangsu
Zheng Ruozeng (1505–1580)		No official career; friend of Mao Kun, Tang Shunzhi; 1560–late 1560/early 1561: Advisor of Hu Zongxian[e]	Kunshan 崑山,Suzhou, Jiangsu
Zheng Shungong (fl. 1523–1566)		1523: Travel to Japan 1555–1556: working with Yang Yi 楊宜 1556–1557: Travel to Japan From 1557: Imprisoned[f]	Xin'an 新安, Guangdong

c For his biography, see Duan Lisheng, "Huang Zhong jiqi *Haiyu*"; Papelitzky, "Editing, Circulating, and Reading Huang Zhong's *Hai yu*", 4–7.

d For his biography, see Goodrich and Fang, *Dictionary of Ming Biography*, 1252–1256.

e For his biography, see Goodrich and Fang, *Dictionary of Ming Biography*, 204–208.

f For his biography, see Kanbe Teruo, "Tei Shunkō to Shō Shū"; Tong Jie 童杰, "Zheng Shungong shengping dayao yu *Riben yijian* de xuanzhu" 鄭舜功生平大要與《日本一鑑》的撰著, *Zhongnan daxue xuebao* (*shehui kexueban*) 中南大學學報(社會科學版) 20, no. 5 (2014), 243–247; Bian Li 卞利, "Mingdai Zheng Shungong jiguan, shengping shiji ji chushi Riben kaobian" 明代鄭舜功籍貫、生平事蹟及出使日本考辨, *Anhui shixue* 安徽史學 no. 6 (2017), 70–76; Masuda Wataru, *Japan and China. Mutual Representations in the Modern Era*, Joshua A. Fogel (trans.) (New York: St. Martin's Press, 2000), 168–171.

TABLE 5.2 The authors (*cont.*)

Author	Degree	Career	Hometown
Xiao Chongye (ca. 1544–1586)	1571 *jinshi*	Several official posts, including: Supervising secretary in the Office of Scrutiny for War, the Office of Scrutiny for Works, and the Office of Scrutiny for Revenue (sent to the Ryūkyūs in this function in 1579) 1580–1581: Vice minister at the Court of Imperial Entertainments 1581–1583: Vice minister at the Court of the Imperial Stud 1583: Superintendent of the *siyiguan* 1583–1585: Chief minister at the Court of the Imperial Stud 1585–1585: Assistant censor-in-chief of the Censorate in Nanjing[g]	Jianshui 建水, Yunnan
Xie Jie (1537–1604)	1574 *jinshi*	Several official posts, including: 1574–?: Messenger (1579 sent to the Ryūkyūs) 1591: Chief minister at the Court of Imperial Entertainments 1592: Governor of Shuntian 順天 1593–1595: Vice censor-in-chief and grand coordinator of Ganzhou 贛州 and Nan'an 南安 (Jiangxi) 1595: Vice minister of justice in Nanjing 1598–1602: Minister of justice[h]	Changle 長樂, Fujian

g For his biography, see Zhu Duanqiang 朱端強, "Mingdai hanghaijia Xiao Chongye" 明代航海家蕭崇業, *Yunnan jiaoyu xueyuan xuebao* 雲南教育學院學報 no. 5 (1993), 54–57. For the dates of his appointments, see *Guochao lieqing ji* 國朝列卿紀 (after 1592), by Lei Li 雷禮, in Xuxiu Siku quanshu (Shanghai: Shanghai guji chubanshe, 1995), 80.4a, 138.4a, 147.6a, 151.5b, 153.10a.

h For his biography, see Fang Baochuan 方宝川, "Xie Jie jiqi zhuzuo kaolüe" 謝杰及其著作考略, *Fujian shifan daxue xuebao (zhexue shehui kexueban)* 福建師範大學學報(哲學社會科學版) no. 2 (2009), 125–131; Xue Xi 薛曦, "Minji Liuqiu cefeng shi Xie Jie qiren qishi qiwen" 閩籍琉球冊封使謝杰其人其事其文, *Ningde shifan daxue xuebao (zhexue shehui kexueban)* 寧德師範學院學報（哲學社會科學版） no. 1 (2012), 76–79. For some of the dates of his appointments, see Zhang Dexin 張德信, *Mingdai zhiguan nianbiao* 明代職官年表 (Hefei: Huangshan shushe, 2009), 922–926, 1205–1207, 2819–2823.

TABLE 5.2 The authors (*cont.*)

Author	Degree	Career	Hometown
Wang Zongzai (fl. 1562–1582)	1562 *jinshi*	Several official posts, including: 1562–1566: Magistrate of Haiyan 海鹽 1578–1579: Superintendent of the *siyiguan* 1579: Vice minister at the court of judicial review 1579–1582: Grand coordinator and assistant censor-in-chief of Jiangxi 1582: Assistant censor-in-chief of the Censorate in Beijing 1583: Cashiered and banished to a frontier guard[i]	Jingshan 景山, Hubei
Deng Zhong (fl. 1576–1614)	1576 military *juren*, 1586 military *jinshi*	Military career, posts include: Assistant Regional Commander in Guangdong Regional Vice Commander in Guangdong (post held in 1607) Regional commander of Guizhou[j]	Jinjiang 晉江, Fujian
Shen Maoshang (fl. 1578–1607)		Low-ranking official in Anzhou 安州, Beizhili[k]	Gui'an 歸安, Zhejiang
Xia Ziyang (fl. 1589–1607)	1589 *jinshi*	1601: Supervising secretary at the Office of Scrutiny for War (sent to the Ryūkyūs) Chief minister at the Court of Imperial Sacrifices[l]	Yushan xian 玉山縣, Jiangxi
Wang Shizhen (fl. 1598–1607)	1598 *jinshi*	1601: Messenger (sent to the Ryūkyūs) Vice minister of the Court of Imperial Entertainments[m]	Sishui 泗水, Shandong

i For his biography, see Goodrich and Fang, *Dictionary of Ming Biography*, 1441f; Papelitzky, *Writing World History*, 42–44. For the dates of his appointments, see *Guochao lieqing ji*, 79.6a, 94.10b, 103.6b, 138.4a, 153.9a, 154.6a.

j For his biography, see *Jinjiang xianzhi* (*Qianlong*), 7.21ab.

k For his biography, see Papelitzky, "An Introduction to *Siyi guangji*", 86f; Papelitzky, *Writing World History*, 41f.

l For his biography, see *Yushan xianzhi* (*Tongzhi*) 玉山縣志 (同治) (1873), in Airusheng – Zhongguo fangzhi ku, 8 上. 8a–9b.

m There is another well-known Wang Shizhen 王士禎 (1634–1711), from Xincheng 新城, Shandong. The last character of his name is written with the radical 示 instead of 木, but

TABLE 5.2 The authors (*cont.*)

Author	Degree	Career	Hometown
Wang Zaijin (1564–1643)	1592 *jinshi*	Several official posts, including: 1612–1619: Surveillance commissioner in Huguang, Zhejiang, and Jiangxi 1620–1622: Vice minister of war 1625–1628: Minister of personnel 1622 and 1628: Minister of war[n]	Taicang 太倉, Jiangsu
Zhang Xie (1574–1640)	1594 *juren*	No official career; writer, poet[o]	Longxi 龍溪, Fujian
Mao Yuanyi (1594–1640)		From 1621: military advisor of Sun Chengzong Regional Vice Commander in charge of the defence of Juehua Island, Liaodong Exiled to Zhangpu, Fujian[p]	Gui'an 歸安, Zhejiang
Zhang Keshi (1591–1654)		No official career; poet; friend of Mao Yuanyi[q]	Xiaogan 孝感, Hubei
Fan Jingwen (1587–1644)	1613 *jinshi*	Several official positions, including: 1629: Governor of Henan 1635–1638: Minister of war in Nanjing 1642–1644: Minister of works 1644: Grand Secretary[r]	Wuqiao 吳橋, Zhili

both in classic sources, as well as in modern secondary literature, the two characters are sometimes confused. Most of the records in the local gazetteers and other sources refer to the later Wang Shizhen. For the biography of the Ryūkyū-envoy Wang Shizhen, see *Sishui xianzhi (Guangxu)* 泗水縣志(光緒) (1892), in Airusheng – Zhongguo fangzhi ku, 11.6ab.

n For his biography, see Arthur W. Hummel (ed.), *Eminent Chinese of the Ch'ing Period (1644–1912)* (Washington: US Government Print, 1943), 839. For the dates of his appointment, see Zhang Dexin, *Mingdai zhiguan nianbiao*, 657, 663, 944–946, 1726–1728, 3523–3530.

o For his biography, see Goodrich and Fang, *Dictionary of Ming Biography*, 77f; Chen Qingyuan 陳慶元, "Zhang Xie nianbiao" 張燮年表, *Nanjing shifan daxue wenxueyuan xuebao* 南京師範大學文學院學報 no. 1 (2013), 182–188.

p For his biography, see Goodrich and Fang, *Dictionary of Ming Biography*, 1053–1054; Ren Daobin 任道斌, "Mao Yuanyi shengping, zhushu chutan" 茅元儀生平、著述初探, *Mingshi yanjiu luncong* 明史研究論叢 no. 3 (1985), 239–264.

q For his biography, see Zhou Yunzhong, "Lun *Wubei zhi* he *Nanshu zhi*", 151.

r For his biography, see Hummel, *Eminent Chinese*, 229f. For the dates of his appointments, see Zhang Dexin, *Mingdai zhiguan nianbiao*, 677–679, 1734–1739, 1959, 2502f, 2890–2892.

6 Conclusion

During the Ming period, sailing routes were a topic that was of little interest to literati. Nevertheless, several authors passed on related information, although none of the authors claims to have produced a book that was useful for sailors. They adapted the information received from seafarers directly or indirectly and produced works that were, in the words of Zhang Xie, "convenient to read", but not useful in actually serving as a guide. The route descriptions were too abbreviated, were changed too much from the original, were scattered throughout the texts and were riddled with errors. Instead, whenever possible, the authors added information that might be of interest to their academic and bureaucratic readers, like the voyage up the Chao Phraya River, but not necessarily of much concern to a sailor.

Most of the books containing information including compass bearings were written during or shortly after the *Wokou* crisis in the mid-sixteenth century, and a large part of them includes routes to Japan. Of the 24 sources described here, thirteen write about Japan, and of these thirteen sources, again more than half (eight) describe *only* routes to Japan, with no descriptions to other places. The influence of the *Wokou* also becomes clear from the authors' respective biographies. Nearly all had some military background, and Hu Zongxian played a role in the lives of several of them, both for good and for ill.

Some of the popularity of routes to Japan, however, seems to be due to the wide circulation of the *Chouhai tubian*. The *Chouhai chongbian*, *Qiantai wozuan*, *Haiyanxian tujing*, *Taicang zhouzhi*, *Haifang zuanyao* and *Siyi guangji* all copied from this work of Zheng Ruozeng. It is doubtful whether, had Zheng Ruozeng not been interested in these routes, so many other authors would have written on this topic.

Those authors who found further information and did not just copy from other written sources tended to be from places close to the coast. They grew up next to the ocean and were interested in topics related to the sea, probably because they were familiar with it. This seems to have resulted in more accurate descriptions, as Zhang Xie's *Dongxiyang kao* has fewer errors than Shen Maoshang's *Siyi guangji*.

Most authors were not motivated to go to great lengths to acquire new, more detailed information on sailing routes. Only those sent on official missions included some first-hand information in their texts. Of course, the ocean and sailing on it were both perceived as intimidating, as Xie Jie showed when he claimed that he still felt uneasy simply thinking about his voyage to the Ryūkyūs years later, even though he had grown up next to the ocean. The majority of surviving texts are based on written sources. The first stage of their knowledge production has long been lost to us.

CHAPTER 6

Diet, Health and Sanitation in the Military and Naval World of Sixteenth-century China: an Analysis of Qi Jiguang's Military Manuals

Mathieu Torck

1 Introduction

In his *Jixiao xinshu* 紀效新書 (New Book of Military Effectiveness) and *Lianbing shiji* 練兵實紀 (Practical Arrangement of Military Training), the Ming dynasty general Qi Jiguang 戚繼光 (1528–1588) treats a wide range of aspects of military organization in great detail. Aimed at maximizing the Ming army's performance in its struggle to ward off external threats of marauding Mongols and pirate incursions, these works signified an important new step in a long tradition of military specialization and innovation that was initiated amidst extraordinary circumstances. While the main emphasis of Qi's manuals lies on key issues such as the training of the troops, discipline, tactical formations, the use of weaponry and naval warfare, he also developed instructions which were obviously intended at maintaining the physical conditions. Within these *high-risk spaces*, to which belong such contexts as battlefields and shipboard environments on the open seas, Qi specifically drew attention to proper food logistics, health care and sanitary measures.

In earlier research I have discussed how ill-managed or disrupted supply lines in early modern China and, in hindsight, nutritionally insufficient rations could severely impact on soldiers' health and ultimately on the outcome of military operations.[1] In addition, clashes on the battlefield were inevitably the cause of a complex traumatology among soldiers. In order to cope with these challenges, the need for medical support was understood among military authorities and writers and gradually evolved into a more institutionalized presence of surgeons in the army. Medical staff were also ideally positioned to monitor general health issues, including any possible outbreaks of epidemic diseases. Qi Jiguang's articulation of stringent measures, including

1 Mathieu Torck, *Avoiding the Dire Straits: An Inquiry into Food Provisions and Scurvy in the Maritime and Military History of China and wider East Asia* (Wiesbaden: Harrassowitz, 2009), 57ff.

 | DOI:10.1163/9789004740556_008

the hierarchically structured monitoring and reporting of disease incidence among the troops, reflects an enhanced awareness of the importance of sanitation and disease control. Following at least in part Pranghofer's insight, one could state that, with Qi Jiguang in early modern imperial China too, "military medicine became an integral part of war planning".[2] While Qi's work is often scrutinized in connection with military tactics and martial arts, he was the first military writer who discussed issues concerning health and sanitation in such a systematic way.[3] This paper presents an attempt to gauge the significance of the respective prescriptions relating to food supply, health care and sanitation as part of military and naval organization in late Ming times.

2 Military Writings in Late Ming Times: a Brief Survey

Having grown out of organized resistance against the Mongol overlords, its victory being fought in no small respect through naval superiority and firepower, the period of the Ming dynasty can hardly be underestimated as an era of military revival and innovation, in spite of setbacks and its eventual downfall.[4] The latter part of the sixteenth century especially offers a fruitful period for study in this respect. In the face of tense relations between the literati and the army officials, the era saw the rise of such outstanding generals as Hu Zongxian 胡宗憲 (1512–1565),[5] Yu Dayou 俞大猷 (1503–1579)[6] and Tan

2 Sebastian Pranghofer, "The Early Modern Medical-Military Complex: The Wider Context of the Relationship between Military, Medicine and the State", *Canadian Journal of History* (2016), Vol. 51 (3), 458.

3 Recent publications on Qi Jiguang include Teddy Y.H. Sim ed., *The Maritime Defence of China: Ming General Qi Jiguang and Beyond*. (Singapore: Springer, 2017); B. Noordam, *The Soldier as a Sage: Qi Jiguang (1528–1588) and the Neo-Confucianization of the Military in Sixteenth-century China* (Dissertation, Leiden University, 2018).

4 Tonio de Andrade, "The military revolution in global history: East Asian perspectives", in Hélder Carvarhal, André Murteira, Roger Lee de Jesus (eds.), *The First World Empire Portugal, War and Military Revolution* (London and New York: Routledge, 2021), 230. On the reevaluation of military power among the later emperors, see e.g. Kenneth M. Swope, "Bestowing the Double-Edged Sword: Wanli as Supreme Military Commander", in David Robinson (ed.), *Culture, Courtiers and Competition: The Ming Court (1368–1644)* (Cambridge, MA: Harvard University Press, 2008), 61–115.

5 See John W. Dardess, *A Political Life in Ming China: A Grand Secretary and his Times*. Lanham: Rowman & Littlefield, 2013, passim; *Mingshi*, vol. 205. See also Ivy Maria Lim, "Qi Jiguang and Hu Zongxian's Anti-wokou Campaign", in Y.H. Teddy Sim, *The Maritime Defence of China: Ming General Qi Jiguang and Beyond* (Singapore: Springer Nature, 2017), 23–42.

6 Lu Zhouxiang, *Politics and Identity in Chinese Martial Arts* (New York/Oxford: Routledge, 2018), passim.

Lun 譚綸 (1520–1577),[7] as well as Qi Jiguang. Clearly, the dynasty was in need of strong military personalities to design solutions to dire crises. Their expertise and performance made a considerable difference in defensive operations against the Mongols and in warding off attacks of the Wokou 倭寇, which soared throughout the sixteenth century with fluctuating levels of hostility and reached an acute crisis in the 1550s. Qi Jiguang became a leading figure in combatting the threat from these Sino-Japanese pirates.[8]

Moreover, these military personalities not only performed on the battlefield, they were also literate and learned men who wrote poetry and more importantly published works concerning their military theories and experience-based practice. These times of intensified military activity and the challenges faced by the Ming empire set the stage for a growing number of military treatises covering a wide range of facets of warfare with the goal of circulating knowledge about the need for the empire's preparedness and performance in facing these various threats.[9] In fact, around that time there was no systematic technical literature which could be resorted to on organizing defense and other urgent military issues. To a large extent, Qi and his fellow military commanders filled that void. The mere numbers of military publications that were compiled and published well into the next century, even while the dynasty was drawing closer to its downfall, remind us of how much military knowledge and know-how was sought after. In the long run this also applied to the Manchu threat on the northeastern borders, when there was no longer a fighting force available with a formation based on Qi's ideas. Among the works that appeared in this period were Qi Jiguang's *Jixiao xinshu* and *Lianbing shiji*, as well as the *Chouhai tubian* 籌海圖編 (Illustrated Compendium of Seaboard

7 Li Kangying, *The Ming Maritime Trade Policy in Transition, 1368–1567* [East Asian Maritime History, 8] (Wiesbaden, Otto Harrassowitz, 2010), passim; *Mingshi*, vol. 222. On Tan Lun's role in military reform operations in the Beijing area, see Lee Hua-yen, "Military Reform around Beijing from the Longqing to the Early Wanli Era (1567–1583)", *Tsinghua Journal of Chinese Studies* 52, no. 3 (2022), 471–506.

8 Defense consisted of the fortification of the coastal areas in order to raise vigilance. Starting from the first emperors of the Ming period, efforts and resources were invested in such projects as the reformation of the army and the reconstruction and armament of the border defenses along the coast. Moreover, the elaboration of a reinforced border defense system was instrumental in maintaining the vigorous maritime proscription policy that targeted private trade. Cf. Mathieu Torck, "Haifang 海防 and the Ming-Qing Transition: A Few Notes on Coastal Defence, Navies and Military Writings", *Crossroads* 11 (2015), 97–114. See also Li Kangying for an analysis of the mentalities and incentives that lay at the bottom of this anti-commercialistic approach. Cf. Li, *The Ming Maritime Tade Policy in Transition*, 2010.

9 One of the most inclusive repositories of military works can be found in Wolfgang Franke, *Annotated sources of Ming history: including Southern Ming and works on neighbouring Lands, 1368–1661*. 2 vols. (Kuala Lumpur: University of Malaya Press, 2011).

Strategies) by the geographer Zeng Ruozeng 鄭若曾 (1505–1580).[10] An outstanding example of an early seventeenth-century work was the monumental *Wubei zhi* 武備誌 (Treatise on Armament Preparations) written by Mao Yuanyi 茅元儀 (1594–1640) in 1621.[11] Among these authors, Qi Jiguang stands out as a figure with an allure and reputation that reverberated into the future. Both his treatises became important references in China and beyond, notably in Choson Korea.[12]

In line with Ray Huang's discussion of the significance of what he calls "the lonely general", the merits of Qi Jiguang's successful tour of duty might not only be sought in the defeat of the *Wokou*, but also in the way Qi dealt with the political challenges he faced in order to achieve his goals.[13] Furthermore, Huang also emphasizes how Qi's sense of detail is telling of the state in which the Ming army found itself around the middle of the century. In that sense, Qi's works are innovative, not so much for their contents as for their systematic inclusion into what became a classical treatise.

In the past few years and decades, these sources have attracted the increased interest of historians in premodern and early modern Chinese military and

10 See e.g. Ho Yi Kai (ed.), *Science in China, 1600–1900: essays by Benjamin A. Elman* (Hackensack (NJ): World Century Publishing and Singapore: World Scientific Publishing, 2015), 55 and passim.

11 *Wubeizhi* 武備誌, by Mao Yuanyi 茅元儀 (1594–1640), 24 vols. (Taipei: Huashi Chubanshe, 1987). For a brief overview of the relevant sources, see Elke Papelitzky, "Naval Warfare of the Ming Dynasty (1368–1644): A Comparison Between Chinese Military Texts and Archaeological Sources", in Rebecca O'Sullivan, Christina Marini, and Julia Binnberg, *Archaeological Approaches to Breaking Boundaries: Interaction, Integration and Division* (Oxford: BAR Publishing, 2017), 129–131. See also Sarah A.G. Basham, *The book multiple: Treatise on Military Preparedness (1621) and encyclopedic practice in seventeenth century China* (Dissertation, University of British Columbia Library, 2019).

12 Still during the Imjin War, the *Jixiao jinshu* reached Korea, where Han Gyo 韓嶠 (1556–1627) turned it into a manual of martial arts techniques – *Muyejeobo Eonhae* 武藝諸譜諺解 (1598) – for practical use during the conflict. Later on, in the seventeenth century, it was condensed and reworked. Cf. Thomas A. Green, Joseph R. Svinth, (eds.), *Martial Arts of the World: An Encyclopedia of History and Innovation* (Santa Barbara/Denver/Oxford: ABC-CLIO, 2010), Vol. 1 "Korea: Kumdo", 187ff; Na Youngil, "The Future of Asian Traditional Martial Arts", *The International Journal of the History of Sport* 33, no. 9 (2016), 893–903. For an analysis of the adaptation of Qi Jiguang's work in Korea, see Felix Siegmund, "The adaptation of Chinese military techniques to Choson Korea, their validation, and the social dynamics thereof" in Kai Filipiak (ed.), *Civil Military Relations in Chinese History: From Ancient China to the Communist takeover* (London and New York: Routledge, 2015), 172–190. Ji Shan 祁山, "Jixiao xinshu chuanru Chaoxian bandao de beijing ji yingxiang 紀效新書傳入朝鮮半島的背景及影響, *Shandong qingnian zhengzhi xueyuan xuebao* 山東青年政治學院學報 29, no. 165 (2013), 137–140.

13 For a lengthy discussion of the headlines and deadlines of Qi Jiguang's career merits and struggles, see Ray Huang's respective chapter in Ray Huang, *1587 – A Year of No Significance* (New Haven and London: Yale University Press), 156–188.

naval history, with various foci, including military institutions, organization, technology, weaponry, strategy, tactics, training, border defense and cartography, as well as aspects of naval performance and warfare.[14] Recent scholarship has described the developments in military strategy and fighting tactics in the course of the Ming dynasty with the advent of the gunpowder age as nothing less than a revolution.[15] The decisive factor in military conflict slowly but surely shifted from mounted cavalry to artillery units, whose performance had a much more destructive effect on the enemy.[16] The sixteenth century ended with the first great East Asian conflict fought on Korean soil, when Ming troops confronted invading Japanese forces under Toyotomi Hideyoshi 豊臣秀吉 (1537–1598).[17] In the latter part of the century, when the first signs of decline had surfaced, the Ming army still displayed its outstanding performance as a result of tight collaborations between military and civil authorities, the circulation of military manuals, and a series of organizational and technological reforms and developments.[18] Apart from these decisive evolutions and groundbreaking shifts, innovation and sophistication may also be sought in developments that are situated outside the main arteries of research in the

14 Examples of recent studies on naval armament and warfare are Elke Papelitzky, "Naval Warfare of the Ming Dynasty (1368–1644): A Comparison Between Chinese Military Texts and Archaeological Sources", in Rebecca O'Sullivan, Christina Marini, and Julia Binnberg, *Archaeological Approaches to Breaking Boundaries: Interaction, Integration and Division.* (Oxford: BAR Publishing, 2017), 129–136; Elke Papelitzky, "Weapons used aboard Ming Chinese ships and some thoughts on the armament of Zheng He's fleet", *China and Asia* 1, no. 2 (December 2019), 192–224. For an earlier article, see Peter Lorge, "Water Forces and Naval Operations", in ed. David A. Graff and Robin Higham (eds.), *A Military History of China* (Kentucky: University Press of Kentucky, 2012), 81–96.

15 Tonio de Andrade, *The Gunpowder Age – China, Military Innovation, and the Rise of the West in World History* (Princeton and Oxford: Princeton University Press, 2016).

16 A number of military historians have argued that the idea that Europe was the heart of military revolution whose accomplishments over time reverberated around the world is misleading and should be replaced by the image of similar but independent developments almost simultaneously taking place in separate cultural areas.

17 For an authoritative study of this major conflict, see Kenneth M. Swope, *A Dragon's Head and a Serpent's tail: Ming China and First Great East Asian War 1592–1598* (Norman: University of Oklahoma Press, 2009). During the conflict Qi Jiguang's *Jixiao xinshu* was relied upon by Ming generals for tactical purposes. Cf. Wanghoon Rhee, Young-jae Kim, "Understanding Gwanghwa Dondae Forts as a Vernacular Model of Construction and Reuse", *Buildings* 12 (2022), 568, 2 (see https://doi.org/10.3390/buildings12050568).

18 On the relations of the civil bureaucracy and the military at the end of the Ming, see Huang, *1587*, 62–63, 100–101, *passim*. See also Kenneth M. Swope, *The Military Collapse of China's Ming Dynasty, 1618–1644*. (London and New York: Routledge), 2, especially Swope's reference to Kai Filipiak, "The Effects of Civil Official Handling Military affairs in Ming Times", *Ming Studies* 66 (2012), 1–15.

military realm. The works of Qi Jiguang and his coverage in them of provisioning, health care and sanitation provide an outstanding example.

3 Qi Jiguang: Background and Career

Born in Dengzhou 鄧州 in Shandong 山東 province, Qi Jiguang grew up in a hereditary military family in the coastal garrison city of Dengzhou. Despite a few setbacks in his experience of the examination system, Qi's talent emerged when leading Shandong troops at the Wall to resist attacks from the Mongols. With the support of prominent bureaucrats such as fellow general Tan Lun and Senior Grand Secretary (*shoufu* 首輔) Zhang Juzheng 張居正 (1525–1582), he made a successful career as a military commander with outstanding tactical qualities. Qi rose to notoriety through his efforts to forge a motivated and effective fighting force involving the use firepower in continental and naval forces, as well as by strengthening the fortifications along the Great Wall and the Chinese coast at a time when coastal defensive facilities were in a deplorable state.[19] Qi's strategy was not to try to take on the enemy in a direct confrontation. Rather, he would lure him into Chinese territory and confront him with a strong force.[20] When Qi wrote his influential *Jixiao xinshu* (*c.*1560) and *Lianbing shiji* (1571), he obviously included a considerable amount of personal experience as a commanding officer in the army and as a weathered warrior in battles with Mongols and Sino-Japanese pirates.[21] *Jixiao xinshu* and *Lianbing shiji* reflect the sense of technicality that characterizes the time in military respects. In these treatises, the emphasis is on discipline, organization, tactics and training, and technology, including firearms.[22] In both works, it is very obvious that Qi strove not to overlook any aspect of military organization and warfare that he deemed essential in strengthening the empire's military effectiveness, instilling a sense of urgency when Ming China came under pressure from external threats. Qi Jiguang wrote his work in the latter decades of the sixteenth century, with the *Jixiao xinshu* originally written in eighteen chapters,

19 Cf. Kai Filipiak, "Technological advance in the war against the Mongols", in Kaushik Roy and Peter Lorge (eds.), *Chinese and Indian Warfare: From the Classical Age to 1870* (London and New York: Routledge, 2015), 121–133.

20 L. Carrington Goodrich and Chao-Ying Fang, *Dictionary of Ming Biography 1368–1644* (New York: Columbia University Press, 1976), 220–224.

21 An excellent study of piracy and contraband in the Fujian area, including in the time of Qi Jiguang, is Paola Calanca, *Piraterie et contrebande au Fujian – L'administration chinoise face aux problems d'illégalité maritime* (Paris: Les Indes Savantes, 2011).

22 A thorough analysis of Qi Jiguang's life and work, see Goodrich and Fang, *Dictionary of Ming Biography*, 220–223.

but several years later it was reworked into a shorter version of fourteen chapters, obviously with slightly differing tables of content.[23]

Chapter 18 of the *Jixiao xinshu* is entirely devoted to the navy and contains Qi Jiguang's views on such issues as naval warfare, the training of marines, naval technology and the use of warships at a time when large-scale naval operations such as Zheng He's Indian Ocean armadas had become a distant and all but forgotten memory.[24] While many facets of Qi's work have received increased scholarly interest, including the enhanced emphasis on the training of the troops and on special training in naval warfare, which have been studied to some extent, other aspects of the military realm remain out of the limelight. Nevertheless, there is an urgent need for a more profound investigation of his work, as this would provide clues to a better understanding of Qi Jiguang successful tour of duty. In order to maximize the army's performance, Qi Jiguang thoroughly elaborates on what appears at first sight to be merely peripheral facets of military organization. Nevertheless, Ray Huang was one of the first scholars who drew attention to Qi's instructions regarding a recipe for food rations. Supplies in this early modern era are an increasingly well-studied subject, yet they usually remain limited to the mechanism and economy of logistics.[25]

4 Food Supply in Chinese Armies: a Historical Overview at a Glance

The success of a military operation has been defined by Martin van Creveld as being tightly connected to "the practical art of moving armies and keeping them supplied".[26] Army life, and especially war conditions, may easily push substantial numbers of troops to their limits. This is what led military servicemen and writers to develop and include practice-based instructions for the preparation of food supplies and other health-related instructions within

23 For a discussion of the chronology of Qi Jiguang's works including both versions of the *Jixiao xinshu*, see Peter Lorge, "The Martial Arts in Qi Jiguang's Military Training", in Teddy Y.H. Sim (ed.), *The Maritime Defence of China: Ming General Qi Jiguang and Beyond.* (Singapore: Springer, 2017), 59–71.

24 *Jixiao xinshu* 紀效新書 by Qi Jiguang (1528–1588), in *Zhongguo bingshu jicheng* 中國兵書集成, vol. 18. (Shenyang: Liaoshen shushe/Beijing: Jiefangjun chubanshe, 1995), 615ff. The fourteen-chapter version has a naval section in Chapter 12, 1029 ff.

25 Huang, *1587*, 159.

26 Martin Van Creveld, *Supplying War: Logistics from Wallenstein to Patton* (Cambridge: Cambridge University Press, 2004) [2nd edition], 1.

the larger framework of military know-how and expertise.[27] Military writings about provisioning continental armies as well as navies, albeit usually a minor chapter, became an area of development, specialization and innovation. Down the centuries, wars in China were fought with an ever-growing number of armies, which created equivalent demands in terms of organizational structures and logistical expertise. Armies and navies, whether standing or in action, confronted the specific challenge of maintaining the performance of their troops, especially in cases when military campaigns shifted into stretched operations in time as well as in space. By and large, army logistics were determined by such factors as troop numbers, distances covered, duration of the campaign, the availability and accessibility of local resources, the operationality of the *tuntian* 屯田 system, geographical and climatological conditions and, more generally, by budgetary means, i.e. the share of state revenue that was reserved for financing armies and wars.[28] Within the area of army logistics, an understudied facet pertains to the soldier's physical performance and health, which directly depended upon the availability of an uninterrupted supply of or access to food resources. Obviously, major breaks in the food logistics were capable of bringing armed conflicts to a standstill, as in the case of the Imjin War (1592–1598), when in 1593 critically depleted supplies triggered, albeit temporarily, the commencement of peace negotiations.[29]

An elaborate discussion of food supplies and medical care in history would go beyond the boundaries of this paper, yet a brief survey of relevant cases may illustrate how Qi Jiguang's inclusion of details about food supplies, health and

27 Mathieu Torck, *Avoiding the Dire Straits: An Inquiry into Food Provisions and Scurvy in the Maritime and Military History of China and wider East Asia* (Wiesbaden: Harrassowitz, 2009), 110.

28 Studies of the role and modes of military supply form a growing subfield in studies in European military history. For a classic work, see Van Creveld (2004) mentioned above; also see Carol B. Stevens "Food and Supply: Logistics and the early modern Russian army", in Brian L. Davies (ed.), *Warfare in Eastern Europe, 1500–1800*. History of Warfare, Vol. 72, Leiden: Brill, 2012, 119–146. Other more recent scholarship on logistics in a naval context includes work on the Spanish navy by Rafael Torres Sánchez, *Military Entrepreneurs and the Spanish Contractor State in the Eighteenth Century*. Oxford: Oxford University Press, 2016. On the *tuntian* system in Ming times, see Gu Cheng 顧誠, *Yinni de jiangtu: weisuozhi yu Ming diguo* 隱匿的疆土：衛所制度與明帝國 (Beijing: Guangming ribao chubanshe, 2012). On Ming financing of the military, see e.g. Ray Huang, "Military expenditures in Sixteenth Century China", *Oriens Extremus* 17, no. 1/2 (1970), 39–62.

29 Kenneth M. Swope, *A Dragon's Head and a Serpent's Tail*, 127. A thorough analysis of seaborne provision during this war is Ku Hong Sung, "Ming dynasty maritime provisions transport during the second stage of the East Asian War (1597–98)", *Chinese Studies in History* 52 (2019), Issue 1: The East Asian War of 1592–98: International Perspectives, 42–58.

sanitation can be understood within a tradition of instructions and references scattered throughout a plethora of sources.[30] Since ancient times, food supplies and the maintenance of supply lines formed obvious and quintessential facets of warfare for the military authorities in order to guarantee the troops' physical condition in the face of the heavy physical demands that warfare exacts on the human body. Early military thinkers such as Sunzi 孫子 understood the fundamental importance of the physical aspects of performance in war. On several locations in the *Sunzi bingfa* 孫子兵法 one can glimpse how much importance was attached to well-provisioned troops ("with provisions enough to carry them a thousand *li*" 千里饋糧). In addition to brief references about food supplies, the text shows glimpses of the organization of the army's baggage train (*zi* 輜). Moreover, food also featured prominently as part of a strategy to weaken the adversary (因糧于敵故軍食可足也). Taking or destroying the enemy's food stores enabled an army to replenish its own food reserves and at the same time substantially jeopardized the health of enemy troops. In so doing, it could easily tip the balance in a military confrontation.[31]

Following the evolution of traditions related to food supplies from a bird's-eye perspective, we can see the appearance in the literature of a wide variety of terms related to armies' food supplies and rations. In Tang times, a growing array of different terms can be found that are related to the food supplies of armies reflecting the degree of sophistication that characterized this process.[32] Coming to the Song dynasty, one of the works that acquired eminent status was the *Liutao* 六韜 (The Six Secret Teachings), a military treatise most probably from the Warring States Period, and perhaps even antedating the *Sunzi bingfa*, but according to tradition attributed to Taigong 太公, ancestor of the ancient state of Qi 齊 and an authority on military affairs. The *Liutao*, written in a question-and-answer style between Taigong, King Wen 周文王 and King Wu 周武王 of the Zhou dynasty (*c.*1050 BCE), is rather unique, since for many aspects of military organization and warfare it goes into much more detail than other works.[33] Chapter 3 provides insights into the organi-

30 A comprehensive survey of medical practices in Chinese armies since classical times is Li Jingwei 李經緯, Lin Zhaogeng 林昭庚, *Zhongguo yixue tongshi* 中國醫學通史 (Beijing: Renmin weisheng chubanshe, 1999).

31 For the relevant passages, see cf. *Sunzi bingfa* 孫子兵法, ch. 2 "Zuozhan 作戰" (Waging War), par. 1, 3 and 4; ch. 3 "Jiudi 九地" (The Nine Situations), par. 3; ch. 7 "Junzheng 軍爭" (Maneuvering), item 2. Cf. https://ctext.org/art-of-war (last accessed December 2022).

32 An excellent reference work concerning terminology in relation to military supplying is Chen Gaochun 陳高春, *Zhongguo gudai junshi wenhua dacidian* 中國古代軍事文化大辭典 (Beijing: Changzheng chubanshe, 1992), 936–995.

33 Together with six other military works it became canonized into the *Wujing qishu* 武經七書. Cf. Ralph D. Sawyer, *The Seven Military Classics of China* (Boulder, CO: Westview Press, 1993), 61.

zational structure of pre-imperial Chinese armies with all the different kinds of personnel and the different duties per category. Among these categories is clearly the position of supply officer tasked with overseeing the provisioning of troops and the transportation of food and water stores (通糧四人：主度飲食蓄積，通糧道，致五穀，令三軍不困乏).[34] Moreover, Taigong's so-called spiritual successor, the military general Sima Rangju 司馬穰苴 (*c.*548–490 BCE) has a biographical entry in the *Shiji* 史記 that reflects the kinds of duties that were performed in an army on the march, including the administration of medicine by physicians (士卒次舍井灶飲食問疾醫藥，身自拊循之).[35] Obviously, the presence of this medical staff at least suggests that at the organizational level important developments had taken place in these early armies with the goal of optimizing the troops' performance.

From the Song dynasty onward, important military works such as the *Wujing zongyao* by Zeng Gongliang 曾公亮 (998–1078) and Ding Du 丁度 (990–1053) and *Huqian jing* 虎鈐經 by Xu Dong 許洞 (976–1018) tend to give more explicitly detailed instructions and discussions concerning food supply, logistical issues, the composition and storage of army provisions and survival techniques in victualling during military operations in difficult geographical terrain.[36] In this respect, the Ming literature may be considered the next level, as by comparison Ming sources contain more systematic references to quantified and calculated rations for soldiers, as well as for fodder for the horses. In memorials to the throne, such as that drawn up by Zeng Xian 曾銑 (?–1548) within the context of the reconquest of the Ordos area around the middle of the 16th century, Ming military diets usually consisted of rice and salted vegetables or, more precisely, soldiers received a salted vegetable issue (*yancai yin* 鹽菜銀) allowing them to

---

34 Cf. *Liutao* 六韜, Ch. 3 "Longtao 龍韜", par. 1 "Wang Yi 王翼", 2.7, see https://ctext.org/liu-tao/wang-yi (last accessed December 2022). Sawyer has the following translation: "Four supply officers responsible for calculating the requirements for food and water; preparing food stocks and supplies and transporting the provisions along the route; and supplying the five grains so as to ensure the army will not suffer any hardship or shortage". Cf. Sawyer, *The Seven Military Classics of China*, 61.

35 Cf. *Shiji* 史記, "Sima Rangju liezhuan 司馬穰苴列傳", 1, see https://ctext.org/shiji (last accessed December 2022). Sawyer translates the passage as follows: "The officers and soldiers next encamped, dug wells, lit the cook fires, and prepared their drink and food. He asked about those with illness, had physicians prescribe medicine and personally looked after them." Cf. Sawyer, *The Seven Military Classics of China*, 114.

36 The instructions concerning provisioning in the *Wujing zongyao* were canonized as one can see them incorporated and thus reiterated in the substantial Ming work *Wubei zhi* 武備誌 of 1621, which also includes many entries on the navy. For a lengthy discussion, see Torck, *Avoiding the Dire Straits*, 2009, 96–99. See also Yves Hervouet, *A Sung bibliography* (Hong Kong: The Chinese University Press, 1978), 235. A thorough study of *Huqian jing* is Li Tianshu 李天舒, "Bei Song Xu Dong "Huqian Jing" yanjiu 北宋許洞《虎鈐經》研究", (Dissertation, Zhengzhou daxue, 2017).

purchase a vegetable component to their staple food. In hindsight, and in view of the hardships of military life, this diet's considerable stability, echoing the composition of ordinary rural diets, cannot have failed to contribute to the soldier's general health condition from a nutritional perspective.[37] As Hasegawa Masato observes in his analysis of the impact of military conflict on the local populations of the Sino-Korean border areas during the Ming-Qing transition, diets that included vegetables were indeed very common in Chinese armies. Mainly through the prism of the *Shizhenglu* 實政錄 (Records of Effective Service) authored by Qi Jiguang's near contemporary Lü Kun 呂坤 (1536–1618), Hasegawa convincingly shows that including a vegetable component or even a variety of greens into the diets of soldiers constituted a common practice in the army, underscored and advised as they were in instructions that formed part of the works of military authorities. Vegetable-inclusive army diets would be continued into the next dynastic period.[38]

To what extent all these instructions also pertained to the food supply of Chinese navies is a chapter that still needs to be written in general terms. In earlier work I showed that sources for Zheng He's expeditions in the early Ming period and premodern naval operations in general remain almost silent about shipboard conditions, let alone the crew's diet. An exception to this is the package of essential livelihood items that eunuchs were entitled to carry with them and share among themselves, since these items appear in one of the edicts of the Yongle 永樂 emperor (r. 1402–1424), who ordered the voyages to take

37 For a more detailed analysis, see Torck, *Avoiding the Dire Straits*, 2009, 100–101. Obviously, the presence of greens in army diets may is far from extraordinary. The prominence of the vegetable component, including the pickled version, in the dietary traditions of China is well-known. Cf. Thomas O. Höllman, *The Land of the Five Flavors: A Cultural History of Chinese Cuisine* (New York: Columbia University Press), 2010, *passim*; Joseph Needham, *Science and Civilisation in China. Vol. 6. Biology and Biological Technology. Part v: Fermentations and Food Science* (by H.T. Huang), (Cambridge: Cambridge University Press, 2000), 402–412 and passim.

38 Cf. Masato Hasegawa, *Provisions and Profits in a Wartime Borderland: Supply Lines and Society in the Border Region between China and Korea 1592–1644* (Dissertation, Yale University 2013), 149–167. See also Hasegawa's lengthy article: "War, Supply Lines, and Society in the Sino-Korean Borderland of the Late Sixteenth Century", *Late Imperial China* 37, no. 1 (June 2016), 109–152. Furthermore, in his research of imperial financial policies concerning the Jinchuan 金川 wars (1746–1749 and 1771–1776), Ulrich Theobald points to the fact that troops received rice as well as a salted vegetable issue (*yancai* 鹽菜銀) and (*kouliangyin* 口糧銀), by means of which they were expected to buy additional foodstuffs on the local markets that were organized for the army: meat, vegetables, tea leaves and some fancy tobacco, and liquor. Cf. Ulrich Theobald, *War Finance and Logistics in Late Imperial China: A Study of the Second Jinchuan Campaign (1771–1776)* (Brill: Leiden, Boston: 2013), 68–72. See also Yingcong Dai, *The Sichuan Frontier and Tibet: Imperial Strategy in the Early Qing* (Seattle: University of Washington Press), 167, 176.

tea leaves, salt, sauce, alcohol, wax and other items (合用盐酱茶酒油烛等件).[39] Additionally, it is noteworthy that Zheng He's shipboard crews included a medical staff (*yishi* 醫士), which highlights an institutionalized approach to health issues in the military, an obvious extension of the organizational structure of land-based troops.[40] Studying the work of Qi Jiguang facilitates a deeper understanding of food supplies, health and sanitary policies in early modern Chinese armies and in navies, almost two centuries after the great ocean-going endeavors of the early Ming emperors.

5 Qi Jiguang on Military Provisioning: Food Supply and Diets

The *Jixiao xinshu* has several references to food supply, yet not all of them are very explicit.[41] Nevertheless, in Chapter 9 Qi Jiguang elaborates on military encampments that are set up in the wilderness. Interestingly, Qi's discourse provides insights into the practices and regulations concerning food and water supplies. As the text relates, soldiers were allowed to go into towns which were located in the vicinity of the encampment (*rucheng* 入城) and had an albeit limited possibility to purchase necessities such as vegetables (*shucai* 蔬菜) and other items (*dengxiang* 等項). In order to have access to drinking water, a difference had to be made between wells that were close by and those that were far off (分別市井遠近).[42] In an earlier passage, Qi also refers to the task of the flag company (*qidui* 旗隊), whose responsibility it was to take care of the food

39 Torck, *Avoiding the Dire Straits*, 224.

40 These basic rations remind us of the kind of diet that Ryukyu students received after they arrived in Qing China for study, as described by Pan Xiang 潘相 (1713–1790) in the *Liuqiu ruxue wenjian lu* 琉球入學聞見錄 (Records of Things Heard and Seen about Students from the Ryukyu Islands). Obviously, this is not a shipboard diet, but it is indicative of the food habits that Ryukyu students connected with when they started their sojourn in Qing China. Cf. Torck, *Avoiding the Dire Straits*, 241–242. The same picture emerges in the *Lidai bao'an* 歷代寶案 (Precious Documents of Successive Generations) that contains descriptions of drifting accidents on the Fujian coast, after which the stranded crews receive supplies from local authorities (rice, salted vegetable pay, meat, liquor, clothing etc.), as was reported on the 26th day of the 8th month of the 36th year of the Qianlong reign (4th October, 1771); or the arrest of pirates and their integration in the ranks of the marines of the coastal patrol, or the rescue operations concerning shipwrecked Japanese in early 19th century. Cf. *Lidai bao'an* 歷代寶案, (Taipei: Guoli Taiwan daxue, 1972), vol. 6, j. 55, coll. 2, 3309, b.11.

41 Food supply features in an entry which deals with the distribution of army provisions (*fen junxiang* 分軍餉), yet the entry basically does not go beyond the practicalities of the core food rations (*yueliang* 月粮), nor does it fundamentally supplement what we know about the contents of the food rations. Cf. *Jixiao xinshu*, ch. 11, 235 (14-chapter version).

42 *Jixiao xinshu*, ch. 9, 194 (14-chapter version).

supplies (*yi shiliang wei chai* 以食糧為差). However, no further explanations are added as to how this team exactly operated.[43]

> 限蔬水每日五更盡，擂鼓已畢，聽掌第一號，各起梳洗。聽掌第二號，各兵通赴木城邊，各擎槍立定發，作守城之勢。各營把門人役赴中軍，報守門無事。訖，聽大吹打，開營門，照場操號令放汲。其汲者限一刻，照場操號令收回。入城市蔬菜等項者，分別市井遠近，[...] 凡地方市賣之人，許於營外三百步內，聚為一處，[...]。

However, in the *Lianbing shiji* written a decade later, Qi provides more details on the soldier's diet that may reflect the adherence to local daily diets. In a short paragraph on dried provisions for the troops, Qi Jiguang stipulates that each camp should have at its disposal 200 *dan* of *qichao* 棋炒, a kind of pastry made of flour, 300 *dan* 石 of rice (*mi* 米) and 500 *dan* of black beans (*heidou* 黑豆).[44] Qi's reference to beans once again provides irrefutable evidence for the fact that there was indeed a vegetable component in the early modern Chinese soldier's diet. This finding has certain implications from a comparative perspective. Data about diets in continental armies invite one to take the issue one step further and also discuss the diet of Chinese marines, or at least soldiers who were selected to serve at sea. On this point Qi is not particularly clear, but another passage in the *Jixiao xinshu* helps us to lift the veil on this issue, at least in part. From this passage, it can also be understood that even the act of supplying was always subject to security measures. Local merchants who traded in food and drink were only allowed to approach the camp at three hundred steps and were concentrated in one location.

6 Camp Latrines in the *Jixiao xinshu*

Traces of sanitary principles in Chinese armies in relevant sources documenting military contexts are relatively rare. There is an early but very concise reference that can be found in the Tang dynasty work *Tongdian* 通典 (Comprehensive Statutes) dealing with administrative history, which documents

43 *Jixiao xinshu*, ch. 1, 9 (14-chapter version).

44 Gao Yangwen 高揚文 et al. describe this as a kind of dry army provision made of flour, sesame oil and sesame seeds. *Qichao* is still available in present-day China. The pastry does not show any resemblance to yet another snack called *guangbing* 光餅, a traditional dish of coastal Fujian named after Qi Jiguang. Cf. *Lianbing shiji* 練兵實紀, ed. by Gao Yangwen 高揚文, Tao Qi 陶琦 et al., (Qi Jiguang yanjiu congshu 戚繼光研究叢書) (Beijing: Zhonghua shuju, 2001), ch. 1, 44, note 3.

digging latrines as one of the duties of an army in setting up camp.[45] In Qi's text, a number of passages seem to suggest that an emphasis was laid on training soldiers into following a routine of personal hygiene. With the beating of the drums around the fifth watch (*wugeng* 五更), soldiers got up and took care of their toilet by brushing and washing themselves (*shuxi* 梳洗).[46] Furthermore, together with a balanced supply of food, Qi Jiguang advocated the strict application of what appears to be a set of sanitary measures when the troops were setting up in the wilds (*yeying* 野营). The 18-chapter edition of the *Jixiao xinshu* has the most elaborate description of this:

> 放廁所　無賊處遠在營外百步間，每一面總開大廁坑二口，營內每一旗於隊后開小坑一口。凡白日登廁員役，由各營門將腰牌懸於門上，方准開門而出；回營到門，將腰牌對認明白，方許放入。夜則大小解俱於營內小廁坑，不許放一人出門。天明吹打時，遇起行則埋之，遇久住則打掃，送出營外坑內。遇賊近或對壘，晝夜皆在營內。[47]

As we can see, Qi develops specific instructions when it comes to setting up latrines (*ce* 廁). He informs his readership about the different sizes of camp latrines and where they were to be set up. In a safe area, with no enemy presence (*zei* 賊), two large latrines (*da cekeng* 大廁坑) on each side of the camp are constructed at a distance of one hundred paces, while inside the camp each division erects one smaller type of latrine (*xiao cekeng* 小廁坑). Furthermore, Qi provides practical details about the daily use of the facility. Soldiers using the outer latrine are expected to hang up their waist badge (*yaopai* 腰牌) to indicate

---

45 The relevant passages read as follows: "諸兵士每下營訖，先令兩隊共掘一廁。" ("Every time all soldiers have completed setting up the camp, two brigades are first ordered to excavate a latrine"). Cf. *Tongdian* 通典 by Du You 杜佑 (735–812), "Bing shi 兵十", "Xiaying chihou bing fanghan ji fenbu chen 下營斥候并防捍及分布陣", par. 18, see https://ctext.org/tongdian (last accessed December 2022). More details about these snacks can be found in a brief article on their globalization: Yan Lin, "Going Global" of Chinese Local Dietary Culture: A Case Study of Traditional Special Snacks Translation", *Journal of Education, Humanities and Social Sciences* Vol. 1, 353–359 (https://doi.org/10.54097/ehss.v1i.683).

46 This is between the third and fifth hour. Cf. Endymion Wilkinson, *Chinese History: A New Manual.* (Cambridge (MS): Harvard University Press, 2015), 538.

47 *Jixiao xinshu*, ch. 9, 196 (14-chapter version). The 18-chapter edition has a similar but shorter entry which omits the details concerning the construction of the toilet. It stipulates that leaving the camp during the night is not allowed. Therefore, anyone who needs to go to the toilet should take care of this within the confines of his own shed. Cf. *Jixiao xinshu* ch. 7, 104. (18-chapter version).

that the facility is presently occupied as well as by whom.[48] Furthermore, the act of attaching the waist badge to the door of the latrine prior to using the facility confirms that the pit had a superstructure, most probably not made of brick, given that a military camp was not a permanent living space. Upon re-entering the camp, the same badge was to be presented for identification. While obviously this was primarily a safety measure, such an approach reveals that the toilet facility could not have been a shared latrine, but one intended for use by one individual at a time. This circumstance invites one to reflect on underpinning notions of personal privacy in this military community, in which for safety reasons identity privacy was sacrificed in favor of physical privacy. At night, soldiers were not allowed to leave the camp and thus could only use the small privy inside the camp, and not the outer latrine. When the signal is blown and beaten and the army prepares for a march, Qi Jiguang instructs that the contents of the latrine should be buried (*mai* 埋). If the troops remain at the specific location for a longer period, then the latrine should be cleaned, and the contents transferred to the outer latrine. If the enemy is approaching or at nightfall, one should remain in the camp at any cost.

While these paragraphs on sanitation in military camps only say so indirectly, Qi Jiguang's text unintentionally signifies a certain shift in writing about military organization by including a focus that at first sight is applied to the sanitary conditions of Chinese army encampments. Never before had a military writer incorporated such detailed practical instructions concerning the installation of latrines in a military treatise. The emphasis on the distance between the encampment and the toilet facility when the surroundings are safe enough to allow movement between them seems obvious: it avoids stench and other inconveniences connected to daily used latrines. In addition, the passage opens up a view on an underlying consideration that may have played in Qi's mind: toilets were a potential source of hazardous disease-carrying germs. Doubtlessly, this approach must have been particularly meaningful when the curbing and preventing of hygiene-related disease patterns for armies on the march or in warzones was at stake.[49]

48 Such an act or habit corresponds to what Gonçalo Santos reported about toilet practices in contemporary rural South China around the turn of the millennium – users of the pit latrine were expected "to leave a hat or some other personal item by the entrance to signal their presence". Cf. see Gonçalo Santos, "Technological Choices and Modern Material Civilization: Reflections on Everyday Toilet Practices in Rural South China", in Johann P. Arnason and Chris Hann (eds.), *Anthropology and Civilizational Analysis: Eurasian Explorations* (Albany: State University of New York Press, 2018), 261.

49 Like the rest of society, at times standing troops took their share in the suffering inflicted by epidemics. According to the *Mingshi* the epidemic that raged in Nanjing in the seventh

7 Health-care Management and Nursing Sick Soldiers

The dangers of such invisible adversaries as epidemic diseases, or, more generally, the variety of risks connected to army life, including those wounded in battle, necessitated the establishment of a system of medical care in the army. First and foremost, we can see the concern about health reflected in the presence of medical doctors, or army surgeons. Indeed, in Chapter one of the *Jixiao xinshu*, "Shuwu 束伍" (Keeping the troops under control), Qi Jiguang refers to medical personnel in his list of miscellaneous craftsmen (*zaliu* 雜流). One physician (*yisheng* 醫生) and one medical assistant (*yisheng jiading* 醫生家丁) were attached to a squad leader (*bazong* 把總).[50] Moreover, a doctor needed to be present in each camp (*ying* 營).[51] While medical officers formed part and parcel of the technical personnel as listed in the *Jixiao xinshu*, the presence of surgeons in Chinese armies, and most probably navies, is certainly not a novel concept that can be credited to Qi.[52] By Ming times, the position of medical officers in the army seems to have been firmly established, and to some extent that also holds true for their more extraordinary presence in the navy. Although textual sources are lacking in clarity on this aspect, the inclusion of medical personnel in the ranks of Zheng He's crew sailing to the Indian Ocean in the first half of the 15th century with a formidable doctor/crew ratio appears to have reflected routine practice.[53]

Elsewhere in his work, namely in the paragraph on "Providing relief to the sick and wounded" (*Xu bing shang* 恤病伤), Qi elaborates in detail on the procedures that need to be followed when soldiers fall ill. He advocates a strict process of reporting among the various army ranks. Sick soldiers are to be

---

month of the second year of the Jiajing 嘉靖 reign (1523) was particularly devastating, as a great number of soldiers perished ("軍民死者甚眾"). Cf. *Mingshi*, vol 28; Cf. Zhang Zhibin 张志斌, *Zhongguo gudai yibing liuxing nianbiao* 中国古代疫病流行年表. (Fuzhou: Fujian kexue jishu chubanshe, 2007), 57. Covering a broad array of cases featuring epidemics affecting armies in a global historical perspective is Rebecca M. Seaman (ed.), *Epidemics and War: The Impact of Disease on Major Conflicts in History*. Santa Barbara CA/Denver CO: ABC-CLIO, 2018).

50 In Ming times a *bazong* was in charge of a smaller military settlement, e.g. a fort. See Hucker, *A Dictionary of Official Titles*. 360–361.

51 *Jixiao xinshu* 紀效新書, by Qi Jiguang 戚繼光 Ed. by Gao Yangwen 高揚文, Tao Qi 陶琦 et al., (Beijing: Zhonghua shuju chubanshe, 2001), (14-chapter version), ch. 1, "Shuwu 束伍", 9.

52 Cf. supra. For a chronological survey of military medicine, including the presence of surgeons in the army, see Li, Lin et al., *Zhongguo yixue tongshi*, passim.

53 Cf. Torck, *Avoiding the Dire Straits*, 164–166; Angela Schottenhammer, Mathieu Torck, Wim De Winter, "Surgeons on the Move in the Asian Waters (15th to 18th centuries)", *Haiyangshi yanjiu* 海洋史研究 18 (2022), 245–302.

taken to a medical ward (遗医胗) to determine the severity of their illness and to receive treatment. Failure to report an illness in the army in due time results in punishments under military law (*junfa* 軍法).

> 凡軍士有疾病， 同火房即報本管隊長，隊長報旗總，驗過，即報百總，徑赴本管主將報知。遺醫胗看病輕重，聽醫官報在營將。營將開來簡易草摺手本，差人即刻直達大將。又百總一面再報該管把總知會。[...] 如有把門人阻攔及將官施行遲誤者，罪坐所由。報病遲過一日者，罪坐報遲之官。若因遲報致病兵身死者，究其遲誤之人已軍法。[54]

Furthermore, Qi addresses the close inspection of sick soldiers by the officers, from low-ranking squad leaders checking upon their sick soldiers every day,up to the generals who only inspect the severely ill who receive medicine (*yao* 藥) and valuables (*zi* 資) in person.

> 凡病兵，隊總則日日視，旗總則兩日視，百總則三日視，把總五日視。主將, 大將惟視病重者，先裹藥資面授之。[55]

These passages suggest an awareness and a sense of vigilance when it comes to keeping track of the incidence of disease among the troops. The fact that low-ranking as well as high-ranking officers were held accountable for regularly visiting the soldier-patients seems to indicate that disease was closely monitored in the army, possibly also including its spread, although the text does not go into this in detail.

8 Diet, Hygiene and Sanitation in Naval Camps and Aboard Warships

While the above passages exclusively concern health, hygiene and sanitation in the military encampments of ground forces, similar such instructions and arrangements concerning the naval forces seem generally to be absent from Qi Jiguang's text. The chapter containing a variety of instructions for marines (*zhoushi* 舟師) mainly provides tactical directives for naval operations against the Wokou, as well as disciplinary measures in case of disobedience of orders in the course of the operation. However, it incidentally also unveils other

54 *Jixiao xinshu*, ch. 11, 234–235 (14-chapter version). See also Fan Zhongyi, *Qi Jiguang bingfa xinshuo*, 229–230.

55 *Jixiao xinshu*, ch. 11, 235 (14-chapter version).

essential aspects of military life, including food supply. The particular chapter entitled "Zhi shuibing bian" 治水兵編 in the 18-chapter edition of the *Jixiao xinshu* has a paragraph describing exercises in and around the naval camps ("Changshi shuizhai zaoxi" 常時水寨操習). At some point soldiers spend the night aboard the ships, and in the morning, on the fifth watch (*wugeng* 五更),[56] at a long blow on the horn, the soldiers get up, tidy up and prepare their own meals (*zuofan* 做飯). With the second blow of the horn, the soldiers eat their breakfast (*shifan* 食飯).[57]

The next paragraph contains an instruction scheme for the launch of a naval operation aimed at chasing and catching pirates. Preparations for such an undertaking require that all naval soldiers arrange their food rations for the numbers of days that the operation will take. At this point in the text, Qi briefly mentions the marines' diet for these short-term expeditions, including dried fish, rice and water (以出洋若干日該備鯗米水數目). Failure in this regard would result in punishment by means of detention and the restriction of food rations (欠者捆打罰工食).

> 一，隔日先行牌諭，將以出洋若干日，該備鯗米水數目，令備完限時點查，欠者綑打，罰工食。[58]

Clearly, this passage expresses a resolve to implement strict measures that guarantee a steady food supply in all circumstances by instilling the troops with a sense of responsibility. Any infringement is penalized accordingly, stressing once more the importance Qi attached to keeping troops well supplied. The naval diet that emerges from the text consists of a simple staple food consisting of dried fish (*xiang* 鯗),[59] which obviously betrays a maritime origin. Here the vegetable component is absent, yet this may be explained by

---

56 The fifth watch approximately equals the time between 03:00 and 05:00 in the morning. Cf. Wilkinson, *Chinese History: A New Manual*, 538.

57 *Jixiao xinshu*, ch. 18, 334 (18-chapter version).

58 *Jixiao xinshu*, ch. 18, 340 (18-chapter version).

59 *Xiang* is dried salted fish; for a survey of references in earlier literature, see *Ciyuan*, vol. 4, 3513.1. In Qi Jiguang's text, this food product features as part of a plain, quotidian diet among marines. However, dried salted fish, especially *xiang* from Tiazhou 台州 (Taixiang 台鯗) made from yellow croaker, emerges in more exquisite dishes, for example, in recipes of the Qing painter and gastronome Yuan Mei 袁枚 (1716–1797). Cf. Yuan Mei, *Recipes of the Garden of Contentment: Yuan Mei's Manual of Gastronomy*. Translated and annotated by Sean J.S. Chen (Great Barrington, MA: Berkshire Publishing Group, 2019), 11, 132, 133, 228.

the fact that for these relatively short naval expeditions the mentioned diet was deemed sufficient to keep the marines in shape.[60]

The references to shipboard provisions for naval troops may be quite scarce, yet data related to sanitation are much more so. Nevertheless, there is little reason to doubt that the strict rules which Qi Jiguang proposes to apply in the camps for land forces deviated very little from similar regulations for naval soldiers. This could especially be inferred given the fact that, except for specific technical naval skills such as tactics, fighting and navigation, there were no very strict boundaries between the two categories of troops. In essence, naval troops were land forces trained to carry out anti-Wokou operations at sea, and it was not uncommon for naval forces to take up the tasks of continental troops, as exemplified by one of Qi's sets of relevant instructions in a paragraph concerned with this particular switch (變水兵為陸兵).[61]

9 Conclusion

The manuals of Qi Jiguang and various other works appeared against the backdrop of the territorial threats that fostered the need for knowledge and know-how about military organization. While these works primarily deal with major foci such as strategy, tactics, training and equipment, Qi Jiguang's inclusion of small chapters and paragraphs on food supplies, sanitation, notions of health care and disease management in military encampments is more than just a peripheral addition to his text. While the scattered references from earlier sources indicate that these practices of camp life in this late Ming military context may not be very innovative, the instructions reflect an inclusive and systematic approach, as well as a talent for detail with which such aspects had never been treated in a military treatise up to that point. A wide range of works predating Qi Jiguang's treatises document the development of logistics, the establishment of sanitary facilities and the organization of medical assistance with growing institutionalization from early on, yet in his writings Qi

60 In his discussion of various ship types active along the Chinese coasts in the *Chouhai tubian* 籌海圖編 Zeng Ruozeng provides details about the *wangsuo* boat (網梭船) which was commonly used in the maritime areas around Dinghai 定海, Linguan 臨觀 and Xiangshan 象山 to harvest of seashell, seaweed and fish (取殼菜、紫菜、打魚之利). In the first place the passage seems to refer to commercial fishing activities, rather than to a way to use these products from the sea to replenish shipboard diets, but the consumption of these products during naval operations is not unlikely. Cf. *Chouhai tubian* 籌海圖編, ch. 13 (*shang* 上), (Beijing: Zhonghua shuju, 2007), 873.

61 Cf. *Jixiao xinshu*, ch. 18, 339 (18-chapter version).

Jiguang took health issues to another level. Clearly, Qi's is a profoundly comprehensive approach. His strict regulations concerning the establishment and use of sanitary infrastructure reflect the weight he gave to factors that were not strictly military, but which he considered vital for the success of military operations. Whether these measures were experience-based or merely related to preventative concerns about the troops' health is hard to ascertain. A strong connection with local, rural practices and traditions seems very obvious, and in this respect, this paper concurs with Geltner's point that military manuals can reflect public health issues.[62]

For lack of a distinctive category of works dealing exclusively with naval organization, this paper has mainly looked at traditional food supplies and sanitary and medical practices from sources that mainly document the perspective of Chinese land-based armies. Whether all the technicalities elaborated by Qi in connection with the sanitary prescriptions for land-based troops also held true for naval soldiers cannot be fully inferred from the text. However, the probability of sharply differing approaches for land-based and sea-borne troops can more or less be ruled out. Moreover, Qi's insistence on the necessity and responsibility of the naval troops on the eve of an anti-*Wokou* expedition to calculate the rations of a basic soldier's diet for the number of days of the operation stands out as one of those rare instructions in the history of the Ming naval realm that go beyond the purely tactical. In this sense, similar to how Richard A. Gabriel assesses the siege of the city of Metz in 1552 as a watershed moment in the history of sanitation in early modern European military conflict, we may consider the systematic way Qi Jiguang approaches the issues of diet, sanitation and medicine in the army as an underestimated moment in military literature from Ming times.[63]

62 G. Geltner, "In the Camp and on the March: Military Manuals as sources for Studying Premodern Public Health", *Medical History* 63, no. 1 (2019), 44–60.

63 During this military operation, the commanders of Charles V's troops appear to have cared little about health and proper sanitation, whereas Francis, Duke of Guise, defended the city of Metz while adopting a very strict sanitary policy. In the end the attacking army had to break up the siege after suffering from epidemic outbreaks, while Francis' forces prevailed without major losses. Cf. Gabriel, Richard A. Gabriel, *Between Flesh and Steel: A History of Military Medicine from the Middle Ages to the War in Afghanistan*. Washington: Potomac Books, 2013, 59–60. Gabriel refers to an old but meaningful paper in this respect, cf. Charles L. Heizmann, "Military Sanitation in the Sixteenth, Seventeenth, Eighteenth Century", *Annals of Medical History* 1 (1917–1918), 281–300 (on the siege of Metz, see 284–287).

CHAPTER 7

The Environment, Perceptions, and Publication of Medical Texts in Fujian during the Ming Period (1368 to 1644)

Xu Zhexin

Traditional Chinese medical texts, such as herbal encyclopedias (*bencao leishu* 本草類書), collections of medical cases (*yi'an* 醫案) and medical formularies (*fangshu* 方書), have attracted increasing attention from historians in recent decades, as scholars have become more attuned to considering these textual materials as important sources and subjects for studies in cultural and social history.[1,2] The regional publication industry of Fujian 福建 during the Ming Dynasty (1368–1644) has also interested many scholars, and a large secondary literature on its organization and bibliographies has accumulated in previous scholarship.[3] By examining the medical texts produced in Ming Fujian, this study aims to contribute to further research by analysing the environmental and social factors in contemporaneous Fujian society that influenced the

1 This chater arises out of the research project "Appraising Risks: Patterns of Major Socio-Economic Risk and Risk Projection in the Indian Ocean World" at McGill University, funded by the Social Sciences and Humanities Research Council of Canada.

2 See Hanson Marta E., *Inventing a Tradition in Chinese Medicine: From Universal Canon to Local Medical Knowledge in South China, the Seventeenth to the Nineteenth Century* (University of Pennsylvania, 1997); Angela Ki Che Leung, "Medical Instruction and Popularization in Ming-Qing China," *Late Imperial China* 24, no. 1 (2003): 130–52; Angela Ki Che Leung, *Leprosy in China: A History* (Columbia University Press, 2012); Han Yi 韩毅, *Zhengfu zhili yu yixue fazhan Songdai yishi zhaoling yanjiu* 政府治理與醫學發展：宋代醫事詔令研究 (Beijing: Zhongguo kexue jishu shubanshe, 2014); Chen Xu 陳旭, *Mingdai wenyi yu Mingdai shehui* 明代瘟疫與明代社會 (Chengdu: Southwestern University of Finance and Economics Press, 2016).

3 See Xie Shuishun 謝水順 and Lin Ting 林珽, *Fujian gudai keshu* 福建古代刻書 (Fuzhou: Fujian renmin chubanshe, 1997); Inoue Susumu 井上進, *Chūgoku shuppan bunka-shi – shomotsu sekai to chi no fūkei* 中国出版文化史：書物世界と知の風景 (Nagoya: Nagoya University Press, 2002); Lucille Chia, *Printing for Profit: The Commercial Publishers of Jianyang, Fujian (11th–17th Centuries)* (Harvard University Asia Center, 2002); Lin Yinglin 林應麟, *Fujian shuyeshi jianben fazhan guijikao* 福建書業史——建本發展軌跡考 (Xiamen: Lujiang chubanshe, 2004); Joseph P. McDermott, *A Social History of the Chinese Book: Books and Literati Culture in Late Imperial China* (Hong Kong University Press, 2006).

 | DOI:10.1163/9789004740556_009

production of medical texts. The main research questions posed in this chapter are therefore as follows:

- Who were the producers and targeted audiences of these texts? What motivated the former to produce such texts within contemporary social contexts?
- What kind of roles did external environmental factors, such as prevalent diseases and natural disasters, play in the production and circulation of these medical texts in the Fujian region during Ming China?
- What perceptions of illness, life and social norms are reflected through those medical texts?

These research questions contextualize these medical texts within the contemporaneous social environment. The prevalence and spread of such texts within and beyond the Fujian region may be considered an example of the transfer of culture and knowledge across various parts of the macro-region.

1 Publication of Medical Texts in Ming-Era Fujian

The earliest preserved written record of commercial printing in Fujian can be traced back to the tenth century. In his poem composed early in the century, Xu Yin 徐寅 (849–938), who fled south to Fujian from the turbulent imperial court, mentioned that there was a local book market where his writings were printed for sale (拙賦偏聞携印賣).[4] In the following Song period (960–1279), Fujian gradually became an important centre of the Chinese printing industry, a reputation it retained for centuries, right up until the modern era. Certain regions in Fujian, especially Jianyang 建陽 in the north, developed as the urban centres of private printing houses and book markets. As stated in the thirteenth-century imperial geography *Fangyu shenglan* 方輿勝覽 (An Overall Survey of the Earth), at that point the entry about Fujian described Jianyang as "the city of books" (號為圖書之府).[5]

While a private printing industry had developed since the Song dynasty, the local authorities played a more active role in producing and editing medical texts. The imperial court of the Northern Song dynasty (960–1127) showed an intense interest in establishing an imperial medical and pharmacy service that offered medical services to the ordinary people, as it also enabled the imperial authority to extend its power at the grassroots and to emphasize the legitimacy

4 Peng Dingqiu 彭定求, ed., *Quan Tangshi Xia* 全唐詩, vol. 3 (Zhengzhou: Zhongzhou guji chubanshe, 1996), 4433.

5 Zhu Mu 祝穆, *Fangyu shenglan* 方輿勝覽 Vol. 1 (Beijing: Zhonghua shuju, 2003), 181.

of its governance by "nurturing the people".[6] With the financial support and political supervision of the imperial court, the official compilation and printing of medical texts flourished during this period, since local administrations were obliged to produce relevant medical treatises.[7] However, at this point in time Fujian was still considered as a relatively "uncultivated" marginal region with poor hygiene practices and medical conditions, given that "only twenty percent of the patients were willing to visit a professional physician rather than a witch doctor" in Fuzhou福州, as recorded in a the preface to a medical treatise written by Cai Xiang 蔡襄 (1012–1067) in 1046 (疾家依巫索祟而过醫門十才二三).[8] In 1178, three types of medical treatise had become popular among physicians in central China, namely the *Hongshi jiyanfang* 洪氏集驗方 (Hong's Collected Empirical Prescriptions), the *Yangshi jiacang* 楊氏家藏 (Yang Family's Heritage Prescriptions) and the *Hushi jingyanfang* 胡氏經驗方 (Hu Family's Tried and Proven Recipes). These texts were reprinted in Fujian by the Fujian *tixingsi* 福建提刑司 (Fujian Provincial Surveillance Commission) under the orders of its supervisor Yanxi 延璽 (date of birth and death unknown). In the preface to the reprinted version, he states that:

> Nowadays most physicians in Jianghuai region use these three formularies as helpful reference books to diagnose and treat diseases, and there is no untreatable case. Fujian is so distant from Jianghuai that these formularies had not been introduced to Fujian before. Therefore, I command that the provincial surveillance commission print those volumes for the sake of public health.
>
> 今江淮間士大夫与醫家多用此三書　對症以治疾　無不取效　闽中相去差遠　猶未之有今刊諸憲司　将以惠眾[9]

Educational institutions also produced medical texts. For instance, in 1264, four types of medical writings in 39 volumes were printed at *Huanxi Shuyuan* 環溪書院 (Huanxi Academy) located in Fu'an County 福安縣 in eastern Fujian,

6 TJ Hinrichs, "Governance Through Medical Texts and the Role of Print," in *Knowledge and Text Production in an Age of Print: China, 900–1400*, ed. Lucille Chia and Hilde De Weerdt (Leiden: Brill, 2011), 217.

7 Li Jingwei 李經緯, "beisong huangdi yu yixue" 北宋皇帝與醫學, *Zhongguo keji shiliao* 10, no. 3 (1989), 3–20.

8 Cai Xiang 蔡襄, *Shenghuifang houxu* 聖惠方後序, in Liu Zaozhuang 劉枣庄 and Liu Lin 劉琳, eds., *Quan Songwen* 全宋文, vol. 24, 24 vols. (Chengdu: Bashu shushe, 1992), 125.

9 Wang Ruixiang 王瑞祥, ed., *Zhongguo guyiji shumu tiyao* 中國古醫籍書目提要, vol. 1, 2 vols. (Beijing: Zhongyi guji chubanshe, 2009), 634.

while the official printing of medical texts was still important in Fujian around the time of the Song dynasty.[10] In the following Yuan dynasty (1271–1368), private publishers started to play an increasingly important role in compiling and printing medical texts, as the local authorities seemed to have become less active in this business by that time. Only two medical treatises were printed by official institutes in Fujian during the Yuan period, both of them by the *guanyi tijusi* 官醫提舉司 (Supervisorate of Medical Schools). One is the *Zhenjing zhinan* 針經指南 (Manual of Acupuncture), printed in Fuzhou in 1295, and the other is the *Shiyi dexiaofang* 世醫得效方 (Effective Prescriptions handed down for Generations of Physicians), printed in Jianning 建寧 in 1343. On the other hand, according to the bibliography of preserved Ming printings, private publishers printed at least 28 types of medical texts in Yuan Fujian, most of which were produced in the Jianyang region.[11]

The printing industry in Fujian continued to develop in the following Ming dynasty. In spite of the turbulent political situation around the late Yuan period, which had a destructive impact upon Fujian, overall its economy and population thereafter. According to the *Mingdai banke zonglu* 明代版刻综录 (Comprehensive Catalogue of the Imprints of Ming China), most of the preserved medical texts that were produced in Fujian during the Ming dynasty were edited and printed by Jianyang private publishers, as they took charge of over 90 percent of the medical texts during this period (see Table 7.1 below). Moreover, the *Zhongguo zhongyi guji zongmu* 中國中醫古籍總目 (Comprehensive Catalogue of Traditional Chinese Medical Texts), published in 2007, lists 112 types of medical books produced by the *shulin* 書林 "publishers" in Jianyang during the Ming dynasty.[12] The recently edited catalogue *Haiwai zhongyi zhenshanben guji congkan tiyao* 海外中医珍善本古籍丛刊提要 (Annotated Bibliography of Overseas Preserved Precious Traditional Chinese Medical Texts), published in 2017, included 38 more titles of medical books produced at Jianyang during the Ming dynasty.[13]

Compared to Jianyang, medical texts produced in other regions of Fujian were relatively scarce. In 1575, the Fujian Provincial Administration Commission (*Fujian buzhengsi* 福建布政司) printed the *Maijing* 脈經 (The Pulse Classic)

10 Xiao Linrong 肖林榕, "Song Yuan shiqi minban yishu de yinshua jiqi yingxiang" 宋元時期閩版醫書的印刷及其影響, Fujian Zhongyiyao 19, no. 1 (1988), 56.

11 Lin, *Fujian shuyeshi jianben fazhan guijikao*, 258.

12 Xue Qinglu 薛清录, ed., *Zhongguo zhongyi guji zongmu* 中國中醫古籍總目 (Shanghai: Shanghai cishu chubanshe, 2007).

13 Zheng Jinsheng 鄭金生 and Zhang Zhibin 張志斌, eds., *Haiwai zhongyi zhenshanben guji congkan tiyao* 海外中醫珍善本古籍叢刊提要 (Beijing: Zhonghua shuju, 2017).

TABLE 7.1 Regional publication of medical texts in Ming China's Fujian province

Fu 府 prefecture-level administrative region	Medical texts produced by private publishers	Medical texts printed by the administration	All texts produced by private publishers	All texts produced by the administration	Total
Fuzhou 福州	4	3	73	50	123
Quanzhou 泉州	0	0	31	16	47
Zhangzhou 漳州	0	0	25	19	44
Tingzhou 汀州	1	0	8	17	25
Xinghua 興化	0	0	39	12	51
Funing 福寧	0	0	3	21	24
Shaowu 邵武	0	0	3	23	26
Yanping 延平	2	0	14	30	44
Jianning 建寧	65	0	1603	67	1670

SOURCE: *MINGDAI BANKE ZONGLU* (1983).
DATA SOURCE: DU XINFU 杜信孚, *MINGDAI BANKE ZONGLU* 明代版刻綜錄, 8 VOLS. (YANGZHOU: JIANGSU GUANGLING KEYINSHE, 1983); LIN YINGLIN, *FUJIAN SHUYESHI JIANBEN FAZHAN GUIJIKAO*.

at Fuzhou, a twenty-volume medical manual on acupuncture treatments.[14] In the same year, during his three-month visit to Fujian, the Spanish Augustinian Priest Martín de Rada (1533–1578) noticed a market at Fuzhou where one could purchase books.[15] During this journey, he collected several types of illustrated Chinese publication, including medical books, which he later took back to Manila.[16] It is possible that he collected them at this local book market in Fuzhou, where he mostly stayed during his journey. For private publishers and book merchants based at Jianyang, neighbouring urban centres with high demands for medical texts were their main target markets, including Fuzhou, Hangzhou 杭州 and Nanjing 南京.[17] Due to the low cost of printing and trans-

14 Du Xinfu, *Mingdai Banke Zonglu*, vol. 5, 32.

15 Galeote Pereira and Gaspar da Cruz, *South China in the Sixteenth Century: Being the Narratives of Galeote Pereira, Fr. Gaspar Da Cruz, O.P. [and] Fr. Martín de Rada, O.E.S.A. (1550–1575)* (Hakluyt Society, 1953): 292.

16 Pereira and Cruz, *South China in the Sixteenth Century*, 295.

17 Wang Taokai 王涛锴, "Heyi chengyi: Ming Qing shidai susongtai diqu de yisheng xunlian he shehui" 何以成醫：明清時代蘇松太地區的醫生訓練和社會, *Zhongguo shehui lishi pinglun* 11 (2010), 170–184, 173.

portation, Fujianese merchants and publishers became the main suppliers of medical treatises and manuals in those markets. To avoid direct competition with their Fujianese counterparts, local private publishers at Hangzhou even had to print books on other subjects.[18] According to Lucille Chia's study of the Jianyang book trade during the Ming dynasty, medicine was the most frequent subject of publication produced by Jianyang publishers in both the earlier and later halves of the Ming dynasty.[19] This also suggests that there was a large demand for texts with medical instructions in contemporary society, which influenced the preferences of book merchants and printers.[20] Medical books printed in Fujian had also been introduced to neighbouring regions beyond China, such as Korea, Vietnam, the Ryukyus and Japan, especially since the late Ming dynasty.[21] In 1528, the Japanese merchant and physician, Asaino Sozui 阿佐井野宗瑞 (1473–1532), reprinted the twenty-four volume Chinese medical treatise *xinbian mingfang leizheng yishu daquan* 新編名方類證医書大全 (Newly Published Categorized Famous Recipes from the Great Compendium of Medical recipes), at the seaport of Sakai 堺 near present-day Osaka 大阪, this being the earliest datable Chinese medical text printed in Japan.[22] In 1617, the *Xinkan wutingzi sujie bashiyi nanjing* 新刊勿聽子俗解八十一難經 (Newly Edited Vernacular Explanation on Eighty-one Difficult Issues by Wutingzi), originally compiled in 1438 in Fujian, was reprinted at Kyōto with Japanese annotations. These examples imply that medical texts printed in Fujian played a leading role in the interregional network of medical knowledge transfer in the contemporary East Asian world.

2 Medical Texts and Environmental Factors

Previous scholars have discussed the roles played by medical texts in aspects of the book trade and of professional medical education in Ming China.[23] This

18 Qi Chenyue 祁晨越, "Mingdai Hangzhou diqu de shuji kanyin huodong" 明代杭州地區的書籍刊印活動, Singapore (Doctoral Thesis, National University of Singapore, 2010), 73.

19 Chia, *Printing for Profit*, 186.

20 Cynthia Joanne Brokaw, *Commerce in Culture: The Sibao Book Trade in the Qing and Republican Periods* (Harvard University Asia Center, 2007), 428–448.

21 Makoto Mayanagi 真柳誠, "Nikkan'etsu no igaku to Chūgoku isho" 日韓越の医学と中国医書, *Nihon ishigaku zasshi* 56, no. 2 (2010), 151–59.

22 Toshiro Kuboo 久保尾俊郎, "Asaino sōzui to 'ishotaizen' no shuppan" 阿佐井野宗瑞と『医書大全』の出版, *Waseda Daigaku Tosyokan Kiyou* 42 (December 31, 1995), 157.

23 See Liang Qizi 梁其姿, *Mianduijibing: chuantong Zhongguo shehui de yiliao guannian yu zuzhi* 面对疾病：傳統中國社會的醫療觀念與組織 (Beijing: Renmin daxue chubanshe, 2012): 181–185; Chia, *Printing for Profit*, 180–192.

study aims to extend the discussion on the relationship between medical texts and coeval environmental factors, especially the diseases that were endemic in the region.

As the demographic and economic centre of the Ming Empire, southeast China was frequently affected by natural disasters and the diseases that spread across the region from them.[24] According to Wang Shuanghuai's statistics on natural disasters in south China during the Ming dynasty, the frequency of *yizai* 疫災 (epidemics) in Fujian was considerably higher than other regions in south China, as it broke out in Fujian 136 times, while Guangdong 廣東 and Guangxi 廣西 had 4 and 47 cases of epidemics in their respective regions during the same period.[25] Additional research on epidemics in China during the Ming and Qing dynasties (1368–1911) also shows that Fujian was among the regions that were most severely affected by epidemics according to records of epidemics in Fujian spanning 122 years.[26] The regional study of epidemics in Ming-era Fujian by Zhang Yiliu further indicated that prefectures in north Fujian, especially Shaowu 邵武, Jianning 建寧 and Yanping 延平, were the most severely affected in the region.[27] However, previous statistical analyses of the frequency of these so-called epidemics could create ambiguity by neglecting the scale of the epidemics and treating all sorts of *yizai* recorded in primary written sources as epidemics.[28] Therefore, this study mainly examines accounts of *dayi* 大疫 ("great prevalent disease") with detailed notes on the casualties in the written sources because they reflect the extent to which these diseases impacted on the local society. Moreover, compared to present-day perceptions of the epidemics, at that time people had different perceptions and understandings of diseases that were prevalent in the region, as physicians, chroniclers and local officials in Ming China usually applied the general term *yi* 疫 to refer to various epidemics and regionally prominent diseases, such as smallpox, cholera and plague, without indicating their exact types.[29] However,

24 Min Zongdian 閔宗殿, "Ming Qing shiqi dongnan diqu yiqing yanjiu" 明清時期東南地區疫情研究, *Xueshu yanjiu*, no. 10 (2003), 109.

25 Wang Shuanghuai 王雙懷, "Mingdai Hua'nan de ziran zaihai jiqi shikong tezheng," 明代華南的自然災害及其時空特征 *Dili yanjiu* 18 (1999), 158.

26 Cheng Yang 程楊, Li Hairong 李海蓉, and Yang Linsheng 楊林生, "Zhongguo Mingqing shiqi yibing shikong fenbu guilü de dingliang yanjiu" 中國明清時期疫病時空分佈的定量研究, *Dili yanjiu* 28, no. 4 (2009), 1063.

27 Zhang Yiliu 張宜镠, "Mingdai Fujiansheng yizai dili guilü yu huanjing jili yanjiu" 明代福建省疫災地理規律与環境機理研究 (Master thesis, Central China Normal University, 2014), 42.

28 Wang Zunwang 王尊旺 and Li Yin 李穎, *Yiliao cishan yu Ming Qing Fujian shehui* 醫療、慈善與明清福建社會 (Tianjin: Tianjin guji chubanshe, 2010), 28.

29 Min, "Ming Qing shiqi dongnan diqu yiqing yanjiu", 110.

in contemporary medical texts, accounts of such diseases can be found in writings of the four types of disease mentioned earlier.

Thus, this study follows the traditional terminology in using the term "prevalent disease" rather than "epidemics" when analysing the relevant primary sources. According to local gazetteers, dynastic chronicles and sourcebooks of natural disasters, the table below charts the total of 87 occurrences of *dayi* in Ming-dynasty Fujian[30] (see Table 7.2). In the temporal aspect, 50 occurrences broke out during the Zhengde 正德 and Jiajing 嘉靖 eras (from 1506 to 1566). The second peak appeared in the second half of the fifteenth century, when there were 16 records of *dayi* during the Chenghua 成化 and Hongzhi 弘治 eras (from 1465 to 1505). In brief, around 76% of the *dayi* in Ming-dynasty Fujian broke out during this century, from 1465 to 1566. In the geographical aspect, the spatial distribution of prevalent diseases in Ming-dynasty Fujian was also relatively unbalanced. Most of them were concentrated on prefectures in north and east Fujian, especially Shaowu 邵武 (19 times), Fuzhou 福州 (17 times), Funing 福寧 (15 times) and Yanping 延平 (8 times), as the density map of prevalent diseases in Ming Fujian shows (see Figure 7.2).

Some of the prevalent regional diseases in Fujian mentioned earlier were caused by military raids. For instance, Funing was severely plundered by the *Wokou* 倭寇 (militarized pirates mostly with Japanese and Chinese backgrounds) three times during the late Jiajing era (in 1559, 1560 and 1561), and the pillage led to the spread of regional diseases that inflicted heavy casualties.[31] Another seaport, Xinghua 興化, faced a similar situation, as it was one of the worst hit areas during the Jiajing *Wokou* raids in Fujian during Ming times (即以吾閩論之其陷興化福清寧德諸郡縣 焚殺一空 而興化尤甚).[32] In the winter of 1560, Xinghua was attacked by the *Wokou* pirates and left further debilitated by the ensuing outbreak of epidemic diseases. Both catastrophes caused heavy casualties in this region (冬倭夷迫城疾癘並臻死者相枕).[33]

---

30 The main sourcebooks on prevalent diseases in Ming China are Li Guoxiang 李國祥 and Yang Chan 楊昶, eds., *Mingshilu leizuan: ziran zaiyi juan* 明實錄類纂：自然災疫卷 (Wuhan: Wuhan Press, 1997); Zhang Zhibin 張志斌, *Zhongguo gudai yibing liuxing nianbiao* 中國古代疫病流行年表 (Fuzhou: Fujian kexue jishu chubanshe, 1997); 张德二, ed., *Zhongguo sanqiannian qixiang jilu zongji* 中國三千年氣象記錄總集 (Beijing: Zhongguo shehui chubanshe, 1999).

31 Zhu Mei 朱梅 et al., eds., *Wangli Fu'ningzhou zhi* 萬曆福寧州志, vol. 7, 32 vols., Riben cang Zhongguo hanjian difangzhi congkan日本藏中國罕见地方志叢刊 (Beijing: shumu wenxian chubanshe, 1990), 409–411.

32 Xie Zhaozhe 謝肇淛, *wuzazu* 五雜俎 (Shanghai: Shanghai shudian chubanshe, 2001), 78.

33 Chen Zhongyu 陳忠瑜, ed., *sanyi jiaozhu xiawuni Lingzi benxing shilu* 三一教主夏午尼林子本行實錄 (Beijing: Beijing Library Press, 1999), 572.

TABLE 7.2 Historical Records of *dayi* 大疫 with casualty accounts in Fujian during the Ming Dynasty

Imperial era	Frequency of *dayi* prevalent diseases	Affected regions (prefecture-level)
Hongwu 洪武 (1368–1398)	1	Funing 福寧 (1369)
Yongle 永樂 (1403–1424)	5	Zhangzhou 漳州 (1405); Jianning 建寧 (1407, 1408); Shaowu 邵武 (1407, 1408, 1410, 1416); Yanping 延平 (1407)
Xuande 宣德 (1426–1435)	1	Zhangzhou 漳州 (1428)
Zhengtong 正統 (1436–1449)	3	Fuzhou 福州 (1442); Xinghua 興化 (ca. 1442); Yanping 延平 (1449); Shaowu 邵武 (1449)
Jingtai 景泰 (1450–1456)	1	Shaowu 邵武 (1455)
Tianshun 天順 (1457–1464)	1	Shaowu 邵武 (1460)
Chenghua 成化 (1465–1487)	13	Shaowu 邵武 (1466, 1475, 1478); Yanping 延平 (1467, 1475, 1476); Zhangzhou 漳州 (1475); Fuzhou 福州 (1477, 1480, 1481, 1485, 1486, 1487); Funing 福寧 (1486, 1487)
Hongzhi 弘治 (1488–1505)	3	Funing 福寧 (1497); Fuzhou 福州 (1498); Xinghua 興化 (1505)
Zhengde 正德 (1506–1521)	22	Shaowu 邵武 (1506, 1507, 1517, 1519); Jianning 建寧 (1506, 1507); Funing 福寧 (1507, 1508, 1509, 1510, 1511); Fuzhou 福州 (1509, 1514, 1516, 1521); Tingzhou 汀州 (1512, 1521); Quanzhou 泉州 (1517)

TABLE 7.2 Historical Records of *dayi* 大疫 with casualty accounts in Fujian (*cont.*)

Imperial era	Frequency of *dayi* prevalent diseases	Affected regions (prefecture-level)
Jiajing 嘉靖 (1522–1566)	28	Shaowu 邵武 (1522, 1544, 1561); Funing 福寧 (1523, 1530, 1535, 1559, 1560, 1561); Fuzhou 福州 (1532, 1542, 1544, 1552); Zhangzhou 漳州 (1537, 1538); Tingzhou 汀州 (1544); Yanping 延平 (1544, 1545, 1556); Quanzhou 泉州 (1562)
Wanli 萬曆 (1573–1620)	5	Jianning 建寧 (1589); Tingzhou 汀州 (1601); Shaowu 邵武 (1609); Quanzhou 泉州 (1615, 1617); Zhangzhou 漳州 (1618)
Chonzhen 崇禎 (1628–1644)	4	Zhangzhou 漳州 (1635, 1640); Fuzhou 福州 (1642); Shaowu 邵武 (1644)

However, most of the prevalent diseases listed above were correlated with seasonal changes and natural disasters. Research on the regional distribution of natural disasters in Fujian during the Ming dynasty shows that the prefectures through which the Min River and its tributaries flow, namely Jianning, Shaowu, Yanping and Fuzhou, suffered most frequently from natural disasters, especially flooding, typhoons and droughts (see Figure 7.1).[34] Due to the mountainous nature of the landscape, most of the major cities and towns in Fujian were along the river valley or near river confluences in the plains and water resources (閩中諸郡大都依兩溪合處為勝).[35] Consequently, in this geographical context human settlements became fragile in face of the threat of certain seasonal natural disasters, such as flooding and typhoons, which inflicted heavy casualties on the local population. Moreover, the extensive river systems, coupled with unhygienic conditions, further facilitated the spread of

34 Wang, "Mingdai Hua'nan de ziran zaihai jiqi shikong tezheng", 158.

35 Wang Shimao 王世懋, *Minbushu* 閩部疏, Zhongguo fangzhi congshu hua'nan difang 中國方志叢書・華南地方243 (Taipei: chengwen chubanshe, 1975), 35.

infectious diseases among these riverside cities and towns. Therefore, severe natural disasters in Ming-dynasty Fujian were usually followed by large-scale outbreaks of disease. For example, the chapter on "Astrology and Weather" (*yinghou* 應侯) in *Jiajing Shaowufu zhi* 嘉靖邵武府志 (Gazetteer of Shaowu Prefecture), edited in 1543, records 11 summer floods hitting the Shaowu region in north Fujian between 1416 and 1541, 9 of them being followed by severe prevalent diseases (*dayi*) with high numbers of victims.[36] Statistical analysis also indicates that the frequency of natural disasters was closely related with outbreaks of disease in both the geographical and chronological aspects. In Ming-era Fujian, Shaowu, Yanping, Jianning and Fuzhou were not only the most severely affected areas by prevalent diseases, but were also impacted by natural disasters like floods, typhoons and droughts. Among these natural disasters, it was the water-related hazards that played the most direct role in causing prevalent diseases, 79.41% of those that hit Fujian during the Ming dynasty being linked to floods and typhoon disasters.[37] The periodic frequencies of prevalent diseases and natural disasters also followed a similar trend. As mentioned above, the regionally prevalent diseases reached their peak in the Zhengde and Jiajing eras, while the frequency of natural disasters in Fujian hit a peak in the 1520s, in the same period, as showed by the decal frequency chart (See Figure 7.1):

Both natural disasters and prevalent diseases caused high levels of disease in local societies, especially in north Fujian. In 1410, the local government of Shaowu reported the high levels of sickness caused by recent prevalent diseases to the imperial court, stating that "over 12,000 households of local inhabitants had died" (福建邵武府言　比歲境內疫　民死絕萬二千餘戶).[38] In 1418, the District Magistrate (*zhixian* 知縣) of Jian'an County 建安縣 under Jianyang also presented an urgent report to Yongle Emperor (r. 1403–1424), indicating that over 174,600 local inhabitants in Jianning, Shaowu and Yanping had died due to prevalent mortal diseases in recent years, i.e. since 1408 (建寧　邵武　延平至永乐六年以来　屢大疫　民死亡十七万四千六百餘口).[39] Contemporary demographic records and statistics in local gazetteers show a fall in population

36 Xing Zhi 邢址 and Chen Rang 陳讓, eds., *Jiajing Shaowufu zhi* 嘉靖邵武府志, vol. 191, 292 vols., Siku quanshu cunmu congshu shibu 四庫全書存目叢書史部 (Ji'nan: Qilu shushe, 1997): 548–549.

37 Wang, "Mingdai Hua'nan de ziran zaihai jiqi shikong tezheng", 158.

38 Li Guoxiang 李國祥 and Yang Chang 楊昶, eds., *Mingshilu leizuan: ziran zaiyi juan* 明實錄類纂：自然災异卷 (Wuhan: Wuhan Press, 1997), 514.

39 Yang Shiqi 楊士奇 et al., eds., *Ming Taizong shilu* 明太宗實錄, vol. 6, 6 vols. (Taipei: Academia Sinica, 1960), 2139.

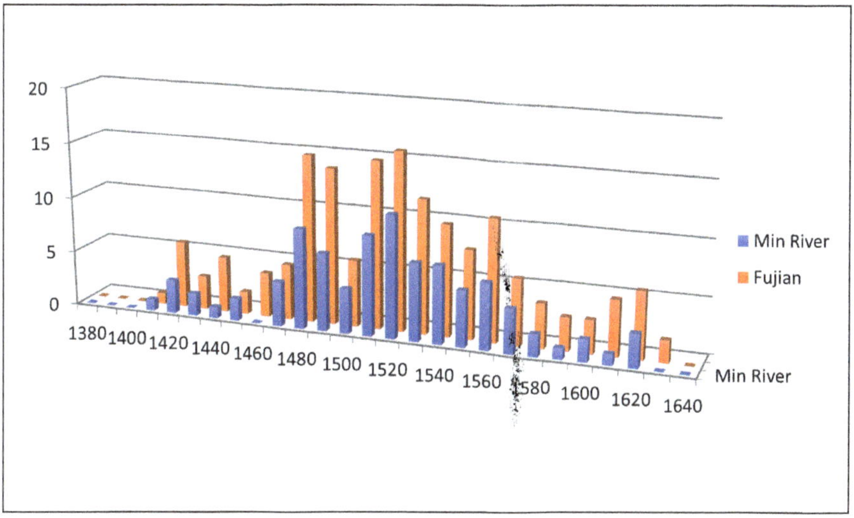

FIGURE 7.1 Decadal frequency of *wenyi* diseases prevalent in Fujian during the Ming period
SOURCE: WANG SHUANGHUAI 王雙懷, "MINGDAI HUANAN DE ZIRAN ZAIHAI JIQI SHIKONG TEZHENG" 明代華南的自然災害及其時空特征, DILI YANJIU 18 (1999): 151–160, AT P. 158.

during this period. For instance, according to *Jianyangxian zhi*建陽縣志 (Gazetteer of Jianyang County), the registered population of Jianyang fell by about 33% during the fifteenth century (see Table 7.3).[40] Similar records can also be found in *Jiajing Shaowufu zhi* 嘉靖邵武府志 (Gazetteer of Shaowu Prefecture), indicating that the registered population of the Shaowu region fell dramatically from 236,710 (in 1391) to 127,891 (in 1412) during the early Ming dynasty.[41] Yanping, another prefecture in north Fujian that suffered frequently from prevalent diseases, also faced population reductions during this period of frequent natural disasters followed by prevalent diseases, since its registered population fell from 300,693 (in 1452) to 230,693 (in 1562), even though it had two more counties during this period.[42]

---

40 Wei Yingshi 魏應時, Tian Juzhong 田居中, and Zhang Bang 張榜, eds., *Jianyangxian zhi* 建陽縣志, vol. 12, 32 vols., Riben cang Zhongguo hanjian difangzhi congkan 日本藏中國罕見地方志叢刊 (Beijing: shumu wenxian chubanshe, 1990), 341–342.

41 Xing Zhi and Chen Rang, *Jiajing Shaowufu zhi*, 644.

42 Fu Ertai 傅尔泰 and Tao Yuanzao 陶元藻, eds., *Qianlong Yanpingfu zhi* 乾隆延平府志, vol. 37, 40 vols., Zhongguo difangzhi jicheng Fujian fuxianzhi ji 中國地方志集成・福建府縣志輯 (Shanghai: Shanghai shudian chubanshe, 2000), 250.

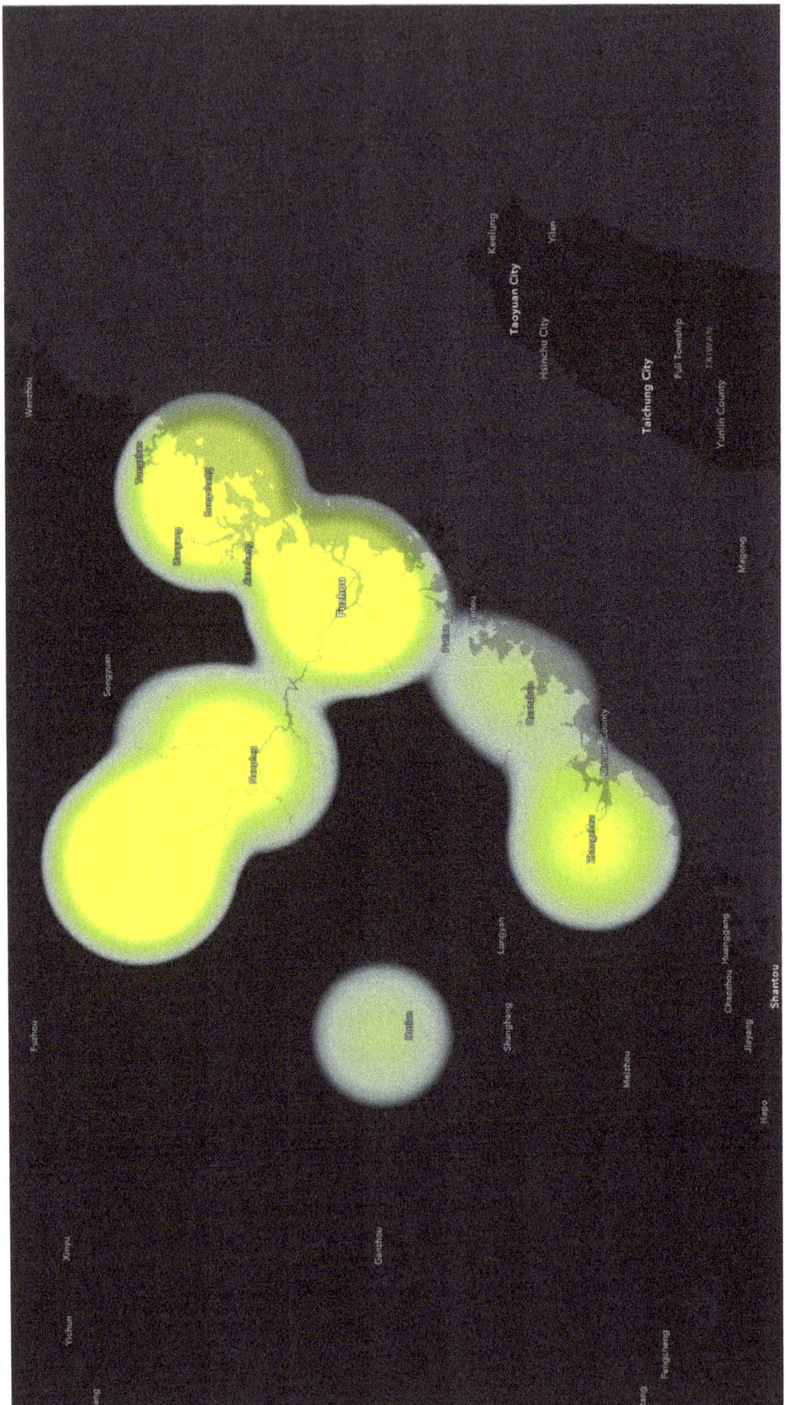

FIGURE 7.2 Density Map of Occurrence of Prevalent Diseases in Ming's Fujian

TABLE 7.3 Selected demographic records of Jianyang during the Ming Dynasty

Year	Female population	Male population	*hu* 户 "households"	*kou* 口 "inhabitant"
1391	59,906	64,361	31,244	124,267
1412	40,436	54,469	29,812	94,985
1432	34,937	53,606	28,381	88,543
1445	31,601	55,963	29,711	87,564
1492	27,438	55,800	24,103	83,238
1532	27,436	55,800	24,731	83,236
1552	29,313	53,970	25,015	83,283
1592	29,352	54,019	25,046	83,371

SOURCE: *WANLI JIANYANGXIAN ZHI* (1601)

In Ming China, medical knowledge and perceptions of regionally prevalent diseases were shaped by geographical perceptions and imagination, which Marta Hanson has called "late Ming medical regionalism".[43] Furthermore, with regard to the extent of epidemiological knowledge, multiple theories based on the traditional Chinese medical system appeared and developed during this period. The perceptions and conceptions of those prevalent infectious diseases in Ming society varied in regions, as Ming physicians and scholars from different regions might introduce and explain similar diseases by using different terms. Moreover, one has to be careful with those medical terms applied by the Ming authors, since their meanings also changed over time. The present study follows the theoretical framework of medical knowledge in Ming China by using these comprehensive medical treatises, which were popular around the late Ming period as major reference works when dealing with terminological issues. This includes texts such as the *Dantai yu'an* 丹臺玉案 (Medical cases from the Dwelling of the Taoist Immortal), compiled in 1636, and the *Jingyue quanshu* 景岳全書 (Comprehensive Collection of the Medical Treaties by Mr Jingyue), compiled in 1624.[44] According to contemporary categorization

43 Marta Hanson, *Speaking of Epidemics in Chinese Medicine: Disease and the Geographic Imagination in Late Imperial China*. (Oxon: Routledge, 2011), 61–65.

44 Sun Wenyin 孫文胤, ed., *Dantai yu'an* 丹臺玉案, 100 種珍本古醫籍校注集成, 100 zhong zhenben guyiji jiaozhu jicheng (Beijing: Zhongyi guji chubanshe, 2012); Zhang Jiebin 張介賓, *jingyue quanshu* 景岳全書, ed. Zhao Lixun 趙立勛, zhongyi guji zhengli congshu 中醫古籍整理叢書 (Beijing: Renmin weisheng chubanshe, 1991).

system of medical treatises around the Ming period, accounts on the regionally prevalent diseases mentioned above can mainly be found in the following four types of medical text:

– *wenyi* 瘟疫 ("pestilence")
– *shanghan* 傷寒 ("cold damage" and *wenbing* 溫病 "warm disease")
– *douzhen* 痘疹 ("smallpox")
– *nüeji* 瘧疾 ("malaria" and *liji* 痢疾 "dysentery")

While contemporary physicians and medical theorists had already linked regionally prevalent diseases to environmental factors, their perceptions of *wenyi* 瘟疫 were considerably different from modern understandings of so-called epidemic diseases. In the preface to his medical treatise *Wenyi lun* 瘟疫論 (Treatise on *Wenyi*), the late Ming physician Wu Youxing 吳有性 (1582–1644) suggested that *wenyi* was caused by there was a specific kind of *qi* 氣 (air) and its prevalence varied by region and season (疫者，感天地之厲氣，在歲運有多寡，在方隅有厚薄，在四時有盛衰，此氣之來，無論老少強弱，觸之者即病).[45] The entry on *wenyi* in the treatise *Dantai yu'an*, mentioned earlier, also declared that *wenyi* was caused by a specific type of *qi*, which chiefly attacked those who had become exhausted by sexual indulgence (有瘟疫，寒疫，此天地不正之氣，多感於房勞辛苦之人).[46] This explanation, blaming a specific type *qi* as the main cause of *wenyi*, was prevalent among Ming-era physicians.[47]

The frequent prevalence of pandemics in Fujian motivated local authorities and officials to produce medical texts to spread medical knowledge and improve local hygiene. In 1584, a two-volume medical treatise, *Huimin zhengfang* 惠民正方 (Authoritative Formulary for Benefiting the People), was printed in Fujian while its author Yang Sizhi 楊四知 (date of birth and death unknown), who had inherited his medical background, was the Regional Inspector of Fujian (*Fujian xun'an yushi* 福建巡案御史). The relatively high quality of its printing also implied that it was directly printed by the local authority, probably at the provincial capital, Fuzhou.[48] While this medical treatise aimed to eradicate so-called *gudu* 蠱毒 disease ("poison of venomous

45 Wu Youxing 吳有性, *Wenyi lun* 瘟疫論, vol. 47, 54 vols., Jingyin wenyuange sikuquanshu zibu bawu yijialei 景印文淵閣四庫全書子部八五醫家類, (Beijing: Zhongyi guji chubanshe, 1986), 3.

46 Sun, *Dantai yu'an*, 50.

47 Chen Guobin 程國斌, "Wenyi zhongde daode xushi" 瘟疫中的道德敘事, *Zhongwai yixue zhexue* 14, no. 1 (2016), 11–33, 18.

48 Yang Sizhi 楊四知, *Huimin zhengfang* 惠民正方, vol. 4, 10 vols., Zhenban haiwai huigui zhongyi guji congshu 珍本海外回歸中醫古籍叢書 (Beijing: Renmin weisheng chubanshe, 2008), 143.

insects") by offering medical instruction, as stated by Yang Sizhi in his preface, the exact definition of *gudu* is unclear. In an official order issued by him in 1584 on preventing the mortal *gudu* disease in Fujian, Yang Sizhi claimed that it spread so severely in Fuzhou, Yanping and Quanzhou, that travellers were unwilling to stay there, and family members were unable to help each other (行旅不敢食宿， 親戚不能相保， 誠地方之大害).[49] This implies that the so-called *gudu* disease was a highly contageous regionally prevalent disease. In 1616, another local official, Nie Shangheng 聶尚恒 (1572–?), the District Magistrate of Ninghua County (*Ninghua zhixian* 寧化知縣) in central Fujian, which was also one of the most severely affected regions of prevalent diseases, completed his two-volume collection of medical cases, namely *Qixiao yishu* 奇效醫述 (Collection of Recipes with Remarkable Effects). In the same year, Jianyang's private publisher Yu Xiangdou 余象斗 (1588–1609) printed this text by the administrative order of the Office of Surveillance Commissioner of Fujian (*Fujian anchashi* 福建按察使司), as is indicated on its title page.[50] This example suggests that the local authority became directly engaged in producing medical texts by assigning such tasks to *shuhu* 書戶 (book households) as the latter's mandatory duty.[51] In the preface to this text about his experience as a part-time physician during his official career, Nie emphasized that "*wenyi* is the most dreadful disease in the world" (瘟疫， 病之最可畏者也).[52] In this text, he also stressed the serious threat to local communities of regionally prevalent diseases. He further explained his motives for writing by arguing that:

> While they seem to be similar, *yi* is different from *shanghan* 傷寒 (cold damage). The ordinary people are unable to tell the difference between these two sorts of diseases, as those charlatans mistakenly treated *yi* as *shanghan*. What a fatal mistake!
>
> 疫瘴皆悍烈之气似傷寒而非傷寒也俗人不知辨白混以傷寒名之俗醫亦以治傷寒方藥混治誤亦甚矣[53]

49 Ibid., 155.

50 Nie Shangheng 聶尚恆, "Qixiao yishu" 奇效醫述, Unknown (1661), Waseda University Library, Japanese and Chinese Classic, URL: http://www.wul.waseda.ac.jp/kotenseki/html/ya09/ya09_00335/index.html (last visited 2019-3-1).

51 Li Zigui discovered that Li Zigui 李子歸, "Mingdai Jianyang de shuhu yu shufang" 明代建陽的書戶與書坊, *Xianggang Zhongwen daxue Zhongguo wenhua yanjiusuo xuebao*, no. 66 (2018), 36.

52 Nie Shangheng 聶尚恆, *Yixue Huihan* 醫學匯函, ed. Fu Haiyan 傅海燕, vol. 2, 3 vols. (Beijing: Zhongguo zhongyiyao chubanshe, 2015), 427.

53 Ibid.

The aforementioned case of the *Qixiao yishu* shows that certain private book publishers were obliged to produce texts, including medical texts, for the local authorities. However, these private commercial printers and intellectuals-cum-physicians also played an active role in compiling and printing medical texts in non-governmental contexts. As shown in previous research, the centre of the printing industry, Jianyang and its neighbouring regions were the areas most severely affected by regionally prevalent diseases. The public pharmacy (*huimin yaoju* 惠民藥局 or the "pharmacy for the benefit of the people") at Jianyang was destroyed in a flood in 1416, being reestablished later in 1481 by a decree of the Ministry of Revenue (*hubu* 戶部).[54] However, it generally remained merely ceremonial, and the building housing it collapsed completely in 1539.[55] In other hinterland prefectures and counties, especially those with large rural populations, such as Shaowu, Yanping and Fu'ning, imperial medical institutes such as the public pharmacies had relatively modest effects on preventing regionally prevalent diseases. According to the chapter on charitable institutions (*xunzheng* 恤政) in Fujian in the *Bamin tongzhi* 八閩通志 (General Gazetteer of Eight Min), edited in 1491, the buildings of local public pharmacies in Zhenghe county 政和 and Shaowu were used as the offices of other government departments.[56] Due to the limited capabilities of government medical institutes during the Ming dynasty, patients had to seek medical assistance from private physicians.[57] Local administrations also needed to seek medical assistance from unofficial physicians when diseases broke out. In 1511, while the *dayi* was striking in Fu'ning, its district magistrate asked a local physician, Xu Qi 許杞 (birth and death date unknown), to provide the patients with herbal medicines, most of whom were saved thanks to his help.[58] Moreover, the prevalence of regional diseases and their disastrous impact

54 Zhao Wen 趙文, Huang Xuan 黃瑄, and Yuan Xian 袁銛, eds., *Jingtai Jianyangxian zhi* 景泰建陽縣志, vol. 176, 292 vols., sikuquanshu cunmu congshu shibu 四庫全書存目叢書史部 (Ji'nan: Qilu shushe, 1996), 83.

55 Feng Jike 馮繼科, ed., *Jianyangxian zhi* 建陽縣志, vol. 31, 68 vols., Tianyige cang Mingdai fangzhi xuankan 天一閣藏明代方志選刊 (Shanghai: Shanghai shudian chubanshe, 2014), 193.

56 Huang Zhongzhao 黃仲昭, ed., *Bamin tongzhi* 八閩通志, vol. 2, 2 vols. (Fuzhou: Fujian renmin chubanshe, 1991), 435.

57 Qiu Zhonglin 邱仲麟, "Yizi yu yaoqian Mingdai de kanzhen wenhua yu minzhong de zhibing fudan" 醫資與藥錢——明代的看診文化與民眾的治病負擔, in Shengmin yiliaoshi yanjiushi 生命醫療史研究室 (ed.), *Zhongguoshi xinlun: yiliaoshi fence* 中國史新論：醫療史分冊 (Taipei: lianjing chuban gongsi, 2015), 382.

58 Chen Menglei 陳夢雷, ed., *Yishu mingliu zhuan* 醫術名流傳, vol. 12, 12 vols., Gujin tushu jicheng yibu quanlu 古今圖書集成醫部全錄 (Beijing: Renmin weisheng chubanshe, 1991), 289.

on local populations prompted the production of medical texts on prevalent diseases by local intellectuals-cum-physicians. In the preface to the medical treaty *huhai qifang* 湖海奇方, "marvelous formulary of folk medicines", written in 1422, its author and editor Xu Hong 許宏 (1341 to 1421), an active local intellectual-cum-physician in Jian'an County 建安縣 (present-day Jian'ou City 建甌市 in Fujian Province) in northern Fujian, stated that "the local poor usually just wait for death when they fell sick, as they cannot afford the medical expenses" (或貧常而無力請醫 或貴料而難為措置 往往束手待斃).[59] He further explained that the purpose of his treatis was to offer practical medical instruction that ordinary people can understand and practice (人人皆可曉用).[60]

Several Jianyang private printers who actively participated in producing medical texts had inherited their backgrounds as medical professionals, which made them capable of compiling and editing medical texts with medical expertise. As one of the leading publishing families, the Xiong 熊 family, had a similar ancestral background, they maintained their interest in producing medical texts, which dominated the lists of Xiong printing houses from the fifteenth century to the end of the Ming Dynasty.[61] Among the Xiong publishers, Xiong Zongli 熊宗立 (1409 to 1482), his son Xiong Yuan 熊瑗 (1436 to 1508) and his sixth-generation grandson Xiong Anben 熊安本 (1594 to 1670) played the most active roles in producing medical texts, as they were not only commercial printers but also authors, editors and experts on medical texts. The *Fujian yiji kao* 福建醫籍考 or "annotated bibliography of Fujian medical texts" recorded 28 titles of preserved medical texts produced at Jianyang during the Ming period by the printing house of the Xiong family, *zhongde tang* 種德堂, 22 of which were printed by one of these three Xiong printers.[62] As the main contributor, the founding printer, Xiong Zongli, edited and printed at least 48 medical treatises from 1437 to 1474, ranging from an encyclopedia of herbal medicines to a formulary on gynaecological diseases.[63] Rather than simply reprinting the original medical texts produced in earlier periods, he illustrated and annotated these medical classics with explanations in simple language, and compiled

59 Xu Hong 許宏, *Quansheng leiyao huhai qifang* 全生類要湖海奇方, vol. 9, 10 vols., Zhenban haiwai huigui zhongyi guji congshu 珍版海外回歸中醫古籍叢書 (Beijing: Renmin weisheng chubanshe, 2008): 1–140, 12.

60 Ibid., 15.

61 Chia, *Printing for Profit*, 167.

62 Wang Zunwang 王尊旺 and Cai Hongxin 蔡鴻新, *Fujian yiji kao* 福建醫籍考 (Xiamen: Xiamen University Press, 2016).

63 Lin, *Fujian shuyeshi jianben fazhan guijikao*, 352.

several new formularies with common ingredients for an ordinary readership.[64] In the preface to his formulary of simple and single-ingredient recipes, *shanju bianyi fang* 山居便宜方 "recipes for convenient use when dwelling in the mountains," written in 1441, Xiong Zongli emphasized his specific concern for the medical conditions of the local population in north Fujian, stating that:

> For those poor households residing in the remote hinterland, they could barely survive from the malignant diseases, since there are no physicians and medical ingredients available to them. [...] I collected those proven, simple, and easily available recipes [in previous formularies], and complied them into this sixteen-volume book, *shanju bianyi*, by categories. [...] For those poor people living in the mountainous hinterland, if they have this book at home when they are sick, the recipes in this book can relieve their pain.
>
> 況窮鄉僻壤貧窶之家有病無醫有方無藥其不罹於夭横者几希……第取其經驗簡直易得之藥積累成編凡十六卷分門析類論證詳明目之曰山居便宜……憫貧居山僻者家置一帙 遇有病之際雖無□元振之可告緩急[65]

The first three *juan* 卷 or "volumes" of this formulary focus on various types of regionally prevalent diseases (*yibing* 疫病). Its second volume on cold-related diseases (*shanghan*) includes 5 recipes against *wenyi*, and the third volume has 45 recipes against regional diseases like malaria, dysentery and cholera. Most of these recipes consist of simple ingredients that were common in northern Fujian, which the editor intentionally collected for the convenience of the poor inhabitants living in the mountainous regions (特為山居貧困者設也).[66]

---

64 For bibliographical study on Xiong Zongli printed medical texts, see Fang Yanshou 方彥壽, "Mingdai keshujia Xiong Zongli shukao" 明代刻書家熊宗立述考, *wenxian*, no. 1 (1987): 222–227; Chen Jihua 陳繼華, "Mingdai Fujian yijia Xiong Zongli yiji bianke ji xueshu sixiang yanjiu" 明代福建醫家熊宗立醫籍編刻及學術思想研究, Fuzhou (Master thesis, Fujian University of Traditional Chinese Medicine, 2012): 11–17; Chen Xi 陳曦, "Xiong Zongli ji mingfang leizheng yishu daquan de yanjiu," 熊宗立及《名方類證醫書大全》的研究 Changchun (Master thesis, Changchun University of Chinese Medicine, 2013): 15–33.

65 Xiong Zongli 熊宗立, *Shanju bianyi fang* 山居便宜方, vol. 7, 12 vols., Haiwai huigui zhongyi shanben guji congshu 海外回歸中醫善本古籍叢書 (Beijing: renmin weisheng chubanshe, 2003): 1–186, 4.

66 Ibid., 40.

Led by Xiong Zongli, printers and physicians from Jianyang and neighbouring regions also started to produce medical treatises and formularies, especially for local rural populations affected by regionally prevalent diseases. Under the management of his son Xiong Yuan, *zhongde tang* printed at least five types of medical texts during the second half of the fifteenth century.[67] During the sixteenth century, another influential Jianyang publishing family, the Yu 余 family, became the main publishers of medical texts at Jianyang. By the end of the Wangli Era, the Ye 葉 family's publishing houses, *guangqin tang* 廣勤堂 and *zuode tang* 作德堂, had printed six types of medical texts at Jianyang.[68] Around the Wangli Era, a local physician called Huang Bingjian 黃秉鍵 (birth and death date unknown) from Pucheng 浦城 in northern Fujian compiled a collection of medical cases recorded by his father, Huang Zhi 黃至 (birth and death date unknown), who "saved a lot of people by offering medicines and herbal tea when severe and deadly infectious diseases prevailed" (歲大疫 死者載道 捐藥施茶 全活甚多).[69] In 1603, the Jianyang publishing house *jingzhao tang* 京兆堂, run by Liu Xishu 劉禧叔 (birth and death date unknown), printed the *jiuji liaopin yijian qifang* 救急療貧易簡奇方, a "simple and useful formulary for helping the poor", at the request of the district magistrate of the neighbouring Wuyuan County 婺源 in southern Jiangxi 江西. As indicated by its title, this text was also aimed at poor households, as it contained 28 simple recipes specifically on *wenyi*.[70] In the same period, another physician based in Xingzhou 信州 (present-day Shangrao City 上饒 in Jiangxi Province) in Jiangxi, Zheng Quanwang 鄭全望 (birth and death date unknown), pointed out in the preface to his *zhangnüe zhinan* 瘴瘧指南 "manual for malaria" (edited in 1609) that it was the prevalence of malarial diseases in neighbouring Fujian and Guangdong that had motivated him to compile this text to offer medical instruction on these diseases to the local population at Xingzhou.[71]

---

67 Lin, *Fujian shuyeshi jianben fazhan guijikao*, 288.

68 Xie and Lin, *Fujian gudai keshu*, 303–305.

69 Sun Erzhun 孫爾準 et al., eds., *Daoguang chongzuan Fujian tongzhi* 道光重纂福建通志, vol. 5, 15 vols., Zhongguo difangzhi jicheng shengzhiji Fujian 中國地方志集成・省志輯・福建 (Nanjing: Fenghuang chubanshe, 2011), 83.

70 Ouyang Zhi 歐陽植, *jiuji liaopin yijian qifang* 救急療貧易簡奇方, vol. 7, 12 vols., *Haiwai huigui zhongyi shanben guji congshu* 海外回歸中醫善本古籍叢書 (Beijing: Renmin weisheng chubanshe, 2003), 203–206.

71 Zheng Quanwang 鄭全望, *zhangnüe zhinan* 瘴瘧指南, vol. 1003, 1800 vols., *Xuxiu siku quanshu* 續修四庫全書 (Shanghai: Shanghai guji chubanshe, 2002), 461.

3 Perceptions and Social Norms as Reflected through Medical Texts

The medical texts produced in Ming China not only reflect contemporary medical conceptions and knowledge, they also describe the social values, worldviews, and perceptions of the body, gender and life. Past studies dealing with Chinese medical history have stressed the links between the Confucian tradition and medical practices, especially through case studies of the *ruyi* 儒醫 or "Confucian physician" in pre-modern China.[72] As a new social notion that emerged in the Song Dynasty, in Ming China the so-called *ruyi* mostly denotes individuals with medical knowledge and official titles, rather than a community with clearly defined boundaries in the legal and institutional aspects.[73] Some scholars suggest that in Ming China the Confucian physician was different from other practicing physicians, especially the so-called *shiyi* 世醫 or "hereditary physician", as the former intentionally followed Confucian traditions in order to establish their moral and intellectual authority over others.[74] However, certain case studies of the *shiyi* in the Fujian and Jiangnan 江南 regions during the Ming Dynasty show that the local *shiyi* also intentionally attempted to establish an identity for themselves as *ruyi* by participating in regional public affairs, fabricating their genealogies so as to show a Confucian ancestral background, and associating with local authorities and intellectual-cum-officials.[75] In respect to the production of medical texts, emphasizing and advocating the dominant social values in medical writings not only indicated obedience to the social order within the empire, but also showed that local medical printers and physicians adopted a practical approach to defend their professional legitimacy and social status.

---

72 For a case study of the place of the Confucian physician in pre-modern China, see Chen Yuanpeng 陳元朋, *Liang Song de shangyi renshi yu ruyi* 兩宋的尚醫人士與儒醫 (Taipei: National Taiwan University Press, 1997); also Zhu Pingyi 祝平一, "Song Ming zhiji de yishi yu ruyi" 宋明之際的醫史與儒醫, *zhongyang yanjiuyuan lishi yuyan yanjiusuo jikan* 77, no. 3 (2006), 401–443; Charlotte Furth, "The Physician as Philosopher of the Way: Zhu Zhenheng (1282–1358)," *Harvard Journal of Asiatic Studies* 66, no. 2 (2006), 423–459; Zhang Li 張莉, "Songdai ruyi yanjiu" 宋代儒醫研究, Changsha (Doctoral Thesis, Hunan University, 2008); Cheng Guobin 程國斌, "Ruyi gainian de wenhua yu zhengzhi yiyun" 儒醫概念的文化與政治意蘊, *zhongwai yixue zhexue* 12, no. 1 (2014), 39–54.

73 Zhu, "Song Ming zhiji de yishi yu ruyi."

74 Yüan-ling Chao, *Medicine and Society in Late Imperial China: A Study of Physicians in Suzhou, 1600–1850* (Peter Lang, 2009), 26.

75 Ding Chun 丁春, "Fujian gudai ruyi zhuanhuan wenti de yanjiu" 福建古代儒醫轉換問題的研究, *Fujian zhongyi xueyuan xuebao*, no. 1 (2001); Wang Min 王敏, "shiyi jiazu yu minjian yiliao: Jiangnan Heshi gean yanjiu" 世醫家族與民間醫療：江南何氏個案研究, Shanghai (Doctoral Thesis, East China Normal University, 2012).

The medical texts produced in Ming Fujian also demonstrate their producers' concerns for moral values and ethical principles. The managers of those Jianyang publishing houses that had a strong preference for printing medical texts openly declared their pursuit of moral virtues through the names of their publishing houses. For instance, the publishing house founded by Xiong Zongli and his son Xiong Yuan was called *zhongde tang* 種德堂 "house of planting the virtues", and it published at least 24 medical texts during the fifteenth century according to surviving editions.[76] Another publishing house belonging to the Xiong publishers, namely *houde tang* 厚德堂 "house of great virtue", also mainly produced medical texts during the sixteenth century, most of its surviving imprints falling under this category. The Ye family's publishing house *zuode tang* 作德堂 or "house practicing the virtues" mainly focused on medical texts as well, and it printed at least six medical tracts during the Jiajing era.[77] These names, which were closely associated with the idea of "virtues", reflect these printers' self-identification as followers, defenders and promoters of the moral virtues through their practice of good deeds, namely producing medical texts and spreading medical knowledge in order to care for the people.[78]

A lofty concept of the value of human life was established among physicians in ancient China.[79] In medical texts produced in Fujian during the Ming period, their authors frequently expressed appreciation for human life, and it almost became a regular pattern for them to emphasize their concern for human life in their prefaces and introductions to their medical tracts. However, such expressions were not simple symbolic gestures showing respect for moral values and ethical principles, as they were related to certain social

76 Xie and Lin, *Fujian gudai keshu*, 285–288; Wang and Cai, *Fujian yiji kao*.

77 Fang Yanshou 方彥壽, "Jianyang keshushi" 建陽刻書史 (Beijing: Zhongguo shehui chubanshe, 2003): 355–351; Shibue Chusai 澀江全善 and Mori Tatsuyuki 森立之, *Jingji fangguzhi* 經籍訪古志, ed. Du Zexun 杜澤遜 and Ban Longmen 班龍門, Ricang Zhongguo guji shuzhi 日藏中國古籍書志 (Shanghai: Shanghai guji chubanshe, 2014): 353; Li Hongtao 李鴻濤 and Zhang Huamin 張華敏, *Guben yiji xuluji* 古本醫籍敘錄集 (Beijing: Zhongyi guji chubanshe, 2016), 250.

78 While the local gazetteers and genealogy had relatively less detailed biographical information about those private medical printers and physicians rooted in north Fujian, the courtesy names chosen by some medical printers and physicians further suggest they might have Daoism 道家 or *Daoxue* 道學 background. The courtesy and art names adopted by Xiong Zongli is Daozong 道宗 and Daoxuan 道軒. Xiong Yuan and Xiong Anben respectively chose Guiheng 貴衡 and Daosheng 道生 as their courtesy names. Another physician rooted in north Fujian, Xu Hong, adopted Zongdao 宗道 as his courtesy name.

79 Zhaojiang Guo, "Chinese Confucian Culture and the Medical Ethical Tradition," *Journal of Medical Ethics*, no. 21 (1995), 243.

issues rooted in Ming-era Fujian society that escalated into ethical crises. One of these issues was the custom of infanticide that was prevalent in Ming-era Fujian, which attracted the concern of local physicians and intellectual–cum-officials. In Ming China, this custom was common among the lower classes in the south of the Empire, especially in Nanzhili 南直隸, Zhejiang 浙江, Jiangxi 江西 and Fujian.[80] Song Yiwang 宋儀望 (1516 to 1580), an official from Zhejiang who once served in Fujian, noted that female infanticide was prevalent in southern China in the Wangli Era.[81] In Fujian itself, this custom mainly prevailed in its mountainous regions in the north, where local families were financially unable to support additional children or afford dowries for their daughters.[82] The district magistrate of Shouning 壽寧 in northern Fujian, Feng Menglong 馮夢龍 (1574 to 1646), pointed out in his *Shouning daizhi* 壽寧待志 "an unfinished gazetteer of Shouning" that he edited in the late Ming Dynasty, that, "similar to other regions in Fujian, Shouning people also preferred sons to daughters, as they would just drown the female newborns" (閩俗重男輕女 壽寧亦然 生女則溺之).[83] The *Min shu* 閩書 "gazetteer of Min" complied in 1620 recorded that parents from Jianning in northern Fujian committed female infanticide to avoid having to pay a large dowry for their daughters in the future.[84] According to the *Fu'anxian zhi* 福安縣志 "gazetteer of Fu'an County", even the ordinary people were unwilling to keep female infants due to the unaffordable dowries they would have to find later (論婚以財 責備筐篚 鬻產妝奩 以致中人之家不敢舉女).[85] In Jianyang, the centre for printing medical texts, similar reasons also led to female infanticide among lower-class households, despite local chroniclers openly condemning the custom in the chapter about local customs in the *Wangli Jianyangxian zhi*

80 Chang Jianhua 常建華, "Mingdai niyin wenti chutan" 明代溺嬰問題初探, *Zhongguo shehui lishi pinglun*, 4 (2002), 121.

81 大江以南 甘心溺女 其殲天地之和 无父子之親 此豈細故也 Song Yiwang 宋儀望, *Huayangguan wenji xukan* 華陽館文獻續刊, vol. 116, 426 vols., Siku quanshu cunmu congshu jibu 四庫全書存目叢書集部 (Ji'nan: Qilu shushe, 1997), 492.

82 For research on dowry and female infanticide in Ming Fujian, see Ann Waltner, "Infanticide and Dowry in Ming and Early Qing China," in *Chinese Views of Childhood*, ed. Anne B. Kinney (Honolulu: University of Hawaii Press, 1995), 193–217.

83 Feng Menglong 馮夢龍, *Shouning daizhi* 壽寧待志, ed. Chen Yukui 陳煜奎 (Fuzhou: Fujian renmin chubanshe, 1983), 51.

84 姻締論財 要責無厭 貧则弃之 故其俗至于溺女 He Qiaoyuan 何喬遠, *Min shu* 閩書, vol. 204, 292 vols., siku quanshu cunmu congshu shibu 四庫全書存目叢書史部 (Ji'nan: Qilu shushe, 1997), 719.

85 Lu Yizai 陸以載, et al., eds., *Fu'anxian zhi* 福安縣志, vol. 12, 32 vols., Riben cang Zhongguo hanjian difangzhi congkan 日本藏中國罕見地方志叢刊 (Beijing: shumu wenxian chubanshe, 1990), 125.

(edited in 1601).[86] The demographic records of Jianyang reveal the unbalanced gender ratio in the area during this period, the male to female ratio of its registered population falling from 0.93 (in 1391) to 0.49 (in 1492), a low level that was maintained until the end of the Ming Dynasty (see Table 7.3). According to the *Wangli Fu'ningzhou zhi* 萬曆福寧州志 "prefectural gazetteer of Fu'ning" (printed in 1616), the male-female ratio of Fu'ning remained at a low level during the Jiajing and Wangli eras, slightly falling from 0.70 (in 1562) to 0.69 (in 1603).[87] This gazetteer also contained evidence of the abnorlality of the female population under the age of 16 (*funü xiakou* 婦女小口) in Fu'ning by 1387, as it was only 50, compared to the figure for the male population of 1,321.[88] These demographic records of the female population in Ming gazetteers were not entirely accurate, since women played a less important role than men in the imperial taxation system based on population registers.[89] However, these numbers still reflected the demographic gender imbalance in Ming-era Fujian, which was partly caused by the custom of female infanticide.

This regional phenomenon received attention from the authorities, intellectuals-cum-officials and religious groups, who condemned the custom in their legal decrees, essays and Buddhist paintings.[90] In respect of medical texts, physicians and printers promoted the ethical principle of valuing human life above the custom of infanticide. In his medical tract on treating smallpox in children, *huoyou xinfa* 活幼心法 "therapies for treating children based on personal experience" (printed in 1616), Nie Shangheng claimed that it would constitute a severe threat to society if people did not value children's lives (夫使兒童夭折　弗遂長年　豈非舉世之大患　而仁者深憂乎).[91] Wang Kentang 王肯堂 (ca. 1552 to 1638), an officer in the Fujian Provincial Admission Commission (Fujian *buzhengsi* 福建布政司), edited the four-volume *yinchan quanshu* 胤產全書 "a comprehensive formulary of pregnancy and childbirth", which was printed by the Liu family's publishing house *qiaoshan tang* 喬山堂

86 婚姻以資財为輕重　要責無厭　致使下户甘心溺女而傷骨肉之情 Wei, Tian, and Zhang, *Jianyangxian zhi*, 286.

87 Zhu and Yin, *Wangli Fu'ningzhou zhi*, 104.

88 Ibid.

89 Wang Xingya 王興亞, "Mingdai renkou tongji zhongde nükou" 明代人口統計中的女口, in *Zhongguo shehui lishi pinglun* 中國社會歷史評論, ed. Zhang Guogang 張國剛, vol. 2 (Tianjin: Tianjin guji chubanshe, 2000), 197.

90 Chen Yunü 陳玉女, "Mingdai duotai chanwang niying de shehui yinying cong sifu fojiao duotai chanwang shuiluhua tanqi" 明代墮胎、產亡、溺嬰的社會因應——從四幅佛教墮胎產亡水陸畫談起, *Chengda lishi xuebao*, no. 31 (2006), 65–112.

91 Nie Shangheng 聶尚恆, *douzhen huoyou xinfa* 痘疹活幼心法, ed. Cai Huazhu 蔡華珠 (Beijing: Zhongguo zhongyiyao chubanshe, 2016), 3.

at Jianyang in the late Wangli period.[92] Like the previous case of *qixiao yishu* printed by Yu Xiangdou under orders from the administration, its fine print quality suggests that this edition might have been an official publication, as the author was also a high-ranking local official. In the preface to this text, he claimed that "nothing is more important than nourishing a newborn and devoting attention to the health of the pregnant woman" (莫若妊婦重也).[93] Meanwhile, this tendency in contemporary society also stimulated the production and dissemination of medical knowledge on pregnancy, including both fertility treatments and methods of contraception.[94] The *shanju bianyifang* edited by Xiong Zongli even includes a recipe for changing the gender of an unborn child from female to male (轉女成男法).[95] at the end of the volume on pregnancy in this formulary, a recipe is also given for carrying out an abortion (未產因他故欲去胎方).[96] While these recipes only contained simple ingredients and even reflected popular religious beliefs in contemporary Fujian society, they still demonstrated the preferences and perceptions of their targeted readership regarding gender. Moreover, the dissemination of recipes for abortion might also have met the needs of those poor households in northern Fujian who were unable to support additional children.

4 Conclusion

The production of medical texts in Ming-era Fujian and the spread of medical knowledge were not only driven by commercial or other personal interests, but were also influenced by the external environment. In Ming-era Fujian, natural disasters like floods, typhoons and droughts, as well as pirate raids, caused many deaths in local communities, especially in northern Fujian during the second half of the Ming Dynasty. Such physical disasters caused severe outbreaks of regionally prevalent diseases in these mountainous regions, with

92 Wang Kentang 王肯堂, *Yinchan quanshu*, ed. Qian Qunying 錢群英, Zhongyi guji zhenben jicheng fukejuan 中醫古籍珍本集成・婦科卷 (Changsha: Hu'nan kexue jishu chubanshe, 2014), 8.

93 Ibid., 12.

94 Li Bozhong pointed out that medical tracts on pregnancy actually offered contraceptive methods for women in Jiangzhe region during the Ming and Qing dynasties. See Li Bozhong 李伯重, "duotai biyun yu jueyu Song Yuan Ming Qing shiqi Jiangzhe diqu de jieyu fangfa jiqi yunyong yu chuanbo" 墮胎、避孕與絕育：宋元明清時期江浙地區的節育方法及其運用與傳播, *Zhongguo xueshu*, no. 1 (2000), 71–99.

95 Xiong, *shanju bianyi fang*, 150.

96 Ibid., 155.

their unhygienic conditions and extensive rivers. Since the imperial medical system based on regional public pharmacies had become merely ceremonial by the middle and late Ming periods, local physicians played a more important role in regions struck by *wenyi*. These external environmental crises therefore also motivated local medical physicians and printers to produce medical texts on treating regionally prevalent diseases in order to satisfy the urgent need to deal with them. In addition to natural disasters, the unbalanced gender ratio and the custom of infanticide, which was commonly practised in northern Fujian, also created ethical and social problems in contemporary society, which prompted the production of medical texts on obstetrics and children's diseases. By means of these medical texts, these intellectuals-cum-official physicians advocated the moral value and ethical principle of valuing human life to defend traditional social norms, while the practical needs of birth control in Ming-era Fujian simultaneously promoted the spread of relevant medical knowledge through medical texts.

The introduction of medical texts produced in Fujian in the Ming era to Japan, the Ryukyus, Korea and Vietnam after the sixteenth century also suggests that these texts played an important role in interregional transfers of culture. The developing maritime commerce after the Zhengde period in Ming-era Fujian introduced a vast number of exotic products to Ming China, including spices, herbal plants and ivory. It is worth noting that these exotic products, such as *Anxi xiang* 安息香 "styrax", *hujiao* 胡椒 "pepper", *longnao* 龍腦 "kapur" and *xiangya* 象牙 "ivory", were commonly associated with medical recipes for trating *wenyi* in formularies and herbal encyclopedias produced in Ming-era Fujian, such as *yixue huihan* 醫學匯函 "comprehensive collection of medical tracts" and *yaoxing huiyuan* 藥性會元 "comprehensive collection of herbal medicines". These descriptions and associations suggest that in Ming China these exotic products had both high economic value and mystical perceptions attached to them. Further investigations are needed to explore the roles of these exotic imports within their contemporaneous medical and cultural contexts.

CHAPTER 8

VOC Mariners' Nautical Investigations and Hydrographical Charting of the Chinese Coast between 1647 and 1668

Cheng Weichung

1 Summary and Suspension of VOC Nautical Investigations, 1622–1647

In the age of sail, Chinese and Dutch mariners engaged with identical restrains of natural forces around the China seas. The remaining Dutch charts, sailing directions, journals and description over the coast therefore became crucial to understand those sailing manners and patterns. In this article the author try to restore a brief history of the Dutch nautical investigations and hydrographical chartings between 1647–1668 as a part of study covering the whole 17th century and all the China's coast visited by the Dutch. It is aim to serve as a guidance for readers who interested about the costal and maritime environment of the East Asian waters during this particular historical times.

The nautical explorations of the Dutch VOC (Vereenigde Oostindische Compagnie) on either side of the Taiwan Straits were usually carried out under the aegis of the governors of Taiwan because the results were to serve military and trading expeditions setting out from Taiwan. The intrusion of the VOC vessels into the Pescadores and along the coast of Fujian between 1622 and 1624 stirred up quite a lot of fear along the Chinese coast, where anxiety was already rife because a group of Chinese pirates also had aspirations to participate in the Sino-Japanese trade, whether legally or illegally. Subsequently, from time to time this triangular relationship between the Dutch, the Chinese authorities and Chinese pirates would cause a series of conflicts that interrupted the trade in Taiwan, where the VOC set up a trading-post after 1624. The VOC swung between trading with the Chinese authorities and trading with the pirates, depending on whom they judged to be the better providers of Chinese commodities at a particular moment. The Dutch East India Company's position in Taiwan had also been weakened by Japanese traders, who presented the VOC administration with a serious challenge in the Bay of Tayouan. The VOC not only levied a tax on the Japanese, it also banned them from the shores of China. It was only after a pirate-turned-navy commander, Zheng Zhilong

 | DOI:10.1163/9789004740556_010

鄭芝龍 (1604–1661), took charge of the Fujian navy and soon afterwards defeated a Dutch fleet under Hans Putmans (?–1654) in Amoy, and after the Japanese shogun started enforcing a policy of seclusion banning all Japanese traders from sailing abroad, that the Dutch felt secure and were content to receive goods shipped on Chinese junks on Taiwan. Once the trade between the Taiwan factory and China had stabilized in the 1640s, nautical explorations to chart the coast of Fujian were also gradually suspended.[1]

Most of the seafaring experiences of the Dutch mariners after 1622 were collected together and compiled into one report written by the Taiwan governor Hans Putmans in about 1636. His work is entitled "A description of the west coast of Taiwan, the coast of China, and the Pescadores, including their rivers, bays, deeps, shallow reefs, sailing courses, latitudes, and estuaries. All have been explored and discovered by particularly experienced mariners commissioned by the Honorable Governor Hans Putmans".[2] This report is about 13,500 words and 17 pages long, and it covers most of the explorations. A brief overview of the contents is given in the table below:

TABLE 8.1 Content of the 'Description of the west coast of Taiwan, the coast of China, and the Pescadores'

Folio number	Subtitle	Coverage
269–271	Coast of Taiwan	N 24 ° 10′ 22 ° 21′
271–281	Chinese coast from Wuqiu (烏坵) Island to Pinghai Bay	22 ° 22′ 25 ° 0′
281–284	Pescadore Islands	23 ° 0′ 24 ° 0′

SOURCE: COLLECTIE AANWINSTEN 119 (1866 A XII), 269–284.

1 Detailed information about earlier nautical expeditions and their results is to be found in my earlier article: Zheng Weizhong [Weichung Cheng] 鄭維中, "Helan dongyindu gongsi renyuan zai taihai lianganjian de shuiwen tance huodong (1622–1636) 荷蘭東印度公司人員在臺海兩岸的水文探測活動", in Liu Xufeng (Liu Shufeng) 劉序楓 (ed.), *Yazhou haiyujian de xinxi chuandi yu xianghu renshi* 亞洲海域間的訊息傳遞與相互認識 (Taibei: Academia Sinica RCHSS, 2018), 385–440.

2 Collectie Aanwinsten 119 (1866 A XII), 269–284.

All these descriptions were also recorded on a chart entitled "Depiction of the Coast of China, beginning from Lantau Nan'ao 南澳 Island, northward, to Shanxiazhen 山霞鎮 Bay".[3]

For security reasons, in the summer of 1640 directions containing new sailing routes were issued to all VOC skippers. For example, when sailing from Batavia bound for Taiwan, the skipper should sail along the coast of Hainan 海南 Island to the estuary of the Pearl River, at which point he should veer to the eastward when the Dangan 擔杆 Islands hoved into sight. This course would bring him to the southwest coast of Taiwan, making landfall at either Xiao Liuqiu 小琉球 Island or the Shoushan 壽山 of Gaoxiong 高雄 (then called the Promontory of Takao). Once he found himself in the seas off Taiwan, he could easily determine his course to the Bay of Tayouan. This route meant that the skipper could avoid the perils of the complex currents that swirl around the Pescadores. It would also minimize the Dutch presence on the coast of China because the nearest point to which they could sail would be located at the outer extremity of the Pearl River estuary at a distance of more than twenty kilometres. The whole Fujian coast would therefore be a closed book to him. The instructions also stipulated that, when a skipper departed from Mejima Island 女島 outside the port of Nagasaki 長崎, he should set a southwesterly course until the Baiquan 白犬, which the Dutch called the "Baboxin" or "Crocodit" Islands, were sighted. He should then turn south and sail until the coast of Taiwan appeared. He should also be able to see the mountainous landscape of the coast of Erlin 二林.[4] From this point, he should proceed with caution along the coast of Taiwan, making for the Bay of Tayouan. Taking this route, the closest point a Dutch vessel would come to the Chinese shore would be at sea near the Baiquan Islands, 23 kilometers from the coast. The instructions also stated that only in an emergency would Dutch vessels be allowed to sail to the shore near the estuary of the Jiulong 九龍 River. In short, the presence of Dutch vessels on the Chinese coast was severely reduced by the introduction of this sailing direction. Usually Dutch nautical explorations were undertaken on other types of mission, military or commercial. Since these sailing routes actually ensured that a ship would not sail within sight of Chinese on-shore lookouts, the number of nautical explorations of Chinese coastal waters declined.

From 1637 to about 1647, the VOC authorities on Taiwan focused their attention on monitoring the Taiwanese coast. It should be pointed out that the

---

3 Österreichische Nationalbibliothek, Van der Hem 41:12; *Grote Atlas van de Oost-Indische Compagnie* (VII), 190.

4 VOC 663 (5 June 1640), not foliated.

compass of the nautical explorations on Taiwan was intricately bound up with Dutch rivalry with the Spanish in Manila and around Luzon. Furthermore, the profound interest in the more distant Chinese coast, in the region of Guangdong and Guangxi, must also be viewed in the context of the VOC's struggles with the Portuguese based in Macau. When the VOC was driven out of Taiwan by the Chinese warlord Coxinga (i.e. Guoxingye 國姓爺, literally "Lord (permitted to carry) the surname of the imperial family", that is *Zheng Chenggong* 鄭成功, 1624–1662) from Amoy in 1662, in a series of counter actions, it took the opportunity to seek a new trading partner in the form of the Manchus (who had become the rulers of China). This led to several harbors near Fuzhou being surveyed between 1663 and 1668. Clearly, these attempts to strike new trade deals would have stimulated a new wave of nautical exploration.

2 Expanding Knowledge about the Guangdong and Guangxi Coast and Hainan Island

As already noted, nautical exploration usually ran in tandem with Dutch-Iberian maritime rivalry. From 1609, VOC vessels began intercepting Portuguese ships at random between Malacca, Macau and Japan. When the Japanese shogunal court (Bakufu 幕府) gradually introduced a policy of seclusion and expelled the Portuguese from Japan from 1633 onwards, the Portuguese-Japan trade withered. This setback compelled the Portuguese in Macau to change their activities to the Macau-Tonkin and Macau-Manila trade. In 1637, the VOC delegate received a warm welcome from the ruler of Tonkin and established a commercial factory there. The Taiwan authorities dispatched a junk, the *Zeelandia*, under the command of Skipper Maarten Gerritsz. de Vries. The crew was composed of 16 Dutch and 25 Chinese mariners, including two Chinese pilots (*Taijcone*), and sailed to Batavia with some complementary goods for the Coromandel Coast. Because Skipper De Vries was reluctant to carry out his mission without the opportunity of intercepting Portuguese vessels, the Taiwan authorities ordered him to sail to Tonkin from the strait between Hainan Island and the coast of China and to take orders from the merchant-in-residence, Carl Harstink (1611–1667). The junk departed in February 1639.[5] This is the earliest record to mention a nautical exploration of Qiongzhou 瓊州 Strait by the Dutch. Later, in December of the same year, Commissariat Nicolaes

5 VOC 1130, 1401–1402.

FIGURE 8.1 Chart of the northern part of the South China Sea with the Gulf of Tonkin and the South Coast of China (part)
SOURCE: NATIONAAL ARCHIEF, VEL0291; *GROTE ATLAS VAN DE OOST-INDISCHE COMPAGNIE* (VII), 84–85

Couckbacker (fl. 1627–1640) proposed a plan to intercept the Portuguese junks sailing from Macau to Tonkin as they entered or sailed out of Qiongzhou Strait. He claimed that, after the Portuguese junks passed through the strait, they would veer toward Vonden Island when Noordwachter Island hove in sight. Vonden Island was located in the eastern quadrant of the Tonkin Gulf. Thereafter the Portuguese junks would be able to reach the islands in a region so-called "Nova Maccau".[6]

The corresponding locations of the Noordwachter and Vonden Islands on a modern map are the Xieyang 斜陽 and Weizhou 潿洲 Islands. A short undated paragraph preserved separately from other sailing instructions briefly describes how to sail from Tonkin to Japan through the Qiongzhou Strait:

> If you choose to sail through the channel between Hainan and the coast of China to the East, you should pass between the southern shoal and Hainan Island according to the Chart. Otherwise you can go through the middle and the southern shoals if conditions permit. But you should know that the middle shoal has grown since 1638 because it is fine sand. After sailing out of the channel, you should follow your course to the north of the *Pulo Taijo* [Qizhou 七洲 Island] closely, and from there you set a course to the southeast, until you find the bottom at a depth of 46 fathoms. Ships sailing from Batavia will usually pass through this stretch of water because of the still unabated southeast wind, which will continue to blow here at the end of monsoon season. From here you can sail to the northern tip of Formosa.[7]

The sailing direction was written by First Mate François Jacobsz. Visscher (fl. 1623–1645) as an official reference for all other mariners. It also refers to Qiongzhou Strait as the Channel of *Mayna*, which does not seem to be a Chinese word. From the remaining archives it is hard to tell whether this route was frequently taken by the VOC's mariners. In 1651, the Taiwan authorities dispatched another expedition on a junk to re-explore the route through the strait, a precautionary measure to check whether it was still secure for the Company's vessels to use. This is a response to an earlier suggestion that VOC officials preferred the route through the strait rather than that south of Hainan

6 VOC 1131, 241–242.

7 Collectie Aanwinsten 1823 (1953I), 7–10.

when they dispatched vessels bound for Taiwan from Tonkin.[8] In the late summer of 1655, a Dutch galliot, the *Rode Vos*, was hit by typhoon in the Taiwan Strait and had to seek shelter on Hainan Island. Some of the crew were sent ashore to seek help and fresh water. On the first day they were treated well by the local Chinese, but the second day, when they anchored their boat closer to the shore, they were slaughtered. Later the surviving crew engaged with some Chinese vessels in the bay and captured one with the required provisions. Thereafter they sailed to Siam and reported to VOC personnel with their prize cargo.[9] During this interlude, the galliot might have done some nautical surveying on the southern shore of Hainan Island.

The truce between the Dutch and the Portuguese ended in 1652, at about the time the Batavian authorities obtained valuable information about Canton. This port was now under the control of the Manchus, who, it was thought, might give permission for trade with the VOC regardless of Portuguese objections. Because the VOC had engaged in indirect trade with China for three decades via Taiwan, in the summer of 1652 the Batavian authorities ordered their subordinates in Taiwan to proceed with this new initiative with the Manchus in Canton.[10] The Taiwan authorities accordingly dispatched an expedition led by Senior Merchant Frederick Schedel (fl. 1642–1658) aboard the yacht the *Bruijnvis* in January 1653 to realize their new project. They embarked in Taiwan on 20 January 1653, with an instruction to investigate the waters in the vicinity of Canton, as yet uncharted by the Dutch. At noon (presumably on 22nd) the yacht arrived in the waters near the Pedro Blanco (Daxing 大星) and sailed on further to Haarlem Bay (Pinghai Bay 平海灣). Here, the Chinese pilot they were carrying with them to navigate into the city of Canton grew reluctant to cooperate, and they had to linger in the same waters for two days (23rd–24th) until Merchant Frederick Schedel decided not to rely on the pilot any longer and began to search for the proper route using an outdated chart that the VOC had captured from the Portuguese a long time earlier, boldly sailing into the estuary of Pearl River on the 25th. They luckily reached Lamtaon Point (Namtou 南頭) at the south-easternmost corner of the Pearl River estuary. They found an anchorage north-northwest about two and a half Dutch miles from the Lema Islands (Dan'gan 擔竿 Islands). They sent the Chinese interpreter on a small boat to contact the Chinese naval post

8 NFJ 284b, 38.

9 VOC 1216, 394^{v}.

10 VOC 876, 465^{r-v}.

and soon received a very positive response, together with a new Chinese pilot, who, on the 26th, guided them up the Pearl River. About noon on the 27th they passed three larger islets on their starboard side and approached the westernmost corner of the western shore of Namtou Point. From there they found an island at distance of about one mile to the north and other island groups in the vicinity of Namtou within a range of twelve miles from north to south and four miles from east to west. On the 29th they reached an island in the middle of the river in the shape of a Mandarin's Hat (probably Lingding 零丁 Island), and soon arrived in the vicinity of *Haijtamon* (Humen 虎門). After a reception provided to them by the commander of Humen, on February 1st they set sail on the flood tide into the Bay of Humen, where the Manchu officials arranged a proper ceremony to welcome them. On the 4th they continued to sail upstream and passed through the Humen Narrows, which had a depth of thirteen fathoms but were only a great musket shot wide, and saw a tall pointed tower on a hill six Dutch miles away on the opposite northwestern shore (probably the Lianhua 蓮花 Pagoda). They remained moored in Humen Bay for a few days, after which Senior Merchant Schedel personally went to Canton and obtained a permit to sail further upstream. On February 7th before daybreak, the yacht the *Bruijnvis* again set sail upstream and passed a lighthouse (Lianhua Pagoda) that could be seen from Humen. At about eight o'clock they reached the eastern boundary of Canton city.[11] It is said that Skipper Andries Wolff (fl. around 1652) and Master's Mate Cornelis Martensz. Rob (fl. around 1652) were in command during the journey from Humen to Canton City. Therefore they might well have recorded the whole journey up the Pearl River and made hydrographical charts.[12] In his report on this expedition, Senior Merchant Frederick Schedel judged the Pearl River suitable for yachts or flute-ships with a draft of twelve to thirteen Dutch feet.[13] He recorded the reason for his assumption in his log, stating that in some places on the route upriver, the river bed near the island could be as shallow as thirteen feet.[14] Such details in sailing up and down the Pearl River might also have been drawn on the VOC charts, as the example below shows:

11 VOC 1197, 643^{v}–656^{r}.

12 VOC 1197, 643^{v}–656^{r}; VOC 1197, 630^{v}.

13 VOC 1197, 630^{v}.

14 VOC 1197, 650^{r}.

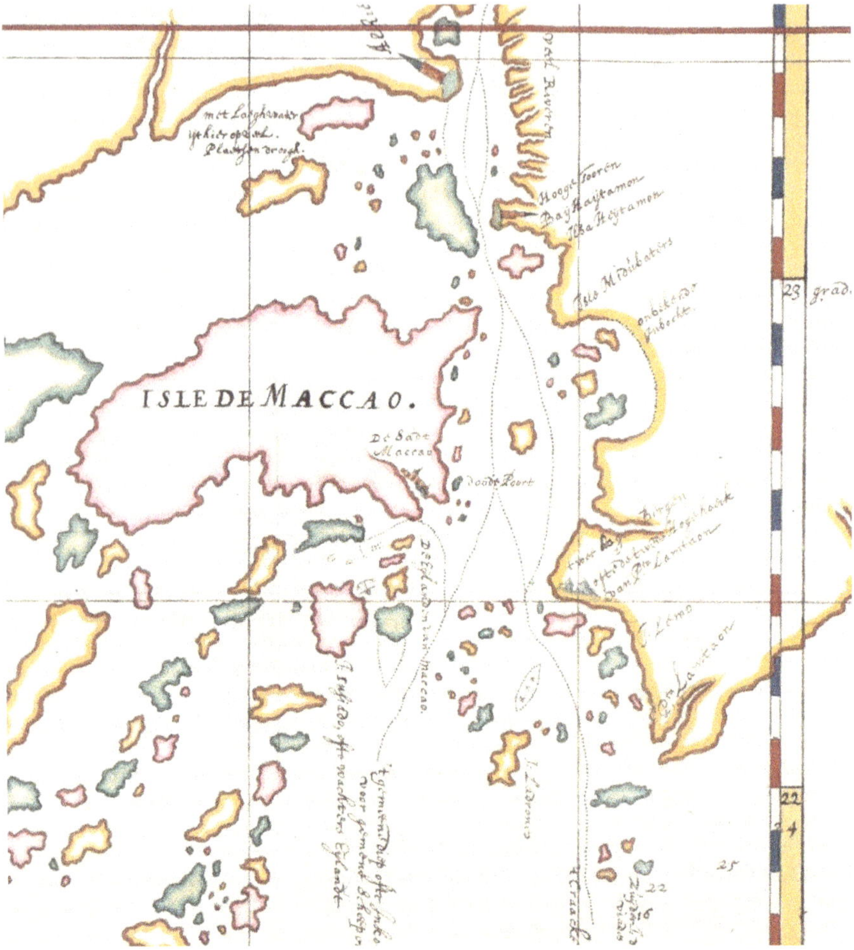

FIGURE 8.2 Chart of the mouth of the Pearl River (part)
SOURCE: ÖSTERREICHISCHE NATIONALBIBLIOTHEK, VAN DER HEM 41:18; *GROTE ATLAS VAN DE OOST-INDISCHE COMPAGNIE* (VII), 89

Senior Merchant Schedel and probably several others serving in this mission remained in Canton until March 1653 and visited it again in July of the same year. Before the party departed in December, they obtained permission for the VOC to participate in a tributary mission to the Beijing court. Hence the first Dutch tributary embassy to China, undertaken by Pieter de Goyer (fl. 1637–1662) and Jacob de Keyser (fl. 1641–1665) in 1655–1656, was organized. After they had established a formal relationship with the Qing court, thereby completing their tributary mission, De Goyer and De Keizer returned to Batavia in March 1657. However, Emperor Shunzhi's decree only allowed them to return again every eight years to pay tribute, an interval that could not be shortened.[15] This state of affairs was unsatisfactory to the Batavian authorities, and in the summer of 1657 they dispatched the yacht the *Zeeridder* to investigate whether they could still proceed with trade under the aegis of the two viceroys in Guangdong.[16] This trading venture was a success, but in the following year, 1658, the Chinese governor in Guangdong took harsh measures to prevent the Dutch from proceeding with any further trade, while the viceroys were busy extracting a generous share of the revenue from the smuggling trade.[17] Although the situation went from bad to worse, in 1659 the Batavian authorities still insisted on dispatching another two yachts to Canton to try their luck. One of the yachts, the *Geelmuyden*, perished in a gale, and only the yacht *Meliskerke* reached Humen Bay outside the estuary of the Pearl River. Unfortunately, the viceroys had earlier been amply furnished with tropical goods provided by Portuguese vessels and were not able to offer attractive prices to purchase the cargo the Dutch had brought. Therefore, the Dutch had to take the cargo further away to Taiwan.[18] Since the attempt to snatch the business from the hands of the Macanese, which had the backing of the two viceroys, had misfired, the Batavian authorities felt an urgent need to take Macau by force. In 1660 they organized an expedition of twelve ships led by Commander Johan van der Laen (fl. 1643–1667) to carry out this long-cherished plan.[19] This action also marked the termination of the VOC's earlier attempts to pursue trade in the estuary of Pearl River. As the Batavian authorities were expecting the results of the epoch-making expedition, one of their merchants resident in Tonkin, Hendrik Baron (fl. 1650–1664), reported some news about a new, hitherto unknown meeting-place on the Chinese coast called "*Lubon*", in the vicinity of the Gulf of Tonkin. His report claimed further:

---

15 For a general evaluation of this embassy, see John E. Wills Jr., *Embassies and Illusions: Dutch and Portuguese Envoys to K'ang-hsi, 1666–1687* (Cambridge, Harvard University Press, 1984), 42–44. The reader should be aware of one error on Wills' account: he states that the first pre-tributary negotiation took place in the summer of 1652, a date which should be 1653 instead. See Leonard Blussé, Margot E. van Opstall, Ts'ao Yung-ho and Wouter. E. Milde (eds.), *De Dagregisters van het Kasteel Zeelandia: Taiwan 1629–1662* ('s-Gravenhage: Nijhoff, II, 1995), vol. II, 327, note 35.

16 *Generaal Missiven* (*III*), 198; Chen Shaogang, *De VOC en Formosa, 1624–1662. Ph. D diss.* (Leiden: Leiden University, 1995), 448–452.

17 *Generaal Missiven* (*III*), 235–237; Chen Shaogang, *De VOC en Formosa*, 454–456.

18 *Generaal Missiven* (*III*), 280–281; Chen Shaogang, *De VOC en Formosa*, 468–469.

19 *Generaal Missiven* (*III*), 360–361; Chen Shaogang, *De VOC en Formosa*, 474–476. Subsequently the fleet was not able to carry out this plan because the governor of Taiwan, Frederik Coyett, insisted on holding the fleet to guard Taiwan as a precautionary measure against and expected assault by Coxinga.

> Lubon is a place located on one of the islands of Nova Macau, in the Gulf of Tonkin, at a distance of twelve Dutch miles from the Arquaron River and within the jurisdiction of Manchu rule. According to hearsay, it is where traders from the Chinese provinces of Guangxi and Yunnan and half-breed Vietnamese meet once a month with commodities like gold, musk, aniseed, raw silk and silk textiles. They carry on a very rich trade.[20]

In order to seize this new opportunity, in the summer of 1661 the Batavian authorities dispatched the yacht the *Meliskerke* to investigate this "Lubon (Longmen 龍門, hereafter written in this form)" via Tonkin.[21] The *Meliskerke* departed from her anchorage in the Red River in Tonkin, near a sand bank called Dome, on 22 June and reached the open sea in the Tonkin Gulf on 28 June.[22] Hugging the shore (of the mainland or of island groups), she sailed north-east until she reached the Tanghhongh ("Thâm Hồng 潭洪" in Vietnamese; see below) ten days later on 8 July.[23] Some details of this voyage were omitted when the report was copied into the diary of Batavia Castle, but they have been preserved in the original letter sent to Batavia from Tonkin on 13 November.[24] The details omitted from the diary of Batavia Castle will be added below when necessary, but the discussions for and against the venture will be omitted if they are irrelevant to the voyage. As mentioned already, the expedition set sail from the estuary of the Red River and set course to the north-east following the coast of Arceqaloe (also written Arcarom or Arquaron).[25] She had to drop anchor for one day on July 6th and set off again setting course for Guangxi Bay, which lay to the north-north-east. It passed over a stretch of low coast called Tinan. Towards evening on July 8th, it eventually sailed into Tanghongh Bay. The crew took two boats to land on the flat land at Vingh ("Vạn Ninh 萬寧" in Vietnamese and "Wanning" in Chinese; when the first syllable is skipped, it is pronounced "Ninh", which is similar to "Vinh") and were welcomed by the officials stationed there. Thereafter, they proceeded overland on their journey. After they had travelled five or six Dutch miles, they eventually

20 VOC 678, not foliated. 9 April 1661; *Dagh-register*, 1661, 72.

21 VOC 678, not foliated. 9 April 1661.

22 *Dagh-register*, 1661, 459.

23 *Dagh-register*, 1661, 459–460; VOC 1236, 845. In the diary there is no mention of where they sailed before the yacht reached Tanghhongh, whereas these details are given in the original letter. See the discussion that follows.

24 VOC 1236, 845.

25 VOC 678, not foliated. 9 April 1661. It is written as "Arquaron"; Kaart van de kusten van Tonkin en Zuid-China Vingboons, Johannes, Van der Hem 41:15. It was written as "Arcarom"; VOC 1236, 845. It is written as "*d'arceqelon*"

reached the Manchu residential camp at Quanteyng (probably "Quan Tái 關塞" in Vietnamese,[26] which means "camp on the border", presumably indicating the camp known as "Fangcheng 防城" in Chinese) or in a reduced form "Teyng", where they arrived on July 13th.[27] The Chinese captain (presumably the "Shoubei 守備", assistant brigade commander, thereafter commander) of Teyng instructed them to proceed further to meet his superior (presumably the "Zhizhou 知州", department magistrate) residing at "Camsiouw" ("Khâm Châu 欽州" in Vietnamese; "Qinzhou" in Chinese).[28] Because the port of Longmen fell under the jurisdiction of the department magistrate, they would have to deal with him in order to request permission to trade freely. Bookkeeper Joan Abbas (fl. around 1661) took Assistant Joan Victory (fl. around 1661) among others on this trip. They carried with them all the gifts and a letter in Chinese. Not long after they were given information by Ming loyalist pirates and realized that, although the Manchus now occupied Qinzhou, the pirates still controlled Longmen. Only if the Dutch were to take measures to chase the pirates away would the Manchus be able to engage in official trade with them in Longmen. Bearing this information in mind, they again consulted the assistant brigade commander. He advised them to head deeper into the hinterland and make contact with the governor at Limtsiouw ("Liêm Châu 廉州" in Vietnamese and Lianzhou in Chinese). Abbas lost no time in leading his team through Qinzhou, where he split it into two halves on August 1st. Joan Abbas and his party were to continue on to Lianzhou, while the other members were to return to the yacht the *Meliskerke* moored in Tanghongh Bay. Abbas arrived in Lianzhou on August 3rd and engaged in a new round of negotiations with the governor (presumably the "Bingbei dao 兵備道", military defense circuit) there.[29] His attempts failed, and he had to return to Qinzhou, where he arrived on August 11th. In the meantime, the other members of this expedition were detained in Fangcheng by the assistant brigade commander. As a result, all the members of the expedition were detained either in Qinzhou or Fangcheng. On September 3rd, the pirates launched a sudden attack on Fangcheng. Two of the expedition members were captured at the height of the raid but were later released and courteously returned on Sept 5th. The pirates retreated to Longmen on September 10th after the helmsman Thomas

26 Although Quanteyng might also be the Vietnamese Phòng Thành signifying Fangcheng (防城) instead of Quan Tái (關塞).

27 VOC 1236, 845.

28 Charles O. Hucker, *A Dictionary of Official Titles in Imperial China* (Taibei: Southern Materials Center, Inc., 1988), 157, 433.

29 Charles O. Hucker, *A Dictionary of Official Titles*, 384.

Pieterskoen (fl. around 1661) of the yacht the *Meliskerke* had sent a letter to Abbas through the pirates reporting on their situation. Once he had received the letter, Abbas quickly replied to Pieterskoen, ordering him to weigh anchor and set sail for Tonkin. While Pieterskoen was waiting for a reply, he sailed the yacht eastwards with the intention of making a hydrographical investigation. He reported that, during this expedition, he discovered Bredams Island[30] and Noorder Wachter Island. He had tried to sail further eastwards after passing Bredams Island, but bad weather prevented him from going any further. The *Meliskerke* left Tanghhongh Bay on October 1st and reached Tonkin on the 28th of the same month.[31]

This record shows that the hydrographic investigation undertaken by the Dutch mariners began in Tonkin and proceeded along the southwestern shore of Guangxi province. Unfortunately, the original journal kept by helmsman Thomas Pieterskoen can no longer be found in the VOC archives, depriving us of further details. An attempt to trace the entire voyage reveals that, from his offshore anchorage in the Red River estuary, Pieterskoen took ten days to reach Tanghhongh Bay during the south monsoon season. From July 8th to September 10th, he and his crew remained moored in Tanghhongh Bay. Thereafter they spent about three weeks (10th Sept.–1st Oct.) carrying out an exploration of the shore between Tanghhongh Bay and Longmen and then a short strip of shore eastwards until Bredams Island and Noorder Wachter Island also hove into their sight. After setting off from Tanghhongh Bay, they took about 28 days to find a route to Tonkin in the north monsoon season. It appears that this expedition can be divided into three zones. The first zone is that between the estuary of the Red River and Tanghhongh Bay; the second between Tanghhongh Bay and Longmen Bay or Nova Macau; and the third between Longmen Bay and Noorder Wachter Island. The chart later produced by the VOC's cartographers presents only the second and the third zones; the first has been totally omitted. When we examine the chart made by the VOC cartographers, for example: "*Kaart van de Kust van Quinam Tonquin en Cochin-China, van P. Cantaon tot aan Punta Lamtaon, benevens het Eyland Aynam en Isla de Pracel* (A chart of the coast of Quinam, Tonkin and Cochinchina, from Lyson Island to Cape Nantou, as well as Hainan Island and the Paracel Islands)" (see Figure 8.3) and measure the distance between the most northerly edge of the estuary of Red River and Longmen Bay or Novo Macau, we find it is about five Dutch miles (about 37 km) according to the scale. This is at odds with the modern distance of about 157 kms. In short,

30 Mentioned as 'Vonden Island' earlier in the article, see above.

31 *Dagh-register*, 1661, 464.

FIGURE 8.3 Chart of the coast of Quinam, Toncquin and Cochin-China, from the River Canton to Punta Lamtaon, the island of Aynam and Isla de Pracel (part)
SOURCE: NATIONAAL ARCHIEF, VEL0269; *GROTE ATLAS VAN DE OOST-INDISCHE COMPAGNIE* (*I*), 348.

100 km of shoreline between the two places were omitted. Meanwhile, the horizontal distance between the east shore of Longmen Bay and Bredam Island is recorded as about 25 Dutch miles (185 km), though the real distance is actually only about 35 km.

The reason why the Dutch cartographer omitted the first zone is probably because Helmsman Thomas Pieterskoen only submitted his findings for the second and third zones, without indicating any proper way of relating their positions to the Tonkin Gulf and the Leizhou 雷州 Peninsula. He was probably also heavily influenced by the *Novus Atlas Sienesis*, which was the most reliable map of China of the time and had been made by the Jesuit Martino Martini from Chinese sources. When we examine the shape of shore between Leizhou Peninsula and Longmen Bay on the map of Guangdong province (including present-day Guangxi) in the *Novus Atlas Sinensis*, there does seem to be a strong similarity to the above-mentioned chart (see Figure 8.4).

Furthermore, the map of Guangdong province locates the border between China and Vietnam (under "*Tungking Confinia*" or "*border with Tonkin*") in the middle of Longmen Bay or Novo Macau (on this map the only river flowing into the bay is called the Longmen River or "Lungmen flu."), and the border touches Longmen Bay at latitude 21 degrees 10 minutes north. According to earlier VOC mariners' bearings, the estuary of the Red River (or, more precisely, the Sông Cấm), where the Dutch vessels usually dropped anchor before sailing upstream to their factory, is also located close to 20 degrees 50 minutes north. Since Longmen Bay and the estuary of the Red River are actually separated by a not inconsiderable distance, the only logical way to situate Longmen Bay was to set it alongside the estuary of the Red River. The VOC cartographer might have made some changes by revising the information given by Martini Martino in 1655 on the basis of the findings provided by the 1661 expedition.

The third reason for the cartographer ignoring the shore between Longmen Bay and the estuary of the Red River in the VOC chart in Figure 8.3 might have been the outcome of confusing textual descriptions of the boundary between China and Vietnam around 1661. During the late Ming period, the land boundary was constantly being moved in the wake of military conflicts. Several villages even subjected themselves to both the Vietnamese and Chinese courts. In the account given by Merchant Joan Abbas, the boundary will not have been located on the shore of Longmen Bay as shown on Martini's map, as it was more likely to have been situated at the border crossing of "Quan Tái" (Fangcheng), because this is where the members of the expedition encountered Chinese Qing officials. On the other hand, Tanghhongh Bay, in which the yacht the *Meliskerke* was moored, most probably then fell under the jurisdiction of Vietnam. According to Abbas's account, in Tanghhongh Bay there were

FIGURE 8.4 Guangdong province, *Novus Atlas Sinensis* (part)
SOURCE: KONINKLIJKE BIBLIOTHEEK, ATLAS VAN DER HAGEN, 1049B13_049

some Vietnamese headmen who had subjected themselves to Manchu rule and about fifty very poor Vietnamese who were making salt there.[32]

The most probable location of "Quan Tái" is Fangcheng, as mentioned earlier. The hierarchical structure extrapolated from Joan Abbass journey shows that it was the final location at the lowest level of the Chinese administrative system. By tracing Abbas's journey on land, it becomes less difficult to identify "Limtsiouw" as "Lianzhou" and "Camsiouw" as "Qinzhou" because they were apparently the most prominent local administrative towns. From Fangcheng

32 *Dagh-register*, 1661, 464.

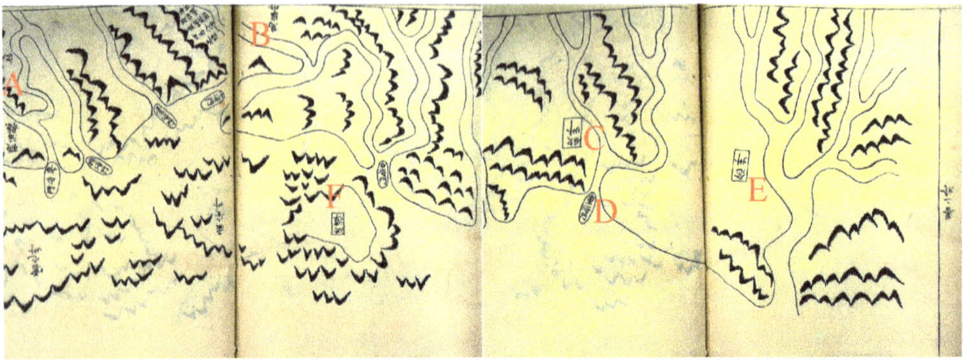

FIGURE 8.5 *Toản tập Thiên Nam tứ chí lộ đồ thư*, 51–52
SOURCE: TŌYŌ BUNKO, Y-X-2-66

to the estuary of the Red River extended a broad zone inhabited by an ethnic minority who frequently paid homage to either the Chinese or the Vietnamese court as the circumstances required.

In the local gazette written in 1637, the land boundary between the jurisdiction of Ming China at Gusendong 古森峝 and of Hậu Lê in North Vietnam was fixed at Wanning or "Vạn Ninh" in Vietnamese.[33] This boundary was drawn by Lin Xiyuan 林希元 (1481–1565) during his term in Quangxi as Zhizhou (sub-prefectural magistrate in Ming or department magistrate in Qing) of Qinzhou from 1538 to 1540 and of the military defense circuit in Lianzhou from 1540 to 1541.[34] A Vietnamese scholar, Nguyễn Văn Siêu 阮文超 (1799–1872), reports that this decision was taken in 1542.[35] This boundary was acknowledged by China and Vietnam in the first half of the eighteenth century. It remained until 1887, when a new boundary was fixed between China and France, which had then become the suzerain of Vietnam.

On a Vietnamese itinerary map, *Toản tập Thiên Nam tứ chí lộ đồ thư* (Collection of the Itinerary Maps in the South), an itinerary from the capital (today Thăng Long, Hanoi) to Qinzhou and Lianzhou was presented by way of illustration. The section on the sea route approaching the Chinese border was adopted as in Figure 8.5. The author added marks from A to F. According to

33 Zhang Guojing 張國經, Zheng Baosu 鄭抱素, *Lianzhou fuzhi* (1637), in Chen Jiang 陳強 *et al.*, *Guangdong lidai fangzhi jicheng · Lianzhoufu buyi* 廣東歷代方志集成 · 廉州府部(一) (Guangzhou: Lingnan meishu chubanshe, 2009), 37.

34 Zhang Guojing, *Lianzhou fuzhi*, 96, 102, 136.

35 Nguyễn Văn Siêu 阮文超, *Phương Đình Địa Chí Loại* 方亭地志類 (Beijing: Renmin chubanshe, 2012 [1900]), vol v, 17.

the Chinese character legends, obviously E: "Niệm Châu 念州 indicates Lianzhou; C: "Khâm Châu 欽州" indicates Qinzhou. D marks the Seagate of the Dragon, which is literally "Longmen", hence it can be taken as certain that D refers to the entrance to Longmen Bay. Mark B is "Vạn Ninh 萬寧" in Vietnamese, which is the Chinese town of Wanning. According to the report written by Nguyễn Văn Siêu cited above, Mark A indicates "Tiên An 先安" in Vietnamese and is identical to the Chinese town of Xin An 新安.[36] F is marked as "Hong Thâm" 洪潭 and cannot yet be identified. However, if we reverse the word sequence it becomes "Thâm Hong" 潭洪 and then fits the Chinese roadstead of Tanhong (Tanghhongh). A and B used to be under Chinese Ming jurisdiction but were came under the North Vietnam court after 1542, when the new boundary was drawn. In the seventeenth century the boundary must have fallen somewhere between Van Ninh in Vietnam and Fangcheng in China. In the early eighteenth century, the frontier must still have existed more or less as it was. Chen Lunjiong 陳倫炯 (fl. 1703–1742), a Qing regional commander in charge of the coastal defence around Gaozhou, Hainan Island and Lianzhou, published a detailed report on the Chinese coast in *Haiguo wenjianlu* 海國聞見錄 (Records of Coastal States), a report on foreign countries in Southwest and South Asia, around 1730. This book was an acknowledged geographical account at that time. A chart presenting the China coast and entitled *Yanhai quantu* 沿海全圖 (Complete Map of the Coastline) was appended to the report. A colourful chart stored in the library of Congress of U.S. (Figure 8.6, entitled *Coastal Map of China* (*Haijiang yangjie xingshi quantu* 海疆洋界形勢全圖) has preserved most of the information given on this chart. The author has added identical English letters to parts of the chart to demonstrate that Hong Thâm was actually located approximately in the vicinity of Tanhong village, which on this chart belongs to Vietnam.

In the red squares on Figure 8.6, the legend states "the boundary with Vietnam". The marks C, D and E are identical to C, D and E in Fig. 8.5. G is Fangcheng, the Chinese border fort and border crossing, which is not shown in Fig. 8.5, while F' clearly refers to the village of Tanhong. Because the F marked in Fig. 8.5 is situated in the border waters, the author has marked F in Fig. 8.6 on the sea beyond all three boundary marks. According to the relative positions of C and D on the boundary, it can be argued that the F (Hong Thâm water) in Fig. 8.5 must be identical with the roadstead of the village of Tanhong (F') in Fig. 8.6.

36 Nguyễn Văn Siêu, *Phương Đình Địa Chí Lo*, 18.

FIGURE 8.6 Coastal map of China (part)
SOURCE: LIBRARY OF CONGRESS, U.S. G7822.C6A5 1801. H31

Furthermore, the explanatory note about the village of Tanhong in Fig. 8.6 states that it belongs to Vietnam, which also tallies with Joan Abbas's report. Assuming the above locations have been currently identified, it is clear that the VOC cartographer who drafted it ignored the zone between Tanhong and the estuary of the Red River (i.e. the Zone 1 mentioned above). This zone was mentioned earlier as "Arceqaloe" and actually covered some of the territory claimed by both China and Vietnam; hence it showed a buffer zone, which confused the cartographers.

3 The North Coast of Fujian and the Putuoshan (普陀山) Islands 1662–1665

On the last day of April 1661, a force dispatched by Coxinga, the erstwhile partner and now competitor of the VOC based on Amoy, launched an attack on Taijouan and landed on the main island of Taiwan (Formosa). The Dutch authorities, led by Governor Frederik Coyett (1615–1687), refused to surrender the fort, so Coxinga laid siege to it for nine months before both sides negotiated a solution. The Batavian authorities heard the news around June and dispatched a rescue fleet that arrived in Taiwan at the end of August 1661, but it was a forlorn hope. The Taiwan authorities decided to foster their burgeoning friendship with the Manchus in the hope that this new ally could break the siege and repel Coxinga's force. Before this idea could be put into action, in February 1662 the Dutch authorities surrendered the fort to Coxinga and returned to Batavia with all the remaining troops, civilians and their moveable property. The Batavian authorities were shocked by this shameful failure but lost no time in realizing a plan to combine direct trade to China with joint naval campaigns with the Manchus, a solution that seemed to them the most reasonable and worthwhile investment.

On 24 June 1662, the newly appointed Admiral Balthazar Bort (1626–1684) led an armada consisting of 12 vessels (8 yachts and 4 flute-ships) from Batavia with the intention of executing this enterprise. According to Admiral Bort's report, the fleet arrived in the Dangan 擔杆 Islands (Lema Islands) in the waters near the Pearl River estuary on July 27. However, as it sailed further north seeking to make the Fujian coast, the weather suddenly turned stormy. The fleet regrouped on the 30th and captured five Chinese fishing junks off the Dangan Islands in the hope of collecting local intelligence.[37] Thereafter the fleet reached Daxing (*Pedro Blanco*) on the 31 July, the Dongshan Islands

37 VOC 1240, 1249–1251.

on 2 August and Weitou 圍頭 Cape (*De Hoek van Puthaij*) on the following day. They almost reached Yongning 永寧 Bay, where Coyett's rescuers had landed during the siege, but lingered in Weitou Bay attempting to make contact with the Manchus at either Jimmen (Quemoy) or Yongning. When this proved impossible, it was decided to sail further north. On the 3rd the fleet passed Meizhou 湄洲 Bay (*De Stormbay*) and on the 4th the most easterly extremity of the Pingtan 平潭 Island (*De hoek van Cavalles*).[38]

Unfortunately, on August 5, the fleet ran into another storm that split it into two parts: four vessels under Vice-Admiral Jan van Kampen (fl. around 1662–1663) and eight vessels under Admiral Bort. According to their original plan, the fleet should all have sailed to 27 ° 30′ north, where it had been calculated that the waters off the estuary of the Min 閩 (alias Fuzhou 福州) River were located.[39] The instruction given by the Batavian authorities had given Yongning Bay as the final destination, but the expedition failed to reach this goal. At this moment their best plan was to look for the Bay of Fuzhou instead. From there they were able reach the city of Fuzhou, where Coyett's messengers were taken to meet the Manchu officials.[40] Bort's report says that Fuzhou had been located at 27 ° 30′ north on the Company chart, so they assembled eight vessels there. However, it did not take him long to realize that this information was wrong because, on the chart made by Father Martino Martini (1614–1661), Fuzhou is correctly put at 26 ° 30′ north. The inventory of the navigational equipment carried on this expedition shows that Admiral Bort had three charts with him covering the Zhangzhou 漳州 River (*Chincheo*, Jiulong 九龍 River), Zhangzhou Bay, Langbai'ao Bay (*Lepuhou*, near Macau) and Gulei 古雷 Bay (alias *Hutoushan*, 虎頭山 *Houtauso*). The inescapable conclusion, however, was that none of them gave really precise information about the coast of Fuzhou.[41] Given that the Taiwan authorities had sent several expeditions to survey Fuzhou waters during the 1630s, this ignorance of earlier nautical knowledge is a mystery.[42] The four vessels in the other branch of the fleet, led by Vice-Admiral Jan van Kampen, gathered off Nanschuang 南礵 Island (*De Ouden Saley*) in the vicinity of 27 ° N on 5th August.[43] Van Kampen decided

38 Olfert Dapper, *Gedenkwaerdig Bedryf der Nederlandsche Oost-Indische Maetschappye, op de Kuste en in het Keizerrijk van Taising of Sina* (Amsterdam: Jabob van Meurs, 1670), 71.

39 VOC 1240, 1249–1251.

40 Olfert Dapper, *Gedenkwaerig Bedryf*, 60.

41 VOC 886, 177.

42 Zheng Weizhong [Weichung Cheng], "Helan dongyindu gongsi renyuan zai taihai lianganjian de shuiwen tance huodong (1622–1636)", 411–421.

43 Olfert Dapper, *Gedenkwaerdig Bedryf*, 72.

to moor at this anchorage for two days, and on August 8th they set sail on course for the coast of China in search of harbours or estuaries.[44]

On the 9th, they were still at a loss about their actual bearings and decided to capture a Chinese fisherman. This expedient worked, and they found themselves near Qitou (*Kitta* 崎頭) Fort, from which the estuary of the Min River (from where the city of Fuzhou lay upstream) was about six or seven Dutch miles to their south. From 5th to 9th August, under the flag of Vice-Admiral Van Kampen, the four vessels surveyed these islands and the coast of China at thirty-minute intervals from 26 ° 30′ N to 27 ° N, covering both the offshore islands and the coast of China. It is possible that the coast of Lutouwei 閭頭尾 was named "Jan van Kampen Promontory" by the Dutch mariners, thereby leaving a trace of the survey carried out by the Vice-Admiral at that time. In Van Kampen's report, he does mention that several uncharted islands were added to the chart, but he does not name them. In the evening of August 10th, this flotilla reached Qitou Bay at 26 ° 27′N.

The following morning it sailed due south, passing three different islands and naming them after their vessels: the *Naerden* (the flag ship of this expedition), the *Zierikzee* and the *Overeen*, now the Gaodeng 高登, Beigan 北竿 and Nangan 南竿 Islands. As they were sending boats to ward off enemy Chinese junks, the main fleet under Admiral Bort was spotted off the shore of China, lying at anchor outside the Min River estuary.[45] The main fleet had arrived in Dinghai 定海Bay (*Tinghaijauo*) and had launched a fierce attack on the enemy's vessels and fort on the 8th.[46] In the following three days, it sailed along the shore to destroy a walled town somewhat further to the north, called Xiao'cheng 筱埕 (*Soothia*). They ransacked the town and burned the junks so that only fishing vessels were left. After the two parts of the fleet regrouped on the 11th, on the 12th they turned about away to the estuary of the Ming River.[47] The nautical survey around Jan van Kampen Promontory is recorded on the chart appended to the journal of First Mate Michiel Gerritsz Boos (fl. 1662–1669), written in 1663 (see Figure 8.7).[48]

On the 14th, the fleet dropped anchor one Dutch mile from the Min River estuary, where the water became shallower because of underwater sandbanks. Admiral Bort dispatched messengers accompanied by a Chinese interpreter

44 Olfert Dapper, *Gedenkwaerdig Bedryf*, 72.

45 Olfert Dapper, *Gedenkwaerdig Bedryf*, 73.

46 John E. Wills Jr., *Pepper, Guns & Parleys: The Dutch East India Company and China 1662–1681* (Cambridge, Mass.: Harvard University Press, 1974), 37–38.

47 Olfert Dapper, *Gedenkwaerdig Bedryf*, 73; VOC 1240, 1252–1253.

48 Collectie Aanwinsten 112 (1866 AIV), not foliated.

FIGURE 8.7 Chart of a Part of the South-east Coast of China with Fuzhou Bay (part)
SOURCE: COLLECTIE AANWINSTEN 112(1866 AIV), NOT FOLIATED; *GROTE ATLAS VAN DE OOST-INDISCHE COMPAGNIE(VII)*, 197

and some deserters from the Manchu army into the Ming River on a barge in the hope of contacting local Manchus officials. The following day (the 15th), Vice-Admiral Van Kampen was ordered to take five Dutch vessels and six captured junks and sail into the estuary of the Min River. Although there is no record of his instructions, apparently the flotilla was sent to survey a fairway leading to an anchorage that would offer shelter from the wind from any direction.[49] It cost him about one day to survey the narrow, tortuous channel between the islands that dotted the estuary of the Min River. The whole fleet under the leadership of Van Kampen sailed to this anchorage on the 16th. As the whole fleet was negotiating the narrowest part of the passage, they encountered three Chinese vessels sent by Manchus officials to welcome them and hence missed the high tide. The yacht carrying Admiral Bort was stranded; all it could do was to wait for the next high tide to sail to the anchorage on the 17th.[50]

On the "Chart of the Harbour and Roadstead before the Min River (Fuzhou River) at Latitude 26 ° 15′ N *et cetera* (Kaart van de reede en haven voor de Hocksiuwse rivier, leggende op 26–15 N.Br. enz)", the voyage of the main fleet under Admiral Bort has been clearly recorded using different letters to mark individual spots around the estuary of the Min River. It gives a picturesque rendering of how the main fleet anchored at the anchorage beyond the fringe of the underwater sandbars and how the narrow channel twisted and turned through the sandbars and islands before reaching the more stable anchorage, as shown below.

On the right-hand side, two anchors are drawn to mark the anchorage of the whole fleet (indicated by the letters "L" and "M"). On the left-hand side, a single anchor is drawn and marked as "The Harbor of the Netherlands Fleet (*De Haven van De Nederlantse Vloot*)". Several smaller vessels marked with the letter "N" indicate the Manchu delegates who came to welcome the Dutch fleet on the 16th.[51] However, the spot at which these vessels are indicated is incorrect: the exact place at which they encountered each other was at the narrowest section of the channel among the islands in the estuary of the Min River. This is as mentioned above and is recorded as "The Channel of the Fuzhou River (*'T Chanael voor de Hocksieuwe River*)". Bort mentions that a yacht, the *Kalf*, which had arrived later, was spotted by the yachts standing guard at the outer

49 John E. Wills Jr., *Pepper, Guns & Parleys*, 31.

50 Olfert Dapper, *Gedenkwaerdig Bedryf*, 75; VOC 1240, 1253.

51 Olfert Dapper, *Gedenkwaerdig Bedryf*, 75. The prominent landmark at the entrance to this water route, Wuhu 五虎 Island, is mentioned here as "The Pyramids".

FIGURE 8.8 Roadstead and anchorage on the River of Fuzhou (part)
SOURCE: NATIONAAL ARCHIEF, VEL0283; *GROTE ATLAS VAN DE OOST-INDISCHE COMPAGNIE* (*VII*), 198–199

anchorage and was guided into the inner anchorage. I presume that by chance it had discovered a reef that lay not far from Nangan Island and was therefore named "Kalf Reef", as shown above in Fig. 8.7.[52]

The negotiations in Fuzhou between the Manchus and the Dutch reached a temporary conclusion in late October.[53] On November 8th, Vice-Admiral Van Kampen was ordered to lead a squadron to patrol further north along the Chinese shore. On the 15th, most of the fleet anchored in a bay to the south of Jan van Kampen Promontory.[54] The crews were gradually mastering the skills they needed to sail against the north monsoon by taking advantage of the ebbs and, slowly but surely, they reached the town of Sansha 三沙 (*Samzwa*) on the 25th. From there they sailed on to reach the waters at 27 ° 37′ N on the 27th.[55] The following day, they spotted Shacheng 沙埕 Bay from a distance of three Dutch miles and moored at 27 ° 39′ N. Vice-Admiral Van Kampen left four vessels of his flotilla anchored at a nearby island and sailed into the estuary with two yachts. Battling heavy contrary winds, on December 1st it was eventually decided to turn about to the south, and not long afterwards they arrived in Qitou or Beijia 北茭 (*Pakka*) Bay on the 11th of December to rejoin with the fleet commanded by Admiral Bort.[56] After this reconnaissance mission came to an end and the Dinghai and Qitou Forts were firmly under the control of the troops led by Admiral Bort, the whole fleet was determined to attack the city of Sacheng, in which Coxinga's people were actively engaging in trade. On the 15th the whole fleet under Admiral Bort returned to where Van Kampen stopped earlier at 27 ° 35′ N, outside Sacheng Bay. The following day, the 16th, the fleet sailed into the bay as far as the outskirts of the city of Sacheng, where it soon engaged in a battle with the garrison troops and inhabitants. On the 17th, after successfully taking the city, the Dutch troops took away all the plundered goods and dispatched one yacht and two flute-ships to sail upstream to give chase to the Chinese junks, which had made themselves scarce during the battle. They returned to the fleet in the evening with captured junks both large and small. On the 18th, Van Kampen took command of a barge to sail upstream again to collect missing soldiers, penetrating as far as the section from which they were not able to navigate any further. The whole action ended on the 22nd. Before Admiral Bort left Sacheng, he ordered Vice-Admiral Van Kampen to continue patrolling against Coxinga's trading junks in this area until the

52 VOC 1240, 1253.

53 John E. Wills Jr, *Pepper, Guns & Parleys*, 40–45.

54 Olfert Dapper, *Gedenkwaerdig Bedryf*, 105.

55 Olfert Dapper, *Gedenkwaerdig Bedryf*, 109.

56 Olfert Dapper, *Gedenkwaerdig Bedryf*, 110–111; John E. Wills Jr., *Pepper, Guns & Parleys*, 45–46.

middle of January 1663.[57] Meanwhile, Bort took the looted goods and some of the captured vessels to the Dinghai and Fuzhou Harbour. Before and after the attack on Shacheng, Van Kampen must have proceeded with repeated nautical investigations. The results can be seen on certain charts like that shown below.

Detailed descriptions of the coast from Jan van Kampen Promontory to the Bay or Estuary of Sacheng have survived in an document entitled "A description of the coast of China from Jan van Kampen Promontory at 26 ° 38′N to the Putoushan Islands at 30 ° 8′–10′N, explored and described by order of Commissariat Constantin Nobel (*Beschrijvinge van China beginnende Van Jan Campenshoek leggende op de N: B-te van 26en g-r 38 mt; tot aan t Papen eijland bij de Chineesen gen-t Houtao en legt op de N B-te van 30 gr-d 8 a 10 mt.ter ordre van de heer Commissaris Constantio Nobel bezeijlt en beschreeven*)" (hereafter "The Description of China's Coast by Nobel").[58] This document consists of sixteen pages in total, the first five of which record the sailing instructions and the profile of this coastal strip. Although this document only achieved its final form after it had been synthesized with the explorations from 1662 to 1665, there is no doubt that the principal initiative for this exploration was that taken by Jan van Kampen. For example, the sailing instructions for sailing into Shacheng Bay, as shown on the chart below (see Figure 8.9), are recorded in this description as follows:

> There are two steep Islands, that we named 'the Lion (de Leeuw) Islands (Deyushan at present)'. There is a small islet just off their eastern point, at a distance of five cannon shots.
>
> … On the northern side of the Lion Islands one comes across another islet. Sailing close to it, it displays a sharply accentuated form along its ridge, scattered with nasty rocks. These rocks lie very close to the shore. One likewise finds a string of broken islands at a distance of one and a half Dutch miles to the east-northeast of the Lion Islands. They are called 'The Thousand Legs (De Duijsende Beenen)' or 'The Thither Islands' (De Derwaarts eijlanden, Taishan 台山 Island, at present). If you want to sail around 'The Thither Islands', you should be on the look-out, because a rock lies to the north of these islands within the compass points between NNW and SSE for one and a half Dutch miles. It is exposed after half-ebb.
>
> ….

57 Olfert Dapper, *Gedenkwaerdig Bedryf*, 112–116; John E. Wills Jr., *Pepper, Guns & Parleys*, 46–48; VOC 1243, 85.

58 Collectie Aanwinsten 553 (1891 19g), not foliated.

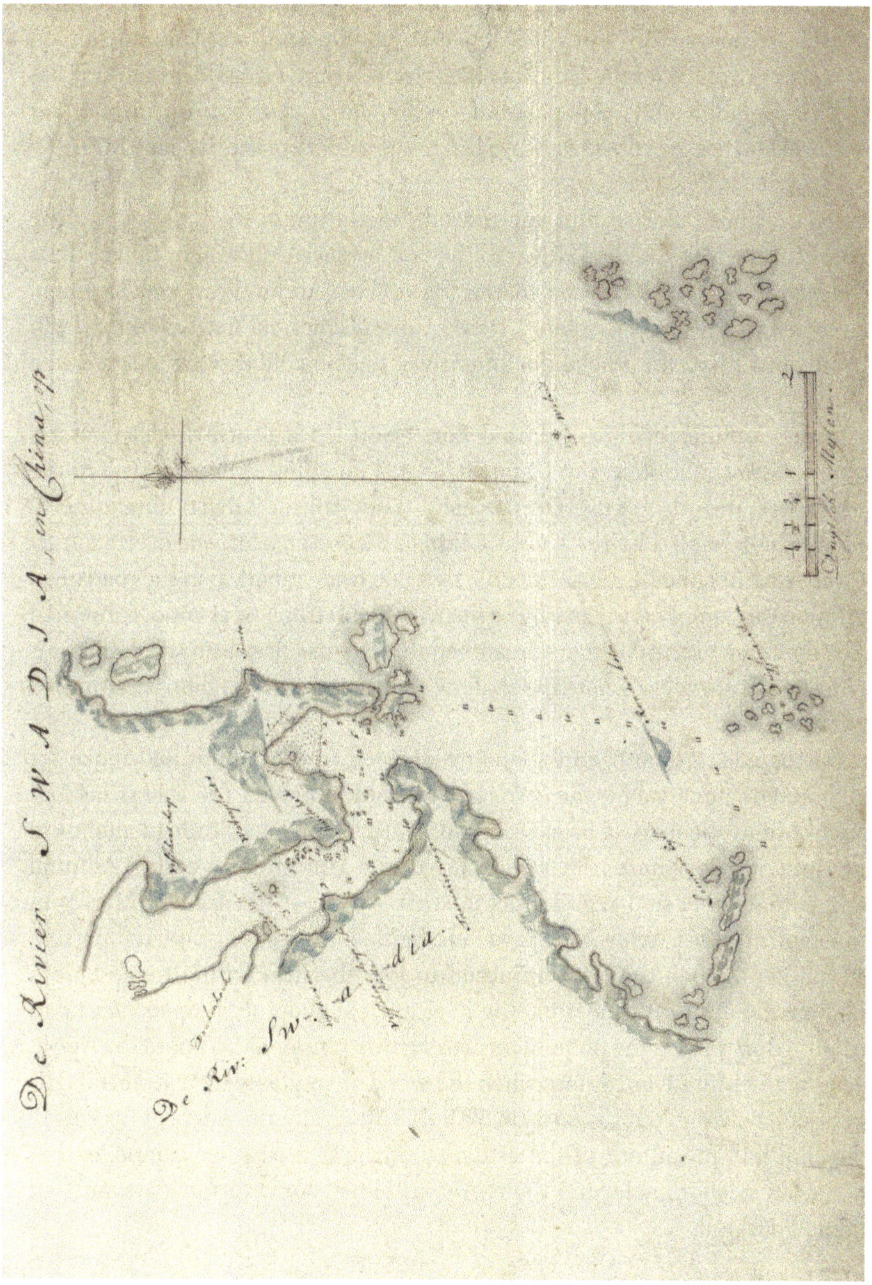

FIGURE 8.9 The River Swadia in China (part)
SOURCE: NATIONAAL ARCHIEF, VEL0279; *GROTE ATLAS VAN DE OOST-INDISCHE COMPAGNIE (I)*, 366

> Keeping the Thousand Legs Islands to your starboard, steer north and, reaching the depth of 8 or 9 fathoms, you find a fairly round-shaped islet to the NW of the Thousand Legs Islands that is called 'The Round Islet (De Ronde Holm)'. Sail past the Round Islet to your port or starboard at will and set the course to N by 1/2 E to the estuary of the Sacheng River.[59]

The author has failed to find any coastal description of the area around the estuary of the Min (Fuzhou) River in the VOC archives. Although similar kinds of descriptions can be found in the log of Vice-Admiral Jan van Kampen, published in the "De Tweede en Derde Gesandschap na het Keyserryck van Taysing of China", no official document was specifically written to serve as a pilot or rutter.[60]

In the summer of 1663, Admiral Bort again led a fleet of twelve vessels from Batavia to the shores of China. It set sail on 20th July and arrived in the Pescadores on 19th August. On the 22nd it set sail for Taiwan, intending to engage the force led by the son of Coxinga. However, as it was overtaken by stormy weather, the fleet was not able to reach its destination in the roadstead of Taijouan. Complicating matters even more, the strong west wind, combined with the force of the current, threatened to drive the fleet into the dangerous strip of coastal waters, where the shallow waters and reefs might have stranded it entirely.

On the 26th Admiral Bort therefore decided to turn about and make for Fuzhou. Only one yacht, the *Zierikzee*, was able to reach the waters off Taijouan, where she made a brief reconnaissance.[61] The fleet dropped anchor in the Netherlander's harbor in the estuary of the Min River on 29th.[62] Admiral Bort immediately sent messengers upstream by boat to summon Merchant Constantin Nobel, who had been left behind there as a contact person. On 3rd September, the latter returned to join the fleet with a request from the Manchu authorities inviting the fleet to Quanzhou 泉州 (*Soanchieu*) Bay. Admiral Bort was on the point of answering this summons on board the *Noortboom* in the Min River Estuary when the weather suddenly turned stormy. His first priority was to put his mission on hold and ensure the safety of his vessel. The ship had to sail out of the estuary, but the bad weather compelled her to cut her anchor cable, and the crew was blown some distance towards an unknown island.

59 Collectie Aanwinsten 553 (1891 19g), not foliated.
60 Olfert Dapper, *Gedenkwaerdig Bedryf*, 74–75.
61 *Dagh-register*, 1663, 602.
62 *Dagh-register*, 1663, 611. On the same day, two yachts were sent to attack any Coxinga vessels that might be lingering around Dinghai. VOC 1244, 2392–2393.

Admiral Bort's first thoughts were to find a sheltered place to drop anchor again until the storm had blown itself out. However, when they approached the shore of this unknown island, it was found to be strewn with rocks and blind reefs and was therefore avoided. He had to sail further driven by the force of the wind. Therefore, the ship passed close to the entrances to two very narrow channels and sailed into a bay that the Dutch had never before visited.

When Admiral Bort approached the two channels, he consulted the Chinese pilot (*taycon*) onboard. The latter replied that the island of Haitan (*Heytan*, present Pingtan 平潭) was located at this point. The Chinese pilot also pointed out that the bottom in the bay (now Haitan 海壇 Strait) was deep enough to take the deep-draft ship. Eventually, they found an anchorage at a depth of twelve Dutch fathoms behind the western promontory of the island. Admiral Bort stayed here for two days and set sail again on the 9th, heading south past various small islands and reaching the southern entrance of this bay on the 10th. The ship the *Noortboom* ran aground and had to be hauled off the sandy bottom three times. In order to sound the channel in the southern entrance, they launched a ship's boat. The results show that only two places were deep enough to allow safe passage, so the Admiral chose the westernmost course and navigated the ship through it. When he endeavored to set course towards the south, the contrary monsoon checked their progress. Admiral Bort had to give up his plan, and he headed back to the northern entrance again on the 11th. In the evening they stopped at the first suitable anchorage they found behind the promontory and stayed there overnight.

Meanwhile, Admiral Bort dispatched a sloop to the estuary of the Min River to summon the rest of the fleet to join him at this anchorage. Five vessels responded and arrived at the place on the 16th.[63] Another two yachts answered his summons but were not able to find the northern entrance to Haitan Strait and therefore sailed to the eastern shore of Pingtan Island. The yacht the *Mars* hit a blind reef off Rugged (*ruijge*) Island (present Niushan 牛山 Island) and had to be pulled on to a beach to be careened.[64] Thereafter, in charge of seven vessels, Admiral Bort set sail and attempted to pass through the southern entrance again on the 23rd. This time two boats were launched on either side of his ship to sound the sea bottom. After dropping anchor near a possible channel, he sent out three boats to make a more precise survey and make sure the fleet could pass safely.[65] Rear Admiral Bartholomeus Verwey (fl. 1664–1667) led the remaining eight vessels to join Admiral Bort in Haitan Strait on the 3rd of October, when repairs to the yacht the *Mars* were scheduled to have

63 *Dagh-register*, 1663, 614–615.

64 *Dagh-register*, 1663, 615.

65 *Dagh-register*, 1663, 616–617.

been completed.[66] This accidental voyage of the VOC vessels along the western and the eastern sides of Pingtan Island produced some nautical survey results that are shown on the chart below:

FIGURE 8.10 The Islands of Haytan on the coast of China, at 25 1/2 degrees North (part)
SOURCE: NATIONAAL ARCHIEF, VEL0279; *GROTE ATLAS VAN DE OOST-INDISCHE COMPAGNIE*(*I*), 366

On the chart, the unnamed places have been given names that tally quite significantly with the known course of this voyage. The northern entrance, the Zhongmen 鐘門 Channel, is marked as "Noortboom's Entrance (*Norteboons ingang*)". The first anchorage off the first western promontory of the island, Shipaiyang 石牌洋, is called "Bort's Harbor (*Borts haven*)", being where the yacht the *Noortboom* found shelter during the initial storm. On the southeastern side of the island, Aodi 澳底 Bay is marked as the Bay of the Careening of the *Mars* (*Baij de Behoude Mars*)", referring to the repair of the yacht the *Mars*.

A first mate on board the yacht the *Naerden*, Michiel Gerritsz. Boos, recorded in his logbook that this bay was given this name on 19 September 1663.[67] The

66 *Dagh-register*, 1663, 618.
67 Collectie Aanwinsten 112 (1866 AIV), 35^{v}.

anchorage next to it, now Haitan Bay, is marked "Verweyts Bight (*Verweijts Bocht*)". Apparently, it refers to the location at which the eight vessels under Rear-Admiral Verwey waited for the yacht the *Mars* to be repaired. The entire fleet of fifteen vessels joined up and sailed from the southern entrance of Haitan Strait, setting a course for the estuary of the Quanzhou River, its original destination one month earlier. They arrived there in the evening of 7th October.[68]

The formal reception and the negotiations to confirm the new alliance were held on land from the 13th to the 22nd when the official agreement was signed by both sides.[69] On the 20th, Admiral Bort gave Rear-Admiral Verwey orders to proceed with the nautical survey of Quanzhou Bay in order to record a precise chart.[70] The only surviving chart is that appended to the logbook or ship's journal of First Mate Michiel Gerritsz. Boos on board the yacht the *Naerden*; this is shown below.

The entry in First Mate Boos's logbook, for 7th October, can be taken as an important reference to this chart:

> This morning we sailed along the shore with our fifteen ships. We sailed all the way with the water at a depth of fifteen fathoms. The wind first blew north-northeast, then shifted to southwest, and we sailed with fine visibility. We sailed along the shore and saw Cape Chongwu 崇武 (*Soumbou*), with its high mountain on a promontory stretching out from the land into sea for about half a Dutch mile. .... We hugged the shore and saw the city of Chongwu. When we sailed into the Quanzhou 泉州 (*Sanseeou*) River, we saw a great tower. In the evening we dropped anchor in the Quanzhou River. When we sailed into the harbour, we kept the somewhat larger island to starboard and the rocks to port. The passage in between has a depth of eleven to thirteen fathoms.[71]

The chart in Figure 8.11 also indicates two anchorages. On the eastern side, the anchorage is located near to the city of Chongwu. Another anchorage is marked in the middle of the chart. Depicted to its southwest is a tall tower. This structure, the Liusheng 六勝 Tower, was built in 1111 as a lighthouse. Along the passage from the first anchorage to the second, a fairway is clearly marked between a small island, Dazhu 大墜, and the rocks opposite it, perfectly matching the description above. A scene of Bort's fleet moored at the anchorage

68 *Dagh-register*, 1663, 618.

69 *Dagh-register*, 1663, 625.

70 VOC 1244, 2470–2471.

71 Collectie Aanwinsten 112 (1866 AIV), 37ʳ.

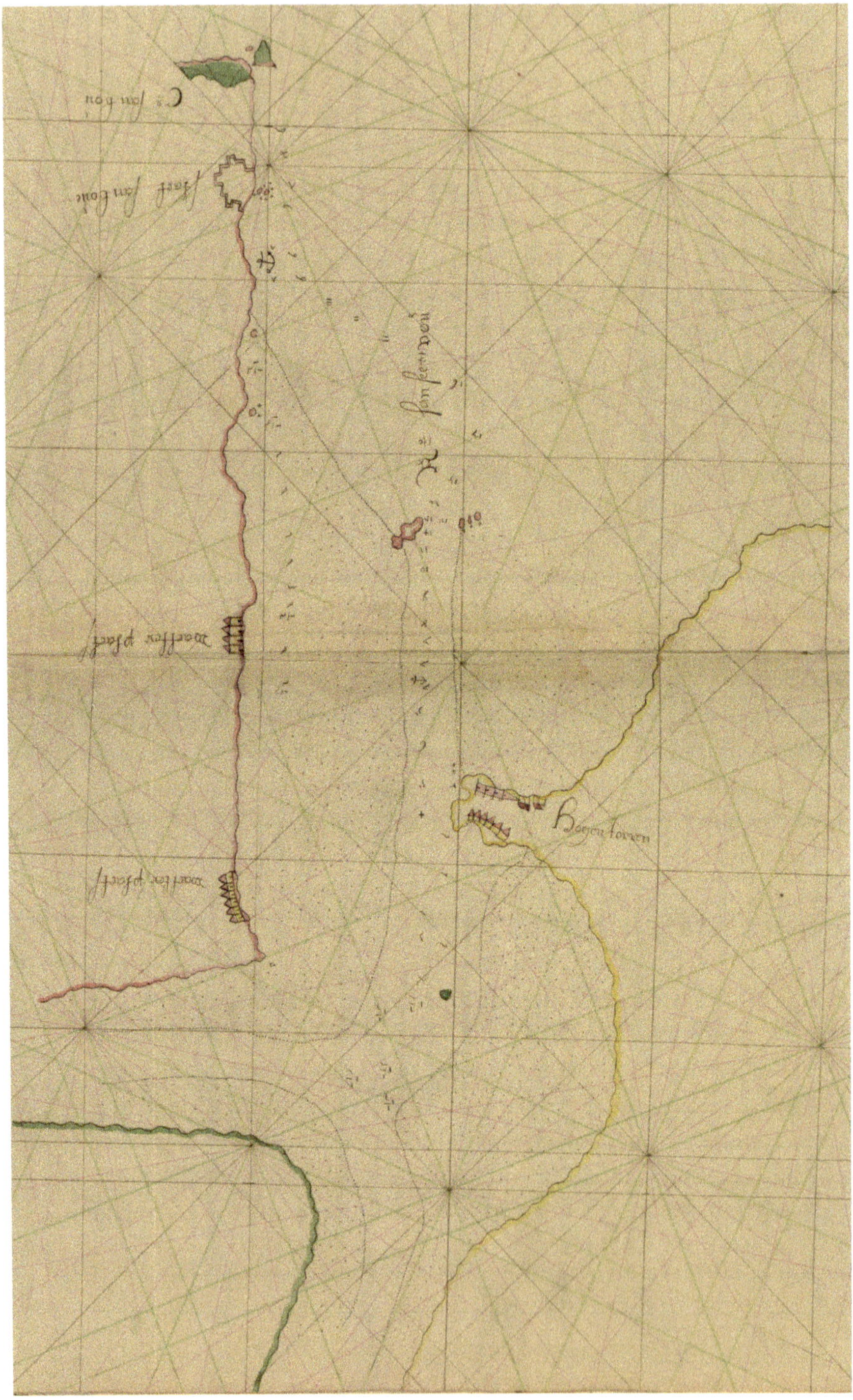

FIGURE 8.11 Chart of Quanzhou Bay
SOURCE: COLLECTIE AANWINSTEN 112 (1866 AIV), NOT FOLIATED; *GROTE ATLAS VAN DE OOST-INDISCHE COMPAGNIE (VII)*, 198–199.

within the estuary of Quanzhou River, the present-day Bay of Quanzhou, can be found in a metrical tale praising Bort's glorious expeditions such as:

FIGURE 8.12 The Bay of Quanzhou
SOURCE: MATTHIJS CRAMER, *BORTS VOYAGIE NAER DE KUSTE VAN CHINA EN FORMOSA* (AMSTERDAM: PIETER DIRCKSZ, 1670), 60

In this picture, the fleet has passed the small island and the rocks to a secure anchorage. The Liusheng Tower is centre left.

As mentioned in the introduction to this chapter, the coast of China was first described by the governor of Taiwan, Hans Putmans, around 1636. In the instructions issued to Admiral Bort by the Batavian authorities on 28 June 1663, it was recommended that Gulangyu 鼓浪嶼, to the west of Amoy (present-day Xiamen), would be the best candidate for a station if they succeeded in driving Coxinga's force away from there, providing the information given by the former governor of Taiwan, Hans Putmans, was correct. The said "description by Putmans" must refer to the coastal description written by Governor Hans Putmans and submitted to the Company in 1636.[72] In t Admiral Bort's diary for

72 VOC 887, 177.

7th October, some records that tally well with those of First Mate Boos can be found, describing how the fleet was piloted to the anchorage in Quanzhou Bay. Having successfully concluded this exploit, Bort refers to Putmans' "description" and comments: "This river and the whole strip of coastline agrees with the description made in 1633 that was handed over to the officials of this fleet as part of their sailing orders."[73] Although he mistakenly dated the document to the year 1633, this line undoubtedly refers to the coastal description compiled and written by Putmans in 1636. The said description records the coast from Wuqio Island to Daxing (Pedro Blanco) in detail. Therefore, after the fleet set off from the southern entrance to Haitan Strait, it soon entered more familiar waters.

Therefore, although most of the crucial events in this expedition occurred in the waters of Zhangzhou Bay, the Taiwan Strait and off the southwestern coast of Taiwan during November and December, the nautical survey of this zone was more a revision of earlier information than a new exploration.[74] These revisions will not be discussed here unless they alter already established facts based on earlier surveys.

On 27 February 1663, Admiral Bort led ten vessels south to Batavia. The other four vessels were to follow after escorting some Manchu soldiers to the Chinese coast.[75] In the summer of 1664, the Batavian authorities dispatched a fleet not to try to recover Taiwan from Coxinga but to occupy Jilong 雞籠, which it was felt might be a useful auxiliary port for the trade in Fuzhou. Although confrontation was not their first priority, they also ordered the patrol to guard the China coast from Coxinga's junks. In the instructions given to Commander Bort by the Batavian authorities, he was ordered to "send 4, 5 or 6 best operated light vessels to patrol around the cape of Songmen 松門 at 28 ° 26′ north during the north monsoon season, their objective being to engage all the Chinese junks from Japan that would be at their most vulnerable there."[76]

On the voyage north, when the whole fleet was anchored off Pulau Tioman, Commander Bort gave each individual vessel her respective orders. Accompanying this order, he distributed an "old description, made by experienced mariners, with confirmed latitude, that also shows all the bays, harbours, islands, rocks, reefs, rivers, shallows, sandbars, depths, from Daxing Island to the island of Wuchiu", that is, the description written by Putmans in 1636. In addition they were also issued with a route "further to Niushan Island from

73 VOC 1244, 2449.

74 A general overview of Dutch activities in the waters of Southeast China during this period from diplomatic and military perspectives can be found in John E. Wills Jr., *Pepper, Guns & Parleys*.

75 Olfert Dapper, *Gedenkwaerdig Bedryf*, 390–391.

76 VOC 888, 220; *Dagh-register*, 1664, 246, 262.

a different description" and "new charts made by Commander Bort in the year 1662 and last year (1663), according to the exploration of the said coastal strip, and especially of the cultivated and inhabited Pingtan Island, further to Fuzhou and Qitou, lying between 26 ° 2′ to 30 ° N". Finally, a description and a new chart covering the region of Shacheng at 27 ° 50′ N was also appended.[77] There is thus irrefutable evidence that the materials gleaned from new nautical investigations had already been synthesized by the summer of 1664. However, as up to that time the expeditions had only reached a short distance to the north of Shacheng Bay, the mariners who would be carrying out patrols around Cape Songmen would also have to proceed with their own nautical explorations.

The patrol was planned to be conducted during the northern monsoon season, usually after November. Therefore, after he set sail from Jilong to China on 27th September, Commander Bort left two yachts, the *Rammekens* and the *Overeen*, in Jilong.[78]According to the orders Bort gave to the first mates of these two yachts, they were to commence this patrol again in early May (1665) if the commander of Jilong considered it advisable. When they parted with the main fleet in Jilong in the late summer of 1664, they each carried sixty mariners and provisions for 15 months.[79] The author has failed to pinpoint the exact period of this expedition. When the *Rammekens* returned to Batavia from the China coast, it carried three different letters signed at different places on different dates. The earliest was dated Jilong February 25th, the second the Jiulong River, October 20.[80] The inference seems to be that they carried out this mission after 25 February and returned to the Min River estuary before the monsoon changed in June. In a letter of 27 June to *Commissariat* Constantin Nobel, the commander of Jilong, Harman de Bitter, wrote that a small hooker had been sent to summon the two yachts from the north. This remark implies they were due to return at the end of June.[81] A short paragraph recorded in the diary of Batavia Castle reveals their work during this expedition:

> Said yachts, the *Rammekens* and the *Overveen*, did not achieve any success in their mission. Those in charge said that they had reached 30 ° N on an island they called the Priests' (*Papen*) Island (now Poutoushan Island) because lots of priests [actually Buddhist monks] were living there. They had been able to take on plenty of provisions of rice and cattle there. They sailed into the Sacheng River and explored there, finding a lot of

77 VOC 1253, 2185–2186.
78 *Dagh-register*, 1664, 515.
79 VOC 1253, 2199.
80 *Dagh-register*, 1665, 386.
81 VOC 1254, 844.

> roof tiles and brickwork in the ruins. On the basis of this intelligence, Merchant Nobel dispatched the yacht the *Overveen* to Shacheng and the hooker the *Poelsnip* to the Priests' Islands in order to fetch some building materials and live cattle for Jilong. They successfully loaded the building materials but failed to obtain cattle because all the priests went to hide in the mountains.[82]

How the results this expedition contributed to nautical exploration is shown on the chart below (Figure 8.13):

FIGURE 8.13 Overveens Islands, China, at 30 degrees north (part)
SOURCE: NATIONAAL ARCHIEF, VEL0279; *GROTE ATLAS VAN DE OOST-INDISCHE COMPAGNIE*(*I*), 366

82 *Dagh-register*, 1665, 388.

A very detailed coastal description is included in the above-mentioned "Description of China's Coast by Nobel", pp. 6 to 11. The following seven pages describe the coast from Poutoushan to Cape Songmen. On page 5, a Chinese pilot is mentioned as being onboard with the team who made a hydrographical survey of the Sacheng River in 1665.[83] This confirms my supposition that most of the information was actually obtained from the expeditions of late spring 1665. On page 8, a description of the sea route to Poutoushan tallies with the chart above:

> From the Jiushan 九山 Islands (*Hooijberg*) to the Poutoushan Islands, the course lies in the direction of north-northeast by half east. This course leads you to Beitingshan 北亭山 Island (*Vogel Eijland*). If you keep this Island to the north-northeast for three Dutch miles, you should be very cautious because there is a blind reef east by north of Zhujiajian 朱家尖 Island, between it and Beitingshan Island, in the middle of the fairway. It protrudes from the water after the half ebb. The depths of the course from the Jiushan to the Beitingshan Island are 15, 14, 16 and 10 fathoms, hard ground. I have called this blind reef 'The Seal' (*de Zeerob*) on the new chart.

Merchant Constantin Nobel (fl. 1650–1678) obtained news that a city called "Mimpo" (now Ningpo 寧波, situated further north) was engaged in the Sino-Japan trade and therefore dispatched the yacht the *Rammekens* to do a reconnaissance. Unfortunately, she failed to reach it. The crews of the *Rammekens* and the *Overveen* caused trouble with the local inhabitants in Zhejiang, and the Manchu governor filed a complaint with the Fujian authorities. They later required the VOC to halt the patrol and hence brought any further nautical explorations to a halt.[84] In the "Description of the route to Poutoushan Island", there is a table marking the latitudes of the locations they surveyed (see Table 8.2, below):

TABLE 8.2 The partial content of the "Description of China's Coast by Nobel"

Placename today	Placename on Dutch chart	North latitude
The coast of Lutouwei	Van Campen Hoek	26° 35′
Sacheng Harbor	De Rivier Swadia	27° 16′
Nanji 南麂 Island	Den Oliphant/Namqum	27° 38′
Shitang 石塘 Peninsula	Cabo Zomber	28° 35′

83 Collectie Aanwinsten 553 (1891 19g), 5.

84 *Dagh-register*, 1665, 388.

TABLE 8.2 the partial content of the "Description of China's Coast by Nobel" (*cont.*)

Placename today	Placename on Dutch chart	North latitude
Yushan 漁山 Islands	Thaijhoeke	28 ° 50′
Jiushan Islands	De Hooijberg	29 ° 27′
Dongting 東亭 Island	T' eijland Ter Goes	29 ° 50′
Nantian 南田 Island	D' Avarel Hoeck	29 ° (7′?)
Poutoushan Island	De Hoek van t Papen Eijland/Poutao	30 ° 10′

SOURCE: COLLECTIE AANWINSTEN 553 (1891 19G), 8V, AS IN FOOTNOTE 56.

A Dutch chart (Figure 8.14), "Chart of a Part of the Southeast Coast of China from the Island of Haitan to the Zhoushan Islands", preserved in the National Library of France, covers all the places mentioned in"The Description of China's Coast by Nobel" mentioned above. Furthermore, the waters near the Fuzhou Estuary, Pingtan Island and northern Taiwan, which were surveyed during the 1662 and 1663 expeditions, are all noted on the chart. Hence this document is a record of the accumulated results of all the hydrographical surveys carried out by the VOC mariners from 1662 to 1665.

4 Conclusion

In 1668, the VOC troops blew up their fort and withdrew from Taiwan because the trade did not look promising enough to justify further actions in Fujian waters: their negotiations with the Manchu (Qing) court did not give them any more liberty than the privilege of being tributary delegates every eight years.[85] The desire to explore the Chinese coast certainly continued, but it had to be put on hold until the 1670s, when the regents of the southern provinces rebelled against the Manchus and invited the Dutch to frequent Chinese ports again.[86] As mentioned above, about 1636, Governor Hans Putmans submitted a detailed description of some of the Chinese coast. The expeditions from 1662 to 1665 allowed the VOC mariners not only to test and complement the descriptions submitted by Putmans, it also enabled them to add new materials

85 John E. Wills Jr., *Pepper, Guns & Parleys*, 138–149.
86 John E. Wills Jr., *Pepper, Guns & Parleys*, 154.

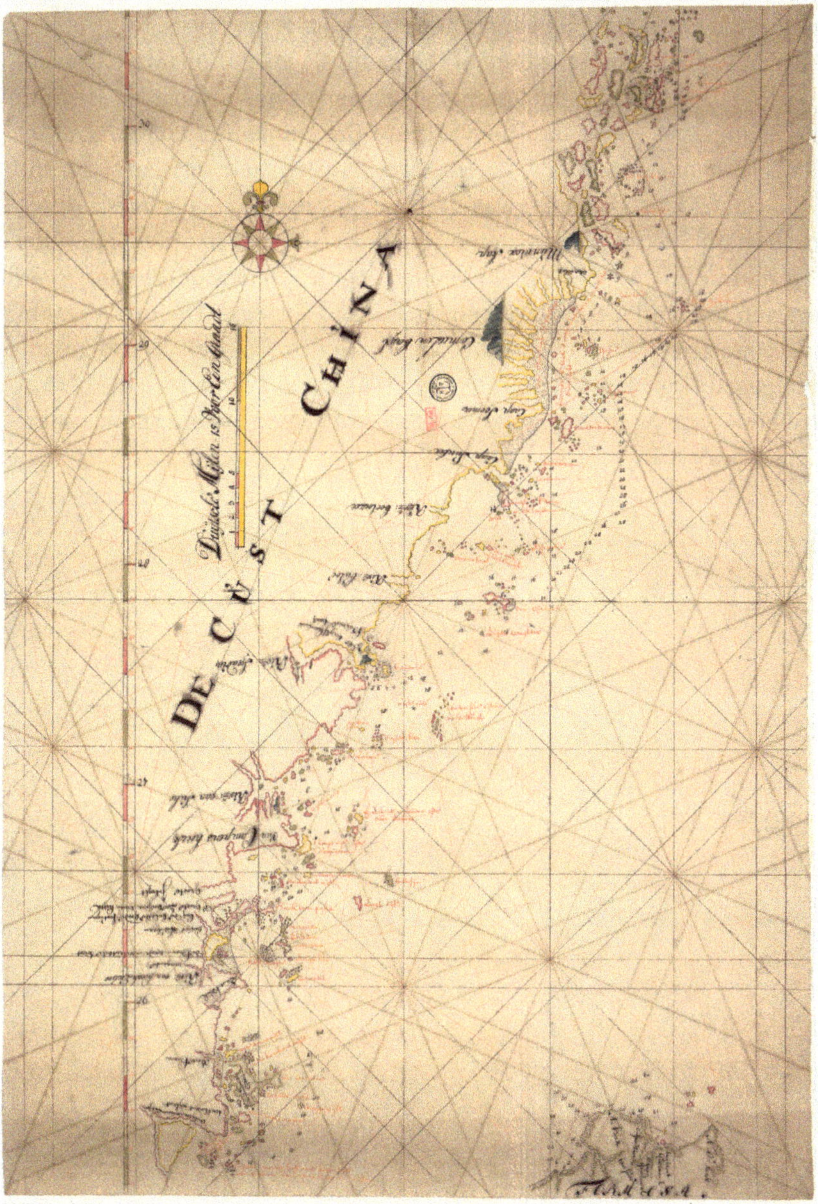

FIGURE 8.14 Chart of a Part of the Southeast Coast of China from the Island of Haitan to the Zhoushan Islands

SOURCE: BIBLIOTHÈQUE NATIONALE DE FRANCE, DCP SH 18 PF 179 DIV 3 P. 4; *GROTE ATLAS VAN DE OOST-INDISCHE COMPAGNIE* (*VII*), 200.

covering the coast from Niushan Island to the Putoushan Islands, a long strip of coast in the northern Fujian and southern Zhejiang provinces.

Between 1638 and 1661, the bulk of the nautical explorations were concentrated in the 1640s because the Company was then using Taiwan as a base from which to launch its forces into the waters of the Philippines and the Gulf of Tonkin. The Qiongzhou Strait, the passage between Hainan Island and the coast of Guangdong province, was the next passage to be explored. Dutch Taiwan also initiated contact with the Manchus in Canton in order to develop a direct trading link with China; this led to a nautical survey of the Pearl River estuary and the border zone between Tonkin and Guangxi. The two waves of Company warfare along the China coast during 1630s and 1660s also greatly stimulated nautical knowledge of the China coast and Taiwan with the help of a great many local pilots, who unfortunately have had to remain anonymous.

CHAPTER 9

The Japanese Missing Link and the Establishment of Dutch-Vietnamese Relations

Leonard Blussé

In the 1920s and 1930s, Japan framed its so-called "peaceful penetration" of Manchuria and its later aggressive expansion into China and Southeast Asia with reference to the ideological concept of establishing the *Daitōa Kyōeiken* 大東亜共栄圏, or the Greater East Asian Co-Prosperity Sphere. Staunch proponents of this propaganda asserted that Japan had as much historic right of access to the resources of the *Nanyō* 南洋 (Southeast Asia) as the Western colonial powers.[1] As the story went at the time, it was all the fault of the *sakoku* 鎖國, the closure of Japan by the Tokugawa 德川 shoguns in the 1630s. If Tokugawa Iemitsu 德川家光 (r. 1623–1651) had not ushered Japan into seclusion, deviating from the commercially oriented path that his grandfather Ieyasu had mapped out, the balance of power in East Asia and Japan's modern fate would have looked totally different in the twentieth century. What these nationalistic firebrands of imperial Japan were referring to was the epochal decision of the *bakufu* 幕府 administration during the reign of Tokugawa Iemitsu to issue the so-called *kaikin* 海禁, or maritime prohibition, which brought to a close the epic era of Japanese merchant adventurers like Yamada Nagamasa 山田長政 (1590–1630), Hamada Yahei 濱田彌兵衛 (fl. around 1628), Suminokura Ryoi 角倉了以 (1554–1614) and his son Sōan (1571–1632), Hirano Tōjirō 平野藤次郎, Suetsugu Heizō 末次平藏 (*c.*1546–1630), Sueyoshi Magozaemon Yoshiyasu 末吉孫左衛門吉康 (1570–1617), his son Nagakata 長方 (1588–1639) and Chaya Shirōjirō Kiyotsugu 茶屋四郎次郎请次 (1584–1622), to name but a few.[2]

Whatever one may think nowadays about the expansive strategies of Imperial Japan on the eve of the Pacific War, it cannot be denied that there were flourishing commercial relations between Tokugawa Japan and Vietnam in the early seventeenth century.[3] The question remains, however, whether these

1 Yano Tōru 矢野暢, *Nihon no Nanyōshikan* 日本の南洋史観 (Tōkyō: Chuō Kōronsha, 1979).

2 Leonard Blussé, "Japanese Historiography and European Sources", Piet Emmer and Henk Wesseling (eds.), *Reappraisals in Overseas History* (Leiden: Leiden University Press, 1979), 193–224.

3 Noël Péri, "Essai sur les relations du Japon et de l'Indochine aux XVIe et XVIIe siècles", *Bulletin de l'École française d'Extrême Orient*, 23 (1923), 1–104. In the autumn of 2020, Pierre-Emmanuel Bachelet defended his doctoral thesis on the Japanese trade with Vietnam at the Université

 | DOI:10.1163/9789004740556_011

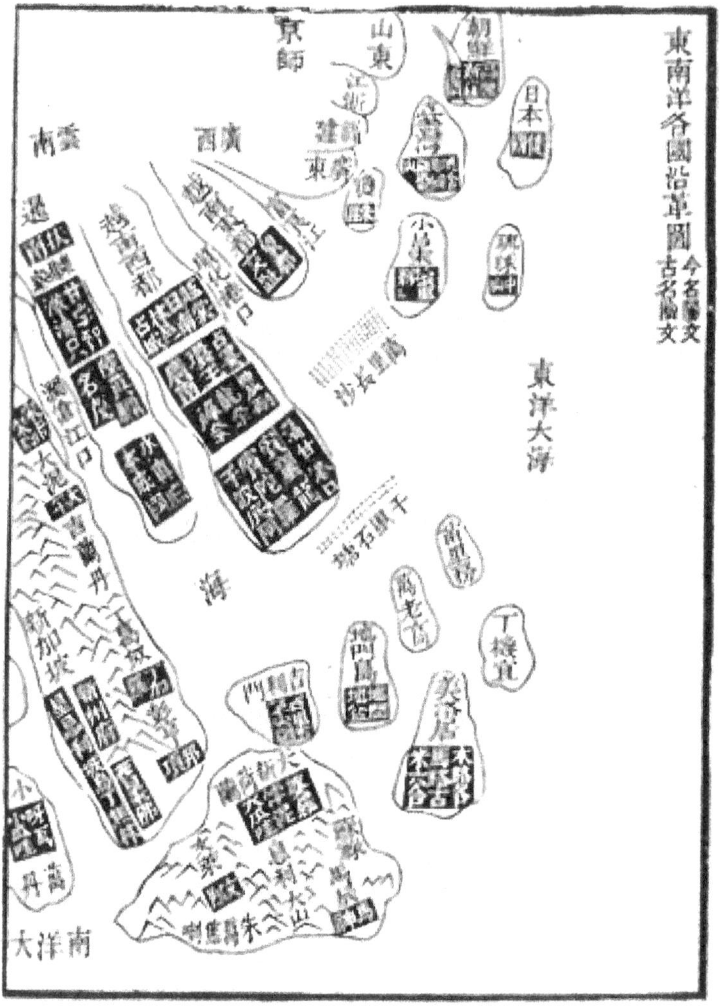

FIGURE 9.1 The East and South China Seas as depicted in Wang Dahai 王大海 Yao Nan 姚楠 (ed.), *Haidao yizhi* [*Island Memories*], 海島逸志 (completed 1791), 香港： 學津書店出版, Hong Kong: Xuejin Bookshop 1992, (first page after the title)

connections between Japan and Tonkin were as completely severed as people have so often suggested. What happened to the communities of Japanese merchants in Southeast Asia, especially in Vietnam (Hội An and Tonkin), who suddenly found themselves stranded on these foreign shores because of the shogunal edict that forbade them to go home?

de Lyon: *Bateaux-pigeons, quartier japonais et cartes nautiques: réseaux marchands et relations interculturelles entre le Japon, le Dai Viêt et le Champa* (*XVIe–XVIIIe siècles*).

1 Nation-Building

At the end of the sixteenth century, after almost a hundred civil wars, the warlords Toyotomi Hideyoshi 豊臣秀吉 (r. 1585–1598) and, in his wake, Tokugawa Ieyasu 徳川家康 (r. 1603–1605) succeeded in uniting the Japanese empire under one ruler and thus started the long process of state formation that in the years that followed created the Tokugawa world order (1600–1870) alongside the Chinese imperial world order. The Ming-Qing 明清 transition may well have eased Japanese attempts to create a self-sufficient economy almost completely divorced from that of its gigantic neighbour. The forty years that it took the Manchu invaders to extend their rule over all of China after they proclaimed the Qing dynasty in 1644 offered breathing room for the Tokugawa *bakufu* to carry out the economic reforms necessary to reach self-sufficiency internationally.[4]

2 Foreign Trade Policies and the Red Seal Trade

In the first two decades of his reign, Tokugawa Ieyasu devised all kinds of stratagems to lessen his dependence on the Portuguese monopoly of the silk for silver trade with China. Because Japanese shipping was not allowed in China and the Ming imperial government still forbade Chinese vessels to sail for Japan, the only way the shogun could acquire Chinese goods was to provide Japanese junks with shogunal passes, or *goshuin* 御朱印 (red seals), so that they could sail to overseas destinations in Southeast Asia and trade with Chinese merchants there. Thus, in the early years of the seventeenth century, temporary and permanent Japanese trading settlements, or *Nihonmachi* 日本町, sprang up to the south of Japan on the island of Formosa, in Manila on Luzon, in the Mekong Delta, in Hội An and Tonkin in Indo-China, and in the capital of Siam, Ayutthaya.

Japan's wide-ranging overseas mercantile expansion in the South China Sea during these years occurred at exactly the same time as the Dutch and English overseas expansion. Yet it was suddenly called to a halt by Tokugawa Ieyasu's grandson only ten years later. As part of his campaign to stamp out the religion

4 Naohiro Asao 朝尾直弘, *Sakoku* 鎖国 (Tokyo: Shōgakukan, 1975). Ronald Toby recapitulated the whole discussion begun by Asao: see Ronald Toby, "Reopening the Question of *Sakoku*: Diplomacy in the Legitimation of the Tokugawa Bakufu", *Journal of Japanese Studies* 3/2 (1977), 323–363. See also his later book, Ronald Toby, *State and Diplomacy in Early Modern Japan: Asia in the Development of the Tokugawa Bakufu* (Princeton: Princeton University Press, 1984).

of the Christians in Japan, whom he considered a dangerous, subversive sect, between 1633 and 1636 Tokugawa Iemitsu promulgated a series of maritime prohibitions, or *kaikin* 海禁. Overseas Japanese navigation was brought to a sudden stop, and Japanese subjects living abroad in the *Nihon machi*, many of them Christian, were not allowed to return home.[5] As a result of these far-reaching decisions, the merchants of the Dutch East India Company trading in Japan immediately saw new commercial opportunities and stepped in to fill in the sudden gap in the island empire's overseas relations.

3 The Dutch Connection

Although a Dutch vessel first appeared on Japan's southern shores in 1600, it was not until 1609 that formal trade relations were initiated at the port of Hirado 平戸, where the Dutch East India Company (VOC) established a trade factory. In the early years, Dutch-Japanese relations were of little economic importance to either party. The VOC was prevented from establishing a trading post on the Chinese coast in the same way that the Portuguese had acquired Macao in the Pearl River estuary, as a result of which they failed to gain a place in the profitable Sino-Japanese trade. In fact, so few Dutch trading ships reached Japan in the first decade of the trade's existence that the Company servants in the Hirado factory even purchased junks to initiate their own commerce with Siam and Vietnam. When a larger number of Dutch and English ships began to frequent Hirado around 1619, they used the port as a base for privateering expeditions against their Spanish and Portuguese enemies in Far Eastern waters, until this piratical behavior was explicitly forbidden by Shogun Hidetada in 1621.[6]

The construction of a Dutch fortress at the entrance to the bay of Tayouan (Formosa) in 1624, following the failed efforts to gain a foothold on the Chinese coast, soon led to such friction between the hot-tempered Dutch governor, Pieter Nuyts (1598–1655), and headstrong visiting Japanese traders under the leadership of Hamada Yahei that the Tokugawa *bakufu* declared a total embargo on Dutch shipping to Japan between 1628 and 1633. After this

5 Iwao Seiichi 岩生成一, *Nan'yō Nihonmachi no kenkyū* 南洋日本町の研究 (Tōkyō: Iwanami shoten, 1966).

6 Leonard Blussé, "Divesting a Myth: Seventeenth Century Dutch-Portuguese Rivalry in the Far East", in Anthony Disney and Emily Booth (eds.), *Vasco da Gama and the Linking of Europe and Asia*, (New Delhi: Oxford University Press, 2000), 387–402.

incident was resolved diplomatically, the VOC directorate in the Netherlands concluded that total subjection to the local rules and customs of Japan was the only option if the Company wished to continue to trade in that proud empire. In his *magnum opus, Van Oud en Nieuw Oost-Indiën*, François Valentijn quotes from VOC sources: "Company officials should above all be provided with modesty, humility, politeness, and friendship, being always very obliging in regard to the Japanese, so that their hearts shall in the end be won over to us."[7]

This implied the complete submission of the Dutch merchants to the Japanese state's regulations. These rules of conduct became the guiding principle for all further action in the years to come and would serve the Dutch well, as we shall soon see. In their competition with the Portuguese to gain part of Japan's foreign trade, the Calvinist Dutch only too gladly played up the Japanese hatred of the Catholic mission.[8] They affirmed to their Japanese hosts that they, like the Japanese, were also involved in a ferocious struggle against Rome's "Popish Plot". As a matter of fact, the Dutch East India Company presented itself to the shogunate as a non-threatening alternative to the Portuguese. The fervent wishes of the Dutch to replace the Portuguese in the profitable silk trade were fulfilled in 1639, when, in the aftermath of the Arima 有馬 and Shimabara peasant rebellions (*Shimabara no ran* 島原の乱), the Portuguese were banished "forever" from Japan. But the real test came in 1640, when the Shogun issued a decree to raze all the Dutch warehouses in Hirado and ordered the Dutch to remove their belongings to the small island of Deshima 出島 in the Bay of Nagasaki 長崎, where the Portuguese had lived during the last few years of their presence in Japan.[9]

When the Dutch conquered Portuguese-held Malacca in 1641 and thereby gained control over the Strait of Malacca, the main thoroughfare between the Indian Ocean and the South China Sea, they became *the* dominant western maritime power in the region. But they were careful not to portray themselves as such to the Japanese, unless it suited them to show that they were fighting as allies against the Spaniards and the Portuguese.[10]

---

7 François Valentijn, *Van Oud en Nieuw Oost-Indiën*, (Dordrecht: Joannes van Braam, 1724–26), vol. 5b, 165. For a recent comment on the Nuyts incident, see Clulow, Adam, *The Company and the Shogun: The Dutch Encounter with Tokugawa Japan*, (New York: Columbia University Press, 2016), 70–100.

8 Blussé, "Divesting a Myth", 387–402.

9 Blussé, "Divesting a Myth", 400.

10 Leonard Blussé and Cynthia Viallé, *The Deshima Daghregisters, 1640–1650* (Leiden: Intercontinental Series XXII), vol. 11.

4 The Consequences of the Maritime Prohibitions

What was the overall effect of the implementation of the Japanese maritime prohibitions? It is well known that Tokugawa Japan's diplomatic relations with Korea to the west and the Ryūkyūs 琉球 to the south remained intact, thanks to the mediating function of the *daimyō* 大名 of Tsushima 対馬 and Satsuma 薩摩. Less generally known, however, is the fact that Chinese and Dutch shipping also carried on Japan's commercial relations with Southeast Asia.

In *The Door Ajar: Japan's Foreign Trade in the Seventeenth Century*, Robert Innes has pointed out how Japan continued to rely on Southeast Asian and Chinese imports until measures to replace these imports with home-grown products bore fruit in the first half of the eighteenth century. The large-scale introduction of the mulberry tree and sericulture in Japanese farming and the development of sugar cultivation in Kyūshū 九州 are well-known examples of these efforts to develop a self-supporting, almost autarkic economy in Japan.[11]

Lately there has been a trend among Japanese historians to deny the seclusive nature of the *Sakoku* period. Yet the attentive reader of the Deshima diaries – in many respects the ideal diagnostic instrument to gauge the general trend of Japan's overseas trade relations over a period of more than two hundred years – will realize that, starting in the second half of the seventeenth and continuing through the eighteenth century, there was a deliberate effort to make Japan economically self-sufficient.[12]

Concerning the short-lived *goshuinsen bōeki* 御朱印船貿易 (red-seal trade) carried out by Japanese junks sailing between Japan and overseas destinations in the first three decades of the seventeenth century, we possess the remarkably detailed and informative research of the late Iwao Seiichi 岩生成一 and, more recently, Nagazumi Yōko 永積洋子.[13] Basing themselves on Chinese and Japanese data, but mostly, oddly enough, on Dutch archival materials from the VOC archives in The Hague, Iwao and Nagazumi reconstructed the overseas trade of the *shuinsen*, the junks that sailed with passes to Southeast Asian destinations, including the *Nihon machi* along the rim of the South China Sea. The data from the VOC archives not only provide quantitative information about that trade, but even reflect on the Japanese living abroad whose return home

11 Robert LeRoy Innes, *The Door Ajar: Japan's Foreign Trade in the Seventeenth Century* (Ann Arbor: University of Michigan, 1980).

12 Paul van der Velde and Rudolf Bachofner, *The Deshima Diaries, 1700–1740* (Tōkyō: The Japan-Netherlands Institute, 1992); Viallé et. al., *The Deshima Diaries, 1740–1780* (Tōkyō: The Japan-Netherlands Institute, 2004).

13 Iwao Seiichi 岩生成一, *Shuinsen bōekishi no kenkyū* 朱印船貿易史の研究 (Tōkyō: Kōbundō, 1958); Iwao, *Nan'yō Nihonmachi no kenkyū*; and Nagazumi, Yōko 永積洋子, *Shuinsen* 朱印船 (Tōkyō: Yoshikawa Kōbunkan, 2001).

FIGURE 9.2
Eighteenth-century wooden block print, depicting the distance from Japan to various ports in China and Tonkin (in the possession of the author)

was forbidden under the maritime prohibitions. Wherever they went, the VOC merchants carefully made notes about the local situation for trade and the middlemen with whom they dealt, but they also commented on their rivals' networks and shipping movements. In the final years of their navigation to Southeast Asian ports, Japanese shipping magnates like Suminokura Ryoi even hired Dutch pilots to navigate their *goshuinsen* with costly cargoes to overseas ports. For this reason, the VOC archives constitute a veritable treasure trove for the student of Japan's commerce with Monsoon Asia in early modern times.

5 The Impact of the Maritime Prohibitions

What was the direct effect of the implementation of the maritime prohibitions of the 1630s? First of all, and as has just been noted, diplomatic relations with Korea to the west and the Ryukyus in the south remained intact, thanks to the mediating function of the *daimyō* of Tsushima and Satsuma. Owing to recent studies by scholars such as Tashiro Kazui 田代和生 and Nakamura Tadashi 中村規, we are gradually gaining greater insights into how much trade may have been carried out via these channels.[14]

14 Fine surveys of these discussions have been given by R.H. Hesselink and Matsui Yōko, and by W.J. Boot, in Blussé et al., *Bridging the Divide, 400 Years The Netherlands-Japan* (Leiden: Hotei, 2000), resp. 33–53 and 73–85.

After the Japanese towns in Siam and Vietnam were cut off from their mother country in 1636, Chinese as well as Dutch merchants saw new business opportunities in connecting with these Japanese expatriate communities and their local networks. They were actually encouraged by the shogunal authorities to do so, and many Japanese moneylenders in Nagasaki who hated to see their investments disappear continued to invest in this trade, even though doing so was strictly forbidden by the shogunal authorities. VOC ships were sent from Taiwan and Nagasaki to Cambodia, Hội An and Tonkin to carry on the trade of the Japanese red-seal ships that had suddenly been interrupted. The same happened to the trade with Ayutthaya in Siam and Tayouan on Formosa, where Dutch and Japanese merchant vessels had previously competed with each other.[15]

Chinese merchants who flaunted their government's ban on sailing to Japan reacted in a similar way, and also hastened to replace Japanese shipping by linking a number of Southeast Asian ports with Nagasaki. The large number of ports of embarkation from which Chinese junks sailed to Nagasaki is illustrated by a scroll in the Matsuura Historical Museum (Matsuura Reksihi Hakubutsukan 松浦史料博物館) in Hirado, which depicts the variety of junks that plied between Japan and Siam, Jakarta, Taiwan, Cochin China and Tonkin in Southeast Asia, and Xiamen 廈門 and Shanghai 上海 in China.[16]

In a different way, but just as illustrative, are the various *Tōsen Fūsetsu-gaki* 唐船風說書 or statements by Chinese captains that were dictated to shogunal interrogators upon the arrival of Chinese junks from foreign destinations.[17]

Supposing that, after the promulgation of the *kaikin*, Chinese and Dutch shipping had continued to sail to and from Japan, unfettered by restrictions on the import of certain commodities or the total volume of imports and exports – Japan could actually have stayed quite open to foreign traffic and the free exchange of goods. This, however, was not the case. The Tokugawa administration continued to experiment with different ways of controlling the nexus between the import and export trades. More specifically, it sought ways to regulate the purchase price of imports and exports and to curtail the volume of bullion exported. While within Japan itself these measures whittled away at

15 George Vinal Smith, *The Dutch in Seventeenth-Century Thailand* (Northern Illinois University: Center for Southeast Asian Studies, 1977).

16 Osamu Ōba, "On *the Scroll of Chinese Ships* in the possession of the Matsuura Museum", *Bulletin of the Institute of Oriental and Occidental Studies, Kansai University*, no. 5 (1972), 13–50.

17 See, for instance, Yoneo Ishii, *The Junk Trade from Southeast Asia, translations from the Tosen Fusetsu-gaki, 1674–1723* (Singapore: ISEAS, 1998).

FIGURE 9.3
Siamese junk (Matsuura Museum, Hirado), reproduced with permission of the owner

the trade, the *Nihon machi* and their local networks were of course gradually dissolved, as they lost their ethnic identity and their *raison d'être*.

6 Restrictions within Japan

Before we focus on the vicissitudes of these overseas settlements as seen through the Dutch sources, let us briefly review here the successive restrictions that were imposed within Japan. In 1672, the so-called *shihō shōhō* 市法商法, or taxation trade, was introduced to prevent the outflow of precious metals. The outcome of this system was that all prices of imported goods were to be set by officials in Nagasaki and representatives of merchant guilds from Edo 江戸, Sakai, Ōsaka 大阪, Kyōto 京都 and Nagasaki, all cities that were under the direct control of the central government. In 1685, this system of taxation was abolished and replaced by *jōdaka* 定高, a 'fixed ceiling', which limited the volume of Chinese and Dutch imports to a total of 150,000 *ryō* 両 of gold (equal to 349,000 taels for the Dutch and 600,000 taels for the Chinese). In addition, the number of Chinese junks entering Nagasaki harbour was limited to seventy per year. Of these, ten junks could come from specific faraway destinations: two from Batavia, one from Cambodia and one from Pattani appeared during the summer season. Three junks from Cochin China, two from Siam and one from Tonkin would show up during the winter season. In 1699, the *Nagasaki kaisho* 長崎会所 (in Dutch *Nagasaki Geldkamer* or treasury) was established, a bank that was to handle all the financial transactions of foreign traders in Nagasaki henceforth.[18]

18 On these various issues, see Hesselink and Matsui in Blussé et al., *Bridging the Divide*, 53.

The restriction of 1685 was further reinforced in 1715 by the *Shōtoku shinrei* 正德新令, the new rules of the Shōtoku reign, which limited the number of Chinese junks annually visiting Nagasaki to thirty, and the Dutch to just two ships. Later in the eighteenth century these quotas were reduced even further. In 1743, the number of Chinese junks was limited to ten a year, and further quotas were imposed on the export of copper. It is important to note three points in particular regarding foreign trade in this period. In the first hundred years of the seclusion polcy, the Japanese were quite successful in finding replacements for expensive foreign consumer goods such as silk and cotton. By replacing silver and gold with copper exports, they rigorously reduced the outflow of precious metals, which threatened the economy because the silver mines were depleted. Moreover, they also replaced these metals in their trade with China in all kinds of edible marine products, like seaweed, trepang, dried sea slugs, dried fish and shark fins.

Japan's foreign trade thus was considerably reduced in scale. Yet although the Dutch trade with Japan shrank in volume dramatically during the eighteenth century, VOC ships continued to provide Japan with commodities in strong demand from all over Asia, and even from as far away as Europe. In addition, the Dutch chief of Deshima had to provide the Japanese authorities with an annual review of "World News", the so called *Oranda Fūsetsugaki* 阿蘭陀風說書.

7 The Industrious National Economy

The great paradox of Tokugawa Japan's overseas relations is that although overseas shipping – that is, long-distance 'ocean' shipping to overseas destinations (apart from Korea and Ryūkyū) – was strictly forbidden to Japanese sailors, at the same time short- and long-distance 'coastal' shipping flourished as never before. The Seto Inland Sea (Seto Naikai 瀬戸内海) developed into a veritable Japanese Mediterranean. The development of so-called *kitamaebune kaiun* 北前船海運 (northwards shipping), which was centered on Ōsaka and sailed via the Sea of Japan as far north as Hokkaidō 北海道, played a crucial role in the spatial expansion of Japanese commercial enterprise within the nation.[19] Cheap and accessible water transport sailing between the extremes of the 2,800-kilometer coastline of the Japanese archipelago, which connected

19 Ryōsei Hokkoku 北国諒星, *Kitamae bune, saredo Kitamaebune, Roman, Goshō Mitsubōeki* 北前船、されど北前船： 浪漫・豪商・密貿易 (Sapporo: Hokkaido Suppan Center, 2017).

the central markets in Honshū 本州 with the cold regions in the north and the subtropical regions in the south, was conducive to the emergence of a highly diversified economy based on regional specialization. The organization of these far-reaching networks centered on the central Kansai 関西 and Kantō 関東 regions, with their teeming urban populations of millions, led to a unique intertwining of interests between the administrative apparatus and the commercial sector, as shown by the various currency reforms and the diversification of agricultural crops.[20]

8 The Overseas World

Let us now address the question of what happened to the overseas Japanese communities and their local networks in Siam and Vietnam, and the extent to which they were integrated into the Dutch and Chinese shipping links. Here, I unashamedly rely on three monographs dealing with VOC relations with Siam and Vietnam by George Vinal Smith, Bhawan Ruangsilp and Hoang Anh Tuan.[21] In addition to these works, for Vietnam there are the excellent PhD thesis by Iioka Naoko 飯岡直子 on Wei Zhiyan 魏之琰 (1617?–1689), a case study of a Chinese entrepreneur engaged in the Tonkin-Nagasaki silk trade, and the useful studies by W.J.M. Buch on the VOC trade with Quinam, as well as Indochina in general.[22] What these works have in common is the argument that, although the first Dutch encounters with these regions occurred very early in the seventeenth century, trade relations with Siam and Indo-China did not become important until the Dutch trade embargo in Japan was lifted in 1632 and the *kaikin* were promulgated in 1636. In other words, Dutch trade relations with Vietnam and Siam were re-opened as a direct result of the *bakufu*'s decisions regarding Japan's international trade.

20 Conrad Totman, *Early Modern Japan* (Berkeley: University of California Press, 1993), 140–160.

21 George Vinal Smith, *The Dutch in Seventeenth-Century Thailand* (Northern Illinois University: Center for Southeast Asian Studies, 1977); Bhawan Ruangsilp, *Perception and Practice: the VOC and the Court Culture of Ayutthaya in the Seventeenth and Eighteenth Centuries* (Leiden: Brill, 2007); Anh Tuan Hoang, *The Dutch East India Company in Tonkin: Political and Commercial Relations, 1637–1700* (Leiden: Brill, 2007).

22 Naoko Iioka, *Literati Entrepreneur: Wei Zhiyan in the Tonkin-Nagasaki Silk Trade* (Singapore: Singapore National University, 2009); W.J.M. Buch, *De Oost-Indische Compagnie en Quinam, de betrekkingen der Nederlanders met Annam in de XVIIe eeuw* (Amsterdam: H.J. Paris, 1929); W.J.M. Buch, "La Compagnie des Indes Néerlandaises et l'Indochine", *Bulletin de l'école Française d'Extrême-Orient*. XXXVI (1936), 100–216.

9 Siam

In Siam, a recognizable Japanese community did not emerge until the last decade of the sixteenth century, during the reign of Naresuan (r. 1590–1605). In the past, traders from Ryūkyū had of course visited the Gulf of Thailand, but the first evidence of a Japanese trading community in Ayutthaya dates to only 1604.[23] Although George Vinal Smith places this emigration within the context of the anti-Christian measures in Japan, there is little doubt that many of these migrants consisted of the flotsam and jetsam from the Japanese civil war, who hired themselves out as mercenaries. We find frequent references to Japanese warrior bands who were locally employed by Thai nobility and the king himself, their most famous leader being Yamada Nagamasa 山田長政 (1578–1633). This warlord, who commanded the strongest military force in Ayutthaya, was finally outmaneuvered by the new king, Prasat Thong (r. 1629–1656), when the latter usurped the throne in 1629: Yamada was appointed governor of Ligor in the south of the kingdom and shortly afterwards poisoned. The Japanese trading network was particularly involved in the collection and shipping of ray skins and deer, cow and buffalo hides, which were in high demand in the home market. Between 1604 and 1636, the *bakufu* issued some fifty-six passports to junks leaving Japan for Ayutthaya, including ships sailing under Dutch or Chinese flags.[24] After the promulgation of the *kaikin*, the Japanese-Thai are said to have continued to play a role in the collection of hides for the Japan trade of the Dutch, and the Thai king actually gave the Dutch the exclusive right to purchase these in 1647. They also continued to trade skins for a considerable time with ports in Cochin China like Hội An, where they sold them to Chinese traders. Smith notes that, by the end of the seventeenth century, the various Japanese communities in Siam had been absorbed into the Thai population without a trace.[25]

10 Quinam (Cochin China, Hội An)

At the beginning of the seventeenth century, the territory of modern Vietnam was basically divided into three parts: the Trịnh-ruled Tonkin in the north, the Nguyễn-ruled Quinam in the centre, and Champa eking out the last years of its independent existence in the south. Dutch relations with the first two

23 Smith, *The Dutch in Seventeenth-Century Thailand*, 9; Jeremias van Vliet, *Historiael Verhael van de sieckte ende doot van Pra Interra-Tsia, 22en Coninck in Siam, ende den Regherenden Coninck Pra Ongh Srij* (1640), edited by Iwao Seiichi (Tōkyō: Tōyō Bunko, 1956), xviii–xxx.

24 Smith, *The Dutch in Seventeenth-Century Thailand*, 76.

25 Smith, *The Dutch in Seventeenth-Century Thailand*, 167n56.

kingdoms were greatly impacted by the ongoing wars between them. In addition, both Faifo (Hội An) in Quinam and Phố Hiến in Tonkin catered to the international trade with Japanese red-seal ships. Hội An was without doubt the more cosmopolitan in outlook and also much larger in terms of trade volumes. Japanese traders came here to trade their silver for Chinese silks brought from southern China by Chinese junks. In that respect it was an emporium of the trading beach sort, which was nonetheless closely monitored by the local rulers. Portuguese ships from Macao also participated in the trade between Hội An and southern China, a connection the Nguyễn rulers used to secure for themselves a constant supply of Western weaponry to repel attacks from the north. Early encounters between the Dutch and the local ruler were characterized by quarrels over shipwrecked Dutch sailors and their confiscated cargoes. A Dutch shipwreck in 1632 also led to the first parleys on the Quinam coast, when two Dutch merchants with great experience of the Chinese and Japanese trade, Paulus Traudenius (?–1643) and François Caron (1600–1673), were sent to establish formal trade relations. The mission failed for two reasons: the local ruler deemed the presents brought by the emissaries too trifling for opening formal negotiations and, more seriously, the visitors discovered that they did not stand a chance in the market place, which was completely dominated by the local Japanese residents and their networks. In fact, the Christian captain or headman of the local Japan town, known as Domingos, acted as the king's *shahbandar*, or harbour master, in Hội An, where he was responsible for dealing with all foreign merchants.

When the Dutch tried to purchase locally produced silk, they found that the entire silk production had been sold in the spring to the visiting Japanese junks. Before the harvest season, Japanese entrepreneurs living in Hội An sent their personnel into the countryside to offer the silk producers there as much as ten to twelve taels. A Dutch merchant, Abraham Duijcker (?–1639), who described this situation in detail, added that he did not see how the Dutch could ever counter the exclusive trading rights enjoyed by the Japanese. When, a year later, the Dutch thought they could find an outlet for a large cargo of *zenes*, Japanese copper coins imported from Japan, in Hội An, they found themselves up against the serried ranks of the local Japanese, who promptly undersold them. The new Japanese harbour master in Hội An, Rockebee (Hiranoya Rokubei 平野屋六兵衛), and a *kongsi* of 42 Japanese even had the temerity to threaten the Dutch traders that unless they were chosen as sole contractors they would make sure that all VOC trade in Quinam would come to naught.[26] The attitude of the Japanese residents in Quinam towards the Dutch

26 W.J.M. Buch, *De Oost-Indische Compagnie en Quinam, de betrekkingen der Nederlanders met Annam in de XVIIe eeuw* (Amsterdam: H.J. Paris, 1929), 31–32.

did not begin to change until the maritime prohibitions were issued in Japan, when they could no longer rely on Japanese shipping to carry their goods. Still, the trading conditions remained so unfavourable that the VOC recalled all its servants stationed in Hội An and decided to throw in its lot with Hội An's mortal enemy, Tonkin.

11 Tonkin

During the seventy-three years of its existence, the Dutch Tonkin trade developed in three consecutive stages: as a transshipment port for Chinese products, as an export port for locally produced silk for the Japanese market, and finally as an export port for products for the Dutch market. Although Tonkin was originally chosen because of its proximity to the Chinese border, so that it could act as a transshipment port for imported Chinese silk and gold, the Dutch soon realized that the Japanese had established a network for buying up locally produced silk. During the Chinese civil war, when very little raw silk was coming out of China, Tonkin provided most of the silk imported by the VOC, and between 1637 and 1654, huge profits were made on this trade with Japan. But silk production in Tonkin was very uneven. Natural disasters like floods and droughts, as well as the ongoing war with Quinam, interrupted the cultivation of silk, which had been introduced on top of a subsistence economy. According to Hoangh Anh Tuan, the economy of Tonkin was fundamentally transformed by its foreign trade with Japan, and it even witnessed the emergence of a manufacturing sector in this period. By the mid-1650s, Tonkinese silk exports to Japan had been replaced by supplies from Bengal, so that the original trading pattern of the former *goshuinsen* came to an end. Yet there were other products, such as the silver exported from Japan, that for many more years continued to link the Japanese and Southeast Asian economies. When, after 1668, exports of silver to purchase Tonkinese silk was forbidden by the shogunal authorities, Japanese copper coins filled the gap to some extent and actually contributed to the monetization of the Tonkin economy. At least until 1677, the VOC trade in copper coins remained highly profitable, showing the continuous resilience of the local Japanese networks in Tonkin, which tightly controlled the cash nexus under the leadership of a certain Japanese merchant and middleman called Resimon. For years on end this man continued to force the Dutch merchants into exclusive contracts. After 1671, no more VOC ships plied between Tonkin and Japan, and this direct shipping link, which had cushioned the repercussions of the *kaikin* edicts, also came to an end.[27] The VOC trade on the Batavia-Tonkin run continued until the middle of the eighteenth century, but this had nothing to do with the original links with Japan.

12 Conclusion

In this chapter I have shown, mainly with the help of Dutch sources from the VOC archives, how, even after they had been cut off from their home country, Japanese overseas settlements, the *Nihon machi*, with their expatriate communities of traders and sailors continued for some time to make an impact on Southeast Asian society by controlling the cash nexus and sericulture. When the links with the homeland were suddenly broken off, the Japanese in Vietnam continued to play a crucial role as middlemen between the Vietnamese and the Dutch. As the years went by, these Japanese middlemen were replaced by overseas Chinese traders, who also pushed the Dutch out of the Tonkin-Nagasaki trade.

Even though Japanese sources for the stranded Japanese communities overseas are lacking, it makes sense to transcend the usual boundaries of national histories by delving into foreign sources (in this case evidence from the VOC archives) and reading them against the grain. In the present case, this has had the effect of bringing back to life the 'banished' Japanese in Southeast Asia so that we may give them the place that they deserve within the larger context of Southeast Asian history.

27 Hoang, *The Dutch East India Company in Tonkin*, 191.

CHAPTER 10

The Sino-Japanese Trade in the Philippines between the Sixteenth and Seventeenth Centuries

Ubaldo Iaccarino

1 Introduction[1]

When the Spanish settled in the Philippines in the late 1560s, traders from China and Japan regularly visited the ports of northern Luzon, from Cagayan to Batangas, where they obtained gold and forestry products.[2] In 1569, Miguel López de Legazpi (d. 1572) ran into a Chinese ship off the coast of Panay (in Capiz) which was probably sailing to Butuan (Mindanao) to buy gold and civet cats. The next year, in Mindoro, Captain Juan de Salcedo (d. 1576) came across "two vessels from China", "large and high", which were carrying silk, cotton, gold thread, musk, earthen jars and porcelain, as well as iron, copper and a small quantity of wax.[3] In Tagalog Maynila, the Master-of-Camp Martín de Goiti (d. 1575) found two other Chinese ships with about forty traders. Along with the Chinese merchants, a group of some twenty Japanese, among them a certain "Pablo", were trading with the natives exchanging gold and silver. The latter had probably come from Kyūshū, Nagasaki or one of the other "Christianized" ports in Japan.[4]

The presence of Chinese ships in the Philippines can be traced back to the middle period. It is a well-known fact that, during the Song 宋 and Yuan 元 dynasties, traders from South China were regularly sailing across the waters of the Eastern Barbarians (*dongfan* 東番), reaching as far as the Moluccas.[5]

1 This study is part of the I+D+i Research Project "El Sudeste Asiático bajo la influencia ibérica en el mundo, 1581–1668," supported by the Ministry of Science and Innovation of the Kingdom of Spain (PID2019-107430GB-100).

2 Letter by Miguel López de Legazpi dated June 23, 1567. Archivo General de Indias (hereafter: AGI), Filipinas 6, n. 7; Blair and Robertson, *The Philippine Islands 1493–1803* (Cleveland, Ohio: The Arthur H. Clark Company, 1903–1909), 55 vols., vol 2, 238.

3 Blair and Robertson, *The Philippine Islands*, vol. 3, 75–76.

4 AGI, *Patronato* 24, r. 17.

5 Zhongshan daxue Dongnanya lishi yanjiusuo 中山大学东南亚历史研究所 (ed.), *Zhongguo guji zhong youguan Feilübin ziliao huibian* 中国古籍中有关菲律宾资料汇编 (Beijing: Zhonghua shuju, 1980), 9–20. Wada Sei, "The Philippine Islands as Known to the Chinese before the Ming Period", *Memories of the Research Department of the Toyo Bunko* 4 (1929),

 | DOI:10.1163/9789004740556_012

In early Ming times, because of the prohibition on maritime activities (*haijin* 海禁), the Chinese had to give up their voyages to the Philippines, and direct trade relations were only kept up through the channels of the tributary system. During the Hongwu 洪武 (r. 1568–1598) and Yongle 永樂 (r. 1402–1424) reign periods, several embassies came to Nanjing 南京 from Luzon (Lüsong 呂宋), Mindoro (Mayi 麻逸, Mait),[6] Sulu and Mindanao bringing letters and tribute to the Son of Heaven, but this had already come to an abrupt end by the second half of the fifteenth century. Despite that, some private trade continued, carried out by both Filipino and Chinese traders in several ports of Southeast Asia through the networks of smugglers and pirates.[7]

As far as the Japanese are concerned, there is no clear evidence of their activities in the Philippines before the arrival of the first Spanish settlers. Legazpi speaks about the presence of Japanese traders in the islands of Luzon and Mindoro,[8] and Captain Juan Pacheco de Maldonado mentions the annual visits of "Japanese ships laden with merchandise".[9] According to this Spanish official, they came to exchange "gold for silver, two to two and a half *marcos* of silver for one of gold".[10]

To arrive at a better understanding of the structure and mechanisms of the Sino-Japanese trade in the Philippines, we need to consider two important factors that affected its development around the middle of the sixteenth century. One factor is related to Japan's commercial isolation and the ending of the

121–166; Wang Zhenping, "Reading Song-Ming Records on the Pre-colonial History of the Philippines", *Journal of East Asian Cultural Interaction Studies* 1 (2008), 249–260.

6 *Gudai Nanhai diming huishi* 古代南海地名匯釋, pp. 740, 988. See also Go Bon Juan, "Ma-I in Chinese Records – Mindoro or Bai? An Examination of a Historical Puzzle", *Philippine Studies* 53/1 (2005), 119–38.

7 Ch'en Ching-ho 陈荆和, *The Chinese Community in the Sixteenth Century Philippines* (Tōkyō: The Centre for East Asian Cultural Studies, 1968); William Henry Scott, *Filipinos in China before 1500* (Manila: China Studies Program, De La Salle University, 1989); Roderich Ptak, "The Northern Trade Route to the Spice Islands: South China Sea – Sulu Zone – North Moluccas (14th to early 16th Century)", *Archipel* 43 (1992), 27–56; *Mingshi* 明史, by Zhang Tingyu 張廷玉 [1672–1755], (Beijing: Zhonghua shuju, 1974 and 1997), 11.8370–8375.

8 AGI, *Filipinas* 6, n. 7.

9 AGI, *Patronato* 24, r. 25, f. 2r. English translation in Blair and Robertson, The Philippine Islands, vol. 3, 298.

10 During the second half of the sixteenth century the ratio between gold and silver in China was 1/5.5, 1/7, or 1/8 (depending on the period) and in foreign countries 1/12. Charles Ralph Boxer, "Plata es Sangre: Sidelights on the Drain of Spanish-American Silver in the Far East, 1550–1700", *Philippine Studies* 18 (1970), 461. This great disparity was extremely advantageous for the Portuguese traders of Macao, who carried Chinese gold to Kyūshū and came back with Japanese silver, as well as for the Fujianese, who sailed illegally to Japan to sell gold and silk in exchange for silver.

tally trade system (*kanhe maoyi* 勘合貿易). Since early Ming times, trade relations between China and Japan had been regulated by a set number of official licenses being issued by the Chinese government and assigned to the Ashikaga shoguns. The system authorized only three Japanese vessels to trade in the port of Ningbo 寧波 – where an Office for Maritime Commerce (*shibosi* 市舶司) was established – once every ten years (at least in theory). However, in 1547/1549, principally because of the raids of the Wokou 倭寇 along the coasts of China, the Ming government decided to put an end to the tally trade and severed all relations and contact with Japan. From that moment on, the Japanese were not permitted to trade in Ningbo, nor in any other port of the Celestial Empire. Later, in 1557, when the Portuguese were granted permission to settle in China, the same kind of prohibition was extended to Macao. Several years before, in 1539, the Korean court had also banned Japanese ships from the ports of South Korea. Trade relations between the two countries were reestablished in 1547 by the treaty of Tenbun 天文, but the Japanese were only permitted to visit the port of Busan, whose trade was quickly monopolized by the lords of Tsushima対馬. In other words, when the Spaniards arrived in the Philippines in 1565 the Japanese had no access to the ports of Korea and China, including the port of Macao.[11]

A second factor influencing the development of the Sino-Japanese trade in the Philippines is related to the *haijin* 海禁 policy. During the first half of the sixteenth century, until 1567, no Chinese trader was allowed to engage in private maritime activities because of the ban on maritime shipping that was in force in all the coastal provinces of China. On Legaspi's arrival in Cebu (1565), the Chinese were still not permitted to sail abroad. It is important to note that, even after the opening of the port of Yuegang 月港 (Haicheng 海澄) to overseas trade, the Fujianese, being the only merchants who were allowed to sail, were still not permitted to visit Japan or trade with the Japanese. As a result, around the middle of the sixteenth century Wokou activities suddenly increased and became a major security problem for Beijing. The Ming court took resolute action against piracy during the 1550s and early 1560s, when several military campaigns were launched against the principal bases of the contraband trade off the coasts of Zhejiang, Fujian and Guangdong. Thus, many bases had to be abandoned in search of new ports to carry on the trade in silk, gold and silver.

11 Wang Yi-tung, *Official Relations between China and Japan, 1368–1549* (Cambridge: Cambridge University Press, 1953); So Kwan-wai, *Japanese Piracy in Ming China during the 16th Century* (Michigan State University Press, 1975); John Whitney Hall (ed.), *The Cambridge History of Japan*. Vol. 4: *Early Modern Japan* (Cambridge: Cambridge University Press, 1991), 235–265.

When the Spanish arrived in the Philippines in 1565, most of the Sino-Japanese pirates and smugglers had been driven away from the Chinese coast, and some of them had moved to the south, to mainland Southeast Asia and the Philippines. We know, for example, of a certain Lin Daoqian 林道乾, who apparently moved to Luzon (and later to Cambodia and the Malay Peninsula),[12] and Lin Feng 林鳳 (alias "Limahón"), who established a temporary base in the south of Taiwan and the Penghu islands before attacking Manila in 1574.[13]

2 The Triangular Network between China, Luzon and Kyūshū and Its Principal Ports

After the arrival of the Spanish in the Philippines in 1565 and the founding of Manila in 1571, an increasing number of Chinese and Japanese ships started to call at the ports of Luzon (mostly at Manila), thus contributing to the exceptional growth in its trade. According to Spanish sources, Manila was visited by 14 Chinese ships in 1574, and 17 ships in 1581. During the 1580s, an average of 20 ships per year continued to call at the capital of the Philippines carrying hundreds of passengers, including traders and settlers. In 1590 the "Pearl of the Orient" was visited by 21 Chinese ships, and in 1595 by up to 50. In 1596 at least 6 ships came from Japan, with a peak in the late 1590s. By 1585 the number of "Sangleys"[14] had already exceeded 4,000 people, and the Japanese traders numbered no less than 1,500 in 1592.[15]

There were several specific reasons for Manila's success as the principal port of call for both Chinese and Japanese ships. Important above all else was its

12 See Igawa Kenji, "At the Crossroads: Limahon and Wakō in Sixteenth-Century Japan", in Robert J. Antony (ed.), *Elusive Pirates, Pervasive Smugglers. Violence and Clandestine Trade in the Greater China Seas* (Hong Kong: Hong Kong University Press, 2010), 80.

13 Tang Kaijian 湯開建, "Ming Longwan zhi ji Yuedong ju dao Lin Feng shiji xiang kao – yi Líu Yáohùi «Dufu shiyi» zhong Ling Feng shiliao wei zhongxin" 明隆萬之際粵東巨盜林鳳事蹟詳考——以劉堯誨《督撫疏議》中林鳳史料為中心, *Lishi yanjiu* 歷史研究, 6 (2012), 43–65; Lin Renchuan 林仁川, *Mingmo Qingchu siren haishang maoyi* 明末清初私人海上貿易 (Shanghai: Huadong shifan daxue chubanshe, Xinhua shudian Shanghai faxingsuo faxing, 1987), 108–111.

14 A Hispanicization of the Hokkienese *sengli* 生理 ("business"), or of the Chinese "*changlai*" 常来 (lit. "those who come regularly"). Some historians also consider it to be a transliteration of the term "*shanglai*" 商来 ("those who come to trade").

15 Pierre Chaunu, *Les Philippines et le Pacifique des Ibériques* (*XVI*^e^*, XVII*^e^*, XVIII*^e^ *siècles*). *Introduction Méthodologique et Indices d'activité* (Paris: S.E.V.P.E.N., 1966), 148–151; Juan Gil, *Los chinos en Manila* (Lisboa: Centro Científico e Cultural de Macau, 2011), 575–580; Iwao Seiichi 岩生成一, *Nanyō Nihonmachi no kenkyū* 南洋日本町の研究 (Tōkyō: Nan-A bunka kenkyūjo, 1940), 257.

geographical position. Ships sailing from the ports of Fujian and Guangdong could reach the city in just two or three weeks sailing time, those from Kyūshū in about a month, depending on winds and currents. The Japanese followed the route that led via the Ryukyu Islands and Taiwan, which gave them at least two advantages: first, they could avoid the danger of sailing too close to China; and second, they could benefit from the black current (*Kuroshio* 黒潮) on the return voyage. Clearly, sailing to Luzon was far more practical and rapid than reaching more distant ports on the Gulf of Siam or the Malay Peninsula. It is still not clear to what extent the Japanese knew the route across the eastern side of Taiwan or whether they were using it at the end of the sixteenth century.

The Sangleys mainly came from Fujian, especially from the region of Minnan 閩南.[16] In fact, most of the residents of the so-called "Parian" and the two Chinese quarters on the other side of the river Pasig, in Binondo and Baybay, were from the prefectures of Zhangzhou 漳州 and Quanzhou 泉州. Of great influence were the Fujianese traders of Haicheng and Anping 安平 (Anhai 安海). The latter were among the richest merchants in Manila, and in 1603 they played an important role in the first Sangley uprising against the Spanish authorities.[17] During the first half of the seventeenth century, the "Anhayes" must have spread their overseas network to Japan and several other countries, as attested by the activities of the Zheng 鄭 family around the middle of the century.[18]

Manila's Parian, located outside the walls of the city, was not the only place where local and foreign traders, including Japanese, could buy silk and other

16 Wang Gungwu, "Merchants without empire: the Hokkien sojourning communities", in James D. Tracy (ed.), *The Rise of Merchant Empires. Long-Distance Trade in the Early Modern World (1350–1750)* (Cambridge: Cambridge University Press, 1990), 400–421; Lin Renchuan, "Fukien's private sea trade in the 16th and 17th centuries", in Eduard B. Vermeer (ed.), *Development and Decline of Fukien Province in the 17th and 18th Centuries* (Leiden: Brill, 1990), 163–215; James K. Chin, "Junk Trade, Business Networks and Sojourning Communities: Hokkien Merchants in Early Maritime Asia", *Journal of Chinese Overseas* 6/2 (2010), 157–215. For an overview on the Ming overseas trade, see Li Jinming 李金明, *Mingdai haiwai maoyi shi* 明代海外贸易史 (Xiamen: Zhongguo shehui kexue chubanshe, 1990); Li Qingxin 李庆新, *Mingdai haiwai maoyi zhidu* 明代海外贸易制度 (Beijing: Shehui kexue wenxian chubanshe, 2007).

17 Bartolomé Leonardo de Argensola, *Conquista de las Islas Malucas* [1609], ed. by Alonso Martín (Madrid: Ediciones Polifemo, 1992), 292ss; James K. Chin, *Merchants and other sojourners: the Hokkiens overseas, 1570–1760*. Ph.D. Dissertation (Hong Kong: University of Hong Kong, 1998), 26.

18 Manel Ollé, "Manila in the Zheng Clan Maritime Networks", *Review of Culture* 29 (2009), 91–103; Patrizia Carioti, *Zheng Chenggong* (Napoli: Istituto Universitario Orientale, 1995); Cheng Wei-chung, *War, Trade, and Piracy in the China Seas 1622–1683* (Leiden: Brill 2013); Xing Hang, *Conflict and Commerce in Maritime East Asia: The Zheng Family and the Shaping of Modern World, c. 1620–1720* (Cambridge: Cambridge University Press, 2016).

products of the Celestial Empire.[19] Throughout the late sixteenth and early seventeenth centuries the Chinese were successful in establishing other "Parianes" in several other places. We know, for example, of the existence of a Chinese Parian in Tondo (to the north of Intramuros), in Pangasinan, and in the cities of Iloilo (Panay), Vigan (Ilocos) and Nueva Segovia (Cagayan). Since most of the Spanish trade was carried out in the city of Manila and a few other places, mostly in the south of the archipelago, we can assume that these places served the overseas trade of other actors. The Japanese must have played an important role in this trade at least until the end of the 1630s.

Unfortunately, little is known about their presence in the north of Luzon, especially in the ports of Pangasinan, Ilocos and Cagayan, which hosted the bases of different groups of pirates in the second half of the sixteenth century. Around the 1560s and 1570s, not few traders and adventurers from the Land of the Rising Sun were visiting indigenous settlements at the mouth of the rivers Agno, Abra, Padsan and Cagayan to trade with the local population. The city of Agoo, for example, on the Gulf of Lingayen, was known to the Spanish as the "Port of Japan" (*Puerto del Japón*) at least from the early 1580s.[20]

It is important to note here that the Spanish presence in the Philippines was concentrated in the cities of Manila and Cebu, which were the two principal settlements on the archipelago. In Northern Luzon the Spanish conquistadors founded only two towns: Vigan (Villa Fernandina) and Lal-lo (Nueva Segovia). At the beginning of the 1580s, no more than thirty Spaniards were living in Fernandina (in spite of it being the political centre of the region) and probably even fewer in Nueva Segovia, which was only founded in 1582. Given that the number of *encomenderos* and royal officials who were in charge of a plethora of villages with several thousands of natives did not reach a few tens of men, we can imagine that a good part of contraband trade must have been carried out in the north of Luzon, far from the eyes of Spanish officials.

Manila's customs accounts registered Chinese ships calling at the ports of Cagayan, Ilocos, Pangasinan, Balayan and Batangas throughout the sixteenth and seventeenth centuries. In 1620 at least twelve Chinese junks anchored in Pangasinan (probably because of the Dutch blockade of the bay of Manila), where they maintained a constant presence in the following years. The growing community of Sangley residents in the regions of Ilocos and Cagayan seems to confirm the prominence of trade in northern Luzon, as well as the Visayas and other small islands of the archipelago. The judge (*oidor*) and former governor of the Philippines, Antonio de Morga, writing around 1609, states that the

19 Alfonso Félix (ed.), *The Chinese in the Philippines: 1570–1770* (Manila: Historical Conservation Society of Manila, 1966), 2 vols., vol. 1, 67–118; Juan Gil, *Los chinos in Manila*, 124–137.

20 AGI, *Patronato* 23.

Sangleys traded throughout the archipelago, "from one island to another, with large and small champans".[21] When sailing across the Philippines, they did not have to pay the *almojarifazgo* tax or the anchorage duties, which is why we can hardly find any evidence of their activities outside the port of Manila and its immediate surroundings. However, we have reason to believe that a considerable number of Chinese vessels arriving from Fujian, Japan and probably mainland Southeast Asia were carrying on a contraband trade in several other ports of the Philippines, especially on Luzon.

The same applies to the Japanese trade. The registers of the red-seal licences (*shuinjō* 朱印状) issued by the Tokugawa shogunate at the beginning of the seventeenth century indicate Luzon (*Ruson, Rusun* 呂宋) and the Visayas (*Misaiya* 密西那) as the destinations of the commercial voyages to the Philippines.[22] It therefore seems reasonable to assume that not all the ships sailing from Japan dropped anchor in the port of Manila.

Between 1616 and 1625, while the Dutch were blockading the entrance to Manila Bay, many Chinese junks and sampans visited and were registered at the ports of Ilocos, Pangasinan, and Mindoro trying to evade the trap set by the officials of the VOC. In 1619, for example, the Dominican missionary Bartolomé Martínez, who was shipwrecked near the coast of Pangasinan while heading for China, took the chance to baptize twenty Chinese merchants who had come there to trade (*que allí avían venido a sus tratos*).[23] Two years later, in 1622, after being informed of the presence of two Chinese junks off the coast of Mindoro,[24] the Dutch sent a squadron against them and were eventually successful at intercepting a "Portingall Junk" and several other smaller ships. However, it was a meagre outcome since most of the cargo had been already shipped to Manila.[25] By the time in question, the Fujianese pirate Li Dan 李旦 (?–1625) was sending his ships back and forth from Hirado calling at several ports in the Philippines. According to the diary of the head of the English factory at Hirado, Richard Cocks (1566–1624), one of his junks sailed to Cagayan

21 António de Morga (1559–1636), *The Philippine islands, Moluccas, Siam, Cambodia, Japan, and China, at the close of the sixteenth century* (London: Printed for the Hakluyt Society, 1868), 348.

22 Murakami Naojirō 村上直次郎 (ed.), *Ikoku ōfuku shokanshū, Zōtei ikoku nikki shō* 異国往復書翰集・増訂異国日記抄 (Tōkyō: Omatsudō shoten, 1966), 278ss.

23 Diego Aduarte, *Historia de la Provincia del Santo Rosario*, vol. 1, 470.

24 There is evidence of Chinese captain-merchants already sailing to Fujian from the ports of Mindoro and of Chinese ships calling at the nearby ports in Batangas at the end of the sixteenth century.

25 Paul Van Dyke, "The Anglo-Dutch Fleet of Defence (1620–1623). Prelude to the Dutch Occupation of Taiwan", in Leonard Blussé (ed.), *Around and about Formosa* (Taipei: Ts'ao Yung-ho Foundation for Culture and Education, SMC Publishing, 2003), 61–81, 78.

and Pangasinan in 1621.[26] A further entry from Cock's diary provides evidence of another voyage by one of his ships from Cagayan to Satsuma.[27]

At the turn of the sixteenth century an increasing number of Japanese ships were reaching the Philippines to trade, taking advantage of the political instability that followed the death of Toyotomi Hideyoshi 豊臣秀吉 (1536–1598) and the end of the war in Korea. In the early years of the seventeenth century, according to a pact between Tokugawa Ieyasu 徳川家康 (1543–1616) and the governors of the Philippines, Francisco Tello de Guzmán (in office from 1598 to 1602) and Pedro de Acuña (in office from 1602 to 1606), only four ships per year were permitted to trade in Manila, a limit which is expressed in the number of annual licenses issued by the Japanese government from 1604 onwards.[28] However, in spite of that, there is evidence of the voyages of several other ships plying from Kyūshū to Luzon, which were not registered by the Spanish authorities. Some of these ships were dispatched from Satsuma 薩摩 by Shimazu Yoshihiro島津義弘 (1535–1619), who even wrote a couple of letters to the Spanish officials in Manila.[29] As a result, we can assume that the share of the "*Bahan* trade",[30] especially in the ports of northern Luzon, must have been considerable.

Ships plying the Kyūshū-Luzon route principally came from the ports of Hirado 平戸, Nagasaki 長崎, Hakata 博多, Kagoshima 鹿児島, Usuki 臼杵, etc. According to a declaration on the state of affairs in the Kingdoms of Japan (*reynos de Japón*) written in 1587 and addressed to the Bishop of Manila, Fr. Domingo de Salazar (1512–1594), most of the merchants trading in the Philippines towards the end of the 1580s were from the ports of Hirado, Hakata, Sakai 堺 and Kyōto 京都 (Miaco), as well as from the provinces of Bungo 豊後 (Ōita prefecture 大分県) and Bingo 備後 (Hiroshima 広島). In the 1590s, ships also sailed to Manila from Nagasaki and several other ports on the western coast of Kyūshū. At the beginning of the seventeenth century, Usuki became the principal port of destination of the official ship sent annually to Japan to buy ammunitions and supplies.[31] That seems to show the existence of a direct

26 Edward M. Thompson (ed.), *Diary of Richard Cocks*, vol. 2, 146.

27 Edward M. Thompson (ed.), *Diary of Richard Cocks*, vol. 2, 334.

28 AGI, *Filipinas* 6, r. 9, n. 161. Cf. Ubaldo Iaccarino, *Comercio y diplomacia entre Japón y Filipinas en la era Keichō (1596–1615)* [East Asian Maritime History, 13] (Wiesbaden: Harrassowitz Verlag, 2017), 47, 51–52.

29 Diego Aduarte, *Historia de la Provincia del Santo Rosario, de la Orden de Predicadores, en Philippinas, Japón y China* (Manila: 1640), vol. 1, 251; Murakami Naojirō, *Ikoku ōfuku shokanshū*, 261–265.

30 The "Bahan trade" (*comercio de bafan*), associated with piracy, takes its name from the god of war Hachiman 八幡.

31 Ubaldo Iaccarino, *Comercio y diplomacia*, 109–113.

trade route between the area around Funai 府内 (Bungo) and the northern Philippines. Nagasaki and Kyōdomari 京泊 (Satsuma) remained the principal ports of departure for the commercial missions to Manila throughout the period of Hispano-Japanese intercourse.

According to Manila's customs records, commercial voyages from Japan continued until 1634, with an average of three to four ships per year under the command of Japanese, Chinese and Iberian captains. The Japanese replaced Chinese exports of ammunitions and supplies to Manila when they were ended at the turn of the 1610s and had the lion's share of the Kyūshū-Manila traffic from then to at least 1624.

3 Commodities of the Sino-Japanese Trade

The Sino-Japanese trade in the Philippines consisted in the purchase of several local products, like gold, cotton, resins, dyewoods, animal hides and horns, as well as silk and silver. According to the *Dongxiyang kao* 東西洋考, the Chinese bought animal hides (*pi* 皮) and horns (*jiao* 角) in Cagayan (Aparri) and Ilocos (Laoag and Vigan), as well as sappan-wood (*sumu* 蘇木), mainly in Pangasinan.[32] In all probability, the Japanese visited the same ports to buy more or less the same products. Their principal purchases, apart from gold, were sappan (*suō* 蘇芳) and deer hides (*shikagawa* 鹿皮). According to the Italian merchant Francesco Carletti (1573–1636), who visited Nagasaki at the end of 1590s, the Japanese used the skin of this Philippine deer to make clothes and saddles:

> [The Japanese] obtain very large numbers of buckskins, which they call *sicino cava* [*shikagawa* 鹿皮], and which they prepare in a curious manner, cunningly painting on them with various designs diverse pictures of animals and other things. And they do this with the smoke from rice straw, which colors the entire skin except that part which has been covered with the form of the pictures, which remain impressed and delineated on the white, unsmoked part of the skin. They use these to make clothing in their own manner and also very handsome horse saddles.[33]

Both sappan wood and deer hides were sold in the ports of the province of Pangasinan, where the Chinese also went to "buy" Zambal slaves from the

32 *Dongxiyang kao* 東西洋考 (ca. 1617), by Zhang Xie 張燮 [1574–1640] (Beijing: Zhonghua shuju, 1981), 95–96.

33 Francesco Carletti, *My Voyage around the World* (London: Methuen & Co., 1965), 130–131.

indigenous population on the coast (in Bolinao), giving in exchange cloth and porcelain.[34] In Manila, they carried principally silk and cotton: velvets, brocades, damasks, satins, taffetas and gorvarans, as well as linen handkerchiefs and tablecloths "of different kinds and sorts".[35] Among these products (the majority of which were destined for the American market), the Japanese principally bought raw silk, which they used to sew kimonos and other clothes according to their tastes. "This silk", wrote the Spanish merchant Bernardino de Ávila Girón (?–1619?) at the beginning of the seventeenth century, "is white silk, raw, and very smooth".[36] Some Japanese clothes and textiles were also sold to the Spanish, who shipped them to Acapulco.[37] In 1574, the Chinese merchant "Sicundey" sold silk in Manila at the following prices:[38]

TABLE 10.1 Price of silks sold at Manila in 1574

Silk	Price
white silk	2.5 *pesos* (*reales de a ocho*)[a]
blue satin	2 *pesos*
broad satin	4 *pesos*
blue damask	3 *pesos*
a catty (*cati*)[b] of colored silk	4 *pesos*
a catty of purple twisted silk (*seda torçida morada*)	2 *pesos*

a A *real* (sometimes translated as "rial") was the eighth part of one *real de a ocho* ("rial of eight", Spanish dollar, piece of eight, etc.). In Manila, the term *peso* generally referred to the *real de a ocho* minted in Mexico.

b Equal to 1 *jin* (斤) or 16 *liang* (兩, taels). A catty was equal to one libra: "Cate es libra de veinte honças". Colín, *Labor evangélica*, vol. 3, 219.

SOURCE: JUAN GIL, *LOS CHINOS EN MANILA* (2011), 562.

34 William Henry Scott, *Barangay. Sixteenth Century Philippine Culture and Society* (Quezon City: Ateneo de Manila University Press, 1994), 248–250.

35 António de Morga, *The Philippine islands*, 338.

36 Bernardino de Ávila Girón, *Relaçión del Reino de Nippón, a que llaman corruptamente Japón* [1615], ed. by Doroteo Schilling, O.F.M., and Fidel de Lejarza, O.F.M. ("Relación del reino del Nippon por Bernardino de Avila Girón"), *Archivo Ibero-Americano* 37 (1934), 5–48, 22.

37 On the Manila galleon trade, see William Lytle Schurz, *The Manila Galleon* (New York: Dutton, 1959); Dennis O. Flynn and Arturo Giráldez, *The Pacific World History: Lands, People, and History of the Pacific, 1500–1900*, vol. 4: *European Entry into the Pacific: Spain and the Acapulco-Manila Galleons* (Burlington, Vermont: Ashgate, 2001); Bernabéu and Shaw (2013).

38 Quantities are indicated as pieces (*pieças*), unless where specified.

A few years later, at the end of the 1570s, Chinese silk was being sold in Manila by Fujianese merchants at the following prices:

TABLE 10.2 Price of silks sold at Manila in the late 1570s

Textiles	Price
One *vara* of damask, of all colors, "as good as those from Spain"	4 reales, or less
One *vara* of taffeta ("better than those from Spain")	2½ *reales*
One *libra* of twisted or untwisted silk [*torçida o floxa*]	15 or 16 *reales*
One *vara* of brocade	10 *reales* ("it has to be very good")
One *libra* of raw silk in a bundle	12 or 13 ("when lacking")
linen [*lienzo*]	"at half a *real* and three *quartillos* per *vara*"
satins of all colors	3 or 4 ("the highest price")
one vara of cotton blanket	1½ *reales*

SOURCE: *RELAÇIÓN DE LO QUE SE ENTIENDE DE LAS COSAS DE LAS YSLAS PHILIPINAS POR PAPELES QUE SE HAN VISTO TOCANTES A ELLAS.* AGI, *PATRONATO* 66, R. 66, F. 8R. SEE ALSO JUAN GIL, *LOS CHINOS EN MANILA* (2011), 62.

The quality of these textiles improved year on year, as soon as competition arose among the Chinese, and probably with the arrival of ships from Japan. As shown in the above table, in the late 1570s one *libra* of raw silk could be sold in Manila for twelve or thirteen *reales*. In the 1610s the price had risen to 200 *pesos* per picul, while in China the price was only 80 *pesos*.[39] That, of course, was due to the presence of too much silver, which flowed into Manila not only from

39 AGI, *Patronato* 24, r. 66. One picul (*pico*) was equivalent to 130 *libras*. Each *tael* was worth ca. 11 *reales* (almost 1 *peso* and a half). According to Spanish sources, one picul of "retro" silk cost 140 *taels* in Guangzhou and was sold in Japan for 370 or even 400 *taels*. AGI, *Patronato*, 46, r. 31. Francesco Carletti, who visited Guangzhou in 1598, gives the price of a "soft and beaten" silk at 150 *taels* per picul. Cf. Carletti, *My Voyage around the World*, 145. At the beginning of the 1610s, according to the diary of John Saris, the price of the best Nanjing silk (called "Howsa") in Nagasaki was 185 reales per picul, and in Guangzhou 80 *reales*. Ernest M. Satow (ed.), *The voyage of Captain John Saris to Japan, 1613* (London: Hakluyt Society, 1900), 224–225.

Mexico but also from Japan.[40] In 1610, the Spanish captain Juan de Cevicos (*c.*1576–?) lamented the high price of silk and criticized the way trade was conducted in Manila. In his view the problem was that, while the Portuguese at Macao regulated the silk-for-silver exchange by means of the *pancada* system (bulk-purchase system), the Spanish allowed the Chinese and the Japanese to trade freely, without any imposition.[41] Moreover, when Cevicos wrote his report, the *almojarifazgo* tax, which had been introduced in the early-1580s under the government of Gonzalo Ronquillo de Peñalosa, was still fixed at a very low tariff of 3%. In that same year (1610) this tariff was raised to 6% for the Chinese but remained the same at 3% for the Japanese traders.[42]

Hence at the beginning of the seventeenth century, especially after the uprising of the *Nihonmachi* 日本町 (Japan-town) of Dilao,[43] the Spanish considered expelling all the Japanese from the Philippines, thus putting an end to their commercial voyages to Manila. The idea, however, soon proved impracticable and was finally abandoned for at least four reasons. First, the Spanish needed metals from the Japanese because, particularly after the Sangley rebellion of 1603, they could not rely exclusively on the imports of the Chinese, whom they did not completely trust. Moreover, since the outbreak of the Imjin War (1592), such strategic products as iron, black powder, saltpetre, etc. had become much more expensive. Second, in 1608/09 the Spanish put an end to the practice of sending a ship to Kyūshū every year from 1602 to buy the products for the royal warehouses. Third, the Japanese presence in the Philippines was needed as a counter to the predominance of its Chinese residents. Fourth, many Japanese "samurai" were fighting with the Spanish as mercenaries in their military campaigns in Southeast Asia. Also significant was the fact that the Spanish had just established an "alliance" (盟, *alianza*) with Tokugawa Ieyasu, to whom they had promised trade not only with the Philippines but also with Mexico (at Acapulco).[44] It goes without saying that Japan was too dangerous a neighbour to reject a formal relationship with.

---

40 The story of the importance of silver to the Chinese economy (especially after the introduction of the 'Single Whip' taxation) is too well known to be repeated here. See especially Richard von Glahn, *Fountain of Fortune: Money and Monetary Policy in China, 1000–1700* (Berkeley: University of California, 1996), 113–141.

41 AGI, *Filipinas* 4, n. 6. The *pancada* had been introduced in the Philippines by royal decree in 1589, but it was never applied.

42 Juan Gil, *Los chinos en Manila*, 50–54.

43 Apart from Dilao, the Japanese also lived in Bagumbayan (Ermita), San Antón (Malate) and later on in San Miguel, as well as in the city of Cavite. "*Nihonmachi* of Dilao" refers here to the Japanese community of Manila as a whole. See Iwao, *Nanyō Nihonmachi no kenkyū* (1940), 212–315.

44 Nakamura Kōya 中村孝也, *Tokugawa Ieyasu monjo no kenkyū* 徳川家康文書の研究 (Tōkyō: Nihon gakujutsu shinkōkai, 1958–1961), 4 vols., vol. 3, 228–229, 235–236.

The Chinese and Japanese also provided Manila with cotton stuff, iron and lead – which were used by the Spaniards in shipbuilding – as well as sulphur, saltpetre and gunpowder (for firearms), copper and tin. They also carried foodstuffs (especially rice and wheat flour) and domestic animals (cows and horses). In addition, the Fujianese shipped porcelain and other ceramics, which were produced in the kilns in the prefecture of Zhangzhou and were destined above all for Mexico and Peru.[45]

Among the products of the Philippines, gold was probably the most important. It was available in many different qualities, from six to more than twenty carats. Two of the best were the *orejeras* (known to the Chinese as "panica") and the *guinoculan*. The Spanish considered the latter to be the "lord of golds" and was highly valued.[46] Good ores were to be found in Camarines (Paracale), Cebu and Mindanao (Butuan), but the best deposits were those on Luzon, in the mountains of the Central Cordillera (especially in the province of Benguet). The Igorot (*Ygolotes*) people carried gold downriver to the regions of Pangasinan, Ilocos and Cagayan following the Agno, Abra and Cagayan rivers, and sold it to the indigenous people on the coast in exchange for pigs, carabaos and pottery. The exchange between the coastal settlers and the mountain dwellers of the Central Cordillera explains why, in the sixteenth century, the Chinese and Japanese concentrated their activities on those provinces, and established trade relations with the coastal settlers, especially in the Gulf of Lingayen.

It is no coincidence that the Chinese pirate Lin Feng 林鳳, after being repulsed from Manila (1574), found protection among the Panganinenses, who eventually helped him to escape from the blockade of the Spanish ships under Captain Juan de Salcedo (1549–1576) that were stopping up the entrance to the Lingayen Gulf. In 1582, a group of Japanese pirates under the leadership of a certain "Taifuza" (Taizufú, etc.) built a fort near the port of Aparri (Cagayan), probably with the intention of taking control of its trade.

During the late *Sengoku* period, and especially under the hegemonic governments of Oda Nobunaga 織田信長 (1568–1582) and Toyotomi Hideyoshi (1582–1598), gold became in Boxer's words "the most compact form in which to keep capital".[47] Carletti states that the Japanese bought it "gladly, so as to have

45 Rita C. Tan, *Zhangzhou ware found in the Philippines: "Swatow" export ceramics from Fujian 16th–17th century* (Manila: Yuchengco Museum, the Oriental Ceramic Society of the Philippines, Artpostasia, 2007).

46 AGI, *Patronato* 46, r. 31.

47 Charles Ralph Boxer, *The Christian century in Japan, 1549–1650* (Berkeley, Los Angeles, Cambridge: University of California Press, 1951), 112.

their property in more manageable shape, if the need should arise to transport it from one place to another because of the fortunes of the war that they wage[d] among themselves".[48] In fact gold was easy to carry and to handle, and it was not subject to being lost in a fire or being damaged in attacks by enemies and rebels. The *Sengoku* daimyos (whose wealth was expressed in *koku* 石 of rice) found gold powder to be a much more practical way of preserving their wealth and maintaining their political power intact. Both Nobunaga and Hideyoshi collected most of their taxes in gold, which thus contributed to the exceptional rise in its value in the second half of the sixteenth century. In Japan gold was also used in the figurative arts (to decorate the golden panels of the Kanō school, 狩野派, for example), in architecture and to embellish clothing and furniture. The Japanese also bought gold from the Sangleys, who generally sold it in powder form.

In Luzon the Japanese also bought the *Ruson tsubo* 呂宋壺, a rough form of earthenware dating back to the Tang and Song dynasties that could be found underground on the north Philippine coast. In the eyes of the assessors these irregular pots were absolutely priceless: Francesco Carletti stated that they were worth "five, six, or ten thousand *scudos* each, though ordinarily one would not say that they were worth a *giulio*", while Antonio de Morga, writing a few years later, remarked that the Japanese were disposed to pay as much as two thousand *taels* each for them.[49]

Both the Chinese and the Japanese sailed to the Philippines to buy forest products like resins, dyewoods and animals. Beeswax, used as a waterproofing agent, was obtained from the honeycombs of various local bees. The Jesuit father Francisco de Alcina describes those of the Visayas, like the *pocoytan* (or *potiocan*) and the *locot* (or *quiut*). According to the Italian merchant and adventurer Giovanni Francesco Gemelli Careri, the *pocoytan* were "bigger than the European [bees]" (*maggiori delle europee*), and their hives, which were almost four palms in length, were resistant to the incessant tropical rains. Alcina states that these bees were by far the best and provided much honey and wax. The little *locot* were instead "small like flies" (*picciole come mosche*) and produced a very sticky black or dark brown wax.[50] According to the *Dongxiyang*

48 Carletti, *My Voyage around the World*, 140.

49 Carletti, *My Voyage around the World*, 100; António de Morga, *The Philippine islands*, 285–286.

50 Gemelli Careri Giovanni Francesco, *Giro del mondo del Dottor Don Gio. Francesco Gemelli Careri* (Napoli: 1699–1700), 6 vols., vol. 5, 181–182; Francisco Ignacio Alcina, S.I., *La Historia de las Islas e Indios Visayas del Padre Alcina*, ed. by M. Luisa Martín-Meras and M. Dolores Higueras (Madrid: Consejo Superior de Investigaciones Científicas, Instituto Histórico de Marina, 1975), Chap. XXVII, f. 240v.

kao, beeswax (*huangla* 黄蠟) came to China from Brunei and the Sulu Islands through the Philippines.[51]

Sappan wood (*caesalpinia sappan*), or *sibucao*, was found in the northern islands of Batanes and Babuyan, but especially in western Luzon.[52] The Spaniards called it "*palo para tintar*" because it was used to dye silks in red and bice. Japanese traders also bought quantities of sappan (蘇芳) in Siam, Cambodia and Patani.

As far as local animals are concerned, the Chinese bought the horns of deer and carabao (a type of buffalo), and the shells of the sea turtles, which were used to prepare medicines and as materials for carving. The Japanese took away principally deerskins, which were used by the samurai for their armour and weapons. Lastly, the Chinese and the Japanese both bought civet cats (*gatos de algalia*) for their musk glands. According to Morga, the natives of Butuan (Mindanao) captured many civet cats and sold them alive in the other islands of the archipelago.[53] Bartolomé de Argensola confirms that these animals were sold in Asia "to different nations" (*a diversas naciones*).[54] In 1593 the "tributary" gift that the Spaniards gathered for Toyotomi Hideyoshi, in addition to five Luzon *tsubo*, two carabaos and some Spanish clothes, included five civet cats.[55] The reason for selling these animals live is explained by Carletti in his *Ragionamenti*:

> The Chinese dilute it [musk] by putting other mixtures into it, and from one sac they make three and four, using the animal's skin to form the others. And those false sacs they sell to the Indians of the region, selling the natural ones to the Portuguese – but even those are falsified in the contents, it being certain that one never finds the musk unadulterated or without admixture if it is not still affixed to the animal's skin. For that reason, among the Chinese musk has its carats just as gold among us, and when it is altogether good it reaches twelve carats, which they call mattes, but one never sees or deals in that sort, as is true of twenty-four-carat

51 Stephen T. Chang, "Commodities Imported to the Chang-chou Region of Fukien during the Late Ming Period. A Preliminary Analysis of the Tax Lists found in T'ung-hsi-yang k'ao", in Roderich Ptak, and Dieter Rothermund (eds.), *Emporia, Commodities, and Entrepreneurs in Asian Maritime Trade, c. 1400–1750* (Stuttgart: Franz Steiner, 1991), 159–194, 176–177.

52 Producono i suoi monti e le campagne [of Ilocos and Pangasinan] quantità di legno del Brasile, per colorire di rosso e turchino, detto dagl'Indiani *Sibucao*". Gemelli Careri (1700), vol. 5, 79–80.

53 Antonio de Morga, *The Philippine islands*, 286.

54 Argensola, *Conquista de las Islas Malucas*, 156.

55 Biblioteca Nacional de España, ms. 13173, f. 93r.

> gold. When musk reaches nine or ten mattes or carats, it is held to be mercantile and good. But at times it is so diluted with the mixture that they add to it that it does not reach to even six or seven mattes. But it does not reach Europe, being consumed among the people of Japan, Siam, Cambodia, Sumatra, and the uncounted other places in India.[56]

The other products purchased in the Philippines by Chinese and Japanese traders included honey, spices (especially cinnamon), palm wine, Spanish glasses, wine and European rarities. In exchange, the Japanese sold manufactured silks and coloured cottons, lacquers, pottery, salted meat, arms, wheat flour, iron, copper and sulphur. They also sold some golden panels, boxes and furniture, which were destined for Mexico, Peru and European courts, as well as larks (*fimbaros*, a Hispanization of *hibari* 雲雀), horses, and of course silver. The Chinese sold a plethora of goods, including silk, cotton, metals, minerals, foodstuffs and animals.

4 The Actors in the Sino-Japanese Trade: Merchants, Smugglers and Pirates

The fulcrum of the Sino-Japanese trade in the Philippines was Manila's Parian, where the silk for silver exchange took place. *El Parián de los Sangleyes* (or simply the *Alcaicería*, "silk market") had its own governor (*gobernadorcillo*), who was appointed by the Spanish and chosen from among the most influential men in the community. In 1590, the "head" (*cabeza*) of the Parian was a Christian Sangley called Francisco Zanco, who was the captain of the junk that Legazpi intercepted in Capiz in 1569.[57] This man had taught the first steps in the Chinese language to the Augustinian friar Martín de Rada (1533–1578), who was eventually dispatched to China in 1575 along with the fleet of the Ming general Wang Wanggao 王望高. After more than twenty years of experience *in loco* he must have been very influential in Manila, and almost certainly he accumulated a great wealth. Bishop Salazar proudly described him as "one of the oldest Christians of the [Philippine] islands".[58]

A few years later, in 1599, the governor of the Parian was a certain Alonso Sauyo, the owner of a ship that had returned to Manila in 1598 from a commercial voyage to Japan. This man was one of the Sangleys who developed the trade

56 Carletti, *My Voyage around the World*, 146.
57 William Henry Scott, *Barangay*, 74.
58 Blair and Robertson, *The Philippine Islands*, vol. 7, 233.

route between Luzon and Kyūshū in the second half of the sixteenth century.[59] Not a few governors of the Parian were smugglers, and some had even been "pirates". The above-mentioned Li Dan (alias Andrea Dittis), for example, is said to have been one of them.[60] He lived in Manila during the difficult years of the war in Korea, and we can imagine him also engaging in contraband activities with China and Japan. It is reasonable to assume that he developed some of his personal power thanks to the Philippine trade. A close relationship with the Spanish officials at Manila may have helped him build his own triangular trade network between China, Japan and Luzon. Li Dan and his followers carried out business in several ports in East Asia and controlled the traffic between Hirado and the province of Cagayan. The Matsura, who were his protectors, had strong interests in the Philippines and were the first daimyos to establish official relations with Manila. In 1607, the year after the rebellion of the Japanese community in Dilao, Matsura Shigenobu 松浦重信 received a red-seal licence for a commercial voyage to Luzon (呂宋, Manila).[61] Interestingly, it seems that Li Dan fled to Hirado from the Philippines that same year, having been condemned by the Spanish to serve as a rower in the royal galleys.[62]

Clearly, the "China Captain" of the English sources was not the only Sangley who traded in Japan. At the turn of the sixteenth century, there is evidence that such voyages were undertaken by the above-mentioned Alonso Sauyo (1598), the Christian captain Gonzalo Aiten (1599) and Lin Yaowu 林耀吾 (Rin Sankan 林三官) (1606). From the diary of the English factor Richard Cocks we know the name "Fingo Shiquan" (Higo Shikan 肥後四管), viz. Guo Binyi 郭濱沂 (d. 1619: "元和己未年仲秋吉旦"), a Fujianese merchant who was trading in Manila in 1618.[63] His gravestone in Ikura 伊倉 (Kumamoto 熊本) lists the names of his two sons, Guozhen 郭國珍 and Guorong 郭國榮, who probably carried on the

---

59 Juan Gil, *Los chinos en Manila*, 579.

60 Iwao Seiichi, "Li Tan. Chief of the Chinese Residents at Hirado. Japan in the Last Days of the Ming Dynasty", *Memoirs of the Research Department of the Tōyō Bunko* 17 (1958), 27–83; Patrizia Carioti, *Cina e Giappone sui mari nei secoli XVI e XVII* (Napoli: Edizioni Scientifiche Italiane, 2006), 121–126.

61 Murakami Naojirō, *Ikoku ōfuku shokanshū*, 291.

62 Chen Kuo-tung, "Manila datusha yu Li Dan chuzou Riben de yige tuice" 馬尼拉大屠殺與李旦出走日本的一個推測 (1603–1607), *Taiwan wenxian* 臺灣文獻, 60/3 (2009), 33–62.

63 Thompson Edward M. (ed.), *Diary of Richard Cocks. Cape-merchant in the English Factory in Japan, 1615–1622* (London: Hakluyt Society, 1883), 2 vols., vol. 2, 83. Nakajima Gakushō, "17 shiji chu Kyushu zhongbu haigang yu Minnan haishang wanglu: Higo diyu zhi Mingren mu yu Tangren ting" 17 世紀初九州中部海港與閩南海商網路：肥後地域之明人墓與唐人町, in Zhu Delan 朱德蘭 (ed.), Disi jie guoji hanxue huiyi: kuayue haiyang de jiaohuan 第四屆國際漢學會議：跨越海洋的交換, Fourth International Conference

family's overseas business. One is tempted to associate the name "Shiquan" (in Minnanhua: Sì-koa^{n}") with one Captain Juan Singuin, who sailed to Manila in 1619 aboard his own ship (*dueño de su navío*). It might have been a member of the same family or group, or Guo Binyi himself, who had travelled abroad one last time before his death.[64] The pilot of the ship, one Domingo Leal, paid 9 *pesos* of *almojarifazgo* tax for five slaves who were brought from Kyūshū (each being worth 60 *pesos*).[65] Juan Singuin appears in Manila's customs records as a Japanese (*japón*), though his name actually looks much more like a Spanish corruption of a Chinese name.[66] He carried merchandize from both Japan and China and paid the *almojarifazgo* tax at 3% or 6% depending on the country of origin of the goods being taxed.

The voyages of Chinese merchants to Japan via Luzon started very early, probably before the arrival of the Spanish. However, the only available evidence dates back to the early 1570s. According to a report by Governor Guido de Lavezaris, a ship sailed to Manila in 1575 to buy carabao horns, tortoiseshell, cotton, beeswax and other products to sell in Japan (*otras cosas para llevar a Japón*).[67] Some years later, in 1592, Gómez Pérez Dasmariñas recorded the arrival of a ship from Japan with a mixed crew of Chinese and Japanese traders.[68] In that same year, the Philippine governor received a letter from Matsura Shigenobu, who declared that several Chinese ships were regularly plying between Manila and Hirado at the turn of the 1580s.[69]

The captain-merchants who sailed to Luzon in the sixteenth and seventeenth centuries were agents of some of the most influential families in southern China, who largely belonged to the gentry and had the power to determine the political choices of the local administrations on matters related

---

on Sinology: The Transoceanic Exchange, 論文集 Book of Abstracts (Taipei: 人文社會科學研究中心, Academia Sinica, 2012).

64 In a copy of the *almojarifazgo* tax records for the years 1620–1681 (AGI, *Filipinas* 24, r. 2, n. 14), his name appears as "Juan Finguin", which sounds very similar to the Hokkien pronunciation of his name: Pin-kî 濱沂.

65 Juan Gil, *Hidalgos y Samurais*, 445.

66 The same can be said about another captain, Husap, who sailed from Japan to Manila in 1629.

67 Manel Ollé, "El factor europeo en la dialéctica entre comercio, contrabando y piratería en las costas de China de los siglos XVI y XVII", in Angela Schottenhammer (ed.), *Tribute, Trade, and Smuggling / Tributo, Comercio y Contrabando* [East Asian Maritime History, 12] (Wiesbaden: Harrassowitz Verlag, 2014), 55–74, here 69–70.

68 AGI, *Filipinas* 18B, r. 2, n. 6.

69 AGI, *Filipinas* 18B, r. 2, n. 12.

to trade and commerce.[70] Without the support of the Sangleys, the Spanish would never have had the chance to visit Fuzhou in 1575 or to establish a base at Piñal for almost one year in 1598/1599.[71] The Chinese merchant Lin Bixiu 林必秀 (Cinçay, Zinçay, etc.; in Chinese *xinshi* 信師?[72]) accompanied the embassy of Martín de Rada and Miguel de Loarca to Zhangzhou in 1575, serving as interpreter for the Spanish, and he translated the letters of Governor Lavezaris into Chinese for the Emperor of China (*Rey de Taybin*) and the governor of Fujian (*Virrey de Hogchiu* [Fuzhou]) Liu Yaohui 劉堯誨. Sinsay had come to Manila in 1574 with a cargo of silk, cloth and porcelain. He also carried iron and gunpowder, whose export abroad was illegal.[73]

The Chinese traders also provided the Spanish with intelligence and helped missionaries be smuggled into China. When in 1604 Captain Marcos de la Cueva's mission arrived in Macao with the news of the Sangley rebellion, three Chinese merchants, whose names appear in Spanish sources as Guansan (關山?), Sinu and Guachuan (or Guanchan), interceded with the local mandarins to have the trade restored. These merchants were among the richest captains in Manila (*los más caudalosos* [...] *en Manila*) and regularly sailed to Luzon around the turn of the sixteenth century.[74] The registers of the Royal Hacienda provide the names of several captains who sailed from China, Japan and mainland Southeast Asia, but it is difficult to determine their identities, since most of these names derive from a Spanish rendering of the local pronunciations of their characters (for example, in Hokkien or in Cantonese).

Some of these merchants, indeed probably many of them, were already carrying on a triangular trade between Fujian, Luzon and Kyūshū at the beginning of the 1570s. As Nakajima Gakushō has pointed out, at that time some Japanese merchants may have reached Manila on the Chinese ships that sailed from Hirado and the other ports of Kyūshū. The Fujianese-built junks and sampans that were destined to ply the waters of the China Seas were lent to the Japanese

70 Chang Pin-tsun, *Chinese Maritime Trade: The Case of Sixteenth-Century Fu-chien (Fukien)*. PhD Dissertation. (Princeton: Princeton University, 1983), 88–102.

71 Paulo Jorge Sousa Pinto, "Enemy at the Gates. Macao, Manila and the 'Pinhal Episode' (end of the 16th Century)", *Bulletin of Portuguese/Japanese Studies* 16 (2008), 11–43.

72 Lee Yu-chung 李毓中, José Luis Caño Ortigosa, "Conociendo China: Investigación del Mapa Topográfico Moderno y Antiguo de la Dinastía Ming (*Ku Chin Hsing Sheng Chih Tu*) obtenido por los españoles en 1574", in Lee Yu-chung and José Luis Caño Ortigosa (eds.), 《古今形勝之圖》研究 *Estudio del mapa "Ku Chin Hsing Sheng Chih Tu"* (Madrid: Ministerio de Educación, Cultura y Deporte, 2016), 65–89, 86; Manel Ollé, *La empresa de China. De la Armada Invencible al Galeón de Manila* (Barcelona: Acantilado, 2002), 267.

73 Juan Gil, *Los chinos en Manila*, 26–27, 561–567.

74 Argensola, *Conquista de las Islas Malucas*, 307.

merchants who traded in Luzon.[75] Some of the crews of these ships could be Chinese, as was the case for the pilots and helmsmen of the "Japanese" ship that reached Manila in 1592 under the command of the envoy-ambassador Harada Kiemon 原田喜右衛門 (Paulo Faranda). Harada's ship, which had a coloured flag on its stern, was probably the first "red-seal ship" (*shuinsen* 朱印船) to sail to the Philippines with a license from Toyotomi Hideyoshi.[76] It should be realized that as late as the end of the sixteenth century the Japanese still lacked the navigational skills required to sail across the South Seas, and most of the time they had to rely on the Chinese or Portuguese nautical knowledge. In 1599, for example, a Chinese pilot was serving on board a "Japanese" pirate ship which came to the Philippines from Kyūshū to attack the local settlements on the northern coast of Luzon.[77] In fact, the triangular route between Fujian, Luzon and Kyūshū was principally used by smugglers, pirates and marauders of all sorts. According to the declarations left in Manila in 1592 by the Japanese captain Pedro "Riochin", a ship belonging to "some Chinese traders" (*unos sangleyes*) was about to sail to Manila from the port of Kushi (久志, in the province of Satsuma) to sell not only wheat flour and other products, but also Chinese weapons (*armas de China*).[78]

The route between Fujian, Luzon and Kyūshū acquired a particular relevance during the Imjin War (1592–1598), when the contraband trade became fundamental to the survival of the Spanish presence in the Philippines. At that time, Sino-Japanese smugglers regularly traded in metals, weapons and other strategic products. We have reasons to assume that the triangular trade through Luzon developed further in those years. The Sangley merchants spread their networks and developed new connections in several ports in Southeast Asia, where they eventually found new sources of contraband. The associations between the owners of capital and the overseas merchants became quite common, and partnerships were formed among different actors.[79] Above all, there were Sino-Japanese smugglers sailing across the waters of the China

75 Nakajima Gakushō 中島楽章, "Jūroku seiki matsu no Fukken – Firipin – Kyūshū bōeki 十六世紀末の福建－フィリピン－九州貿易", *Shien* 史淵 144 (2007), 55–92, 67, 71–75.

76 Francisco Colín, *Labor evangélica*, vol. 2, 62; Blair and Robertson, *The Philippine Islands*, vol. 9, 54–55. On the *shuinsen* system: Nagazumi Yōko 永積洋子, *Shuinsen* 朱印船 (Tōkyō 東京: Nihon rekishi kaikan, 2001).

77 Blair and Robertson, *The Philippine Islands*, vol. 10, 212–213.

78 Francisco Colín, *Labor evangélica*, vol. 2, 50.

79 Oka Mihoko 岡美穂子 and François Gipouloux, "Pooling Capital and Spreading Risk: Maritime Investment in East Asia at the beginning of the Seventeenth Century", *Itinerario* 37:3 (2013), 75–91.

Seas and the most powerful lords of Kyūshū. By the early seventeenth century, the Sangleys had also established private companies with Spanish officials at Manila to purchase silks and other commodities from China.

It is interesting to note here that, among the reasons for the *pancada* system not being introduced in Manila was the fact that the free purchase of silk was advantageous to too many people, including the richest merchants in the city, the agents of the Mexican and Portuguese investors, and the missionaries of the three Mendicant Orders (Augustinians, Franciscans and Dominicans). The latter not only took part in the Galleon trade with their own quotas, they also strengthened their ties with Christian traders and opened up new possibilities for the evangelization and development of their own missions. All these people, of course, took advantage of their personal connections and of their close relations with the Chinese residents of the Parian, as well as benefitting from the Fujianese and Cantonese overseas networks in East and Southeast Asia.[80]

Thanks to the silver wealth of the Spanish and the Portuguese, as well as their investments in China and Japan, the Sangleys increased their own trading activities year after year and expanded their overseas networks. While benefitting from a monopoly on the route from Luzon to Fujian, the Chinese also had access to the Mexican market, since they invested money in the transpacific voyages of the Manila Galleons. Being allowed to transship a part of their silks to Acapulco, they thus enjoyed a double profit.

At the end of the 1620s, after the severance of Hispano-Japanese relations (1623/1624), the Chinese started to control the maritime route between Kyūshū and Luzon, acting as mediators and brokers for the Spanish merchants in Manila. According to the records of the Royal Hacienda, an average of two ships per year reached Luzon from Japan from 1629 to 1634, until the decrees issued by the Tokugawa *Bakufu* between 1633 and 1635 put an end to these voyages.[81] Below is a table of the Japan-Luzon traffic from 1624 to 1634, showing the increasing preponderance of Chinese shipping after 1624.

80 On the interconnected system of ports of the so-called "Asian Mediterranean", see François Gipouloux, *La Méditerranée asiatique, villes portuaires et réseaux marchands en Chine, au Japon et en Asie du Sud-est, XVIe–XXIe siècle* (Paris: CNRS, 2009); Angela Schottenhammer (ed.), *The East Asian "Mediterranean": Maritime Crossroads of Culture, Commerce and Human Migration* [East Asian Maritime History, 6] (Wiesbaden: Harrassowitz, 2008); Roderich Ptak, "Ming Maritime Trade to Southeast Asia, 1368–1567: Visions of a 'System'", in Claude Guillot, Denys Lombard, and Roderich Ptak (eds.), *From the Mediterranean to the China Sea: Miscellaneous Notes* (Wiesbaden: Harrassowitz Verlag, 1998), 157–192.

81 AGI, *Filipinas* 24, r. 2, n. 14; Pierre Chaunu, *Les Philippines et le Pacifique des Ibériques*, 153–159; Juan Gil, *Los chinos en Manila*, 592–599.

TABLE 10.3 Ships sailing to the Philippines from Japan between 1620 and 1635

Year	Captains of the ships from Japan	*Almojarifazgo* tax[a]
1624–1628	No ship sailed from Japan in these years.[b]	
1629	Husap (*japón*)	9 p. (the ship was a sampan)
	Hantion (*sangley*)	91 p., 4 g.
1630	Diego Simba [Diego Simbo][c]	447 p., 11 g. (the ship was a champan)
	Teng Siau [Tengçiao] (*sangley*)	12 p. (the ship was a sampan)
	Binbay [Vingay]	11 p., 3 t., 11 g.
1631	Gousan [Gusan]	42 p., 4 t., 9 g. (a sampan)
	Siansed	6 p. ("a ship with supplies")
	Manuel Álvarez de Orego	–
	Miguel Victoria	671 p., 3 t., 7 g.
	Secua [Sequa] (四管?)	188 p., 6 t., 6 g.
1632	Manuel Álvarez [de Orego]	313 p., 1 g.
	Mataymodono (又右衛門? • 殿)	324 p., 7 t., 8 g.
	Yaoyoc [Yanyog] (*sangley*)	3 p., 6 t., 7 g. ("with supplies")
	Chagay [Chapay] (*sangley*)	310 p., 6 t., 4 g.
	Quinsin [Qumsin] (*sangley*)	44 p., 3 t., 9 g. (the ship anchored in Balayan)
1633	Chiquan [Chinquan] (*sangley*) (七管?)	6 p. (a sampan)
	Siquan [Sinquan] (*sangley*) (四管?)	62 p., 3 t., 2 g.
	Hunqua (*sangley*)	72 p., 4 t., 9 g. (a sampan)
1634	Bitquan (*chino*)	87 p., 6 t.

a Expressed in *pesos* (p.), *tomines* (t.), and *granos* (g.).

b In 1624, under the third shogun Tokugawa Iemitsu 徳川家光 (1604–1651), the diplomatic relations between Edo and Manila were frozen. However, Manila customs records register one ship in 1627, captained by Juan Antonio de Vega, "governor of the Japanese", and three other ships in 1628, captained by Miguel Yaumis, Tomé Choyamu, and Miguel Coroue, respectively.

c The names between square brackets are those given by J. Gil in *Los chinos en Manila*, 594–599.

SOURCE: AGI, *FILIPINAS* 24, R. 2, N. 14, FF. 34V–53V

After 1634 the traffic in Japanese commodities to Manila was partly diverted to Macao, where duties and taxes were lighter, and partly to Taiwan, where the Spanish had established an outpost in 1626.[82] Finally, when the Portuguese were expelled from Nagasaki in 1639, it fell into the hands of Chinese traders, who continued to sail to Japan throughout the Edo period.

Like Chinese merchants, the Japanese sailed to Luzon on behalf of the agents of the most powerful lords of Kyūshū, who controlled the principal ports on the island and had access to the overseas trade. Around the middle of the sixteenth century several groups of merchants from the Kinai area established branch offices in Kyūshū, in the ports of Hakata, Hirado, Usuki, Kagoshima, etc. Their ships and crews were put at the disposal of the local daimyos, and several merchants sailed from their territories. At the turn of sixteenth century, the principal families investing in the Philippine trade were the Shimai 島井, Itami 伊丹, Itoya 糸屋 and Sueyoshi 末吉 (Hirano 平野). The latter operated in Manila by means of their principal agent, Tanabeya Matazaemon 田那邊屋又左衛門, whose name appears in several red-seal licences issued in the early years of the seventeenth century. The Sakai-born Nishi Sōshin (西宗眞, or Nishi Ruisu 西類子), who was known in Manila by his Christian name, Luis Melo, became the principal agent of the Philippine government at the end of the 1610s, providing the royal warehouses with iron, copper, sulphur, gunpowder, hemp and other articles. According to Juan Gil, one of his ships managed to evade the Dutch blockade at the entrance of Manila Bay in 1618.[83] The ship, which is described as a "junk" (*junco*), carried on board a quantity of ammunition concealed inside some wheat flour bags. In the following years, "Melo" continued to supply the royal customs with metals and ammunition, taking advantage of the presence of the Anglo-Dutch fleet of Defense off the Philippine coasts, which targeted the Fujianese ships en route to Manila.[84]

Many Japanese merchants had moved to Manila in the 1580s to serve as agents of the Matsura, Ōmura and Shimazu families. They contributed to the population of the Japanese quarter in Dilao and pursued connections with the Chinese merchants in Manila and other ports on Luzon. Moreover, many

---

82 Juan Gil, *Hidalgos y Samurais*, 443, 445; José Eugenio Borao, *Spaniards in Taiwan* (Taipei: SMC Publishing, 2001–2002), 2 vols., vol. 1, 62. See also Van Dyke "The Anglo-Dutch Fleet of Defence", 78. Some ships had sailed to the Philippines from Japan, via Macao, already in the 1620s. See Ubaldo Iaccarino, "The Macao-Manila Route under the Iberian Union", *Review of Culture, International Edition*, 60 (2019), 117–120.

83 Juan Gil, *Hidalgos y Samurais*, 439–442.

84 Reinier Hesselink, "A metal dealer and spy from Nagasaki in Manila in the first quarter of the seventeenth century", in Jane Kate Leonard and Ulrich Theobald (eds.), *Money in Asia (1200–1900): Small Currencies in Social and Political Contexts* (Leiden: Brill, 2015), 489–510.

of them converted to Christianity and strengthened their personal ties with the Spanish missionaries, which eventually opened the path to the despatch of Spanish ships to Kyūshū in the first years of the seventeenth century. The Spanish appointed a "Governor of the Japanese" (*governador de los japones*) in Dilao, who was generally a Japanese Christian and was chosen from among the most influential men of the community.

In 1585, Matsura Takanobu 松浦隆信 and his son Shigenobu sent an embassy to Manila asking for the despatch of Franciscan and Dominican missionaries to Hirado, and the following year (1586) eleven Japanese "pilgrims" arrived from the province of Hizen in the name of the Lord of Ōmura 大村. The missions were sent off to the Philippines after the visits to Hirado of two Franciscan friars and the Prior of the Augustinian convent of Manila in the early 1580s. In fact, in Guangzhou in 1582 (that is, immediately before their first visit to Japan) the Franciscans had met some retainers of the Ōmura and Ōtomo 大友 families, who had invited them to meet their lords, the Christian daimyos Ōmura Sumitada 大村純忠 (Dom Bartolomeu) and Ōtomo Sōrin 大友宗麟 (Yoshishige 義鎮, or Dom Protasio), in Japan. However, the two Franciscans, instead of reaching the bay of Ōmura, ended up in the port of Hirado.

As it is well known, the Matsura were one of Japan's principal "pirate lords" (*kaizoku daimyō* 海賊大名), and Hirado was one of the most visited ports in East Asia. At the end of the sixteenth century not a few daimyos of Kyūshū were supporting the activities of the Sino-Japanese pirates in Philippine waters, and the Matsura were surely among them. The pirates infested the northern coast of Luzon and attacked the merchant ships bound for Manila. In 1574 the Spaniards experienced the attack of a certain "Sioco" (小哥? 莊公?),[85] one of the generals of Lin Feng. A few years later, in 1582, Captain Juan Pablo de Carrión (1513–?) almost lost his life in Cagayan trying to expel a community of Japanese pirates who were under the leadership of the above-mentioned "Taifuza". Spanish documents reveal that he had come from Japan (from Satsuma?) to Cagayan "to settle down" (*con intento de poblar*) with a thousand settlers, who were still awaiting the arrival of others.[86]

The problem of the Japanese pirates was partly resolved in 1602, when Tokugawa Ieyasu had sixty-one of them crucified in Satsuma, another forty in Kinai and twenty in Nagasaki in order to please the governor of the Philippines, Francisco Tello de Guzmán (1532–1603), and establish an "alliance" with the

85 See Tang Kaijian, "Ming Longwan zhi ji", 54.

86 Gaspar de San Agustín, *Conquistas de las Islas Filipinas (1565–1615)* Ed. Manuel Merino, O.S.A. (Madrid: CISC, 1975), 544; AGI, *Filipinas* 6, r. 5, n. 53.

Spanish.[87] However, these marauders continued to infest the China Seas throughout the seventeenth century. The lineage of the Zheng 鄭 family is just one example of the influence that the Sino-Japanese pirates acquired during the first half of the seventeenth century.

5 Conclusion

After Tokugawa Iemitsu adopted the *kaikin* 海禁 policy in the early 1630s, the voyages of Japanese merchants to the Philippines were abruptly ended. Despite this, the Chinese continued to ply between Manila and Nagasaki throughout the Edo period (1603–1867), and around the middle of the seventeenth century they extended their trade networks in Southeast Asia to include new ports and markets. We have reason to assume that the trade route between Fujian, Luzon and Kyūshū fell under the control of the Zheng family, who established a sort of informal maritime state across the East China seas and in 1662 established a base in Taiwan. While the Japanese merchants, who had sailed to Manila under the protection of the Tokugawa *Bakufu*, had to give up their overseas ventures, the Chinese successfully invigorated the collateral branches of their own maritime networks. Around the Philippines, they revalorized the eastern route to the Spice Islands thanks to the flow of silver bullion from Mexico, and extended their trade routes to the Gulf of Siam and the Malay Peninsula. The high level of interaction and interdependence between the actors in the Sino-Japanese trade, not only in the Philippines, but also in many other countries of East and Southeast Asia, determined the establishment of a regional system that scholars have described in several ways and given various names to.

As the examples of the "Japanese" captain-merchants "Juan Singuin/Funguin" and "Husap" have shown, the transcultural identities of the traders who sailed to the Philippines make it extremely difficult to determine their nationalities, as it is hard to place their permeable natures in any one specific category. Traders could at one and the same time be smugglers, pirates and local potentates. In Manila, they could act as "governors" of the local foreign communities, help the Spaniards maintain law and order, or be the ringleaders of revolts and uprisings. Similarly, they could receive the privilege to participate in the transpacific trade of the Manila Galleons while engaging in piratical actions and smuggling activities.

87 AGI, *Filipinas* 27, n. 35; Archivum Romanum Societatis Iesu, *Jap.-Sin.* 13 II.

After the severance of diplomatic relations between Edo and Manila (1623/24) and the withdrawal of Japanese merchants from the seas (early 1630s), the Sino-Japanese trade in the Philippines changed its structure, thus paving the way for the exceptional rise of the Chinese overseas expansion of the early Qing period (1644–1912).

CHAPTER 11

Negotiations over the Translation of the Dutch Letter of Credence to the Qianlong Emperor in 1794

Ellen Xiangyu Cai

1 Introduction

In the first year of the Shunzhi 顺治 emperor's reign (1644), the Qing government issued the following decree on the tribute system: "Foreign countries should be allowed to pay a tribute with the certificate of a letter of credence and presents that are verified by the governor-general and governor (of a relevant province)."[1] Great importance was attached to the letter of credence and the presents brought by ambassadors, these should usually be well prepared before sending an embassy to China. Even though several Dutch embassies had been sent to Beijing during the seventeenth century, the inexperience of the Dutch East India Company in preparing the 1794 Beijing embassy was obvious. The content of the Dutch letter to the Qianlong 乾隆 emperor (r. 1733–1796) led to a series of negotiations between the Chinese authorities and the Dutch ambassadors, and resulted in the letter's revision under the former's supervision. With the aim to perseverantly confirm the content of this letter of credence, several versions in French, Chinese and Latin languages were brought into existence when the embassy stayed in Canton and Beijing. The presents, which also ought to have been well prepared before the arrival of Isaac Titsingh (1745–1812), had to be collected anew from Canton. Most of the members of the embassy were also recruited on the spot except for Titsingh and André Everard Van Braam Houckgeest (1739–1801), who had been designated ambassadors by the Commissioners-General in Batavia. The revision of the letter of credence, the fresh acquisition of presents and the recruitment of embassy members were the Dutch ambassadors' crucial activities during their stay in Canton between September 17th and November 22nd 1794, before they set off to Beijing. This chapter will analyse the negotiations over the translation of the Dutch letter of credence to the Qianlong Emperor that occurred in Canton.

1 Liang Tingnan 梁廷枏, *Haiguo sishuo* 海国四说 (Beijing: Zhonghua shuju, 1999), 165.

 | DOI:10.1163/9789004740556_013

2 Academic Background and Versions of the Letter of Credence

Upon receiving two letters which were successively written by Van Braam Houckgeest at the request of the embassy dated April 6th and 12th,[2] the Commissioners-General in Batavia accepted his proposal and drew up two letters, one for the Qianlong Emperor, the other for Changlin 长麟, Governor-General of the Guangdong and Guangxi. Each letter was attached to a Chinese translation by a Chinese resident living in Batavia, most probably the secretary of the Chinese Council (*gongguan* 公馆) of Batavia. The two Dutch letters with their Chinese translation were brought to China by Isaac Titsingh, the newly appointed ambassador to the Qing court. Titsingh called both letters "*brief*" in Dutch, and in French diplomatic language that for the Emperor was called "*la lettre de créance hollandaise*" (the Dutch letter of credence),[3] while Van Braam called it an "*adresse*" (address) or "*dépêche*" (dispatch).[4] Van Braam had intentionally pointed out to the Commissioners-General that the letter of credence should be titled "*compliment*", but his suggestion was not adopted.

Neither the Dutch nor the Chinese letters for Governor-General caused any dispute, but the Chinese letter to the Qianlong Emperor attracted much attention on the part of the Cantonese authorities because of its problematic wording and content. Governor-General Changlin, Hoppo Suleng'e 苏楞额 and Governor Zhu Gui 朱珪 (1731–1806) held a joint meeting to discuss the letter and asked the Dutch ambassadors to make a new translation immediately. J.J.L. Duyvendak attached the four letters to Qianlong and Changlin, in both Dutch and Chinese versions, to his related article in 1938, and paid special attention to the texts of the Chinese letters. However, he did not fully reconstruct the process of negotiation between the Chinese and Dutch parties.[5] Cai Hongsheng discussed the meanings of several confusing words in 1997.[6]

2 The first letter is compiled as supplément A in Andre Everard van Braam Houckgeest, *Voyage de l'Ambassade de la Compagnie des Indes Orientales Hollandaises, vers l'Empereur de la Chine, dans les Années 1794 & 1795* (Philadelphia, 1797), vol. 2, 357–364. While the second one is not available so far.

3 Chrétien-Louis-Josephe de Guignes, *Voyages à Peking, Manille et L'Île de France, faits dans l'Intervalle des Années 1784 à 1801* (Paris: De L'Imprimerie Impériale, 1808). Tome 1, Voyage à Peking pendant les Années 1794 et 1795 (1808), vol. 1, 258.

4 Andre Everard van Braam Houckgeest, *Voyage de l'Ambassade de la Compagnie des Indes Orientales Hollandaises, vers l'Empereur de la Chine, dans les Années 1794 & 1795* (Philadelphia, 1797), vol. 1, 7; vol. 2, 357–364.

5 Duyvendak, J.J.L., "The Last Dutch Embassy to the Chinese Court (1794–1795)", *T'oung Pao*, no. 34, (1938), 1–137.

6 Cai Hongsheng, "Wang Wengao helanguo gongshi jishishi shizheng" 王文诰荷兰国贡使纪事诗释证, in Cai Hongsheng 蔡鸿生, *Zhongwai jiaoliu shishi kaoshu* 中外交流史事考述 (Zhengzhou: Daxiang chubanshe, 2007), 363–364.

However, there is still a need to fully reconstruct the process of the Sino-Dutch negotiations and to conduct a more complete textual analysis of the various versions of the letter of credence. The new sources available are the new rendering of the Chinese letter of credence collected in Liang Tingnan's (梁廷枏) book *Four Tales on Maritime Countries* (*Haiguo sishuo* 海国四说), and a long letter dated November 26th 1794 written by Titsingh to the Commissioners-General in Batavia while the embassy was passing by Yingde 英德 county in the north of Guangdong province. This letter contains useful information on the process of negotiation. Together with the journals of Titsingh, Van Braam and the French secretary De Guignes, these records could help to clarify how and why the various versions of the letter to the Qianlong emperor, whether in Dutch, Chinese, French or Latin (see table 11.1 below), were shaped.

TABLE 11.1 Dutch and Chinese letters brought to Canton by Isaac Titsingh and the relevant versions in French, Chinese, Latin

To	Letter	Language	No. ※	Writer/ translator	Date of Issue	Source
Emperor Qianlong	**Original letter of Credence**	Dutch	1	Commissioners-General, Secretary E. Daniels	July 26th, 1794	Duyvendak's paper
		French	5	Van Braam/ De Guignes	Sept. 24th–27th, 1794/Jan. 11th, 1795	Appendix D in Van Braam's journal
		Chinese	6	Hong Merchants, Chinese Lingua Carlos, Buzheng Shi and Ancha Shi	Sept. 27th–Oct. 7th, 1794	*Four Tales on Maritime Countries*
	Chinese copy	Chinese	3	Anonymous Fujianese translator in Batavia	July 26th, 1794	Original copy in the main library of Leiden University
		Latin	7	A certain missionary in Beijing	Not known; Titsingh received it after May 10th, 1795	Appendix G1 in Titsingh's journal
		Dutch	8	Translator unknown, may be Titsingh?	After May 10th, 1795	Appendix G3 in Titsingh's journal

TABLE 11.1 Dutch and Chinese letters brought to Canton (*cont.*)

To	Letter	Language	No. ⁕	Writer/ translator	Date of Issue	Source
Governor-general Changlin	**Original letter**	Dutch	2	Commissioners-General, Secretary E. Daniels	July 26th, 1794	Original copy in the main library of Leiden University
		French	9	Van Braam	Which Van Braam planned to publish in his journal in the US	Appendix C in Titsingh's journal
	Chinese copy	Chinese	4	Anonymous Fujianese translator in Batavia	July 26th, 1794	Original copy in the main library of Leiden University

⁕ listed chronologically

In his letter, Van Braam reminded the Commissioners-General that the Qing government attached much importance to etiquette. Therefore, the Dutch ambassador should try to avoid irritating the Chinese as the British had done the previous year, when Lord Macartney (1737–1806) had refused to kow-tow nine times to the Qianlong Emperor. Van Braam made three suggestions for preparing the letters to Qianlong and Changlin. First, the *compliment* to Qianlong should bear the signature of the Stadtholder, Prince Willem Orange-Nassau, for the Chinese officials regarded the Dutch Republic as a kingdom. This suggestion inadvertently undermined the authority of the Commissioners-General in Batavia because it seemed to imply that the VOC had no right to substitute the 'King' (*Stadhouder*) of the Netherlands in issuing the letter of credence. Second, the letter addressed to the Governor-General should make it clear that the objective of the embassy was to celebrate the sixtieth anniversary of Qianlong's enthronement: the fact that the embassy had been dispatched at the request of Governor-General Changlin should not be mentioned. This suggestion might have been the idea of the Hong merchant Monqua (Cai Shiwen 蔡世文) in order to conceal the leading role Changlin had played in this event and to maintain the dignity of the Celestial Empire. Thirdly, both letters should be written in either Dutch or Latin. Although Van Braam showed he knew the significance of etiquette to the Chinese government when he said "le moindre oubli des formes pourrait produire de grandes conséquences, principalement chez une nation qui a porté le cérémonial à un point de raffinement inouï, comme l'a récemment prouvé le mauvais succès de l'ambassade anglaise",[7] he still could not anticipate what problems would confront the embassy in China. Van Braam concluded his letter by saying that, if the three suggestions were adopted, the mission would be carried out smoothly. The Commissioners-General in Batavia adopted most of the suggestions, and thus the letters to Qianlong and Changlin were drawn up together with their Chinese translations. Even though the contents of the two letters are quite similar, they had totally different fates due to the status of their respective recipients: the Dutch and Chinese letters to the Governor-General were accepted without any dispute, but the Chinese letter of credence to Qianlong, with their content and form, aroused unease and dissatisfaction among the Cantonese authorities, causing them to be written anew in Canton.

The letters to the Governor-General were presented to Changlin by Titsingh personally on the occasion of the audience that took place in the Honam Temple (i.e., Hai Zhuang Si 海幢寺) on October 13th 1794. Reading the Chinese version, Changlin seems to have been deeply touched by the consideration of the Batavian authorities. The Commissioners-General asked Changlin to provide assistance to the Dutch embassy, and the latter promised Titsingh that he would endeavor to provide the embassy with all the provisions that would be indispensable for the trip to Beijing.[8] Changlin did not look at the Dutch letter, suggesting that the Chinese version was sufficiently satisfactory to fulfill the procedure of receiving the letters addressed to him and the emperor, and so the audience was concluded. Changlin himself had suggested such a mission and on April 2nd had dispatched Zhao Hongwen 赵鸿文, the Magistrate of Nanhai 南海 county, and the senior Hong merchant Monqua to urge the chiefs of the English and Dutch factories to carry out his plan. As the originator of the scheme, he knew very well what was stated in the letter. The audience welcoming the arrival of Titsingh was probably a mere formality for the Governor-General. The next day, a newly arrived vessel brought the duplicates of the letters to the Emperor and Governor-General, having been sent to Van Braam in case the vessel *Siam* with Titsingh on board suffered shipwreck. When the Governor-General learned of the existence of these duplicates, he proposed to send the duplicate of the Dutch letter of credence to Beijing by express mail at a speed of 500 *li* (*c.*250 km) per day, together with a memorial

7 Van Braam, *Voyage*, Vol. 2, 357–364. "The slightest ignorance to the forms could induce great consequences, mainly among a nation that has brought the ceremonial to an incredible point of refinement, as has recently been proved by the failure (ill success) of the English Embassy." (Own translation, Cai Xiangyu).

8 Van Braam, *Voyage*, vol. 1, 15.

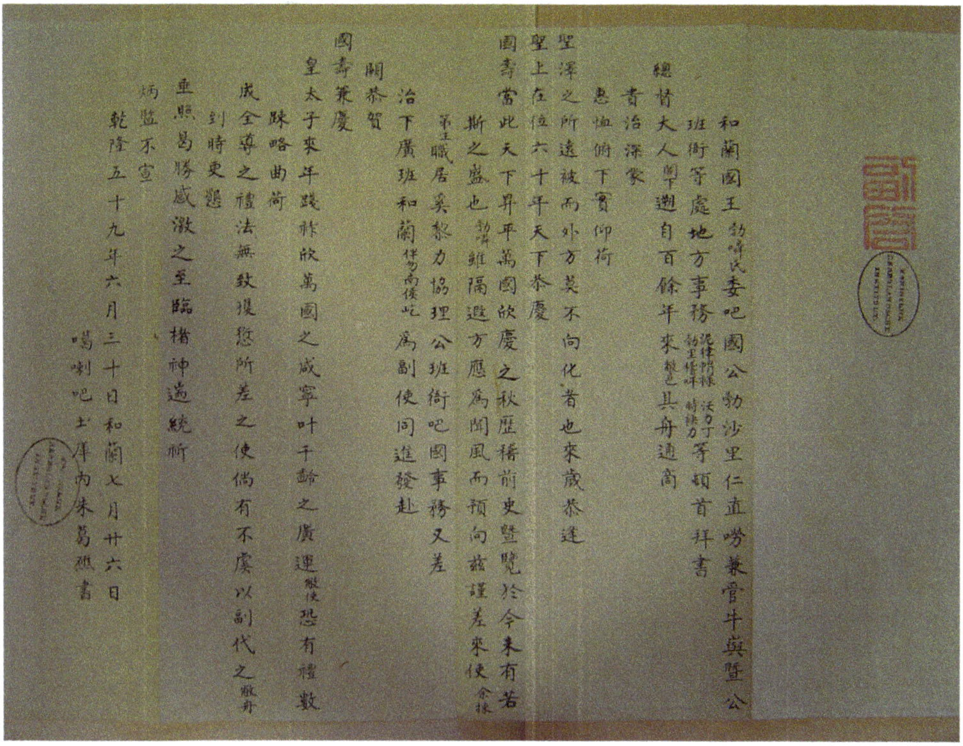

和蘭國王勃嚐氏委吧國公勃沙里仁直嘮兼管牛與暨公
班衙等處地方事務等頓首拜書
總督大人閣下邇自百餘年來具舟通商
貴治深蒙
恩恤俯下實仰荷
聖澤之所遠被而外方莫不向化者也來歲恭逢
聖上在位六十年天下恭慶
國壽當此天下昇平萬國欣慶之秋歷稽前吏暨覽於今未有若
斯之盛也雖隔遐方應爲聞風而預向茲謹差來使
第一職居吳黎力協理公班衙吧國事務又差
治下廣班和蘭爲副使同進發赴
闕恭賀
國壽兼慶
皇太子來年踐祚欣萬國之咸寧叶千齡之廣運恐有禮數
疏略曲荷
成全尊之禮法無致謬悞所差之使倘有不虞以副代之
到時吏題
垂照曷勝感激之至臨楮神遊統祈
炳鑒不宣
乾隆五十九年六月三十日和蘭七月廿六日
噶喇吧土庫內朱葛礁書

FIGURE 11.1 The Chinese Letter of Credence to the Qianlong Emperor (the following copies are all in the Special Collection of the main Library of Leiden University)

(*zouzhe* 奏折) stating his support of the Dutch embassy. As for the original Dutch letter of credence, he believed it would be better for Titsingh to bring it personally to the court.[9] From the four duplicates, i.e., the letter of credence in Dutch and Chinese, and the letter to Changlin in Dutch and Chinese, only the first one was received by the Chinese government, the other three being sent back to the Netherlands together with a copy of Titsingh's journal of the embassy and several Chinese documents. Today these documents are kept in the special collection of the University Library of Leiden. Prof. Duyvendak included photographs of the three letters to his afore-mentioned article. When I had the chance to read them in 2009, these documents were still in very good condition, and only a library seal had been added to them. In 2017 when I checked these documents once again, the Chinese documents attached to Titsingh's journal were gone, the librarian explained that they were moved to the Chinese collection of the East Asian Library.

9 Ibid., 19, October 14, 1794.

FIGURE 11.2 Exterior of the letters to Governor-General Changlin, both in Dutch (left) and Chinese (right)

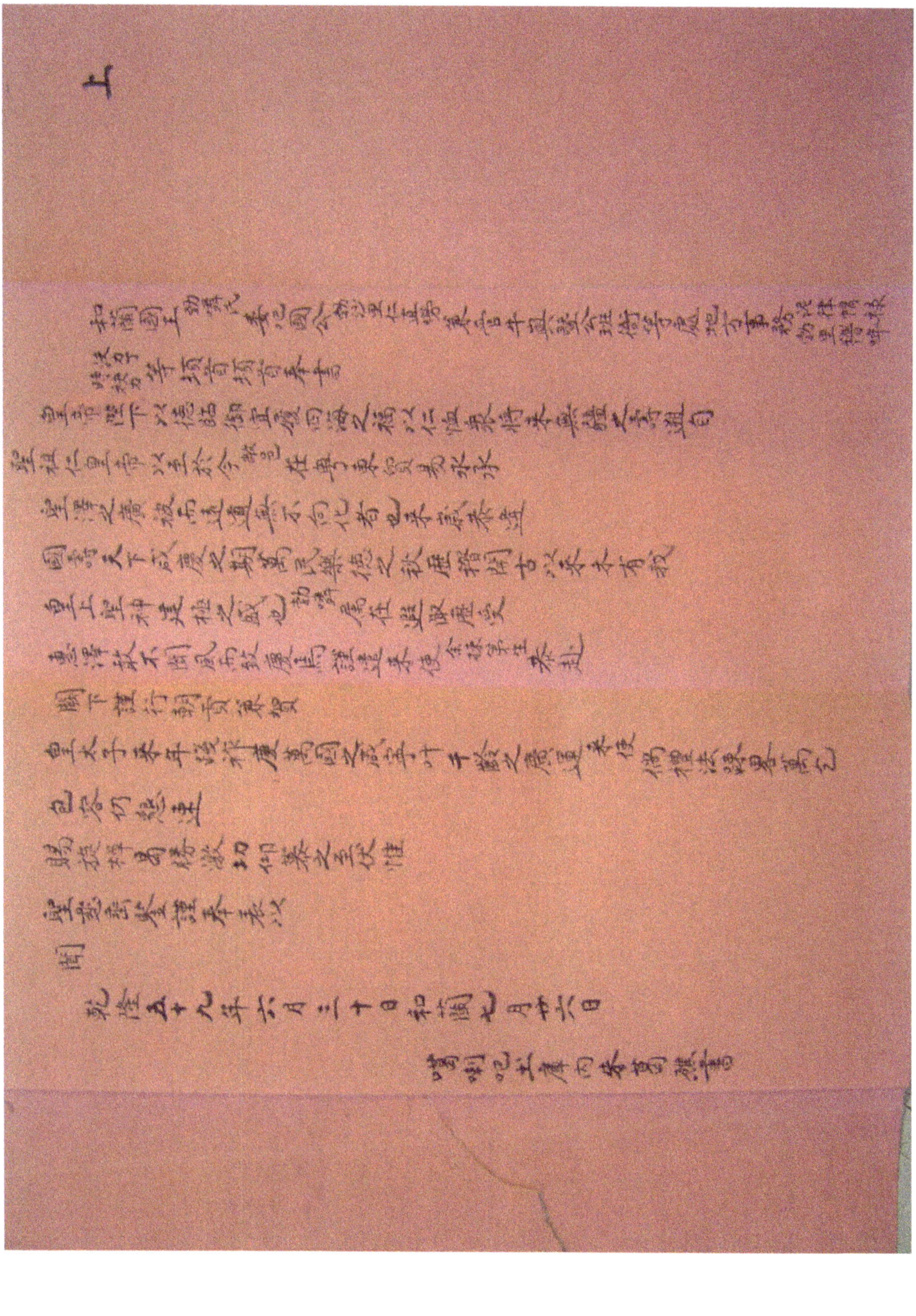

FIGURE 11.3 Chinese letter to the Governor-General

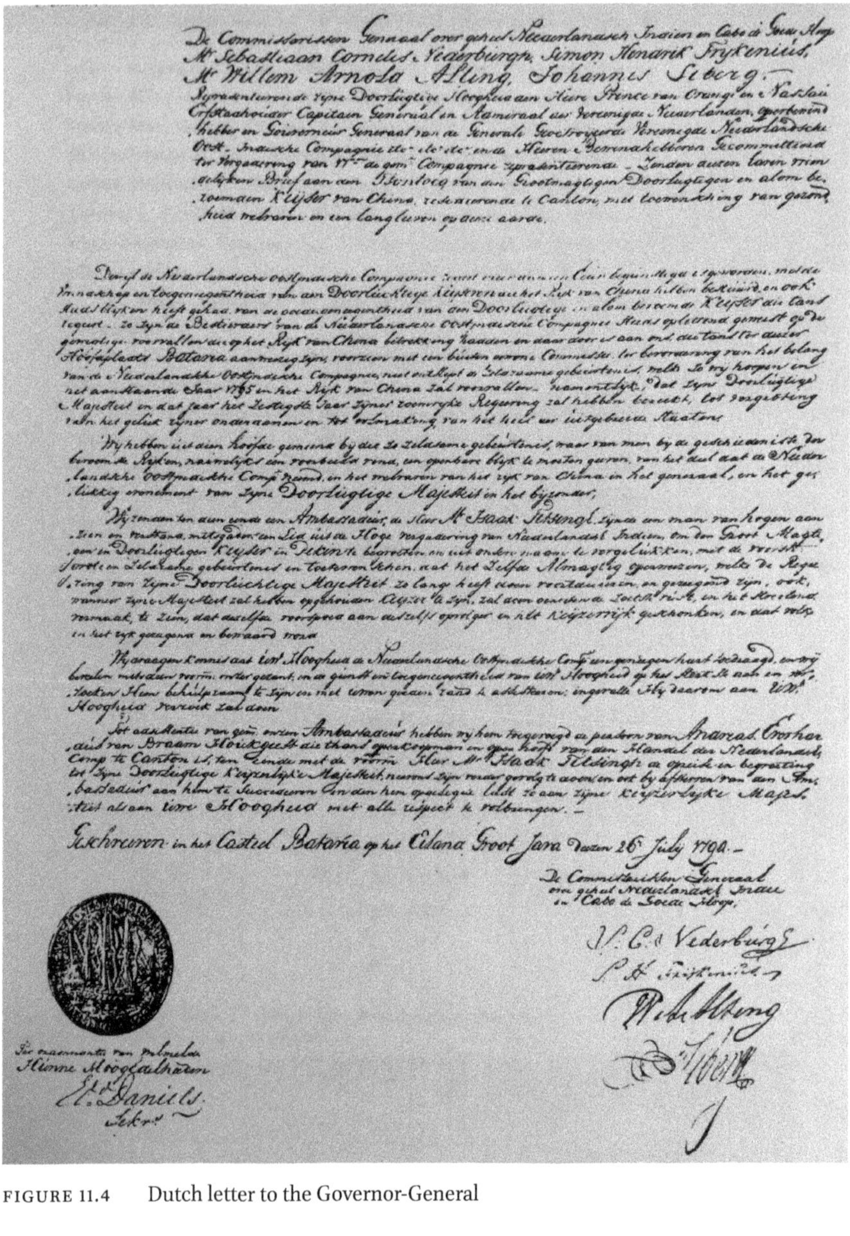

FIGURE 11.4 Dutch letter to the Governor-General

3 The Process of Negotiation (between September 24th and October 12th 1794)

When Titsingh and the Dutch fleet arrived at the Whampoa roadstead near Canton on September 24th 1794 the Hoppo Suleng'e came on board the ship *Siam* to welcome Titsingh and examine the letter of credence. After paying his compliments, the Hoppo wanted to know the real objective of this embassy:

> inquireerde voorts naauwkeurig of ik ook eenige versoeken of klagten aan het Hof had te doen. daar ik wel sag waar dit heen wilde, en het gevaarlijk was hem te seggen, dat men klagten had over den vorigen Hoppo (i.e. Sheng Zhu, 盛住), 't geen dit Gesantschap meede aan tegenkantingen en verneedering had blood gesteld, betuijgde ik hem dat de vergelukking van den Kijser het eenig doelwit was. Hij begeerde hiervan de kragtigste verseekering, wijl het mij niet zou vergund zijn iets anders ten Hove te mogen voordragen dan wat ik hem hier zoude bekend maken, waarvan het Hof terstond moest worden verwittigd. [Ik] antwoorde dat de Hollanders steeds getoond hadden in haar handel en wandel opregt te werk te gaan, dat de Chineesen moesten overtuijgd zijn dat zij zig met geene onwaarheeden ophielden, en dat ik hem op het plegtigst versekerde dat dit Gesantschap geen ander oogmerk als de begroeting van zijn Majesteid bedoelde, dit stelde hem gerust, in zijn gelaat en gesprek, zoals dat zijner versellende mandarijns straalde een bijsonder genoege door.[10]

From the above quotation, we can see that Titsingh still had another objective in mind, one had been proposed by Van Braam in his letter to the

10 Frank Lequin, *Isaac Titsingh in China: het Onuitgegeven Journaal van Zijn Ambassade naar Peking 1794–1796* (Alphen aan Den Rijn: Canaletto/Repro-Holland, 2005), 233. A similar record could be found in Titsingh's journal dated September 24th, 1794, see ibid., 75–76. "Inquired furthermore carefully whether I also had some requests or complaints to lodge in the court. Since I anticipated where this would lead to, and it was dangerous to tell him that people had complaints about the previous Hoppo (i.e., Shengzhu, 盛住), by which this embassy had been exposed to resistance and humiliation, (therefore) I declared to him that congratulating the emperor was the one and only purpose. He demanded the strongest confirmation of this, while I would not be allowed to propose in the court anything else than what I would disclose to him here, of which the Court had to be notified immediately. [I] replied that the Dutch had always shown honesty in their dealings, that the Chinese must be convinced that they busy themselves with no falsity, and that I assured him most solemnly that this embassy has no other purpose than to greet his Majesty, this reassured him, and in his face and conversation as well as in that of his accompanying mandarins an exceptional satisfaction shone through." (Own translation, Cai Xiangyu).

Commissioners-General in Batavia to safeguard the interests of the VOC: "Il y aurait l'espoir de demander, par une requête mesurée, une satisfaction des traitements arbitraires du précédent hou-pou, à l'égard de la détention du navire le *Zuiderberg*."[11] This incident occurred in December 1792. Faced with Suleng'e's enquiry, Titsingh realized the danger in telling him the potential objective of his expedition. Due to the fact that Lord Macartney had lodged a complaint to Qianlong against the excessive extortions of the Customs House in Canton and caused anger among the Emperor and his officials at the court, Suleng'e took the first opportunity to ask the newly arrived Dutch ambassador whether he was also planning to make a complaint, and to avoid any such unwelcome event ever happening again. Titsingh understood that it would be better to conceal the real aim of asking compensation for the ship *Zuiderburg* so as to ensure the success of the mission. He therefore assured Suleng'e that the one and only objective of the embassy was to congratulate the Emperor on the sixtieth anniversary of his enthronement, with which the Hoppo and the accompanying officials seemed entirerly satisfied. Then followed the procedure of examining the letters brought by Titsingh:

> bood hem (Hoppo) den brief van Heeren Comm: Gen[l] aan. zy kwam hem te eenvoudig voor. hy insteerde op dies opening, als moetende vooraf door den Tsontok worden geleesen, en dies inhoud aan het Hof bedeeld. aan zyn versoek voldoende, betuygde hy zyne verwondering dat de brief enkel op papier in het Hollands geschreven, en er eene vertaling in het Chinees was bygevoegd, onder het leesen van welke, hy diverse keeren bedenkingen scheen te maken, en het hoofd schudde. verstond dat de brief door Lord Macartney aangebragt op parkament en in het Latyn was gecoucheerd, en deeze meede in het Latyn of Fransch had behoren te zyn, om door de Missionarissen te kunnen worden vertaald. Liet hem voorhouden dat men daarvan op Batavia was onkundig geweest, en vertrouwde dat onse Linguas dies inhoud behoorlyk in het Chinees konden overbrengen. dat het Chinees geschrift niet zo zeer eene vertaling, als wel een kort verslag van dies voorname inhoud behelsde, wyl de Chinesen aldaar te onkundig waren in de Hoftaal om zulks na vereisch te verrigten.[12]

11 See Van Braam, *Voyage*, vol.2, 359. "There would be hope of asking, by a measured application, a compensation of the arbitrary treatments of the previous Hoppo, with respect to the detainment of the ship Zuiderberg." (Own translation, Cai Xiangyu).

12 Lequin, *Isaac Titsingh in China*, September 24th, 1794, 76. "Presented him (Hoppo) the letter from the gentlemen Commissioners-General. It turned out to be too simple for

Van Braam, who was also present and witnessed their conversation, complained in his journal that Titsingh should not trust Suleng'e with the revision of the Chinese letters of credence at his entire disposal. Titsingh could not even guarantee the accuracy of the Chinese translation, which had been made by an anonymous South Fujianese translator in Batavia, so he took the risk of asking the Hoppo for his assistance in working out a better Chinese version.[13]

That evening, in Van Braam's apartment in the Dutch factory at Canton, the host tried to make a new Chinese version based on the Dutch letter of credence together with four Hong merchants (Khequa / Pan Youdu 潘有度, Ponqua / Ni Bingfa 倪秉发, Pouayqua / Wu Bingjun 伍秉钧 and Kiouqua / Wu Guozhao 伍国钊), trading partners of the VOC that year.[14] They noticed that "The Chinese translation carries less than one quarter portion of what the Dutch letter contains. (het Chinees translaat geen vierde gedeelte inhield van wat die brief behelsde)". This might have been judged merely from the length of both letters, but this is subjective and incorrect, as we can see from the textual analyses of the letters in the next part of this chapter. Making the revisions was attended with many difficulties, for Titsingh noticed two days later that Van Braam and the Hong merchants were still working late into the night preparing a detailed explanation of the content of the Dutch letter of credence. The Governor-General, Governor and Hoppo held a meeting on September 27th and came to the decision that a new Chinese letter of credence should be translated on the spot. Khequa passed the news to Van Braam, and together with Ponqua, Pouayqua and Kiouqua, they met again in Van Braam's apartment. Van Braam dictated the letter in English, the four Hong merchants took it down, and the revisions were finished by midnight.[15] In the afternoon of September 28th, the Governor-General sent an official to the Dutch factory

---

him. He insisted to open it, as must be read in advance by the Tsontok, and to share its content with the Court. When his request was satisfied, he expressed his surprise at the letter having been written on paper in Dutch only, and there was a Chinese translation attached, while reading it, he seemed to make consideration several times, and shook his head. Learnt that the letter brought by Lord Macartney was written down in Latin on parchment, and this same letter should have been in Latin or French, so that it could be translated by the missionaries. Let him be told that the Chinese people in Batavia were incompetent, and believed that our Linguas could translate the content decently into Chinese. That the Chinese text was not so much a translation, just contained a short report of the main content, since the Chinese there were too ignorant in the court language to fulfill this requirement" (own translation, Cai Xiangyu).

13 Van Braam, *Voyage*, vol. 1, September 24th, 1794, 7–8.

14 The identities of these four Hong merchants are recorded in Van Braam's journal dated September 27th, ibid., 10.

15 Ibid.

asking Van Braam to explain some of the terms used in the letter.[16] Van Braam's record of the process of negotiation ends here, and no further information can be found in his journal.

The process of re-rendering, however, was not as simple as mentioned by Van Braam. Titsingh revealed a more complicated process in his letter to the Commissioners-General dated November 26th during the trip to Beijing. In the evening of September 24th, the four Hong merchants came to the Dutch factory in the names of Governor-General, Governor and Hoppo. Their duty was to work out a new Chinese version based on the Dutch letter of credence together with Van Braam:

> de laaste (i.e. the Dutch letter of credence) had in het Latijn moeten geschreeven zijn, eeven als die van den Koning van Engeland, om door de Missionarissen aan het Hof in het Chinees te worden vertaald; daar dit niet viel te herdoen moest men op een ander middel bedagt zijn, ZE. (i.e. Van Braam) seide hem sin voor sin in het portugeesch voor, zij poogden dit in het Chinees na te volgen, dog verklaarden na een arbeid van vier uuren, geene bewoordingen kragtig genoeg te weeten, om daaraan na behoore te voldoen, en dat het Chinees translaat geen vierde gedeelte inhield van wat die brief behelsde, dat het door een Chin Chouer [a native from Zhangzhou, Fujian province] was opgemaakt, een gemeen mensch dat er veele van die woorden en spreekweisen in voorkwamen die aan de zeekusten, als te Aijmuij, Quemuij, en elders, in gebruijk waren, en geheel moest worden veranderd. toen translateerde ZEd: den brief in het Fransch, met verklaring, van hierin zelf verre te kort te schieten, om de volle kragt van de verpligtende en verheevene steil te kunnen uitdrukken. een Chinees, in name Carlos, die ruijm twintig jaren zo te Rome als te Parijs had gestudeerd, dus het Fransch grondig verstond, en door den Tsontok steeds wierd g'emploijeerd, zou het in het Chinees overbrengen. toen dit na eenige dagen was verrigt, had de Tsontok zelf verbeeteringen gemaakt, waarna het translaat ter beoordeeling aan de geleerdste mandarijns wierd aangeboden: deeze, na Conferentie met Carlos, vonden nog kragtiger uijtdrukkingen voor zommige characters, het blijkt hieraan hoe bezwaarlijk het is om de Hoftaal grondig te verstaan, en zig in de schrijfstijl na dies smaak te kunnen rigten, zo dus immer een dierlijk voorval weeder exteerd, moet men zig op Batavia van het versenden van Chineese translaten sorgvuldig wagten. den 3. Octb: kreeg ik een besoek

16 Ibid., September 28th, 1794, 10–11.

van den [...] zij begeerden te weeten waarom het Chinees geschrift bij den brief was gevoegd. Antwoorde hen dat het in het kort de voornaamste sin moest inhouden, dog dat Heeren Commissarissen Generaal wel weetenden, dat de Chineese te Batavia van te geringe afkomst waren, om onder hen geletterden te vinden, die daaraan na behoore konden voldoen, mij hadden gelast, den Tsontok te versoeken de vertaling aan een kundig perzoon te willen opdragen, om hare diepe eerbied en hoogagting aan den Keijser na waarheid te kunnen uitdrukken; zij informeerden zig meede na onsen Vorst, en wie de Heeren waaren die den brief hadden onderteekend, dit baarde mij bedenking of de inboesemingen der Engelsen ook eenige inpressie maakte, gaf hen van het een en ander een volleedige uijtlegging, waarmeede zij voldaan vertrokken.[17]

---

17 Lequin, *Isaac Titsingh in China*, 234–235. "The latter (i.e. The Dutch Letter of Credence) should have been written in Latin, the same as the one from the King of England, to be translated into Chinese by the missionaries; in order not to rewrite it, they had to consider a different way. Rev. (i.e., Van Braam) told them (the content of the Dutch letter) sentence by sentence in Portuguese, they tried to follow this in Chinese, but after four hours of labor, they stated they knew no wording potent enough to meet it properly, and that the Chinese translation contained less than one quarter of the content of this letter, that it had been made up by a Chin Chouer [A Native From Zhangzhou, Fujian Province], a common man, that many of those words and expressions featured in it which were used along the coasts, as in Amoy, Quimoy, and elsewhere, and had to be changed completely. Then Rev. (i.e., Van Braam) translated the letter into French, stating he fell far too short of expressing the full cogency of the requisite and elegant style. A Chinese, named Carlos, who had studied about twenty years both in Rome and in Paris, so understood French thoroughly, and had been employed by the Tsontok all the time, would translate it into Chinese. When this was carried out for a few days, then (the translation) was improved by the Tsontok himself, after which the translation was offered to the learned mandarins for assessment: these men, after discussing with Carlos, still found more potent expressions for some characters, this proves how difficult it is to understand the court language thoroughly, and to conform to the taste of this writing style, therefore if ever a similar case occurs again, in Batavia one must be careful about sending Chinese translations. On October 3rd I received a visit from the [...] they desired to know why the Chinese text was attached to the letter. Responded to them that it had to contain the most principal points briefly, yet the gentlemen Commissioners-General well recognized, that the Chinese in Batavia were of humble birth, (it was difficult) to find men of letters among them, who could satisfy the decency of the letter, they had ordered me, to entreat the Tsontok to entrust the translation to a skilled person, to be able to express in sincerity their deep reverence and esteem to the Emperor; they also asked about our Sovereign, and who were the gentlemen who had signatures on the letter, this made me to think whether the inculcations of the English also made some impression, (I) gave them a thorough explanation about a few matters, with which they were satisfied and left." (Own translation, Cai Xiangyu).

Although this paragraph records the negotiation between September 24th and October 3rd, Van Braam dates the process to between September 24th and 28th. Some of the records of Titsingh and Van Braam seem to contradict each other. For instance, Van Braam said he dictated the Dutch letter in English and that the Hong merchants noted it down in Chinese. Titsingh recorded two attempts being made: the first was in the evening of September 24th, when Van Braam dictated the Dutch letter to the Hong merchants in Portuguese; this took four hours and did not produce any result. The second time Van Braam translated the letter into French, and a certain Carlos, a Chinese who had received many years of education in Rome and Paris, then translated the French version into Chinese. Regardless of these contradictions, either method may have been adopted. Since Dutch was not well known in the port city of Canton, the Cantonese authorities would have required the Dutch letter of credence to be translated into English and French so they could compare their Chinese versions with both translations so as to guarantee the accuracy and completeness of the contents of the original Dutch version. It is quite possible and reasonable that Van Braam, with the aim of minimizing any criticism, intentionally noted down a simpler process for the recasting of the text in his journal. Besides, although Van Braam said he dictated the letter in English, while Titsingh said he did so in Portuguese, there was not necessarily much difference because Van Braam may have dictated the letter in "Canton English", a kind of pidgin English mixed with Portuguese vocabulary. "Canton English", spoken orally, was widely used in conducting commercial transactions between Chinese and foreigners in the port of Canton. As a newcomer, Titsingh was not familiar with this kind of lingua franca and therefore may have thought Van Braam was speaking Portuguese.

Titsingh's record revealed that four categories of people were involved in the process of negotiation: 1) the officials in Canton, including the Hoppo, Governor-General, Governor, *Financieel Commissaris* (Provincial Administration Commissioner, i.e. Buzhengshi 布政使), *Juridisch Commissaris* (Surveillance Commissioner, Anchashi 按察使), *Zout Controleur* (Salt Distribution Commissioner, or Salt Controller, Yanyunshi 盐运使) and *Graan Intendant* (Grain Tax Circuit Intendant, or Tax Circuit, Liangdao 粮道);[18] 2) Van Braam, Chief of the Dutch factory and deputy ambassador; 3) four Hong merchants who were partners of the Dutch China trade; and 4) Carlos, the Chinese translator or *lingua* (*tongshi* 通事) who had spent twenty years in Rome and Paris and

---

18 Lequin, *Isaac Titsingh in China*, 80, footnotes 5 to 8; Charles O. Hucker, *A Dictionary of Official Titles in Imperial China*, Taiwan Edition, (Taipei: Southern Materials Center Inc., 1985), 88–89, 103, 310, 391, 581.

was employed by the Governor-General for his service. All of them worked together to bring out a new Chinese version, so that "the letter was translated anew in elegant terms by two of the most learnt mandarins (de vertaling van den brief opnieuw door twee der geleerdste Mandaryns in cierlyke termen wierd overgebragt)".[19] The identities of both mandarins, as mentioned by Van Braam, were the *Financieel Commissaris* (Chen Dawen 陈大文) and *Juridisch Commissaris* (Woshibu 倭什布); they discussed the translation with Carlos and made some improvements to the wordings of the text (see Version 6).[20]

Driven by jealousy, some Europeans in Canton circulated rumours that Titsingh had not been appointed and dispatched by the ruler of the Netherlands, and that this ruler was not a king, while the ambassador was not an official of high rank either. The Chinese authorities attached so great a concern to these rumors that Governor-General Changlin sent the four officials mentioned above to verify this information. They repeatedly asked Titsingh the following questions: 1. Wat is de naam van onse Vorst? 2. Waarom de brief voor den Keiser niet door hem was geteekend? 3. Wie de Commissarissen Generaal waaren? 4. Waarom haar Cachet niet neevens hare handteekening stond? 5. Waarom eene Chinese vertaling by den brief was gevoegd?[21] The answers given by Titsingh were brought back to the Governor-General by these officials and were integrated into the new Chinese version of the letter of credence. Both the original Chinese version (version 3) and this new Chinese version (version 6) were included in the *Four Tales on Maritime Countries* edited by Liang Tingnan 梁廷枏.[22] It is noteworthy that, when the Dutch embassy arrived in Beijing on January 10th 1795, He Shen 和珅 (1750–1799), the first minister, asked the embassy to provide a French version of the Dutch letter of credence the next day. Van Braam thought this request obviously revealed that the first minister planned to ask the French missionaries in the court to translate it into Chinese, so that it could be compared with the new Chinese version that had been

19 Ibid., 79, October 3rd, 1794.

20 Van Braam, *Voyage*, 79, October 3rd, 1794.

21 Lequin, *Isaac Titsingh in China*, 78, 3 October 1794. "1. What is the name of our Sovereign? 2. Why the letter for the Emperor was not signed by him? 3. Who were the Commissioners-General? 4. Why their cachet was not next to their signature? 5. Why a Chinese translation was attached to the letter?" (Own translation, Cai Xiangyu). Van Braam only recorded three questions in his journal: "ces quatre mandarins demandèrent, au nom du tsong-tou, pourquoi l'on avait ajouté à Batavia, à la lettre pour l'empereur, une traduction en chinois (question 5 as mentioned by Titsingh); pourquoi notre monarque n'avait pas signé la lettre (question 2); & enfin pourquoi l'on n'y trouvait que le sceau de la Compagnie des Indes hollandaises, sans que le cachet des quatre mandarins (les quatre commissaires-généraux) qui l'avaient signée y eût été apposé (question 4)." Vol. 1, 12–13.

22 Liang Tingnan, *Haiguo sishuo*, 211–212.

translated in Canton.[23] This episode reveals the extreme caution exercised by the high officials in the court in checking the accuracy of the content of the original Dutch letter. Both Van Braam and De Guignes mentioned in their journals that the French version had been worked out respectively by themself, though it was probably based on the French version translated by Van Braam at Canton and was then revised by De Guignes, since he was French and had worked as Chinese interpreter for many years in the French Consulate at Canton. A French version is available in Van Braam's journal.[24] De Guignes also mentioned a trick plotted by himself when preparing the French version: he signed his name and the date "January 11th, 1795" instead of "July 26th, 1794" at the bottom of the letter, so as to let the French missionaries know that he was now in Beijing and wanted them to take the opportunity to visit the Dutch embassy. However, no news was received from them, for such visits were forbidden by the Chinese government. In order not to arise suspicion among the Chinese, neither Van Braam nor De Guignes dared to meet the missionaries anymore.[25] Actually it was the missionaries at the court who worked out a Latin version of the original Chinese version of the letter. Titsingh was given it by a missionary who visited Canton after he had returned there.[26] The Latin version may also have been created at the request of He Shen with the aim of comparing different versions of the letter and guaranteeing the accuracy of the information contained in the Dutch letter of credence.

4 Textual Analysis

In this section, I will compare four versions of the letter of credence, i.e. the original Dutch letter (Version 1), the original Chinese version worked out in Batavia (Version 3), the French translation of the Dutch letter (Version 5) and the new Chinese version drawn out by Van Braam, Hong merchants and Carlos (the *lingua*) and improved by the Cantonese authorities (Version 6). In doing so, we shall be able to determine what information is missing, what terms were considered unsuitable in Version 3, and therefore what had to be replaced with other expressions in Version 6.

Among the four versions, most of the sentences in the Dutch and French versions coincide, and it is obvious that the original and new Chinese versions had far fewer words than the Dutch and French versions. Besides the lack of certain

23 Van Braam, *Voyage*, Vol.1, 140, January 11th, 1795.
24 Ibid., Vol.2, Appendix D, 371–374.
25 De Guignes, *Voyages à Peking, Manille et L'Île de France*, January 11th, 1795.
26 Lequin, *Isaac Titsingh in China*, Appendix G., 223.

information, the manners of expression in the two Chinese versions are also different: the original version uses a written form of expression, while the new one is more oral in kind. While the original Dutch letter has four paragraphs, the French version has seven, presumably having been redivided by Van Braam and De Guignes for convenience of translation (the following Paragraphs 2, 3, 4 and 5 are combined into a single long paragraph in the Dutch version).

For the Chinese authorities, the problems with the original Chinese version were as follows. First, it had less than one quarter the length of the Dutch letter at first glance, suggesting that some important information might have been omitted. Second, as the Chinese secretary in Batavia came from Fujian province, he had adopted the pronunciation and vocabulary of the South Fujianese dialect in rendering the proper nouns (i.e. personal names and place names) phonetically in the letter. This was not readable by the mandarins neither in Canton nor Beijing because they did not understand the dialect, and was thus considered improper by the Cantonese authorities. Third, the wordings and expressions used should be replaced with more elegant vocabularies and a more solemn style of writing. And fourth, the crucial problem, was who had actually dispatched the Dutch ambassador? Under the tribute system, no organization or individual but a monarch had the right to dispatch an embassy to the court of China, the so-called Celestial Empire and Middle Kingdom.

The first sentence of Version 6, "至大普惠仁慈中外洋溢天朝大皇帝陛下", agrees with "De Grootmagtige Doorlugtige en alomme beroemde Keijzer van China" at the beginning of Version 1, while Version 3 lacks this expression. The sentence "皇帝陛下以德临御，宜履四海之福；以仁恤众，将来无疆之寿" [May Your Majesty the Emperor, reigning by virtue, walk in the happiness of (all within) the Four Seas; cherishing the multitudes with benevolence, may Your Majesty reach a boundless age] agrees with the sentence "toegewenscht (e)en bestendig genot van alle Zeegeningen die het geluk van de bevoorregtste Sterveling op deeze aarde kunnen Volmaken", while Version 6 translated it as "保佑天朝大皇帝万事遂心，吉祥如意。天降征祥，从心所欲". The latter version is more accurate, but neither the expression nor parallel structure is as elegant and concise as in Version 3.

As for the names of the Commissioners-General, Version 6 changes the South Fujianese pronunciation into Cantonese so as to correspond with the conventional expression that would be used by the Cantonese authorities. For instance, "泥律帽禄" (Nederburgh) is changed into "呢（口德）啵", "勃里稽（口年）" (Frikenius) to "啡呢（口坚）（口尔）吐", "沃力丁" (Althing) to "（口压）喇（口打）", and "时袂力" (Siberg) to "（口施）啤喱". "勃嶙氏" (Willem, Version 1, mentions "Prince van Orange en Nassau", without "Willem") was changed into "喊咻・哗（口兰）咥・哪嗖" (Willem Orange en Nassau). It should be mentioned that the Radical "口" ("mouth" in Chinese) is added to

TABLE 11.2 Comparing four versions of the Letter of Credence

Paragraph 1	Version 1-Dutch	Aan den Keijzer van China De Grootmagtige Doorlugtige en alomme beroemde Keijzer van China word door Mr Sebastiaan Cornelis Nederburgh Simon Hendrik Frijkenius Mr Willem Arnold Alting en Johannes Siberg Commissarissen Generaal over geheel Neederlandsch Indiën en Cabo de Goede Hoop, repraesenteerende Zijne Doorluchtige Hoogheid den Heere Prince van Orange en Nassau, Erfstadhouder Capitain Generaal en Admiraal der Vereenigde Neederlanden, Opper Bewindhebber en Gouverneur Generaal van de Generaal geoctroijeerde Neederlandsche Comp: etc: etc: etc: en de heeren Bewindhebberen gecommitteerd ter Vergadering van 17en de gem: Comp: representeerende toegewenscht (e)en bestendig genot van alle Zeegeningen die het geluk van de bevoorregtste Sterveling op deeze aarde kunnen Volmaken.
	Version 3-Chinese (English translation by Duyvendak, with slight revision by Cai Xiangyu)	上 和兰国王勃嶙氏，委吧国公勃沙里仁直唠兼管牛屿暨公班衙等处地方事务泥律帽禄、勃里稽（口年）、沃力丁、时袂力等顿首顿首奉书： 皇帝陛下以德临御，宜履四海之福；以仁恤众，将来无疆之寿。 Presented to … Delegated by the King of Holland, by the name of Pu-lien (Willem), Cong-pu-sha-li jen-chih-lao (Commissarissen Generaal) of the country of Pa (Batavia), also having the administration of the local affairs of the island of Niu and Kung-pan-ya and other places, Ni-lü-mao-lu (Nederburgh), Pu-li-ki-nien (Frykenius), Yao-li-ting (Alting), Shih-mei-li (Siberg), knocking their hands (sic. heads) to the ground, humbly present this letter. May Your Majesty the Emperor, reigning by virtue, walk in the happiness of (all within) the Four Seas; cherishing the multitudes with benevolence, may Your Majesty reach a boundless age.

TABLE 11.2 Comparing four versions of the Letter of Credence (*cont.*)

Version 5-French	Dépêche des Commissaires-Généraux de Batavia, à Kien-Long, Empereur de la Chine. Messieurs Sebastien Cornelis Neederburch; Simon Henri Frykenius; Guillaume Arnold Alting; & Jean Siberg: Représentans ladite Compagnie: Souhaitent au Très-Puissant & par tout Célèbre Empereur de la Chine, la jouissance durable de toute la félicité que le plus heureux des mortels puisse goûter sur la terre.
Version 6-Chinese	至大普惠仁慈中外洋溢天朝大皇帝陛下： 呢（口德）啵、啡呢（口坚）（口尔）吐、（口压）喇（口打）、（口施）啤喱四人，专主办理（口贺）（口兰）国事务，恭代国王嘁啉哗（口兰）咥哪嗖具奏：保佑天朝大皇帝万事遂心，吉祥如意。天降征祥，从心所欲。因为声教覃敷，天下一人。圣明睿智，天下无不感颂。

each character in one's name, a phonetic principle used in Canton in rendering foreigners' names into Chinese.

"和兰" is changed into "（口贺）（口兰）", the Chinese appellation of the Netherlands used among the merchants in Canton. Soon, at the end of 1794, Qianlong issued an edict to change "（口贺）（口兰）国" into "荷兰国", literally "the country of the lotus and orchid".[27] Cai Hongsheng has noted that there were several expressions in Chinese for the country of the Netherlands in the Ming and Qing dynasties, such as 贺兰, 和兰, 阿兰陀 and 尼特兰.[28] Koos Kuiper has discussed the time, area and context in which the names和兰, 荷兰 and 贺兰 were each adopted. He points out that the three names were shown at the same time in Changlin's memorial to Qianlong dated October 15th 1794 – i.e. "和兰" in Version 3 (prevailing in Batavia) and "（口贺）（口兰）" in Version 6 (prevailing among the Cantonese merchants), both as attachments – while "荷兰" was adopted by Changlin in his own report (widely accepted by the Chinese authorities). This may explain why Qianlong issued an edict to standardize the Chinese appellation of the Netherlands (荷兰 was chosen).[29]

27 Liang Tingnan, *Haiguo sishuo*, 202. Recently I have found in the VOC archives that 河兰 is also adopted by the Hong merchants at Canton in 1760s. See NL-HaNA 1.04.02 4384, pp. 186, 187, 189, 191, 198, 199; NL-HaNA 1.04.02 4387, p.153.

28 Du Zongyu 杜宗预, *Yinghuan yiyin yiming ji* 瀛寰译音异名记 (Records on Different Translations of the Names of Countries of the World), quoted from Cai Hongsheng, *Zhongwai jiaoliu shishi kaoshu*, 343–344.

29 Koos Kuiper, "The Chinese Name for "Holland": 和兰，荷兰，贺兰 – A Historical Survey", in Xu Quansheng 许全胜, Liu Zhen刘震 eds., *Neilu ouya lishi yuyan lunji: Xu*

In fact, the three names remained current in different countries, areas and contexts from then on, and the name 荷兰 was eventually adopted as the formal name of this country in 1944.[30]

The beginning of Version 1 makes it clear that the four Commissioners-General had been representing the Prince of Orange and Nassau, "Capitain Generaal en Admiraal der Vereenigde Neederlanden, Opper Bewindhebber en Gouverneur Generaal", in writing the letter and dispatching the embassy. Although Version 5 only mentioned that the Commissioners-General were representatives of the VOC, this suited the views of De Guignes and the English merchants, who were hostile to Van Braam. They insisted that Titsingh had been sent by the company, not by the King of the Netherlands. Version 6 changes the expression into "恭代国王喊咻哗（口兰）哑哪嗖具奏" (to report on behalf of King Willem of Orange and Nassau), which shows that the Commissioners-General were the representatives of Willem of Orange and Nassau, the King of the Netherlands. This is the only expression that was acceptable to the Chinese government. As to the territorial jurisdiction of the Commissioners-General, Versions 1 and 3 both refer to the whole of the Dutch Indies and the Cape of Good Hope, while Version 5 does not mention it at all, and Version 6 describes it as "专主办理（口贺）（口兰）国事务" (primarily in charge of the affairs of the country of the Netherlands). The aim here was to conceal the status of the Commissioners-General as administrators of the VOC (they were still merchants in the eyes of the Chinese authorities), and to give them new identities as officials of the Dutch government. Such changes could help to avoid institutional conflicts and remove the Chinese authorities's suspicions.

P2	V1-D	Daar de roem van Uw Majesteit wijze Regeering zich over de voornaamste gewesten van den aardbol heeft verspreid en de Neederlandsche Compagnie het Streelend Geluk geniet zeedert zij in het Rijk van China heeft handel gedreeven, met de onwaardeerbaare Vriendschap van Uwe Majesteits Doorlugtige Voor vaderen en ook van Uwe Majesteits begunstigd te worden, hebben ook de bestierders van de Neederlandsche Oost Indische Compagnie steeds de vuurigste zucht voor de voorspoed en het Heil van het Chinasche Rijk gekoesterd. Dit heeft hun dan ook bestendig oplettend doen zijn op de gewichtige gebeurtenisse die op het zelve betrekking hadden,

Wenkan xiansheng guxi jinian 内陆欧亚历史语言论集——徐文堪先生古稀纪念 (Lanzhou: Lanzhou University Press, 2014), 87–88.

30 Ibid., 95.

(*cont.*)

V3-C/E	溯自圣祖仁皇帝（康熙）以至于今，敝邑在粤东贸易，永承圣泽之广被，而远迩无不向化者也。 We recall how our city from the days of the Emperor Sheng-tsu (K'ang-hsi) till now has traded in Kuang-tung and has always received the wide-reaching tokens of the Sacred blessings, so that everyone far and near has submitted to (China's) civilising influence. (quotation of translation by Duyvendak)
V5-F	La gloire du sage gouvernement de Votre Majesté étant connue des plus vastes Empires de l'Univers, & la Compagie des Indes Orientales Hollandaises, ayant joui, depuis qu'elle a commencé à commercer avec l'Empire de la Chine, du bonheur de recevoir des preuves inappréciables d'affection, tant de la part de Votre Majesté, que de celles de ses illustres Ancêtres, les Directeurs de cette Compagnie, animés à leur tour, par un sentiment qui les porte à désirer ardemment tout ce qui peut tendre à la prospérité & à la tranquillité de l'Empire de la Chine, n'ont pas cessé d'avoir les yeux continuellement fixés sur les circonstances propres à intéresser ce double objet.
V6-C	再，（口贺）（口兰）国来广东贸易，感沐天朝列祖大皇帝、天朝大皇帝格外施恩。缘本国王同公班衙世代沾恩感激，本国王久有心输诚，命专主国事呢（口德）啵四人，在叭哋（口末）就近探听，

Version 6 adopts the Cantonese pronunciation "叭哋（口末）" to translate "Batavia" instead of "Kelapa" (噶喇吧, which means "coconut" in Malay), as shown at the end of Version 3. The expressions and meanings of Version 1 and 6 are quite similar, while Version 3 just expressed the main idea of Version 1 more concisely – it could not be regarded as a missing translation. The last sentence of Version 6, "本国王久有心输诚，命专主国事呢（口德）啵四人，在叭哋（口末）就近探听" (the King, who has wished to express his sincerity for a long time, asked the four people, who were in charge of the country's affairs and stationed in Batavia nearby, including Nederburgh, to find out a good opportunity), is not shown in either Version 1 or 5 and according to Titsingh must have been added by the Cantonese officials. The reason for this was to give the impression that the Commissioners-General, who signed the bottom of the letter, had been entrusted by the King of the Netherlands to conduct Chinese affairs.

P3	V1-D	en daar door is aan ons die tans ter deeser Hoofdplaats Batavia aanweezig zijn, voorzien met een buijtengewoone commissie ten einde het belang der Neederlandsche Oost Indische Compe te bevorderen niet ontslipt een der Zeldzaamste gebeurtenissen waar van men bij de geschiedenisse der beroemste rijken naauwelijk een voorbeeld vind, het tijdstip namentlijk dat Uw Majesteit in het aanstaande Jaar 1795 het Zestigste jaar zijner Loffelijke Regeering zal hebben bereikt tot vergroting van het geluk zijner onderdanen, tot Volmaking van het Heil zijner uitgebreide Staten.
	V3-C/E	来岁恭逢国寿，天下咸庆之期，万民乐德之秋，历稽开古以来，未有我皇上圣神建极之盛也。 Next year we shall respectfully witness Your Majesty's Anniversary, an occasion on which All-under-Heaven jubilates, and a period in which all the people rejoice over (the Imperial) virtue. Examining (the records) from the beginning of antiquity there has never been such a glorious reign as that of our Emperor.
	V5-F	Il n'a donc pas échappé à nous Commissaires actuels de la capitale de Batavia, chargés de diriger cette Compagnie, qu'un grand événement, dont les plus célèbres Empires offrent à peine l'exemple, est au moment d'arriver, puisque Votre majesté va entrer, pendant l'année prochaine 1795, pour l'accroissement du bonheur de ses sujets & la prospérité de ses vastes États, dans la soisantième année de son règne si glorieux.
	V6-C	闻得明年恭逢天朝大皇帝六十年大庆，普天同庆。

While Versions 1 and 5 are identical, here too Version 3 expresses the main idea of Version 1 concisely and in parallel style. Conversely, Version 6 contains neither the meanings "unprecedentedly" nor "do not want to miss the great event", etc. Version 1 mentions that "ten einde het belang der Neederlandsche Oost Indische Compe te bevorderen", which does not fit Titsingh's aim of congratulating Qianlong on the 60th anniversary of his enthronement. This expression can therefore not be found in the other three versions.

P4	V1-D	De erkentenis die de Neederlandsche Oost Indische Compe voor zo langjaarig(e) en meenigvuldige weldaden gevoeld, heeft ons aangespoord, een plegtig gezandschap te benoemen om Uwe Doorlugtige Majesteit met die zigtbaare blijk der bescherming van den Heemel te vergelukken.

(cont.)

	V3-C/E	勃（口粦）属在遐陬，历受惠泽，敢不闻风而致庆焉。 I, William, although I have territories in remote parts, yet have I often received Your Majesty's bounties; should I then, hearing these tidings, venture not to come and congratulate!
	V5-F	La reconnaissance dont de nombreux bienfaits ont rempli la Compagnie des Indes Hollandaises depuis longues années, nous a déterminés à charger une Ambassade solennelle, d'aller féliciter Votre Illustre Majesté, à l'occasion de cette preuve manifeste de la protection du Ciel.
	V6-C	本国王同公班衙十分欢喜，一面启知本国王，一面专差贡使嘚（口胜），赍表到京叩贺。(N.B: This sentence was added by the Cantonese authorities according to Titsingh, but could not be split into two parts and is therefore listed as Paragraphs 4 and 5.)

This paragraph is mostly the same in Versions 1 and 5, while Version 3 still expresses the main idea in Version 1 more concisely. The subject of Version 1 and 5 is "the Dutch East India Company", but Version 3 changes it into "William, the King of the Netherlands" to make it acceptable within the framework of the system of tribute. By comparison, the subject of Version 6 is presented as "The King, together with the company" (本国王同公班衙), and a sentence is added, viz.: "(the Commissioners-General) report to the King on the one hand, and dispatch Titsingh as tribute ambassador on the other, to fetch the letter of credence to Beijing to address congratulations …) (一面启知本国王，一面专差贡使嘚（口胜），赍表到京叩贺). The insertion of this sentence was presumably the idea of the Cantonese authorities, the aim being that, although, due to the limitations on his time and the long distance between China and the Netherlands, Titsingh could not be dispatched directly by the King, the Commissioners-General have still taken measures to inform the King about this mission. Comparing Versions 1 and 6, the meaning of "de Neederlandsche Oost Indische Compe voor zo langjaarig(e) en meenigvuldige weldaden gevoeld" in the former is missing in the latter, thus concealing the fact that the VOC was really the subject of the letter.

P5	V1-D	waar toe Wij tans afvaardigen den persoon van Mr Isaac Titsingh, een Man van aanzien en een Lid uit de Hoge vergadering van Neederlandsche Indien Wie wij in de bezondere toegeneegentheid van Uwe Majesteit aanbeveelen.

(*cont.*)

V3-C/E	谨遣来使余悚第生，恭赴阙下， I am now respectfully sending Ambassador Yu-shu-ti-sheng to proceed reverently to the Palace-gates (quotation of translation by Duyvendak)
V5-F	En conséquence nous envoyons vers vous Titsingh, homme de considération & membre de la Haute Assemblée des Indes Orientales Hollandaises, que nous recommandons à la protection particulière de Votre Majesté.
V6-C	专差贡使嘚（口胜），赍表到京叩贺。务求天朝大皇帝赏脸。

Version 1 and 5 are comparable, while Version 3 removes the explanation for Titsingh's position as member of the high government in the Dutch Indies. Besides, the meaning "Wie wij in de bezondere toegeneegentheid van Uwe Majesteit aanbeveelen" is missing is Version 3, Version 6 expresses it in the sentence "务求天朝大皇帝赏脸" (wish the great emperor of the Celestial Empire to do us a honour), which is satisfactory.

P6 V1-D	Deeze onze ambssadeur zal Uwe Majesteit uit onze naam bij welke thans, als daar toe gecommitteerd door Hoogst gemelde Zijne Doorlugtige Hoogheid den Heere Prince van Orange en Nassau, en de aanzienlijke vergadering van 17en het opperste bestuur over de Neederlandsche Oost Indische Compagnie in deese gewesten word uitgeoeffend, met de gevoeligste deelneeming, en diepen eerbied vergelukken met die groote en Zeldsame gebeurtenis en toewenschen dat het Almagtig opperweezen door welk de Regeering van Uwe majesteit zo lange heeft voortgeduurd, en gezeegend is met Vreede, Luijster, en Welvaart, in de geheele uitgestrekheid van het Rijk – Ja zo, dat uwe Majesteit het waarlijk voor een Regeerder groot genoegen gevoeld, van de bewustheid dat desselves beveelen en schikkingen steeds gestrekt hebben tot bevordering van het wel zijn van het Rijk den luijster haerer Regeeringen, en de welvaard haarer onderdanen, dat datzelfde Almachtig opperweezen, na dat uwe Majesteit navolgens desselves verlangen zal hebben opgehouden keijzer te zijn, Uwe Majesteit zal doen genieten de Zoetste Rust, met het Streelend vermaak, te zien, dat dezelfde voorspoed waarmeede uwe Majesteit begunstigd is gebleeven, aan de opvolger in het Keijzerrijk geschonken, en dat volk in het Rijk gezeegend en bewaard word.

(*cont.*)

V3-C/E	谨行朝贡，兼贺皇太子来年践祚，庆万国之咸宁，叶千龄之广运。 in order humbly to appear at an audience and present tribute, and at the same time to congratulate the Heir-apparent (and express the wish that), when next year he will ascend the throne he may be congratulated on the universal peace of all the countries and may equal the grand good fortune of a long life (with slight revision by Cai Xiangyu).
V5-F	Cet Ambassadeur ira, avec le plus profond respecte, féliciter Votre Majesté en notre nom, nous qui sommes dépositaires de l'autorité de Son Altesse Sérénissime Monseigneur le Prince d'Orange & de Nassau, ainsi que de celle de la haute Assemblée des Dix-Sept, qui représentent & exercent la souveraineté de la Compagnie des Indes Orientales Hollandaises dans cette région. Il assurera en outre Votre majesté du vif intérêt que nous prenons à ce grand événement, & lui dira que nous faisons les voeux les plus ardens pour que l'Être Suprême qui a accordé à Votre Majesté un long règne couvert de bénédictions, & remarquable par la paix, l'éclat & la prospérité de tout l'Empire; qui a permis que Votre Majesté goûtât la plus vive satisfaction que peut éprouver celui qui gouverne, celle de se rendre ce témoignage que ses volontés & ses vues ont continuellement servi à accroître la félicité publique, à illustrer son gouvernement & à rendre ses peuples heureux, veuille ajouter à tant de bienfaits, lorsque Votre Majesté jugera à propos d'abandonner les rênes de l'Empire, celui de la laisser jouir d'un doux repos, & d'être témoin que les mêmes principes auront pour son successeur les mêmes résultats, & que le Peuple & l'Empire soient également bénis & conservés.
V6-C	今贡使嘚（口胜）恭代国王来京虔诚叩首，恭贺千载难逢之盛典，即如本国王亲来叩贺一样。贡使叩见天朝大皇帝面奏，惟愿上苍庇祐，岁岁天下太平，长生万万岁，将来天朝大皇帝亲见皇太子受天庇祐，万事如意，均同天朝大皇帝一样。

Versions 1 and 5 are almost the same in this long paragraph, while most of the information is missing in Version 3,which it simply uses the phrase "humbly to appear at an audience and present tribute" (谨行朝贡) to cover all the missing information. The parallel style "he may be congratulated on the universal peace of all the countries and may equal the grand good fortune of a long life" (庆万国之咸宁，叶千龄之广运, N.B.: the subject "He" refers to "the Heir-apparent", i.e. the succeeding emperor Jiaqing, not Qianlong) agrees with "toewenschen dat het Almagtig opperweezen door welk de Regeering van Uwe majesteit zo lange heeft voortgeduurd, en gezeegend is met Vreede, Luijster, en Welvaart, in de geheele uitgestrekheid van het Rijk". Also, the sentence "惟愿上苍庇祐，岁岁天下太平，长生万万岁" in Version 6 (N.B. the subject in Versions 1 and 6 is Qianlong) is colloquial and could not be judged to be as elegant and solemn as required by the Cantonese authorities. As for the sentence "To congratulate the Heir-apparent (and express the wish that) when next year he will ascend the throne" (兼贺皇太子来年践祚) in Version 3, though it was widely known all over China that Qianlong would pass the throne to his son the next year, to mention this in an official document like a letter of credence was still considered inappropriate. Furthermore, the phrase "next year" (来年) in Version 3 does not appear in Version 1, but instead "uwe Majesteit … zal hebben opgehouden keijzer te zijn". Therefore in Version 6 the sentence was changed to "将来天朝大皇帝亲见皇太子受天庇祐，万事如意，均同天朝大皇帝一样" (in the future the great emperor of the Celestial Empire will see that the Heir-apparent enjoys the same blessings from Heaven, everything goes as he wishes, just as all has been enjoyed by you, the great emperor of the Celestial Empire), which agrees well with "dezelfde voorspoed waarmeede uwe Majesteit begunstigd is gebleeven, aan de opvolger in het Keijzerrijk geschonken". However, the sentence "en dat volk in het Rijk gezeegend en bewaard word" is still missing from Version 6. It should be pointed out here that the subject in Versions 1 and 5 is "Deeze onze ambssadeur zal … uit onze (Commissioners-general's) naam", while version 6 changes it into "The tribute ambassador Titsingh on behalf of the King", still with the aim of avoiding institutional conflict. As to Titsingh's name, the Cantonese pronunciation "嘚（口胜）" – again with the radical "口" (mouth) being attached to the left of each character – was adopted instead of the Fujianese rendering "余悚第生".

P7 V1-D Wij verlangen zeer na het bericht, dat dit gezandschap aan Uwe Majesteit aangenaam is geweest en desselves verlangens in onze voor aangehaalde wenschen voor de Welvaart en het genoege van Uwe Majesteit vervuld zijn, en het zal ons om die reedenen ook aangenaam zijn, dat voorm: onzen gezant bij Uwe Majesteit een spoedig gehoor verleen(d) word.

V3-C/E 来使倘礼法疏略，万乞包容。仍恳速赐旋棹，曷胜激切仰慕之至。伏惟圣慈垂鉴。谨奉表以闻。

In case my Ambassador may not be sufficiently versed in the etiquette, I earnestly pray that Your Majesty will graciously pardon him and will

(*cont.*)

	permit him a speedy return in his ship. I find no words to express my feelings and my desire to see (Your Majesty). Prostrating myself I hope that Your Sacred Kindness will deign to glance at this and respectfully I present this document for Your Majesty's information.
V5-F	Nous désirons fortement que cette Ambassade obtienne l'approbation de Votre majesté, & que nos vœux pour son bonheur soient exaucés. C'est avec ces sentiments que nous sollicitons Votre Majesté d'accorder une prompte audience à notre Ambassadeur.
V6-C	贡使嘚（口胜）来京叩贺，定邀天朝大皇帝喜欢优容。惟愿贡使回国时，面述天朝盛典，更加舞蹈欢呼。

Versions 1 and 5 are still comparable, while the sentence "In case my Ambassador may not be sufficiently versed in the etiquette, I earnestly pray that Your Majesty will graciously pardon him" (来使倘礼法疏略，万乞包容) in Version 3 does not appear in Version 1. Cai Hongsheng points out that the word "etiquette" (礼法，礼数) is mentioned in both of the original Chinese letters to Qianlong and Changlin, a reference to the ritual of kowtowing, which caused a great sensation when it was refused by the Macartney embassy.[31] Received twice in the Honam Temple by Changlin before leaving for Beijing, as requested by the Chinese authorities, Titsingh kowtowed to the tablet of Qianlong in both audiences. The appearance of "etiquette" in Version 3, even though it does not exist in Version 1, indicates that Titsingh would be obedient and well behaved enough to win the favour of the Chinese authorities. In fact, as far back as the seventeenth century the VOC had issued instructions to its officials to follow the rules of the country they were in. Titsingh did not, unlike Macartney, regard kowtowing as a humiliation, therefore, when he learnt that he should follow this etiquette before the tablet of Qianlong when meeting the Hoppo on September 24th 1794, he agreed to do so. On this etiquette he wrote to the Commissioners-general that "ik in een vreemd Land komende mij na de gebruijken moest schikken".[32]

The words "Permit him a speedy return in his ship" (速赐旋棹) in Version 3 does not exist in Version 1 either, which only mentions "onzen gezant bij Uwe Majesteit een spoedig gehoor verleen(d) word". Version 6 goes on to say "惟愿贡使回国时，面述天朝盛典，更加舞蹈欢呼" (only wish the tribute ambassador

31 Cai Hongsheng, *Zhongwai jiaoliu shishi kaoshu*, 364.

32 Lequin, *Isaac Titsingh in China*, 232.

to report vis-à-vis the illustrious ceremony of the Celestial Empire, even dance and hurrah because of happiness). From "quickly granted our ambassador an audience" to "permit him a speedy return in his ship" to "wish the tribute ambassador to report vis-à-vis the illustrious ceremony of the Celestial Empire", we can see that logically Version 3 still has impact on Version 6.

Given the help of all the people involved, Version 6 eventually came into existence. Then followed the technical problems of decoration and package. Titsingh mentioned in his letter dated November 26th that:

> Het sakje van geel satijn waarin de brief beslote was wierd meede afgekeurd, en diende voor die van den Tsontok, de Heer Van Braam liet terstond een ander vervaardigen van wit satijn met goude draken en coleuren in haar fantestique smaak superbe geborduurd, zomeede een houte versilverde doos met verguld lofwerk. Wijl de brief der Engelsen op parkement beschreeve was, moest dit meede veranderd, hiertoe wierd een groot vel in het vierkant gesneede en na het afmeeten van den brief de overschietende breede van den keurig met bloemwerk en vercierselen beschilderd, waarna er de brief wierd opgeplakt, na lang sukkelens kreeg dit een en ander den 12: (October) zijn beslag.[33]

Van Braam simply wrote in his journal dated September 28th:

> Et comme l'on avait marqué beaucoup d'étonnement de ce qu'au lieu d'être, comme la commission de l'ambassadeur, sur du parchemin, elle

33 Ibid., 235. "The little sack of yellow satin in which the letter was enclosed was also rejected, and served for that of the Tsontok, Mr. Van Braam immediately had another handicraft of white satin with gold dragons and colors in fantastic taste superbly embroidered, as well as a silver plated wooden box with gilt foliage. While the letter of the English was written on parchment, this also had to be changed, for this purpose a big sheet of parchment was tailored in square and according to the measure of the letter, the side spaces were painted neatly with flowers and (other) decorations, after which the letter was pasted on it, after enduring setbacks these matters were brought to a conclusion on October 12th." (Own translation, Cai Xiangyu). Titsingh recorded in his journal dated September 26th as follow: "het Opperhoofd van Braam besorgde verders wat na begeere der Chineesen omtrend den brief wierd vereischt, als een vel parkament aan de randen ter breedte van circa drie duymen met leeuwen en bloemwerk beschilderd, waarbinne de brief wierd vastgeplakt. een sakje van geel zatyn met den Keiserlyken Draak in goud geborduurd. een houte vergulde doos waarop de Draak meede was uytgewerkt." See Isaac Titsingh, *Relaas mijner Ambassade naar China in 1794–1795*, BPL 2177, Special Collection, Leiden University Library, (date unknown), 77–78. According to both records by Titsingh, it is clear that what was rejected by the Chinese is the white satin envelope, not the yellow one.

> n'avait été écrite que sur du simple papier, je pris, pour remédier à cet inconvénient, une grande feuille de parchemin, sur laquelle je fis peindre une bordure festonnée en fleurs & deux lions debout. Je collai ensuite la lettre sur ce parchemin, ce qui satisfit entièrement pour cet objet.[34]

Van Braam's record is simpler than Titsingh's, as he did not want to mention this annoying episode, which could lead him to be criticized by the authorities in Batavia for not providing useful instructions in preparing a qualified letter of credence, regardless of its language, contents or packaging.

5 Conclusion

Although Van Braam Houckgeest provides some suggestions for the Commissioners-General in Batavia in how to draw up the letter of credence, the Chinese letter to Qianlong that was translated by a Fujianese translator in Batavia still aroused great sensation among the Chinese officials in Canton. The main reason for this was that the preparations for the content (in terms of proper names, expressions and institutional background) and the form (the appearance and decoration) of a proper Chinese letter of credence were beyond the practical knowledge of foreigners. Van Braam, who had been working in the Dutch factory for a long period and was entirely confident that he was familiar with the customs and rules of Chinese society was quite aghast at the emergence of so many unexpected problems. His suggestion that the letter should be issued in the name of the King, for example, did not take into consideration the fact that the Commissioners-General in Batavia had no right to dispatch an embassy on behalf of the stadhouder. Nor was a dispatch in the name of the company acceptable to the Chinese authorities. The question of who had dispatched the embassy was the central problem in this controversy: it made the Chinese officials suspicious and then led to the joint decision by the Cantonese authories to require the Chinese letter of credence to be rewritten. Changlin, the Governor-General, was the wire-puller behind the curtain. He knew very well that the ambassador had been dispatched from Batavia,

34 Van Braam, *Voyage*, 12–13. "And as a lot of astonishment was noticed about what had happened, while the commission of the ambassador was written on parchment, it had been written simply on paper, I took, to remedy this disadvantage, a large sheet of parchment, on which I had painted a bordure decorated with flowers & two standing lions. I then pasted the letter on this parchment, which satisfied entirely for this object". (Own translation, Cai Xiangyu).

the VOC headquarters in Asia, for he himself urged Van Braam to dispatch a Dutch embassy to Beijing. In his memorial to the court dated October 14th, he stated that "Now that the Netherlands have dispatched an ambassador to pay tribute, I have examined the letter of credence (and found that) this ambassador (i.e., Titsingh) was dispatched by Nederburgh and the other Commissioners-General of the company, which seems not conform to the regulations. After inquiring repeatedly, (Titsingh) states that the King, being sincere and earnest indeed, has wished to pay tribute for a long time. Because it was quite late when Nederburgh was informed (about the matter of paying tribute), there was no time for him to travel home and have the letter of credence issued and signed (by the King). Nederburgh himself, indeed, dared not arbitrarily make such a determination on behalf of the King. If (Titsingh) is blessed by the grace and is allowed to come to the court to pay congratulation (to the Emperor), then not only would the King of this country be blessed with grace, but also the foreigners (or barbarians) of all nations who are doing business in Canton would even respect and jointly share the benevolence of (the Emperor)."[35] This paragraph showed that Changlin was keen on maintaining the tribute system of the Celestial Empire and on putting Qianlong's idea of "cherishing men from afar" into practice.

The process of negotiation and the textual analysis of the letter of credence make it clear that the Latin and French languages were much more important in East Asian diplomacy, even though "Canton Portuguese" and "Canton English" were successively adopted in oral communications within the circle of commercial transactions. As for the records of commercial activities, different European countries used their own languages. Without doubt the primacy of Latin and French in the diplomatic domain was connected with the presence of a group of French Catholic missionaries who served in the Court of Beijing at that time. Carlos, the Chinese *lingua*, who was proficient in both languages, was recruited by Governor-General Changlin to assist in foreign affairs in the port city of Canton. Had Van Braam realized the significance of Latin in the Qing government's foreign affairs, he would have suggested that the Batavian authorities write the letter straight in Latin. If they had done so, there might have been less friction in negotiating and recasting the Dutch

35 The original Chinese text is: "今荷兰国遣使进贡，臣等查其表文，系公班大臣呢（口德）啵等恭代国王出名，似与体制不符。但经臣等再三盘诘，据称该国王实在诚心，早要纳贡，呢（口德）啵等因得信已迟，计算日期，不及回国缮表属实。并非呢（口德）啵等敢替国王擅作主意等语。倘蒙圣恩准其趋诣阙廷，随班叩祝，不惟该国君臣幸叨恩宠，即在广贸易之各国夷人，亦必更深钦仰，共戴宽仁。" See Liang Tingnan, *Haiguo sishuo*, 213–214.

letter of credence. The Chinese authorities, bearing in mind the bold requests and offensive behavior of the Macartney embassy, embarked on this tortuous and burdensome process of negotiation either to assist, and discipline, the Dutch embassy, or simply because it was part of an inevitable process of integrating the activities of the Dutch embassy into the Qing Empire's system of tribute. The Titsingh embassy was only accepted as trustworthy by the Qing government when it decided to observe all these disciplinary actions regarding discourse and etiquette.

CHAPTER 12

Comparing the Ostend Company's Worlds

the Formation of the GIC's Trade Communities through Intercultural Interactions in Eighteenth-Century China and Bengal

Wim De Winter

1 Introducing the GIC or "Ostend Company"

During the first half of the eighteenth century, agents of the Austrian Netherlands became engaged in Europe's overseas expansion into Asia, using the port of Ostend as their departure point. They thereby followed in the footsteps of joint-stock trading companies such as the British East-India Company (EIC) in 1600, the Dutch Verenigde Oost-Indische Company (VOC) in 1602 and the French Compagnie des Indes in 1664, which established a commercial presence in factories and trading settlements in the Indian Ocean world.[1] As a result, the General Imperial India Company or GIC was officially founded as a licensed joint-stock trading company in December 1722, ratified with a license for the Austrian-Netherlands Asia trade by the Austrian Emperor Charles VI. The company's foundation had been preceded by a series of individual initiatives and attempts by merchants to expand their capital through private maritime expeditions following the War of the Spanish Succession.[2] Organizationally it took the GIC an average of six to nine months to reach Asia, and a full trade cycle between the purchasing of Asian commodities and their resale in Europe could easily take two years. As this was a long-term and risky investment for private merchants, the joint-stock trading company became their preferred organizational form.[3] Within Asia, other European companies noticed the arrival of the newly founded GIC. The British EIC's "Materials for a

1 Om Prakash, "The European Factories in India: A Blessing or a Curse?", in John Everaert and Jan Parmentier (eds.), *International Conference on Shipping, Factories and Colonization* (Brussel: Koninklijke academie voor overzeese wetenschappen, 1996), 14–15.

2 Karel Degryse, "Zuid-Nederlands kapitaal in de VOC en de voorcompagnieën", in Jan Parmentier (ed.), *Noord-Zuid in Oost Indisch perspectief* (Zutphen: Walburg Pers, 2005), 82.

3 Femme S. Gaastra, and Jaap R. Bruijn, "The Dutch East India Company's Shipping, 1602–1795, in a comparative perspective", in Femme Gaastra and Jaap R. Bruijn (eds.), *Ships, Sailors and Spices. East India Companies and Their Shipping in the 16th, 17th and 18th century* (Amsterdam: NEHA, 1993), 177.

 | DOI:10.1163/9789004740556_014

History of Trade with China" mention a strategic note of internal communication within the Company, written in 1719 as a response to the Ostenders' role as newcomers to the China trade. The note clearly considered them to be interlopers to British commerce, as it mentioned that "we must try to make these Interlopers sick of their voyages for Tea".[4] The 1723 "Diary & Consultation Book of William Fazakerley et. al." pointed out how news of the Ostenders reaching China travelled via British contacts with "country ships" in the Straits of Banca and led the EIC merchants at Canton to fear that "if the Chineese would know of their being so near at our heels it would infallably raise the price of Goods".[5]

Despite the GIC directors' official instructions to limit intercultural contacts to strictly necessary commercial or diplomatic purposes,[6] the practices of individual agents on the ground and the GIC's local organization show that reality was different at sea, especially in Asia, than officially described on paper in Europe. A "global microhistorical"[7] look at Armenian intermediaries' letters or GIC captains' diaries enables us to uncover the local entanglements in which the company agents were involved in Asia. As Jan Parmentier has pointed out, although the VOC and the Southern Netherlandish sailors were officially competitors and even enemies, interpersonal and commercial boundaries were often crossed in practice, as shadowy private trade deals could and were made "behind the scenes".[8] This became particularly apparent in collaboration over smuggling in Bengal during the period 1720–1744. Parmentier has shown in great detail how GIC personnel engaged in alliances with the Dutch and French company directors Sichterman (1692–1764) and Dupleix (1697–1763), who collaborated informally in order to undertake intra-Asian trade, and has

4 Peter Pratt (ed.), *Materials for a History of the Rise and Progress of the Trade to China* (British Library London: India Office Records, 1821), G/12/8, 1367–1368.

5 Peter Pratt (ed.), *Materials for a History of the Rise and Progress*, G/12/24 – "Diary & Consultation Book", 16.

6 "Instructies aan Kapitein De Winter", in SAA (Stadsarchief Antwerpen) GIC (Generale Indische Compagnie) 5665 *Copijboek der orders gegeven voor Bengalen, Cabulon, China aan residenten, scheepskapiteins, enz. 1721–1730*.

7 This phrase denotes a qualitative method of detailed, source-based analysis yielding qualitative insights into individuals or crews' strategies, and pointing to the relationship between local social practices and global historical processes, as mentioned in Colin Heywood, "Microhistory/Maritime History: Aspects of British Presence in the Western Mediterranean in the Early Modern Period", in Bernard Heyberger and Albrecht Fuess (eds.), *La frontière méditerranéenne du XVe au XVIIe siècle: échanges, circulations et affrontements* (Turnhout: Brepols, 2014), 82–83.

8 Jan Parmentier, "Vriend en Vijand – De Zuid-Nederlanders en de VOC tijdens de achttiende eeuw", in Jan Parmentier (ed.), *Noord-Zuid in Oost-Indisch perspectief* (Zutphen: Walburg Pers, 2005), 149.

underlined the opportunities for smuggling and personal enrichment this involved. One may argue that these enterprises even formed the lifeline or main motivation for GIC personnel to remain engaged in Asia, even beyond the company's definitive official abolition in 1731–1732.[9] A degree of acculturation was required in order to maintain this presence and to acquire permits and permissions from foreign authorities. This process dictated the need for a specific use of language and etiquette in order to negotiate trading and diplomatic contacts, for which intercultural linguists and writers often fulfilled a crucial role as mediators. These mediators included a heterogenous group of agents, including Armenian or Persian merchants and *vakils* (courtiers) in Bengal, and merchants or officials in China, whose relations were marked by commercial and political obligations, as well as informal intercultural contacts. The particular enforcement of these relations depended on policies and authorities enabling interaction, which often referred back to earlier customs and precedents, and which defined the spaces for both commercial and non-commercial exchanges in China and Bengal. Comparing the two contexts reveals different local forms of agency in response to this power, as well as paying due attention to the local interactions and influences that have often eluded earlier GIC historians. Hence, it was important for the GIC's agents in Asia to establish and maintain their presence in sustained trading communities in both Canton and Bengal, for which they needed the crucial mediation of local merchants and courtly agents. This urges us to replace the perspective of "Empire" with the image of a layered, multi-sited historical anthropology which, in Jerry H. Bentley's terms, broadens the historical focus "from a narcissistic Eurocentric study of European travelers to the analysis of cross-cultural interactions as historical processes."[10]

2 The GIC's Trade Communities in Canton

In the context of the GIC's interactions in Canton, Chinese foreign policy towards European agents focused on the maritime domain. The GIC and earlier Southern Netherlandish expeditions never travelled inland beyond the port city of Canton on the Pearl River, and only dealt with local Mandarin officials such as customs officers and provincial governors. No courtly interactions took

9 This was initially GIC governor Alexander Hume's plan, according to Parmentier; see Jan Parmentier, *De holle compagnie* (Hilversum: Verloren, 1992), 38–44.

10 Jerry H. Bentley, "Hemispheric Integration, 500–1500 CE", *Journal of World History* 9:2 (1998), 251.

place beyond occasional meetings with these officials, or with Chinese merchants with official ties. Yet the framework of the "Canton System",[11] through which the GIC trade and its encounters would take place, was strongly statist in the maritime domain, in line with Qing foreign policies emanating from the imperial centre in Beijing. For Qing China, recent scholarship by Angela Schottenhammer, Ronald Po and Matthew Mosca has argued that the maritime context was of greater importance to Qing foreign policies than had hitherto been recognized.[12] As Leonard Blussé indicates in *Visible Cities*, the "Canton system" was a matter of managing trade across cultures, in which regulations were designed to keep all interactions between foreigners and Chinese merchants as far removed from the Imperial administration as possible.[13] To achieve this, the Qing administration licensed foreign trade through a limited group of merchants, while keeping firm control over customs duties and anchorage fees through its officials.[14] In total, this made for an accumulation of procedures which, over time, had been refined and attuned to local conditions.[15] Paul Van Dyke compares the concrete constellation of interactions that took place as "The Canton System" to "a huge machine, with thousands of little parts that worked independent of, but in concert with, each other to move trade forward".[16] The foreign-policy aspect of this system was placed firmly in the hands of the local authorities, especially the *hoppo* (Yuehai guanbu 粵海關部) or customs officials. As Weng Eang Cheong notes, the inadequacies of the *hoppo*'s administration had become clear during the 1720s, after which it was restructured. The GIC therefore entered China at a time when new trade policies were being installed. The Chinese authorities felt the need to regulate the behaviour of bureaucrats in order to prevent exploitation, personal gain and corruption. Chenog states that where *hoppo* officials had previously had one year to raise revenue quotas and line their pockets under an arbitrary

11 See Paul Van Dyke, *The Canton Trade. Life and Enterprise on the China Coast, 1700–1845* (Hong Kong: Hong Kong University Press, 2005), 1.

12 As argued in Angela Schottenhammer, "Characteristics of Qing China's Maritime Trade Politics, Shunzhi through Early Qianlong reigns", in Angela Schottenhammer (ed.), *Trading Networks in Early Modern East-Asian Maritime History* (Wiesbaden: Harrassowitz, 2010), 101–154; Ronald Po, *The Blue Frontier. Maritime Vision and Power in the Qing Empire* (Cambridge: Cambridge University Press, 2018); Matthew Mosca, *From Frontier Policy to Foreign Policy: The Question of India and the Transformation of Geopolitics in Qing China* (Stanford: Stanford University Press, 2013).

13 Leonard Blussé, *Visible Cities: Canton, Nagasaki, and Batavia and the Coming of the Americans* (Cambridge, MA: Harvard University Press, 2008), 53.

14 Blussé, *Visible Cities*, 33.

15 Blussé, *Visible Cities*, 52.

16 Van Dyke, *The Canton Trade*, 165.

administration, the twelve-yearly appointments of a *Fuyen* (*fuyuan* 撫院) or Viceroy led to their having quasi-seigneurial rights over trade.[17] Even when this system changed over time, and grew more bureaucratic rather than seigneurial appearances, GIC merchants and captains' logbooks would continue to show a similar and unchanged perception on perceived customs impositions to their trade. Regardless of changes or forms in the system, the GIC would always continue to designate customs supervision as 'tyranical'. They showed limited awareness of institutional changes or functions on the Chinese side, except when replacements occurred or governor changed, which they tried to use as occasions to renegotiate tariffs.

The journals of GIC captains on their return to Ostend reveal the conditions and procedures of their operations in Canton. Nicolas Carpentier's 1724 journal of the ship *L'Aigle* clearly states how the supercargoes (or chief merchants) first came on land at Macao to inform themselves about "Chinese affairs", which "they found very different from previous times by the change that had been done of a hoppo and replacement by a viceroy who in Chinese is called Fouin (Fuyen) and governs the whole province of Canton".[18] The replacement Carpentier is alluding to was in fact an attempt by the Qing court to strengthen the hoppo's position by combining his role with that of provincial governor or Fuyen, in the period between 1724 and 1729. This led to the appointment of Yang Wenqian 楊文乾 (died 1728) in a double role as governor and customs official, which Cheong states "excited fear and resentment" among the merchants.[19] Even beyond Yang Wenqian 楊文乾's passing, and the administrative changes this entailed, Carpentier and the GIC agents continued to express a sense of resentment or insecurity established by his earlier appointment. Yang Wenqian had enforced strict control over trade, increased the quota of tax revenue, and thereby set a higher precedent for subsequent *hoppos*, to the detriment of the Canton merchants.[20] Chinese sources in Lo-Shu Fu's *Documentary Chronicle* seem to portray how Yang Wenqian was eventually impeached in 1727, through memorials claiming corruption and extortion in the illegal collection of taxes of which the Imperial Court was unaware.[21] This was also the view that GIC and EIC sources ascribed to in portraying the interests of European and Chinese

17 Weng Eang Cheong, *The Hong Merchants of Canton: Chinese Merchants in Sino-Western Trade* (Richmond: Curzon, 1997), 196.

18 SAA GIC 5655 "Journaux et Rapports au retour des Capnes" 1724–1728 – "Rapport au retour du cap N. Carpentier China L'aigle".

19 Cheong, *The Hong Merchants*, 196.

20 Cheong, *The Hong Merchants*, 196.

21 Lo-Shu Fu, *A Documentary Chronicle of Sino-Western Relations (1644–1820)* (Tucson: University of Arizona Press, 1966), 159.

merchants. Instead, Cheong seems to attribute this to a plot by Yang's political opponents, coupled with Chinese merchants' dissatisfaction with the efficient institutional changes Yang had made as Fuyen.[22] The replies that GIC captains and merchants attempted to make to such changes was the nearest they came to courtly or diplomatic negotiations in Qing China.

Having arrived at Canton, Captain Nicolas Carpentier and the GIC merchants made their arrival known by sending their interpreter or "linguist" to the Fuyen in order to request an audience.[23] That the Fuyen could impose his power strictly was very clear to the European merchants, as the 1727 "Diary and Consultation Book" of the British EIC also testified when mentioning how the Fuyen "threatens merchants with chains" if they are not compliant with his authority.[24] In that same year, GIC captain Carpentier, this time commanding the ship *Hope* (*L'espérance*), discovered this for himself when he was kept under arrest following the obligatory inspection of his ship. Moreover, he complained about this in an angry letter to the Fuyen or viceroy,[25] written while he was forcibly detained on board his ship despite suffering illness and fever.[26] Just as the commercial process of the European Canton trade was streamlined by the introduction of a clear procedure, it was made crystal clear that authority and punishment also lay only in the hands of the Fuyen.

As for daily life at the GIC's Canton factory or *hong*, Jan Parmentier describes how European merchants were only allowed to stay on the outskirts of Canton's walled city, where privileged Chinese merchants built warehouses and shops near the foreigners' *hong*s. The Chinese authorities turned a blind eye to the large number of illegal Chinese shops, bars and craftsmen established in the streets and alleys around these *hong*s, where foreign sailors and traders could find everything they needed. Occasionally problems were caused in these quarters by drunken Flemish sailors, some of whom died from drinking badly prepared Chinese punch.[27] As soon as their factory was set up and the ship's cargo of silver had been placed under guard, Chinese merchants began visiting

---

22 Cheong, *The Hong Merchants*, 135–201.

23 SAA GIC 5655 "Journaux et Rapports au retour des Capnes 1724–1728" – "Carpentier", 12.

24 Peter Pratt (ed.), *Materials for a History of the Rise and Progress*, G/12/27 – "Diary and consultation Book of the Transactions of Peter Godfrey, Richard Newman et al.", 7.

25 The GIC sources alternately label this Chinese officer a viceroy and a governor, partly due to the office itself being in a state of flux or reorganization under Wenqian's tenure.

26 Algemeen Rijksarchief Brussel (ARA), Departement voor de Nederlanden van de Hof- en Staatskanselarij te Wenen, nr. 639 – "Extrait du Journal tenu par le Capne Nicolas Carpentier, command le vaisseau de la compe imple l Esperance 1727".

27 Jan Parmentier, *Tea Time in Flanders: The Maritime Trade between the Southern Netherlands and China in the 18th Century* (Gent: Ludion, 1996), 99.

their European counterparts and soliciting their wares. European merchants could in turn visit the Chinese merchants and make their personal *pacotille* (personal tsrade) deals.[28] Cheong mentions that the functions of up-country suppliers, linguists, compradors and shopkeepers were legally defined and that they were placed under the surveillance and had the backing of security merchants. Shops were required to register and underwrite each other's debts.[29] However, local authorities might have allowed a wider margin of informal initiatives to take place, besides these official procedures.

The "resolution books" of GIC merchants in Canton mention how a house or *hong* was usually rented through one of the GIC's preferred China merchants or trading partners. For instance, Canton merchant Cudgin was contracted for a *hong* in 1727: "Contracted with Cudgin alias Quique for his Hong called Chin Ching Hong for four hundred tales Canton August the 20th 1726".[30] Once the *hong* had been rented, the supercargoes started a round of consultations with the Chinese merchants on tea prices, during which the GIC merchants chose their preferred trading partners. In 1726 they settled on the merchants Suqua[31] (alias Cumshaw) and Cudgin (alias Quequa) as "two persons who are well known by Experience and who we look upon as capable to Comply with their Contracts and at this time much more capable than any other Merchants in this place".[32] According to Van Dyke, Cudgin and Suqua would be the main merchants to supply the GIC throughout the 1720s.[33]

To acquire porcelain or Chinaware, the merchants mostly decided to trade with a merchant called Tinqua. Van Dyke mentions Tan Tinqua, or Chen Tengguan 陳騰觀 as another of the VOC's main suppliers.[34] Hence we see that Suqua and Cudgin were to be the GIC's main commercial contacts in 1726, and they even decided to put a "very Large Sum of Money" into their hands for safekeeping, as "Wee think to much to trust in the factory for fear of fire or any

28 Parmentier, *Tea Time in Flanders*, 98–100.

29 Cheong, *The Hong Merchants of Canton*, 187.

30 SAA GIC 5752 "Resolutions & Contracts for Sundry Merchandise Bought at Canton for the Cargoes of the Ships Lyon, Tiger & Eagle, belonging to the Imperial & Catholick Company Established In the Austrian Netherlands. By Robert Hewer, Jacobus de Meyer, Charles Morford, Peter de Boubereel & Joan de Jong jr. Sup Cargoes for the account of said Company. Canton Anno 1726", fo. 1.

31 Although GIC sources consequently mention this as one name and one word, as they did with other Chinese names, one may point out that the designation qua/quan (觀) indicates a respectful honorific, in a similar sense to the use of the word *khoja* in Bengal.

32 SAA GIC 5752 "Resolutions & Contracts for Sundry Merchandise Bought at Canton", fo. 2.

33 Paul Van Dyke, *Merchants of Canton and Macao. Politics and Strategies in Eighteenth-Century Chinese Trade* (Hong Kong: Hong Kong University Press, 2011), 20.

34 Van Dyke, *Merchants of Canton and Macao*, 20.

other accidents".[35] Van Dyke mentions Tan Suqua or Chen Shouguan 陳壽觀 as an influential figure at the centre of Canton's commerce from 1716 to 1778, someone who was generally considered very trustworthy and as delivering top-quality merchandise. He had been contracted with the British EIC since 1716, and was still serving as its main supplier of tea and silk in 1722, under the alias "Suqua" or "Cumshaw". He traded with the Austrian-Netherlandish GIC since the beginning of its China trade in 1719, in addition to his arrangements with Portuguese, Spanish, French, Muslim and Armenian merchants.[36] In addition, Cheong even mentions Suqua as the leader of the Canton trade between 1720 and 1725, someone who was even appointed as chief merchant by Yang Wengqian during his 1725 reforms.[37] Cudgin is mentioned by Van Dyke as belonging to the Ye 葉 family of merchants, who traded from the Duanhe Hang 端和行 and was presumably involved in the Fujian junk trade. The GIC would also have traded with him while also supplying the British EIC, as Suqua did. Van Dyke emphasizes the great volumes of goods he traded, and hence his reliance on foreign capital. By 1728, he is mentioned by the English as no longer appearing in business himself, having turned his trade over to his family, and having been appointed a "mandarin". He apparently purchased this title from the emperor, giving himself social status and enhancing his legal protection.[38] Regardless of whether or not he purchased the title, Cheong also mentions that he made it into "mandarin ranks" as a result of successfully defending Yang Wenqian against the claims of political rivals over the illegality of his 10% custom levies.[39] Cheong considers Cudgin's rise from trader to mandarin to be "a model of the making of a merchant prince in the early Canton trade", thus demonstrating the potential for "upward mobility in a merchant class which held disdain for its own profession".[40] Although official competitors, multiple European companies therefore had alliances with the same merchants. GIC accounts and logbooks also show how their supercargoes dealt with other Chinese merchants beyond their primary merchants and landlords, though to a less frequent extent. The 1727 journals of the ships *Concordia* and *Marquis de Prié* mention interactions with Honqua, "Quycon alias mandarin" for piasters

35 SAA GIC 5752 "Resolutions & Contracts for Sundry Merchandise Bought at Canton", fo. 9.

36 Van Dyke, *Merchants of Canton and Macao*, 79–80.

37 Cheong, *The Hong Merchants*, 135.

38 Cheong, *The Hong Merchants*, 181–182.

39 Cheong, *The Hong Merchants*, 196.

40 Cheong, *The Hong Merchants*, 145.

or capital, Tomsay for rhubarb, Gonqua and Teyqua, although they still identified Tinqua as their main trading partner.[41]

3 Chinese Merchants as Mediators with the Official Authorities

Despite the reliance on a fixed number of trusted merchants, commercial disputes could lead to conflicts with the authorities at Canton. One such occasion was sparked by the death of a Chinese merchant called Barrowla in January 1727, when his Chinese business partners complained to the Fuyen that the GIC had an unpaid contract with him for the delivery of green tea. Following the complaint, the Fuyen immediately had the GIC's linguist or translator arrested: "Upon which our Linguist was immediately put in Chains and brought to the factory to examine our Accounts. They positively insisted on their pretentions."[42] In this state of emergency, the GIC merchants immediately turned to their close connections and main trading partners Suqua and Quinqua, who in turn summoned their four colleagues, the Hong merchants. Together, they went to register their protest collectively to the Fuyen:

> We sent for Suqua and Quinqua and acquainted them with this affair, who immediately sent for the other four Merchants and went all into the City to acquaint the Foyen with the injustice these Villains would impose on us.[43]

As Governor Yang Wenqian fostered stricter controls on trade and doubled the quota for tax revenues in his attempts to improve the system created by his dual Hoppo/Fuyen role,[44] European and Chinese merchants considered him "more avaricious". This image played into pre-existing biases regarding Asian corruption and covetousness already held by the GIC agents:

> But he being more avaricious then Just would not Clear ye affair but rather seemed inclined to the other party and this day Stoped our Shiping off and declared that we should not have our Chop till cleard that affair with those Merchants alias Villains who this afternoon demanded that

41 SAA GIC 5700 "Journal of Groot Boeck van de supercargos op de schepen de Concordia en de Marquis de Prié" (Canton 1727), 2.
42 SAA GIC 5752 "Resolutions & Contracts for Sundry Merchandise Bought at Canton", fo. 32.
43 SAA GIC 5752 "Resolutions & Contracts for Sundry Merchandise Bought at Canton", fo. 32.
44 Cheong, *The Hong Merchants*, 196.

> we should take our Oaths before Pater Guigue we accordingly went to his house.[45]

Suqua then attempted to intervene by asking the claimants to be more considerate, whereas they replied that their ties with the Fuyen would enable them to have the GIC forced to pay:

> Upon which Suqua asked them what they could desire more; they then positively insisted on some consideration and declared otherwise they had interest enough with the Foyen to Stop us and force us to do it.[46]

To the affair, the supercargoes were advised by the merchants Suqua, Quique and Tinqua to pay up and settle the debt so that they would not lose the seasonal rhythm of their trade. As a result, the *supercargoes* (principal GIC traders) decided to have these merchants settle the affair by paying the claimed debt for them against an advance on the next season's order of tea, "knowing the Tea would be worth the money and much better than any other green tea we had on board".[47]

The GIC's interactions at Canton confirm Cheong's point that the "Canton System" was therefore not merely a set of ancient Chinese regulations imposed by officials, but had also been shaped by local practices and repeated adjustments from 1684.[48] By its presence among other European companies, the GIC also played a role in shaping and influencing these official practices, as well as the business of Chinese merchants. The circumstances of the GIC's interactions at Canton, which formed their local trade community, depended entirely on their relations with a limited number of Chinese merchants acting as their commercial partners. These Chinese merchants were attracted individually to and dealt simultaneously with multiple European companies, while occasionally operating as one body if their collective interests were at stake. On behalf of the GIC, they even spoke to officials, whether through the mediation of the company's own linguist or directly by themselves as merchants. In addition, the GIC's suppliers or compradors, attracted by these same merchants, guaranteed the commercial infrastructure and daily livelihoods. The GIC therefore had to establish and maintain commercial relations as the entire grounds for their continued presence at Canton and had to comply fully with the local

45 SAA GIC 5752 "Resolutions & Contracts for Sundry Merchandise Bought at Canton", fo. 32.
46 SAA GIC 5752 "Resolutions & Contracts for Sundry Merchandise Bought at Canton", fo. 32.
47 SAA GIC 5752 "Resolutions & Contracts for Sundry Merchandise Bought at Canton", fo. 32.
48 Cheong, *The Hong Merchants*, 207.

authorities' disciplinary arrangements for regulating these procedures. Both taxation and limits on interaction were imposed by protocol and precedent. In their local power relations, company agents had to submit themselves to the *hoppo* authorities responsible for customs and the disciplinary framework of the Fuyen as viceroy of Canton, or the combined role embodied by the same person as under Yang Wenqian's local regime. Different GIC merchants and captains attempted to negotiate this narrow context of interactions, which was limited by security concerns, yet also enabled by commercial gain and taxation. They thus shared the same fate of other European companies in whose footsteps they had followed.

4 The GIC's Trade Communities in Bengal

Just as Canton presented a context in which GIC merchants had to engage with a limited number of trusted merchants, so Bengal formed a rural economy supported by a complex system of socio-political institutions governing relations between artisans, merchants and the authorities.[49] As a *subah* or province within the centralized and bureaucratic Mughal Empire, Bengal faced taxation problems which required the use of financial intermediaries to transform the in-kind revenue into cash.[50] As a consequence, economic logic relied on the structure of peasant production, transport technologies and local identities that were continually being eroded and reshaped by the social and political forces that articulated the rural economy or connected it to towns and cities.[51] As Irfan Habib points out, the resulting distinction between an agricultural sphere and an exchange economy based on the disposal of surplus led to a differentiation in commodity production and its corresponding division of labour.[52] As a consequence of this division of labour, Sushil Chaudhury mentions how, during the first half of the eighteenth century, the commercial life of Bengal was dominated by merchant princes who controlled the money market by which both trade and government were financed. In their role as creditors, these merchant princes had a close relationship with foreign merchants, including the European trading companies. Their political role as creditors to

49 Kirti N. Chaudhuri, *Asia before Europe: Economy and Civilisation of the Indian Ocean from the Rise of Islam to 1750* (Cambridge: Cambridge University Press, 1990), 39.

50 Chaudhuri, *Asia before Europe*, 39.

51 Chaudhuri, *Asia before Europe*, 40.

52 Irfan Habib, *Essays in Indian History: Towards a Marxist Perception* (New Delhi: Tulika, 1995), 34.

the courts also determined their position and influence at Murshidabad.[53] In contrast, Ashin Das Gupta downplayed the extent of these merchants' influence at court, merely considering them as "part of 18th century India's system of checks and balances".[54] Sanjay Subrahmanyam and Christopher A. Bayly use the term "portfolio capitalists" to designate those merchants who straddled the worlds of commerce and political participation, thereby removing the barrier between mercantile activity and military-political power.[55] Their role and intercession would directly shape the conditions for the GIC's interactions and commercial opportunities. Due to the nature of the agricultural economy and its organization, land-ownership and its diplomatic acquisition constituted an important factor in the GIC's settlement process, as well as its relations with local merchants.

In establishing their India trade and associated settlements, two fundamental roles European companies such as the VOC or GIC engaged with in Bengal were those of the *vakil* or courtly agent, and the *dalals* or commission agent. The latter were given an amount of money with which to procure goods for export against an *arhat* or commission of 2%. This commission was often presented by the *gomashta*s or company bankers.[56] *Dalal*s were also engaged by the EIC or GIC to approach the weavers and other local artisans directly. In this way, the GIC had their local business arranged by a *banyan* merchant acting as a broker, who would deal with weavers and producers for a fee or salary.[57] Ashin Das Gupta confirms the importance of such "dalals or Gentile brokers", whose employment was deemed essential by European merchants in India ever since they were mentioned in the travelogue of the French India traveller Jean-Baptiste Tavernier (1605–1689). Taking a view fed by early-modern orientalist bias, Tavernier emphasized that a broker should be a "native of the country, an idolater and not a Mohammadan, because all the workmen with whom he will have to do are idolaters".[58] The GIC also established their

53 Sushil Chaudhury, *From Prosperity to Decline: Eighteenth Century Bengal* (New Delhi: Manohar, 1995), 109.

54 Ashin Das Gupta, "The Maritime Merchant, c. 1500–1800", in Uma Das Gupta (ed.), *The World of the Indian Ocean Merchant 1500–1800: Collected Essays of Ashin Das Gupta* (Oxford: Oxford University Press, 2001), 11.

55 Christopher A. Bayly and Sanjay Subrahmanyam, "Portfolio Capitalists and the Political Economy of Early Modern India", *The Indian Economic and Social History Review* 25:4 (1998), 418.

56 Om Prakash, *The Dutch East-India Company and the Economy of Bengal, 1630–1720* (Princeton: Princeton University Press, 1985), 106–107.

57 Parmentier, *De holle compagnie*, 19.

58 Jean-Baptiste Tavernier cited in Ashin Das Gupta, *Indian Merchants and the Decline of Surat: c. 1700–1750* (Wiesbaden: Franz Steiner Verlag, 1979), 188.

factories or settlements with the aid of such *dalal*s, as we find in an agreement between GIC governor Alexander Hume and a Bengali "Gentile" merchant called Chieramra, who was appointed for the initial development of settlement and commerce at Banquibazar, which became the GIC's main textile factory in Bengal. His Bengali contract stipulated that he would arrange for the settlement of the newly developed trading post, for which he would provide building materials and hire all the necessary servants and workers, being able to "reliably deal with his own People".[59] In connection with this, GIC ambassador Jacques-André Cobbé (–1724) also mentioned that the Company would be obliged to spend resources in attracting people to their establishment, which had to be solid in commerce, as otherwise "there would be but poor and indigenous people who would establish themselves in the hopes of a better fortune".[60]

In contrast to Canton, the GIC's establishment in Bengal required a more elaborate process of creating a suitable social and commercial environment. Multiple levels of authority, multiple creditors and a variety of commercial policies involved GIC agents entering into a greater diversity of personal and territorial relations. Production relations were also more diversified, as well as more directly connected to the company's claims for a local terrain due to the process of settling both local labourers and merchants. In the organization of commerce, the availability of credit and capital depended on both individual "merchant princes" and the wider mercantile communities, which required constant interactions in respect of the shifting constellations of power and alliance affecting GIC agents. The potential for different territorial, political and commercial claims created frictions and potential conflicts on a local scale. As Subrahmanyam has pointed out, this was not necessarily a matter of incommensurability,[61] but of a "complex mixture of commerce, diplomacy and violence".[62] In this process, a crucial role was played by "merchant princes" and intermediaries. In Bengal the GIC's settlement was established due to the combined brokerage of the Persian and Armenian merchants of Saïdabad, the local aristocracy and the support of powerful bankers such as Fatechand Jagat Seth (–1744). The diplomatic and commercial support of Armenian

59 SAA GIC 5782 "Papieren A. Hume Banquibazar" – "Conditien gemaakt op 't engagement van Chieramra als Benjaan en coopman over des keyserlijcke Compagnies nu zijnde of naast komende handel &c", fo. 1.

60 SAA GIC 5772 "Papieren en Brieven Cobbé" – "Memoire de ce qui serroit necessaire pour mentenir le Terrein", fo. 1 verso.

61 Sanjay Subrahmanyam, *Courtly Encounters: Translating Courtliness and Violence in Early Modern Eurasia* (Cambridge MA: Harvard University Press, 2012), 24–25.

62 Subrahmanyam, *Courtly Encounters*, 32.

merchants was especially crucial to the GIC's communications and their establishment of commercial networks in eighteenth-century Bengal.

5 The GIC's Armenian Merchants as Commercial Partners and Mediators

As a commercial presence, Armenian merchants proved vital to the GIC's commerce in Bengal. They operated on a specific communal and operational basis throughout the early-modern world, while keeping their trade networks focused on a central node in New Julfa (Isfahan), through which they had also established themselves in Bengal since the seventeenth century.[63] The Armenian merchants in Bengal spontaneously offered their services to the newly arriving Austrian-Netherlandish company. On 3 June 1725, a patent by GIC merchant Vincent Parraber affirmed that "Khoja Saffar, Armenian & inhabitant of said Ballacore", had approached the company on his own initiative and made it known that he would take care of arranging pilots for the GIC ships, supplying them by sloop and procuring victuals at Ballasore.[64] In addition, multiple Armenian merchants or *khojas* would become deeply involved in the organization of the GIC's commerce in Bengal, particularly at Dacca.

At Banquibazar, location of the GIC's main textile factory in Bengal, the company's 1727–1729 accounts indicate the central role played by an Armenian merchant, Khoja Aga Mallick, whom they even engaged as a factor to organize their trade and settlement at this site, and with whom they held relations of credit and debt. Mallick operated in tandem with Khoja Alexander, who would be one of the creditors responsible for the GIC's acquisition of trading rights and a territory. At the factory in Dacca, the Armenian merchants would be almost entirely responsible for the organization of GIC trade: the priest and merchant Agha Petrus Arrakiël was indicated as organizing the trade, while Khoja Minas served as the GIC's central factor there. Minas belonged to the Minassian family, one of New Julfa's leading merchant families operating out of Isfahan, who owned a fleet of merchant vessels plying their trade into the South China Sea and to Manila.[65] In addition to their commercial role in

63 Sebouh David Aslanian, *From the Indian Ocean to the Mediterranean. The Global Trade Networks of Armenian Merchants from New Julfa* (Berkeley: University of California Press, 2011), 3.

64 SAA GIC 5782 "Brieven Hume Banquibazar / Hollandsen 1732 / Stukken betreffende bedienden" – "1725 3 Juin v Parrabere Copie de la patente de Coje Safar agent pour la Compagnie a Ballasore".

65 Aslanian, *From the Indian Ocean to the Mediterranean*, 159–162.

the GIC's factories, Armenian merchants would also become involved in the intra-Asian trade of both the French and GIC companies,[66] just as Chinese merchants traded simultaneously with multiple European partners. In addition to this commercial role, they also had an important diplomatic role as cultural mediators for GIC agents at the Bengali court of Murshidabad.

For the initial courtly negotiations whereby the GIC attempted to acquire a site for itself and trading rights, in 1723 an embassy was sent to the court of Murshidabad under the leadership of "ambassador" Jacques-André Cobbé. An alternative perspective on this visit to what we are told in Cobbé's own diary is provided by the correspondence between an Armenian merchant and *vakil*, Khoja Delaune, and GIC chief merchant Alexander Hume. This allows us to see the GIC's negotiations through Armenian eyes, through the correspondence of this *vakil*. As Hume was one of the key persons employing Khoja Delaune in this affair, possibly through his brother Khoja Alexander (see below), Khoja Delaune kept him updated about the progress of courtly affairs. The GIC had engaged Khoja Delaune as *vakil*, as they believed him "to be of Confidence and particularly adept in the Routines of the Nawab's Court, with whom he has previously treated several similar affairs, to help in the voyage and to instruct usefully by his advice".[67] Khoja Delaune himself indicated in a letter from the Armenian quarter at Seïdabad that he had been at the court of the Nawab for 24 years and was therefore well versed in such affairs.[68] Using this letter, Khoja Delaune effectively applied for a position as *vakil* or courtly mediator for the GIC.

Previously, English sources had already mentioned this "Cojah Delaune" as a merchant at Surat in 1676.[69] Presumably he was an affluent merchant who had gathered some political capital along with his commercial capital, and thus hoped to prosper by introducing the GIC as a new agent for the Bengali trade. Khoja Delaune delivered his letters by means of his brother Khoja Alexander, whom the GIC was also involved with commercially. Delaune told his brother that he had translated the letter to Hume, as Delaune was surrounded by at least forty spies, "& because of this I cannot write in Bengali nor in Persian, I must absolutely write in Armenian, there is no other remedy".[70] On some

66 Parmentier, *De holle compagnie*, 43–54.

67 SAA GIC 5772 "Papieren en Brieven Cobbé" – "Danemarnagor, 13 7bre 1723", fo. 2 vo.

68 SAA GIC 5772 "Papieren en brieven Cobbé" – "Letter from Khoja Dilon, written from Seydabad".

69 Vahe Baladouni and Margaret Makepeace (eds.), *Armenian Merchants of the Seventeenth and Early Eighteenth Centuries* (Philadelphia: American Philosophical Society, 1998), 81.

70 SAA GIC 5772 "Papieren en brieven Cobbé" – "Letter from Khoja Dilon, written from Seydabad".

occasions, Delaune's use of the Armenian language (in its Julfan dialect), coupled to his mastery of the Persian language used by the court, formed a particular strategic asset the *vakil* could use to deliver his messages "in code".

On 16th October 1723, Khoja Delaune wrote that it had been ten days since he had arrived at Murshidabad, and that he found himself inconvenienced by not having had one moment of rest. He also mentioned how the conditions for the GIC's acceptance would depend on earlier proceedings between the Bengali court and other European companies:

> I have been four times to the Nawab and I have said what until present no one dared say in front of the Nawab (…) he has ordered that their books are checked on the way accommodations and conditions had been made with the English, Dutch and French, and that this article is presented to him.[71]

Delaune also mentioned that Fatechand Seth would be in favour of the GIC if they had the goodness to send two "livres of Portuguese tobacco, as he asked for it himself".[72] This intervention and involvement of the "House of the Jagat Seths" was not a coincidence, as by the eighteenth century its bankers had become a permanent presence at the *darbar* and had great influence at the Nawab's court. Originally a migrant from Marwar, Fatechand Seth received the title of "Banker of the World" (Jagat Seth) from the Mughal emperor in 1723, and was placed in control of the Murshidabad mint and exchange rates.[73] As such, he belonged to the non-Muslim elites that were employed in the revenue and executive branches of the Nawab Murshid Quli Khan's court. As the richest merchant-banker in Bengal and with a personal guard numbering two thousand soldiers, the Jagat Seth oversaw Murshidabad's annual transfers of rent to the imperial court at Delhi and provided loans to the Mughal aristocracy.[74] He was therefore an unavoidable figure at the centre of power, authority and capital in eighteenth-century Bengal. As Chaudhury mentions, both the Nawab and the merchants in Bengal benefitted from his credit and

71 SAA GIC 5772 "Copie de translate des Lettres envoyé pr Coje Delon a mrs Hume & Harrisson", fo. 2 – "13 Octob a mestre Hume & Capiteyn Harrisson".

72 SAA GIC 5772 "Copie de translate des Lettres envoyé pr Coje Delon a mrs Hume & Harrisson", fo. 2 – "13 Octob a mestre Hume & Capiteyn Harrisson".

73 Sushil Chaudhury, "Merchants, Companies and Rulers: Bengal in the Eighteenth Century", *Journal of the Economic and Social History of the Orient* 31:1 (1988), 92.

74 Robert Ivermee, *Hooghly: The Global History of a River* (Oxford: Oxford University Press, 2020), 48.

presence.[75] Jagat Seth's specific request for a gift of Portuguese tobacco was highly significant. The GIC could not possibly grant a gift worthy of one of the wealthiest men in the world in terms of its actual value, so it was presumably a token gift whose specific meaning was derived from its possible scarcity. The power he showed in his ability to request exactly that item served as confirmation of his importance and status.

On 22nd October 1723, Khoja Delaune mentioned that the Bengali government would no longer reply to their demands as long as the offered sum was not increased. He mentioned how the court continuously delayed and postponed the affair, as the Nawab told Delaune that he had asked for 75,000 rupees, 30,000 in advance and 45,000 by the arrival of the next GIC ships.[76] Jagat Seth Fatechand also advised them to give that sum, as the Nawab had his accounts checked and claimed that the Dutch had previously given 90,000 rupees in cash, two elephants, four horses, quantities of cloves and cinnamon, and scarlet textiles, the whole of which would amount to 150,000 rupees. Khoja Delaune warned that, compared to this sum, "we would have to follow suit so that they don't mock us, because the Dutch are ready to pay 50,000 rupees for our affairs to fail, [and] as well … 25,000 rupees is not much for the treasury".[77] However, regardless of whether the other companies could even raise that sum, Khoja Delaune reported that the Nawab was favourably disposed towards the establishment of a GIC settlement. He also mentioned that, "after talking with him for about two hours, he says that he is also a servant and also has to respond to his master, after which I tell him that if we knew that we would have consulted at Hughli".[78] Delaune went further into the specific difficulties of his position as mediator or *vakil*, reporting that "whether at day or night, each time I meet with the Nabab and the way I speak – I don't know if others would have done as much – he replies that money is needed and the officers here dare not write one word without the Nabab's consent".[79]

Having lost his patience, Cobbé decided to force the matter by presenting himself as a general raising an army, with which he could potentially engage in direct conflict with the authorities. He gathered an army of sixty to seventy

75 Chaudhury, "Merchants, Companies, and Rulers", 91–94.

76 SAA GIC 5772 "Copie de translate des Lettres envoyé pr Coje Delon a mrs Hume & Harrisson", fo. 2 vo., "22 Octobre".

77 SAA GIC 5772 "Copie de translate des Lettres envoyé pr Coje Delon a mrs Hume & Harrisson", fo. 2 vo., "22 Octobre".

78 SAA GIC 5772 "Copie de translate des Lettres envoyé pr Coje Delon a mrs Hume & Harrisson", fo. 2 vo., "22 Octobre".

79 SAA GIC 5772 "Copie de translate des Lettres envoyé pr Coje Delon a mrs Hume & Harrisson", fo. 2 vo., "22 Octobre".

local soldiers, which thoroughly horrified Khoja Delaune in his position as a diplomat. On 13th November, Delaune wrote to Alexander Hume in order to express his anxiety at the turn of events:

> You know well that I am a weak man and [that] that man is a prompt man and not of the same humour as he was at Hughli. At present he is a brute general, he has nearly 60 to 70 peons and musketeers of the country, the orders and commands are in another way … while I try to hold unto my Credit by the honour I Received from you Sirs … for your affairs I would shed my blood … in my life I have not seen the like of that man … I would rather become the servant of your servants than [be] the friend of this man … he has spoiled the whole Court.[80]

On 17th November, Khoja Delaune wrote that Cobbé's posturing had backfired spectacularly, as

> all the people of the Darbar … are in Hope of having 10 000 to 15 000 rupees worth of presents in gold or in Merchandise, and as he has published that he is a General of Allemagne they believe themselves assured of having that sum.[81]

Khoja Delaune's documents also contained a copy of a courtly letter translated from Persian, in which Nawab Murshid Quli Khan declared having understood the GIC's intention of freely conducting trade in the country, without their goods being impounded by customs officials, which he promised to ensure:

> Esteemed by Jesus Christ, my great merchants and all others to messieurs Hume and Harrison. I hope you are well and in good health according to your desires. I heard from Haji Abdullah, Khoja Bellal and Khoja Delon that your intention is that your merchandise would not be arrested in this country, and the trade would run its course. I promise you that there will not be any hindrances.[82]

80 SAA GIC 5772 "Copie de translate des Lettres envoyé pr Coje Delon a mrs Hume & Harrisson", fo. 2 vo., "22 Octobre", fo. 3 – "13 9bre".

81 SAA GIC 5772 "Copie de translate des Lettres envoyé pr Coje Delon a mrs Hume & Harrisson", fo. 4 vo., "le 17 9bre".

82 SAA GIC 5772 "Copie de translate des Lettres envoyé pr Coje Delon a mrs Hume & Harrisson" – "copie d'une lettre translaté hors de langue Persien en langue François par sn Ignace".

Apart from negotiations, possible obstructions by rivals and differences in negotiating style, the Nawab's added suspicions regarding previously malicious affairs complicated matters at the outset. Delaune insisted on the difficulty of being caught between the Nawab and Cobbé. As he stated, "me, I am a poor man, I have to look at Two Sides to conduct the affair".[83] He noted that he had advised Cobbé that his plans were unsuitable, at which Cobbé "stamped his feet against the earth with threatening eyes against me, accusing you that you didn't want a lodge, sometimes in the presence of the Nachoda or the other Haji [Mecca pilgrim]".[84] While Delaune and Hume's primary focus was to conduct trade and establish a settlement for that purpose, Cobbé apparently considered himself the main person in charge of claiming some land for the Austrian Netherlands. This motivation seemed more important to him than smoothing relations or peacefully conducting trade. The double identity of soldier and merchant would frequently cause frictions in Mughal India, as the GIC's history of interactions with others repeatedly testifies. GIC ambassador Cobbé's 1723 diplomatic diary of his visit to the Murshidabad court mentioned how the Nawab sent an aristocrat to check whether the GIC embassy looked like soldiers or merchants:

> The Moor Sich Tahameth came, who we welcomed and who, after some impartial discourse, made us understand that he had been sent from the Nabab to See if His Honour [Cobbé himself] resembled a Soldier rather than a Merchant, and to Inquire if among those Same people there were no merchants, as he had said that the Hollanders and the English had circulated rumours that his Honour had come with other designs than those apparent, which would be to the Nabab's disadvantage.[85]

Cobbé eventually decided to raise an army of hirelings, which sparked a conflict which the residents of the temporary GIC settlement could not possibly win, and in which he lost his own life. GIC captain Cayphas best summed up the events of this conflict in a letter to GIC director and shareholder Louis Beernaert, where he mentioned how the "war" waged by Cobbé had caused

83 SAA GIC 5772 "Copie de translate des Lettres envoyé pr Coje Delon a mrs Hume & Harrisson" – "copie d'une lettre translaté hors de langue Persien en langue François par sn Ignace".

84 SAA GIC 5772 "Copie de translate des Lettres envoyé pr Coje Delon a mrs Hume & Harrisson" – "copie d'une lettre translaté hors de langue Persien en langue François par sn Ignace".

85 SAA GIC 5772 "Dagboek en klad van M. Cobbé juli 1723–febr. 1724" – "14 october".

much damage to the company's relations. In a sober and lucid perspective, Cayphas mentioned how

> it has led here to wonderment of many of our party all that has said to have happened in the war … in such occasion to make war with few people and less ammunition of war, as one Comes in another man's country to buy a place, for the negotion of which already 70 000 Rupees had been paid in advance, which, as I am said, has been presented again by the Nabab for the death of Cobbé to be resolved of all unrest and difficulties in this land, and I am being told now by many different persons that sir Cobbé has never wanted to Listen to that, as now being at war by forcing the same moors to grant his Provana and firman which cannot be obtained so swiftly and sometimes takes a while for it as has happened for the other nations … meanwhile there are many friends which work for us through mr Humes and Harrisson though everything proceeds as low-key as possible so as not to give cause to other parties to know about it or to hinder us.[86]

Some of the low-key proceedings by which GIC agents attempted to re-establish both political and commercial relations following Cobbé's conflict consisted of an extensive exchange of Persian correspondence undertaken by Basque GIC merchant Vincent Parraber in 1724. As for the scribes or *munshi*s who composed such letters, Bayly mentions them as a professional class which, in a commercial context, entailed clerks being employed by the large merchant houses to write in Persian and local languages, while junior partners had been taught to do Hindi accounts in family or merchant schools.[87] Subrahmanyam and Alam note that these *munshi*s were especially trained in *akhlaq*, or the Mughal system of norms. This entailed listening to elders and adopting the proper codes of respect, as well as studying works such as Saadi's *Gulistan* or *Bustan* or Mulla Jami's letters in order to "accumulate one's own capital and gain the virtue of knowledge" in one's code of conduct.[88] *Munshi*s were also instructed to read books on norms and ethics, and to study the collections and *masnavi*s of Persian master-poets such as Hakim Sana'ī, Farid al-Din Attar,

86 UBG (Ghent University Library) HS.1970 "Een relais ofte copie van vier brieven gheschreven door eenen pater discals, uyt het werelds deel Affrica en Asea aen syne auders tot Ghendt woonende – Arnoldus Luck, Michiel Cayphas, J.J. Hye-Hoys, 1724", fo. 4–5.

87 Christopher A. Bayly, *Empire and Information: Intelligence Gathering and Social Communication in India, 1780–1870* (New York: Cambridge University Press, 1996), 41.

88 Sanjay Subrahmanyam, and Muzaffar Alam, "The Making of a Munshi", *Comparative Studies of South Asia, Africa and the Middle East* 24:3 (2004), 62.

Khwaja Hafiz, Amir Khusraw and Mulla Rumi. In total, Subrahmanyam and Alam show that their written education was formed by a diverse but coherent programme of Persian texts, ranging from statecraft and accountancy to poetry and historiography. From these works, they acquired a whole range of Perso-Islamic expressions as well as attitudes.[89] These indispensable attitudes were required by *vakil*s as well as *munshi*s while acting as intermediaries for merchants such as Parraber, the latter having to attune themselves to the register and requirements of such an Indo-Persian courtly culture.

On 21st August 1724, chief GIC merchant Vincent Parraber sent a letter to Muhammad Ahsanullah Khan, *faujdar* or governor of Hughli, to assure him that the GIC's only purpose was to come to Bengal for trade. He attempted to convince the governor that "general Cobbé" was only supposed to come to Bengal to establish a settlement, and would have returned after concluding his trade, under the assurances of having been given a *parvannah* and land to establish a settlement, "the same as the other nations".[90] However, Parraber also indicated that, after his arrival, he discovered that "Cobbe has rather loved to make war against the orders he had from the Emperor, our august master, than to satisfy to manage your good friendship and that of the Nawab to obtain the *parvannah* and terrain which had been promised to him".[91] Parraber repeatedly insisted that *faujdar* Assanullah Khan had procured the *parvannah* and terrain "on the footing of the Dutch and French so that we can conduct our affairs". In doing so he used the argument of friendship, as "we have so much confidence in your friendship that we are persuaded it will not depend on you if we should not have as earliest as possible all the satisfaction we can wish".[92]

Parraber also attempted to re-engage a second network, that of the merchants and aristocrats of Hughli, and especially those who had occasion to travel to Murshidabad. To that end, he wrote to merchant Hadji Muhammad Sallé of Hughli, whom he informed that the GIC had not written him "a letter of friendship" since his arrival at Murshidabad. He also stated, in a flattering but formal way, that "I pray you in quality of a friend to write me of your good success, I pray God accomplishes all your Desires".[93] To this he added that Hadji

89 Subrahmanyam and Alam, "The Making of a Munshi", 63.

90 SAA GIC 5577 "Translat des lettres Persiennes en Français. Araabsche tekst met vertaling" – "3. 3724 Aoust 21 Letre au Gouverneur de Bengalle Assanouacan".

91 SAA GIC 5577 "Translat des lettres Persiennes en Français. Araabsche tekst met vertaling" – "3. 3724 Aoust 21 Letre au Gouverneur de Bengalle Assanouacan".

92 SAA GIC 5577 "Translat des lettres Persiennes en Français. Araabsche tekst met vertaling" – "3. 3724 Aoust 21 Letre au Gouverneur de Bengalle Assanouacan".

93 SAA GIC GIC 5577 "Translat des lettres Persiennes en Français. Araabsche tekst met vertaling" – "1724 Xbre 13 Agi Mahamet Sallé a Ougly a present a Maxoudabat".

Muhammad's knowledge and contacts at the *darbar* or court could be useful in re-opening the GIC's trade: "and as you find yourself at Court presently I have the confidence that you would have the goodness to search some means to open the Way for us, as you know me only from merchant to merchant".[94] The identity of Haji Muhammad Saleh proved difficult to determine: he may have formed part of a so-called "Turkish merchant community" with ties to Jeddah and the pilgrimage route to Mecca,[95] or could have been the same Haji Saleh who was sent to the Mughal Emperor Farrukhsiyar on behalf of the *sharif* of Mecca in 1716,[96] and he may have served as governor of Bihar in the early eighteenth century.[97] He might also have formed part of the merchant community around the Persian merchant Aga Motahar.[98] In any case, he was clearly identified as an influential merchant with direct connections to the Murshidabad court and treasury.

Parraber also tried to rekindle former relations with powerful courtiers and merchants who had previously been of benefit or support to the company. To this end, he again wrote to request the services of Chidiserour, who had served as the GIC's second *vakil* next to Delaune: "since he has retaken you in his grace (to our great joy), we hope that you could well want to undertake our affairs and help us to obtain our Terrain and Pravana, and that You take a hand in our Interests near the Nabab".[99] He also asked for Chidiserour's advice, asking that, "if you judge on behalf that we should write a letter to the Nabab on this Subject, have the goodness to warn us".[100]

The establishment of the GIC's trade communities in Bengal and the diplomatic and courtly relations required to do so show us how their presence involved changing and shifting allegiances through which its agents attempted to acquire a piece of land. To do this, as well as for the sake of their commerce itself, they had to engage with a world shaped by cosmopolitan constellations of Armenian, Jain, Persian and other merchants and interest groups. Within

---

94 SAA GIC GIC 5577 "Translat des lettres Persiennes en Français. Araabsche tekst met vertaling" – "1724 Xbre 13 Agi Mahamet Sallé a Ougly a present a Maxoudabat".

95 Ruquia Kazim Hussain, "Armenian, Iranian and Turkish Merchants in India 1550–1800" (PhD dissertation, Aligarh Muslim University, 2005), 300–301.

96 Hussain, "Armenian, Iranian and Turkish Merchants in India", 304.

97 Syed Husain Askari, "Bihar in the 1st Quarter of the 18th Century", *Proceedings of the Indian History Congress* 5 (1941), 394.

98 As mentioned throughout: Bengal Revenue Department, *Collection of Papers Relating to the Hooghly Imambara* (Calcutta: Bengal Secretariat Book Depot, 1914).

99 SAA GIC GIC 5577 "Translat des lettres Persiennes en Français. Araabsche tekst met vertaling" – "Xbre 19 1724 Mr Chidiserour à Mexoudabat".

100 SAA GIC GIC 5577 "Translat des lettres Persiennes en Français. Araabsche tekst met vertaling" – "Xbre 19 1724 Mr Chidiserour à Mexoudabat".

these constellations, Armenian merchants formed a particularly important mediating factor in all domains, from their role as *vakil*s in courtly ceremonies to their organizational role in trade. Likewise, the extensive diplomatic correspondence that GIC agents had to undertake in Bengal required the use of highly skilled Persian writers, who performed the task of linguistic mediation.

6 Conclusion

Instead of static systems or procedures, the formation of this smaller European trading company's trading communities and interactions shows how Bengal and Canton were both examples of trading contexts in motion, even during the limited period from 1723 to 1731. In both Bengal and Canton, the GIC relied on Asian merchants to foster their trade as well as their political alliances. In China, we see figures such as Cudgin or Suqua playing the role of "political merchants" or "merchant princes" and therefore mixing commerce with politics, although to a lesser extent than the merchants the GIC interacted with in Mughal India. Bengal presented a context of constantly shifting constellations and allegiances, which involved numerous mercantile and diplomatic contacts. As a consequence, the GIC's trading communities in Bengal were based on relations that covered more than mere commerce. The communications used to support these relations were based on an Indo-Persian courtly culture. The process of acquiring proficiency at navigating this culture required the active involvement of scribes and intermediaries as agents, such as Armenian merchants, who straddled the gulf between the political or diplomatic and commercial realms. The GIC's *vakil*s or intermediaries, such as Khoja Delaune, understood these subtleties and indicated their fraught position between different cultural contexts through their correspondence. While GIC merchants had to adopt a subordinate attitude marked by long negotiations in "courtly encounters", both in their performative behaviour at court[101] and in their textual communications, this often contrasted with their commercial motivations concerning the free flow of trade. The GIC's courtly interactions were generally marked by an impatient attitude which refused to recognize procedures of interaction or the time needed in making alliances and influencing the process of negotiation. Some of the GIC's captains and their Armenian *vakil*s clearly understood this process better. A global microhistorical approach of

101 For more on this aspect, see Wim De Winter, "Perspectives for a Comparative Cultural History of the Ostend Company Interactions in Bengal and China", *Crossroads: Studies on the History of Exchange Relations in the East Asian World* 11 (2015), 115–129.

GIC sources has allowed us to look in detail at the processes required for these interactions, the diversity of actors they involved and the identities of the GIC's trusted trading partners among Armenian, Bengali, Persian and Chinese merchants. Unlike earlier GIC historiography,[102] this perspective hints at wider cosmopolitan worlds marked by commercial interactions at Canton and Bengal, which branched out across the Indian Ocean and beyond.

---

102 As I have argued in Wim De Winter, "Hofrituelen en koloniale recuperatie van de Oostendse Compagnie in 18e eeuws Bengalen en China", *Handelingen: Koninklijke Zuidnederlandse Maatschappij Voor Taal- En Letterkunde En Geschiedenis* 68 (2015), 119–138.

CHAPTER 13

The Founding of the Nagasaki Tōjin Yashiki 長崎唐人屋敷 in 1689 in Light of Early Tokugawa Foreign Policy

Patrizia Carioti

1 The Historical Premises: the So-Called sakoku 鎖国 Policy

The rise to power of the Tokugawa shogunate in Japan led to the reunification of the archipelago, which, during the claim period, needed a strong push towards cohesion, as well as a decisive intervention in making the government of Edo effective and stable. For this reason, Tokugawa Ieyasu 徳川家康 (r. 1603–1605), first *shōgun* 将軍 and founder of the Tokugawa *bakufu* 徳川幕府, promoted a foreign policy based on peaceful cooperation. Nevertheless, the complex international situation of the first decades of the seventeenth century required careful and continuous scrutiny.

The simultaneous presence of four European countries, divided on two fronts – the Catholic Iberians and the Protestant English and Dutch companies – though not free from mutual rivalries even on the same side, was undoubtedly a destabilizing element, albeit at the same time a great stimulus to the East Asian maritime trade. Moreover, Japanese sea-traders, often financed by the coastal *daimyō* of Kyūshū, had benefited from the trade introduced by the arrival of the Europeans. The second half of the sixteenth century had seen the emergence of numerous *Nihon machi* 日本街 or "Japanese quarters" in Siam, Cambodia, Vietnam, and the Philippines.[1] Due to the political instability of those years of civil war, the *Sengoku jidai* 戦国時代, Japanese maritime and commercial activities were able to develop without restrictions. Those were the years of the *wakō* 倭寇 (in Chinese *wokou*) and *kaikō* 海寇 (in Chinese *haikou*), pirate-adventurers and sea-merchants of the Japanese archipelago who had shared routes and trade with their Chinese counterparts and

1 On *Nihon machi*, see Iwao Seiichi 岩生成一, *Shuinsen bōekishi no kenkyū* 朱印船貿易史の研究 (Tōkyō: Kōbundō, 1958); Iwao Seiichi 岩生成一, *Shuinsen to Nihon machi* 朱印船と日本町 (Tōkyō: Shibundō, 1962).

 | DOI:10.1163/9789004740556_015

quarters (*Tōjin machi* 唐人街). Nor was there any lack of alliances and groupings based on dual nationalities.[2]

However, the seventeenth century opened up about an extremely complex situation internationally, and Japanese maritime activities were gradually subjected to the *bakufu* directives. Tokugawa Ieyasu cautiously continued in the process of centralization: the aim was not to repress or stop the expansionism of the archipelago's sea trade, but to control it under the auspices of the government: the *shuinsen* 御朱印船 system was enacted. The shogunal licenses were mainly issued to authorized Japanese merchants for a period of time between 1605 and 1633.[3] The tacit message of the *bakufu* was clear: overseas trade is welcome, as long as it takes place under Japanese sovereignty and brings real advantages to the country.[4]

The gradual hardening of the Tokugawa *bakufu* had precise motivations, both ideological and economic. The need to put Japan's foreign trade under the control of the central authorities stemmed from the excessive drainage mainly of silver, but also of gold and copper, which drove the country's economy. Despite the attempt to channel the flow of imports and exports under central government directives through a conciliatory policy of the formal endorsement of trade, other measures were needed to better control the balance of payments with foreign countries.[5]

---

2 Patrizia Carioti, (2014), "Japan behind the Curtains: The Matsuura Clan of Hirado among haikou, wokou, and Europeans", in Michèle Battesti (ed.), *La piraterie au fil de l'histoire: Un défi por l'état* (Paris: Presses de L'Université Paris-Sorbonne, 2014), 161–184; Patrizia Carioti, *Cina e Giappone sui mari nei secoli XVI e XVII* (Napoli: Edizioni scientifiche italiane, 2006), 107–164.

3 Nagazumi Yōko 永積洋子, *Kinsei shoki no gaikō* 近世初期の外交 (Tōkyō: Sobunsha, 1990); Nagazumi Yōko 永積洋子, *Shuinsen* 朱印船 (Tōkyō: Yoshikawa Kōbunkan, 2001); Iwao, *Shuinsen bōekishi no kenkyū*; Iwao, *Shuinsen to Nihon machi*. See also: Nagazumi Yōko, "The Japanese Go-shuinjo (Vermilion Seal) Maritime Trade in Taiwan", in Leonard Blussé (ed.), *Around and about Formosa* (Taipei: Ts'ao Yung-ho Foundation for Culture and Education, 2003), 27–41; Iwao Seiichi, "Japanese Foreign Trade in the 16th and 17th Centuries", *Acta Asiatica* 30 (1976), 1–18.

4 For the Japanese sea-merchants, who in previous years had become accustomed to running their activities completely independently, this had in any case been a setback. Moreover, unlike Chinese mercantilism, which was based on trade and strong group cohesion (elements that were repeated in the structure of Overseas Chinese communities), the Overseas Japanese were often hired as mercenaries, either by the Europeans or by local potentates in the host country. The VOC itself had repeatedly used Japanese soldiers in various locations. Their recognized ability to use weapons, and the *samurai* martial tradition, turned the Japanese fighters into the bravest and most gifted: there were many incidents involving the Japanese mercenaries. In the eyes of the *bakufu* authorities, all these elements worked against the free activity of the Japanese sea-traders.

5 See Arano Yasunori 荒野泰典, Ishii Masatoshi 石井政敏, and Murai Shōsuke 村井章介 (eds.), *Kinseiteki sekai no seijuku, Nihon no taigai kankei* 近世的世界の成熟，日本の対外

The presence and activities of the four European countries had to be regulated. In 1612, a formal veto was issued against the Christian religion; in 1622 the bloody episode of the 22 martyrs of Nagasaki took place. After the withdrawal of the English East India Company (EIC) from Hirado in 1623, the Spaniards were expelled in 1624, given the overly aggressive religious proselytism of their missionaries. In 1636, the *bakufu* decided to transfer the Portuguese to Deshima (Dejima 出島) – although this never happened – and construction of an artificial islet located in Nagasaki Bay was started. However, as we shall see, in 1637–1638 the uprising of Shimabara (*Shimabara no ran* 島原の乱) exploded violently at probable Portuguese instigation. In 1639, the Portuguese were finally removed from the archipelago. The VOC, the Dutch East India Company, was the only European presence allowed to remain on Japanese territory.[6]

関係, 7 vols., VI (Tōkyō: Yoshikawa kōbunkan, 2010); Arano Yasunori 荒野泰典, *Edo bakufu to Higashi Ajia* 江戸幕府と東アジア (Tōkyō: Yoshikawa kōbunkan, 2003); Arano Yasunori 荒野泰典, *Kinsei Nihon to Higashi Ajia* 近世日本と東アジア (Tōkyō: Tōkyō daigaku shuppankai, 1988); Arano Yasunori 荒野泰典, *Rettōnaigai no kōtsū to kokka* 列島内外の交通と国家 [Nihon no shakaishi 日本の社会史1] (Tōkyō: Iwanami shoten, 1988); Arano Yasunori 荒野泰典, Ishii Masatoshi 石井政敏, and Murai Shōsuke 村井章介 (eds.), *Ajia no naka no Nihonshi* アジアの中の日本史, 6 vols. (Tōkyō: Tōkyō daigaku shuppankai, 1992–1993); Kishi Toshihiko 貴志俊彦, Arano Yasunori 荒野泰典, and Kokaze Hidemasa 小風秀雅, *Higashi Ajia no jidaisei* 東アジアの時代性 (Hiroshima: Keisuisha, 2005); Nagazumi, *Kinsei shoki no gaikō*; Sone Yūji 曽根勇二 and Kimura Naoya 木村直也, *Atarashii kinseishi II. Kokka to taigai kankei* 新しい近世史 II. 国家と対外関係 (Tōkyō: Shin jinbutsu ōraisha, 1996); Iwao, "Japanese Foreign Trade"; Derek Massarella, *A World Elsewhere. Europe's Encounter with Japan in the Sixteenth and Seventeenth Centuries* (New Haven and London: Yale University Press, 1990); Nakane Chie and Ōishi Shinzaburō (eds.), *Tokugawa Japan. The Social and Economic Antecedents of Modern Japan* (Tōkyō: Tōkyō University Press, 1991); Ronald Toby, *State and Diplomacy in Early Modern Japan* (Princeton: Princeton University Press, 1984).

6 Charles Ralph Boxer, "The Swan Song of the Portuguese in Japan, 1635–1639", *Transactions and Proceedings of the Japan Society* (*London*) 17 (1929–30), 4–11; Charles Ralph Boxer, *The Christian Century in Japan, 1549–1650* (Berkeley, Los Angeles, and London: University of California Press, 1951); Charles Ralph Boxer, *The Great Ship from Amacon: Annals of Macao and the Old Japan Trade, 1555–1640* (Lisbon: Centro de Estudos Historicos Ultramarinos, 1963); Patrizia Carioti, "The International Setting of Far Eastern Seas during the First Half of the 17th Century: A New Balance of Power", in Jorge Manuel Dos Santos Alves (ed.), *Portugal e a China: Conferências no III Curso de Livre de História das Relaçãos entre Portugal e a China* (Lisboa: Fundaçao Oriente, 2001), 35–60; Roberto Carneiro and A. Teodoro de Matos (eds.), *O século Cristão do Japão* [Actas do Colóquio Internacional Comemorativo dos 450 Anos de Amizade Portugal-Japão, 1543–1993) (Lisboa: Centro de Estudos dos Povos e Culturas de Expressão Portuguesa da Universidade Católica Portuguesa, 1994); A.H. de Oliveira Marques, *História dos Portugueses no Extremo Oriente, Vol. I, Part I: Em torno de Macau* (Lisboa: Fundação Oriente, 1998); A.H. de Oliveira Marques, *História dos Portugueses no Extremo Oriente, Vol. I, Part II: De Macau à periferia* (Lisboa: Fundação Oriente, 2000). See also: Shimizu Hirokazu 清水紘一, *Kirishitan kinseishi* キリシタン禁制史 (Tōkyō: Kyōikusha,

Other measures were more closely concerned with the regulation of foreign trade, in particular the Chinese trade, and the connected inner market. In 1616 it was decided to limit the foreign trade to Hirado 平戸 and Nagasaki 長崎: the port of Hirado was still considered a leading port. However, already with the first *sakoku* ordinance of 1633, Hirado also had to submit to national regulations and wait for the price of goods to settle in Nagasaki according to the *itowappu* 糸割符 system (*pancado*) before proceeding with the trade.

The ordinances issued by the Tokugawa *bakufu* between 1633 and 1639 (more precisely in 1633, 1634, 1635, 1636, and 1639), which fall under the name of *sakokurei* 鎖国令 (*sakoku* ordinances), are generally divided into three groups. Composed of seventeen basic articles, to which, over time, no substantial changes were made, these orders were focused on:

1) travel abroad by the Japanese (Articles 1 to 3): the Japanese were forbidden to leave the country, and those who were living abroad temporarily or permanently were ordered to return immediately to Japan.
2) the Christian religion (Articles 4 to 8): the ban on Christian belief was reaffirmed, and mixed unions between foreigners and Japanese were prohibited. In 1639, in addition to the previous articles, the final removal of the Portuguese was decreed.
3) foreign trade (Articles 9 to 17): the rules and regulations relating to international trade were established in considerable detail at the two ports of Hirado and Nagasaki – from 1635, only in Nagasaki – and delegated exclusively to the merchants authorized by the *bakufu* for the management of such trade, from the moment that imported goods arrive until their distribution on the internal market, including their registration and evaluation.

In 1635, the *shuinsen* system was abolished, and the landing of Chinese ships was limited to Nagasaki port. The Tokugawa *bakufu* in fact decreed Japan's withdrawal from the Asian sea routes and, just as importantly, placed under its direct control the commercial activities of the Chinese presence in Japan. This measure deeply affected the interests of the island of Hirado, and therefore of the local headquarters of the VOC, which drew much of their livelihood from the Chinese mediation. In 1641, the Dutch East India Company was transferred to the artificial islet of Deshima and the Chinese and Dutch were placed under the direct control of the Tokugawa *bakufu*. Hirado was replaced in its

---

1981); Mitsui Rokurō 満井緑郎, Doi Shin'ichirō 土井進一郎, *Shin Nagasaki nenpyō* 新長崎年表 (Nagasaki: Nagasaki bunkensha, 1974); *Tokugawa Ieyasu monjo no kenkyū* 徳川家康文書の研究 (Tōkyō: Nihon gakujutsu shinkōkai, 1960); *Tokugawa Iemitsu kōden* 徳川家光公伝 (Nikkō: Nikkō tōshogu, 1963).

official role as an international post by the city of Nagasaki. The measures taken were designed to protect and safeguard the country's economy. Under the third *shōgun*, Tokugawa Iemitsu 徳川家光 (r. 1623–1651), Japan entered the so-called *sakoku*.[7]

The Dutch East India Company was heavily involved in the political choices of the Japanese archipelago.

2 Consequences for the VOC: Misunderstandings and Suspicion

In the early decades of the seventeenth century, during the entire period of the VOC presence in Hirado (1609–1641), the Dutch East India Company faced significant changes in its relations with the Tokugawa *bakufu*, both in the political climate that gradually took shape in the archipelago and in more specific situations. The beginning of the relationship had developed most auspiciously, thanks in part to the special friendship that had bound together two strong personalities, each in his own way, the first *shōgun* Tokugawa Ieyasu and the English William Adams (1564–1620), pilot of *De Liefde*.[8] Certainly, Ieyasu had

7 Anno Masaki 安野眞幸, *Kōshiron: Hirado, Nagasaki, Yokoseura* 港市論。平戸, 長崎, 横瀬浦 (Tōkyō: Nihon editā sukūru shuppanbu, 1992); Kamiya Nobuyuki 紙屋敦之 and Kimura Naoya 木村直也, *Kaikin to sakoku* 海禁と鎖国 [Nihon Rekishi 日本歴史, 14] (Tōkyō: Tōkyōdō shuppansha, 2002); Kato Eiichi 加藤栄一 and Yamada Tadao 山田忠雄, *Sakoku* 鎖國 (Tōkyō: Yūhikaku, 1981); Kawakatsu Mamoru 川勝守, *Nihon kinsei to Higashi Ajia sekai* 日本近世と東アジア世界 (Tōkyō: Yoshikawa kōbunkan, 2000); *Nagasaki kenshi* 長崎県史 (*Hanseihen* 藩政編) (Tōkyō: Yoshikawa Kōbunkan, 1973); Nakamura Tadashi 中村質, *Kinsei Nagasaki bōekishi no kenkyū* 近世長崎貿易史の研究 (Tōkyō: Yoshikawa Kōbunkan, 1988); Oda Fujio 小田富雄, Arikawa Yoshihiro 有川宜博, Yonezu Saburō 米汁三郎, and Kanzaki Yoshio 神崎義夫, *Kita Kyūshū no rekishi* 北九州の歴史 (Fukuoka: Ashi shobō, 1979); Ōta Katsuya 太田勝也, *Sakoku jidai Nagasaki bōekishi no kenkyū* 鎖国時代長崎貿易史の研究 (Kyōto: Shibunkaku shuppan, 1992); Ozawa Toshio 小澤敬夫, *Nagasaki nenpyō* 長崎年表 (Nagasaki: Guroria shobō, 1935); Nagazumi Yōko, 永積洋子, *Sakoku wo minaosu* 鎖国を見直す [*Kokusai bunka kōryū shuishin kyōkai* 國際交流国際文化交流推進協会] (Tōkyō: Yamakawa shuppansha, 1992). Yamamoto Hirofumi 山本博文, *Sakoku to kaikin no jidai* 鎖国と海禁の時代 (Tōkyō: Azekura shobō, 1995); Carioti, *Cina e Giappone sui mari*, 153–164; George Bryan Souza, *The Survival of Empire. Portuguese Trade and Society in China and the South China Sea, 1630–1754* (Cambridge: Cambridge University Press, 1986).

8 A.L. Sadler, *The Maker of Modern Japan. The Life of Tokugawa Ieyasu* (Rutland, VT/Tōkyō: Tuttle, 1989); Conrad Totman, *Tokugawa Ieyasu: Shōgun* (Torrance CA: Heian International, 1983); *Sunpuki* 駿府記 in *Dai Nihon shiryō* 大日本史料 (Tōkyō: Shiryō Hensanjo, 1901 ~), 12, X; *Tokugawa Ieyasu monjo no kenkyū*, III/I (Keichō, 15th year, 12th month, 16th day), 641–644; *Da Asia. Decada XII* (1645), by Diogo de Couto [ca. 1542–1616] (Lisboa, 1788), 451; J. Murdoch, Yamagata I., *A History of Japan*, 3 vols. (New York: Greenberg, 1926), II, 400–471; George Sansom, *A History of Japan*, 3 vols. (Tōkyō: Tuttle, 1987), II, 402–403.

wanted and carefully protected the settlement of the VOC in Hirado in 1609, as well as that of the EIC in 1613, continuing to look favourably on the Dutch presence until the end of his life: a functional and intelligent foreign policy moved Japan to conquer the seas under the aegis of the *shuinsen*. Yet, in 1616, with the death of Ieyasu and the consequent acquisition of full powers by Tokugawa Hidetada 徳川秀忠, *shōgun* from 1605 to 1622, the political climate in Japan changed.

That same year 1616, with the decree limiting international trade to the sole ports of Hirado and Nagasaki, the VOC had perceived a hardening in the attitude of the Japanese authorities.[9] Perhaps feeling the changing context as less welcoming, the Dutch Company made a serious diplomatic mistake. Armed with Ieyasu's permission to keep a seat in Hirado, the VOC delegates petitioned Hidetada, requesting that this permission be renewed. In the eyes of the Edo authorities it was an inappropriate gesture, as the request itself was seriously contrary to protocol and was seen as a lack of respect for the new *shōgun*. It was also deeply offensive in content, as it cast doubt on Hidetada's feelings of filial piety towards Ieyasu, and implicitly asserted the possibility that the *shōgun* could alter or even rescind what his father had decided. For the *bakufu* this was unacceptable and insulting behaviour: already the VOC began to experiment with the first sanctions and to experience a climate that was not entirely benevolent.[10]

Things were certainly no better in the 1620s: since Hirado, as we know, housed both the offices of the VOC and those of the EIC, nothing was more natural for the two leaders than to station the Defense Fleet (1620–1622) in the local bay.[11] But the menacing presence of European warships did not please the Japanese authorities at all, especially when ships of the Anglo-Dutch alliance began to patrol the seas, attack enemy merchants and then re-enter the waters of the archipelago. Immediately the *bakufu* veto was triggered: the Anglo-Dutch fleet had to find a different location than in the Japanese bay of

9 Nagazumi, *Kinsei shoki no gaikō*; Leonard Blussé, Willem Remmelink, and Ivo Smith (eds.), *Nichi-Ran kōryū 400nen no rekishi to tenbō* 日蘭交流400年の歴史と展望 (Tōkyō: Nichi-Ran gakkai, 2000); Patrizia Carioti, *Guardando al "Celeste Impero" ... L'avventura della VOC in Asia Orientale* (Trento: Centro Studi Martino Martini, 2012).

10 Fiorella Leemhuis, "Gli Olandesi a Deshima", *Il Giappone* 11 (1971), 63–84; Charles Ralph Boxer, *Jan Compagnie in Japan, 1600–1850* (The Hague: Martinus Nijhoff, 1950); Boxer, *The Great Ship from Amacon*.

11 The *Fleet of Defence* was a military alliance between the VOC and the EIC formed in 1620–1622 and ending with the attack on Portuguese Macau in 1622. See Paul Van Dyke, "The Anglo-Dutch Fleet of Defence (1620–1622): Prelude to the Dutch Occupation of Taiwan", in Leonard Blussé (ed.), *Around and about Formosa* (Taipei: Ts'ao Yung-ho Foundation for Culture and Education, 2003), 61–81.

Hirado.[12] Moreover, the intervention of Edo's government was even more peremptory in condemning the attacks that the Dutch ships launched against the Chinese ships leaving Nagasaki in order to plunder their cargo of silver. The Tokugawa authorities would not have tolerated such piratical behaviour by the Company, which was forced to review its conduct in the seas of Japan.[13]

The period between the late 1620s and early 1630s was even more difficult. The so-called "Nuyts incident" of 1628 had poisoned relations, and it was proving very difficult to regain mutual trust.[14] In addition, although the headquarters at Hirado had resumed conducting international trade regularly in 1632, the Company's delegates had now been placed under close supervision by the local authorities. The year 1633 had marked the enactment of the first decree of the *sakoku*: the VOC was required to sell raw silk at the same price as that set for the Portuguese in Nagasaki, and other products, which were also to be sold at a defined price, could only be put on the market after the price of raw silk had been fixed.[15]

Nicolaes Koeckebaker (fl. 1627–1639), Governor of Hirado from 1633 to 1639, tried in vain to evade the *bakufu*'s impositions, but was severely reprimanded by the Matsuura *daimyō* 松浦大名. More and more restrictions were imposed on the Company's delegates regarding both their commercial activities and their personal freedom. In those years, the atmosphere of distrust was intensified by the day: after the expulsion of the Spaniards in 1624 the Portuguese had been placed under close surveillance, and by 1636 Portuguese ships could no longer stop at the port of Nagasaki, being allowed to remain there just long enough to unload their goods. By 1635, all Chinese ships, *Tōsen* 唐船, had to use Nagasaki as their only port of entry, while Hirado was cut off from the international network and trades. This was close to the expulsion of the Portuguese in 1639, which would mark a turning point in relations with Europe. Indeed, the permanence of the VOC in the Japanese archipelago also appeared to be in question.[16]

---

12 Van Dyke, "The Anglo-Dutch Fleet".

13 Nagazumi Yōko 永積洋子, *Tōsen yūnyū shutsuhin suryō ichiran 1633–1685* 唐船輸入出品数量一覧一六三三 ~ 一六八五 (Tōkyō: Sobunsha, 1988), 6–13, at p. 9.

14 Leonard Blussé, "Bull in a China Shop, Pieter Nuits in China and Japan (1627–1636)", in Leonard Blussé (ed.), *Around and about Formosa* (Taipei: Ts'ao Yung-ho Foundation for Culture and Education, 2003), 95–110.

15 Nakamura, *Kinsei Nagasaki bōekishi no kenkyū*; Arano, Ishii, and Murai, *Kinseiteki sekai no seijuku*; Arano, *Edo bakufu to Higashi Ajia*; Arano, Ishii, and Murai, *Ajia no naka no Nihonshi*; Nagazumi, *Kinsei shoki no gaikō*.

16 Blussé, Remmelink, and Smith, *Nichi-Ran kōryū 400nen no rekishi*; Charles Ralph Boxer, *The Dutch Seaborne Empire* (London: Penguin Pelican, 1965) [repr. 1973]; Boxer, *Jan Compagnie in Japan*; Charles Ralph Boxer, *Jan Compagnie in War and Peace, 1602–1799* (Hong Kong, Singapore, Kuala Lumpur: Heinemann Asia, 1979).

3 Shimabara no ran, 1637–1638

By 1612, the veto against the Christian religion had been decisively reaffirmed, and the relations of the Iberian countries with the Japanese authorities had begun to break down. Nevertheless, Spanish and Portuguese missionaries continued to profess their religion, ignoring the orders of the *bakufu*. In 1614, there was the first bloody cases of crucifixion, to be followed in 1616 by the expulsion of several Christian missionaries, who had to escape and take refuge in Macau. However, these serious changes in the political climate were not enough to curb missionary activity: in 1622, the martyrdom of Nagasaki was the prelude to the expulsion of the Spaniards in 1624. Abjuration and the *fumie* 踏み絵or "walking on sacred images" were imposed on all converts, proving that the Christian religion had been disavowed.[17]

The Portuguese had less and less freedom of action and pressed their Spanish allies to stop smuggling missionaries from the Philippines, but in vain: the Spanish had nothing left to lose in Japan and continued to oppose the *bakufu*'s veto in trying to get back into the archipelago unofficially.[18] This was undoubtedly of extreme harm to the Portuguese: in 1636, the construction of the artificial islet of Deshima meant the forced transfer of Portuguese to Nagasaki Bay, in total isolation from the rest of the country. The tension was spasmodic: in 1637, a new edict forbade all foreigners to travel in Japan, a move designed to prevent the Portuguese from moving within the archipelago using Dutch passports.[19]

In the same year, 1637, the Shimabara uprising erupted violently, and the Tokugawa authorities thought they saw the Portuguese acting in its background. The revolt was intended as a Christian rebellion, since in fact most of the rebels professed the Catholic religion, but it had its origins mainly, in the extreme poverty of large sections of the population.

The rebels took refuge in Hara Castle 原城 (*Harajō*), and the *bakufu* militias launched repetitive assaults against its walls, but in vain. The situation threatened to go on for a long time: the siege had lasted for over a month. It was at this point that the Tokugawa authorities called for the intervention of the Dutch artillery, both to speed up the solution of the problem and to test, this time in fact, the loyalty of the VOC towards the *shōgun*, which was repeatedly

17 Boxer, "The Swan Song of the Portuguese in Japan"; Boxer, *The Christian Century in Japan*; Shimizu, *Kirishitan kinseishi*; Mitsui and Doi, *Shin Nagasaki nenpyō*.

18 Mitsui and Doi, *Shin Nagasaki nenpyō*; Juan Gil, *España y Japón en los siglos XVI y XVII* (Madrid: Alianza Editorial, 1991).

19 Boxer, "The Swan Song of the Portuguese in Japan"; Boxer, *The Christian Century in Japan*; Shimizu, *Kirishitan kinseishi*; Mitsui and Doi, *Shin Nagasaki nenpyō*; Seno Seiichirō 瀬野精一郎, *Nagasakiken no rekishi* 長崎県の歴史 (Tōkyō: Yamakawa Shuppansha, 1972).

expressed, but had never concretely been demonstrated. Nicolaes Koeckebaker, governor of Hirado, was uncertain what to do and wanted to consult with the High Council of Batavia, but there was no time. The Nagasaki *bugyō* 奉行 (commissioner) instructed him to send the requested help as soon as possible, and Koeckebaker sent Shimabara a ship equipped with twenty guns.[20]

The Dutch ship remained in the service of the *shōgun* for about twenty days, during which it fired against the rebel-held fortress before being sent back to Hirado. Word had spread that the besieged had no more supplies, so the VOC's support was no longer necessary. Japanese troops took the fortress and massacred the survivors, some 37,000 civilians, including the elderly, women, and children. The same leader who had supported the siege for three months was only 15–16 years old: he was known as Amakusa Shirō 天草四郎 (*c.*1621–1638) and baptized as Geronimo Francis. The rebellion and its ferocious repression came to be called the "Shimabara massacre". In Europe, the VOC was long blamed for its participation, as the Dutch soldiers had had fight against fellow Christians. Certainly, in such a hostile climate, Nicolaes Koeckebaker had made the only possible choice: disobeying the *shogun*'s orders would have meant certain death for himself and his men and the loss of the VOC's important commercial base in Japan. In 1639, in the aftermath of the bloody events just described, the Portuguese was permanently expelled from Japanese territory.[21]

4 Deshima no Oranda yashiki 出嶋のオランダ屋敷

The military support given to the Japanese militias during the Shimabara uprising did not mean that the VOC were granted any favours: the prospects of the Dutch staying in Japan did not seem at all guaranteed. In fact, the Japanese authorities held a heated debate about the VOC's presence in Japan. Nevertheless, the years 1638–1640 had been the most profitable for the Dutch East India Company: the VOC was now the only European presence still tolerated in the archipelago. One idea that was gaining ground among the *bakufu* authorities was to move the VOC headquarters from Hirado to Deshima, which was certainly not very welcome to the Dutch officials. In a secret meeting held

20 Blussé, Remmelink, and Smith, *Nichi-Ran kōryū 400nen no rekishi*; Boxer, *The Dutch Seaborne Empire*; Shimizu, *Kirishitan kinseishi*, 156–165; Boxer, *The Christian Century in Japan*, 362–397.

21 Grant K. Goodman, *Japan: The Dutch Experience* (London and Dover: Athlone Press, 1986), 9–17, at p. 14. Boxer, "The Swan Song of the Portuguese"; Shimizu, *Kirishitan kinseishi*, 156–165; Boxer, *The Christian Century in Japan*, 362–397.

in 1640, the Matsuura *daimyō* and the Dutch governor of Hirado, Francois Caron, expressed fears about the Company's imminent transfer to Deshima and looked for a possible way of avoiding it.[22]

However, it was the Dutch delegates themselves who provided the pretext for the Tokugawa *bakufu* to implement this move. After completing the construction of a new building for the VOC quarters in Hirado, on the facade they wrote the date of completion in Latin, in accordance with the usual custom: *Anno Domini MDCXLI*. This mistake proved fatal: the Japanese authorities ordered the immediate removal of the Christian date and the destruction of all VOC edifices in Hirado. The experienced governor, François Caron, did not hesitate and immediately proceeded to demolish the VOC's buildings. In that situation of cold hostility and mistrust, a single objection by Governor Caron could result in the immediate expulsion of the VOC from the archipelago. In 1641, the headquarters of the Dutch East India Company were relocated to the artificial island of Deshima.[23] Hirado was replaced by Nagasaki in its official international position. With the third *shōgun*, Tokugawa Iemitsu, Japan had entered the so-called *sakoku*.

In this situation of forced isolation, the only information the VOC could obtain, at least officially, came from the Dutch interpreters, who were among the few to be allowed to go to the *Oranda yashiki* (Dutch residence) on occasion.[24] Surrounded by an impenetrable Iron Curtain – or at least such was the intention of the Japanese authorities – the Dutch delegates were not allowed to leave Deshima, and, if they needed to do so, they needed a special pass. Strict and comprehensive control was exercised on all those who came to or left the island. They had access to Deshima, the *bugyō* of Nagasaki, the high magistrate of the area, and those who worked at his offices, the authorized merchants, suppliers of basic daily necessities. Prostitutes carefully selected by the local authorities were also provided.[25]

---

22 "Nōson shihai no henka to gaikoku bōeki" 農村支配の変化と外国貿易, *Hiradohan* 平戸藩, in *Nagasaki kenshi* 長崎県史 (*Hanseihen* 藩政編) (Tōkyō: Yoshikawa kōbunkan, 1973), 403–412.

23 Blussé, Remmelink, and Smith, *Nichi-Ran kōryū 400nen no rekishi*; Boxer, *The Dutch Seaborne Empire*; Goodman, *Japan*, 9–17, 18–24.

24 See: Isabel Tanaka Van Daalen, "Communicating with the Japanese under Sakoku: Dutch Letters of Compliant and Attempts to Learn Japanese", in Nagazumi Yōko (ed.), *Large and Broad: The Dutch Impact on Early Modern Asia. Essays in Honor of Leonard Blussé* (Tōkyō: Tōyō bunkō, 2010), 100–129.

25 Cynthia Viallé and Leonard Blussé (eds.), *The Deshima Dagregisters, XI: 1641–1650* (Leiden: Institute for the History of European Expansion, 2001); Niwa Kankichi, *The Dutch Settlement at Dejima* (*Dejima Oranda yashiki*) (Nagasaki: Nagasaki Bunkensha, s.d).

However, in the years to come, the VOC would never give up: using informants and trusted agents, the Dutch tried to obtain any information that might prove useful in understanding, following and directing the development of Japan's internal market to their own advantage.[26] The VOC delegates were very interested in the events related to the Ming – Qing transition, as well as to the Zheng's activities, trades and connections in Japan.[27]

During the entire period of the VOC remaining on Japanese territory, the small island of Deshima served as a vital bridge between Japan and Europe: distinguished names such as Engelbert Kaempfer (1651–1716), Carl Peter Thunberg (1743–1828), Isaac Titsingh (1745–1812), and Philipp Franz von Siebold (1796–1866) indelibly marked the technical, scientific, and cultural dialogue. European knowledge was introduced into the archipelago, just as studies of Japan entered Europe, through that small outpost of the European presence in the country. In particular, medical knowledge became the subject of careful studies and fruitful exchanges. The "Dutch studies", or *Rangaku* 蘭学, spread to Edo and Kyōto among Japanese intellectuals, and the medical school of the archipelago was enriched by the novelties of European surgery. At the same time, the first knowledge of Chinese medicine, mediated by Japanese scholars *Yōgakusha* 洋学者, penetrated Europe as well. The role of the VOC in Deshima, rather than being economic in nature, proved to be invaluable in the priceless sharing of information, ideas and knowledge that it allowed between "East and West".[28]

At the time of their transfer from Hirado to Deshima, the VOC delegates, although completely unaware of the cultural and scientific role that history would call them to play, understood perfectly that the VOC's freedom of maneuver had been drastically reduced, and that even trade would be partly affected by this event. Nagasaki became, at least formally, the only gateway to international trade, the *sakoku no mado* 鎖国の窓 ("A window of the closed country"). The Dutch settlement and the Chinese presence, on which the Zheng 鄭 exerted a significant influence, coexisted in Nagasaki, being forced

26 The international trade made a substantial profit for both the Japanese and Dutch actors: in 1638 imports from Japan alone generated a profit of 2.5 million forints for the VOC, while between 1651 and 1675, the average annual gain was around 900,000 forints.

27 In 1682, the Japanese authorities formally prohibited, subject to death, any information about Nagasaki's trafficking. This highlights the enormous strategic importance of keeping the reunited Company as much as possible in the dark about the archipelago's trades, while at the same time being a clear demonstration of the partial futility of those precautions that were taken. See Tanaka van Daalen, "Communicating with the Japanese under Sakoku".

28 Blussé, Remmelink, and Smith, *Nichi-Ran kōryū 400nen no rekishi.*

into a close and contradictory coexistence. The sharp rivalry between the Zheng organization and the VOC was re-enacted on Japanese territory.

Despite having created a policy of defense and restraint in foreign trade, the Japanese archipelago had not yet been able to free itself from the need for imports involving heavy outlays. By restricting international trade from 1641 to the port of Nagasaki and allowing access to the Chinese and the Dutch, it had in fact found itself officially hosting two conflicting powers in its territory, which were therefore undergoing intense competition, especially since the organizations of the Zheng and the VOC imported the same goods into Japan, that is to say, essentially silks.[29] Moreover, the first decades had seen a decisive Chinese supremacy, partly favored also by the *bakufu*, which certainly had less distrust of the Chinese. Not surprisingly, the *bakufu* had hosted the Chinese presence in the city of Nagasaki but relegated the headquarters of the Dutch Company to the small artificial island of Deshima, granting Chinese interpreters – who were responsible for any commercial, civil and criminal relations between the Chinese community and the Japanese authorities – much more latitude than that given to the Dutch interpreters, who were among the very few who had access to Deshima and were subject to strict control.[30]

The Dutch East India Company and the maritime organization of Zheng Chenggong 鄭成功 (1624–1662) therefore found themselves lined up against each other, initially commercially, but not only. And this economic clash took place and was repeated at all the stops on the East Asian routes from Indonesia to Japan, which were common to them both.[31] It is clear that this harsh rivalry could only escalate. The Zheng conquest of Taiwan 臺灣 on the 1st February 1662, after nine months of siege, and the VOC's consequent surrender and expulsion from Fort Zeelandia (Tainan) were the unavoidable

29 Henriette Bugge, "Silk to Japan: Sino Dutch Competition in the Silk Trade to Japan, 1633–1685", *Itinerario* 13, no. 2 (1989), 25–44.

30 Patrizia Carioti, "Focusing on the Overseas Chinese in Seventeenth Century Nagasaki: The Role of the Tōtsūji in the Light of the Early Tokugawa Foreign Policy", in Nagazumi Yōko (ed.), *Large and Broad: The Dutch Impact on Early Modern Asia: Essays in Honor of Leonard Blussé* (Tokyo: Toyo Bunko, 2010), 62–75.

31 At its base in Batavia, for example, the Reunited Company had established a monopoly on maritime trade (1652), preventing the Chinese of the local community from carrying out this activity. However, in 1654 and 1655 a fleet of eight vessels arrived in Batavia from Fujian, all belonging to Zheng Chenggong, who was completely indifferent to this type of imposition, of which, not wrongly, the authority recognized. Leonard Blussé, *Strange Company: Chinese Settlers, Mestizo Women and the Dutch in VOC Batavia* (Dordrecht: Foris Publications, 1988), 117; Coolhaas, W. Ph. (ed.), *Generale Missiven van Gouverneurs-Generaal en Raden van Indië aan Heren XVII der Verenigde Oostindische Companie 1610–1671*, 13 vols. ['s Gravenhage: Rijks Geschiedkundige Publicatiën, n. 112, 1960–2007], Vol. II, 1964, 824.

results of decades of rivalry, commercial hostilities and military conflict that had existed since Zheng Zhilong 鄭之龍 (1604–1661) times, between the Zheng regime and the Dutch East India Company.[32]

5 In the Shadow of the Zheng Regime

The Manchu conquest of Beijing in 1644 gave rise to the complex and exhausting dynastic transition from the Ming to the Qing. The Ming-Qing conflict, as is well known, lasted until 1662, when the Qing captured Yongli 永曆 (r. 1646–1662), the last emperor of the Southern Ming 南明 (1644–1662), and put him to death.

During the years of the Ming-Qing dynastic transition and military conflicts, many requests for military support were forwarded to the Tokugawa *bakufu* by the Ming loyalists: for the most part, they were directly or indirectly sent by the Zheng group, and in a few cases by other loyalist forces as well. It was exactly thorough the activities of the Chinese literati – and more in general of the Ming loyalists – that a link with the *Tōjin* 唐人 in Nagasaki proved to be a key element in this relationship: the *Kokusen'yasen* 國姓爺船 (Guoxingye: Zheng Chenggong's ships) brought many refugees escaping from the Manchu to Nagasaki, that is to say, many Ming loyalists, literati and Buddhist monks wanting to take refuge in Japan.[33] The Chinese settlement of Nagasaki, on which the Zheng organization could exert such a deep influence, played a fundamental role in the economic, political, and military decisions taken by the Tokugawa *bakufu*. The requests sent by the Zheng – or by other Ming

32 Patrizia Carioti, "Higashi Indokaisha no nigai haiboku: Tei Seikō ni yoru Taiwan seifuku, 1661–1662" 東インド会社の苦い敗北。郑成功による台湾征服、 1661–1662, in Arano Yasunori 荒野泰典 (ed.), *Kinsei Nihon no kokusai kankei to gensetsu* 近世日本の国際関係と言説 (Hiroshima: Keisuisha, 2017), 63–81.

33 In this regard, the role attended by the literati in support of the Ming resistance was indeed very significant, although not so incisive: Huang Zongxi 黃宗羲 (1610–1695) and Zhu Shunshui 朱舜水 (1600–1682) can be cited as examples. We also have to remember that Zheng Chenggong had received a traditional Confucian education at the Nanjing Imperial Academy, although he was compelled to interrupt his studies because of the war. See Patrizia Carioti, "Echoes of the Ming-Qing Conflict: Notes on the Political Role of the Overseas Chinese in Nagasaki", in Magda Abbiati and Federico Greselin (eds.), *Il liuto e i libri Studi in onore di Mario Sabattini, vol. 1, Sinica venetiana* (Venezia: Edizioni Ca' Foscari, 2014), 137–156.

supporters – to the *bakufu* for Japanese military intervention in favor of the Ming were sent to Japan for more than forty years, until 1686.[34]

The influence of Zheng Chenggong on Japan's foreign trade, and therefore on its inner market as well, was substantial, and the *bakufu* could not ignore this. This in itself was reason enough not to make relations too strained by issuing rigid or ostentatious refusals. In answer to his requests, Zheng Chenggong obtained metals, medicines, and armaments to strengthen his armies, but no Japanese troops were sent to swell the loyalist ranks.[35] Thus, Japan sought to support Zheng Chenggong without compromising itself: more than once, acting on explicit orders, the Japanese officials responsible for vessels in transit in the port of Nagasaki turned away those few Chinese traders who owed allegiance to the Manchu, thereby in practice granting Zheng's ships a monopoly. This discriminating caution was an accurate reflection of the delicate circumstances in which the archipelago found itself.

34 Twelve of the twenty-two total requests were sent in the late '40s, immediately after the Manchu conquest of Beijing (1644) and Nanjing (1645). This is quite comprehensible, as the entire world of Chinese literati, officials, gentry and upper classes were attempting to confront the Manchu advancing troops. In those years, the loyalist force was extremely active, although since the beginning in a very disordered way. During the '50s, the appeals to the Tokugawa *bakufu* were few: Zheng Chenggong was absorbed by the war against the Qing, alternating military conflicts and apparent attempts at dialogue while preparing the final assault (1659) – and his terrible defeat, as we know – on the core of the Chinese Empire, namely Nanjing. Those were the years of the saying "*fu Ming da Qing*" 複明打清. The beginning of the '60s still witnessed a few attempts to obtain Japanese support. Although already settled in Taiwan from 1661, and after having expelled the VOC on 1st February 1662, in 1663 the Zheng (Zheng Jing) were still defending their bases in Xiamen and Jinmen, but in vain: the Sino-Dutch attack compelled the Zheng regime to retire definitively, at least for the moment, from the Chinese continent. The '70s saw a recrudescence of the conflict: the so-called "Rebellion of the Three Feudatories" was shaking the recently established Qing Empire. Zheng Jing, after re-conquering Xiamen, tried once again to get some support from the Tokugawa government. The last appeal of 1686, as we have seen, is quite surprising, as it was – at least apparently – completely un-contextual. Cf. Patrizia Carioti, "The Zheng Regime and Tokugawa Japan: Asking for the Japanese Intervention", in Tonio Andrade and Hang Xing (eds.), *Sea Rovers, Silver, and Samurai: Maritime East Asia in Global History, 1550–1700* (Honolulu: University of Hawai'i Press, 2016), 156–180. See also: Bai Di 白蒂 (Patrizia Carioti), "Shiqi shiji Zhengshi haishang jituan zai dongya de guoji jiaose" 17世紀鄭氏海上集團在東亞的國際角色, in Zhu Chengru 朱成如 and Wang Tianyou 王天有 (eds.), *Ming Qing luncong* 明清論, vol. 12 (Beijing: Gugong chubanshe, 2012), 221–246; Bai Di 白蒂 (Patrizia Carioti), *Yuandong guoji de wutaishang de fengyun renwu Zheng Chenggong* 遠東國際舞臺上的風雲人物鄭成功 (Guangxi: Guangxi renmin chubanshe, 1997).

35 Carioti, "The Zheng Regime and Tokugawa Japan".

During Zheng Jing's 鄭經 (1642–1681) leadership as well, the economic influence on the Japanese market was still significant, while the contrast between the Zheng and the VOC was even sharper. The Dutch sided with the Qing fleet in 1663, succeeding in expelling Zheng Jing from Xiamen 廈門 and Jinmen 金門: for the Zheng Regime, this was the first time it had been completely estranged from mainland China. Nevertheless, during the "Revolt of the Three Feudatories" (*Sanfan zhi luan* 三蕃之亂, 1673–1681), Zheng Jing was back again in Fujian 福建, and Xiamen became once more an important center of the international sea-trade network. It is worth noting that in those years the EIC, as a direct rival of the VOC, reappeared in East Asian seas, opening offices first in Taiwan in 1670, and few years later, in 1675, in Xiamen as well, with Zheng Jing's consent and support. Yet, as we know, the turning point came with the end of the Revolt in 1681 and with Zheng Jing's death that same year. The collapse of the Zheng Regime was unavoidable: in 1683 Admiral Shi Lang's 施琅 (1621–1696) fleet landed on Taiwan's shores, and Zheng Keshuang 鄭克爽 (1670–1707) capitulated to the Qing without conditions. Under the bright guidance of Emperor Kangxi 康熙 (r. 1661–1722), a new era was starting, and the long and complex Ming-Qing dynastic transition came to an end.[36]

In 1684, the Kangxi Emperor launched the "Open Port Policy". Soon afterwards, in 1689, the *Tōjin yashiki* of Nagasaki took shape.

6 1689: the Tōjin yashiki of Nagasaki

With the final pacification of the Chinese south, the Qing Empire finally considered the long process of conquering China to be at an end. Nevertheless, the new dynasty did not cease paying attention to its coasts, where it rather it looked with interest at their economies. Thanks to the enlightened leadership of the Kangxi Emperor, the central authorities distanced themselves from the policy of their Ming predecessors and worked to satisfy the needs of coastal areas.[37] In 1684, the Qing authorities overturned the prohibition on navigation

36 Ibid.

37 Lawrence D. Kessler, *K'ang-hsi and the Consolidation of Ch'ing Rule, 1661–1684* (Chicago and London: The University of Chicago Press, 1976), 81–90; Tsao Kai-fu, "K'ang-hsi and the San-fan War", *Monumenta Serica* 31 (1974–75), 108–130; Zhuang Guotu, "Canton System: China's Reaction to European Commercial Expansion in 18th Century", *Ming Qing Yanjiu* 2, no. 1 (1993), 127–163; Deng Gang, *Maritime Sector, Institutions, and Sea Power of Premodern China* (Westport, CT and London: Greenwood Press, 1999); Deng Gang, *Chinese Maritime Activities and Socioeconomic Development* (Westport, CT and London: Greenwood Press, 1997).

for the Chinese sea-traders and opened four ports to international trade, allowing the landing of European ships.[38] The international maritime trade was brought under direct control by the authorities through the creation of offices and the appointment of officials with specific posts for this task.[39] The Chinese sea-traders regained their vigor and once again embarked on their conquest of the seas, which they developed considerably. Their relative freedom allowed the *Tōjin* to strengthen ties with Chinese communities scattered throughout the coasts of Southeast Asia, especially in Nagasaki, and to expand and increase the international maritime trade.[40]

In Japan, the very rich Genroku period 元禄時代 (1688–1704) was marked by unbridled consumerism: although it flourished culturally, its life style was expensive, and the economic balance of the country was unstable: the influence of Chinese commerce on the Japanese economy was still significant.[41]

38 Canton (Guangzhou), Amoy (Xiamen), Ningbo, and Yuntaishan 雲台山. To distinguish Chinese ships by place of origin, the Chinese authorities imposed an explicit diversification of their colours: for example, Fujian ships had green trees and red identification marks; the ships coming from Guangdong were blue, with the characters of the writings in red. Crews also varied in number based on the size of the vessels, according to specific rules and regulations. See Blussé, *Strange Company*, 121–122.

39 The tax on the maritime trade was an important entry for the treasury's coffers, as was the massive silver lining for the purchase of Chinese artisanal products; Moreover, although the Manchu were in favour of the private management of international trade, the autonomy of these activities was well defined and had to meet the requirements imposed by the authorities. The official post of supervisor of private merchant trades, conducted in the permitted Chinese ports, was entrusted to a local merchant of proven experience chosen from among the richest and most trusted: it was a customary practice, which recalled the traditional criterion of mutual responsibility. The *guanshang* 官商 system of merchant-officials was in place and was already the embryonic system of the *hong* merchants (*hang* 行), the only ones authorized to pose as interlocutors and intermediaries of trade with Europeans (*yanghuohang* 洋貨行). Cf. Weng Eang Cheong, *Hong Merchants of Canton: Chinese Merchants in Sino-Western Trade, 1684–1798* (Richmond, Surrey: Curzon, 1997), 30.

40 Zhuang, "Canton System"; Ng Chin-keong, *Trade and Society: The Amoy Network on the China Coast 1683–1735* (Singapore: National University of Singapore Press, 1983); Weng, *Hong Merchants of Canton*, 7–11; Nagazumi Yōko, "From Company to Individual Company Servants: Dutch Trade in Eighteenth-century Japan", in Leonard Blussé and Femme S. Gaastra (eds.), *On the Eighteenth Century as a Category of Asian History: Van Leur in Retrospect* (Aldershot: Ashgate, 1998), 147–172, here 152–155; *Nagasaki kenshi* (*Hanseihen*); Yamamoto Kitsuna 山本紀綱, *Nagasaki Tōjin Yashiki* 長崎唐人屋敷 (Tōkyō: Kenkōsha, 1983).

41 Already around the year 1676 the *bakufu* was in debt because of the fluctuations in imports and exports of commodities, and for the excessive exports of precious metals, especially silver. See Suzuki Yasuko, "Changes in the Nagasaki Governorship System, 1680–1690", in Nagazumi Yōko (ed.), *Large and Broad: The Dutch Impact on Early Modern Asia. Essays*

Under the fifth *shōgun*, Tokugawa Tsunayoshi 徳川綱吉, who ruled from 1680 to 1705, many changes were undertaken in the *bakufu* policy, as Tsunayoshi was determined to be an absolute ruler. New political trends were applied to the governance structure, and the administrative system of the *bakufu* – the *buke shohatto* 武家諸法度 – was revised in respect of both agricultural improvements and economic policies.[42]

The central authorities paid particular attention to Nagasaki. In 1685, the Japanese authorities launched the *gojōdaka* 御定高 system (fixed-ceiling trade) and re-introduced the *itowappu* 糸割符 system (yarn guild): the limit was 6,000 *kanme* 貫目 of silver for the Chinese merchants, and 50,000 gold *ryō* 両 for the VOC, as the Dutch had prohibited exports of silver since 1664. Several reforms and restrictions were put into effect with the precise aim of limiting and regulating the Nagasaki trade, with direct consequences for Chinese commercial activities and for their lives in Japan. Contextually, after the *gojōdaka* system was established, several reforms were implemented: in 1688 coastal control was enforced around Nagasaki Bay, and in the following year 1689 the number of the *Tōsen* permitted each year was limited to seventy cargos. It appears evident that the founding of the *Tōjin yashiki* in 1689 was perfectly consistent with the severe restrictions placed on Chinese activities and the wider economic policies promoted by the Edo authorities.[43] Also in 1695, the *Nagasaki kaisho* 長崎会所 (the *bakufu* trading office) was established in Nagasaki. In 1715 new limitations on the number of Chinese ships were issued, a new ordinance of the Shōtoku Era (*Shōtoku no shinrei* 正徳の新令, 1711–1716).

The Japanese authorities were particularly concerned about the significant amount of smuggling, illegal and unofficial trade being carried out in the city of Nagasaki, both through the VOC in Deshima, thanks to the connivance of Dutch officials, and more particularly through the *Tōsen*, these Chinese merchants being free to circulate in Nagasaki and thus well placed to establish direct contact with their Japanese partners.[44]

---

in Honor of Leonard Blussé (Tōkyō: Tōyō Bunkō, 2010), 76–99, here 78; Nagazumi, "From Company to Individual Company Servants", 148–149.

42 Being a convinced Confucian, Tokugawa Tsunayoshi greatly appreciated Zhu Xi 朱熹 (1130–1200), and under his guidance, ethics and morality were strongly reaffirmed, while Chinese culture and civilization were again largely spread among the Japanese intellectuals.

43 See the interesting analysis by Suzuki, "Changes in the Nagasaki Governorship System".

44 Although the 1635 restrictions had already limited the activities of the *Tōjin*, an enormous flux of business carried out in Nagasaki was on the "black market" and completely hidden from the Japanese officials, who could not control it at all. This meant also a significant

From 1684 onwards, after the Kangxi Emperor had lifted the ban on the Chinese maritime trades, the number of *Tōsen* entering the port of Nagasaki increased more and more.[45] In 1688, there were more than nine thousand *Tōjin* in Nagasaki, while in the following year, 1689, the Japanese population totaled around fifty thousand.[46] Indeed, this was an impressive number, making it necessary to gather the Chinese sea-traders together in a specific and delimited quarter on Nagasaki's hill in order to interrupt the smuggling and to avoid possible subversive military actions. Moreover, the 1680s were also an era when Japanese foreign policy was again agitated by the potential revival of *kirishitan* キリシタン (i.e. Christian) subversion from abroad. The alarming news that Christians now had the ear of the emperor of China was indeed one of the reasons that motivated the founding of the *Nagasaki Tōjin yashiki*.[47]

As we understand, several motivations and different circumstances led to the *bakufu*'s definite decision to build the *Tōjin yashiki*, the most significant of which was to free the Japanese economy from Chinese influence.

The construction took shape in 1688–1689, and the established place for the Chinese settlement became a park area in a small village near the Temple of Jūzenji 十善寺, on the Nagasaki hill.[48] The costs of the construction of the Chinese compound were partly covered by the Nagasaki authorities and partly taken from public revenues: actually, in a few years, the costs were paid back by

---

loss of profit for the *bakufu*, which had no means of obtaining an income from taxing the illicit commerce. Nagazumi, "From Company to Individual Company Servants", 148–149.

45 Due to the impressive number of Chinese ships, even some fears of invasion from Manchu China rose among the Japanese officials: the overwhelming fluctuations in *Tōsen* landing in Nagasaki might reveal to be an implicit way for the Qing to conquer the Japanese archipelago. Although the danger of a Manchu invasion was unlikely, the *bakufu* was in evident need to affirm its control over Chinese activities in Nagasaki with regard to both hypothetical political or military actions from the continent, and the illegal and uncontrolled fluctuations of trades.

46 Nakamura, *Kinsei Nagasaki bōekishi no kenkyū*, 208.

47 Many were in fact the books entering Nagasaki via the *Tōsen*, and the checking of the contents related to the Christian religion was one of the most important tasks attended by the *Tōtsūji* 唐通事together with the *machidoshiyori* 町年寄, the Japanese officials. Also, contemporary Dutch sources marked the beginning of renewed Japanese anxiety regarding issues related to Catholicism: Matsukata Fuyuko 松方冬子, *Oranda fūsetsugaki to kinsei Nihon* オランダ風説書と近世日本 (Tōkyō: Tōkyō daigaku shuppansha, 2007); Matsukata, Fuyuko, "From the Threat of Roman Catholicism to the Shadow of Western Imperialism: Changing Trends in Dutch News Reports Issued to the Tokugawa Bakufu, 1690–1817", in Nagazumi Yōko (ed.), *Large and Broad: The Dutch Impact on Early Modern Asia. Essays in Honor of Leonard Blussé* (Tōkyō: Tōyō bunkō, 2010), 130–146.

48 See: *Nagasaki kenshi* 長崎県史 (*Kōshōhen* 交渉編) (Tōkyō: Yoshikawa Kōbunkan, 1985), 511–524.

the Chinese merchants in the form of rent for their accommodation. From 1689 onwards, the Chinese merchants entering the port of Nagasaki had to reside in the *Tōjin yashiki* for the entire period of their stay in Japan, that is to say, for the time they needed to complete all the procedures relating to their business. The dimension of the *Nagasaki Tōjin yashiki* was around 30,000 square meters, and it was a closed district, with a main entrance and two smaller gates: as in Deshima, access to it was controlled by Japanese officials. During the construction of the *Tōjin yashiki*, those living in proximity to it were moved away, as was the Satsuma *yashiki* 薩摩屋敷, which was situated almost in front of the Chinese compound. The aim, we can easily understand, was to keep the *Tōjin* isolated from the local population.[49]

Permission to reside permanently in Nagasaki had been almost abolished since 1635, with very rare exceptions; therefore, the Chinese compound housed the Chinese sailors and sea-traders who arrived in Nagasaki's port with their ships and cargos and stayed there only temporarily. The crew could stay in the *Tōjin yashiki* for the entire period they need to sell their goods and complete all the related procedures.[50] For the *Tōjin*, the medium period of their stay in the *Tōjin yashiki* went from few months to one year (the maximum recorded was almost two years). This depended on the efficiency of the *Nagasaki kaisho* officials in providing the Chinese with their due payments in copper as fixed during the commercial transactions. Once the entire process had been completed, but before leaving from Japan, the *Tōjin* had to obtain the formal permission from the Japanese official in order to be allowed to come back to Nagasaki again the following year.[51]

---

49 Compared with the VOC settlement in Deshima, the Chinese settlement was more than double the size, and of course it was not surrounded by the sea. Yamamoto, *Nagasaki Tōjin yashiki*; Yokoyama Hiroaki 横山宏章, *Nagasaki Tōjin yashiki no nazo* 長崎唐人屋敷の謎 (Tōkyō: Shin'eisha, 2011).

50 The limitations imposed by the *bakufu* in 1685 on the export of 6,000 *kanme* of silver according to the *gojōdaka* system caused several *Tōsen* to leave Nagasaki without being able to sell their merchandise, in spite of the established limits of seventy ships per year. Suzuki, "Changes in the Nagasaki Governorship System".

51 The entire process was quite long and complex, as the Japanese officials of the *Nagasaki kaisho*, together with the *Tōtsūji*, had to inspect the cargo and check the merchandise; then the most beautiful and precious items among the goods had to be selected and kept apart, in order to be sent to Edo and be presented with to the *shōgun* and other high officials. It was necessary to write the complete and exact list of all the merchandise, its condition, and its value. Finally, after a detailed examination of each item, it was necessary to establish the price according to market trends and to establish the government's rules and limits: in this negotiation with the Japanese officials, the *Tōtsūji* could be active and try to get a better price for the Chinese merchants. When agreement was reached on the prices of the merchandise, again a precise list of the items with the agreed prices

The *Tōjin yashiki* had twenty residential buildings, built on two floors, where the Chinese could live and sleep: the second floor was more comfortable and was generally reserved for the captains and the high officials of the *Tōsen*, while the first floor was used by the ordinary crew members: some of the richest even took two or more rooms for their single use. Within the Chinese compound, the *Tōjin* tried to reproduce the Chinese lifestyle has much as possible, with their habits, ceremonies and rituals, as well as their foods and cuisine, according to their region of origin.[52] In the square outside the two gates of the *Tōjin yashiki* was a market where the *Tōjin* could go in order to buy fish, vegetables and other food products, while inside the *Tōjin yashiki* there were other shops where the *Tōjin* could purchase what they needed.[53]

In 1702, a new part was built, the *shinchi* 新地, an island in front of the Chinese settlement that was used to deposit the merchandise, with many storerooms for the Chinese goods. Many checks and controls were needed, and many duties and functions had to be attended to, with many actors involved on both sides. The *Tōtsūji* 唐通事 or "Chinese interpreters" performed several functions among the Chinese residents, while at the same time acting on behalf of the Japanese authorities, acting as bridge between the two. One of the most important tasks of the *Tōtsūji* was to check the cargos upon the arrival of the Chinese ships in the presence of the Japanese inspectors, the *machidoshiyori* 町年寄 ("Elders" or "officials of the city").[54]

Inside the *Tōjin yashiki*, there were the Shrine to the Local Deity (*Dojindō* 土神堂) and another to the Goddess Mazu 媽祖 (*Tenkōdo* 天后堂), where the *Tōjin* usually went to pay their respects soon after docking in Nagasaki bay,

had to be prepared because all the goods had to be precisely listed: this was a necessary procedure before the goods could be finally purchased and the definitive negotiation completed. Then the *Tōjin* had to wait for the due payment: if there was a shortage of copper in Nagasaki, they were forced to stay longer. If the *Nagasaki kaisho* officials were not efficient enough in carrying out the procedures or lacking in their tasks in this complex process, they could even be found directly responsible and be compelled to refund a certain sum from their own money. Yokoyama, *Nagasaki Tōjin Yashiki no nazo*, 147–186; Yamamoto, *Nagasaki Tōjin yashiki*.

52 Actually, the *Tōjin* applied the same distinctions and hierarchies as they were enacted on board of the ships. Just to give an example, in 1705, according to the official registers, there were 2,236 *Tōjin* residing in the Chinese compound, that meant an average of more than 110 people for each residence: Yokoyama, *Nagasaki Tōjin yashiki no nazo*, 43–44.

53 With regard to a detailed description of the *Tōjin yashiki*, see the interesting pictorial source of mid-eighteenth century: *Tōkanzu Rankanzu emaki* 当館図蘭館図絵巻 (mid-18th century), by Ishizaki Yushi 石崎融思, edited by Harada Hiroji 原田博二 (Nagasaki: Bunkensha, 2005).

54 Carioti, "Focusing on the Overseas Chinese in Seventeenth Century Nagasaki".

as the Goddess Mazu was a protector of sailing and sailors: the *Tōjin* transported the statue of Mazu, which was on board the ship, to the Mazu Shrine in the *Tōjin yashiki* in a sort of procession. When the *Tōjin* had completed all their business and the ship was ready to leave, the statue of Mazu was removed from the Mazu Shrine and placed back on the ship.[55]

The restrictions on the number of *Tōsen* allowed to dock in Nagasaki each year, the fixed amounts that limited the export of precious metals, and the strict control of Chinese activities in Nagasaki had as their primary aim precisely to reduce the excessive exports of precious metals, to prevent smuggling and illicit trading, to control the activities of the *Tōjin* and, last but not least, to keep the peace and order in Nagasaki. The *Tōjin yashiki* lasted until the beginning of the Meiji Era 明治時代 (1868–1912), when a completely new international situation arose in the East Asian seas.

7 Some Closing Remarks

The label "closed country" has for long time influenced studies and research concerning the defensive policy of the Tokugawa *bakufu*, resulting in rather limited interpretations of the measures taken by the Japanese government in the seventeenth century. The drastic removal of Iberians from the national territory (the Spanish in 1624 and the Portuguese in 1639), as well as the restriction of the Chinese trade to the sole port of Nagasaki in 1635, followed in 1641 by the transfer of the VOC from Hirado to Deshima, have long been interpreted with reference to religious and ideological causes. Only in recent decades have the Tokugawa's political choices been examined in the light of their wider economic policy. Arano Yasunori 荒野泰典 was the first scholar to seriously question the old-style Eurocentric interpretation of the so-called "*sakoku*" policy.[56]

Consequently, historians of the early Edo period began to move towards an innovative interpretation of the history of the Tokugawa period: the foreign policy of Japan was taken into account and examined in light of the wider international context of East Asia. At the same time, the rigid label *sakoku* was also re-examined. The economic aspect of the measures taken by the

55 This was the last ritual accomplished by the *Tōjin* before the ship left Nagasaki, symbolizing their wish and pray to come back again to Nagasaki the following year. This ritual was very impressive for the Japanese population, and the scene has been often reproduced on paintings, scrolls, etc. related to the Chinese lifestyle.

56 Arano, *Kinsei Nihon to Higashi Ajia*; Arano, *Rettōnaigai no kōtsū to kokka*.

Tokugawa government were considered more carefully, and together with the term *sakoku*, a new term, *kaikin* 海禁 (*haijin*, "veto on the seas", of Chinese origin), entered the debate, only to be discussed, criticized, and dismissed in its turn.[57]

The so-called *sakoku*, or rather the defensive policy of the Tokugawa *bakufu*, had as its primary goal the freeing of the Japanese market from its economic dependence on China due to the huge imports of silks, paid for by the equally heavy exports of precious metals. Consistently with this, Tokugawa monetary policy was used to enforce the central government's power: the *bakufu* unified the currency on a national basis through the creation of a state mint, the *Ginza* 銀座, in Edo and Nagasaki, while promoting the Japanese production of silks to be sold in the internal market as an alternative to the Chinese silks. Many of the so-called *sakoku* ordinances issued by the Tokugawa *bakufu* were closely concerned with the *Tōjin* and their trading activities in Japan. In this sense, the founding of the *Nagasaki Tōjin yashiki* in 1689 was directly connected to the Tokugawa *bakufu*'s attempts to reduce the impact of the Chinese commerce on the national economy as much as possible.

The turning point was the 1635 decree, when the Tokugawa *bakufu* restricted the arrival of Chinese ships to the port of Nagasaki and imposed stricter control over the Chinese in the city. From that moment onwards, the *Tōjin* coming to Japan were effectively compelled to enter the Japanese archipelago via Nagasaki, where they were gradually made to live apart from the Japanese people and to reside together in their own separate quarter. These impositions were the preconditions for the very founding of the *Tōjin yashiki* as a delimited and closed area.

In 1641, the VOC was moved from Hirado to Deshima. As a result, Japan was linked, albeit for different reasons, to two conflicting powers: the Zheng family, which in the 1640s had firmly asserted total supremacy over the Chinese trade, on which it depended commercially; and the VOC, an indispensable protective screen to the expansionism of conquest by Europeans and still an important commercial interlocutor. In its forced neutrality, Japan did not participate directly in the confrontation, but became the scene of heated commercial rivalries in what was a ruthless Cold War over markets, which took the form of just two interlocutors: the Chinese sea-traders, tied to the Zheng regime; and the Dutch delegates of the VOC.

The Chinese empire, for its part, following the decline of the Ming dynasty, completely lost control over its coastal trade and overseas activities, was faced

57 Kamiya and Kimura, *Kaikin to sakoku*; Yamamoto, *Sakoku to kaikin no jidai*.

with threats on its northern frontiers from the Manchu, and entered the long transition from the Ming to the Qing dynasty. Many Chinese refugees moved to Japan in order to escape the disorders in China and to avoid being subjugated by the Manchu. In doing so, they attempted to attract the attention of Japanese intellectuals and to obtain concrete support from the Tokugawa *bakufu*. The requests for military support forwarded to the Tokugawa *bakufu* were for the most part sent directly or indirectly by the Zheng, and in few cases by other loyalist forces.[58]

The Chinese settlement of Nagasaki, on which the Zheng organization was able to exert such a deep influence, played a fundamental role in the economic, political and military decisions taken by the *bakufu*. Between 1645 and 1686, the requests sent by the Zhengs – or by other Ming supporters – for Japanese military intervention in favor of the Ming totaled twenty-two. The Tokugawa *bakufu* never sent soldiers to support the Ming loyalists, but on several occasions it provided the Zheng regime with gold, precious metals, medicines, and armaments. With great skill and foresight Japan pursued its policy of equilibrium, refusing to intervene in the military struggle on the continent.[59]

In 1683, after the Qing conquest of Taiwan by Shi Lang and the collapse of the Zheng regime on the island, China was definitely pacified under Manchu rule. Once the civil war had been decided and the Qing empire pacified, the lifting of the ban on China's seas by Emperor Kangxi in 1684 opened up an innovative age for the Chinese empire and led to a veritable invasion of *Tōsen* to the port of Nagasaki. In 1689 the *Tōjin yashiki* of Nagasaki took shape.

The Chinese settlement of Nagasaki was a key element in the extremely complex situation in East Asia: the *Tōjin* in Nagasaki played a significant role in the historical intercourse between China and Japan, and exerted a profound influence on Japan's foreign policy, first of all with regard to China, and more generally on its political and economic strategies.

58 See: *Cixing shimo* 賜姓始末, by Huang Zongxi 黃宗羲, in Taiwan wenxian congkan 台灣文獻叢刊 (Taibei: Taiwan yinhang jingji yanjiushi, 1959); *Haiwai tongkuji* 海外慟哭記, Taiwan Zhengshi jishi 台灣鄭氏紀事, by Huang Zongxi 黃宗羲, in Taiwan wenxian congkan (Taibei: Taiwan yinhang jingji yanjiushi, 1961); *Zheng Chenggong zhuan* 鄭成功傳, by Huang Zongxi 黃宗羲, in Taiwan Wenxian congkan (Taibei: Taiwan yinhang jingji yanjiushi, 1959); *Zhu Shunshui ji* 朱舜水集, by Zhu Zhiyu 朱之瑜 (ed.) (Taibei: Hanjing wenhua shiye youxian gongsi chubanshe, 1985).

59 Ishihara Michihiro was the first and the most eminent scholar who researched the Zheng's deep ties and connections with Japan in detail. See: Ishihara Michihiro 石原道博, *Kokusen'ya* 國姓爺 (Tōkyō: Yoshikawa kōbunkan, 1959); Ishihara Michihiro 石原道博, *Shu Shunsui* 朱舜水 (Tōkyō: Yoshikawa kōbunkan, 1961); Ishihara Michihiro 石原道博, *Minmatsu Shinsho Nihon kisshi no kenkyū* 明末清初日本乞師の研究 (Tōkyō: Fuzanbō, 1945).

We can therefore conclude that the so-called *sakoku* policy was a defensive economic policy and not a policy of "isolation". During the first decades of the seventeenth century, Tokugawa political choices certainly took religious matters into account, but the policy that was pursued had as its primary aim to free the Japanese economy from severe international competition and, above all, to protect the national market from its economic dependence on the fluctuations in the Chinese import and export trade and its consequent political influence. Throughout the seventeenth century, the *Tōjin* were gradually placed under stricter control: the founding of the *Nagasaki Tōjin yashiki* in 1689 was the last step in the coherent and long-term policy pursued by the Japanese authorities. The *bakufu* had succeeded in its objective of freeing Japanese economy from dependence on China, thus bring the long seventeenth century to its end: Tokugawa Japan had entered a new era.

Conclusion

Angela Schottenhammer

Already in 1960, the famous historians John K. Fairbank and Edwin Reischauer expressed their doubts about writing history by strictly sticking to dynastic cycles. They considered the concept of a dynastic cycle as "a major block to the understanding of the fundamental dynamics of Chinese history".[1] Since then, more and more attention has been paid to *longue-durée* developments and transitions among not only Western but also Chinese and Japanese historians.[2]

Strictly speaking, a dynasty rules over a country or region in the person of representatives of the same family or clan. It immediately springs to mind that brothers or a father and a son do not necessarily share the same interests and that their politics can consequently differ greatly. The theoretical framework of a dynastic cycle is seen as a gradual rise to an economic peak and an eventually gradual decline accompanied by moral decay and corruption, which finally resulted in the loss of the Heavenly Mandate. This would then justify the fall of the dynasty and the establishment of a new one. However, this does not say anything about political goals or a *raison d'état* of the rulers of a dynasty. What does this mean for maritime politics and commerce? How much do dynastic cycles and transition periods matter?

The establishment of the Song, Yuan, and Ming dynasties, for example, all went along with a different *raison d'état* which had partly far-reaching consequences for the development of the maritime trade. The decision of early Song rulers to treat their maritime trade as a source to be tapped for government income or the initiation of the maritime proscription policy (*haijin* 海禁) in the early Ming had a significant influence on China's maritime commerce. We therefore cannot deny that dynastic changes did matter. However, to what extent they mattered in a specific case needs examining. We cannot sufficiently understand developments in Chinese history and maritime politics by restricting ourselves to the events and decisions of a single dynasty, and should move

1 John K. Fairbank and Edwin O. Reischauer, *East Asia: The Great Tradition* [A History of East Asian Civilization, 1] (Boston: Houghton Mifflin Company. 1960), 115.

2 It is not the purpose of this conclusion, or this volume, to introduce to the reader the meanwhile large amount of scholarship on this topic, let alone, for example, for the Tang-Song transition. For a discussion of the latter, I would like to refer the interested reader to Luo Yinan's article, "A Study of the Changes in the Tang–Song Transition Model", in *Journal of Song-Yuan Studies* 35 (2005), 99–127, with rich references to Chinese and Japanese scholarship.

 | DOI:10.1163/9789004740556_016

from dynastic approaches to a 'dedynasticization'. In most cases, we observe gradual transitions.

Moreover, we should critically assess constraints in terms not only of time and dynastic cycles, but also of space, locality and centrality, domestic and foreign, and land and maritime borders. We should also examine specific decisions and developments by not only considering the political but also the socio-economic context. This means that we should leave Euro- and Sino-centric approaches behind and move to polycentric approaches, which consider developments, encounters, and events from various perspectives.

Stocking with the examples of the Song and Ming, it is clear that the decisions they made were the result of changing geopolitical, social, and economic situations, and not just of personal arbitrariness. As mentioned in the introduction, in order to examine how land and sea trade were interconnected and how the latter influenced the former and *vice versa*, we have to thoroughly consider developments in Central Asia and along China's continental borders. In other words, to write global history, we need to consider the wider geopolitical situation, which combines local and central, domestic and foreign policies.

One example: the decision to impose restrictive control and administration on China's maritime borders was not only based on the experiences of the former Yuan court with influential, wealthy merchants such as Zhang Shicheng 張士誠 and Fang Guozhen 方國珍 (1319–1374), which obviously significantly influenced Hongwu's assessment of the maritime frontier and his fears concerning the increasing influence of merchants and pirates. Early Ming China also found itself confronted with an unstable geopolitical situation with various maritime neighbours, from Japan to Korea to Annam, as a kind of crisis situation. The political instability in various parts of maritime Asia also alarmed the emperor. In such a politically insecure and tricky situation, Hongwu considered it the best option to put maritime trade under the strict control of a state monopoly and manipulate it for the state's purposes. A correct understanding of the prohibition on the private maritime trade is, consequently, only possible when considering the wider historical context of this political decision.

What does this mean for future research?

In general terms, we will need to pay even more attention to inter- and transdisciplinary, global, and 'interactive' scientific approaches. We discussed this in detail during our two-day conference in Ghent in 2017. Participants and discussants agreed that this refers especially to interactions between local, regional, and central, as well as domestic and foreign developments. It also means a stronger focus on micro-histories and cross-cultural relations (in contrast to more national histories), together with an increasing interest in formerly marginalized aspects, events, or people. It also includes a more careful consideration of foreign influences and relations, meaning here especially the maritime realm, in contrast to the long-maintained stress on China's overland relations, This does not mean that continental frontiers, borders, and relations are suddenly marginalized, nor that macro-historical questions are neglected. In addition, we need to give due respect to the environmental aspects. In this context, most scholars attending the above-mentioned conference supported fluid and open boundaries and networks. This tendency towards global history, fluid boundaries, global, cross-cultural, and interdisciplinary integration and interaction, in terms of both time and space, regardless of the specific focus of the research, was interestingly very obvious also during the 3rd 'Middle Period Chinese Humanities, 200–1600' Conference, convened at Yale University from 22 to 25 June 2023.

Such an 'open', 'global' and 'fluid' approach is of course especially important for the study of foreign, cross-cultural relations. And it opens up various new perspectives for our studies. It will allow students to understand world cultures and histories in a connected way, instead of limiting their views to pure national histories and perspectives, thus blurring the diversity, dynamics, and interactivity of what happened in the past.

Bibliography

Charts

Anonymous, "Chart of a Part of the Southeast Coast of China from the Island of Haitan to the Zhoushan Islands", ca. 17th century, Bibliothèque nationale de France, Paris, Département Cartes et Plans (DCP), SH18PF.179DIV P. 4.

Anonymous, "Chart of the Northern Part of the South China Sea with the Gulf of Tonkin and the Souch Coast of China", ca. 18th century, Nationaal Archief, The Hague, VEL0291.

Anonymous, "Coastal Map of China" (Haijiang yangjie xingshi quantu 海洋疆界形勢全圖), 1787–1801, Library of Congress, Washington, D. C., G7822.C6A5, 1801.H31.

Blaeu, Joan, "Guangdong province", *Novus Atlas Sinensis*, 1655, Koninklijke Bibliotheek, The Hague, Atlas van der Hagen,1049B13–049.

Boos, Michiel Gerritsz., "Chart of a Part of the South-east Coast of China with Fuzhou Bay", ca. 1668, Nationaal Archief, The Hague, Collectie Aanwinsten 553 (1891 19g), not foliated.

Boos, Michiel Gerritsz., "Chart of Quanzhou Bay", ca. 1668, Nationaal Archief, The Hague, Collectie Aanwinsten 553 (1891 19g), not foliated.

De Graaf, Isaac., "Chart of the coast of Quinam, Toncquin and Cochin-China, from r. Cantaon to Punta Lamtaon, the island of Aynam and Isla de Pracel", ca 1700, Nationaal Archief, The Hague, VEL0269.

De Graaf, Isaac," Overveens Islands, in China, at 30 degrees North", ca. 1700, Nationaal Archief, The Hague, VEL0279.

De Graaf, Isaac, "The River Swadia in China", ca. 1700, Nationaal Archief, The Hague, VEL0279.

De Graaf, Isaac, "The Islands of Haytan on the coast of China, at 25 1/2 degrees North", ca. 1700, Nationaal Archief, The Hague, VEL0279.

Tim, Jan Hendriksz., "Roadstead and Anchorage on the River of Fuzhou", 1662, Nationaal Archief, The Hague, VEL0283.

Vingboons, Johannes, "Chart of the Mouth of the Pearl River", 1665–1670, Österreichische Nationalbibliothek, Vienna, Van der Hem 41:18.

Vingboons, Johannes, "Depiction of the Coast of China, beginning from Lantau (Nan'ao 南澳) Island, northerward, to Shanxiazhen 山霞鎮 Bay)", 1665–1670, Österreichische Nationalbibliothek, Vienna, Van der Hem 41:12.

Published Primary Texts

Aduarte, Diego, O.P., *Historia de la Provincia del Santo Rosario, de la Orden de Predicadores, en Philippinas, Japón y China* (Manila: 1640).

Aḫbār aṣ-Ṣīn wa l-Hind, by Abū Zayd Ḥasan ibn Yazīd al-Sīrāfī [fl. 916] (French translation: Jean Sauvaget (tr., ed.). *Aḫbār aṣ-Ṣīn wa l-Hind Relation de la Chine et de L'Inde redigee en 851* [Paris: Belles Lettres, 1948]. Chinese translation: Mu Genlai 穆根來, Wen Jiang 汶江, Huang Zhuohan 黄倬漢 (trs.), *Zhongguo yindu jianwenlu* 中國印度見聞錄 [Beijing: Zhonghua shuju, 1983]).

Annan tuzhi 安南圖誌 (1608), by Deng Zhong 鄧鐘, in Sibu congkan xubian 四部叢刊續編 (Taibei: Taiwan shangwu yinshuguan, 1976).

Argensola, Bartolomé Leonardo de, *Conquista de las Islas Malucas* [1609], ed. by Alonso Martín (Madrid: Ediciones Polifemo, 1992).

Bamin tongzhi 八閩通志, ed. Huang Zhongzhao 黄仲昭 (1435–1508), vol. 2, 2 vols. (Fuzhou: Fujian renmin chubanshe, 1991).

Bili zacun 碧里雜存 (Wanli), by Dong Gu 董穀 (Shanghai: Shangwu yinshuguan, 1937).

Bisonglou cangshu zhi 皕宋樓藏書志, by Lu Xinyuan 陸心源 (1834–1894). In Xuxiu siku quanshu 續修四庫全書 (Shanghai: Shanghai guji chubanshe, 2002).

Cefu yuangui 冊府元龜, by Wang Qinruo王欽若 (962–1025), Zhou Xunchu周勛初 et al. [eds.] (Nanjing: Fenghuang chubanshe, 2006).

Chaoxian shilue 朝鮮史略. In Jingyin Wenyuange Siku quanshu 景印文淵閣四庫全書 (Shanghai: Shanghai guji chubanshe, 1987).

*Chaxiang shi cong*chao 茶香室叢鈔, by Yu Yue 俞樾 (1821–1907), in Zhen Fan 貞凡, Gu Sheng 顧馨 and Xu Minxia 徐敏霞, annotated version of *Chaxiang shi congchao* 茶香室叢鈔 (Beijing Zhonghua shuju. 2006).

Chijs, J. A. van der (ed.), *Dagh-Register gehouden int Casteel Batavia vant passerende daer ter plaetse als over geheel Nederlandts-India., Anno 1661.* ('s Hage: M. Nijhoff, 1889).

Chijs, J. A. van der (ed.), *Dagh-Register gehouden int Casteel Batavia vant passerende daer ter plaetse als over geheel Nederlandts-India., Anno 1663.* ('s Hage: M. Nijhoff, 1891).

Chijs, J. A. van der (ed.), *Dagh-Register gehouden int Casteel Batavia vant passerende daer ter plaetse als over geheel Nederlandts-India., Anno 1664.* ('s Hage: M. Nijhoff, 1893).

Chijs, J. A. van der (ed.), *Dagh-Register gehouden int Casteel Batavia vant passerende daer ter plaetse als over geheel Nederlandts-India., Anno 1665.* ('s Hage: M. Nijhoff, 1894).

Chouhai chongbian 籌海重編 (1592), by Deng Zhong 鄧鐘, in Siku quanshu cunmu congshu 四庫全書存目叢書 (Jinan: Qilu shushe, 1997).

Chouhai tubian 籌海圖編 (1562), by Zheng Ruozeng 鄭若曾 (1505–1580), Li Zhizhong 李致忠 (ed.) (Beijing: Zhonghua shuju, 2007).

Cixing shimo 賜姓始末, by Huang Zongxi 黃宗羲 (1610–1695), in Taiwan wenxian congkan 台灣文獻叢刊 (Taibei: Taiwan yinhang jingji yanjiushi, 1959).

Coolhaas, W. P. (ed), *Generale Missiven van gouverneur-generaal en raden aan Heren XVII der Verenigde Oostindische Compagnie* ('s-Gravenhage: Rijks Geschiedkundige Publicatiën, III, 1968) 1656–1674.

Cramer, Matthijs, *Borts Voyagie Naer de Kuste van China en Formosa.* (Amsterdam: Pieter Dircksz, 1670).

Da Asia. Decada XII (1645), by Diogo de Couto (ca. 1542–1616) (Lisboa, 1788).

Dantai yu'an 丹臺玉案, ed. Sun Wenyin 孫文胤 (fl. 17th cent.), 100 zhong zhenben guyiji jiaozhu jicheng 100 種珍本古醫籍校注集成 (Beijing: Zhongyi guji chubanshe, 2012).

Daoguang chongzuan Fujian tongzhi 道光重纂福建通志, eds. Sun Erzhun 孫爾準 (1770–1832) et al., vol. 5, 15 vols., Zhongguo difangzhi jicheng shengzhiji Fujian 中國地方志集成・省志 輯・福建 (Nanjing: fenghuang chubanshe, 2011).

Daoyuan lei gao 道園類稿, by Yu Ji 虞集 (1272–1348), in Yuanren wenji congkan 元人文集珍本叢刊 (Taibei: Xinwenfeng chuban, 1985).

Dapper, Olfert, *Gedenkwaerdig Bedryf der Nederlandsche Oost-Indische Maetschappye, op de Kuste en in het Keizerrijk van Taising of Sina* (Amsterdam: Jabob van Meurs, 1670).

Da Qing lichao Shengzu Renhuang shilu 大清歷朝聖祖仁皇實錄 (Kangxi) (Taibei: Huawen shuju, 1964).

de Guignes, Chrétien-Louis-Josephe, *Voyages à Peking, Manille et L'Île de France, faits dans l'Intervalle des Années 1784 à 1801* (Paris: De L'Imprimerie Impériale, 1808). Tome 1, Voyage à Peking pendant les Années 1794 et 1795.

Dongxi yangkao 東西洋考 (c. 1617), by Zhang Xie's 張燮 (1574–1640).

Dongxiyang kao 東西洋考 (c. 1617), by Zhang Xie 張燮, Xie Fang 謝方 (ed.) Zhongwai jiaotong shiji congkan 中外交通史籍叢刊 (Beijing: Zhonghua shuju, 2000 [1981]).

Dushi zhaji 讀史札記 (late 18th century), by Lu Wenchao 盧文弨, in Xuxiu Siku quanshu 續修四庫全書 (Shanghai: Shanghai guji chubanshe, 2002).

Douzhen huoyou xinfa 痘疹活幼心法, by Nie Shangheng 聶尚恆 (b. 1572), ed. Cai Huazhu 蔡華珠 (Beijing: Zhongguo zhongyiyao chubanshe, 2016).

Fu'anxian zhi 福安縣志, eds. Lu Yizai 陸以載, et al., vol. 12, 32 vols., Riben cang Zhongguo hanjian difangzhi congkan 日本藏中國罕見地方志叢刊 (Beijing: shumu wenxian chubanshe, 1990).

Gaubil, S. J., Antoine, *Correspondance de Pékin, 1722–1759 (Geneva: Librairie Droz, 1970).*

Guangdong tongzhi (*Wanli*) 廣東通志(萬曆) (1602). In Airusheng – Zhongguo fangzhi ku 愛如生 – 中國方志庫.

Guochao lieqing ji 國朝列卿紀 (after 1592), by Lei Li 雷禮 (1505–1581), in Xuxiu Siku quanshu 續修四庫全書 (Shanghai: Shanghai guji chubanshe, 1995).

Haidao yizhi 海島逸志 (completed 1791) by Wang Dahai 王大海 (19th cent.), edited by Yao Nan 姚楠 *et al.*, (Hong Kong: Xuejin Bookshop, 1992).

Haifang zuanyao 海防纂要 (1613), by Wang Zaijin 王在晉 (1570–1643). In Siku jinhui shu congkan 四庫禁燬書叢刊 (Beijing: Beijing chubanshe, 2000).

Haiwai tongkuji 海外慟哭記, *Taiwan Zhengshi jishi*台灣鄭氏紀事, by Huang Zongxi 黃宗羲 (1610–1695), in Taiwan wenxian congkan 台灣文獻叢刊政 (Taibei: Taiwan yinhang jingji yanjiushi, 1961).

Haiyanxian tujing 海鹽縣圖經 (1624). In Airusheng – Zhongguo fangzhi ku 愛如生 – 中國方志庫.

Haiyu 海語 (1536), by Huang Zhong 黃衷, Lingnan yishu 嶺南遺書 edition in Zhongguo shixue congshu xubian 中國史學叢書續編 (Taibei: Taiwan xuesheng shuju, 1975).

*Han Changli wenji jiaozhu*韓昌黎文集校注, by Han Yu韓愈 (768–824), Ma Qichang 馬其昶 (ed.), (Shanghai: Shanghai guji chuban she, 1986).

Haotaiwang bei yuanta ben 好太王碑原拓本. Collection of the Liaoning Provincial Museum, China.

Huayangguan wenji xukan 華陽館文獻續刊, by Song Yiwang 宋儀望 (1516–1580), vol. 116, 426 vols. In Siku quanshu cunmu congshu jibu 四庫全書存目叢書集部 (Ji'nan: Qilu shushe, 1997).

Huang Zongxi quanji 黃宗羲全集, by Huang Zongxi黃宗羲 (1610–1695) (Hangzhou: Zhejiang guji chubanshe, 1985).

Huangchao zhanggu huibian 皇朝掌故彙編, by Zhang Shouyong 張壽鏞 (1876–1945) (Beijing: Qiushi shushe, 1902).

Huimin zhengfang 惠民正方, Yang Sizhi 楊四知 (fl. 16th cent.), vol. 4, 10 vols., Zhenben haiwai huigui zhongyi guji congshu 珍本海外回歸中醫古籍叢書 (Beijing: renmin weisheng chubanshe, 2008).

Jiajing Ningbofu zhi 嘉靖寧波府志 (1560), by Zhou Xizhe 周希哲 et al. In Zhongguo fangzhi congshu: Huazhong difang 中國方志叢書：華中地方 (Taibei: Chengwen chubanshe, 1983).

Jiajing Shaowufu zhi 嘉靖邵武府志, eds. Xing Zhi 邢址 and Chen Rang 陳讓, vol. 191, 292 vols., Siku quanshu cunmu congshu shibu 四庫全書存目叢書史部 (Ji'nan: Qilu shushe, 1997).

Jiaqing chongxiu yitong zhi 嘉慶重修一統志, by Mu, Zhang'a 穆彰阿 et al. In Sibu congkan xubian 四部叢刊續編 (Shanghai: Shangwu yinshuguan, 1934).

Jianyangxian zhi 建陽縣志, ed. Feng Jike 馮繼科, vol. 31, 68 vols., in Tianyige cang Mingdai fangzhi xuankan 天一閣藏明代方志選刊 (Shanghai: Shanghai shudian chubanshe, 2014).

Jianyangxian zhi 建陽縣志, eds. Wei Yingshi 魏應時, Tian Juzhong 田居中, and Zhang Bang 張榜, vol. 12, 32 vols., Riben cang Zhongguo hanjian difangzhi congkan 日本藏中國罕見地方志叢刊 (Beijing: shumu wenxian chubanshe, 1990).

Jinjiang xianzhi (*Qianlong*) 晉江縣志 (乾隆) (1765), in Airusheng – Zhongguo fangzhi ku 愛如生 – 中國方志庫.

Jintai ji 金臺集 (1638), by Nai Xian 迺賢, in Haiwang cun guji congkan 海王邨古籍叢刊 (Beijing: Zhongguo shudian, 1990).

Jintai ji 金臺集, by Na Xin 納新. In Siku quanshu zhenben shiyi ji 四庫全書珍本十一集 (Taibei: Tanwan shangwu yinshuguan, 1981). Also published in Jingyin chizaotang siku quanshu huiyao 景印摛藻堂四庫全書薈要 (Taibei: Shijie shuju, 1988).

Jintai ji 金臺集, by Na Yan 納延. In Jingyin Wenyuange Siku quanshu (Taibei: Taiwan shangwu yinshuguan, 1985).

Jingtai Jianyangxian zhi 景泰建陽縣志, eds. Zhao Wen 趙文, Huang Xuan 黄璿, and Yuan Xian 袁銛, vol. 176, 292 vols., Siku quanshu cunmu congshu shibu 四庫全書存目叢書史部 (Ji'nan: Qilu shushe, 1996).

Jingyue quanshu 景岳全書, by Zhang Jiebin 張介賓, ed. Zhao Lixun 趙立勛, Zhongyi guji zhengli congshu 中醫古籍整理叢書 (Beijing: renmin weisheng chubanshe, 1991).

Jiu Tangshu 舊唐書, by Liu Xu 劉煦 (Hou Jin) (Beijing: Zhonghua shuju, 1997).

*Jiu Wudaishi*舊五代史, by Xue Juzheng薛居正 (912–981), (Beijing: Zhonghua shuju, 1976).

Jiuji liaopin yijian qifang 救急療貧易簡奇方, by Ouyang Zhi 歐陽植, vol. 7, 12 vols. In Haiwai huigui zhongyi shanben guji congshu 海外回歸中醫善本古籍叢書 (Beijing: renmin weisheng chubanshe, 2003).

Jiuling shanfang ji 九靈山房集, by Dai Liang 戴良 (1317–1383). In Sibu congkan chubian 四部叢刊初编 (Shanghai: Shangwu yinshuguan, 1936).

Jiuling shanfang ji 九靈山房集, by Dai Liang 戴良. In Jingyin Wenyuange Siku quanshu (Shanghai: Shanghai guji chubanshe, 1987).

Jixiao xinshu 紀效新書, by Qi Jiguang 戚繼光 (1528–1588), in Zhongguo bingshu jicheng 中國兵書集成. Vol. 18. (Shenyang: Liaoshen shushe/Beijing: Jiefangjun chubanshe, 1995).

Koryŏsa 高麗史 (1451), by Chŏng In-ji 鄭麟趾 (1396–1478) et al. Collection of the Gyujanggak 奎章閣, Korea.

Koryŏsa chŏryo 高麗史節要 (1452), by Kim Chong-sŏ 金宗瑞 (1383–1553). Collection of the Gyujanggak, Korea.

*Haiguo sishuo*海国四说 (1846), by Liang Tingnan梁廷枏 (1796–1861), (Beijing: Zhonghua shuju, 1999).

Lianbing shiji 練兵實紀, ed. by Gao Yangwen 高揚文, Tao Qi陶琦 et al., *Qi Jiguang yanjiu congshu* 戚繼光研究叢書 (Beijing: Zhonghua shuju, 2001).

Lianzhou fuzhi 廉州府志 (1637), by Zhang Guojing張國經, Zheng Baosu 鄭抱素, in Chen Jiang 陳強 et al., Guangdong lidai fangzhi jicheng – Lianzhoufu buyi 廣東歷代方志集成·廉州府部（一）(Guangzhou: Lingnan meishu chubanshe, 2009).

Lidai bao'an 歷代寶案 (Taipei: Guoli Taiwan daxue, 1972).

Liutao 六韜 , anon., https://ctext.org/liu-tao/.

Lu Xuangong quanji 陸宣公全集 by Lu Zhi陸贄 (754–805), (Shanghai: Shijie shuju, 1936).

Mao Lumen xiansheng wenji 茅鹿門先生文集 (1588), by Mao Kun 茅坤 (1512–1601), in Zhang Dazhi 張大芝 and Zhang Mengxin 張夢新 (eds.), *Mao Kun ji* 茅坤集 (Liangzhe zuojia wencong 兩浙作家文叢), (Hangzhou: Zhejiang guji chubanshe, 1993).

Min shu 閩書, by He Qiaoyuan何喬遠 (10558–1632), vol. 204, 292 vols., Siku quanshu cunmu congshu shibu 四庫全書存目叢書史部 (Ji'nan: Qilu shushe, 1997).

Minbushu 閩部疏, by Wang Shimao 王世懋 (1536–1588). In Zhongguo fangzhi congshu hua'nan difang 中國方志叢書・華南地方 243 (Taipei: Chengwen chubanshe, 1975).

Ming shilu 明實錄, *Taizong shilu* 太宗實錄 (Taibei: Zhongyang yanjiuyuan lishi yuyan yanjiusuo, 1966), 133 vols.

Ming Taizu shilu 明太祖實錄 (Taibei: Taiwan zhongyang yanjiu yuan shiyu suo, 1962).

Mingshi shilu 明氏實錄, by Yang Xueke 楊學可, in Xuehai leibian 學海類編 (Shanghai: Shanghai hanfenlou, 1920).

Mingshi shilu 明氏實錄, by Yang Xueke 楊學可, in Xuxiu Siku quanshu 續修四庫全書 (Shanghai: Shanghai guji chubanshe, 1996).

Mingshi 明史, by Zhang Tingyu 張廷玉 (1672–1755) et al., (Beijing: Zhonghua shuju, 1974).

Nanhan ji 南漢記, by Wu Lanxiu吳蘭修 (*juren* 1808), Wudai shishu huibian 五代史書彙編, vol. 10 (Hangzhou: Hangzhou chubanshe, 2004).

Nanhan shu 南漢書, by Liang Tingnan梁廷枏 (1796–1861) (Guangzhou: Guangdong renmin chubanshe, 1981).

Nanhan shu 南漢書, by Liang Tingnan梁廷枏 (1796–1861), *Wudai shishu huibian* 五代史書彙編, vol. 10 (Hangzhou: Hangzhou chubanshe, 2004).

Nanshu zhi 南樞志 (c.1635–1638), by Fan Jingwen 范景文 (1587–1644) and Zhang Keshi 張可仕, in Zhongguo fangzhi congshu 中國方志叢書 (Taibei: Chengwen chubanshe, 1983).

Nian'er shi zhaji: buyi 廿二史劄記：補遺, by Zhao Yi 趙翼 (Beijing: Zhonghua shuju, 1984).

Pingzhou ketan 萍洲可談, by Zhu Yu 朱彧 (1075 – after 1119), (Shanghai: Shanghai guji chubanshe, 1989).

Qixiao yishu 奇效醫述, by Nie Shangheng 聶尚恆, (1572–?), Waseda University Library, Japanese and Chinese Classic, URL:
http://www.wul.waseda.ac.jp/kotenseki/html/ya09/ya09_00335/index.html (last access 2019–3-1).

Qianlong Yanpingfu zhi 乾隆延平府志, eds. Fu Ertai 傅尔泰 and Tao Yuanzao 陶元藻 (1716–1801), vol. 37, 40 vols.. In Zhongguo difangzhi jicheng Fujian fuxianzhi ji 中國地方志集成・福建府縣志輯 (Shanghai: Shanghai shudian chubanshe, 2000).

Qianqingtang shumu 千頃堂書目 (17th century), by Huang Yuji 黃虞稷 (1629–1691), (Shanghai: Shanghai guji chubanshe, 1990).

Qiantai wozuan 虔臺倭纂 (1595), by Xie Jie 謝杰 (1537–1604), in Xuanlantang congshu xuji 玄覽堂叢書續集 (Nanjing: Guoli zhongyang tushuguan, 1947).

Qinding gujin chu'er jinjian 欽定古今儲貳金鑒, in Jingyin Wenyuange Siku quanshu 景印文 淵閣四庫全書 (Shanghai: Shanghai guji chubanshe, 1987).

Quansheng leiyao huhai qifang 全生類要湖海奇方, by Xu Hong 許宏, vol. 9, 10 vols., in Zhenban haiwai huigui zhongyi guji congshu 珍版海外回歸中醫古籍叢書 (Beijing: renmin weisheng chubanshe, 2008).

Quan Songwen 全宋文, ed. by Zeng Zaozhuang 曾棗莊, Liu Lin 劉琳 (Shanghai: Shanghai cishu chubanshe and Anhui jiaoyu chubanshe, 2006).

Quan Tangshi Xia 全唐詩, ed. Peng Dingqiu 彭定求, vol. 3 (Zhengzhou: Zhongzhou guji chubanshe, 1996).

Quan Tang wen 全唐文, by Dong Gao 董誥 (1740–1818) (Beijing: Zhonghua shuju, 1983).

Riben yijian 日本一鑑 (c. 1566), by Zheng Shungong 鄭舜功 (Shanghai: Shangwu yinshuguan, 1936).

Riben yijian: Qionghe huahai 日本一鑑：窮河話海, by Zheng Shungong鄭舜功 (1939).

*Sanshan zhi*三山志, by Liang Kejia 梁克家 (1128–1187), Fuzhou shi difangzhi bianzuan weiyuanhui 福州市地方志編纂委員會 [eds.] (Fuzhou: Haifeng chubanshe, 2000).

Shanju bianyi fang 山居便宜方, by Xiong Zongli 熊宗立, vol. 7, 12 vols., Haiwai huigui zhongyi shanben guji congshu 海外回歸中醫善本古籍叢書 (Beijing: renmin weisheng chubanshe, 2003), 1–186.

Shenghuifang houxu 聖惠方後序, by Cai Xiang 蔡襄 (1012–1067), in Quan Songwen 全宋文, eds. Liu Zaozhuang 劉枣庄 and Liu Lin 劉琳, vol. 24, 24 vols. (Chengdu: Bashu shushe, 1992).

Shi Liuqiu lu 使琉球錄 (1579), by Xiao Chongye 蕭崇業 (?–1588) and Xie Jie 謝杰, in *Shi Liuqiu lu sanzhong* 使琉球錄三種 (Taiwan wenxian congkan 台灣文獻叢刊), (Taibei: Taiwan yinhang, 1970).

Shi Liuqiu lu 使琉球錄 (1607), by Xia Ziyang 夏子陽 (1522–1610) and Wang Shizhen 王士楨 (1634–1711), in Shi Liuqiu lu sanzhong 使琉球錄三種 (Taiwan wenxian congkan 台灣文獻叢刊), (Taibei: Taiwan yinhang, 1970).

Shiguo chunqiu 十國春秋, by Wu Renchen吳任臣 (1628–1689), (Beijing: Zhonghua shuju, 1983).

Shiji 史記, by Sima Qian司馬遷 (145–86 BCE), https://ctext.org/shiji.

Shouning daizhi 壽寧待志, by Feng Menglong 馮夢龍 (1574–1646), ed. Chen Yukui 陳煜奎 (Fuzhou: Fujian renmin chubanshe, 1983).

Shunfeng xiangsong 順風相送 (late 16th century), in Xiang Da 向達 (ed.), *Liangzhong haidao zhenjing* 兩種海道鍼經. In Zhongwai jiaotong shiji congkan 中外交通史籍叢刊 (Beijing: Zhonghua shuju, 2000).

Shuyu zhouzilu 殊域周咨錄 (completed 1574, printed 1583), by Yan Congjian 嚴從簡 (*jinshi* 1559). In Zhongwai jiaotong shiji congkan 中外交通史籍叢刊, ed. by Yu Sili 余思黎 (Beijing: Zhonghua shuju, 2000).

Sishui xianzhi (*Guangxu*) 泗水縣志 (光緒) (1892), in Airusheng – Zhongguo fangzhi ku 愛如生– 中國方志庫.

Siyi guangji 四夷廣記 (ca.1601–1603), by Shen Maoshang 慎懋賞 (fl. 1553–1607), in Xuanlantang congshu xuji 玄覽堂叢書續集 (Nanjing: Guoli zhongyang tushuguan, 1947).

Siyiguan kao 四夷館考 (1580), by Wang Zongzai 王宗載 (fl. 1562–1582), in Zhongguo shaoshu minzu guji jicheng 中國少數民族古籍集成 (Chengdu: Sichuan minzu chubanshe, 2002).

Song huiyao jigao 宋會要輯稿, by Xu Song 徐松 (1781–1848) et al., comp. (Taibei: Shijie shuju, 1964).

Song xueshi wenji 宋學士文集, by Song Lian 宋濂 (1310–1381). In Sibu congkan chubian (Shanghai: Shangwu yinshuguan, 1929).

Songshi 宋史, by Tuo Tuo 脫脫 (1311–1355), (Beijing: Zhonghua shuju, 1977).

Suishu 隋書, by Wei Zheng魏徵 (580–643), (Beijing: Zhonghua shuju, 1973).

Sunzi bingfa 孫子兵法, by *Sunzi* 孫子 (fl. 6th cent. BCE), https://ctext.org/art-of-war.

Taicang zhouzhi (*Chongzhen*) 太倉州志(崇禎) (1642 [1678]), in Airusheng – Zhongguo fangzhi ku 愛如生– 中國方志庫.

*Taiping guangji*太平廣記, by Li Fang李昉 (925–996), (Beijing: Zhonghua shuju, 1961).

Taizu Zhu Yuanzhang 太祖朱元璋 (1328–1398, r. 1368–1398), *Huang Ming zuxun* 皇明祖訓, in Xuxiu Siku quanshu, fasc. 264.

Titsingh, Isaac, *Relaas mijner Ambassade naar China in 1794–1795*, BPL 2177, Special Collection, Leiden University Library, [date unknown].

Tōkanzu Rankanzu emaki 当館図蘭館図絵巻 (mid-18th century), by Ishizaki Yushi石崎融思 (1768–1846), ed. Harada Hiroji 原田博二 (Nagasaki: Bunkensha, 2005).

Tongdian 通典, by Du You 杜佑 (735–812), https://ctext.org/tongdian.

Tongguk Yi Sang-guk chip 東國李相國集 (1241) by Yi Kyubo 李奎報 (1168–1241). Collection of Waseda University Library, Japan.

Valentijn, F., *Van Oud en Nieuw Oost-Indiën* (Dordrecht, 1724–26).

van Braam Houckgeest, Andre Everard *Voyage de l'Ambassade de la Compagnie des Indes Orientales Hollandaises, vers l'Empereur de la Chine, dans les Années 1794 & 1795* (Philadelphia, 1797).

Wangli Fu'ningzhou zhi 萬曆福寧州志, eds. Zhu Mei 朱梅 et al., vol. 7, 32 vols., in Riben cang Zhongguo hanjian difangzhi congkan 日本藏中國罕见地方志叢刊 (Beijing: Shumu wenxian chubanshe, 1990).

Weizhai ji 畏斋集, by Cheng Duanli 程端禮 (1271–1345), in *Jingyin Wenyuange Siku quanshu* (Shanghai: Shanghai guji chubanshe, 1987).

Weizhai ji 畏斋集, by Cheng Duanli 程端禮, in *Siming congshu* 四明叢書 (Ningbo: Zhangshi yueyuan, 1932).

Wenxian tongkao 文獻通考, by Ma Duanlin 馬端臨 (1254–1323) (Beijing: Zhonghua shuju, 1986).

Wu Wenzheng ji 吳文正集, by Wu Cheng 吳澄 (1249–1333), in *Jingyin Wenyuange Siku quanshu* (Shanghai: Shanghai guji chubanshe, 1987).

Wenyi lun 瘟疫論, by Wu Youxing 吳有性 (1582–1652), vol. 47, 54 vols., in Jingyin Wenyuange Sikuquanshu zibu bawu yijialei 景印文淵閣四庫全書子部八五醫家類, (Beijing: Zhongyi guji chubanshe, 1986).

Wubei zhi 武備志 (1621), by Mao Yuanyi 茅元儀 (1594 – c.1640), facsimile edition, in *Siku jinhuishu congkan* 四庫禁燬書叢刊 (Beijing: Beijing chubanshe, 2000).

Wubian 武編 (mid-16th century, printed 1618), by Tang Shunzhi 唐順志, in Zhongguo bingshu jicheng 中國兵書集成 (Beijing: Jiefang jun chubanshe, Shenyang: Liaoshen shushe, 1989).

*Wudai huiyao*五代會要, by Wang Pu王溥 (922–982) (Shanghai: Shanghai guji chubanshe, 1978).

Wuzazu 五雜俎, by Xie Zhaozhe 謝肇淛 (Shanghai: Shanghai shudian chubanshe, 2001).

*Xin Wudai shi*新五代史, by Ouyang Xiu歐陽修 (1007–1072), (Beijing: Zhonghua shuju, 1974).

Xin Yuanshi 新元史, by Ke Shaomin柯劭忞 (1848–1933), (Changchun: Jilin renmin chubanshe, 1996).

Xin Yuanshi 新元史, by Ke Shaomin 柯劭忞 (Shanghai: Kaiming shudian, 1935).

Xinshu jiaozhu 新書校注, by Jia Yi 賈誼 (c. 200–168 BCE), Yan Zhenyi 閻振益, Zhong Xia鍾夏 (eds.) (Beijing: Zhonghua shuju, 2000).

Xiyang chaogong dianlu 西洋朝貢典錄 (1520), by Huang Xingzeng 黄省曾, as *Xiyang chaogong dianlu jiaozhu* 西洋朝貢典錄校注, Xie Fang 謝方 (ed.). In Zhongwai jiaotong shiji congkan 中外交通史籍叢刊 (Beijing: Zhonghua shuju, 1982).

Xu zizhi tongjian changbian shibu 續資治通鑑長編拾補, by Huang Yizhou黄以周 (1828–1899) (Beijing: Zhonghua shuju, 2004).

Xu zizhi tongjian 續資治通鑒, by Bi Yuan 畢沅 (1730–1797), (Beijing: Zhonghua shuju, 1957).

Yanyou Siming zhi 延祐四明志 (1320), by Yuan Jue 袁桷 (1266–1327), in Song Yuan fangzhi congkan 宋元方志叢刊 (Beijing: Zhonghua shuju, 1990).

Yanzhou shiliao 弇州史料 (1614), by Wang Shizhen 王世貞 (1526–1590), in Siku jinhui shu congkan 四庫禁燬書叢刊 (Beijing: Beijing chubanshe, 2000).

Yibin ji 伊濱集, by Wang Yi 王沂 (*jinshi* 1315). In Jingyin Wenyuange Siku quanshu (Shanghai: Shanghai guji chubanshe, 1987).

Yixue huihan 醫學匯函, by Nie Shangheng 聶尚恆 (b. 1572), ed. Fu Haiyan 傅海燕, vol. 2, 3 vols. (Beijing: Zhongguo zhongyiyao chubanshe, 2015).

Yinchan quanshu, by Wang Kentang 王肯堂 (1552–1639), ed. Qian Qunying 錢群英, *Zhongyi guji zhenben jicheng fukejuan* 中醫古籍珍本集成・婦科卷 (Changsha: Hu'nan kexue jishu chubanshe, 2014).

Yingya shenglan jiaozhu 瀛涯勝覽校注, by Ma Huan 馬歡 (1414–1451), Feng Chengjun 馮承鈞 (ed.) (Beijing: Zhonghua shuju, 1955).

Yuanshi 元史, by Song Lian 宋濂 (1310–1385), (Beijing: Zhonghua shuju, 1976).

Yuanying Wu xiansheng ji 淵穎吳先生集 (1577), by Wu Lai 吳萊 (1297–1340). In Sibu congkan chubian (Shanghai: Shangwu yinshuguan, 1929).

Yuding zizhi tongjian gangmu sanbian 御定資治通鑑綱目三編, by Zhang Tingyu (1672–1755). In Jingyin Wenyuange Siku quanshu (Shanghai: Shanghai guji chubanshe, 1987).

Yupi lidai tongjian jilan 御批歷代通鑑輯覽, by Fu Heng 傅恆 (1722–1770) et al. In Jingyin wenyuange Siku quanshu (Shanghai: Shanghai guji chubanshe, 1987).

Yushan xianzhi (*Tongzhi*) 玉山縣志 (同治) (1873). In Airusheng – Zhongguo fangzhi ku 愛如生– 中國方志庫.

Yusi ji 玉笥集, by Zhang Xian 張憲 (?– 926). In Yue yatang congshu 粵雅堂叢書 (1851). Also reprinted in Congshu jicheng chubian 叢書集成初編 (Beijing: Zhonghua shuju 1985).

Zhangnüe zhinan 瘴瘧指南, by Zheng Quanwang 鄭全望 (fl. early 17t cent.), vol. 1003, 1800 vols., *Xuxiu siku quanshu* 續修四庫全書(Shanghai: Shanghai guji chubanshe, 2002).

Zhao'an xianzhi (*Kangxi*) 詔安縣志(康熙) (1874 reprint). In Airusheng – Zhongguo fangzhi ku 愛如生– 中國方志庫.

Zheng Chenggongzhuan 鄭成功傳, by Huang Zongxi黃宗羲 (1610–1695). In Taiwan wenxian congkan 台灣文獻叢刊 (Taibei: Taiwan yinhang jingji yanjiushi, 1959).

Zheng Kaiyang zazhu 鄭開陽雜著 (Kangxi), by Zheng Ruozeng 鄭若曾 (1503–1570), in Wenyuange Siku quanshu 文淵閣四庫全書 (Taibei: Taiwan shangwu yinshuguan, 1983).

Zhizheng Siming xuzhi 至正四明續志 (1342), by Wang Yuangong 王元恭. In Song Yuan fangzhi congkan 宋元方志叢刊 (Beijing: Zhonghua shuju, 1990).

Zhu Shunshui ji 朱舜水集, by Zhu Zhiyu 朱之瑜 (1600–1682), (Taibei: Hanjing wenhua shiye youxian gongsi chubanshe, 1985).

Zhufan zhi jiaoshi 諸蕃志校釋, by Zhao Rukuo 趙汝適 (1170–1231), Yang Bowen 楊博文 [ed.] (Beijing: Zhonghua shuju, 1996).

Zixi wengao 滋溪文稿, by Su Tianjue 蘇天爵 (1294–1352). In Congshu jicheng xubian 叢書集成續編 (Shanghai: Shanghai shudian, 1994).

Zizhi tongjian 資治通鑒, by Sima Guang司馬光 (1019–1086), Hu Sanxing胡三省 (ed.), (Beijing: Zhonghua shuju, 1956).

Unpublished Archival Sources

Algemeen Rijksarchief Brussel (ARA), Departement voor de Nederlanden van de Hof- en Staatskanselarij te Wenen, nr. 639 – 'Extrait du Journal tenu par le Capne Nicolas Carpentier, command le vaisseau de la compe imple l Esperance 1727'.

Collectie Aanwinsten 112(1866 AIV), *Journaal, gehouden door de opperstuurman Michiel Gerritsz. Boos van de schepen Maarsseveen, Naarden, Vlaardingen, Nieuwenhoven, Durgerdam, Diemermeer en Nusenborch 1662–1669*, fos. 1–130.

Collectie Aanwinsten 119 (1866 A XII), *Beschrijvinge van de westcust van Formosa, de cust van China en Pehu ofte Pescadores, met haere riveren, baijen, diepten, droochten clippen, droogten segge coursen, hoochten ende inhammen, alles door verscheijden ervaren stuerluijden daertoe expresselijck gecommitteert, gedurende het gouvernement van E Hans Putmans ondersocht en bevonden*, fols. 269–284.

Collectie Aanwinsten 1823 (1953I), *Beschrijvingh vande vaart uijt Tonkin, tusschen t naau van Maijna door, na door Firando so int passeren den cust van China, Pehoe , de galf als het aandoen vant lant Japan bijden stierman Frans Jacobz Visscher, door lang ervaren tot en opmercking bevonden, en tot gerief en tot geraf der genen die sulx noodigh hebben ten dienst van de Generale Compagnie uit cort vervat, en voortgebracht*, fols. 7–8.

Collectie Aanwinsten 553 (1891 19g), *Beschrijvinge van China beginnende van Jan Campenshoek leggende op de N: B-te van 26en g-r 38 mt; tot aan t Papen eijland bij de Chineesen gen-t Houtao en legt op de N B-te van 30 gr-d 8 a 10 mt.ter ordre van de heer Commissaris Constantio Nobel bezeijlt en beschreeven*, not foliated.

NFJ 284b, *Copie Instructie door den H-r gouverneur [Nicolaes] Verburgh aen den oppercoopman Sr. Jan de Groot [in Toncquin] verleent*, Taiwan, 6 Jan. 1651 fos. 33–42.

SAA (Stadsarchief Antwerpen) GIC (Generale Indische Compagnie) 5665 'Copijboek der orders gegeven voor Bengalen, Cabulon, China aan residenten, scheepskapiteins, enz. 1721–1730' - 'Instructies aan Kapitein De Winter'.

SAA GIC 5577 'Translat des lettres Persiennes en Français. Araabsche tekst met vertaling'

SAA GIC 5655 'Journaux et Rapports au retour des Capnes' 1724–1728 – Rapport au retour du cap N. Carpentier China L'aigle'.

SAA GIC 5700 'Journal of Groot Boeck van de supercargos op de schepen de Concordia en de Marquis de Prié (Canton 1727).

SAA GIC 5752 'Resolutions & Contracts for Sundry Merchandise Bought at Canton for the Cargoes of the Ships Lyon, Tiger & Eagle, belonging to the Imperial & Catholick Company Established In the Austrian Netherlands. By Robert Hewer, Jacobus de Meyer, Charles Morford, Peter de Boubereel & Joan de Jong jr. Sup Cargoes for the account of said Company. Canton Anno 1726'.

SAA GIC 5772 'Copie de translate des Lettres envoyé pr Coje Delon a mrs Hume & Harrisson'.

SAA GIC 5772 'Dagboek en klad van M. Cobbé juli 1723 – febr. 1724' – '14 october'.

SAA GIC 5772 'Papieren en Brieven Cobbé' – 'Memoire de ce qui serroit necessaire pour mentenir le Terrein'.

SAA GIC 5782 'Brieven Hume Banquibazar / Hollandsen 1732 / Stukken betreffende bedienden' - '1725 3 Juin v Parrabere Copie de la patente de Coje Safar agent pour la Compagnie a Ballasore.

SAA GIC 5782 'Papieren A. Hume Banquibazar' – 'Conditien gemaakt op 't engagement van Chieramra als Benjaan en coopman over des keyserlijcke Compagnies nu zijnde of naast komende handel &c'.

UBG (Ghent University Library) HS.1970 'Een relais ofte copie van vier brieven gheschreven door eenen pater discals, uyt het werelds deel Affrica en Asea aen syne auders tot Ghendt woonende – Arnoldus Luck, Michiel Cayphas, J.J. Hye-Hoys, 1724'.

VOC 1130, *Missive van gouverneur Jan van der Burch naer Batavia aen gouverneur generael Anthonio van Diemen,*Taiwan, 16 Feb 1639, fols. 1401–1404.

VOC 1131, *Rapport [van Nicolaes Couckebacker] aen den gouverneur generael Anthonio van Diemen ende de raeden van India, nopende Couckebacker's besendinge naer Tonckin ende gedaene visite des Comptoirs ende verderen ommeslag uijt Tayouan, gelegen op het eijlandt Formosa, in the fluitship de Rijp,* 8 Dec. 1639, fols. 222–315.

VOC 1197, Copie daghregister van den coopman Fredrick Schedel, Conton, 20 Jan. 1653–6 May 1653, fols. 643–729.

VOC 1197, *Copie rapport van den coopman Fredrick Schedel, Canton,* 9 May 1653, fols. 612–642.

VOC 1216, *Originele missive door Volckerius Westerwolt en raad aen de Ed. heer Joan Maatsuijcker gouverneur generael ende Ed. heeren raaden van India tot Batavia,* Siam, 16 Feb. 1656, fols. 392–403.

VOC 1236, *Missive door den koopman Hendrick Baron aen haer Ed. Heer Joan Maetsuijcker gouverneur general ende Ed. Heeren raaden van India tot Batavia,* Tonkin, 13 Nov. 1661, fols. 829–855.

VOC 1240, *Missive van commandeur Balthasar Bort naar Batavia aan haar Ed. Joan Maetsuijcker gouverneur generael,* Dinghai, 5 Nov 1662, fols. 1247–1282.

VOC 1243, *Copie missive door den Ed. commandeur Balthasar Bort aen haer Eds. tot Batavia geschreven,* Canton, 23 Jan. 1663, fos. 80–88.

VOC 1244, Daghregister van 't voorgevallene ende tweede uijtgeruste vlote nae China ende Formosa, China and Taiwan, 1 July 1663–27 Oct., fols. 2343–2488.

VOC 1253, *Order voor de respective opperhoofden vande schepen bescheijden onder de vlaggge vanden Heer Command- Balthasar Bort,* Paulu Tioman, 17 July 1664, fols. 2185–2186.

VOC 1253, *Verbael van den edelen commandeur Balthasar Bort dienende voor rapport wegens sijn verrichtingh om de Noort,* China and Taiwan, 7 July 1664 – Mar. 1665, fols. 2162–2251.

VOC 1254, *Missive van Commandeur Harman de Bitter op Quelangh naer Commissaris Constantin Nobel*, Jilong, June 27, 1665, fols. 844–846.

VOC 663, *Kopie-resolutië van gouverneur-generaal en raden in de serie overgekomen brieven en papieren uit Indië aan de heren XVII en de kamer Amsterdam*, Batavia, whole volume (1640 Jan. 21-Nov. 17).

VOC 678, Kopie-resolutië van gouverneur-generaal en raden in de serie overgekomen brieven en papieren uit Indië aan de heren XVII en de kamer Amsterdam, whole volume (1658 Jan. 2–1663 Dec. 7).

VOC 876, *Missive van Batavia [van Carel Reniersz.] naer Tayouan aen den E. Heer gouvernuer Nicolaes Verburch en sijnen raet, per 't Witte Paert geschreven*, Batavia, 25 Julij 1652, fos. 457–472.

VOC 886, *Register der Tayouanse Papieren uijt de generaele secretarie geligt ende aen den commandeur Balthasar Bort ter handt gestalt, om op sijn wedercomste getrstitueert te worden [dato 21 Junij 1662]*, Batavia, fols. 177–178.

VOC 887, *Instructie [van Joan Maetsuijcker] voor d' E. Balthasar Bort gaende van hier als commandeur over de vlote ende het volck van oorloge, gedestineert nae de custe van China, tot herstelinge van Compagnies vervalle saecken om de Noord, waernaer hij hem met sijn bijgevouchden raedt, in 't bevorderen ende uijtvoeren van die gewichtige commissie sal hebben te reguleren*, Batavia, 28 Junij 1663, fols. 166–189.

VOC 888, *Instruactie [van Joan Maetsuijcker] voor d' E Balthasar gaende als Commandeur over de vlote ende het volck van orloge, gedestineert near de custe van China, waerna hij ende sijnen bijgevouchden raad hun in 't bevorderen en uijtvoeren van Compagnies desseijnen aldaer sullen hebben te reguleeren*, Batavia, 6 Julij 1664, fos. 203–228.

General Bibliography

Abu-Lughod, Janet, *Before European hegemony: The world system A.D. 1250–1350* (New York and Oxford, 1989).

Alcina, Francisco Ignacio, S.I., *La Historia de las Islas e Indios Visayas del Padre Alcina, 1668*. Ed. by M. Luisa Martín-Meras and M. Dolores Higueras (Madrid: Consejo Superior de Investigaciones Científicas, Instituto Histórico de Marina, 1975).

Allsen, Thomas T., "Mongolian Princes and Their Merchant Partners, 1200–1260", *Asia Major*, Third Series, 2.2 (1989), 83–126.

Allsen, Thomas T., *The Steppe and the Sea* (Philadelphia: University of Pennsylvania Press, 2019).

Anderson, J. (ed.), *The Tongking Gulf through History* (Philadelphia: University of Pennsylvania Press, 2012).

Anderson, J., "Slipping through Holes: The late tenth century and early eleventh century Sino-Vietnamese Coastal Frontier as Subaltern Trade Network", in Anderson (2012), 87–100.

Anno Masaki 安野眞幸, *Kōshiron: Hirado, Nagasaki, Yokoseura* 港市論：平戸，長崎，横瀬浦 (Tōkyō: Nihon editā sukūru shuppanbu, 1992).

Arano Yasunori 荒野泰典, *Edo bakufu to Higashi Ajia* 江戸幕府と東アジア (Tōkyō: Yoshikawa kōbunkan, 2003).

Arano Yasunori 荒野泰典, Ishii Masatoshi 石井政敏, and Murai Shōsuke 村井章介 (eds.), *Ajia no naka no Nihonshi* アジアの中の日本史, 6 vols. (Tōkyō: Tōkyō daigaku shuppankai, 1992–1993).

Arano Yasunori 荒野泰典, Ishii Masatoshi 石井政敏, and Murai Shōsuke 村井章介 (eds.), *Kinseiteki sekai no seijuku, Nihon no taigai kankei* 近世的世界の成熟，日本の対外関係, 7 vols., VI (Tōkyō: Yoshikawa kōbunkan, 2010).

Arano Yasunori 荒野泰典, *Kinsei Nihon to Higashi Ajia* 近世日本と東アジア (Tōkyō: Tōkyō daigaku shuppankai, 1988).

Arano Yasunori 荒野泰典, *Rettōnaigai no kōtsū to kokka* 列島内外の交通と国家 [*Nihon no shakaishi* 日本の社会史 I] (Tōkyō: Iwanami shoten, 1988).

Asao Naohiro 朝尾直弘, *Sakoku* 鎖国 (Tōkyō: Shōgakukan, 1975).

Asao, Naohiro, *State and Diplomacy in Early Modern Japan. Asia in the Development of the Tokugawa Bakufu* (Princeton: Princeton University Press, 1984).

Askari, Syed Husain, "Bihar in the 1st quarter of the 18th Century", *Proceedings of the Indian History Congress*, vol. 5 (1941), 394–405.

Aslanian, Sebouh David, *From the Indian Ocean to the Mediterranean. The Global trade Networks of Armenian Merchants from New Julfa* (New York: University of California Press, 2011).

Avila, Girón Bernardino de, O.F.M., *Relaçión del Reino de Nippón, a que llaman corruptamente Japón* [1615], ed. by Doroteo Schilling, O.F.M., and Fidel de Lejarza, O.F.M. ("Relación del reino del Nippon por Bernardino de Avila Girón"), *Archivo Ibero-Americano* 36 (1933), 481–531; 37 (1934), 5–48, 259–275, 392–434, 493–554; 38 (1935), 103–130, 216–239, 384–341.

Azuma Yoshimochi 東喜望. "Chūgoku to Ryūkyū no kokkō II: sakuhōshi no rūto" 中国と琉球の国交 II：冊封使のルート. *Shiraume gakuen tanki daigaku kiyō* 白梅学園短期大学紀要 31 (1995), 29–49.

Bachelet, Pierre-Emmanuel, *Bateaux-pigeons, quartier japonais et cartes nautiques: réseaux marchands et relations interculturelles entre le Japon, le Dai Viêt et le Champa (XVIe-XVIIIe siècles)*. Unpublished PhD thesis (Université de Lyon, 2020).

Bai Di 白蒂 (Patrizia Carioti), "Shiqi shiji Zhengshi haishang jituan zai dongya de guoji jiaose" 17世紀鄭氏海上集團在東亞的國際角色, in Zhu Chengru 朱成如 Wang Tianyou 王天有 (eds.), *Ming Qing luncong* 明清論, vol. 12 (Beijing: Gugong chubanshe, 2012), 221–246.

Bai Di 白蒂 (Patrizia Carioti), *Yuandong guoji de wutaishang de fengyun renwu Zheng Chenggong* 遠東國際舞臺上的風雲人物鄭成功 (Guangxi: Guangxi renmin chubanshe, 1997).

Baladouni, Vahe, and Margaret Makepeace (eds.), *Armenian Merchants of the Seventeenth and Early Eighteenth Centuries*, (Philadelphia: American Philosophical Society, 1998).

Baldanza, Kathlene. *Ming China and Vietnam. Negotiating Borders in Early Modern Asia* (Cambridge: Cambridge University Press, 2016).

Barendse, René J., *The Arabian Seas. The Indian Ocean World of the Seventeenth Century* (New York, London: M. A. Sharpe, 2002).

Basham, Sarah A.G., *The book multiple: Treatise on Military Preparedness (1621) and encyclopedic practice in seventeenth century China*. PhD thesis (University of British Columbia Library, 2019).

Batchelor, Robert. "The Selden Map Rediscovered: A Chinese Map of East Asian Shipping Routes, *c*.1619". *Imago Mundi* 65:1 (2013), 37–63.

Batchelor, Robert. *London. The Selden Map and the Making of a Global City, 1549–1689* (Chicago and London: The University of Chicago Press, 2014).

Bayly, Christopher A. and Sanjay Subrahmanyam, "Portfolio Capitalists and the political economy of early modern India", *The Indian Economic and Social History Review*, 25:4 (1998), 401–424.

Bayly, Christopher A., *Empire and information: intelligence gathering and social communication in India, 1780–1870*, (New York: Cambridge University Press, 1996).

Bellwood, P., Cameron, J., Viet, V. N., and Liem, V. B., "Ancient Boats, Boat Timbers, and Locked Mortise-and-Tenon Joints from Bronze/Iron-Age Northern Vietnam", *The International Journal of Nautical Archaeology* 36:1 (2007), 2–20.

Bengal Revenue Department, *Collection of papers relating to the Hooghly Imambara*, (Calcutta: Bengal Secretariat Book Depot, 1914).

Bentley, Jerry H., "Hemispheric Integration, 500–1500 CE", *Journal of World History*, 9:2 (Fall 1998), 237–254.

Bernabéu, Albert Salvador, and Carlos Martínez Shaw (eds.), *Un océano de seda y plata: el universo económico del Galeón de Manila* (Sevilla: Consejo Superior de Investigaciones Científicas, 2013).

Bernholz, Peter and Hans Gersbach, "Gresham's Law: Theory", in *The New Palgrave Dictionary of Money and Finance*, vol. 2 (London and Basingstoke: Macmillan, 1992), 286–288.

Bian Li 卞利. "Mingdai Zheng Shungong jiguan, shengping shiji ji chushi Riben kaobian" 明代鄭舜功籍貫、生平事蹟及出使日本考辨, *Anhui shixue* 安徽史學 6 (2017), 70–76.

Blair, Emma Helen, and James Alexander Robertson (eds.), *The Philippine Islands 1493–1803* (Cleveland, Ohio: The Arthur H. Clark Company, 1903–1909), 55 vols.

Blussé, Leonard and Viallé, Cynthia. *The Deshima Daghregisters, 1640–1650*. Vol. 11, (Leiden: Intercontinental Series XXII, 2001).

Blussé, Leonard, "Bull in a China Shop, Pieter Nuits in China and Japan (1627–1636)", in Leonard Blussé (ed.), *Around and about Formosa* (Taipei: Ts'ao Yung-ho Foundation for Culture and Education, 2003), 95–110.

Blussé, Leonard, "Divesting a Myth: Seventeenth Century Dutch-Portuguese Rivalry in the Far East", in Disney and Booth (2000), 387–402.

Blussé, Leonard, "Japanese Historiography and European Sources", in Emmer and Wesseling (1979), 193–224.

Blussé, Leonard, *Visible Cities: Canton, Nagasaki, and Batavia and the Coming of the Americans*, (Harvard: Harvard University Press, 2008).

Blussé, Leonard, Remmelink Willem and Smits Ivo (eds.), *Bridging the Divide, 400 Years The Netherlands-Japan* (Leiden: Hotei, 2000).

Blussé, Leonard, *Strange Company: Chinese Settlers, Mestizo Women and the Dutch in VOC Batavia* (Dordrecht: Foris Publishers, 1986).

Blussé, Leonard, *Strange Company. Chinese Settlers, Mestizo Women and the Dutch in VOC Batavia* (Dordrecht: Foris Publications, 1988).

Blussé, Leonard, Willem Remmelink, and Ivo Smith (eds.), *Nichi-Ran kōryū 400nen no rekishi to tenbō* 日蘭交流400年の歴史と展望 (Tōkyō: Nichi-Ran gakkai, 2000).

Blussé, Leonard; Margot E. van Opstall, Ts'ao Yung-ho and Wouter E. Milde (eds.), *De Dagregisters van het Kasteel Zeelandia: Taiwan 1629–1662* ('s-Gravenhage: Nijhoff, II, 1995).

Boot, W. J., "Japan, China and the West", in Leonard Blussé *et al.* (2000), 73–85.

Borao, José Eugenio, *Spaniards in Taiwan* (Taipei: SMC Publishing, 2001–2002), 2 vols.

Boxer, Charles Ralph, "Plata es Sangre: Sidelights on the Drain of Spanish-American Silver in the Far East, 1550–1700", *Philippine Studies* 18 (1970), 457–475.

Boxer, Charles Ralph, "The Swan Song of the Portuguese in Japan, 1635–1639", *Transactions and Proceedings of the Japan Society* (London) 17 (1929–30), 4–11.

Boxer, Charles Ralph, *Jan Compagnie in Japan, 1600–1850* (The Hague: Martinus Nijhoff, 1950).

Boxer, Charles Ralph, *Jan Compagnie in War and Peace, 1602–1799* (Hong Kong, Singapore, Kuala Lumpur: Heinemann Asia, 1979).

Boxer, Charles Ralph, *The Christian century in Japan, 1549–1650* (Berkley, Los Angeles, Cambridge: University of California Press, 1951).

Boxer, Charles Ralph, *The Christian Century in Japan, 1549–1650* (Berkeley, Los Angeles, and London: University of California Press, 1951).

Boxer, Charles Ralph, *The Dutch Seaborne Empire* (London: Penguin Pelican, 1965 [repr. 1973]).

Boxer, Charles Ralph, *The Great Ship from Amacon. Annals of Macao and the Old Japan Trade, 1555–1640* (Lisbon: Centro de Estudos Historicos Ultramarinos, 1963).

Brokaw, Cynthia Joanne *Commerce in Culture: The Sibao Book Trade in the Qing and Republican Periods* (Harvard University Asia Center, 2007).

Brook, Timothy. *Mr. Selden's Map of China. Decoding the Secrets of a Vanished Cartographer* (New York et al.: Bloomsbury Press, 2013).

Buch, W. J. M., "La Compagnie de Indes Néerlandaises et l'Indochine", *Bulletin de l'École Française d'Extrême-Orient.* XXXVI (1936), 100–216.

Buch, W. J. M., *De Oost-Indische Compagnie en Quinam, de betrekkingen der Nederlanders met Annam in de XVIIe eeuw* (Amsterdam: H.J. Paris, 1929).

Bugge Henriette, "Silk to Japan. Sino Dutch Competition in the Silk Trade to Japan, 1633–1685", *Itinerario* 13:2 (1989), 25–44.

Cai Hongsheng 蔡鸿生, "Wang Wengao helanguo gongshi jishishi shizheng"王文诰荷兰国贡使纪事诗释证, in Cai Hongsheng (2007), 363–364.

Cai Hongsheng 蔡鸿生, *Zhongwai jiaoliu shishi kaoshu*中外交流史事考述 (Zhengzhou: Daxiang chubanshe, 2007).

Calanca, Paula, *Piraterie et contrebande au Fujian – L'administration chinoise face aux problems d'illégalité maritime* (Paris: Les Indes Savantes, 2011).

Carioti Patrizia, "Focusing on the Overseas Chinese in Seventeenth Century Nagasaki: The Role of the *Tōtsūji* in the Light of the Early Tokugawa Foreign Policy", in Nagazumi Yōko (ed.), *Large and Broad. The Dutch Impact on Early Modern Asia. Essays in Honor of Leonard Blussé* (Tokyo: Toyo bunko, 2010), 62–75.

Carioti Patrizia, "The Zheng Regime and Tokugawa Japan: Asking for the Japanese Intervention", in Tonio Andrade and Hang Xing (eds.), *Sea Rovers, Silver, and Samurai: Maritime East Asia in Global History, 1550–1700* (Honolulu: University of Hawai'i Press, 2016), 156–180.

Carioti, Patrizia, "Echoes of the Ming-Qing Conflict: Notes on the Political Role of the Overseas Chinese in Nagasaki", in Magda Abbiati and Federico Greselin (eds.), *Il liuto e i libri Studi in onore di Mario Sabattini* [Sinica venetiana 1] (Venezia: Edizioni Ca' Foscari, 2014), 137–156.

Carioti, Patrizia, "Higashi Indokaisha no nigai haiboku. Tei Seikō ni yoru Taiwan seifuku, 1661–1662" 東インド会社の苦い敗北。郑成功による台湾征服、1661–1662, in Arano Yasunori 荒野泰典 (ed.), *Kinsei Nihon no kokusai kankei to gensetsu* 近世日本の国際関係と言説 (Hiroshima: keisuisha, 2017), 63–81.

Carioti, Patrizia, "Japan behind the Curtains: The Matsuura Clan of Hirado among *haikou, wokou,* and Europeans", in Michèle Battesti (ed.), *La piraterie au fil de l'histoire. Un défi pour l'état* (Paris: Presses de L'Université Paris-Sorbonne, 2014), 161–184.

Carioti, Patrizia, "The International Setting of Far Eastern Seas during the First Half of the 17th Century: A New Balance of Power", in Jorge Manuel Dos Santos Alves (ed.), *Portugal e a China. Conferências no III Curso de Livre de História das Relaçaos entre Portugal e a China* (Lisboa: Fundaçao Oriente, 2001), 35–60.

Carioti, Patrizia, *Cina e Giappone sui mari nei secoli XVI e XVII* (Napoli: Edizioni scientifiche italiane, 2006).

Carioti, Patrizia, *Cina e Giappone sui mari nei secoli XVI e XVII* (Napoli: Edizioni Scientifiche Italiane, 2006).

Carioti, Patrizia, *Guardando al "Celeste Impero" … L'avventura della VOC in Asia Orientale* (Trento: Centro Studi Martino Martini, 2012).

Carioti, Patrizia, *Zheng Chenggong* (Napoli: Istituto Universitario Orientale, 1995).

Carletti, Francesco, *My Voyage around the World* (London: Methuen & Co., 1965). English translation of *Ragionamenti di Francesco Carletti, fiorentino, sopra le cose da lui vedute ne' suoi viaggi si dell'Indie Occidentali e Orientali come d'altri paesi*, Firenze, 1701.

Carneiro, Roberto and A. Teodoro de Matos (eds.), *O século Cristão do Japão* [Actas do colóquio internacional comemorativo dos 450 anos de amizade Portugal-Japão, 1543–1993] (Lisboa: Centro de Estudos dos Povos e Culturas de Expressão Portuguesa da Universidade Católica Portuguesa, 1994).

Carrington Goodrich, Luther and Chao-Ying Fang, *Dictionary of Ming Biography 1368–1644* (New York: Columbia University Press, 1976), 2 vols.

Carvarhal, Hélder; André Murteira, Roger Lee de Jesus (eds.), The First World Empire Portugal, War and Military Revolution (London and New York: Routledge, 2021).

Ch'en Ching-ho 陈荆和, *The Chinese Community in the Sixteenth Century Philippines* (Tōkyō: The Centre for East Asian Cultural Studies, 1968).

Chen Gaochun 陳高春, *Zhongguo gudai junshi wenhua dacidian* 中國古代軍事文化大辭典 (Beijing: Changzheng chubanshe, 1992).

Chaffee, John W., "Introduction: Reflections on the Sung", in John W. Chaffee and Paul J. Smith (eds.) *The Cambridge History of China*, vol. 5, part Two, *Sung China, 960–1279*. Cambridge: Cambridge University Press, 2014), 1–18.

Chaffee, John W., "Song China and the multi-state and commercial world of East Asia", *Crossroads – Studies on the History of Exchange Relations in the East Asian World* 1.2 (2010), 33–54.

Chang Jianhua 常建華, "Mingdai niyin wenti chutan" 明代溺嬰問題初探, *Zhongguo shehui lishi pinglun*, 4 (2002), 121–136.

Chang, Pin-tsun, *Chinese Maritime Trade: The Case of Sixteenth-Century Fu-chien (Fukien)*. PhD thesis (Princeton: Princeton University, 1983).

Chang, Stephen T., "Commodities Imported to the Chang-chou Region of Fukien during the Late Ming Period. A Preliminary Analysis of the Tax Lists found in T'ung-hsi-yang k'ao", in Roderich Ptak, and Dieter Rothermund (eds.), *Emporia, Commodities, and Entrepreneurs in Asian Maritime Trade, c. 1400–1750* (Stuttgart: Franz Steiner, 1991), 159–194.

Chao, Yüan-ling, *Medicine and Society in Late Imperial China: A Study of Physicians in Suzhou, 1600–1850* (Peter Lang, 2009).

Chaudhuri, Kirti N., *Asia before Europe: economy and civilisation of the Indian Ocean from the Rise of Islam to 1750* (New York: Cambridge University Press, 1990).

Chaudhury, Sushil, "Merchants, Companies and Rulers: Bengal in the Eighteenth Century", *Journal of the Economic and Social History of the Orient*, 31:1 (1988), 74–109.

Chaudhury, Sushil, *From Prosperity to decline: eighteenth century Bengal* (New Delhi: Manohar, 1995).

Chaunu, Pierre, *Les Philippines et le Pacifique des Ibériques* (*XVIe, XVIIe, XVIIIe siècles*). *Introduction Méthodologique et Indices d'activité* (Paris: S.E.V.P.E.N., 1966).

Chen Gaohua 陳高華, "Yuandai shiren Nai Xian shengping shiji kao" 元代詩人迺賢生平事蹟考, *Wenshi* 文史 32 (1990), 247–268.

Chen Guobin 程國斌, "Wenyi zhongde daode xushi" 瘟疫中的道德敘事, *Zhongwai yixue zhexue* 中外醫學哲學 14:1 (2016), 11–33.

Chen Jiarong 陳佳榮, "Zaishuo *Shunfeng xiangsong* yuanzi Wu Pu de *Duhai fangcheng*" 再說《順風相送》源自吳朴的《渡海方程》, *Haiyangshi yanjiu* 海洋史研究 10 (2017), 354–364.

Chen Jiarong 陳佳榮 and Zhu Jianqiu 朱鑒秋 (eds.), *Duhai fangcheng jizhu* 渡海方程輯注 (Shanghai: Zhongxi shuju, 2013).

Chen Jiarong 陳佳榮, Xie Fang 謝方, and Lu Junling 陸峻嶺 *Gudai Nanhai diming huishi* 古代南海地名匯釋 (Beijing: Zhonghua shuju, 1986).

Chen Jiarong 陳佳榮, "'Mingmo jiangli ji Zhang Quan hanghai tongjiao tu' bianhui shijian, tese ji haiwai jiaotong diming lüexi" 《明末疆裡及漳泉航海通交圖》編繪時間、特色及海外交通地名略析, *Haijiaoshi yanjiu* 海交史研究 2 (2011), 52–66.

Chen Jiarong 陳佳榮, "*Shunfeng xiangsong* zuozhe ji wancheng niandai xinkao"《順風相送》作者及完成年代新考. Nanmingwang 南溟網, 2011. http://www.world10k.com/blog/?p=2028.

Chen Jiarong 陳佳榮 (eds.), *Zhongguo lidai hailu zhenjing* 中國歷代海路針經. 2 vols. (Guangzhou: Guangdong keji chubanshe and Quanguo youxiu chubanshe, 2016).

Chen Jihua 陳繼華, *Mingdai Fujian yijia Xiong Zongli yiji bianke ji xueshu sixiang yanjiu* 明代福建醫家熊宗立醫籍編刻及學術思想研究. Master thesis (Fuzhou : Fujian University of Traditional Chinese Medicine, 2012).

Chen Kuo-tung 陳國棟, "Manila datusha yu Li Dan chuzou Riben de yige tuice" 馬尼拉大屠殺與李旦出走日本的一個推測 (1603–1607), *Taiwan wenxian* 臺灣文獻, 60/3 (2009), 33–62.

Chen Maoheng 陳懋恒, *Mingdai wokou kaolüe* 明代倭寇考略 (Beijing: Beijing renmin chubanshe, 1957).

Chen Menglei 陳夢雷 (ed.), *Yishu mingliu zhuan* 醫術名流傳, vol. 12, 12 vols., gujin tushu jicheng yibu quanlu 古今圖書集成醫部全錄 (Beijing: renmin weisheng chubanshe, 1991).

Chen Qingyuan 陳慶元, "Zhang Xie nianbiao" 張燮年表. *Nanjing shifan daxue wenxueyuan xuebao* 南京師範大學文學院學報 1 (2013), 182–188.

Chen Wenshi 陳文石, *Ming Hongwu Jiajing jian de haijin zhengce* 明洪武嘉靖間的海禁政策 (Taibei: Guoli Taiwan daxue wenxueyuan, 1966).

Chen Xi 陳曦, *Xiong Zongli ji mingfang leizheng yishu daquan de yanjiu* 熊宗立及《名方類證醫書大全》的研究. Master thesis (Changchun: Changchun University of Chinese Medicine, 2013).

Chen Xu 陳旭, *Mingdai wenyi yu Mingdai shehui* 明代瘟疫與明代社會 (Chengdu: Southwestern University of Finance and Economics Press, 2016).

Chen Yuanpeng 陳元朋, *Liang Song de shangyi renshi yu ruyi* 兩宋的尚醫人士與儒醫 (Taipei: National Taiwan University Press, 1997).

Chen Yunü 陳玉女, "Mingdai duotai chanwang niying de shehui yinying cong sifu fojiao duotai chanwang shuiluhua tanqi" 明代墮胎、產亡、溺嬰的社會因應——從四幅佛教墮胎產亡水陸畫談起, *Chengda lishi xuebao* 31 (2006), 65–112.

Chen Zhongyu 陳忠瑜, ed., *Sanyi jiaozhu xiawuni Lingzi benxing shilu* 三一教主夏午尼林 子本行實錄 (Beijing: Beijing Library Press, 1999).

Cheng Guobin 程國斌, "Ruyi gainian de wenhua yu zhengzhi yiyun" 儒醫概念的文化與政治意蘊, *Zhongwai yixue zhexue* 12:1 (2014), 39–54.

Cheng Wei-chung, *War, Trade and Piracy in the China Seas 1622–1683* [TANAP Monographs on the History of Asian-European Interaction, 16] (Leiden: E. J. Brill, 2013).

Cheng Yang 程楊, Li Hairong 李海蓉, and Yang Linsheng 楊林生, "Zhongguo Mingqing shiqi yibing shikong fenbu guilü de dingliang yanjiu" 中國明清時期疫病時空分佈的定量研究, *Dili yanjiu* 地理研究 28:4 (2009), 1059–1068.

Cheng, Shaogang, *De VOC en Formosa, 1624–1662*. Ph. D diss. (Leiden: Leiden University, 1995), 2 vols.

Cheng, Wei-chung, *War, Trade, and Piracy in the China Seas 1622–1683* (Leiden: Brill, 2013).

Cheong, Weng Eang, *The Hong Merchants of Canton: Chinese merchants in Sino-Western Trade*, (Richmond: Curzon, 1997).

Chia, Lucille, *Printing for Profit: The Commercial Publishers of Jianyang, Fujian (11th–17th Centuries)* (Harvard University Asia Center, 2002).

Chin, James K. 錢江, "Merchants, Smugglers, and Pirates: Multinational Clandestine Trade on the South China Coast, 1520–50". In Robert J. Antony (ed.), *Elusive Pirates, Pervasive Smugglers: Violence and Clandestine Trade in the Greater China Seas* (Hong Kong: Hong Kong University Press, 2010), 43–57.

Chin, James Kong, "Junk Trade, Business Networks and Sojourning Communities: Hokkien Merchants in Early Maritime Asia", *Journal of Chinese Overseas* 6/2 (2010), 157–215.

Chin, James Kong, *Merchants and other sojourners: the Hokkiens overseas, 1570–1760*. Ph.D thesis (Hong Kong: University of Hong Kong, 1998).

Chown, John, *A History of Money: From AD 800* (London and New York: Routledge / Taylor & Francis, 1994/1996).

Ciyuan 辭源, 4 vols. (Beijing: Shangwu yinshuguan, 1983).

Clark, Hugh, "The Southern Kingdoms between the T'ang and Sung", in vol. 5, part One, Denis Twittchett and Paul J. Smith (eds.) *The Five Dynasties and Sung China, 960–1279* (Cambridge: Cambridge University Press, 2009), 133–205.

Clulow, Adam, *The Company and the Shogun: The Dutch Encounter with Tokugawa Japan* (New York: Columbia University Press, 2016).

Colín, Francisco, S.I., *Labor evangélica, ministerios apostólicos de los obreros de la Compañía de Jesús, fundación y progresos de su provincia en las islas Filipinas* [1663]. Ed. by Pablo Pastells. 3 vols. (Barcelona: Imprenta y Litografía de Henrich y Compañía, 1900–1902).

Coolhaas, W. Ph. (ed.), *Generale Missiven van Gouverneurs-Generaal en Raden van Indië aan Heren XVII der Verenigde Oostindische Companie 1610–1671*, 13 vols. ('s Gravenhage: Rijks Geschiedkundige Publicatiën, 1960–2007), Vol. II (1964).

Dai Nihon Shiryō 大日本史料 (293 vols.) (Tōkyō: Shiryō Hensanjo, 1901 ~).

Dai, Yingcong, *The Sichuan Frontier and Tibet: Imperial Strategy in the Early Qing* (Seattle: University of Washington Press).

Dardess, John W., *A Political Life in Ming China: A Grand Secretary and his Times* (Lanham: Rowman & Littlefield, 2013).

Dars, Jacques, "Les jonques chinoises de haute mer sous les Song et les Yuan", *Archipel* 18 (1979), 41–56.

Das Gupta, Ashin, *Indian Merchants and the Decline of Surat: c. 1700–1750*, (Wiesbaden: Franz Steiner Verlage, 1979).

Das Gupta, Ashin, Uma Das Gupta (ed.), *The world of the Indian Ocean merchant 1500–1800: collected essays of Ashin Das Gupta*, (Oxford: Oxford University Press, 2001).

Davies, Stephen. "On Course and Course Keeping in Ming Dynasty Seafaring. Probabilities and Improbabilities". In Hong Kong Maritime Museum (ed.), *Mapping Ming China's Maritime World* (*Zhenlu lanlü* 針路藍縷), 289–336 (Hong Kong: Zhonghua shuju, 2015).

Davies, Stephen, "Routes, Rutters, Navigational Techniques and the Development of Navigational Aids in Traditional Chinese", *Artefact. Techniques, Histoire et Sciences Humaines* 8 (2018), 141–182.

de Andrade, Tonio, *The Gunpowder Age – China, Military Innovation, and the Rise of the West in World History* (Princeton and Oxford: Princeton University Press, 2016).

de Andrade, Tonio, "The military revolution in global history: East Asian perspectives", in Hélder Carvarhal, André Murteira, Roger Lee de Jesus (eds.), *The First World Empire Portugal, War and Military Revolution* (London and New York: Routledge, 2021).

de Morga, António (1559–1636), *The Philippine islands, Moluccas, Siam, Cambodia, Japan, and China, at the close of the sixteenth century* (London: Printed for the Hakluyt Society, 1868).

De Oliveira Marques, A. H., *História dos Portugueses no Extremo Oriente*, Vol. I, Part I: *Em torno de Macau* (Lisboa: Fundação Oriente, 1998).

De Oliveira Marques, A. H., *História dos Portugueses no Extremo Oriente*, Vol. I, Part II: *De Macau à periferia* (Lisboa: Fundação Oriente, 2000).

De Winter, Wim, "Hofrituelen en koloniale recuperatie van de Oostendse Compagnie in 18e eeuws Bengalen en China", *Handelingen: Koninklijke Zuidnederlandse Maatschappij Voor Taal- En Letterkunde En Geschiedenis*, vol. 68 (2015), 119–138.

De Winter, Wim, "Perspectives for a Comparative Cultural History of the Ostend Company Interactions in Bengal and China", *Crossroads: Studies on the History of Exchange Relations in the East Asian World*, vol. 11 (April 2015), 115–129.

Degryse, Karel, "Zuid-Nederlands kapitaal in de VOC en de voorcompagnieën ", in: J. Parmentier (ed.), *Noord-Zuid in Oost Indisch perspectief* (Zutphen: Walburg Pers, 2005), 81–98.

Deng Gang, *Chinese Maritime Activities and Socioeconomic Development* (Westport, CT and London: Greenwood Press, 1997).

Deng Gang, *Maritime Sector, Institutions, and Sea Power of Premodern China* (Westport, CT and London: Greenwood Press, 1999).

Ding Chun 丁春, "Fujian gudai ruyi zhuanhuan wenti de yanjiu" 福建古代儒醫轉換問題的研究, *Fujian zhongyi xueyuan xuebao* 福建中醫學院學報1 (2001).

Disney, Anthony and Booth, Emily (eds.), *Vasco da Gama and the Linking of Europe and Asia* (New Delhi: Oxford University Press 2000).

Đỗ, T. G., Suzuki, T., Nguyun, V. Q., and Yamagata, M., "Champa Citadels: An Archaeological and Historical Study", *The Asian Review of World Histories* 5:2 (2017), 70–105.

Du Xinfu 杜信孚, *Mingdai banke zonglu* 明代版刻綜錄, 8 vols. (Yangzhou: Jiangsu guangling keyinshe, 1983).

Duan Lisheng 段立生, "Huang Zhong jiqi *Haiyu*" 黃衷及其《海語》. *Dongnanya Nanya yanjiu* 東南亞南亞研究 3 (1984), 48–52.

Duyvendak, J. J. L. *Ma Huan Re-Examined* [Verhandelingen Der Koninklijke Akademie van Wetenschappen Te Amsterdam] (Amsterdam: Noord-Hollandsche Uitgeversmaatschappij, 1933).

Duyvendak, J. J. L., "The Last Dutch Embassy to the Chinese Court (1794–1795)", *T'oung Pao* 34, (1938), 1–137.

Elisonas, Jurgis, "The Inseparable Trinity: Japan's Relations with China and Korea". In John Whitney Hall and James L. McClain (eds.), *The Cambridge History of Japan, Vol. 4. Early Modern Japan*, 235–300 (Cambridge: Cambridge University Press, 1991).

Elliott, Mark C., *Emperor Qianlong. Son of Heaven, Man of World* [Library of World Biography, ed. by Peter N. Steams] (New York, San Francisco, Boston: Longman, 2009).

Emmer, P. C. and Wesseling, H. L. (eds.), *Reappraisals in Overseas History* (Leiden: Leiden University Press 1979).

Endicott-West, Elizabeth, "Merchant Associations in Yuan China: The "Ortoy", *Asia Major* Third Series 2.2 (1989), 127–154.

Fan Wentao 范文濤, "*Zheng He hanghai tu* diming kaoshi" 《鄭和航海圖》地名考釋. In Jinian weida hanghaijia Zheng He xiaxiyang 580 zhounian choubei weiyuanhui 紀念偉大航海家鄭和下西洋580週年籌備委員會 and Zhongguo hanghaishi yanjiuhui 中國航海史研究會 (eds.), *Zheng He yanjiu ziliao xuanbian* 鄭和研究資料選編, 216–241 (Beijing: Renmin jiaotong chubanshe, 1985).

Fan Zhongyi 范中義 and Tong Xigang 仝晰綱, *Mingdai Wokou shilue* 明代倭寇史略 (Beijing: Zhonghua shuju, 2004).

Fang Baochuan 方宝川, "Xie Jie jiqi zhuzuo kaolüe" 謝杰及其著作考略. *Fujian shifan daxue xuebao* (*zhexue shehui kexueban*) 福建師範大學學報(哲學社會科學版) 2 (2009), 125–131.

Fang Jun, "The Military Functions of the Southern Capital in Ming China", *Monumenta Serica* 55 (2007), 133–155.

Fang Yanshou 方彥壽, "Mingdai keshujia Xiong Zongli shukao" 明代刻書家熊宗立述考, *Wenxian* 文獻1 (1987), 222–227.

Fang Yanshou 方彥壽, *Jianyang keshushi* 建陽刻書史 (Beijing: Zhongguo shehui chubanshe, 2003).

Félix, Alfonso (ed.), *The Chinese in the Philippines: 1570–1770* (Manila: Historical Conservation Society of Manila, 1966), 2 vols.

Filipiak, Kai, "The Effects of Civil Official Handling Military affairs in Ming Times", *Ming Studies* 66 (2012), 1–15.

Filipiak, Kai, *Civil Military Relations in Chinese History: From Ancient China to the Communist takeover* (London and New York: Routledge, 2015).

Filipiak, Kai, "Technological advance in the war against the Mongols", *in* Kaushik Roy and Peter Lorge (eds.), *Chinese and Indian Warfare – From the Classical Age to 1870* (London and New York: Routledge, 2015), 121–133.

Fitzpatrick, Merrilyn, "Local Interests and the Anti-pirate Administration in China's South-East 1555–1565", *Ch'ing-shih wen-t'i* 4:2 (1979), 1–50.

Flecker, Michael, *The Archaeological Excavation of the 10th century Intan Shipwreck* (Oxford: Archaeopress, 2002).

Flynn, Dennis O., and Arturo Giráldez (eds.), *The Pacific World History. Lands, People, and History of the Pacific, 1500–1900*, vol. 4: *European Entry into the Pacific: Spain and the Acapulco-Manila Galleons* (Burlington, Vermont: Ashgate, 2001).

Forte, Antonio, *The Hostage An Shiguo ad His Offsprings* [Italian School of East Asian Studies, Occasional Papers, 6] (Kyōto: Italian School of East Asian Studies, 1995).

Franke, Herbert, "Sung Embassies: Some General Observations", in Morris Rossabi (ed.), *China Among Equals: The Middle Kingdom and Its Neighbors, 10th–14th Centuries* (Berkeley: University of California Press, 1983), 116–148.

Franke, Wolfgang, and Foon Ming Liew-Herres, *Annotated Sources of Ming History. Including Southern Ming and Works on Neighbouring Lands 1368–1661.* 2 vols. (Kuala Lumpur: University of Malaya Press, 2011).

Fu, Lo-Shu, *A documentary chronicle of Sino-Western relations (1644–1820)*, (Tucson: University of Arizona Press, 1966).

Fujita Kayoko (ed.), *Asian Empires and Maritime Contacts before the Age of Commerce.* 2009–2011, JSPS Grants-in-Aid for Scientific Research (B) No. 90454983, Empires, Systems, and Maritime Networks: Reconstructing Supra-Regional Histories in Pre-19th Century Asia, Working Paper Series 1 (Osaka, 2010).

Fujita Motoharu 藤田元春, "Chukai zuhen Nihon kōro kō (1)" 籌海圖編日本航路考 (一). *Jikyū* 地球 24:2 (1935), 135–145.

Fujita Motoharu 藤田元春, "Chukai zuhen Nihon kōro kō (2): tsuke gōresu kō" 籌海圖編日本航路考(二)： 附ゴーレス考. *Jikyū* 地球 24:6 (1935), 439–452.

Fujita Tatsuo 藤田達生, *Hideyoshi to kaizoku daimyō: umi kara mita sengoku shūen* 秀吉と海賊大名： 海から見た戦国終焉 (Tōkyō: Chūkō shinsho, 2012).

Furth, Charlotte, "The Physician as Philosopher of the Way: Zhu Zhenheng (1282–1358)," *Harvard Journal of Asiatic Studies* 66:2 (2006), 423–59.

Gaastra, Femme S., and Jaap R. Bruijn, "The Dutch East India Company's Shipping, 1602–1795, in a comparative perspective", in F. Gaastra and J. R. Bruijn (eds.), *Ships, Sailors and Spices. East India Companies and Their Shipping in the 16th, 17th and 18th century* (Amsterdam: NEHA, 1993), 177–208.

Gabriel, Richard A., *Between Flesh and Steel: A History of Military Medicine from the Middle Ages to the War in Afghanistan* (Washington: Potomac Books, 2013).

Galeote Pereira, Galeote and da Cruz, Gaspar, *South China in the Sixteenth Century: Being the Narratives of Galeote Pereira, Fr. Gaspar Da Cruz, O.P. [and] Fr. Martín de Rada, O.E.S.A. (1550–1575)* (Hakluyt Society, 1953).

Gao Rongsheng 高榮盛, "Yuandai 'wokou' lun" 元代"倭寇"論, in: *Yuanshi qianshi* 元史淺識 (Nanjing: Fenghuang chubanshe, 2010), 247–266.

Gao Rongsheng 高榮盛, *Yuandai haiwai maoyi yanjiu* 元代海外貿易研究 (Chengdu: Sichuan renmin chubanshe, 1998).

Geiss, James, "The Chia-ching Reign, 1522–1566", in Frederick W. Mote and Denis Twitchett (eds.), *The Cambridge History of China, Vol. 7, The Ming Dynasty, 1368–1644, Part 1* (Cambridge: Cambridge University Press, 2008), 490–510.

Geltner, G., "In the Camp and on the March: Military Manuals as sources for Studying Premodern Public Health", *Medical History* 63:1 (2019), 44–60.

Gemelli Careri, Giovanni Francesco, *Giro del mondo del Dottor Don Gio. Francesco Gemelli Careri* (Napoli: 1699–1700), 6 vols.

Gil, Juan, *Hidalgos y samurais. España y Japón en los siglos XVI y XVII* (Madrid: Alianza Editorial, 1991).

Gil, Juan, *Los chinos en Manila* (Lisboa: Centro Científico e Cultural de Macau, 2011).

Gipouloux, François, *La Méditerranée asiatique, villes portuaires et réseaux marchands en Chine, au Japon et en Asie du Sud-est, XVIe-XXIe siècle* (Paris: CNRS, 2009).

Go, Bon Juan, "Ma-I in Chinese Records – Mindoro or Bai? An Examination of a Historical Puzzle", *Philippine Studies* 53/1 (2005), 119–38.

Goddio, F., Crick, M., Lam, P. Pierson, S. and Scott, R., *Lost at Sea: the strange route of the Lena Shoals junk* (London: Periplus Publishing, 2002).

Gommans, Jos *et al* (eds.), *Grote Atlas van de Verenigde Oost-Indische Compagnie* (Voorburg: Atlas Maior, 2010), vol. 7.

Goodman, Grant K., *Japan: the Dutch Experience* (London and Dover: Athlone Press, 1986).

Goodrich, L. Carrington and Chaoying Fang (eds.), *Dictionary of Ming Biography. 1368–1644* (New York and London: Columbia University Press, 1976).

Green, Thomas A. and Joseph R. Svinth, (eds.), *Martial Arts of the World: An Encyclopedia of History and Innovation* (Santa Barbara/Denver/Oxford: ABC-CLIO, 2010), Vol. 1.

Gu Cheng顧誠, *Yinni de jiangtu: weisuozhi yu Ming diguo* 隱匿的疆土：衛所制度與明帝國(Beijing: Guangming ribao chubanshe, 2012).

Gu Sili 顧嗣立 (ed.), *Yuanshi xuan chuji* 元詩選初集 (Beijing: Zhonghua shuju, 1987).

Guida, Donatella, "Ming Images of Nanyang. Some Stories from *Haiyu* (Words of the Sea) [1536]". *Annali / Università Degli Studi Di Napoli l'Orientale* 54 (1994), 389–399.

Guo Yunjing, "Views of Japan and Policies Toward Japan in the Early Qing", in Joshua Fogel (ed.), *Sagacious Monks and Bloodthirsty Warriors: Chinese Views of Japan in the Ming-Qing Period* (Norwalk: EastBridge, 2002), 88–108.

Guo Yusheng 郭育生, and Liu Yijie 劉義杰. "*Dongxiyang hanghai tu* chengtu shijian chutan" 《東西洋航海圖》成圖時間初探. *Haijiaoshi yanjiu* 海交史研究 2 (2011), 67–81.

Guo, Zhaojiang, "Chinese Confucian Culture and the Medical Ethical Tradition," *Journal of Medical Ethics* 21 (1995), 239–246.

Guy, John, "China in India: Porcelain trade and attitudes in collecting in early Islamic India", in Geoff Wade, James K. Chin (eds.), *China and Southeast Asia: Historical Interactions* (London, New York: Routledge, 2019), 44–84.

Habib, Irfan, *Essays in Indian History: Towards a Marxist Perception*, (New Delhi: Tulika, 1995).

Haijun haiyang cehui yanjiusuo 海軍海洋測繪研究所 and Dalian haiyun xueyuan hanghaishi yanjiushi 大連海運學院航海史研究室 (eds.), *Xinbian Zheng He hanghaitu ji* 新編鄭和航海圖集 (Beijing: Renmin jiaotong chubanshe, 1988).

Hall, John Whitney (ed.), *The Cambridge History of Japan*. Vol. 4: *Early Modern Japan* (Cambridge: Cambridge University Press, 1991).

Hall, K.R., "Revisionist study of Cross-Cultural Commercial Competition on the Vietnamese coastline in the fourteenth and fifteenth centuries and its wider implications", *Journal of World History* 24:1 (2013), 71–105.

Han Yi 韩毅, *Zhengfu zhili yu yixue fazhan Songdai yishi zhaoling yanjiu* 政府治理與醫學發 展:宋代醫事詔令研究 (Beijing: Zhongguo kexue jishu shubanshe, 2014).

Hanson Marta, *Inventing a Tradition in Chinese Medicine: From Universal Canon to Local Medical Knowledge in South China, the Seventeenth to the Nineteenth Century* (University of Pennsylvania, 1997).

Hanson, Marta, *Speaking of Epidemics in Chinese Medicine: Disease and the Geographic Imagination in Late Imperial China.* (Oxon: Routledge, 2011).

Hasegawa, Masato, *Provisions and Profits in a Wartime Borderland – Supply Lines and Society in the Border Region between China and Korea 1592–1644.* PhD thesis (Yale University 2013).

Hasegawa, Masato, "War, Supply Lines, and Society in the Sino-Korean Borderland of the Late Sixteenth Century", *Late Imperial China* 37:1 (June 2016), 109–152.

He Guanbiao 何冠彪, "Qianlong chao chongxiu Liao Jin Yuan sanshi pouxi" 乾隆朝重修遼、金、元三史剖析, *Menggu xue xinxi* 蒙古學信息 1 (1997), 26–34.

Heibonsha 平凡社, (ed.), *Nihon shi daijiten* 日本史大事典 (Tokyo: Heibonsha, 1994).

Heizmann, Charles L., "Military Sanitation in the Sixteenth, Seventeenth, Eighteenth Century", *Annals of Medical History* 1 (1917–1918), 281–300.

Hervouet, Yves, *A Sung Bibliography* (Hong Kong: The Chinese University Press, 1978).

Hesselink, Reinier H. and Matsui Yôko, "'Sakoku', or Japan "Closed Off" from the World. A new stage: the second half of the seventeenth century", in Blussé *et al.* (2000), 33–53.

Hesselink, Reinier H., "A Metal Dealer and Spy from Nagasaki in Manila in the First Quarter of the Seventeenth Century", in Jane Kate Leonard and Ulrich Theobald (eds.), *Money in Asia (1200–1900): Small Currencies in Social and Political Contexts* (Leiden: Brill, 2015), 489–510.

Heywood, Colin, "Microhistory / Maritime History: Aspects of British Presence in the Western Mediterranean in the Early Modern Period", In: B. Heyberger and A. Fuess (eds.), *La frontière méditerranéenne du XVe au XVIIe siècle: échanges, circulations et affrontements* (Turnhout: Brepols, 2014), 82–111.

Higgins, Roland L., *Piracy and Coastal Defense in the Ming Period, Government Response to Coastal Disturbances, 1523–1549.* PhD thesis (University of Minnesota, 1981).

Higgins, Roland L., "Pirates in Gowns and Caps: Gentry Law-breaking in the Mid-Ming", *Ming Studies* 1 (1980), 30–37.

Hinrichs, T. J. "Governance Through Medical Texts and the Role of Print," in Lucille Chia and Hilde De Weerdt (eds.), *Knowledge and Text Production in an Age of Print: China, 900–1400* (Leiden: Brill, 2011), 215–238.

Hirth, Frederick and Rockhill, W. W. (trans.), *Chau Ju-kua: His Work on the Chinese and Arab Trade in the Twelfth and Thirteenth Centuries, Entitled* Chu-fan-chi (St. Petersburg: Imperial Academy of Sciences, 1911; reprinted: Taibei: Ch'eng-wen Publishing Company, 1971).

Ho, Yi Kai (ed.), *Science in China, 1600–1900: essays by Benjamin A. Elman* (Hackensack, NJ: World Century Publishing and Singapore: World Scientific Publishing, 2015).

Hoang Anh Tuan, *The Dutch East India Company in Tonkin: Political and Commercial Relations, 1637–1700*, Tanap Monograph Series No. 6 (Leiden: Brill, 2007).

Hokkoku Ryōsei 北国諒星, *Kitamae bune, saredo Kitamaebune, Roman, Goshō Mitsuboeki* 北前船、されど北前船：　浪漫・豪商・密貿易 (Sapporo: Hokkaido Shuppan Center, 2017).

Höllman, Thomas O., *The Land of the Five Flavors: A Cultural History of Chinese Cuisine* (New York: Columbia University Press, 2010).

Hong Fuzhong 洪富忠 and Wang Liyuan 汪丽媛, "Yuanchao haijin chutan" 元朝海禁初探, *Qiannan minzu shifan xueyuan xuebao* 黔南民族师范学院学报 5 (2003), 59–63.

Horridge, G. A., *The lashed-lug boat of the eastern archipelagoes, The Alcina MS and the Lomblem whaling boats. Maritime Monographs and Reports* (London: Trustees of the National Maritime Museum, 1982).

Hostetler, Laura, *Qing Colonial Enterprise. Ethnography and Cartography in Early Modern China* (Chicago: University of Chicago Press, 2001).

Huang, Ray, "Military expenditures in Sixteenth Century China", *Oriens Extremus* 17:1/2 (1970), 39–62.

Huang, Ray, *1587, A Year of No Significance – The Ming Dynasty in Decline* (New Haven and London: Yale University Press, 1981).

Huang Runhua 黃潤華 and Xue Ying 薛英 (eds.), *Guojia tushuguan zang Liuqiu ziliao huibian* 國家圖書館藏琉球資料匯編 (Beijing: Beijing chubanshe, 2000).

Hucker, Charles O., *A Dictionary of Official Titles in Imperial China* Taiwan Edition, (Taipei: Southern Materials Center Inc., 1985).

Hucker, Charles O., *A Dictionary of Official Titles in Imperial China* (Taibei: Southern Materials Center, Inc., 1988).

Hummel, Arthur W. (ed.). *Eminent Chinese of the Ch'ing Period (1644–1912)* (Washington: US Government Print, 1943).

Hummel, Arthur W., *Eminent Chinese of the Ch'ing Period.* 2 vols. (Taiwan: SMC Publishing, 1991), 2 vols.

Hussain, Ruquia Kazim, *Armenian, Iranian and Turkish Merchants in India 1550*–1800, Aligarh Muslim University (Ph.D) – 2005 (supervisor Shireen Mosvi). Unpublished PhD. thesis.

Iaccarino, Ubaldo, "The Macao-Manila Route under the Iberian Union", *Review of Culture, International Edition*, Instituto Cultural do Governo da Região Administrativa Especial de Macau, 60 (2019), 104–123.

Iaccarino, Ubaldo, *Comercio y diplomacia entre Japón y Filipinas en la era Keichō (1596–1615)* [East Asian Maritime History, 13] (Wiesbaden: Harrassowitz Verlag, 2017).

Igawa Kenji, "At the Crossroads: Limahon and Wakō in Sixteenth-Century Japan", in Robert J. Antony (ed.), *Elusive Pirates, Pervasive Smugglers. Violence and Clandestine Trade in the Greater China Seas* (Hong Kong: Hong Kong University Press, 2010), 73–84.

Iioka Naoko, *Literati Entrepreneur: Wei Zhiyan in the Tonkin-Nagasaki Silk Trade*. PhD thesis (Singapore: National Singapore University 2009).

Inoue Kiyoshi 井上清, *Riben lishi* 日本歴史, translated by Tianjin shi lishi yanjiu suo 天津市歴史研究所 (Tianjin: Tianjin renmin chubanshe, 1974).

Inoue Susumu 井上進, *Chūgoku shuppan bunka-shi – shomotsu sekai to chi no fūkei* 中国出 版文化史: 書物世界と知の風景 (Nagoya: Nagoya University Press, 2002).

Ishihara Michihiro 石原道博, *Kokusen'ya* 國姓爺 (Tōkyō: Yoshikawa kōbunkan, 1959).

Ishihara Michihiro 石原道博, *Minmatsu Shinsho Nihon kisshi no kenkyū* 明末清初日本乞師の研究 (Tōkyō: Fuzanbō, 1945).

Ishihara Michihiro 石原道博, *Shu Shunsui* 朱舜水 (Tōkyō: Yoshikawa kōbunkan, 1961).

Ishii, Yoneo, *The Junk Trade from Southeast Asia, translations from the Tosen Fusetsu-gaki, 1674–1723* (Singapore: ISEAS, 1998).

Ivermee, Robert, *Hooghly: The Global History of a River* (Oxford: Oxford University Press, 2020).

Iwao Seiichi 岩生成一, "Li Tan. Chief of the Chinese Residents at Hirado. Japan in the Last Days of the Ming Dynasty", *Memoirs of the Research Department of the Tōyō Bunko* 17 (1958), 27–83.

Iwao Seiichi 岩生成一, *Nanyō Nihonmachi no kenkyū* 南洋日本町の研究 (Tōkyō: Nan-A bunka kenkyūjo, 1940).

Iwao Seiichi 岩生成一, *Shuinsen bōekishi no kenkyū* 朱印船貿易史の研究 (Tōkyō: Kōbundō, 1958).

Iwao Seiichi 岩生成一, *Shuinsen to Nihon machi* 朱印船と日本町 (Tōkyō: Shibundō, 1962).

Iwao Seiichi, "Japanese Foreign Trade in the 16th and 17th Centuries", *Acta Asiatica* 30 (1976), 1–18.

Iwao Seiichi岩生成一, *Nan'yō Nihonmachi no kenkyū* 南洋日本町の研究 (Tōkyō: Iwanami shoten 1966).

Ji Shan 祁山, "Jixiao xinshu chuanru Chaoxian bandao de beijing ji yingxiang ji 紀效新書傳入朝鮮半島的背景及影響, *Shandong qingnian zhengzhi xueyuan xuebao* 山東青年政治學院學報 29:165 (2013), 137–140.

Jin Xin 金鑫, Qianlong chao gaiding Liao Jin Yuan sanshi yiming tanxi 乾隆改定遼金元三史譯名探析. *Manyu yanjiu* 滿語研究1 (2009), 58–62.

Kamiya Nobuyuki 紙屋敦之 and Kimura Naoya 木村直也, *Kaikin to sakoku* 海禁と鎖国 [Nihon Rekishi 日本歴史 14] (Tōkyō: Tōkyōdō shuppansha, 2002).

Kanbe Teruo 神戸輝夫, "Tei Shunkō cho *Nihon ikkan* ni tsuite (sei). *Fukai zukyō* to *Zettō shinpen*" 鄭舜功著『日本一鑑』について（正）:「ふ海図経」と「絶島新編」. *Ōita daigaku kyōiku fukushi kagakubu kenkyū kiyō* 大分大学教育福祉科学部研究紀要 22:1 (2000), 15–31.

Kanbe Teruo 神戸輝夫, "Tei Shunkō to Shō Shū. Ōtomo Sōrin to atta futari no Minjin" 鄭舜功と蒋洲:大友宗麟と会った二人の明人. *Ōita daigaku kyōiku fukushi kagakubu kenkyū kiyō* 大分大学教育福祉科学部研究紀要 21:2 (1999), 109–124.

Kato Eiichi 加藤栄一 and Yamada Tadao 山田忠雄, *Sakoku* 鎖國 (Tōkyō: Yūhikaku, 1981).

Kawakatsu Mamoru 川勝守, *Nihon kinsei to Higashi Ajia sekai* 日本近世と東アジア世界 (Tōkyō: Yoshikawa kōbunkan, 2000).

Kessler, Lawrence D., *K'ang-hsi and the Consolidation of Ch'ing Rule, 1661–1684* (Chicago and London: University of Chicago Press, 1976).

Kikuchi Seiichi 菊池誠一, "Betonamu kaiiki no chinbotsusen" ベトナム海域の沈没船, in Kikuchi Seiichi 菊池誠一, Abe Yuriko 阿部百里子 (eds.), *Umi no michi to kōkogaku: Indoshina hantō kara Nippon e* 海の道と考古学: インドシナ半島から日本へ (Tōkyō: Koshi shoin, 2010), 127–138.

Kikuchi Seiichi 菊池誠一, Abe Yuriko 阿部百里子 (eds.), *Umi no michi to kōkogaku: Indoshina hantō kara Nippon e* 海の道と考古学: インドシナ半島から日本へ (Tōkyō: Koshi shoin, 2010).

Kimura, J. and Pollack, J., "Preliminarily study on Van Don: Lost ports and lost fleets in northern Vietnam", in Tan (2015), 385–393.

Kimura, J., Staniforth, M., Le, T. L., and Sasaki, R., "Naval battlefield archaeology of the Lost Kublai Khan Fleets", *The International Journal of Nautical Archaeology* 43:1 (2014), 76–86.

Kishi Toshihiko 貴志俊彦, Arano Yasunori 荒野泰典, and Kokaze Hidemasa 小風秀雅, *Higashi Ajia no jidaisei* 東アジアの時代性 (Hiroshima: Keisuisha, 2005).

Ku, Hong Sung, "Ming dynasty maritime provisions transport during the second stage of the East Asian War (1597–98)", *Chinese Studies in History* 52:1 (2019): The East Asian War of 1592–98: International Perspectives, 42–58.

Kuiper, Koos "The Chinese Name for "Holland" : 和兰，荷兰，贺兰 – A Historical Survey", in Xu Quansheng and Liu Zhen (2014).

Lacsina, L., "The Butuan Boats of the Philippines: Southeast Asian edge-joined and lashed-lug watercraft", *Journal of the Australasian Institute for Maritime Archaeology* 39 (2015), 126–132.

Le, T.L., Dinh, T.N., Sheppard, R., Briles, C., O'Toole, P., Kimura, K., and Staniforth, M., *Recent research into the ancient port of Van Don.* Proceedings of *the second SEAMEO SPAFA International Conference on Southeast Asian Archaeology* (Bangkok: SEAMEO SPAFA Regional Centre for Archaeology and Fine Arts, 2017).

Lee, Hua-yen, "Military Reform Around Beijing from the Longqing to the Early Wanli Era (1567–1583)", *Tsinghua Journal of Chinese Studies* 52:3 (2022), 471–506.

Lee Yu-chung 李毓中, José Luis Caño Ortigosa, "Conociendo China: Investigación del Mapa Topográfico Moderno y Antiguo de la Dinastía Ming (*Ku Chin Hsing Sheng Chih Tu*) obtenido por los españoles en 1574", in Lee Yu-chung and José Luis Caño Ortigosa (eds.), 《古今形勝之圖》研究*Estudio del mapa "Ku Chin Hsing Sheng Chih Tu"* (Madrid: Ministerio de Educación, Cultura y Deporte, 2016), 65–89.

Leemhuis, Fiorella, "Gli Olandesi a Deshima", *Il Giappone* 11 (1971), 63–84.

Lequin, Frank, *Isaac Titsingh in China: het Onuitgegeven Journaal van Zijn Ambassade naar Peking 1794–1796* (Alphen aan Den Rijn: Canaletto/Repro-Holland, 2005).

LeRoy Innes, Robert, *The Door Ajar: Japan's Foreign Trade in the Seventeenth Century*. PhD thesis (Ann Arbor: University of Michigan, 1980).

Leung, Angela Ki Che, "Medical Instruction and Popularization in Ming-Qing China," *Late Imperial China* 24:1 (2003), 130–152.

Leung, Angela Ki Che, *Leprosy in China: A History* (Columbia University Press, 2012).

Li Bozhong 李伯重, "Duotai biyun yu jueyu Song Yuan Ming Qing shiqi Jiangzhe diqu de jieyu fangfa jiqi yunyong yu chuanbo" 墮胎、避孕與絕育:宋元明清時期江浙地區的 節育方法及其運用與傳播, *Zhongguo xueshu* 中國學術 1 (2000), 71–99.

Li Bozhong, "Was There a 'Fourteenth-Century Turning Point'? Population, Land, Technology and Farm Management", in Smith and von Glahn (2003), 135–175.

Li Guoxiang 李國祥 and Yang Chang 楊昶, eds., *Mingshilu leizuan: ziran zaiyi juan* 明實錄類纂: 自然災异卷 (Wuhan: Wuhan Press, 1997).

Li Hongtao 李鴻濤 and Zhang Huamin 張華敏, *Guben yiji xuluji* 古本醫籍敘錄集 (Beijing: Zhongyi guji chubanshe, 2016).

Li Jingwei 李經緯, "Beisong huangdi yu yixue" 北宋皇帝與醫學, *Zhongguo keji shiliao* 中國科技史料10:3 (1989), 3–20.

Li Jingwei 李經緯, Lin Zhaogeng 林昭庚, *Zhongguo yixue tongshi* 中國醫學通史 (Beijing: Renmin weisheng chubanshe, 1999).

Li Jinming 李金明, *Mingdai haiwai maoyi shi* 明代海外贸易史 (Xiamen: Zhongguo shehui kexue chubanshe, 1990).

Li Kangying 李康英, *The Ming Maritime Trade Policy in Transition, 1368 to 1567* (Wiesbaden: Harrassowitz, 2010).

Li Kangying, *The Ming Maritime Trade Policy in Transition, 1368–1567* [East Asian Maritime History, 8] (Wiesbaden, Otto Harrassowitz, 2010).

Li Qingxin 李庆新, *Mingdai haiwai maoyi zhidu* 明代海外贸易制度 (Beijing: Shehui kexue wenxian chubanshe, 2007).

Li Tianshu 李天舒, *Bei Song Xu Dong "Huqian Jing" yanjiu* 北宋許洞《虎鈐經》研究. PhD thesis (Zhengzhou daxue, 2017).

Li Zhi'an 李治安, "Yuandai ji Ming qianqi shehui biandong chutan" 元代及明前期社會變動初探, *Zhongguo shi yanjiu* 中國史研究, special issue (2005), 83–98.

Li Zigui 李子歸, "Mingdai Jianyang de shuhu yu shufang" 明代建陽的書戶與書坊, *Xianggang Zhongwen daxue Zhongguo wenhua yanjiusuo xuebao* 香港中文大學中國文化研究所學報 66 (2018), 23–45.

Li, Tana, "Jiaozhi (Giao Chi) in the Han period – Tongking Gulf", in J. Anderson (2012), 39–52.

Liang Qizi 梁其姿, *Miandui jibing: chuantong Zhongguo shehui de yiliao guannian yu zuzhi* 面对疾病： 傳統中國社會的醫療觀念與組織 (Beijing: Renmin daxue chubanshe, 2012).

Liebner, Horst Hubertus, *The Siren of Cirebon: A Tenth-Century Trading Vessel Lost in the Java Sea*. PhD thesis (University of Leeds, 2014).

Lim, Ivy Maria, *Lineage Society on the Southeastern Coast of China. The Impact of Japanese Piracy in the 16th Century* (New York: Cambria, 2010).

Lim, Ivy Maria, "Qi Jiguang and Hu Zongxian's Anti-wokou Campaign", in Y.H. Teddy Sim, *The Maritime Defence of China: Ming General Qi Jiguang and Beyond* (Singapore: Springer Nature, 2017), 23–42.

Lin Meicun 林梅村, "*Zheng Zhilong hanghai tu* kao. Niujin daxue Bodeli tushuguan cang *Xueerdeng Zhongguo ditu* mingshi bian" 《鄭芝龍航海圖》考. 牛津大學博德利圖書館藏《雪爾登中國地圖》名實辯. *Wenwu* 文物 9 (2013), 64–82.

Lin Renchuan 林仁川, "Fukien's private sea trade in the 16th and 17th centuries", in Eduard B. Vermeer (ed.), *Development and Decline of Fukien Province in the 17th and 18th Centuries* (Leiden: Brill, 1990), 163–215.

Lin Renchuan 林仁川, *Mingmo Qingchu siren haishang maoyi* 明末清初私人海上貿易 (Shanghai: Huadong shifan daxue chubanshe, Xinhua shudian Shanghai faxingsuo faxing, 1987).

Lin, Yan, "Going Global" of Chinese Local Dietary Culture: A Case Study of Traditional Special Snacks Translation", *Journal of Education, Humanities and Social Sciences* 1, 353–359 (https://doi.org/10.54097/ehss.v1i1.683).

Lin Yinglin 林應麟, *Fujian shuyeshi jianben fazhan guijikao* 福建書業史——建本發展軌跡 考 (Xiamen: Lujiang chubanshe, 2004).

Liu Hsü-feng (Liu Xufeng) 劉序楓, "Qing Kangxi~Qianlong nianjian yangtong de jinkou yu liutong wenti 清康熙~乾隆年間洋銅的進口與流通問題", in T'ang Hsi-yung 湯熙勇 (ed.), *Zhongguo haiyang fazhan shilun wenji* 中國海羊發展史論文集, vol. 7, *j*. shang (Taibei: Zhongyang yanjiuyuan, 1999), 93–144.

Liu Shufen, "Jiankang and the Commercial Empire of the Southern Dynasties: Change and Continuity in Medieval Chinese Economic History", in Scott Pearce, Audrey Spiro, and Patricia Ebrey (eds.), *Culture and Power in the Reconstitution of the Chinese Realm, 200–600* (Cambridge and London: Harvard University Asia Center, 2001), 35–52.

Liu Xufeng [Liu Shufeng] 劉序楓 (ed.), *Yazhou haiyujian de xinxi chuandi yu xianghu renshi* 亞洲海域間的訊息傳遞與相互認識 (Taibei: Academia Sinica RCHSS, 2018).

Liu Yijie 劉義傑 and Wang Ningjun 王寧軍, "Haidao zhenjing shulun" 海道針經述論. *Guojia hanghai* 國家航海 14 (2016), 52–63.

Lo Jung-pang, "Maritime Commerce and its Relation to the Sung Navy", *Journal of the Economic and Social History of the Orient* 12 (1969), 57–101.

Lo Jung-pang, *China as a Sea Power, 1127–1368: A Preliminary Survey of the Maritime Expansion and Naval Exploits of the Chinese People during the Southern Sung and Yuan Periods*, Bruce Elleman (ed.), (Hong Kong: Hong Kong University Press, 2012).

Lo Jung-pang, *China as a Sea Power, 1127–1368: A Preliminary Survey of the Maritime Expansion and Naval Exploits of the Chinese People During the Southern Song and Yuan Periods*, edited by Bruce A. Elleman (Singapore: National University of Singapore Press, 2011).

Lorge, Peter, "Water Forces and Naval Operations", in David A. Graff and Robin Higham (eds.), *A Military History of China* (Kentucky: University Press of Kentucky, 2012).

Lu Zhouxiang, *Politics and Identity in Chinese Martial Arts* (New York/Oxford: Routledge, 2018).

Ma Guang, "Re-evaluating the *Wokou* Problem in East Asia During the 1220s and 1390s from the Perspective of Environmental History", *Journal of Asian History* 54:2 (2020), 261–280.

Makoto Mayanagi 真柳誠, "Nikkan'etsu no igaku to Chūgoku isho" 日韓越の医学と中国医書, *Nihon ishigaku zasshi* 56:2 (2010), 151–59.

Manguin, Pierre-Yves, "Trading ships of the South China Sea: Shipbuilding Techniques and their Role in the Development of Asian Trade Networks", *Journal of the Economic and Social History of the Orient* 36 (1993), 253–280.

Marx, Karl, *Capital. A Critique of Political Economy* (London: Lawrence & Wishart, 1959), Books I, II and III.

Massarella, Derek, *A World Elsewhere. Europe's Encounter with Japan in the Sixteenth and Seventeenth Centuries* (New Haven and London: Yale University Press, 1990).

Masuda Wataru. *Japan and China. Mutual Representations in the Modern Era*. Joshua A. Fogel (trans.) (New York: St. Martin's Press, 2000).

Matsukata Fuyuko 松方冬子, "From the Threat of Roman Catholicism to the Shadow of Western Imperialism: Changing Trends in Dutch News Reports Issued to the Tokugawa *Bakufu*, 1690–1817", in Nagazumi Yōko (ed.), *Large and Broad. The Dutch Impact on Early Modern Asia. Essays in Honor of Leonard Blussé* (Tōkyō: Tōyō bunkō, 2010), 130–146.

Matsukata Fuyuko 松方冬子, *Oranda fūsetsugaki to kinsei Nihon* オランダ風説書と近世日本 (Tōkyō: Tōkyō daigaku shuppansha, 2007).

McDermott, Joseph P., *A Social History of the Chinese Book: Books and Literati Culture in Late Imperial China* (Hong Kong University Press, 2006).

Mills, J. V. G., "Arab and Chinese Navigators in Malaysian Waters in about A.D. 1500". *Journal of the Malaysian Branch of the Royal Asiatic Society* 47:2 (226) (1974), 1–82.

Mills, J. V. G., "Chinese Navigators in Insulinde about A.D. 1500", *Archipel* 18:1 (1979), 69–93.

Mills, J. V. G., *Ma Huan. Ying-Yai Sheng-Lan. The Overall Survey of the Ocean's Shores* [*1433*] (Cambridge: University Press, 1970).

Min Zongdian 閔宗殿, "Ming Qing shiqi dongnan diqu yiqing yanjiu" 明清時期東南地區疫 情研究, *Xueshu yanjiu* 學術研究 10 (2003), 109–115.

Mitsui Rokurō 満井緑郎 and Doi Shin'ichirō 土井進一郎, *Shin Nagasaki nenpyō* 新長崎年表 (Nagasaki: Nagasaki bunkensha, 1974).

Momoki, Shiro, "Dai Viet and the South China Sea Trade: from the 10th to the 15th century", *Crossroads: An Interdisciplinary Journal of Southeast Asian Studies*. 12:1 (1998), 1–34.

Momoki, Shiro 桃木至朗, "Vietnam hokubu to kitachuubu ni okeru minatoshi no ichi" ベトナム北部・中北部の港湾都市の位置, in Murai Shōsuke 村井章介 (eds.), *Rekishigaku kenkyukai* 歴史学研究会 (2005), 179–205.

Mosca, Matthew, *From Frontier Policy to Foreign Policy: The Question of India and the Transformation of Geopolitics in Qing China*, (Stanford: Stanford University Press, 2013).

Mukai Masaki 向正樹, "The Interests of the Rulers, Agents and Merchants Behind the Southward Expansion of the Yuan Dynasty", *Journal of the Turfan Studies: Essays on The Third International Conference on Turfan Studies, The Origins and Migrations of Eurasian Nomadic Peoples* (Shanghai: Shanghai guji chubanshe, 2010), 428–45.

Mukai Masaki, "Contacts between Empires and Entrepots and the Role of Supra-regional Network: Song-Yuan-Ming Transition of the Maritime Asia 960–1405", in *Empire, Systems, and Maritime Networks: Reconsidering Supra-regional Histories in Prenineteenth Century Asia Working Paper Series* (2010), 1–24.

Murakami Naojirō 村上直次郎 (ed.), *Ikoku ōfuku shokanshū, Zōtei ikoku nikki shō* 異国往復書翰集・増訂異国日記抄 (Tōkyō: Omatsudō shoten, 1966).

Murdoch, J. and Yamagata I., *A History of Japan*, 3 vols. (New York: Greenberg, 1926).

Na, Youngil, "The Future of Asian Traditional Martial Arts", *The International Journal of the History of Sport* 33:9 (2016), 893–903.

Nagasaki kenshi 長崎県史 (*Hanseihen* 藩政編) (Tōkyō: Yoshikawa Kōbunkan, 1973).

Nagasaki kenshi 長崎県史 (*Kōshōhen* 交渉編) (Tōkyō: Yoshikawa Kōbunkan, 1985).

Nagazumi Yōko 永積洋子, *Kinsei shoki no gaikō* 近世初期の外交 (Tōkyō: Sobunsha, 1990).

Nagazumi Yōko 永積洋子, *Shuinsen* 朱印船 (Tōkyō: Nihon rekishi kaikan, 2001).

Nagazumi Yōko 永積洋子, *Shuinsen* 朱印船 (Tōkyō: Yoshikawa kōbunkan, 2001).

Nagazumi Yōko 永積洋子, *Tōsen yūnyū shutsuhin suryō ichiran 1633–1685* 唐船輸入出品数量一覧一六三三 ~ 一六八五 (Tōkyō: Sobunsha, 1988).

Nagazumi Yōko 永積洋子 *Sakoku wo minaosu* 鎖国を見直す, *Kokusai bunka kōryū shuishin kyōkai* 國際交流国際文化交流推進協会 (Tōkyō: Yamakawa shuppansha, 1992).

Nagazumi Yōko, "From Company to Individual Company Servants: Dutch Trade in Eighteenth-century Japan", in Leonard Blussé and Femme S. Gaastra (eds.), *On the Eighteenth Century as a Category of Asian History. Van Leur in Retrospect* (Aldershot: Ashgate, 1998), 147–172.

Nagazumi Yōko, "The Japanese Go-shuinjo (Vermilion Seal) Maritime Trade in Taiwan", in Leonard Blussé (ed.), *Around and about Formosa* (Taipei: Ts'ao Yung-ho Foundation for Culture and Education, 2003), 27–41.

Nakajima Gakushō 中島楽章, "Jūroku seiki matsu no Fukken – Firipin – Kyūshū bōeki 十六世紀末の福建ーフィリピンー九州貿易", *Shien* 史淵 144 (2007), 55–92.

Nakajima Gakushō, "17 shiji chu Kyushu zhongbu haigang yu Minnan haishang wanglu: Higo diyu zhi Mingren mu yu Tangren ting" 17世紀初九州中部海港與閩南海商網路：肥後地域之明人墓與唐人町, in Zhu Delan朱德蘭 (ed.), Disi jie guoji hanxue huiyi: kuayue haiyang de jiaohuan第四屆國際漢學會議：跨越海洋的交換, Fourth International Conference on Sinology: The Transoceanic Exchange, 論文集 Book of Abstracts (Taipei: 人文社會科學研究中心, Academia Sinica, 2012), 1–24.

Nakamura Kōya 中村孝也, *Tokugawa Ieyasu monjo no kenkyū* 徳川家康文書の研究. 4 vols. (Tōkyō: Nihon gakujutsu shinkōkai, 1958–1961).

Nakamura Tadashi 中村質, *Kinsei Nagasaki bōekishi no kenkyū* 近世長崎貿易史の研究 (Tōkyō: Yoshikawa Kōbunkan, 1988).

Nakane Chie and ōishi Shinzaburō (eds.), *Tokugawa Japan. The Social and Economic Antecedents of Modern Japan* (Tōkyō: Tōkyō University Press, 1991).

Naniek, Harkantiningsih, Sonny Chr Wibisono and John Norman Miksic, *Catalogue of the Cirebon Wreck, Sunken Treasures from the Tenth Century* (*Five Dynasties or Early Northern Song*), National Committee for Salvage and Utilization of Valuable Objects from Sunken Ships (PANNAS BMKT, 2010).

Needham, Joseph, *Science and Civilisation in China. Vol. 4. Physics and Physical Technology. Part I: Physics* (Cambridge: Cambridge University Press, 1962).

Needham, Joseph, *Science and Civilisation in China. Vol. 4. Physics and Physical Technology. Part III: Civil Engineering and Nautics* (Cambridge: Cambridge University Press, 1971).

Needham, Joseph, *Science and Civilisation in China. Vol. 6. Biology and Biological Technology. Part V: Fermentations and Food Science* [by H.T. Huang] (Cambridge: Cambridge University Press, 2000).

Ng, Chin-keong, *Trade and Society. The Amoy Network on the China Coast 1683–1735* (Singapore: National University of Singapore Press, 1983).

Nguyễn Văn Siêu 阮文超, *Phương Đình Địa Chí Loại: Đại Việt Địa Dư Toàn Biên* 方亭地志類大越地輿全篇 (Beijing: Renmin chubanshe, 2012 [1900]), vol v.

Nguyen, V. K., "Hệ thống thương cảng Vân Đồn qua các nguồn tư liệu lịch sử, điền dã và khảo cổ học (The Harbor System of Van Don as Seen through Historical and Archaeological Materials), *Khảo cổ học* (Journal of Archaeology) 4 (2006), 48–65.

Nishimura, Masanari, "Reexamination of the Lung Khê Citadel in the Red River Delta", *Southeast Asia: History and Culture* 30 (2001), 46–71.

Nishino, Noriko; Aoyama, Toru; Kimura, Jun; Nogami, Takenori; Le, Thi Lien, "Nishimura Masanari's Study on the Oldest Known Shipwreck Ever Found in Vietnam", *The Asian Review of World Histories* 5:2 (2017), 106–122.

Niwa Kankichi, *The Dutch Settlement at Dejima* (*Dejima Oranda yashiki*) (Nagasaki: Nagasaki Bunkensha s.d.).

Noordam, Barend, *The Soldier as a Sage – Qi Jiguang and the neo-Confucianization of the military in sixteenth-century China*. PhD thesis (Leiden University, 2018).

Nōson shihai no henka to gaikoku bōeki 農村支配の変化と外国貿易, *Hiradohan* 平戸藩, in *Nagasaki kenshi* 長崎県史 (*Hanseihen* 藩政編) (Tōkyō: Yoshikawa kōbunkan, 1973), 403–412.

Ōba, Osamu, "On *the Scroll of Chinese Ships* in the possession of the Matsuura Museum", *Bulletin of the Institute of Oriental and Occidental Studies, Kansai University* 5, March 1972, 13–50.

Oda Fujio小田富雄, Arikawa Yoshihiro 有川宜博, Yonezu Saburō 米汁三郎, and Kanzaki Yoshio 神崎義夫, *Kita Kyūshū no rekishi* 北九州の歴史 (Fukuoka: Ashi shobō, 1979).

Oka Mihoko 岡美穂子 and François Gipouloux, "Pooling Capital and Spreading Risk: Maritime Investment in East Asia at the beginning of the Seventeenth Century", *Itinerario* 37:3 (2013), 75–91.

Ollé Manel, "El factor europeo en la dialéctica entre comercio, contrabando y piratería en las costas de China de los siglos XVI y XVII", in Angela Schottenhammer (ed.), *Tribute, Trade, and Smuggling / Tributo, Comercio y Contrabando* [East Asian Maritime History, 12] (Wiesbaden: Harrassowitz Verlag, 2014), 55–74.

Ollé, Manel, "Manila in the Zheng Clan Maritime Networks", *Review of Culture* 29 (2009), 91–103.

Ollé, Manel, *La empresa de China. De la Armada Invencible al Galeón de Manila* (Barcelona: Acantilado, 2002).

ōta Katsuya 太田勝也, *Sakoku jidai Nagasaki bōekishi no kenkyū* 鎖国時代長崎貿易史の研究 (Kyōto: Shibunkaku shuppan, 1992).

Ōtomo Shin'ichi 大友信一 and Liu Zhenyu 刘震宇, "Nihon ikkan no banri chōka. Honyaku to oboekaki" 「日本一鑑」の「万里長歌」. 翻訳と覚え書き. *Okayama daigaku bungaku bu kiyō* 岡山大学文学部紀要 4 (1984), 83–97.

Ozawa Toshio 小澤敬夫, *Nagasaki nenpyō* 長崎年表 (Nagasaki: Guroria shobō, 1935).

Papelitzky, Elke, "An Introduction to *Siyi guangji* 四夷廣記". *Crossroads. Studies on the History of Exchange Relations in the East Asian World* 11 (2015), 85–95.

Papelitzky, Elke, "Sea Routes to Thailand Described in Chinese Texts of the Ming Dynasty". In Chinese Maritime Museum 上海中國航海博物館 (ed.), *Silu de yanshen. Yazhou haiyang lishi yu wenhua. Guoji xueshu taolunhui lunwenji* 絲路的延伸：亞洲海洋歷史與文化國際學術研討會論文集 (Shanghai: Zhongxi shuju, 2015), 249–275.

Papelitzky, Elke, "Naval warfare of the Ming Dynasty (1368–1644): A Comparison Between Chinese Military Texts and Archaeological Sources", in Rebecca O'Sullivan, Christina Marini, and Julia Binnberg (eds.), *Archaeological Approaches to Breaking Boundaries: Interaction, Integration and Division* (Oxford: BAR Publishing, 2017), 129–136.

Papelitzky, Elke, "Editing, Circulating, and Reading Huang Zhong's *Hai yu*. A Case Study in the History of Reading and the Circulation of Knowledge in Ming and Qing China", *Ming Qing Yanjiu* 23:1 (2019), 1–38.

Papelitzky, Elke, "Weapons used aboard Ming Chinese ships and some thoughts on the armament of Zheng He's fleet", *China and Asia* 1:2 (December 2019), 192–224.

Papelitzky, Elke, "Gui'an as a Centre for Writing about the World during the Late Ming Dynasty", *Monumenta Serica* 68:1 (2020), 107–135.

Papelitzky, Elke, *Writing World History in Late Ming China and the Perception of Maritime Asia* [East Asian Maritime History 15] (Wiesbaden: Harrassowitz, forthcoming 2020).

Papelitzky, Elke, "Shallow Water at China's Coast: Depicting Dangers on Early Modern Chinese Maps", *Isis* 112 (2021), 111–121.

Parmentier, Jan, "Vriend en Vijand – De Zuid-Nederlanders en de VOC tijdens de achttiende eeuw", in J. Parmentier (ed.), *Noord-Zuid in Oost-Indisch perspectief* (Zutphen: Walburg Pers, 2005), 149–166.

Parmentier, Jan, *De holle compagnie* (Hilversum: Verloren, 1992).

Parmentier, Jan, *Tea Time in Flanders: the maritime trade between the Southern Netherlands and China in the 18th century*, (Gent: Ludion, 1996).

Pelliot, Paul, "Les grands voyages maritimes chinois au début du XVe siècle". *T'oung Pao* 30:3/5 (1933), 237–452.

Peng Xinwei 彭信威, *Zhongguo huobi shi* 中國貨幣史 (Shanghai: Shanghai renmin chubanshe, 1958).

Péri, Noël, "Essai sur les relations du Japon et de l'Indochine aux XVIe et XVIIe siècles", *Bulletin de l'École française d'Extrême Orient* 23 (1923), 1–104.

Po, Ronald, *The Blue Frontier. Maritime Vision and Power in the Qing Empire* (Cambridge: Cambridge University Press, 2018).

Prakash, Om, "The European Factories in India: A Blessing or a Curse ?", in J. Everaert and J. Parmentier (eds.), *International conference on shipping, factories and colonization* (Brussel: Koninklijke academie voor overzeese wetenschappen, 1996), 13–20.

Prakash, Om, *The Dutch East-India Company and the Economy of Bengal, 1630–1720* (Princeton: Princeton University Press, 1985).

Pranghofer, Sebastian, "The Early Modern Medical-Military Complex: The Wider Context of the Relationship between Military, Medicine and the State", *Canadian Journal of History* 51:3 (2016), 451–472.

Pratt, Peter (ed.), *Materials for a history of the rise and progress of the trade to China* (British Library London: India Office Records, 1821), G/12/8.

Pratt, Peter (ed.), *Materials for a history of the rise and progress of the trade to China* (British Library London: India Office Records, 1821), G/12/24 'Diary and Consultation Book of William Fazakerley Esq.

Pratt, Peter (ed.), *Materials for a history of the rise and progress of the trade to China* (British Library London: India Office Records, 1821), G/12/27 'Diary and consultation Book of The Transactions of Peter Godfrey, Richard Newman et. Al.'

Ptak Roderich, "Ming Maritime Trade to Southeast Asia, 1368–1567: Visions of a 'System'", in Claude Guillot, Denys Lombard, and Roderich Ptak (eds.), *From the Mediterranean to the China Sea: Miscellaneous Notes* (Wiesbaden: Harrassowitz Verlag, 1998), 157–192.

Ptak Roderich, "Sino-Japanese Maritime Trade, circa 1550: Merchants, Ports and Networks", in Roberto Carneiro and A. Teodoro de Matos (eds.), *O século cristão do Japão. Actas do Colóquio Internacional Comemorativo dos 450 Anos de Amizade Portugal-Japão (1543–1993)* (Lisboa: Universidade Nova de Lisboa, 1994), 281–311.

Ptak Roderich, "The Northern Trade Route to the Spice Islands: South China Sea – Sulu Zone – North Moluccas (14th to early 16th Century)", *Archipel* 43 (1992), 27–56.

Ptak, Roderich, "Jottings on Chinese Sailing Routes to Southeast Asia, Especially on the Eastern Route in Ming Times". In Jorge Manuel dos Santos Alves (ed.), *Portugal e a China. Conferências nos encontros de história luso-chinesa*, 107–131 (Lisbon: Fundação Oriente, 2001).

Qi Chenyue 祁晨越, *Mingdai Hangzhou diqu de shuji kanyin huodong* 明代杭州地區的書籍刊印活動. PhD thesis (National University of Singapore, 2010).

Qi Gong 啟功 and Wang Jingxian 王靖憲 (eds.), *Zhongguo fatie quanji* 中國法帖全集 (Wuhan: Hubei meishu chubanshe, 2002).

Qian Jiang [James K. Chin] 錢江, "Yifu xinjin faxian de Mingchao zhong ye caihui hanghaitu" 一幅新近發現的明朝中葉彩繪航海圖. *Haijioashi yanjiu* 海交史研究 1 (2011), 1–7.

Qiu Zhonglin 邱仲麟, "Yizi yu yaoqian Mingdai de kanzhen wenhua yu minzhong de zhibing fudan" 醫資與藥錢——明代的看診文化與民眾的治病負擔, in Shengmin yiliaoshi yanjiushi 生命醫療史研究室 (ed.), *Zhongguoshi xinlun: yiliaoshi fence* 中國史新論：醫 療史分冊 (Taipei: Lianjing chuban gongsi, 2015), 337–386.

Ren Daobin 任道斌, "Mao Yuanyi shengping, zhushu chutan" 茅元儀生平、著述初探. *Mingshi yanjiu luncong* 明史研究論叢 3 (1985), 239–264.

Rhee, Wanghoon and Young-jae Kim, "Understanding Gwanghwa Dondae Forts as a Vernacular Model of Construction and Reuse", *Buildings* Vol. 12 (2022), 568, 2. (https://doi.org/10.3390/buildings12050568).

Rong Xinjiang, *Zhonggu Zhongguo yu wailai wenming*中古中国与外来文明 (Beijing: Sanlian shudian, 2011).

Rong Xinjiang 荣新江, *Sichou zhi lu yu Dongxi wenhua jiaoliu* 丝绸之路与东西文化交流 (Beijing: Beijing daxue chubanshe, 2015).

Ruangsilp, Bhawan, *Perception and Practice: The VOC and the Court Culture of Ayutthaya in the Seventeenth and Eighteenth Centuries*, Tanap Monograph Series No. 8 (Leiden: Brill, 2007).

Sadler, A. L., *The Maker of Modern Japan. The Life of Tokugawa Ieyasu* (Rutland, VT/ Tōkyō: Tuttle, 1989).

San Agustín, Gaspar de, O.S.A., *Conquistas de las Islas Filipinas (1565–1615)* Ed. by Manuel Merino, O.S.A. (Madrid: CISC, 1975).

Sansom, George, *A History of Japan*, 3 vols. (Tōkyō: Tuttle, 1987).

Santos, Gonçalo, "Technological Choices and Modern Material Civilization – Reflections on Everyday Toilet Practices in Rural South China", in Johann P. Arnason and Chris Hann (eds.), *Anthropology and Civilizational Analysis: Eurasian Explorations* (Albany: State University of New York Press, 2018), 259–280.

Satow, Ernest M. (ed.), *The voyage of captain John Saris to Japan, 1613* (London: Hakluyt Society, 1900).

Sawyer, Ralph D., *The Seven Military Classics of China* (Boulder, CO: Westview Press, 1993).

Sawyer, Ralph D., *The Tao of Deception: Unorthodox Warfare in Historic and Modern China* (New York: Basic Books, 2007).

Sawyer, Ralph D., *The Tao of Spycraft: Intelligence Theory and Practice in Traditional China* (New York: Basic Books, 2004).

Schilder, Günter (ed.), *Grote Atlas van de Verenigde Oost-Indische Compagnie.* (Voorburg: Atlas Maior, 2006), Vol. I.

Schottenhammer, Angela (ed.). *The East Asian "Mediterranean": Maritime Crossroads of Culture, Commerce and Human Migration* [East Asian Maritime History, 6] (Wiesbaden: Harrassowitz, 2008).

Schottenhammer, Angela, "'Peruvian balsam': an example of transoceanic transfer of medicinal knowledge", *Journal of Ethnobiology and Ethnomedicine* 16:69 (2020), 1–20, https://doi.org/10.1186/s13002-020-00407-y.

Schottenhammer, Angela, "Characteristics of Qing China's Maritime Trade Politics, Shunzhi through Early Qianlong reigns", in: A. Schottenhammer (ed.), *Trading Networks in Early Modern East-Asian Maritime History*, (Wiesbaden: Otto Harrassowitz, 2010), 101–154.

Schottenhammer, Angela, "Characteristics of Qing China's Maritime Trade Politics, *Shunzhi* through Early *Qianlong* Reigns", in A. S. (ed.), *Trading Networks in Early*

Modern East Asia [East Asian Maritime History, 9] (Wiesbaden: Harrassowitz, 2010), 101–154.

Schottenhammer, Angela, "China's Gate to the Indian Ocean – Iranian and Arab Long-distance Traders", *Harvard Journal of Asiatic Studies* 76:1–2 (2016), 135–179.

Schottenhammer, Angela, "China's Gate to the South: Iranian and Arab Merchant Networks in Guangzhou During the Tang-Song Transition (c.7 50–1050), Part 2: 900 – c. 1050", *AAS Working Papers in Social Anthropology/ÖAW Arbeitspapiere zur Sozialanthropologie* 29 (2015), 1–30.

Schottenhammer, Angela, "China's Increasing Integration into the Indian Ocean World Until Song 宋 Times: Sea Routes, Connections, Trades", in Angela Schottenhammer (ed.), *Early Global Interconnectivity Across the Indian Ocean World* [Palgrave Series in Indian Ocean World Studies], 2 vols. (London: Palgrave Macmillan), vol. I, *Commercial Structures and Exchanges*, 21–52.

Schottenhammer, Angela, "China's Rise and Retreat as a Maritime Power", in Robert Antony, Angela Schottenhammer (eds.), *New Discourses on China's Role in East Asian Maritime History* (Wiesbaden: Otto Harrassowitz, 2017), 189–211.

Schottenhammer, Angela, "Empire and Periphery? The Qing Empire's Relations with Japan and the Ryūkyūs (1644 – c. 1800), a Comparison", *The Medieval History Journal* 15, no .2 (2012), 139–196.

Schottenhammer, Angela, "Foreign Trade, 1000–1800", in Debin Ma, Richard von Glahn (eds.), *The Cambridge Economic History of China* (Cambridge: Cambridge University Press, 2021), forthcoming.

Schottenhammer, Angela, "Imperial Maritime China", in *Oxford Research Encyclopedia, Asian History*, https://oxfordre.com/asianhistory/view/10.1093/acrefore/9780190277727.001.0001/acrefore-9780190277727-e-209.

Schottenhammer, Angela, "Japan – the tiny Dwarf? Sino-Japanese Relations from the Kangxi to the Early Qianlong Reigns", in Angela Schottenhammer (ed.), *The East Asian Mediterranean – Maritime Crossroads of Culture, Commerce, and Human Migration* [East Asian Maritime History, 6] (Wiesbaden: Otto Harrassowitz, 2008), 331–388.

Schottenhammer, Angela, "Quanzhou's Early Overseas Trade: Local Politico – Economic Particulars During its Period of Independence", *Journal of Song-Yuan Studies* 29 (1999), 1–41.

Schottenhammer, Angela, "The Emergence of China as a Maritime Power", chapter 7 of vol. 5 of *The Cambridge History of China*, vol. 5, part Two, *The Five Dynasties and Sung China, 960–1279*, ed. by John W. Chaffee und Paul J. Smith (Cambridge: Cambridge University Press, 2014), 437–525.

Schottenhammer, Angela, "The Song 宋 Dynasty (960–1279) – A Revolutionary Era Turn?", in Kósa Gábor (ed.), *China across the Centuries* [Budapest Monographs in East Asian Studies] (Budapest: ELTE University, Department of East Asian Languages, 2017), 133–173.

Schottenhammer, Angela, *China's Historical Access to the Silk Roads and the Outside World: Role and Content* (Cambridge: Cambridge University Press, forthcoming).

Schottenhammer, Angela, *Das songzeitliche Quanzhou im Spannungsfeld zwischen Zentralregierung und maritimem Handel. Unerwartete Konsequenzen des zentralstaatlichen Zugriffs auf den Reichtum einer Küstenregion* [Münchener Ostasiatische Studien, 80] (Wiesbaden: Otto Harrassowitz, 2002).

Schreibweis, Maria, "Der Seeweg China – Ryūkyū am Beispiel des Gesandtschaftsberichts *Shi Liuqiu lu* 使琉球錄 von Chen Kan 陳侃 (1489–1538)", in Angela Schottenhammer (ed.), *Trade and Transfer Across the East Asian "Mediterranean"*, 11–74 [East Asian Maritime History 1] (Wiesbaden: Harrassowitz, 2005).

Schurmann, Franz, *Economic Structure of the Yuan Dynasty* (Cambridge, MA: Harvard-Yenching Institute, 1956).

Schurz, William Lytle, *The Manila Galleon.* (New York: Dutton, 1959).

Scott, William Henry, *Barangay. Sixteenth Century Philippine Culture and Society* (Quezon City: Ateneo de Manila University Press, 1994).

Scott, William Henry, *Filipinos in China before 1500* (Manila: China Studies Program, De La Salle University, 1989).

Seaman, Rebecca M. (ed.), *Epidemics and War: The Impact of Disease on Major Conflicts in History* (Santa Barbara CA/Denver CO: ABC-CLIO, 2018).

Sen, Tansen, "The formation of Chinese maritime networks to Southern Asia, 1200 to 1450", *Journal of the Economic and Social History of the Orient.* 49:4 (2006), 421–53.

Sen, Tansen, "The Yuan Khanate and India: Cross-Cultural Diplomacy in the Thirteenth and Fourteenth Centuries", *Asia Major*, Third Series 19 (2006), 299–326.

Sen, Tansen, "The Yuan Khanate and India: Cross-Cultural Diplomacy in the Thirteenth and Fourteenth Centuries", Asia Major, 3rd Series, 1/2:19 (2006), CHINA AT THE CROSSROADS: A FESTSCHRIFT IN HONOR OF VICTOR H. MAIR, 299–326.

Sen, Tansen, *Buddhism, Diplomacy, and Trade: The Realignment of Sino-Indian Relations, 600–1400* (Honolulu: University of Hawaii Press, 2003), 177–178.

Seno Seiichirō 瀬野精一郎, *Nagasakiken no rekishi* 長崎県の歴史 (Tōkyō: Yamakawa shuppansha, 1972).

Seyock, Barbara, "Pirates and Traders on Tsushima Island During the Late 14th to Early 16th Century: As Seen from Historical and Archaeological Perspectives". In Angela Schottenhammer (ed.), *Trade and Transfer Across the East Asian "Mediterranean"* (Wiesbaden: Harrassowitz, 2005), 91–124.

Shanghai bowuguan 上海博物館 (ed.), *Zhongguo shuhuajia yinjian kuanshi* 中國書畫家印鑒款識 (Beijing: Wenwu chubanshe, 1987).

Shen Dengmiao 沈登苗, "Mingdai wokou jianji Aomenshi yanjiu zhongwen lunzhu suoyin" 明代倭寇兼及澳門史研究中文論著索引, *Aomen yanjiu* 澳門研究 30 (2005), 208–229.

Shibue Chusai 澀江全善 and Mori Tatsuyuki 森立之, *Jingji fangguzhi* 經籍訪古志, ed. by Du Zexun 杜澤遜 and Ban Longmen 班龍門, *Ricang Zhongguo guji shuzhi* 日藏中國古籍書 志 (Shanghai: Shanghai guji chubanshe, 2014).

Shimizu Hirokazu 清水紘一, *Kirishitan kinseishi* キリシタン禁制史 (Tōkyō: Kyōikusha, 1981).

Siegmund, Felix, "The adaptation of Chinese military techniques to Choson Korea, their validation, and the social dynamics thereof" in Kai Filipiak (ed.), *Civil Military Relations in Chinese History: From Ancient China to the Communist takeover* (London and New York: Routledge, 2015), 172–190.

Smith, Adam, *An Inquiry into the Nature and Causes of the Wealth of Nations* (MetaLibri: Amsterdam, Lausanne, Melbourne et al., 2007), Book III, Chapter III, 313–314 (G.ed. p. 407).

Smith, George Vinal, *The Dutch in Seventeenth-Century Thailand* Special report No.16, (Northern Illinois University: Center for Southeast Asian Studies, 1977).

Smith, Paul Jakov, Richard von Glahn (eds.), *The Song-Yuan-Ming Transition in Chinese History*. (Cambridge: Harvard University Press, 2003).

S.n., "First wrecked now pillaged: Vietnam's underwater treasure", *The Conversation*, November 8, 2012.

http://theconversation.edu.au/first-wrecked-now-pillaged-vietnams-underwater-treasure-10219

So Kwan-wai 蘇均煒, *Japanese Piracy in Ming China During the 16th Century* (East Lansing: Michigan State University Press, 1975).

Sone Yūji 曽根勇二 and Kimura Naoya 木村直也, *Atarashii kinseishi* 新しい近世史, II, *Kokka to taigai kankei* 国家と対外関係 (Tōkyō: Shin jinbutsu ōraisha, 1996).

Sonnendecker, Klaus, *Huang Xingzeng. Verzeichnis der Akteneinträge zu Audienzen und Tributen vom Westlichen Meer* (*Xiyang chaogong dianlu*) [黄省曾, 西洋朝貢典錄, 1520 n. Chr.] PhD thesis (Freie Universität Berlin, 2005).

Sousa, Pinto Paulo Jorge, "Enemy at the Gates. Macao, Manila and the 'Pinhal Episode' (end of the 16th Century)", *Bulletin of Portuguese/Japanese Studies* 16 (2008), 11–43.

Souza, George Bryan, *The Survival of Empire. Portuguese Trade and Society in China and the South China Sea, 1630–1754* (Cambridge: Cambridge University Press, 1986).

Spence, Jonathan, *The Search for Modern China* (New York: W. W. Norton & Company, 1990).

Staniforth, Mark, "First wrecked, now pillaged: Vietnam's underwater treasure", *The Conversation*, 2012. Available from http://theconversation.edu.au/first-wrecked-now-pillaged-vietnams-underwater-treasure-10219.

Staniforth, Mark; Kimura, Jun, and Le, Thi Lien, "Defeating the fleet of Kublai Khan: the Bach Dang River and Van Don Naval battlefields research project", *Archeologia Postmedievale* 18 (2014), 29–44.

Stevens, Carol B., "Food and Supply: Logistics and the early modern Russian army", in Brian L. Davies (ed.), *Warfare in Eastern Europe, 1500–1800. History of Warfare*, Vol. 72 (Leiden: Brill, 2012), 119–146.

Subrahmanyam, Sanjay, and Muzaffar Alam, "The Making of a Munshi", *Comparative Studies of South Asia, Africa and the Middle East* 24:3 (2004), 61–72.

Subrahmanyam, Sanjay, *Courtly Encounters: translating courtliness and violence in early modern Eurasia* (Cambridge: Harvard University Press, 2012).

Suganuma, Unryu, *Sovereign Rights and Territorial Space in Sino-Japanese Relations. Irredentism and the Diaoyu/Senkaku Islands* [Asian Interactions and Comparisons] (Honolulu: University of Hawai'i Press, 2000).

Sun Guangqi 孫光圻, *Zhongguo gudai hanghaishi* 中國古代航海史 (Beijing: Haiyang chubanshe, 1989).

Sunpuki 駿府記 in *Dai Nihon shiryō* 大日本史料 (Tōkyō: Shiryō hensanjo, 1901 ~), 12, x.

Suzuki Yasuko, "Changes in the Nagasaki Governorship System, 1680–1690", in Nagazumi Yōko (ed.), *Large and Broad. The Dutch Impact on Early Modern Asia. Essays in Honor of Leonard Blussé* (Tōkyō: Tōyō Bunkō, 2010), 76–99.

Swope, Kenneth M., "Bestowing the Double-Edged Sword: Wanli as Supreme Military Commander", in David Robinson (ed.), *Culture, Courtiers and Competition: The Ming Court (1368–1644)* (Cambridge, MA: Harvard University Press, 2008).

Swope, Kenneth M., *A Dragon's Head and a Serpent's Tail – Ming China and the First Great East Asian War, 1592–1598* (Norman: University of Oklahoma Press, 2009).

Swope, Kenneth M., "Naval Technology, State Power and the Influence of Qi Jiguang in the Ming", in Kenneth M. Swope, *The Maritime Defence of China* (Singapore: Springer, 2017), 201–216. https://doi.org/10.1007/978-981-10-4163-1_12.

T'ien Ju-K'ang, "The First Printed Chinese Rutter: Duhai Fangcheng 渡海方程". *T'oung Pao*, Second Series, 68:1/3 (1982), 76–90.

Tan, N. H. (ed.), *Advancing Southeast Asian Archaeology 2013: Selected papers from the first SEAMEO SPAFA International Conference on Southeast Asian Archaeology* (Bangkok: SEAMEO SPAFA Regional Centre for Archaeology and Fine Arts, 2015).

Tan, Rita C., *Zhangzhou ware found in the Philippines: "Swatow" export ceramics from Fujian 16th–17th century* (Manila: Yuchengco Museum, the Oriental Ceramic Society of the Philippines, Artpostasia, 2007).

Tanaka Takeo 田中健夫, *Wokou: Haishang lishi* 倭寇：海上歷史, Yang Hangqiu 楊翰球 (trans.) (Wuhan: Wuhan daxue chubanshe, 1987).

Tanaka Van Daalen, Isabel, "Communicating with the Japanese under *Sakoku*: Dutch Letters of Compliant and Attempts to Learn Japanese", in Nagazumi Yōko (ed.), *Large and Broad. The Dutch Impact on Early Modern Asia. Essays in Honor of Leonard Blussé* (Tōkyō: Tōyō Bunkō, 2010), 100–129.

Tang Kaijian 湯開建, "Ming Longwan zhi ji Yuedong ju dao Lin Feng shiji xiang kao – yi Liu Yaohui « Dufu shiyi » zhong Ling Feng shiliao wei zhongxin" 明隆萬之際粵東巨盜林鳳事蹟詳考—以劉堯誨《督撫疏議》中林鳳史料為中心, *Lishi yanjiu*歷史研究 6 (2012), 43–65.

Taylor, K.W., *A History of the Vietnamese* (Cambridge: Cambridge University Press, 2013).

Thompson, Edward M. (ed.), *Diary of Richard Cocks. Cape-merchant in the English Factory in Japan, 1615–1622*. 2 vols. (London: Hakluyt Society, 1883).

Tibbetts, G. R. "Comparisons between Arab and Chinese Navigational Techniques". *Bulletin of the School of Oriental and African Studies, University of London* 36:1 (1973), 97–108.

Toby, Ronald, "Reopening the Question of *Sakoku*: Diplomacy in the Legitimation of the Tokugawa Bakufu", *Journal of Japanese Studies* 3/2 (1977), 323–363.

Toby, Ronald, *State and Diplomacy in Early Modern Japan* (Princeton: Princeton University Press, 1984).

Toby, Ronald, *State and Diplomacy in Early Modern Japan: Asia in the Development of the Tokugawa Bakufu* (Princeton: Princeton University Press, 1984).

Tokugawa Iemitsu kōden 徳川家光公伝 (Nikkō: Nikkō Tōshogu, 1963).

Tokugawa Ieyasu monjo no kenkyū 徳川家康文書の研究 (Tōkyō: Nihon Gakujutsu Shinkōkai, 1960).

Tong Jie 童杰, "Zheng Shungong shengping dayao yu *Riben yijian* de xuanzhu" 鄭舜功生平大要與《日本一鑑》的撰著. *Zhongnan daxue xuebao* (*shehui kexueban*) 中南大學學報(社會科學版) 20:5 (2014), 243–247.

Toshiro Kubō 久保尾俊郎, "Asaino sōzui to 'ishotaizen' no shuppan" 阿佐井野宗瑞と『医書大　全』の出版, *Waseda daigaku toshokan kiyō* 早稲田大学図書館紀要 42 (December 31, 1995), 157–176.

Totman, Conrad, *Early Modern Japan* (Berkeley: University of California Press 1993).

Totman, Conrad, *Tokugawa Ieyasu: Shōgun* (Torrance CA: Heian International, 1983).

Tremml-Werner, Birgit, *Spain, China, and Japan in Manila, 1571–1644* (Amsterdam: Amsterdam University Press, 2015).

Tsao, Kai-fu, "K'ang-hsi and the San-fan War", *Monumenta Serica* 31 (1974–75), 108–130.

Twitchett, Denis and Janice Stargardt, "Chinese Silver Bullion in a Tenth-Century Indonesian Wreck", *Asia Major* (*third series*), 15:1 (2002), 23–72.

Theobald, Ulrich, *War Finance and Logistics in Late Imperial China – A Study of the Second Jinchuan Campaign* (*1771–1776*) (Brill: Leiden, Boston: 2013).

Torck, Mathieu, *Avoiding the Dire Straits: An Inquiry into Food Provisions and Scurvy in the Maritime and Military History of China and wider East Asia* [East Asian Maritime History 5] (Wiesbaden: Harrassowitz, 2009).

Torck, Mathieu, "Haifang 海防 and the Ming-Qing Transition: A Few Notes on Coastal Defence, Navies and Military Writings", *Crossroads* 11 (2015), 97–114.

Torres Sánchez, Rafael, *Military Entrepreneurs and the Spanish Contractor State in the Eighteenth Century* (Oxford: Oxford University Press, 2016).

Van Creveld, Martin, *Supplying War: Logistics from Wallenstein to Patton* (Cambridge: Cambridge University Press, 2004) [2nd edition].

van der Velde, Paul and Bachofner, Rudolf, *The Deshima Diaries, 1700–1740* (Tōkyō: The Japan-Netherlands Institute, 1992).

Van Dyke, Paul A., *Merchants of Canton and Macao*, vol. 2, *Success and Failure in Eighteenth-Century Chinese Trade* (Hong Kong, Hong Kong University Press, 2016).

Van Dyke, Paul, "The Anglo-Dutch Fleet of Defence (1620–1623). Prelude to the Dutch Occupation of Taiwan", in Leonard Blussé (ed.), *Around and about Formosa* (Taipei: Ts'ao Yung-ho Foundation for Culture and Education, SMC Publishing, 2003), 61–81.

Van Dyke, Paul, "The Anglo-Dutch Fleet of Defence (1620–1622): Prelude to the Dutch Occupation of Taiwan", in Leonard Blussé (ed.), *Around and about Formosa* (Taipei: Ts'ao Yung-ho Foundation for Culture and Education, 2003), 61–81.

Van Dyke, Paul, *Merchants of Canton and Macao. Politics and Strategies in Eighteenth-Century Chinese Trade*, (Hong Kong: Hong Kong University Press, 2011).

Van Dyke, Paul, *The Canton Trade. Life and Enterprise on the China Coast, 1700–1845* (Hong Kong: Hong Kong University Press, 2005).

van Vliet, Jeremias, *Historiael Verhael van de sieckte ende doot van Pra Interra-Tsia. 22en Coninck in Siam, ende den Regherenden Coninck Pra Ongh Srij* (1640), edited by Iwao Seiichi (Tōkyō: Tōyō Bunko, 1956).

Viallé, Cynthia and Leonard Blussé (eds.), *The Deshima Dagregisters*, XI: 1641–1650 (Leiden: Institute for the History of European Expansion, 2001).

Viallé, Cynthia, Leonard Blussé, van Daalen Isabel, and Remmelink Willem, *The Deshima Diaries, 1740–1800* (Tōkyō: The Japan-Netherlands Institute, 2004).

von Glahn, Richard, "Imagining Pre-modern China", in Paul Jakov Smith, Richard von Glahn (eds.), *The Song-Yuan-Ming Transition in Chinese History* (Cambridge: Harvard University Press, 2003), 35–70.

von Glahn, Richard, *Fountain of Fortune: Money and Monetary Policy in China, 1000–1700* (Berkeley: University of California, 1996).

Wada, Sei, "The Philippine Islands as Known to the Chinese before the Ming Period", *Memories of the Research Department of the Tōyō Bunko* 4 (1929), 121–166.

Wade, Geoff, "The Patani Region in Chinese Texts of the 6th to 19th Centuries". In Patrick Jory (ed.), *Ghosts of the Past in Southern Thailand. Essays on the History and Historiography of Patani* (Singapore: NUS Press, 2013), 53–84.

Waltner, Ann, "Infanticide and Dowry in Ming and Early Qing China," in Anne B. Kinney (ed.) *Chinese Views of Childhood* (Honolulu: University of Hawaii Press, 1995), 193–217.

Wang, Gungwu, "Ming Foreign Relations: Southeast Asia", in Denis Twitchett and Frederick Mote (eds.), *The Ming Dynasty, 1368–1644*, Part 2, vol. 8 of *The Cambridge History of China* (Cambridge: Cambridge University Press, 1998), 301–332.

Wang Min 王敏, *Shiyi jiazu yu minjian yiliao: Jiangnan Heshi gean yanjiu* 世醫家族與民間醫療:江南何氏個案研究. PhD thesis (Shanghai: East China Normal University, 2012).

Wang Ruixiang 王瑞祥 (ed.), *Zhongguo guyiji shumu tiyao* 中國古醫籍書目提要, vol. 1, 2 vols. (Beijing: Zhongyi guji chubanshe, 2009).

Wang Shuanghuai 王雙懷, "Mingdai Hua'nan de ziran zaihai jiqi shikong tezheng", 明代華南的自然災害及其時空特征, *Dili yanjiu* 地理研究 18 (1999), 152–160.

Wang Taokai 王涛锴, "Heyi chengyi: Ming Qing shidai susongtai diqu de yisheng xunlian he shehui" 何以成醫:明清時代蘇松太地區的醫生訓練和社會, *Zhongguo shehui lishi pinglun* 中國社會歷史評論 11 (2010), 170–184.

Wang Ting 王頲, "Wokou gonglue" 倭寇攻掠, in *Shengwang zhaoye: Han Ri Zhong jiaosheshi kao* 聖王肇業:韓日中交涉史考 (Shanghai: Xuelin chubanshe, 1998), 241–259.

Wang Wenchu 王文楚, "Mingchao yu Liuqiu de haishang hanglu" 明朝與琉球的海上航路, *Shilin* 史林 1 (1987), 29–34.

Wang Xingya 王興亞, "Mingdai renkou tongji zhongde nükou" 明代人口統計中的女口, in *Zhongguo shehui lishi pinglun* 中國社會歷史評論, ed. Zhang Guogang 張國剛, vol. 2 (Tianjin: Tianjin guji chubanshe, 2000).

Wang Yuquan 王毓銓 and Cao Guilin 曹貴林 (eds.), *Zhongguo lishi da cidian: Mingshi juan* 中國歷史大辭典:明史卷 (Shanghai: Shanghai cishu chubanshe, 1995).

Wang Zhenping, *Tang China in Multi-Polar Asia. A History of Diplomacy and War* (Honolulu: University of Hawai'i Press, 2013).

Wang Zhongge 王忠閣, "Jiuling shanfang ji banben yuanliu kao" 九靈山房集版本源流考, *Wenxian* 文獻 1 (2001), 171–176.

Wang Zunwang 王尊旺 and Cai Hongxin 蔡鴻新, *Fujian yiji kao* 福建醫籍考 (Xiamen: Xiamen University Press, 2016).

Wang Zunwang 王尊旺 and Li Yin 李穎, *Yiliao cishan yu Ming Qing Fujian shehui* 醫療、 慈善與明清福建社會 (Tianjin: Tianjin guji chubanshe, 2010).

Wang, Gungwu, "Merchants without empire: the Hokkien sojourning communities", in James D. Tracy (ed.), *The Rise of Merchant Empires. Long-Distance Trade in the Early Modern World (1350–1750)*. (Cambridge: Cambridge University Press, 1990), 400–421.

Wang, Yi-tung, *Official Relations between China and Japan, 1368–1549* (Cambridge: Cambridge University Press, 1953).

Wang, Zhenping, "Reading Song-Ming Records on the Pre-colonial History of the Philippines", *Journal of East Asian Cultural Interaction Studies* 1 (2008), 249–260.

Weng Dongling, "Overseas Circulation of Ancient Chinese Currency on the Silk Road and Its Enlightenment", *Journal of Shihezi University (Philosophy and Social Sciences)* 32:6 (2018), 84–93.

Weng Eang Cheong, *Hong Merchants of Canton. Chinese Merchants in Sino-Western Trade, 1684–1798* (Richmond, Surrey: Curzon, 1997).

Whitmore, J. K., "The Rise of the Coast: Trade, State and Culture in Early Dai Viet", *Journal of Southeast Asian Studies* 37:1 (2006), 103–122.

Wicks, Robert S., "Monetary Developments in Java Between the Ninth and Sixteenth Centuries: A Numismatic Perspective", *Indonesia* 42 (1986), 43–77.

Wicks, Robert S., *Money, Markets, and Trade in Early Southeast Asia: The Development of Indigenous Monetary Systems to A.D. 1400* (Ithaca: Cornell University Press, 1992).

Wilkinson, Endymion, *Chinese History: A New Manual* (Cambridge, MS: Harvard University Press, 2015).

Wills, John E. Jr., *Embassies and Illusions: Dutch and Portuguese Envoys to K'ang-hsi*, 1666–1687. (Cambridge, MS: Harvard University Press, 1984).

Wills, John E. Jr., *Pepper, Guns & Parleys: The Dutch East India Company and China 1662–1681* (Cambridge, MS.: Harvard University Press, 1974).

Wisseman Christie, Jan, "Money and Its Uses in the Javanese States of the Ninth to Fifteenth Centuries A.D.", *Journal of the Economic and Social History of the Orient* 39:3 (1996), 243–86.

Wu Enrong 吳恩榮, "Mingdai liangjing guanshu zhi de zuanxiu jiqi zhengzhi wenhua jiedu" 明代兩京官署志的纂修及其政治文化解讀. *Lishi dang'an* 歷史檔案 2 (2015), 52–62.

Xia Zhengnong 夏征農 (ed.), *Da cihai: Zhongguo gudaishi juan* 大辭海：中國古代史卷 (Shanghai: Shanghai cishu chubanshe, 2005).

Xiang Da 向達 (ed.), *Zheng He hanghai tu* 鄭和航海圖 [Zhongwai jiaotong shiji congkan 中外交通史籍叢刊] (Beijing: Zhonghua shuju, 2000 [1961]).

Xiang Da 向達, "Yingya suozhi. Ji Bali ben Wang Zongzai Siyiguan kao" 瀛涯瑣志. 記巴黎本王宗載四夷館考. *Tushu jikan* 圖書季刊 Xin 新2:2 (1940), 181–186.

Xiao Linrong 肖林榕, "Song Yuan shiqi minban yishu de yinshua jiqi yingxiang"宋元時期閩　版醫書的印刷及其影響, *Fujian Zhongyiyao* 福建中醫藥大學 19:1 (1988), 56–57.

Xiao Qiqing 蕭啟慶, "Yuandai Menggu semu jinshi beijing de fenxi" 元代蒙古色目進士背景的分析, *Hanxue yanjiu* 漢學研究 18:1 (2000), 101–128.

Xie Fang 謝方 (ed.), *Xiyang chaogong dianlu jiaozhu* 西洋朝貢典錄校注 [Zhongwai jiaotong shiji congkan 中外交通史籍叢刊] (Beijing: Zhonghua shuju, 2000 [1982]).

Xie Shuishun 謝水顺 and Lin Ting 林珽, *Fujian gudai keshu* 福建古代刻書 (Fuzhou: Fujian renmin chubanshe, 1997).

Xing Han 星漢, "Nai Xian shengping kaolüe" 迺賢生平考略, *Xinjiang daxue xuebao (zhexue shehui kexue ban)* 新疆大學學報 (哲學社會科學版) 4 (1998), 77–82.

Xing, Hang, *Conflict and Commerce in Maritime East Asia: The Zheng Family and the Shaping of Modern World, c. 1620–1720* (Cambridge: Cambridge University Press, 2016).

Xu Quansheng 许全胜, Liu Zhen刘震 (eds.), *Neilu ouya lishi yuyan lunji: Xu Wenkan xiansheng guxi jinian*内陆欧亚历史语言论集——徐文堪先生古稀纪念 (Lanzhou: Lanzhou University Press, 2014).

Xu, Zhexin, "The Environment, Perceptions, and Publication of Medical Texts in Fujian during the Ming Period (1368 to 1644)", in Angela Schottenhammer, Mathieu Torck and Wim De Winter (eds.), *Seafaring, Trade, and Knowledge Transfer. Maritime Politics and Commerce in Early Middle Period to Early Modern China* (Leiden: E. J. Brill, 2026), 154–179.

Xue Qinglu 薛清录 (ed.), *Zhongguo zhongyi guji zongmu* 中國中醫古籍總目 (Shanghai: Shanghai cishu chubanshe, 2007).

Xue Xi 薛曦, "Minji Liuqiu cefeng shi Xie Jie qiren qishi qiwen" 閩籍琉球冊封使謝杰其人其事其文. *Ningde shifan daxue xuebao* (*zhexue shehui kexueban*) 寧德師範學院學報 (哲學社會科學版) 1 (2012), 76–79.

Yamamoto Hirofumi 山本博文, *Sakoku to kaikin no jidai* 鎖国と海禁の時代 (Tōkyō: Azekura shobō, 1995).

Yamamoto Kitsuna 山本紀綱, *Nagasaki Tōjin yashiki* 長崎唐人屋敷 (Tōkyō: Kenkōsha, 1983).

Yamamoto Tasuro山本達郎, "Annan no bōekiko Unton" 安南の貿易港雲屯, *Tōho Gakuhō* 東方学報 9 (1939), 277–309.

Yan Xuanjun 晏選軍, "Dai Liang Shandong Changle, Yidu xingji kaobian" 戴良山東昌樂、益都行跡考辨, *Wenxian* 文獻 3 (2008), 178–179.

Yang Fuyou 楊富有 and Shi Haiguang 石海光, "Nai Xian de yishou shi yu Yuandai Zhong Ri guanxi jiqi yiyi" 迺賢的一首詩與元代中日關係及其意義, *Yuwen xuekan* 語文學刊 5 (2013), 1–2.

Yang Shiqi 楊士奇 et al. (eds.), *Ming Taizong shilu* 明太宗實錄, vol. 6, 6 vols. (Taipei: Academia Sinica, 1960).

Yano Tōru 矢野暢, *Nihon no Nanyōshikan* 日本の南洋史観 (Tōkyō: Chūō Kōronsha, 1979).

Yokkaichi Yasuhiro, "The Structure of Political Power and the Nanhai Trade: From the Perspective of Local Elites in Zhejiang in the Yuan Period". Paper presented to the annual meetings of the Association for Asian Studies, San Francisco, March 2006.

Yokoyama Hiroaki 横山宏章, *Nagasaki Tōjin yashiki no nazo* 長崎唐人屋敷の謎 (Tōkyō: shin'eisha, 2011).

Yu Xiangdong 於向東 and Cheng Sijia 成思佳, "Zheng Ruozeng yu *Annan tushuo* lüelun" 鄭若曾與《安南圖說》略論, *Zhongguo bianjiang shidi yanjiu* 中國邊疆史地研究 26:3 (2016), 96–110.

Yuan, Mei, *Recipes of the Garden of Contentment: Yuan Mei's Manual of Gastronomy*. Translated and annotated by Sean J.S. Chen (Great Barrington, MA: Berkshire Publishing Group).

Zhang Caixia 張彩霞 and Lin Renchuan 林仁川, "Lun Zhang Xie 'Dongfan kao' de ziliao laiyuan" 論張燮《東番考》的資料來源, *Zhongguo shehui jingqi shi yanjiu* 中國社會經濟史研究 2 (2009), 64–66.

Zhang Deren 张德二 (ed.), *Zhongguo sanqiannian qixiang jilu zongji* 中國三千年氣象記錄總集 (Beijing: Zhongguo shehui chubanshe, 1999).

Zhang Dexin 張德信, *Mingdai zhiguan nianbiao* 明代職官年表 (Hefei: Huangshan shushe, 2009).

Zhang Li 張莉, *Songdai ruyi yanjiu* 宋代儒醫研究. PhD thesis (Changsha: Hunan University, 2008).

Zhang Rong 張榮 and Liu Yijie 劉義傑, "*Shunfeng xiangsong* jiaokan ji biancheng niandai xiaokao" 《順風相送》校勘及編成年代小考, *Guojia hanghai* 國家航海 2 (2012), 78–96.

Zhang Tingyu 张廷玉 (1672–1755) *et al.*, *Mingshi* 明史 (Taibei: Dingwen chubanshe, 1975~).

Zhang Wende 張文德, "Cong Xianluoguan de shili kan Mingchao houqi yu Xianluo de wenhua jiaoliu" 從暹羅館的設立看明朝後期與暹羅的文化交流, *Dongnanya zongheng* 東南亞縱橫 11 (2009), 116–122.

Zhang Wende 張文德, "Wang Zongzai ji qi *Siyiguan kao*" 王宗載及其《四夷館考》, *Zhongguo bianjiang shidi yanjiu* 中國邊疆史地研究 3 (2000), 89–100.

Zhang Xie 張燮 (1574–1640), *Dongxiyang kao* 東西洋考 [c. 1617]. (Beijing: Zhonghua shuju, 1981).

Zhang Yiliu 張宜镠, "Mingdai Fujiansheng yizai dili guilü yu huanjing jili yanjiu" 明代福建省疫災地理規律与環境機理研究. Master thesis (Central China Normal University, 2014).

Zhang Zhejun 張哲俊, *Zhongguo gudai wenxue zhong de Riben xingxiang yanjiu* 中國古代文學中的日本形象研究 (Beijing: Beijing daxue chubanshe, 2004).

Zhang Zhibin 張志斌, *Zhongguo gudai yibing liuxing nianbiao* 中國古代疫病流行年表 (Fuzhou: Fujian kexue jishu chubanshe, 1997).

Zhao Gang [Zhao Gang 趙岡], *The Qing Opening to the Ocean: Chinese Maritime Policies, 1684–1757* (Honolulu: University of Hawai'i, 2013).

Zhao Lingyang 赵令扬 *et al.* (eds.), *Ming shilu zhong zhi Dongnanya shiliao* 明實錄中之東南亞史料. 2 vols. (Hong Kong: Hsüeh-tsin Press, 1968, 1976).

Zhao Shiyu 趙世瑜, "Ming qingshi yu Song Yuan shi: shixue shi yu shehui shi shijiao de fansi" 明清史與宋元史：史學史與社會史視角的反思, *Beijing shifan daxue xuebao (shehui kexue ban)* 北京師範大學學報 (社會科學版) 5 (2007), 87–95.

Zheng Jinsheng 鄭金生 and Zhang Zhibin 張志斌 (eds.), *Haiwai zhongyi zhenshanben guji congkan tiyao* 海外中醫珍善本古籍叢刊提要 (Beijing: Zhonghua shuju, 2017).

Zheng Liangsheng 鄭樑生, *Zhong Ri guanxi shi yanjiu lunji* 中日關係史研究論集, vols. 1–11 (Taibei: Wenshizhe chubanshe, 1990–2001).

Zheng Liangsheng 鄭樑生, *Mingdai Zhong Ri guanxi yanjiu* 明代中日關係研究 (Taibei: Wenshizhe chubanshe, 1985).

Zheng Tianting 鄭天挺 *et al.* (eds.), *Zhongguo lishi da cidian* (*Yinxu ben*) 中國歷史大辭典 (音序本) (Shanghai: Shanghai cishu chubanshe, 2007).

Zheng Weizhong [Weichung Cheng] 鄭維中, "Helan dongyindu gongsi renyuan zai taihai lianganjian de shuiwen tance huodong (1622–1636) 荷蘭東印度公司人員在臺海兩岸的水文探測活動", in Liu Xufeng (Liu Shufeng) 劉序楓 (ed.), *Yazhou haiyujian de xinxi chuandi yu xianghu renshi* 亞洲海域間的訊息傳遞與相互認識 (Taibei: Academia Sinica RCHSS, 2018), 385–440.

Zheng Yongchang 鄭永常, "Zheng Shungong Riben hanghai zhi lü" 鄭舜功日本航海之旅, *Guojia hanghai* 國家航海 9 (2014), 144–165.

Zhongguo guji zongmu bianzuan weiyuanhui 中國古籍總目編纂委員會, *Zhongguo guji zongmu* 中國古籍總目 (Beijing, Shanghai: Zhonghua shuju, Shanghai guji chubanshe, 2009–2012).

Zhongshan daxue Dongnanya lishi yanjiusuo 中山大学东南亚历史研究所 (ed.), *Zhongguo guji zhong youguan Feilübin ziliao huibian* 中国古籍中有关菲律宾资料汇编 (Beijing: Zhonghua shuju, 1980).

Zhou Yunzhong 周運中, "Lun *Wubei zhi* he *Nanshu zhi* zhong de *Zheng He hanghai tu*" 論 《武備志》和《南樞志》中的《鄭和航海圖》, *Zhongguo lishi dili luncong* 中國歷史地理論叢 22: 2 (2007), 145–152.

Zhou Yunzhong 周運中, "The Retrogression in Overseas Geographical Knowledge during the Mid-Ming Period". In Y. H. Teddy Sim (ed.), *The Maritime Defence of China. Ming General Qi Jiguang and Beyond* (Singapore: Springer, 2017), 145–161.

Zhou Yunzhong 周運中, *Zheng He xiaxiyang xinkao* 鄭和下西洋新考 (Beijing: Zhongguo shehui kexue chubanshe, 2013).

Zhu Duanqiang 朱端強, "Mingdai hanghaijia Xiao Chongye" 明代航海家蕭崇業. *Yunnan jiaoyu xueyuan xuebao* 雲南教育學院學報 5 (1993), 54–57.

Zhu Jianqiu 朱鑑秋, "*Riben yijian fuhai tujing* ji Mingdai ZhongRi haishang hanglu de yanjiu" 《日本一鑑桴海圖經》及明代中日海上航路的研究, *Haijiaoshi yanjiu* 海交史研究 2 (2002), 31–38.

Zhu Mu 祝穆, *Fangyu shenglan* 方輿勝覽 Vol. 1 (Beijing: Zhonghua shuju, 2003).

Zhu Pingyi 祝平一, "Song Ming zhiji de yishi yu ruyi" 宋明之際的醫史與儒醫, *Zhongyang yanjiuyuan lishi yuyan yanjiusuo jikan* 中央研究院歷史語言研究所集刊 77:3 (2006), 401–443.

Zhuang, Guotu, "Canton System: China's Reaction to European Commercial Expansion in 18th Century", *Ming Qing Yanjiu* 2:1 (1993), 127–163.

Index